1 MONTH OF
FREE
READING

at

www.ForgottenBooks.com

By purchasing this book you are eligible for one month membership to ForgottenBooks.com, giving you unlimited access to our entire collection of over 1,000,000 titles via our web site and mobile apps.

To claim your free month visit:

www.forgottenbooks.com/free965117

ISBN 978-0-260-70150-3
PIBN 10965117

REPORT OF CASES

DECIDED IN THE

COURT OF QUEEN'S BENCH.

BY

JAMES LUKIN ROBINSON, Esq.,

BARRISTER-AT-LAW AND REPORTER TO THE COURT.

VOL. XII.

CONTAINING THE CASES DETERMINED
FROM HILARY TERM, 17 VICTORIA, TO HILARY TERM, 18 VICTORIA,
WITH A TABLE OF THE NAMES OF CASES ARGUED,
AND DIGEST OF THE PRINCIPAL MATTERS.

SECOND EDITION.

TORONTO:
ROWSELL & HUTCHISON.
1872.

JUDGES

OF

THE COURT OF QUEEN'S BENCH,

DURING THE PERIOD OF THESE REPORTS:

THE HON. SIR JOHN BEVERLEY ROBINSON, BART., C. J.
"   WILLIAM HENRY DRAPER, J.
"   ROBERT EASTON BURNS, J.

———

Attorney-General.
HON. JOHN A. MCDONALD.

———

Solicitor-General.
HON. HENRY SMITH.

A

TABLE

OF THE

NAMES OF CASES REPORTED IN THIS VOLUME.

REPORT OF CASES

COURT OF QUEEN'S BENCH.

HILARY TERM, 17 VIC.

Present :

THE HON. JOHN BEVERLEY ROBINSON, C. J.
" WILLIAM HENRY DRAPER, J.
" ROBERT EASTON BURNS, J.

REYNOLDS V. WADDELL.

Detinue for a deed—Evidence—Measure of damages.

Detinue for an indenture of bargain and sale. *Pleas*—1. Non detinet; 2. That the deed was not the plaintiff's. The jury found that the indenture was delivered by one A. to the defendant, to be delivered to the plaintiff after A.'s death, on condition that he (the plaintiff) should keep A. until his death, and should pay his debts :—and that the plaintiff had not maintained A. but after his death was ready to pay his debts. The defendant, who was one of A.'s creditors, had refused to accept his debt from the plaintiff, and had destroyed the deed.

Held, that on these facts and pleadings the plaintiff could not recover :— for, as to the first plea, the writing being delivered to the defendant merely as an escrow, was not in fact a deed as described in the declaration; and, as to the second plea, the plaintiff had forfeited his right by a breach of one of the conditions.

Semble, that in such cases, where the plaintiff shews himself entitled to the deed, but the defendant, intending to do right, has given it up to another, the damages should be left as a question for the jury under the circumstances, and should not, as of course, be the value of the land.

This was an action for detaining from the plaintiff an indenture of bargain and sale, executed by one Abraham Brown to the plaintiff, for the north-west quarter of lot No. 21, in the 3rd concession of the township of Cartwright.

The defendant pleaded—1st. *Non detinet;* and 2ndly. That the indenture was not the plaintiff's.

At the trial, at the last assizes held at Peterborough, before *Burns*, J., the facts appeared to be these :—

Abraham Brown had been the owner of the land mentioned in the indenture, and had bargained to sell it jointly to one David Holmes and a son of Holmes. The son died before the bargain was completed by payment of the purchase money, and David Holmes went into possession. The date of the indenture was not shewn, but it was in the winter of 1850. In consequence of an understanding between the plaintiff (who was a nephew of David Holmes) and his uncle, that he should keep and maintain him, he (the plaintiff) was to have a conveyance of the land. He applied to Brown for it, and Brown appointed a day and place to execute it. The defendant David Holmes and Brown met together at the place appointed, but the plaintiff did not attend. Brown executed the conveyance, as he proved, upon the request of David Holmes, and delivered it to the defendant, who was to keep it; and the understanding upon which it was delivered was, that the plaintiff should pay what remained due to Brown on the land, which was a small sum, and should keep and maintain his uncle, and should pay to the defendant a debt due to him from David Holmes of about £30, and any other debts the uncle owed. Brown stated that David Holmes had often, both before the deed was executed and afterwards, told him the conditions upon which the plaintiff was to have the land, but he was not present at any time when the matter was discussed between the plaintiff and his uncle. The plaintiff lived in another part of the country, and shortly after the deed was executed the plaintiff sent his brother to make some arrangements about taking care of the uncle, but he staid only one night, and then left, and the plaintiff took no further steps toward maintaining the old man, and the old man removed from the land to Brown's house, where he lived until he died, in the month of June afterwards. Brown stated that David Holmes told him after the deed was executed that he had sold the land to one Collins, who was in possession before the old man died, and that his nephew never should have the land. After the old man died the plaintiff offered and tendered to the defendant the amount due to him, and at that time the defendant had the indenture in his possession. At first the defendant made no objection to delivering the deed to the plaintiff upon receiving the amount due to him ; but when the amount was afterwards made up, the defendant then stated that the plaintiff had not performed the agreement to keep his uncle and take care of him. Upon the application subsequently of John Holmes, another son of David Holmes, Brown executed a conveyance of the land to him; and his deed, which had been placed in the hands of the defendant, was destroyed.

The jury found the facts specially thus—that the indenture was delivered conditionally to Waddell ; that the plaintiff was to maintain his uncle, and also to pay the uncle's debts, but was not to have the deed till his uncle's death and after the debts had been paid that the plaintiff did not perform the condition of maintaining his uncle but was ready and willing after his death to pay his debts, and did all he could to accomplish that object ; that when the deed was demanded from the defendant he informed the plaintiff that he (the plaintiff) had not performed the agreement on his part as to the maintenance of his uncle, and he was indemnified for refusing him the deed. They found the land to be worth £125.

Upon this finding a verdict was entered for the plaintiff subject to the opinion of the Court with the understanding that if the plaintiff was entitled to recover and for more than nominal damages, then the verdict to be entered for £125 ; and if the plaintiff was not entitled to recover, then a verdict to be entered for the defendant.

Weller for the plaintiff.

Richards, contra, cited Cruise Dig. vol. iv., pp. 29, 30 ; Com. Dig. Fait A. 4, Shep. Touch 59 ; Hooper v. Ramsbottom, 6 Taunt 12 ; Johnson v. Baker 4 B. & Al. 440.

ROBINSON, C. J., delivered the judgment of the court.

If the plaintiff in this case were in our opinion entitled to sustain his action notwithstanding the facts found by the jury we should then have to consider the point referred to us upon

the proper measure of damages.   That is a question not easy
to answer satisfactorily in all such cases.   In trover for a
deed or in detinue the damage sustained by the plaintiff does
not necessarily amount to the value of the estate conveyed by
the deed, because the plaintiff's interest in the estate is not
lost to him by the detention of the title-deed; and it would be
unreasonable that he should recover the value while he still
holds the property itself, and while he may be well able,
notwithstanding the detention of the deed, to maintain his
title.

In Loosemore v. Radford (9 M. & W. 659), Baron Alderson
observes, that in an action of trover for title-deeds the jury
may give the full value of the estate to which they belong by
way of damages although the damages are generally reduced
to forty shillings on the deeds being given up.   There the
principle may be that a wrong-doer has no right to insist upon
the jury going into a nice scrutiny of the damages which the
plaintiff may possibly sustain from the inconvenience of being
without his title deeds and on that account less able to convince a third party that he has a good title, and less able to
shew his right if any occasion arises.   When the verdict is
merely intended to be used as a means of compelling the
defendant to surrender the deed which he still wrongfully
detains, there is less reason for attempting to arrive at any
exact measure of actual damage.

But in a case like the present when the defendant, meaning as we may suppose to do what was right under the
circumstances as he understood them, returned the deed to
the heir of the grantor, and has it no longer in his power to
hand it over to the grantee, he would have no means of relieving himself from the verdict, but must satisfy the judgment
that would be entered upon it ; and in such case we are by
no means satisfied that the plaintiff should as of course
receive a verdict for the value of the land.   We do not mean to
say that it would in every such case be deemed improper in
the jury to give damages to the value of the estate, but that
the question of the amount of damages should be left to them
as one requiring to be considered with reference to all the
circumstances proved and that it would not be proper to

direct them that as a matter of right the plaintiff is entitled to recover damages equal to the value of the land.

But here the plaintiff, we think, has no right to a verdict for any amount. The defendant has pleaded—1st. *Non-detinet;* and, 2dly, that the indenture was not the property of the plaintiff. Upon the first plea nothing but the detention is in issue under the new rules of pleading; and according to Jones v. Dowle (9 M. & W. 19), the plaintiff is entitled to succeed upon that issue if he shows the article detained to have been in the possession of the defendant, although the defendant may not have had it still in his possession at the time of commencing the action. Neither the property of the plaintiff in the goods, nor the right of the defendant to detain them, comes in issue upon the plea of *non-detinet;* but, whether the plaintiff is therefore entitled to a verdict upon the plea of *non-detinet,* does not seem to depend solely upon the defendant's right to put the plaintiff to proof of property upon that issue, or to give in evidence the defendant's own right to detain. There still remains the onus upon the plaintiff to prove the affirmative upon the issue of *non-detinet,* which he cannot do in this case without proving that the defendant did detain "an indenture of bargain and sale made between Brown and the plaintiff;" and the plaintiff, we think, failed in that, if the writing was never delivered except to a stranger as an escrow, for then it was no *indenture of bargain and sale made* between the parties: it was in fact no deed.

And at any rate, on the second plea, which denies that the indenture was the property of the plaintiff, the defendant was clearly entitled to succeed at the trial upon the finding of the jury, which was well supported by the evidence.

The defence was, that the deed, though signed and sealed by Brown, was not delivered to the plaintiff, who was not present at its execution, and that it was not intended to be delivered, but, on the contrary, was placed in the hands of this defendant, a third party, with the express injunction that it should not be delivered to the plaintiff (the grantee), but should be held in the hands of this defendant until the plaintiff should pay the balance still due to Brown upon the land, and should pay other debts due by the grantor Holmes; and subject to the further condition that the plaintiff should maintain Holmes upon the place during his life. Whether the deed was delivered as an escrow, and conditionally upon that understanding, and whether the conditions had been performed, were questions for the jury. They found that the deed had been delivered to the defendant only as an escrow, and upon the conditions we have mentioned, and that those conditions had not been fully performed. The evidence we think, shewed the fact to be so. The plaintiff has not in fact paid or done anything, though he shewed himself ready to comply with part of the conditions. The failure to support Holmes upon the place was clearly proved, and it was an important and substantial part of the condition. He did not live long; and therefore, as it turned out, that condition would not have formed, perhaps, by any means as large a proportion of the value to be given for the place as Holmes and the plaintiff may have contemplated; but it was, nevertheless, at the time of the transaction in all appearance a very material part, and most important for Holmes to insist on. He did, as it seems, insist on it, and was not willing to vest the title in the plaintiff and take his chance of that condition being performed, but thought it safer to deliver the deed to this defendant as an escrow, not to be delivered to the plaintiff till he had performed the condition;—in other words, till it was seen whether, besides paying such debts as he undertook to pay, he had also faithfully performed his engagement to support Holmes on the farm till he died. So far as appears in evidence he paid no attention to that condition, but left Holmes to be supported by others, or to support himself as he could; and, in consequence, Holmes declared on his death-bed that the plaintiff should never have the land. If the plaintiff had duly observed this condition as well as the others, then the writing would have become a valid deed by relation back to the time of the delivery, and no difficulty would have arisen from the fact of Holmes's death.

This is a case in which there is the least color for complaining of the condition being insisted upon, for Brown was conveying to the plaintiff land which he was bound to convey to Holmes; and though he had the authority of Holmes for doing so, yet the authority was a qualified one. The land was only to be conveyed to the plaintiff in a certain manner and upon certain conditions, and Brown was in effect in the position of a person executing a power.

Postea to defendant.

LOGAN V. STRANAHAN ET AL.

Sub-contract for work on railroad—Extra work—Reference to original contract.

The defendants, with other persons, had entered into an agreement with the Great Western Railway Company to make and complete certain sections of the railway. Their agreement was to do the several descriptions of work in accordance with the plans and specifications furnished by the Company's engineer, and for the prices contained in a schedule, all of which were annexed to the agreement. In these were contained, among other things, a full detail of the manner in which the culverts were to be made, and the kind of stone to be used, &c. It was also provided that, if the engineer should so direct, embankment might be substituted for trestle work or piling, at any point, and *vice versa*, without any extra allowance therefor. The plaintiff afterwards entered into an agreement under seal with the defendants to furnish all materials necessary to build and complete all the arched culverts required on one of the sections included in their contract with the Company; "and that the same shall be done in strict accordance with the plans, specifications, and directions of the engineer of the Great Western Railway Company having charge of the same." This agreement was signed "S. Farwell & Co." by Farwell, one of the defendants. The plaintiff was proceeding with the construction of the culverts, when the Company's engineer in charge decided upon having a description of mason work superior to and different from that specified in the defendants' original contract with the Company, and one of the defendants then desired the plaintiff to go on with the work as required, and promised to pay the additional expense incurred by the change. The plaintiff sued on the common counts for the value of the work as done upon that undertaking, not under the contract.

Held, that, although it was stipulated that he should abide by the directions of the engineer, the plaintiff might refer to the defendants' original contract with the Company, to shew what kind of work was contemplated by his agreement, and that he was entitled to recover under the common counts for extra work; for, as the plaintiff's contract was evidently made with reference to that under which the defendants were acting, it would be impossible, without looking at both, to put a just construction on their agreement.

Quære, whether the contract with the plaintiff, as executed by Farwell, could bind the other defendants.

DEBT on simple contract—Common counts for work and labor and materials, for money paid, and on account stated.

Pleas—1. *Nunquam indebitati.*

2.—As to £933 7s. 3d., payment.

At the trial at Hamilton, before *McLean*, J., it appeared that the defendants, Stranahan, Farwell, and Zimmerman, had on the 22nd of January, 1848, in conjunction with seven other persons, entered into a sealed contract with the Great Western Railway Company, to make and complete certain sections of the railway, according to certain specifications referred to. Their agreement was, that they would, under the inspection and direction of the Company's engineer, in a good, substantial, and workmanlike manner, construct, and in every respect complete the road bed on the said sections, and the clearing, grubbing, grading, and excavating, and the ditches, *the box and arched culverts, &c.*, and every other matter and thing incident to the said road bed, together with the bridges and superstructure, exclusive of the furnishing of the iron spikes and chairs; and these contractors were at their own costs and charges to provide the best materials of every kind for the said work; *the whole in strict conformity with the engineer's specifications* of the said work, which were annexed to this contract and signed by the parties, and with such plans, sections, and drawings, as should from time to time be furnished by the engineer of the Company for the guidance of the contractors. The whole work was to be done in two years from the commencement, to the satisfaction of the Company's engineer, to be by him certified to the Company. The Company bound themselves to pay to the said contractors the rates and prices specified in the annexed proposals.

It was one of the conditions of this contract, that "if the engineer should so direct, changes should be made, substituting embankment for trestle work or piling, and in like manner trestle work or piling for embankment, at any point which he may deem proper, and no claim for damages or allowances shall be made for such changes." And also it was provided "*that if any work shall be done by the contractors which is not included in this contract, the price and value of such work shall be determined by the engineer,* and that the work during its progress shall be subject to the supervision and inspection of the engineer, *and shall be made to conform in every respect to his directions.*"

And it was further agreed, with a view of preventing all disputes and misunderstandings, that the chief engineer should determine the amount or quantity of the several kinds of work so contracted to be done, and *should decide every question which could or might arise* relating to the execution of the work under this contract, on the part of the said contractors, and that his decision should be final and conclusive. No part of the work was to be sub-contracted for, except with the sanction of the engineer.

In the proposals of the contractors, which, being accepted by the company, formed the basis of the contract, and were annexed to and referred to in it, the contractors agreed to do the several descriptions of work on the several sections *agreeably to the plans and specifications furnished by the engineer of the said Company,* for the prices contained in a schedule, which prices were stated in reference to the description of the different kinds of work, as given in a printed paper also annexed. In this, among other things, a very particular detail was given of the manner in which the culverts were to be made, the kind of stone to be used, the method of dressing it, &c.

A long delay, it seemed, occurred after this contract was entered into before the Company were prepared to go on with the work. On the 24th of February, 1852, an agreement under seal was executed, between the present plaintiff Logan of the one part, and " Samuel Farwell & Co.," of the other part, whereby the plaintiff agreed to furnish all materials necessary to build and complete all the *arch culvers* required in section No. 4, one of those included in the Company's contract above recited. The plaintiff engaged to commence thereon " as soon as Farwell & Co. may require, *and that the same shall be done in strict accordance with the plans, specifications, and directions of the engineer of the Great Western Railway Company having charge of the same.*" And "Farwell & Co." agreed to pay the plaintiff for furnishing sand, cement, stone, and labor, for doing the above named work as might be required, the sum of three dollars and 12½ cents per cubic yard, measured in the work.

It was provided in this contract, that if the plaintiff should not execute his work faithfully, *or conform to the conditions of this contract,* Farwell & Co. might treat the contract as abandoned, and might agree with others to execute it, and the estimate of the engineers was to decide the quantity of yards to be paid for under this contract.

This agreement was signed and sealed by the plaintiff Logan, and opposite another seal was written, "*Samuel Farwell & Co.*," which was in the hand-writing of Samuel Farwell, one of the ten persons with whom the Company made the original contract of the 22nd of January, 1848.

The plaintiff's counsel, in opening the case to the jury on the common counts for work and labor, and materials, &c., stated that the plaintiff's claim was grounded on the following facts; namely, that the plaintiff had begun to make the arched culverts, and was proceeding with them, when the Company's engineer in charge of the work, decided upon having a different and superior description of mason work from that specified in the original contract of January, 1848, and directed the plaintiff to conform to this alteration, which would have compelled him to do the work in a manner quite different from, and much more expensive than, the description of work contemplated by the original contract; that the plaintiff in consequence stopped the work, insisting that he could not execute such work for the prices which he had agreed to accept for the other work; and that Farwell thereupon desired him to go on with the work as required by the engineer, and promised to pay him the difference of expense occasioned by the change. This action was in consequence brought to recover the value of the work as done upon that undertaking, and not under the special contract.

It was objected by the defendants' counsel, that the contract with this plaintiff, made on the 24th February, 1852, though signed "Samuel Farwell & Co.," was in its legal effect only a contract with Farwell who executed it, and that the order to execute the work mentioned in that contract in a superior manner, if made at all, was only made by Farwell, and was binding on him alone, and could give no right of action against others; that at any rate the plaintiff having undertaken by his written contract to do all the work in strict accordance with the plans and directions of the Company's engineer, he had only done what he had bound himself to do, and could have no claim for extra work ; that it was not competent for the plaintiff to refer to the original contract of these defendants and others with the Railway Company, with a view to shew what the plaintiff could be required to do under his own contract with Farwell & Co.—the latter being independent of the former, and having no reference to it; and that he could not be allowed to attempt to shew by parol evidence that his own contract was different in its terms or effect from what it appeared to be by its own language.

The learned judge held that the two contracts must be treated as independent of each other, and that the plaintiff being bound by his new agreement to do the work as the Company's engineer should direct, could not be allowed to refer to the first contract between the Company and other parties, in order to shew what kind of work was contemplated at the time he took his contract.

The plaintiff was on this ground nonsuited.

Freeman obtained a rule nisi to set aside the non suit He cited Story on Partnership, sec. 122 ; Bloomley v. Grinton and Watkins, 9 U. C. R. 455.

Connor, Q.C., shewed cause, and cited Harris v. Goodwyn, 2 M. & G. 417 ; West v. Blakeway, Ib. 729 ; Gwynne v. Davy et al., 1 M. & G. 857 ; Tay. Ev. secs. 820-1-2-3.

ROBINSON, C. J., delivered the judgment of the court.

In the first place it is to be considered that the plaintiff has to overcome the objection raised by the defendants, that he is proceeding against Farwell and two others to recover upon a contract made in point of law by Farwell alone ; and to support that objection the defendants have insisted that the execution of the sealed contract by Farwell alone, subscribing to it " Farwell & Co.," and placing a seal opposite, is not such an execution of a speciality as can bind any one but Farwell himself. But, without pronouncing an opinion how far that method of execution could be allowed, with or without other evidence, to make all or any of Farwell's partners liable as well as himself, it does not appear to us that if the case had been suffered to go on that question was likely to have arisen ; for the plaintiff founds his claim, not on the

contract, but on the implied, and even upon an express promise of Farwell to pay him the value of work done, which
the plaintiff contends was beside the contract.

At the conclusion of the case the questions would have
been, whether on a comparison of the contract with the
work done the plaintiff's claim could properly be entertained
under the common counts, as for work done beside and independent of his contract, which could not be determined
without shewing both the original contract and the sub-
contract; and, in the next place, whether as to any promise
expressly made by Farwell, or as to any work done at his
request upon the culverts in question, there was sufficient
in the evidence to make the other two defendants liable;
or whether, for all that appeared, he must be looked upon
as having acted for himself only in the matter.

How the case might have stood in these respects if the
whole evidence had been received we cannot tell, because the
case was prevented from going to the jury in consequence of
the learned judge at the trial taking a view of it in which
we are not able to concur. It seemed to him that he was not
at liberty to look at the original contract in order to determine what description of work this plaintiff had reason to
suppose he was undertaking to do, but that he and the jury
must confine their view entirely to the contract between these
parties, and not look at anything out of it. But we think the
nonsuit was ordered in this respect on insufficient ground,
and that the learned judge would most probably have changed
his opinion if he had had time to reflect more maturely on
the circumstances. It appears to us that it is impossible to
determine the just claims of these parties without referring
to the terms of the original contract with the Company,
which the plaintiff had engaged with Farwell to execute.

The plaintiff, as a sub-contractor, engaged to build *all the
arch-culverts required* on section No. 4, finding all the materials, and to build them in strict accordance with the plans
and specifications and directions of the engineer in charge of
the work, and he undertook to do this for 3 dollars and 12½
cents per cubic yard (of masonry). Now we must know
something of the public work with reference to which this

agreement was made, before we can understand what the plaintiff could be expected to do under it at the price named. If nothing had been added to the word " culverts," we should not have known by the agreement whether they were to be wooden box culverts, or of stone. We may understand, I suppose, from the word *arched culverts,* and from the price being fixed per cubic yard, that they were to be made of stone, but of what kind of stone, and what description of work, we could learn nothing, without looking out of the agreement ; and yet it is certain that stone culverts may be of kinds altogether different as to the nature and value of the materials and the manner in which they are to be prepared and placed in the work. When this plaintiff entered into this contract, we cannot suppose he entered into it blindly without reference to a knowledge of the kind of culverts which the defendants were to build. It is very true that the Company were at liberty to make changes in regard to the work, but yet not without limit, and the very condition in the original contract, that they should be allowed to substitute embankment for trestle-work or piling, and *vice versá,* implies that there was not to be an unlimited power to change the description of work, and yet hold the defendants to their contract. The reasonable construction to give to the original contract in that respect is, that in carrying out the kind of work contracted for, the directions of the engineers were to be obeyed. The plaintiff had, for all that appears, full opportunity of seeing what kind of culverts were being made upon the work ; and, if so, he would naturally suppose that he would be required to complete that part of the contract upon the same scale of work. In his contract with the defendants there is no such stipulation as there is in the first contract with the Company, about doing work not included in the contract. Let us suppose that Farwell & Co. had made a contract with the Company to supply all the wooden ties that they should require, and that they were directed by the specifications to be of hemlock, and to be eight feet long, and that after the work had been begun, the Company had made a change in their gauge, and required the ties to be twelve feet long, and had also determined that they must be of oak.

Could it be said that this plaintiff, if he had agreed with Farwell & Co. to find all the ties required in this section at so much a hundred, must under that contract provide them of oak, and twelve feet long, at the price named in his agreement? We must, as courts have said, receive evidence of the surrounding circumstances in order to assist us in putting a just construction on a contract, and unless we were to do so, we should frequently find that we were doing the greatest injustice. It is not to vary or contradict the clear import of the words of the contract that we can admit such evidence, but to enable us to fix with precision what has not been described with distinctness, because the parties were evidently contracting with reference to something which they themselves well understood, though they omitted to repeat it; so that strangers looking at their agreement, without the knowledge of facts which they had, would not be able to comprehend clearly what was meant. We think there should be a new trial without costs.

Rule absolute.

NELSON V. COOK.

Brantford & Buffalo R. R. Co.—Construction of deed taken by—Right to enter upon lands—License not revocable—Plaintiff not in a position to maintain trespass—12 Vic. ch. 84, 16 Vic. ch. 45.

On the 26th of October, 1852, the Buffalo and Brantford Joint Stock Railroad Company took a deed from the plaintiff's father, by which, in consideration of the benefits which would result to him from the construction of the road, and of £27 10s., he agreed "to allow and permit the said Company forthwith to take, occupy, possess and enjoy of and through" the land in question. It appeared that the plaintiff had no title to the land, but had merely been allowed by his father to occupy it; that he had admitted in presence of his father, that it was with his father and not with him that the Company must settle; and that he had worked under the defendant, a contractor with the Company, in making the fence along the line through this land. After the deed the plaintiff and his father forbade the defendant from entering. The defendant entered in December, 1852, for the purpose of making the railway, and the fences along the line being insufficient, the plaintiff's wheat was injured by cattle getting in. For these injuries he sued in this action of trespass *quare clausum fregit.*—The jury found for the plaintiff, and £25, on the ground, as they stated, that the defendant had been forbidden to enter upon the premises before any work was done.

The Company was established under the general act 12 Vic. ch. 84, and the deed was taken while under that act; but before entering they were placed under "The Railway Clauses Consolidation Act" by 16 Vic. ch. 45.

Held (treating the question as between the Company and the owner)—
First, That, the deed taken was more than a mere agreement as to the price; the effect of it was to give the Company permission forthwith to take and occupy a right of way through the land, of the ordinary width of the road.

Secondly, That the Company, having, by their agreement previously made, a right to enter *forthwith,* the 14 & 15. Vic. ch. 51, sec. 11, sub-sec. 2. would not apply.

Thirdly, That the Company could enter forthwith, though they had not paid or tendered the money ; that not being a condition precedent according to the deed, and there being nothing in the 12 Vic. ch. 84, to prevent it ; and therefore that they could not be considered trespassers.

Held, also, as to the plaintiff, that the verdict was wrong, taking the reasons given by the jury ; for, looking upon the deed merely as a license, it was acted upon the moment the Company entered into contracts for the work, on which they would be liable to others, and was therefore not revocable.

Secondly, That on legal grounds, independently of his own conduct, which in justice should estop him, the plaintiff could not maintain trespass against any one claiming under the Company ; for he was not at any time more than a tenant at will, and the deed determined the will and left him tenant at sufferance only, with a right to enter and remove the crop.

TRESPASS, *qu. cl. fr.* upon the close of the plaintiff, being lot 5 *in* the 2nd concession of Seneca,—destroying fences trampling down the crops, and cutting down and convert-, ing to the defendant's use the trees and underwood, &c.

The defendant pleaded, " by statute," not guilty.

At the trial at Cayuga, before *McLean,* J., it appeared that the plaintiff complained in this action of trespasses committed by the defendant, a contractor with the Buffalo and Brantford Railway Company, in throwing down his fences and entering into a small field which he had enclosed, and in which he had some wheat growing. He proved that the defendant, for the purpose of making the railway, which was laid out through that field, entered and cut down trees in the autumn of 1852, (in December), and in the following spring and summer, and that the fences put up along the line of railway being insufficient, the cattle got in and consumed and spoiled the wheat growing there.

The defendant having pleaded not guilty, by statute, gave evidence that the land in question was not the property of the plaintiff, but of his father, John Nelson, who had conveyed no interest in it to the plaintiff, but had merely allowed him to occupy it ; that the plaintiff, in the presence of his father, admitted that it was with his father and not with him that the Company must settle for the land ; that after the line had been staked out, and some trees cut down, the plaintiff and his father objected to their going on, and the Company were referred to for instructions, and the party was instructed to proceed with the work. On the 26th of October, 1852, the Company, through their agent, had made an agreement with the plaintiff's father and taken from him a deed, by which, " in consideration of the benefits and advantages which will result to him by the construction of the Brantford and Buffalo Railroad, and for the further consideration of £27 10s., the said John Nelson" (father of the plaintiff and owner of the land,) " did, for himself and his heirs, &c., covenant, promise, and agree with the Brantford and Buffalo Joint Stock Railroad Company to allow and permit the said Company *forthwith* to take, occupy, possess, and enjoy *of and through a lot of land* bought of Paul and Adah Park, and being part of a lot of land in the township of Seneca, granted to William Young of the township of Oneida." And he did thereby further covenant with the said Company to convey by deed the said land to the said Company, free from all incumbrances, so soon as the construction of the said railroad should be commenced.

It was objected at the trial that this action could not be maintained, because the defendant, on behalf of the Company, had authority by law to enter upon the land and construct the railway, and could not be made a trespasser in doing so ; (the statute 14 & 15 Vic. ch, 51, sec. 11, sub-secs. 2, 6, 7, 9, & 19, and sec. 20, were referred to) ; and that, at any rate, the deed taken from the owner, John Nelson, gave the Company and their agents and workmen the right to enter and take possession.

It was proved that John Nelson had, after the making of the deed, forbidden the defendant from entering on the land ; but, according to the weight of evidence, this was after the trees had been cut along the line. The plaintiff was not living on the property at the time of the alleged trespass. It was proved that he had assisted in making the fence along the line of railway through the field in question, and had been paid by the defendant for doing so ; also, that eight dollars had been tendered to the plaintiff as compensation for any damage done to the wheat which he had growing, but he

declined accepting it. It was admitted that the £27 10s.
mentioned in the deed had never been paid or tendered to
John Nelson, and that no deed had ever been made of the
land to the Company. This land was proved to be the same
land described in the deed made by the plaintiff's father to
the Company, which deed, it was contended on the part of the
defendant, constituted a license under seal not revocable by
parol, and especially after the defendant had entered and
done work.

The jury found for the plaintiff £25, on the ground as they
stated, that the defendant had been forbidden to enter upon
the premises before any work was done.

There was much evidence to the contrary, however, and the
defendant contended that he could by law enter for the purpose for which he did enter, without any license of the party ;
that there was, however, this license from the owner and that
being under seal it could not be revoked by parol, and
certainly not after work had been done under its authority.

Martin obtained a rule *nisi* for a new trial on the law and
evidence, and for misdirection.   He cited Doe dem. Davenish
v. Moffatt, 13 Q. B. 257 ; Taplin v. Florence, 10 C. B. 744.

Freeman showed cause.

The statutes referred to are noticed in the judgment.

ROBINSON, C. J., delivered the judgment of the court.

This undertaking to make a railway between Buffalo and
Goderich through Brantford was commenced under the authority given by the general statute respecting roads, 12 Vic.
ch. 84, amended by statute 13 & 14 Vic. ch. 72 ; and by the
statute 16 Vic. ch. 45, sec. 4, the company was brought
under the operation of "The Railway Clauses Consolidation
Act," 14 & 15 Vic. ch. 51, as regards those provisions in the
last-mentioned act which relate to the powers of the Company,
and to "lands and their valuation."   But it was in November,
1852, that the statute 16 Vic. ch. 45, was passed, and we
could not hold that any acts which had been done by the
Company, or their servants and agents, before the passing of
this latter act, and under the powers which they possessed

under the statute 12 Vic. ch. 84, could be held to have been exercised under or with any view to the Railway Clauses Consolidation Act. It does not appear to us, however, that the case would be materially affected by our having to apply the provisions of one of these statutes rather than of the other. The plaintiff at the trial gave no evidence of any interference with his occupation till December, 1852, and what he claimed damages for was the injury done to his wheat in the spring and summer of 1853—chiefly in the summer—by the defendant letting down the fences in order to go on with the work, and also by his neglecting to keep up a sufficient fence to separate the plaintiff's wheat field from the railway. It was in *November*, 1852, that the statute 16 Vic. ch. 45 was passed, which extended the Railway Clauses Consolidation Act to this work. Before that act was passed, and while this Company was still proceeding only under the powers given by the act 12 Vic. ch. 84, they took from the father of this plaintiff, the actual proprietor of this land, the deed of the 26th of October, 1852. The first clause of the statute 12 Vic. ch. 84 provided that no company should construct a road through or over any private property without having first obtained the permission of the owner ; and by other clauses of the act provision is made for enabling the company when they cannot agree with the owner to have it settled by arbitration what damages they shall pay him, and the sum awarded must be paid or tendered before the company can legally take possession of the land. There was no resort to the arbitration clauses in this case, because the owner of the land had agreed to accept a certain sum ; and there having been no arbitration, this provision as to paying or tendering the sum awarded before taking possession could not apply.

Then, before anything was done of which the plaintiff complains, according to the evidence produced by him upon the trial, this Company had by the statute 16 Vic. ch. 45 been brought under the operation of the Railway Clauses Consolidation Act, which must govern as to anything done after the 10th of November, 1852, except in so far as the operation of any of those clauses may be deemed to be necessarily affected by anything that had taken place while this Company was still acting under the statute 12 Vic. ch. 84.

We have then to consider what bearing the railway consolidation clauses must have upon anything done by this Company after the 10th of November, 1852, of which this plaintiff has complained.

The Company had already acquired by deed from the owner of the land in question "permission *forthwith*" to take and occupy a right of way through his land,—for that we take to be the reasonable construction and effect of the very slovenly and imperfectly drawn instrument taken by the Company's agent. This writing is something more than a mere agreement as to the price : it gives a right to take possession *forthwith* for the considerations expressed—namely the benefits and advantages to accrue to the proprietor from the railway (which has, perhaps doubled the value of his land), and the further consideration of £27 10s., not stating whether that sum had been paid or not: it is admitted, however, that the £27 10s. is not yet paid. Whether it was paid or not, we perceive nothing in the act 12 Vic. ch. 84, that makes the right to enter depend upon the previous payment or tender of the sum settled by agreement between the parties. The only restrictions that we find in that act are—that there can be no entry upon the land without leave of the owner until the amount, in case of disagreement, has been settled by arbitration; in which case (which is not the present case) the amount awarded must be paid or tendered before entry. If the deed of the 26th of October, 1852, gives permission to enter and occupy (so far as the proprietor is concerned)—which we think it does, but only to the extent of the ordinary width of the road—then for anything contained in the act the Company was at liberty to enter at once, though they had not paid or tendered the £27 10s. But it seems that before they did enter they had been placed under the conditions of the general railway clauses by the statute 16 Vic. ch. 45. Then how would those clauses affect them if the question were between them and the proprietor ?

The parts of the General Railway Act 14 & 15 Vic. ch. 51, which it seems necessary to consider are sec. 4; sec. 9. sub-secs. 4, 12; sec. 10, sub-secs. 8 & 9; sec. 11, sub-secs. 1, 2, 5, 7, 19; and sec. 13, sub-sec. 2, which relates to fencing in the line; and we think the question arising upon these, as regards the right to enter before paying or tendering the sum fixed by agreement between the parties, depends upon the effect to be given to the second sub-section of the 11th clause. Whether that clause should be taken to extend to a case where the price had been fixed by agreement between the parties, as this was (we are speaking now only with reference to the proprietor), before the Company was placed under the influence of the general railway clauses, has seemed to us to be a question which affords much room for difference of opinion. The opinion that we have formed is, that it does not, and more specially when it was part of such agreement previously executed that the Company should be permitted to enter and occupy *forthwith*. If those words had been wanting we should have more doubt.

Then, as we view the case, the Company were entitled, so far as the proprietor was concerned, to enter forthwith, though they had not paid or tendered the money, there being nothing in the 12th Vic. ch. 84 to prevent it, and the deed allowing it—that is, the deed as we construe it; for, admitting that there is nothing in the deed to estop John Wilson from saying that the £27 10s. is yet unpaid, yet it does not form the whole consideration, as the deed recites; and, permission being expressly given to enter and occupy forthwith, we should not hold, we think, that the payment of the money was, upon the principles of the common law, a condition precedent to the right of taking possession. Our conclusion therefore is, that as against John Nelson, the owner of the land, the Company had a right to enter and construct the road without first paying or tendering the money, and that they could not be held to be trespassing upon him by doing the acts complained of as having been done between March last and the time of harvest, in respect to which acts the damages were principally, if not exclusively, given.

Still the jury gave a verdict of £25 against this defendant a servant or agent of the Company, for the damage done to the plaintiff, not as owner, but as a person occupying with permission of the owner and having on the ground a field of wheat which by reason of the entry of the Company, and their proceedings in the construction of the railway was exposed to injury, and they gave their verdict upon the ground, as they stated, that after the owner of the land had given the deed of the 26th of October, which at the trial was treated as a license, he revoked such license by forbidding the defendant to enter before any work had been done. But the owner could not, we think, recall the right which he had conveyed to the Company by his deed under seal for a consideration expressed, and which was in part paid by whatever the Company had then done towards constructing the railway; and besides, the evidence was strong, we think, to shew that before the owner of the land forbad the defendant from proceeding, there had been work done by cutting down trees upon the land in question, though the jury have found otherwise. In addition to this, if we look upon the deed of the 26th of October, 1852, as being a license and nothing more, it was as much acted upon the moment the Company made contracts for the work relying upon the permission given to take possession, and make themselves of course liable to others upon such contracts, as it would have been by any amount of work laid out upon the road.

We think therefore that the verdict which the jury found against this defendant was found upon an error, taking their own explanation of their reasons.

Still it remains to be considered that this is not an action by the proprietor who signed the instrument of the 26th of October, but by an occupant who claims on a distinct ground —not for the land taken, but for damage done to wheat which he had put in on the same farm by permission of the proprietor; and the question is, whether he may not be in a position to maintain an action, though the proprietor, John Nelson, may be unable to do so. To ascertain the precise position of the plaintiff, William Nelson, has appeared to us the most difficult part of this case. All we hear of his interest in the premises is that his father had bought the property, intending to give it to him; but, though he had allowed him to cultivate it for four or five years, he had given him no title, and

nothing in writing had passed between them.   There is no
proof either that any rent was paid or agreed upon, or any
term created by verbal contract.   The relation of landlord
and tenant in its proper sense therefore did not exist.   The
plaintiff was at the utmost only tenant at will at any time.
Great doubts have been expressed by a very learned judge in
England whether, since the passing of the new statute of
limitations, a tenancy at will can be recognized as subsisting
for any purpose after the lapse of the first year; and in the
case before us, if we look upon the plaintiff as being tenant
at will to his father during the whole time of his occupation
up to the making of the deed of the 26th of October, 1852,
that act of the owner must surely have terminated the tenancy
at will—as to what part of the land, at least, which that deed
gave the company permission to enter and occupy forthwith.
Admitting, then, that the plaintiff was tenant at will up to
the execution of the deed, he could after that be but tenant
at sufferance, with the right we suppose which a tenant at
will has to the emblements, when the will is terminated not
by an act of the tenant, but of the owner.   That claim to
the emblements would amount only to a legal right to enter
for the purpose of reaping and taking away the crop.   It
would not put the tenant at sufferance in a position to maintain trespass against the owner of the land, or any one holding
a right of possession under him, whatever might be the case
as between him and a mere stranger.   And this action is not
for taking the plaintiff's wheat : it is strictly an action of
trespass *quare clausum fregit,* charging the prostrating the
fences and destroying the crops as a matter of aggravation
The gist of the action we take to be the alleged illegal entry
upon the land which in our opinion was not, under the
circumstances illegal.   This applies to the plaintiff's strict
right to recover upon technical grounds.   But against the
plaintiff's right in justice to recover there were also these
strong objections appearing in the evidence, and not contradicted : that he had himself held out his father as the
person with whom the Company was to settle, and had so
far acquiesced, to all appearance, in possession being taken
by the Company, and he took himself, under this defendant,

as their contractor, the job of putting up the fences which were to secure the wheat, and was paid by him for doing it.

This action, too, as was properly insisted upon by the defendant's counsel at the trial, is not an action for negligence in not putting up fences or keeping them in repair; if it were, then it would be necessary to consider that under the general railway clauses, sec. 13, sub-sec. 2, before the obligation to enclose could be held to have attached, it would be necessary to shew that the proprietor of the land had required the Company to do it.

Unless the jury wholly disbelieved the evidence, which stood uncontradicted, that this plaintiff had held out his father as the person who was to be settled with, and that he had himself worked under the contractor upon the land after the Company had made their agreement with his father, that surely should have been held sufficient to relieve the Company from the necessity of settling separately with him before they took possession; and it would seem doubly hard that the plaintiff should be allowed to turn upon the contractor under whom he had himself been working upon the place, and who could not be supposed to know the particular situation in which the Company stood with regard to the persons interested in the land through which they were making their railway. The hardship and inconvenience would be great of holding contractors and laborers liable in such cases as trespassers, for they could never think it necessary to enquire whether the Company had or had not acquired their right of way in each individual case. That they would not be liable for negligence in not keeping up fences, but the Company only, we think we should be obliged to hold, upon the principle of *respondeat superior;* and it is really for not keeping up fences that damages are sought here, rather than for any direct trespass. The jury not having been misdirected, as it appears to us, gave the plaintiff the value of his wheat as if all had been lost by the acts or the negligence of this party: whereas there was much room afforded by the evidence for ascribing the loss in part to the crops being badly inclosed in other parts besides that contiguous to the railway, which the plaintiff himself had been paid by the defendant for inclosing;

and they found their verdict upon the ground that the Company held nothing more than a revocable license, which had been legally revoked.   We think they came in that respect to a wrong conclusion, and that there should therefore be a new trial, with costs to abide the event.

It is much to be regretted that room should be left in these cases for litigation, which must throw a considerable expense upon one or other of the parties, and which by a little caution and consideration could in general be avoided.   The writing taken in this case is most carelessly and imperfectly framed, and was evidently done in haste.   It is more than a mere agreement about the amount to be paid, and yet it is not stated clearly in it what present or future right it was intended to confer; and, whatever might be the legal right of the Company to enter under it before paying the sum mentioned in it, they ought to have felt it just and reasonable to pay the £27 10s. before taking possession, and ought to have taken some pains to ascertain their exact position when a difficulty was first started.   In these cases it is better to offer to do whatever is fair, than to embark in a contention about a trifle.

Rule absolute.

In re Dulmage v. The Judge of the County Court of Leeds and Grenville.

Jurisdiction of Division Courts—13 & 14 Vic. ch. 53.

The jurisdiction of the Division Courts does not extend to persons residing out of the county.

A. McLean moved for a mandamus to the Judge of the County Court of Leeds and Grenville to try a case brought at the suit of this plaintiff, which he declined to do on the ground that the defendant in the case, being resident at Chatham, in the County of Kent, was served with a summons from a Division Court in Leeds and Grenville to appear in such Division Court, which the judge considered to be illegal, and that he could not take cognizance of the case.

Cur adv. vult.

Robinson, C. J., delivered, the judgment of the court.

We think the doubt of the learned judge as to his right to

entertain this case well founded ; and unless we thought it quite clear that he would be right in proceeding to trial, we ought not to command him to do it. Upon general principles, the jurisdiction of these inferior courts and the authority of their process must be taken to be confined to the locality within which they have power to act; and if for any purposes they can exercise authority in matters or over persons out of such limits, it can only be under some express legislative provisions giving them such authority. We find nothing in the statute authorizing service of summons not merely out of the division, but of the county, and there are several provisions of the statute which are quite inconsistent with any such extension of jurisdiction ; for if a plaintiff in the County of Leeds can summon a defendant residing in the County of Kent to appear and answer in a Division Court in the County of Leeds, it would in many cases be impossible for the defendant served with process in so remote a county to conduct his defence within the time and in the manner prescribed by the statute. Some of the provisions would require to be altered, or the defendants would in such cases lose the privileges and opportunities of defence which the act is intended to secure to them.

Rule refused (a).

THROOP AND WIFE V. EDMONDS.

Ejectment—Construction of deed—Revocation of will—Misdirection.

In January, 1841, B. made his will, devising to his daughter, the wife of the defendant, the land in question, in fee. In July following B., and the defendant and his wife, executed a deed reciting the will, and stating that the parties had mutually agreed that the defendant and his wife should come upon the land, and have, hold, occupy, possess and enjoy it, without the interruption or denial of him the said B., his heirs or assigns as long as the defendant and his wife should support the said B. and his wife in the manner described. The deed then set out that in consideration of the will, and that the said B. did put the defendant and his wife in possession, they had agreed to maintain the said B, and his wife during their natural lives ; and that if the defendant and his wife should keep their agreement then the land was to become the property of the said defendant and his wife, their heirs and assigns for ever. B. lived with and was supported by the defendant and his wife until his wife died in 1847. He afterwards married again, and in July, 1850, a few days before his death, made another will revoking all former wills, and directing his executors to sell all his land and divide the proceeds equally among his four daughters.

(a) See 13 & 14 Vic. ch. 53, secs. 23, 24, 25, 29, 32, 43, 45, 46, 48, 55, 60, 64.

The defendant had made considerable improvements on the farm during his occupation.

Held, On ejectment brought by one of the four daughters, that the deed passed no estate of inheritance, and that nothing contained in it could operate as an estoppel on the devisees under the second will. It gave only a right to occupy until the testator's death, with the assurance that if the agreement were kept by defendant and his wife, he would make no alteration in his first will.

Held, also, That it should not have been left to the jury to find whether the testator was of sound mind when he made the second will, or whether any coercion had been used in obtaining it, for there was no evidence to impeach the will on either of these grounds.

Quære, Whether the defendant, having kept the condition on his part, would have any remedy against B.'s representative for breach of the agreement.

EJECTMENT for an undivided fourth part of the west half of fifteen, in the first concession of Windham.

At the trial at Simcoe, before *McLean, J.*, it appeared that Hannah Throop, one of the plaintiffs, claimed an interest in this land, as one of four daughters, and co-heiresses of Joseph Button, who, it was admitted, was seized of the premises.

On the 25th of January, 1841, Joseph Button made a will, by which he devised " to his daughter Abigail Edmonds, wife of the defendant George Washington Edmonds, the west half of lot fifteen in the first concession of Windham, to have and to hold the same to her, and her heirs and assigns forever."

When Button made this will he was living on the premises thus devised, with his first wife Elizabeth Button ; and the defendant George W. Edmonds, who had married his daughter, was living on other land in the neighborhood.

On the 5th day of July, 1841, until which time Button and his son-in-law, the defendant, continued to reside apart, Button and the defendant executed an instrument under their seals, by which it was recited that Button had by his last will given to his daughter, Abigail Edmonds, the west half of fifteen in the first concession of Windham ; and in this deed it was stated that " the said Joseph Button and the said Abigail Edmonds, together with her husband George W. Edmonds, have mutually agreed that the said Abigail and George W. Edmonds shall come upon the premises (meaning the land devised), and have, hold, occupy, possess, and enjoy it, without the interruption or denial of him the said Joseph Button his heirs or assigns, *as long as the* said Abigail and George W. Edmonds shall find a fit and comfortable support for him the said Joseph Button, and Elizabeth Button his wife, in meat, drink, washing, lodging, and apparel,—subjecting him, the said George W. Edmonds, to the payment of all taxes and the repairs of what may be necessary on the premises; and the said Joseph Button reserves to himself the privilege of keeping one horse, one cow, and three sheep, on the produce of the premises." And the deed proceeded thus: "Now, know ye, that for and in consideration of the said Joseph Button having willed the above named premises to the said Abigail Edmonds, and doth put into possession thereof the said Abigail and George W. Edmonds, they the said Abigail and George W. Edmonds have agreed and undertaken to keep and maintain the said Joseph Button and Elizabeth Button his wife, during their natural lives. If, therefore, the said Abigail and George W. Edmonds, their heirs, executors, or administrators, do and shall from time to time and at all times hereafter, during the natural lives of the said Joseph and Elizabeth Button, well and sufficiently maintain and keep, or cause to be well and sufficiently maintained and kept, in some convenient part of the house on the premises, with meat, drink, clothes, and all other things fit and convenient for their support, during their natural lives, then and in that case the above mentioned premises with the appurtenances is to become the property of the said Abigail and George W. Edmonds, their heirs and assigns for ever.'

This deed was registered in the county register, on the 15th of August, 1850.

Elizabeth, the wife of Joseph Button, mentioned in this instrument, died in 1847 or 1848.

The defendant Edmonds and his wife, about the time of this deed being executed, in July, 1841, removed from their own farm and went to live in Joseph Button's house, and maintained him and his wife there, upon the premises now in question, until the death of the latter in 1848. Whether the defendant, in his treatment of Joseph Button and his wife up to that time, had punctually fulfilled what he undertook to do by the deed, was not quite clear upon the evidence. There was some proof of unkind and rough treatment on the part of Mrs. Edmonds; but on the other hand, it was proved that

Button after his wife's death had declared that he was well satisfied with what Edmonds and his wife had done.

But not long after his wife's death, Button who was then about 75 years old, married a young woman of indifferent character, which annoyed his family, and Edmonds and his wife refused to receive her into the family, in consequence of which Button left them in the spring of 1849, and went to live on another lot of land in which he had some interest. He continued to live in a small shanty on that lot, with his second wife, till he died in July or August, 1850. A few days before his death, on the 24th of July, 1850, Button made another will, which was prepared by the medical man attending him, and was duly executed. By this will he expressly revoked all former wills, and directed that his debts and funeral expenses should be paid out of his personal property if sufficient; "and my will" (he said) "likewise is, that my executors shall sell my estate, as soon as convenient after my death —that is, my landed estate, lot number 15 in the first concession of Windham—and the proceeds to be equally divided among my four daughters, Elizabeth Heron, Olive Daniels, Hannah Throop, and Abba Edmonds. If my personal property should not be sufficient to pay off my debts, the residue shall be taken from my landed property above mentioned." The will appointed certain persons to be executors.

It was proved that the defendant Edmonds had made considerable improvements on the farm during his occupation.

There was no proof of any influence or constraint being used by Button's second wife, or by any one, to induce him to make the last will. He had before made a will which would have had substantially the same effect in giving to his daughters equally the proceeds of this land. There was really no proof of Button not being of sound disposing mind when he made his will, nor indeed at any time, farther than might be accounted for by occasional illness. The evidence that he was able perfectly to understand his will when he did execute it, and that it was read over to him before execution, was distinct and positive, and was uncontradicted.

The learned judge directed the jury that if the last will

was executed by Button, while in the possession of his proper faculties, without coercion or undue influence it must operate as a revocation of the former will, under which the defendant's claim was in part founded, and would leave the defendant nothing but the agreement of the 5th of July, 1841, to support his right to the possession. That if that deed conveyed no legal estate in the land, then, as the will last executed only amounted to a power to the executors to sell the land would descend to the four daughters as co-heiresses.

With regard to the performance by Edmonds of the conditions mentioned in the deed of the 5th of July, 1841, the learned judge thought that the evidence preponderated in Edmonds's favour, though there might have been some slight differences which were reconciled. Button seemed satisfied with his treatment till he departed. He concluded by leaving to the jury to find—1st, Whether the will set up by the plaintiff as a revocation of the first will was duly executed by Button without coercion or improper influence, and while in the full possession of his mental faculties: and 2ndly, Whether the agreement of the 5th of July, 1841, had been duly performed by the defendant Edmonds and his wife.

The jury found that the agreement was duly performed by Edmonds and his wife, and that, the last will was not executed by Joseph Button while of sound and disposing mind, and they rendered a verdict for the defendant.

Freeman moved for a new trial, on the grounds that the verdict was rendered perversely, and against law and evidence and the judge's charge, and for the reception of improper evidence.

Read shewed cause, and cited 12 Vic. ch. 71, secs. 8, 14; Co. Lit., 42 *a*, 216 *b*; 1 Roll. Abr. 845; Freeman dem. Vernon v. West, 2 Wils. 165; 1 Leon 129; 3 Bulst. 252; doe dem. Jackson v. Ashburner, 5 T. R. 163; Alderman v. Neate, 4 M. & W. 704.

Freeman, contra, cited Vin. Abr. "Deeds" I., page 412.

ROBINSON, C. J., delivered the judgment of the court.

We think there should be a new trial, with costs to abide the event. The learned judge, it appears, did incline so

strongly against the sufficiency of the evidence to set aside
the last will on the ground of the testator's mental incapacity
that the verdict is complained of as having been perversely
rendered against his charge ; but it appears to us that there
was an error in submitting to the jury any question upon that
point, and more especially in submitting to them any question
as to whether there had been improper coercion or constraint
used in obtaining the will.   There really was no evidence
whatever on which to rest a verdict against the will on either
ground.   The testator was an old man but it was not shewn
that his mind was gone or even shaken, while there was clear
and direct evidence of his sanity ; and as to constraint, we see
no grounds for suspecting it.   It was not shewn that the
second wife in any way interfered, even by persuasion, and
the will makes no provision for her.   It may be conjectured
that the second wife resented her not being received by Mrs.
Edmonds, but surely the jury were not at liberty to act upon
such a conjecture without evidence, and to infer from it constraint of which there was no evidence, and constraint sufficient in a court of law to amount to a proof that a testator
could not and did not exercise his own will—when it was
abundantly proved by disinterested witnesses that the testator
was in every way capable of directing his own conduct, and
when this testimony was uncontradicted.

It is to be remembered, too, that the testator by this will
makes such a disposition of his estate as placed Mrs. Edmonds
on the same footing with his other daughters ; in fact, a
will of the same kind as one he made long before he contracted his second marriage.

The case necessarily turns, we think, altogether on the
validity of the second will for the deed of July, 1841, gave
no estate of inheritance in the property to Edmonds and his
wife or to either of them.   Independently of the technical
difficulty of the necessity of words of grant sufficient to pass
a present estate and of the impossibility of creating by deed
a fee simple estate that shall commence *in futuro*—for this
is no case of a remainder limited after a particular estate to
some other party—it was the plain intent of this instrument,
shewn by its reference to the then existing will, that the tes-

tator meant only to give an assurance that he would leave that will to operate, and would not change the disposition which he had made therein of his property, provided Edmonds and his wife should maintain the testator and his wife in comfort so long as they lived; and the testator for that purpose agreed to allow them to come upon the place and hold it, and support him there in the meantime—that is, until they could take the estate under his will.

It is not necessary now to determine whether any remedy could not be had against the representative of the testator for a breach of this agreement, if it be true, as the jury found, that the condition had been fulfiled. That is quite another question. We have at present only to determine where the legal estate is. It certainly cannot be in Edmonds and his wife by virtue of the first will, if that will has been revoked. The writing could not and did not convey an estate in fee simple, to vest *in futuro*. It merely gave a right to occupy till the testator's death, and nothing contained in it, unless it amounts to a legal conveyance of an estate in fee simple, can operate as an estoppel upon the devices in the second will from asserting their right. Those cases which were cited where a plaintiff in ejectment has been prevented from recovering possession against his own covenant for quiet enjoyment, do not apply to such a case. Estoppels *in pais* arising from the conduct and declarations of parties, do not operate upon estates so as to bind the rights of other parties, though they disable the party himself from acting inconsistently with his own former conduct.

Rule absolute.

COMMERCIAL BANK V. MUIRHEAD.

Principal and surety—Discharge of surety—Pleading.

Debt on bond against a surety for the performance by W. R. of his duties as agent for the plaintiffs. *Breach*, the conversion by W. R. to his own use of money received for the plaintiffs. *Plea*—That, after the breach the plaintiffs and W. R. accounted together respecting the indebtedness of the said W. R. to the plaintiffs *as such agent and otherwise*, and on such accounting the said W. R. was found indebted to the plaintiffs, *as such agent*, in £4462 8s. 1d.; that the said W. R. then immediately executed and delivered to the plaintiffs a mortgage of certain lands to secure the payment of his said indebtedness, in which said mortgage the said W. R. convenanted to pay the plaintiffs the said sum on certain days and times therein mentioned, whereby the said indebtedness of W. R. became merged in the said specialty, and the time of payment thereof postponed and

delayed withont the consent of the defendent ; by reason whereof the
defendant became absolutely discharged 'from the said debt above
demanded, and damages, &c.

Held, on demurrer, plea bad, as not showing that the consideration for which
the mortgage was taken would include everything that could be proved
under the declaration against the defendant as surety.

This was an action of debt brought against the defendant
as surety in a bond for the faithful performance by one
William Richardson of his duties as agent for the Commercial
Bank at Brantford. *Breach*—That the said William Richardson misspent and unlawfully took away and appropriated to
his own use a large sum of money received by him for the
plaintiffs ; by means whereof, and by the misbehaviour and
neglect of the said William Richardson, the said Bank sustained and suffered great loss and damage and prejudice.

Sixth Plea—That after the making of the writing obligatory, and after the breach of the condition thereof above in
the said declaration mentioned—to wit, on the 1st December,
1838—the plaintiffs and the said W. R. accounted together
respecting the indebtedness of the said W. R. to the said
plaintiffs *as such agentand otherwise* and upon such accounting it was found that the said W. R. was indebted to the said
plaintiffs, *as such agent* as aforesaid, in the sum of £4462
8s. 1d. ; and the said W. R. then immediately after such
accounting made and executed in favour of the said plaintiffs
a certain indenture, sealed with the seal of the said W. R.,
&c., and thereby conveyed certain lands therein mentioned
and described to the said plaintiffs as security for the payment by the said W. R. of his indebtedness to the said
plaintiffs ; and the said W. R. did in and by the said indenture convenant to and with the plaintiffs to pay them the said
sum of £4462 8s. 1d. on certain days and times, and in manner as in the said indenture was and is particulary mentioned;
and the said W. R. then delivered the said indenture, duly
executed, to the plaintiffs, and the plaintiffs then excepted the
same from the said W. R., whereby the said indebtedness of
the said W. R. became merged in the said specialty, and the
time of payment thereof postponed and delayed without the
consent of the defendant ; by reason whereof the defendant
became and is fully and absolutely discharged and exonerated
from the said debt above demanded, and all damages sus-

tained by the plaintiffs by reason of the breach of the condition of the said writing obligatory in the said declaration mentioned.

Demurrer—assigning for cause that the said plea contains no sufficient defence to the cause of action alleged in the declaration : that there was no such merger as is alleged in the plea ; and that there is no valid discharge of the defendant from his liability shewn therein.

Cameron, Q. C., for the demurrer, cited Davey v. Prendergrass, 5 B. & A. 187 ; Field v. Robins, 8 A. & E. 90 ; Ashbee v. Neame, 1 M. & W. 564 ; Aldridge v. Harper, 10 Bing. 118.

M. C. Cameron, contra, cited Mattheson v. Brouse, 1 U.C.R. 272 ; Chy. on Con. 460; McPherson v. Dickson, 8 U.C.R. 29.

ROBINSON, C. J., delivered the judgment of the court.

The questions which present themselves upon this plea are —1st. Does it sufficiently shew that for and in respect of all the causes of action which the bank might have had against Mr. Richardson, and for which the defendant could be held liable in this action, a sum was settled by agreement between them, and a mortgage taken, giving time to Mr. Richardson, the principal, to pay such sum; so that until that time arrived (if indeed at any time) the bank could have had no action against the principal by reason of any misconduct or default, or in respect of anything which, under the condition of the bond, could bring a liability upon the defendant as surety?

2ndly. If the plea does sufficiently shew that, then is the defendant thereby discharged from his bond upon the principle of what civilians call a novation of contract between the principal and the obligee, which in such cases has been held to have discharged the surety ?

The mere giving of time by a creditor to his debtor will not discharge a surety who has become bound in a bond for the debt, whatever ground it may afford for obtaining relief in equity, when the extension of time was given without the consent of the surety, and has been or may have been prejudicial to his interests. The cases cited in the argument on the part of the plaintiffs went principally to that point.

f—VOL. XII. Q. B.

Neither will an absolute agreement by parol to give time to the principal, which is something stronger than the mere fact of a mission to sue, discharge the surety at law from his obligation, where the debt of the principal was of that nature that the parol agreement to give time would not be binding at law, so that the surety would not be thereby disabled from proceeding against the principal in the name of the creditor notwithstanding the parol agreement.   Further than this perhaps, the cases have not gone; and if this were the case of a plain debt existing between Mr. Richardson and the bank, for which this defendant had become surety by bond that it should be paid on a particular day, then if the bank had afterwards, without the assent of the defendant, taken the bond of Mr. Richardson to pay his debt at a more distant day (and perhaps without any extension of time, the effect would be the same), the cases of Rees v. Berrington (2 Ves. Jr. 542) and of Orme v. Young (Holt, N. P. C. 86) are authorities for holding that the defendant could be no longer held liable upon his bond, because he would not be surety for the performance of the only contract which in such a case would be subsisting between the bank and their debtor.   It is the same principle, though applied in rather a different manner, on which the case of Whitcher v. Hall was decided (5 B. & C. 277).

But upon the first point—that is, whether the plea sufficiently shews that there was nothing for which this defendant could otherwise have been held liable under the condition of his bond, which was not, as between the bank and Richardson compromised by the mortgage—we do not see that our way is clear in determining that this does appear by the plea.

The allegations are, that after the breach of the condition in the declaration mentioned, not after all the breaches, the bank accounted with Richardson respecting *his indebtedness to them as such agent and otherwise* (which, we take it, means his indebtedness as agent and his indebtedness on his private account with them) ; that he was found indebted *as agent* in a certain sum, and that a mortgage was taken from him to pay that sum on certain days and times, not saying expressly that any time was given, if that were material ; and this, it is insisted in the plea, operates as a merger of the indebtedness of Richardson, and as a discharge of the defendant from his debt, and from all damages sustained by means of the breach of the condition of the bond.   Now the question on this part of the case is, whether a mortgage for the sum in which Richardson was found indebted *as agent* necessarily concludes the bank as to any complaint they might otherwise have against him for anything that is in the declaration charged as a breach of the condition of the defendant's bond.   For all that appears, he might have been *indebted* to the bank as their agent upon causes of action not involving an unlawful conduct of his part, such as the declaration charges ; for unlawfully mis-spending and taking and appropriating the bank money to his own use, would be something more than mere *indebtedness*.   Suppose, for instance, that Mr. Richardson had rendered his account to the bank, admitting himself to be indebted by bad debts incurred contrary to their instructions, or otherwise, in a certain sum, which he felt it just to assume, and that the bank, believing his account of his indebtedness to be correct, had given him time to pay the money, and had taken his mortgage ;—if they had afterwards discovered that he had in other cases where he had no such excuse · either taken their money and applied it to his own use, or had by his neglect occasioned them great damage, surely their having taken the mortgage for the balance of his mere *debt* as agent would not have disabled them from proceeding for the defalcation and misappropriation which they had afterwards discovered.   On that ground—that this plea does not shew a complete identity between what may have formed the consideration of the mortgage and all that could be proved under this declaration, as imposing a liability on the defendant as surety—We think the plea is insufficient.   If the plea had shewn the identity clearly and to the full extent, I am at present disposed to think that the defence would be good ; I mean, if the plea had stated that the bank had accounted with the defendant of all causes of action which they had, or might or could at any time thereafter have against him, by reason of any such breaches of duty as are averred in the declaration, and had then shewn that the mortgage was taken in full satisfaction of all such breaches of duty and causes of action, then the case would stand on other ground, though such a plea would still be liable to be met by an averment on the other side that the breaches of duty stated in the declaration were not included in the alleged accounting, as indeed they could not be unless they had been all then discovered.

The plaintiffs are in our opinion entitled to judgment on this demurrer.

Judgment for plaintiffs on demurrer.

McGILL v. THE MUNICIPAL COUNCIL OF PETERBOROUGH AND VICTORIA.

Taxes—16 Vic. ch. 183, sec. 11, construction of—"Herein contained" in the last cause construed to apply to that clause only—Money had and received.

The plaintiff paid certain taxes imposed by a by-law of a district council. This by-law was afterwards decided to be illegal in an ejectment brought by this plaintiff to contest the validity of the sale of his lands for these taxes, but it was not quashed by the court, because before the application was made for that purpose it had been repealed by the council who passed it. The plaintiff then brought this action for money had and received, &c., to recover back what he had paid.

During the pendency of this suit a statute was passed (16 Vic. ch. 183) which enacted that taxes imposed under certain by-laws, of which this was one, should be valid, and that any such taxes that had been paid should not be recovered back and notwithstanding the informality of the by-law, should remain chargeable against the land; and (in the eleventh clause) that when lands, had been sold for such taxes, and the owner should neglect to redeem them under the privilege given by the act, the sale should be confirmed—"Provided that nothing *Herein contained* shall be held to make valid the title to any lands which shall have been adjudged to be invalid by any court of competent jurisdiction, or in any way to make void any judgment in any of the superior courts of Upper Canada, or to affect any suit pending therein in which the validity of any such by-law may have been called in question."

Held, that the words "herein contained" must be applied only to the clause in which they occur, and not to the whole act—that being in this case the reasonable, and in general the more obvious, though not the inevitable construction; for otherwise, either the absurdity would result, that as the plaintiff's recovery back would cancel the payment, the land under the provisions of the statute would become chargeable with the same sum:— or the plaintiff having paid the taxes to avoid a sale, would be in a better position than those who had not paid, or whose lands had been sold, which could not have been intended.

The action being defeated by the statute, it was unnecessary to determine the point argued—whether money had and received would lie under the circumstances in which the payment was made.

Debt on simple contract for £1000 : On the common counts, for money had and received—money lent—money paid for interest—and on account stated.   Damages £100.

Plea—Nunquam indebitati.

The sum paid by the plaintiff to the treasurer of the United Counties of Peterborough and Victoria, on the 22nd of February, 1850, and which the plaintiff sought to recover back in this action, consisted, first, of an arrear of taxes accrued between the 1st of July, 1840, and the 1st of January, 1843, under the statutes of the province 59 Geo. III. caps. 7 & 8 ; and secondly, of arrears accrued between the 1st of January, 1843, and the 1st of July, 1848, under a by-law of the Municipal Council of the District of Colborne, passed on the 11th of November, 1842.

A special case was stated for the opinion of the court, of which the material facts are fully set out in the judgment of the Chief Justice.

Hagarty, Q. C., for the plaintiff, cited Doe McGill v. Langton, 9 U. C. R. 91 ; Baldwin v. Johnson, 2 U. C. R. 475 ; Shuter v. Leonard, 3 O. S. 314 ; Knibbs v. Hall, 1 Esp. 84 ; Valpy v. Manley, 9 Jur. 452 ; Kearns v. Durell, 6 C. B. 596 ; Morgan v. Palmer, 2 B. & C. 729 ; Parker v. The Great Western Railway Co., 7 M. & G. 253 ; Atlee v. Backhouse, 3 M. & W. 633 ; Close v. Phipps, 7 M. & G. 586 ; Wakefield v. Newbon, 8 Jur. 735 ; Hills v. Street, 5 Bing. 37.

Wallbridge (with him *Bell*), for the defendants, cited Brown v. McKinally, 1 Esp. 279 ; The Duke de Cadaval v. Collins, 4 A. & E. 866, 867.

The above cases bear only upon the question whether money had and received would lie, under the circumstances of the case ; and this point, as will be seen by the judgment, was not decided.   16 Vic. ch. 183, was referred to, but the case was not argued upon the effect of that statute.

ROBINSON, C. J.—With respect to the first portion of the amount—namely, that accruing up to the 1st of January, 1843, under the provincial statutes—there can be no question that the plaintiff has no claim to have that repaid to him. It cannot be said that that was money to which the defen-

dants were not justly and legally entitled, and which therefore, they ought not in good conscience to retain. On the
contrary, it was both justly and legally due. It ought to
have been paid in each year, as it accrued, without compulsion,and the circumstance of its having been paid in at the
same time with other money to which the defendants were
not entitled (admitting the fact to be so),can give no pretence
for suing for it back. As regards the other portion, this
action raises a question of considerable difficulty, as it seems
to me, and one certainly of much delicacy and importance.

In October, 1849, the plaintiff's lands having been returned as being in arrear for taxes from the 1st of July, 1840, to
the 1st of July, 1848, were sold under the authority of the
Municipal Council; and, what has a singular appearance,
while unexplained, were bought in by themselves at the sale.

The portion of arrears claimed for the period between the
1st of January, 1843, and the 1st of July, 1848, was claimed
as having accrued under a by-law of the defendants, the
Municipal Council of Peterborough and Victoria, passed on
the 11th of November, 1842, which by-law was plainly on
the face of it illegal, for reasons stated in the judgment
given in this Court in Trinity term, 15 Vic., in an ejectment brought by the present plaintiff, in order to test the
validity of the sale for taxes (9 U. C. R. 91). In the Hilary
term after that judgment was given, by which the plaintiff
recovered the land in question in that action, on the ground
that this court held the sale to be illegal.

We were applied to by the plaintiff to quash the by-law,
but we declined doing so, because the illegal by-law had
been long ago repealed by the council themselves, by a by-
law passed on the 8th of February, 1848, which was to take
effect on the 5th of July, 1848—See 9 U. C. R. 562.

. This portion then of the taxes which the plaintiff paid in
February,1850,had accrued under a by-law passed in November, 1842, which this court, after the plaintiff had paid the
taxes, viz., in Trinity term, 1852, determined to have been
from the first void and illegal, as being beyond the authority
of the District Council of Colborne to pass, but which by-law
had never been quashed because it had never been moved

against until after it was no longer in force, having been repealed in February, 1848, or rather from the 5th of July, 1848.

. None of the proceedings towards the sale of the lands in December, 1849, were taken under the by-law of November, 1842, for that perscribed no method of proceeding for collecting the taxes further than by directing that they should be levied in the manner prescribed by law, which could only have been intended, I suppose to refer to the provisions of 4 & 5 Vic. ch. 10. Whether the Municipal Council of the County could legally sell the land for payment of taxes imposed by the by-law, was discussed by this court on the ejectment case already referred to (9 U. C. R. 98–9), but we did not find it necessary to determine the point; nor is it material now in order to dispose of any question before us, especially since the passing of the late statute 16 Vic. ch. 183, which was meant to prevent as far as possible any litigation on that point.

. If the by-law of November, 1842, were wholly void from its inception as we must now take it to have been, and as it undoubtably was then it must follow in my opinion, that the taxes imposed by the provincial statutes 59 Geo. III caps. 7 & 8, were not superseded by anything provided by that by-law, and that the one fifth or one-eighth of a penny in the pound of the assessed value of lands, must be held to have been payable under those statutes throughout the whole period in question, viz. to the 1st of July, 1848 ; for the District Council only intended to impose by their law certain rates in lieu of and exceeding those imposed by the statute—they did not intend to abolish the former rates and impose none other in lieu, if they could have done so. I think, therefore, that £126 16s. 6d. was rightly charged against the plaintiff's lands, if that be a correct calculation of the amount he would have had to pay up to the 1st of July, 1848, under the provincial statutes. This would leave the portion of the rates about which there is still a legal question to be determined, £81 10s. 6d. ; and before we examine upon what footing the plaintiff's action to recover back that amount can be held to rest according to the principles of the common law, it is necessary that we should consider carefully what effect, if any, the late statute 16 Vic. ch. 183, should have in disposing of the question.

This action was commenced on the 12th of November, 1852. The first, second, fourth, fifth, eighth, tenth, and eleventh, clauses of the statute require to be considered.

It seemed to be assumed in the argument of this case last term, that that statute did not affect the questions to be determined in this action. In some respects and as to some purposes that may appear to be so, for this by-law of November, 1842, has neither been disallowed by the government, nor been quashed by any court and we must always bear that in mind in applying the several clauses of the statute. This action, it is true, was pending before and when the statute was passed, but it does not therefore follow that the provisions of that statute cannot interfere with the plaintiff's right to recover back the money which he has paid under the by-law, and this independently of the principle that the money having been paid with a knowledge of the facts cannot, as it is contended, be recovered back.

The statute had several objects in view First to make by-laws legal which had been open to exception as being contrary to the terms of the statute under which the district councils derived their authority. These the Legislature determined to maintain, even as regarded their future operation, provided they had not been disallowed or quashed, and provided they did not impose a larger tax than might legally have been imposed. These the Legislature upheld, but with certain restrictions which it is not necessary to dwell upon, because the by law in question having been repealed by the council which passed it there can be nothing further done under it, so that this object of the statute has no application in regard to this by-law.

Then by the fourth clause of the act provision is made in regard to taxes that had been charged under any of these irregular by-laws, which, like that in question, have not been disallowed or quashed ; and the provision is that such taxes as have been paid under the by-law, illegal though it was, shall not be recovered back, and where they have not been paid, they shall (notwithstanding the informality of the by-law) remain chargeable against the land—with a certain restriction as to the amount which this statute imposes.

Then, as to the lands sold for the payment of any taxes accrued under illegal by-laws, opportunity is given to the owner to redeem them, under certain equitable conditions, notwithstanding they had been conveyed to the purchasers (sec. 9). We need not consider this part of the statute, because the plaintiff's lands were redeemed by his paying the amount charged against them, and they were not conveyed.

The last provision of the statute applies to those cases in which lands had been sold to pay taxes that had been charged wholly or in part under illegal by-laws, and had been conveyed to the purchasers at such sales—and which the former owner should fail to redeem under the privilege given to him by this statute. The Legislature in such cases confirms the titles made under the sales for taxes, where the former owner shall neglect to redeem them; but with this proviso (in the 11th clause), "that nothing *herein contained* shall be held to make valid the title to any lands which shall have been adjudged to be invalid by any court of competent jurisdiction, or in any way to make void any judgment in any of the superior courts of Upper Canada, *or to affect any suit pending therein, in which the validity of any such by-law may have been called in question.*"

It has perhaps been assumed that this proviso prevents anything which is contained in the second and fourth clauses of the act from affecting this suit, but I do not take that to be the legal effect of the proviso, or the reasonable construction of the act. The question arises wholly under the last two lines, which we must read as follows : " Provided also, that nothing *herein contained* shall be held to affect any suit pending in any of the superior courts of Upper Canada, in which the validity of any such by-law may have been called in question." If the words *"herein contained"* as here used should be taken by us to refer to the whole statute, and not merely the eleventh clause, then it is clear that nothing in the second or fourth clause, or in any other part of the act, could be allowed to affect the plaintiff's right to recover in this action, and we must then dispose of it as we should have done if no such statute had been passed. But I consider that the proper grammatical construction to be given to the word "herein" confines it to the clause in which it is used, and that the word does not over-ride the entire act.

In the second clause there is a proviso that nothing *in the act* contained shall be held to make lawful any by-law that had already been disallowed or quashed. That, of course, must be applied to the whole act, but it is different where the word "herein" is used, and not the words "in this act." There the proviso may be properly confined to anything contained in the clause, though I do not consider that we must inevitably so confine the meaning, if the giving the more extended construction to the word "herein" would better comport with the evident intention of the Legislature (a). I mean only to say that the applying the word to the clause and not to the whole act, would be in general the more obvious and the safer construction; that it is in the case before us the more sensible and reasonable construction, taking into view all the provisions of the act; and that we should therefore so understand it. The Legislature surely never could have meant that those whose lands had been sold and conveyed away because they had not paid these taxes should lose their lands forever, unless they should redeem them by paying what the statute exacts; and that those whose lands had not been sold, should still hold them chargeable with these taxes; and yet that those who had paid the taxes in order to prevent a sale should be allowed to recover them back, and this perhaps years after the councils had spent the money.

I think, if we read the eleventh clause carefully, we shall see that the Legislature have said nothing more in it than this—that if the owners of lands which have been sold to pay these illegal taxes, or these taxes irregularly imposed, shall omit to take advantage of the power of redeeming them which this act gives, by paying what the act directs, they shall lose their lands and the sales shall be confirmed; but, with this exception, that notwithstanding this general enactment that such sales shall be confirmed, those cases

---

(a) See Becke v. Snith 2 M. & W. 195 ; Stracey v. Nelson, 12 M. & W. 544.

shall be excepted in which the sale of any particular lands has been held invalid by judgment of a court in an action brought to try the right as regarded such lands, or to make void any judgment of a superior court which stands opposed 'to the confirmation of a title under such sale; as, for instance, where the effect of such sale may have been otherwise called in question, as in actions of covenant or trespass brought to try the right; nor shall the provision in this clause *confirming the sales,* or in other words, nor shall "anything herein contained, affect any suit pending in which the validity of any by-law may have been called in question." They felt it necessary not only to prevent the statute from reversing judgments that had been already pronounced, which judgments were inconsistent with the sales referred to being held valid, but also to prevent this clause of the statute from having the effect of confirming such sales in a manner that might change the rights of parties in any suit which was then pending.

Further than that I think the proviso in the eleventh clause does not go, and was not intended to go; and indeed, if we were to take the words "herein contained" to apply to all the clauses of the statute, as well as to the eleventh clause, then it would remain to be considered, that if in consequence of that construction we should hold the plaintiff entitled to recover back the taxes which he had paid, then the effect of such recovery would be to cancel the payment and leave the taxes yet in arrear,—and the lands, as it seems to me, would then remain chargeable with the tax under the express words of the 4th clause, just as they would have been if they had never been paid to the treasurer, which would make the recovery back in this action an absurdity. It could never be held that by the operation of the proviso in the eleventh clause, and its effect upon the fourth clause, a person in the situation of the present plaintiff could defeat the payment that had been made by him, and yet not be obliged to pay again, for then he would be in a situation unlike that of every other person who had not paid the taxes.

For these reasons, I think the plaintiff cannot recover; for it would be repugnant to reason to allow him to recover

back the taxes, if they must in consequence be chargeable
on his land—it would be creating trouble and confusion to
no purpose.   If we did not take this view of the statute, it
would be necessary to go into the consideration of the other
question—whether money paid as this was could or could
not be recovered back.   But for the reasons I have stated,
the statute, in my opinion, settles the question, and renders
the consideration of this other point immaterial.

BURNS, J.—It is unnecessary to consider the question upon
which this case was rested in the argument, for it must be
decided upon another ground, which I think fatal to the
plaintiff.   The difficulty in his way is created by the effect of
the statute 16 Vic. ch. 183.   It is true that this statute was
passed after these parties were at issue, and there is no plea
subsequently bringing the matter to the notice of the court.
I do not conceive that, however, to be necessary in the case
of a public act of Parliament, which the court is bound to
notice.   In Todd v. Emly (9 M. & W. 606), it was held that
where the subject matter arose at Nisi Prius in the presence
of the judge, and so became a fact within his own personal
knowledge, it was not necessary that a plea *puis darrein
continuance* should be accompanied by an affidavit, which
in ordinary cases appears to be indispensable, unless the
court order otherwise.   It appears to me that an act of
Parliament of this description altering the law, is much
stronger ; and that in such cases, not only need there be no
affidavit accompanying a plea setting up the altered law,
but there need be no plea for the purpose, and the court
must judicially take notice of the fact.

The statute mentioned legalizes the rates imposed under
the by-law which had been held to be illegal, and the fourth
section declares that where the money has been paid it shall
not be recoverable back, and further enacts that the lands
shall be chargeable with such tax as was intended to be
imposed.   Other sections provide for enforcing payment.
If the plaintiff must succeed in this action, it would then
follow that the taxes have not been paid, and in such case he
would be obliged to repay all the taxes, or the land would be

sold. The principle upon which the action for money had and received is based fails in a case where, if the court allow it to be sustained, it follows that the money can be obtained back again by some other means or process. A strong instance of this is the case of Simpson v. Swan (3 Camp. 291). This view will dispose of the demand for the return of the amount of the taxes, unless there be anything in the eleventh section which saves the plaintiff's right. I do not look upon the proviso in the eleventh section as over-riding the whole act, but consider that it applies only to the matters contained in that section. If it be read to over-ride the whole act, the result would then be to place those who happened to be fortunate enough to have commenced an action before the act passed to recover the money paid for taxes back, either upon the footing of being exempt from the taxes altogether, or of a right to receive the amount and afterwards repay it. The latter is an absurdity, and we cannot suppose that was intended. If the other were intended, or whether intended or not, if that be the meaning of the words, we should have to construe it so, then one class would stand on a different footing from others. The fourth section contains no exception, and by its provisions all lands are to be chargeable with the taxes. To be consistent, the proviso in the eleventh section must mean something else than to exempt the lands of those who may have commenced actions to recover back the money paid, and the only way to render the whole consistent is to read the words *herein contained* as applying to the section itself and not to the whole act. The same words are used in other sections, where clearly the expression is confined to the section. If the context, however, shewed the intention to be that the words *herein contained* required the wider interpretation to be given, of course it would be done; but in this case the context is otherwise, and the section itself contains sufficient to give effect to the expression without going outside of it.

In this case it may be said the plaintiff has paid money before the time he would have been obliged to pay it, had it not been for the illegal by-law, and so having lost the use of his money in the meantime, therefore he ought to be entitled to recover the interest. Here there is no contract to pay interest—the demand for it is incidental to the claim for the principal, and as that fails the adjunct must share the same fate. With regard to the expenses paid to the sheriff, I do not see that the plaintiff can recover. If the by-law were illegal, then the taxes remained as provided for under the former statutes, and the lands had become liable to be sold. The plaintiff should then at least have offered to pay such amount when the lands were liable to be sold. I have had more doubt respecting the sum of 20 per cent. paid by the plaintiff as redemption money than the others. If the lands had been purchased by some purchaser on his own account, and though the money were paid upon an illegal demand for it, yet by the 6th Geo. IV. ch. 7, which imposes the penalty, the purchaser would receive the redemption money; and in such case I do not well see how the plaintiff could recover it from the corporation. In this case Messrs. Langton and Shandan purchased in their names in behalf of and as trustees for the corporation. It is far from creditable to the corporation thus to speculate upon the lands of individuals, while the lands are taxed by the corporation, and to pay those taxes the land is being sold. That is a matter, however, between Messrs. Langton and Shandan and the corporation, and cannot affect legal liability of the plaintiff to pay something for redemption, because a portion of the taxes paid were legally imposed. It is a matter of indifference to him who pockets that portion of the money. I apprehend that the effect of 16 Vic. ch. 183, prevents any claim to recover back any portion of the redemption money.

Judgment for plaintiff.

FISHER V. THE MUNICIPALITY OF VAUGHAN.

Obstruction of Road—Pleading—Evidence.

In an action on the case for obstructing a road, the plaintiff declared that he was possessed of a certain close, and *by reason thereof* was entitled to a certain way, and he charged the defendant with obstructing the said way while he, the plaintiff, was so possessed of the said close, and so entitled to the said way as aforesaid. The defendants traversed the right of way set up.

Held, that upon these pleadings the plaintiff was bound to show an easement as alleged in the declaration, and could not proceed for the obstruction of a public highway; and even if he could, it would have been fatal to his case that no special damage was alleged, without which he could have no right of action as a private individual.

This was an action on the case for nuisance in obstructing a road.

The plaintiff alleged in his declaration that he was possessed of a certain close in the Township of Vaughan, and that *by reason thereof* he had, and of right ought to have, a certain way from his said close towards certain other closes in the said township, and through and over the same, towards a certain common and public highway in the township aforesaid, and into the same, and back again from the said common and public highway towards the said closes, and over the same to the closes of the plaintiff; and he charged the defendant with having obstructed the said way, while he, the plaintiff, was *so possessed* of the said close *and so entitled* to the said way as aforesaid.

There was no particular damage stated in the declaration to have been suffered by the plaintiff from the obstruction of the way, such as might entitle an individual to an action for obstructing a *common and public highway,* if the plaintiff could be understood as complaining of a nuisance of that kind.

The defendant pleaded a special plea, setting up that the way mentioned in the declaration was a *common* public highway, such as the defendants were by law authorized, upon a proper proceeding, to close and stop up, if they saw cause for doing so; and that, before the injury complained of, they had, by a by-law duly passed, closed and shut up the said highway. This plea was demurred to, and was held to be bad, on the ground that the plaintiff was not complaining of the obstruction of a common public high-way, such as the Municipal Council of the township could in their dis-

cretion direct to be closed, but of an obstruction to a right
of way which he had *by reason of his possession of a certain close*, which description of the road conveyed the idea
of a private easement, and not a common public highway;
that the council had no authority to close up any but common public highways; and that, if the way in question was
not one which the plaintiff could claim by reason of any
peculiar right and privilege, the defendant should have
traversed that he had such an easement as that which he
claimed; for if he had, then the council could not extin-
guish his private easement, though they might have provided that it should no longer be a common or public highway, if it had by any means acquired that right (*a*).

Besides this plea, which was held bad upon demurrer, the
defendants had pleaded a plea, simply traversing the right
of way set up in the declaration; and upon that defence,
and the plea of not guilty, the case went down to trial at
the last assizes. Upon the plaintiff's statement of the case
to the jury, the learned judge held that he could not sustain his action, and the defendants submitted to a nonsuit,
with liberty to move against it.

Dempsey moved accordingly, citing Johnson v. Boyle, 11
U. C. R. 101; Regina v. Spence et al., 11 U. C. R. 45;
Greasly v. Codling, 2 Bing. 263; Wilks v. Hungerford
Market Co., 2 Bing. N. C. 281.

ROBINSON, C. J., delivered the judgment of the court.

We think there is no room for doubt as to the propriety of
the nonsuit, upon the double ground that the plaintiff shewed
no special damage which should entitle him to maintain an
action, if we could regard the plaintiff as complaining of a
public nuisance; and upon the further ground, that upon the
pleadings, the plaintiff was bound to shew an easement such
as he had alleged, and could not rest his case upon proof of a
common public highway, when his alleged easement had been
denied. If he could have been allowed to show a common
public highway, and not a highway which he enjoyed merely

(*a*) The case referred to by the Chief Justice is not reported. The plea
was decided to be bad at the argument, without time taken to consider.

by reason of his possession of a certain close, then it must have followed that the defendants should be permitted to shew that there was no common public right of way existing at the time of the alleged injury, because a by-law had before been passed for closing the road.

The plaintiff, at the trial, rested his case upon its being a public highway, which was inconsistent with his own declaration, and with the ground upon which he obtained judgment on the demurrer ; and if, after the plea traversing the easement which he had alleged, he could have proceeded as for an injury arising from the obstruction of a common public highway, then it was fatal to his case that he had alleged no special damage which could give him a right to sue individually for his share of the injury arising from a public nuisance. Not having alleged any such special damage, he could not be allowed to give evidence of any. In Greasly v. Codling (2 Bing. 263). and Wilks v. The Hungerford Market Co. (2 Bing. N. C. 281), which were cited by Mr. Dempsey, the declaration contained particular allegations of special damage, on which ground expressly the actions were upheld. There is nothing of the kind in this case.

Rule refused.

REGINA V. ORR.

Quarter Sessions—Order to pay costs of appeal—Indictment for disobedience of.

The Court of Quarter Sessions have no authority to order a person to pay any part of the costs of an appeal to them from a conviction, after he has been acquitted on such appeal, or to convict him of an offence for disobeying such order.

The defendant Orr had been convicted before a justice of the peace upon some charge, the nature of which was not stated either in the indictment placed before the court, or in the case stated; and having appealed to the Quarter Sessions from the conviction, he was tried by a jury upon the charge at last April sessions, and was acquitted. The court thereupon made an order, taxing the costs of the appeal and trial at £3 3s. 5d., and directing that "each party shall pay one-half of the above costs." An indictment was afterwards preferred against Orr, at the instance of the clerk of the peace, for non-payment of his costs according to the order.

The indictment stated that, at the General Quarter Sessions of the Peace, holden for the United Counties of Lanark and Renfrew on the 5th of April, 1853, at Perth, before &c. it was ordered by the same justices and court there, in the appeal, Robert Orr, appellant, John Elliot, respondent—the jury having quashed the conviction—that each party shall pay one-half of his costs, viz; that is to any (setting out the items), as by the said order, reference being had thereto, will more fully appear; of which said order the said Robert Orr, appellant aforesaid, in the order aforesaid named, afterwards, to wit, on, &c., was duly and personally served with a copy ; nevertheless, the said Robert Orr unlawfully and contemptuously, upon being served with said order, did neglect and refuse to pay his portion of said costs, to wit, the sum of £1 11s. 8½d., as by the said order he, the said Robert Orr, was required to do : nor hath he, the said Ropert Orr, at any time since complied with the said order, although often requested so to do, in contempt of our Lady the Queen and her laws, to the evil example of all others in like case offending, and against the peace of our said Lady the Queen, her crown and dignity.

The defendant was found gulty ; and the question as to the sufficiency of the indictment to sustain a conviction was reserved for the opinion of this court.

No counsel appeared to argue the case on either side.

ROBINSON, C. J., delivered the judgment of the court.

We do not know on what principle this indictment for not paying costs has been preferred, nor on what authority the Quarter Sessions may have supposed they could order a defendant charged with an offence to pay costs, notwithstanding he had been acquitted by the jury who tried him.

The indictment, of which a copy has been transmitted to us, does not charge the refusal or neglect to pay costs to be an offence against any statute ; and certainly the common law gives no authority to the Court of Quarter Sessions to convict a person of an offence in not obeying an order to pay the costs of an appeal from a conviction after he has been acquitted on his trial which followed the appeal.

We should have been informed by the case, on what principle or under what statute, the indictment was attempted to be supported.   I suppose it must have been under the statute 13 & 14 Vic. ch. 54, but there is nothing in that statute to authorize an order that a defendant who has appealed and been acquitted by a jury upon his trial shall pay the costs of the appeal and trial, or any portion of them.

The act plainly imports the contrary, for it provides that in case of the *affirmance* of the conviction, the court shall order the offender to be punished according to the conviction, and to pay such costs as shall be awarded.   Besides, there is nothing in the order directing to whom the costs are to be paid.   There is nothing in the statute to make the non-payment of them an indictable offence ; and if there were, still the indictment does not profess to be founded upon any statute ; and if an indictment would lie in such a case, the one before us is altogether imperfect and defective.

We must therefore direct (under statute 14 & 15 Vic. ch. 13) that judgment arrested.

Judgment arrested.

DOUGALL v. THE SANDWICH AND WINDSOR PLANK AND
GRAVEL ROAD COMPANY.

Sandwich and Windsor Road Company—Limits of their road.

Held, upon the special case stated below, that the defendants, a joint stock road company, incorporated under 12 Vic. ch. 84, had no authority to construct their road through the town of Windsor, or beyond the entrance of the town from Sandwich—the road which they were authorized to make being described in their instrument of incorporation filed under the act as a road *from the town of Sandwich to the town of Windsor.*

Secondly—That as no limits had been assigned to the town of Windsor when the defendants were incorporated, the court would look to what the proprietor of land on which a part of what was commonly called Windsor stood, had designated Windsor on a plan which he had filed in the Registry office, and referred to in giving deeds ; and to the popular understanding as to what constituted Windsor ; and that, taking these facts as guides, it was quite clear that the road had been extended into the town and a toll-gate placed within the limits.

Thirdly—That it was immaterial that at a public meeting held in Windsor it had been resolved to make no opposition to the road, for this could not bind the plaintiff.

ASSUMPSIT money for had and received. Plea, Non-assumpsit.

The following special case was agreed upon, and submitted for the opinion of the court :—

"We the attorneys of the plaintiff and defendants, respectively, do, as such attorneys, hereby undertake, promise, and agree, each to and with the other, that, in order to save the expense of the production of witnesses and documents on the trial of this cause, we will consent that a verdict shall be taken on the occasion in favor of the plaintiff, for one shilling damages, the said verdict to stand or be set aside, and a verdict thereupon entered for the defendants, according to the opinion of the court above, upon the following facts of the case, which are agreed upon between us, viz. :—

"*Firstly.* It is admitted on behalf of the defendant at the instance of the plaintiff, that 'The Sandwich and Windsor Plank and Gravel Road Company' was, on the third day of February, 1852, incorporated 'for the construction of a road from the town of Sandwich to the town of Windsor,' as stated in their 'instrument' of association or charter, filed according to law, in the register office of the county on the organization of the said company ; a true copy of which said 'instrument' is hereto annexed, marked (No. 1).

"*Secondly.* That the said company have since constructed a gravel road from a point 'commencing at Detroit Street in the said town of Sandwich,' at the corner of the property there belonging to Miss Hall, and continuing up to, and through, the town of 'Windsor,' to lot No. eighty-six (township of Sandwich), owned by Arthur Rankin, Esquire, —the distance being about two and a half miles from one extreme point to the other ; the said road thus extending over, across, and through the said place called 'Windsor,' to McDougall Street, in the town plot called and known as 'South Detroit.'

"*Thirdly.* That in the said place called 'Windsor,' to wit, at a point near the limit between lots numbers eighty-two and eighty-three, the said company have erected a toll-gate, whereat they did, prior to the first day of October instant collect, and have subsequently collected, tolls from the plaintiff as well as others, for passing over with their animals and vehicles that portion of the said road, which they have so constructed, being within the place so called the 'town of Windsor' in the said registered instrument of association or charter.

"*Fourthly.* That a map or plan of a portion of the said place called 'Windsor' (composed of the front part of lots numbers seventy-nine and eighty in the first concession of the said township of Sandwich), as laid out by the late François Baby, Esquire, and by him designated as a portion of the town of 'Windsor,' has been, since the commencement of the construction of the said gravel road, filed, with some alterations upon his original plan, in the register office of the said county.

"*Fifthly.* That a deed from the said late François Baby to the plaintiff dated on the 24th day of June, 1845, conveying portions of part of the said lot number seventy-nine forming a portion of 'Windsor' aforesaid), was registered on the 17th day of July following; that in the register book there is appended at the foot of the registry of the said deed a map or sketch of a portion of the said place called 'Windsor,' which map or sketch is referred to in the said memorial in the following terms to wit, 'Which said sketch of the town of "Windsor" in the said indenture of bargain and sale mentioned and which is to the said indenture annexed, and forms a part of the same, being dated on the 24th day of June, 1845, and as the same was made by Alexander Wilkinson, Esquire, a deputy provincial surveyor, is in the words and figures following, to wit,' (here follows the sketch or plan).

"*Sixthly.* That the said place called 'Windsor' is, and has been for many years known and recognized in the post-office department by that name; and that the name of a place in Whitby, formerly called 'Windsor,' was changed in order to avoid confusion in the names of the two places.

"*Seventhly and lastly.* That the said plaintiff paid the said tolls amounting to one shilling at the least, under protest, contending that the said defendants could not lawfully exact tolls for the use of the portion of the said road which they had so constructed within the said place called 'Windsor;' the said portions of road being as he contended, beyond and without the *terminus* indicated by the defendants' instrument filed, or charter for their road."

And it is admitted by the plaintiff, at the instance of the defendants :—

"*Firstly.* That the limits of the said place called 'Windsor' had not, prior to the construction of the said road, been defined by statute or proclamation, and that no map or plan thereof, or of any portion thereof, had, up to that time, been filed in the register office of the county, in pursuance of the provision of law for that purpose, excepting always the sketch forming a portion of the said deed, from the said late François Baby to the said plaintiff, referred to.

"*Secondly*. That, at a meeting of the inhabitants of 'Windsor,' held in the spring of the present year at which the directors of the said road company were present, a resolution having been proposed that a petition should be gotten up to the Township council praying that the said company might be prohibited from constructing their then contemplated road inasmuch as they declined pledging themselves not to erect a toll-gate within the town of 'Windsor,' an amendment to such resolution was proposed and carried, to the effect that there had not been sufficient cause shewn to the meeting to warrant the intended opposition to the contemplated road.

"*Thirdly*. That the distance from the easterly boundary of the town of Sandwich (the point mentioned in the said instrument as the point of commencement of the said road, and which is the site of the western toll-gate on the said road) to the eastern extremity of the said gravel road, as constructed by the said defendants (McDougall Street in 'South Detroit' aforesaid), is about 152 chains and 10 links; that the distance from the said easterly boundary of Sandwich to the westerly terminus of the said road as constructed (Miss Hall's corner, hereinbefore mentioned), is about 36 chains and 50 links; and that the distance from the toll-gate at the said eastery limit of Sandwich to lot number seventy-nine in the said township of Sandwich, and which lot (being a portion of the property of the said late François Baby, so laid out by him as a part of 'Windsor' as aforesaid the) plaintiff contends is within 'Windsor,' is about 110 chains and 60 links.

"*Fourthly and lastly*. That the paper hereto annexed, and marked (No. 2) is really and truly what it purports to be."

It is also agreed by and between the said parties—

"That nothing contained in the admissions of the plaintiff shall be construed into an admission on his part that the village of 'Windsor' does not extend further westward than lot number seventy-nine aforesaid, or even so far as its westerly limit as lately proclaimed.

"It is further agreed that the said company's contract with the contractors for making the said road with the plan thereto annexed, or copies of them, verified by affidavit, may be filed at Nisi Prius or in Banc., and upon which the several different points in the said road, hereinbefore mentioned. may be indicated."

(No. 1).

"Be it remembered that, on this 3rd day of February, 1852, we, the undersigned stockholders, met at Sandwich, in

the county of Essex and Province of Canada, and resolved
to form ourselves into a company, to be called 'The Sandwich and Windsor Plank and Gravel Road Company,' according to the provisions of a certain act of the Parliament of
this province entitled 'An act to authorize the formation of
joint-stock companies for the construction of roads and other
works in Upper Canada,' for the purpose of constructing a
plank road *from the town of Sandwich to the town of Windsor*, along the now travelled road—the greater part of the said
road being on the top of the bank running along the river
'Detroit;' and we do hereby declare that the capital stock
of the said company shall be one thousand pounds, to be
divided into two hundred shares, at the price or sum of five
pounds each; and we, the undersigned stockholders do
hereby agree to take and accept the number of shares set by
us opposite our respective signatures: and we do hereby
agree to pay the calls thereon, according to the provisions of
the said in part recited act, and of the rules, regulations,
resolutions and by-laws of the said company, to be made or
passed in that behalf: and we do hereby nominate Arthur
Rankin, Esq., Josiah Strong, Esq., Thomas Woodbridge,
Esq., Elam Beeman, and Charles Baby, to be the first directors of the said company.

Names.	No. of shares.	Amount.
A. Rankin	100	£500
Josiah Strong	30	150
Elam Beeman	30	150
Thos. Woodbride	20	100
Chas. Baby	20	100

"Witness—JAMES WOODBRIDGE, Junr."

(No. 2).

"Copy of a resolution passed at a meeting of the directors
of 'The Sandwich and Windsor Plank and Gravel Road
Company,' held at Sandwich on the 14th day of February,
1852:—

'That a competent engineer shall be immediately employed to survey and lay out the road extending from Detroit
Street in the town of Sandwich to McDougall Street in the
town of Windsor, and to furnish the directors with plans and
specifications, in order that the grading and planking may
be contracted for with as little delay as possible: the plans
and specifications to give all necessary instructions, so that
the work may be effectually carried on and completed; and

that Arthur Rankin, Esquire, be empowered to employ such engineer on the part of the company.'

"(Copy).

"CHAS. BABY, Secretary."

Prince for the plaintiff.

Cooper for the defendants.

ROBINSON, C. J., delivered the judgment of the court.

This case presents a single point for our decision, and I think we are much indebted to the counsel who settled and prepared the statement for the careful and clear manner in which everything is brought before us that it can be material to consider.

Our conclusion is, that the undertaking for which the defendants were incorporated being plainly described in the instrument filed by them under the statute as an undertaking to construct a road "*from the town of Sandwich to the town of Windsor,*" they have no authority to construct a road through the town of Windsor, or beyond the entrance of the town from Sandwich—the word "to" being clearly not inclusive, but exclusive.

We are also of opinion that,—as it is admitted that at the time of the instrument being registered and the Company formed, there were no limits assigned to the town of Windsor by any statute or proclamation,—there is nothing to guide us but the two facts, of what Mr. Baby, the proprietor of this land on which a part at least of what is called *Windsor* stands, is known to have designated *Windsor* in a plot which he had referred to—or the popular understanding in respect to what constituted "Windsor;" and it seems to us abundantly clear that if we are governed by either of these facts, the road has been made far beyond the Western or Sandwich end of Windsor, and the toll-gate has been placed in the town, and where the company have no right to place it.

It was rightly, we think, contended on the argument, that the admissions made on the part of the defendants in the case stated, cut away all ground for argument, by shewing that, if there was any such place as Windsor at all, the road has been carried not merely to it, but into and through it.

It can make no difference, we think, that at a public meeting of the inhabitants of Windsor, held last spring, it was resolved to forbear for the time to make any opposition to the contemplated road, which it then appeared the company were making, with the intention, as it was surmised of placing a toll-gate within the town of Windsor. Any number of the inhabitants in terms agreeing to it, could have no legal effect on the competence of the company to go beyond the purpose for which they were associated. Any one individual was at liberty at any time to question their right, notwithstanding; and the question, when raised, must be determined by the instrument of association.

Besides, in reason, no weight can be given to the amended resolution, carried at the meeting referred to; for the inhabitants, for all that we can tell, might have withdrawn their opposition, from being advised or convinced that if the company should make such a road as they intended, they could still not claim a right to exact a toll within the town, or in respect to any part of the line beyond the western limit of Windsor.

We determine that the plaintiff is entitled to the postea.

Judgment for plaintiff.

OSBORNE V. WRIGHT.

Arbitration—Appointment of third arbitrator.

A submission under a rule of reference was to K. and M., and such person as they should appoint. The affidavits were contradictory as to the fact of a verbal appointment of C. as third arbitrator, and there was no proof of any appointment in writing; but it was sworn that he was chosen by the defendant, as one of two persons proposed by the plaintiff, and that he sat with the others, and voted in the defendant's presence without objection The court, under these circumstances, refused to interfere against an award made by K. and C.

Wilson, Q. C., obtained a rule *nisi* that the plaintiff and Robert Kerr, one of the arbitrators between the parties, should shew cause why the verdict for the plaintiff rendered subject to a reference, and the award subsequently made, should not be set aside on these grounds,—

1st. That there was no appointment in writing of one Isaiah Clarke, who has executed the award, as the third arbitrator.

i—VOL. XII. Q. B.

2ndly. That he was not in fact appointed an arbitrator by the other two arbitrators, Kerr and McMichael.

3rdly.   That Kerr and Clark, without notice to or knowledge of McMichael and the defendant, held a meeting as arbitrators, and made their award.

4thly. That the award is unjust and partial.

. And why the plaintiff, or Kerr, the arbitrator, should not pay the costs of the day, and of the reference, and of this application.

Richards shewed cause, and cited Oliver v. Collings, 11 East, 367.

Wilson, Q. C., contra, cited Carpenter v. Vanderlip, E. T. 3 Vic.; Still v. Halford, 4 Camp. 17 ; Routledge v. Thornton, 4 Taunt. 704.

The facts are stated in the judgment.

ROBINSON, C. J., delivered the judgment of the court.

The rule of reference was upon a submission to two persons, Kerr and McMichael, and such person as they should appoint, so as they, or any two of them, should make their award by a day named.

There is no proof that Clarke, the third arbitrator, was appointed in writing by the other two ; but it is positively sworn that he was chosen by the defendant as one of two whom the plaintiff had proposed, and that he sat with the others, and acted in the presence of the defendant without objection,   The submission is precisely in the same terms as that in Still v. Halford (4 Camp. 17).   That case goes no further than to require that some proof of the appointment of the third arbitrator under such a submission should be given, and that it will not do in an action upon the award to rely upon the mere fact that he sat with the others and joined in making the award.   To that extent the case seems to be recognized as authority.

There is an actual verbal appointment sworn to in this case in the affidavits filed on the part of the plaintiff; and though the defendant contradicts that statement, yet we should not determine in a summary manner between these conflicting statements.   And, indeed, upon considering the affidavits, we do not think we can with propriety make the rule absolute upon any of the exceptions taken. The allegations on the defendant's part are so far repelled as not to leave sufficient ground for interference.

Rule discharged.

NIGH v. SOWERWINE.

Case for overflowing land—Pleading—Evidence.

CASE for overflowing the plaintiff's land, by penning back the water of a stream running through it, and thence over the land of the defendant.

The second count charged that one H. wrongfully erected a dam across the stream, on the defendant's land, which occasioned it to overflow the plaintiff's land, and that the defendant wrongfully kept up the said dam so wrongfully erected by H., whereby the water had been injuriously penned back upon the plaintiff's land.

The third count stated that one H. had erected a dam ten feet high on defendant's close. (not alleging this to be a wrongful act): that one T, wrongfully raised and increased in height and width the dam built by H., by means whereof the water was obstructed and penned back on and overflowed the plaintiff's land; and that the defendant had wrongfully kept up and maintained the dam so wrongfully increased by T.

The defendant pleaded not guilty to the whole declaration, and to the second count a prescriptive right, for the use of a certain mill on his lot. The jury found for the defendant.

Held, that on these pleadings the defendant was entitled to retain his verdict on the third count, as well as on the second; for the plea of not guilty put in issue the erection of a dam by H., charged in the second count, as well as the continuance of it by the defendant; and the gist of the action, and the substantial point involved in both counts, was not the erection of the dam, but the wrongful penning back of the water, which was decided in the defendant's favor by the verdict on the third count.

CASE for overflowing the plaintiff's land.

In the first count the plaintiff charged, that he, being possessed of lot 15, in the second concession of Bertie, and the defendant possessed of lot 16 in the same concession, there was a stream of water running through and over the plaintiff's land, and thence to the land of the defendant: that on the first of August, 1833, one Matthias Hawn erected a dam on the said close of the defendant of the height of ten feet, and that the stream used to run and flow, and of right ought to run and flow, from the plaintiff's land to and through the defendant's close, in its natural course, except so far as it might be interrupted and hindered by the said dam. Yet that the defendant, viz., on the first of May, 1850, and on divers days between that and the commencement of this suit, wrongfully built upon, and raised and increased in length and width, the *said dam,* so built (by Hawn); whereby the water could not flow as it before had been used to do, but was penned back, and overflowed the plaintiff's land.

The second count charged, that on the first of August, 1833, Hawn wrongfully erected a dam across the stream on the land of the defendant, which obstructed the stream, and prevented its flowing in its natural course, and occasioned it to overflow the plaintiff's land, and that the defendant wrongfully kept up and continued the said dam so wrongfully erected by Hawn, for a long time, viz., from the first of May, 1850, hitherto; whereby the water had been injuriously penned back upon and over the plaintiff's land.

In the third count the plaintiff stated, as in the first, that Hawn, on the first of August, 1833, had erected a dam ten feet high on the close of the defendant (not alleging that to have been a wrongful act) and from that time to the committing of the grievance, &c., the stream continued to flow in its natural course to and over the defendant's land, except so far as it was obstructed by Hawn's dam. That one Benjamin Throop, viz., on the first of January, 1850, and on divers days between that and the committing of the grievances now complained of, wrongfully raised and increased in height, and length, and width, the dam built by Hawn, by means whereof the water was obstructed and could not flow as before through the defendant's land, but was penned back on the plaintiff's land, and overflowed the same; and that the defendant, on the first of May, 1850, and from thence hitherto has wrongfully kept up and maintained the dam so wrongfully increased by Throop, &c.

The defendant pleaded—1st, not guilty, to the whole declaration. 2ndly, to the second count, a prescriptive right for twenty-five years to keep the water of a certain height, to wit, of the height of ten feet above the level of the stream, &c., and thereby to pen back the water to such extent as was necessary to enable the occupiers of lot 16 for the time being to use a mill which they had used and enjoyed upon the said close for twenty years, &c.; wherefore the defendant, being the owner and occupier of lot 16, and of the said mill and premises, as of right did keep and maintain the said dam so erected, and being of the height, viz., of ten feet, and thereby necessarily obstructed the water of the said stream "for the purpose of making full and proper use of the said mill, and *no greater*, as he lawfully might for the cause aforesaid," &c.

The plaintiff replied to the second plea, that the respective owners and occupiers of lot 16 did not, for the full period of twenty-five or twenty years next before this suit, actually use and enjoy as of right, and without interruption, the right of placing, erecting, and raising the said dam, as in the second plea mentioned, in manner and form, &c.

The case was tried at Niagara before *Macaulay*, C. J., and a verdict found for the defendant.

Eccles moved for a new trial without costs, for misdirection, and on the law and evidence.

Vankoughnet, Q. C., shewed cause.

ROBINSON, C. J.—I think the learned Chief Justice of the Common Pleas was right in considering, as he did at the trial, that the merits of the case were involved in the second count, and the plea of prescription which applies to that count; because, unless it were made to appear upon the trial that the water had for twenty years next preceding the bringing of this action been kept up as high as the defendant has kept it up by the dam complained of and continued by him, the plea of prescription must have been found against the defendant. The jury by their verdict found that there had been no raising of the water by the defendant higher than it had been for forty years back or more, which is clearly inconsistent with the dam having been raised, as is alleged in the third count, by Throop.

And if, after giving proof of an injury which would come clearly under the second count, and to which the defence pleaded to that count must apply, the plaintiff should nevertheless be allowed to confine his case to the third count, because he thinks the injury stated in that count is not so fully answered, still, in my opinion, if the jury believed the testimony given on the part of the defence, the verdict might properly be rendered for the defendant, on the plea of not guilty to that count, as it has been. The charge against the defendant in the third count is, that he kept up Throop's dam; *and that he, the defendant, thereby and therewith wrongfully penned back and obstructed the water, and prevented it from flowing as it was wont and accustomed to do* before the dam was raised by Throop, and that *the said* water was penned back, and forced out of *its said course ;* that is, out of its course as it existed before Throop's time.

The gist of the action is the actual *penning back of the water by the defendant* beyond the extent to which it had been kept back before Throop's time. The mere making the dam higher, or longer, or wider, is no grievance by itself, unlesss by keeping it up as Throop made it the defendant did in fact overflow the plaintiff's land to a greater extent than had been done before; and of this the defendant pleads that he is not guilty, and the fact that he did keep back the water has not been established to the satisfaction of the jury.

BURNS, J.—I think the Chief Justice was right in declining to tell the jury that the plaintiff should have a verdict upon the third count on the ground that there was an allegation therein contained, not traversed, which upon the evidence would entitle the plaintiff to a verdict. I consider the plea of not guilty in this case does put in issue the question whether there was a wrongful erection of the dam since Hawn's time. If the allegation had been that it was the defendant who wrongfully raised the dam, instead of stating that it was done by Throop, then it could not be questioned that not guilty would put the whole in issue. The question between these parties is not whether one person or another person did it, but whether it was wrongfully done to the injury of the plaintiff. If the plaintiff had alleged that Throop merely raised the dam, then not guilty would have admitted that fact; but the allegation is that Throop wrongfully and unjustly built upon, raised and increased the dam in height, length, and breadth, and that the defendant, to injure the plaintiff, kept, continued, and maintained the same so wrongfully raised, heightened, and lengthened. It is clear, I think, that what Throop is alleged to have done is descriptive of the defendant's act, and is nothing more than if the same had been described to have been done by the defendant himself. The dispute between the parties, as the pleading shew, is not whether Throop, as a matter of fact, did or did not raise the dam, but the question is, whether it was wrongfully raised. If the defendant had pleaded that Throop did not wrongfully raise the dam, the plaintiff might well have said, I think, that such an answer would be an argumentative denial that he himself did not keep, continue, and maintain the dam so wrongfully raised. The effect of not guilty to this declaration, I think, is just this—the defendant says, "I am not guilty of keeping up, continuing, and maintaining a dam so wrongfully raised upon to your injury;" and I think, according to common sense, that involves the wrongful raising, as well as the keeping, continuing, and maintaining; for if it had never been wrongfully raised, it is impossible that it could be continued. See Norton v. Scholefield (9 M. & W. 665); Grew v. Hill (3 Ex. 801).

DRAPER, J., concurred.

Rule discharged.

MAIR v. CULY.

Libel on title to land—Pleading—Justification—Estoppel.

CASE for libel, in publishing a printed notice denying the plaintiff's title to certain land, of which the declaration alleged that he was seized in fee, and which he had advertised for sale, and stating that one C. J. had the title, and that a suit was pending in Chancery to establish her undoubted right.

Second plea—That the plaintiff was not, at the said time, when, &c., seized as of fee of or in the land, or any part thereof.

Third plea—That the matters published by the defendant were at the said times when, and still are true in substance and effect.

Fourth plea—That the said C. J. had, and still has, an undoubted right to the land; and that the defendant so believing, as her agent, and at her request, published the notice, to protect her right, and without malice.

The *fifth plea* alleged that the plaintiff's only title was by virtue of an indenture of mortgage executed to him by one K., who was then seized in fee; that the said indenture was given to secure usurious interest; that the said K. died intestate; and his heir gave to the said C. J. full license to enter on and occupy the said land during her life, and thereupon the defendant, as her agent, published, &c., (as in the fourth plea.)

The plaintiff replied, by way of estoppel, a verdict and judgment in au action of ejectment brought by him against the defendant and one E. Y., to recover possession of this land, in which it was found by the jury that the said indenture was not illegal or usurious.

Held, on demurrer, second plea good. Third plea bad, as too general. Fourth and fifth pleas bad, for omitting to justify the statement that a Chancery suit was pending, that being a very material part of the libel.

Semble, that the replication to the fifth plea shewed an estoppel.

CASE for libel. The declaration averred that the plaintiff was seized in fee of certain land, and charged the defendant with being guilty of a malicious libel, by publishing a printed notice denying that the plaintiff had a title to such estate, which he had advertised for sale on a particular day, and stating in the notice that he could not give a title, for that one Catharine John had the title to the land, and that a suit was pending in Chancery to establish her undoubted right.

The defendant, in his second plea answered the declaration by alleging that the plaintiff was not, at the said time when, &c., seized as of fee of or in the land in the declaration mentioned, or in any part thereof.

The third plea set up as a defence, that the matters published by the defendant were at the said times when, &c., and still are true in substance and effect.

The fourth plea was, that the said Catharine John, at the said several times when, &c., had, and still has, an undoubted right to the land ; whereupon the defendant, believing that the said Catharine John had such right, he, the defendant, as the agent and servant of the said Catharine John, and at her instance and request, composed and published, &c., for the purpose of protecting the said Catharine John in her right, and without any malicious or other unlawful motive whatever.

The plaintiff demurred to each of these pleas.

In a fifth plea the defendant averred that one William Johnson Kerr, before the said times when, &c., was seized in fee of the land, and being so seized, by a certain indenture then made between the said William Johnson Kerr of the first part, and the defendant of the second part—after reciting that the said Kerr, by his bond, bearing even date therewith, was bound to the plaintiff in £1250, with a condition that the said bond should be void on payment by the said Kerr to the plaintiff of £625 within one year from the date thereof—certain lands therein described, being, &c., being the same as the lands in the declaration maintained, were pretended to be conveyed by the said Kerr to the plaintiff, subject to redemption on payment of the said £625, which said pretended indenture, with the patent from the crown to the said Kerr, formed the only title or claim of the plaintiff to the said land; that the said bond and indenture were given to secure the payment of £500 then advanced, and also of £125; being the interest thereon for a year, being at a rate exceeding six per cent., contrary to the statute ; that the said Kerr afterwards, and before the said time when, &c., died intestate and seized in fee of the said land, leaving William Kerr, his eldest son him surviving; that the said William Kerr granted to the said Catharine John full license to enter upon and occupy the said lands during her life ; and thereupon as the agent and servant of the said Catharine John, and at her instance and request, and to protect her rights, he, the defendant, composed and published the matters complained of, without any malicious or unlawful motive.

To this plea the plaintiff replied, by way of estoppel, that before the committing of the said grievance, &c., the defendant and one Edward Young were in possession of the said land, and the said plaintiff then impleaded the said defendant and the said Edward Young in an action of ejectment for the recovery of the possession of the said lands ; that the said defendant and the said Edward Young pleaded that the said plaintiff was not entitled to such possession and issue was thereupon joined; that at the trial of the said issue the plaintiff made title under and by virtue of the said indenture in the said fifth plea mentioned that the jury were charged to enquire, and did enquire whether the said indenture was given to secure the said loan and usurious interest, and that they found the said issue in favor of the plaintiff, and that the said indenture was not given upon such illegal and usurious consideration; and that afterwards, by the judgment of the court the plaintiff recovered against the said defendant and the said Edward Young his possession of the said lands, which said judgment still remains in full force, &c.

The defendant demurred to this replication as shewing no estoppel.

Cameron, Q. C., for the defendant cited Malachy v. Soper, 3 Bing. N. C. 371; Brook v. Rawl. 4 Ex. 521 ; Hanna v. DeBlaquiere, 11 U. C. R. 310.

M. C. Cameron, for the plaintiff, cited J'Anson v. Stuart, 1 T. R. 748 ; Hickinbotham v. Leach, 10 M. & W. 361 ; Clubine v. McMullen, 11 U. C. R. 250 : Doe v. Wright, 10 A. & E. 763 ;

ROBINSON, C. J., delivered the judgment of the court.

I thought at first that the second plea might be insufficient, in not shewing who was seized if the plaintiff was not, or pointing out any defect in his title. It is a principle that pleas of justification must be particular and specific, not vague and general. Viewing this plea as in effect a plea of justification, I was inclined to think that the defendant should have set out such facts as would shew that what he did publish is true ; that is that Mrs. John had the right which he had stated she had, and was proceeding to establish it. But we are now satisfied that the plea is good, and that it is a mere traverse of the plaintiff's alleged interest in the estate which forms the foundation of his claim to sue for the alleged injury.

The third plea we take to be clearly insufficient. The plea, when it is intended as a justification of the alleged slander, must justify specially, stating the particular facts which evince the truth of the imputation—1 Saund. 130, note 1 ; Jones v. Stevens (11 Price 283), 1 Ch. Pl. 522, Rowe v. Roach (1 M. & S. 304).

The fourth plea seems to us to admit of more doubt. It is not, we think, double. It merely alleges Catharine John's title, in order to shew a good ground for acting in the matter by her authority, and for the protection of her interests. Such a defence may be pleaded specially, though it would be available under the general issue, as tending to disprove malice, which the plea of not guilty puts in issue. We incline, however, against the plea, on the ground that it does not go far enough. It ought to have averred that a suit in Chancery was pending, in order to shew that the notice in that respect was no malicious invention, for that specific assertion might have a strong effect in deterring bidders.

As to the replication to the fifth plea, we do not at present see, as the action of ejectment was between these parties, and not in the old form, why, if the question of usury did come up in it, as is averred, and was tried and determined, the judgment entered upon the verdict, which in effect decided that question, should not, with the aid of proper averments, estop the said party from asserting the usury as a fact in this action. Whether the judgment in that action of ejectment would estop the defendant in another action to try the right of possession at another time, would be a different question. However, we do not express a positive opinion on that point. The plea, we think, is bad, because it does not justify a very material part of the libel—namely, that a suit in Chancery was pending, which, for all that is stated in this plea, may have been a mere malicious invention, and as injurious a slander in its effects as anything that is charged. It is of little moment, in fact, whether the plea is sufficient or not, further than as regards costs, for the defence intended to be set up is one of privileged communication, denying malice, and would be admissible under the plea of not guilty, which is on the record.

> Judgment for defendant on demurrer to second plea, and for plaintiff on the demurrer to the third and fourth pleas, and on the demurrer to the replication to the fifth plea.

YOUNG v. THE GRAND RIVER NAVIGATION COMPANY.

Grand River Navigation Company—Liability of, for consequential injuries—
2 W. IV. ch. 13.

The Grand River Navigation Company, under their act of incorporation, are not liable in an action at law for consequential injuries arising from works erected by them on the Grand River, or on lands in the vicinity of the persons injured.

This was an action on the case. In the first count the plaintiff alleged that the defendants had erected certain dams and works, &c., upon land adjacent to and above the plaintiff's close and dwelling house, whereby large quantities of the water of a certain stream, which ought to have flowed to and past the said close and dwelling house of the plaintiff, was penned back, and stopped and turned away, and thereby the said quantities of the water of the said stream became tainted und unhealthy, and generated offensive smells, &c.

Having stated this injury, he then proceeded to charge further that, by reason of the improper construction and management of the said dams, &c.; divers large quantities of the said water burst through and escaped, and were forced with increased violence upon and over the plaintiff's close, washing away the soil and obstructing the dams. And further, that the defendants, by stopping the stream below the plaintiff's close with stone and rubbish, &c., had penned back the water on his close, and forced it to accumulate there, &c.

The last count stated the incorporation of defendants by 2 W. IV. ch. 13, the erection of the dams, &c., and the consequential injury; and averred that the defendants so erected and continued the said dams, &c., because they considered the same to be necessary and convenient for the purposes of the navigation, for the effecting of which they were incorporated: that before the commencement of this suit, to wit, on, &c., the damages suffered by the plaintiff, by reason of the premises, amounted in the whole to £250; that the plaintiff t$_h$en gave notice to the defendants, and the defendants well knew that he, the plaintiff, had suffered such damages, and that the plaintiff was then wholly unremunerated therefor; that the plaintiff then requested the defendants to remunerate him in a reasonable manner, and although a reasonable time within which the defendant could have made such satisfaction, to wit, twenty-four hours from making such request, had elapsed before the commencement of this suit, yet the defendants well-knowing the premises, but not regarding their duty in that behalf, and the said statute, and contriving, &c., to injure the plaintiff, and to defraud and deprive him of all remuneration for the said damages, wholly neglected and refused to remunerate, or to satisfy the plaintiff in any manner whatever, contrary to their said duty and the said statute; and the plaintiff still remains wholly unsatisfied, to his damage of £300.

The defendants demurred to the declaration, alleging several special causes of demurrer, which are not material to be mentioned, as the judgment was given only upon the substantial question, whether, with reference to the statute incorporating the defendants, the injuries stated would be sufficient to sustain an action.

Connor, Q. C., for the defendant. *Martin*, contra.

The clauses of the statute which are material, are noticed in the judgment.

ROBINSON, C. J., delivered the judgment of the court.

In the case of Kerby v. The Grand River Navigation Company, we had occasion to consider the substantial question upon which this case must necessarily turn. The 2nd, 3rd, 4th, 5th, 7th, 8th, and 34th clauses of the act of incorporation of that company, 2 Wm. IV. ch. 13, are all that it appeared to us required to be considered in that case; and we think it is upon these clauses that we must form our opinion upon the sufficiency of either of the two counts in this declaration which are demurred to, for sustaining such an action as has been brought. The conclusion which we then formed, upon a careful examination of the statute, was, that a person whose lands have not been taken possession of or entered upon by the company, but who complains of damages sustained by him in consequence of any dams or other works erected by the company on the Grand River, or on lands in the vicinity of such person, within the limits of the charter, and erected or continued for purposes allowed by the statute, cannot sue the company in an action for *tort*, as if they had acted wrongfully in erecting or continuing such works.

The law gives them authority to do what they are in this case charged with doing; it makes the act therefore lawful, and we cannot allow an action to be sustained for it as for a wrong done. The statute does not, in respect to such consequential damages, provide that the company shall not do the act till they have made compensation, as it does in respect to the taking possession of lands which they may require to occupy.

Such a provision would indeed have been unreasonable and inconvenient, because it could not be known with any certainty what extent of consequential injury would follow till the improvement had been completed; and, at any rate, it is clear that the statute allows the company to go on and do all such things as are complained of here, without first making compensation; so that the wrong, if there be any, does not consist in their putting up dams or piers, or cutting ditches upon lands, or near the river, adjacent to or above the plaintiff's land, without first making him compensation for any consequential damage occasioned to his property, of which he had not been deprived.

There are then but these two considerations —1st, Has the plaintiff a claim to compensation; And 2ndly, Is the plaintiff in a condition, upon what he has shewn, to sue the company in tort, as for a breach of duty in not having made him compensation? It is the last count only that could sustain an action upon that ground. The first is not framed with such a view, but treats the erection and continuing of the dams as giving a ground of action in tort, merely by reason of the consequential injury. In our opinion, the company are under no obligation to compensate the plaintiff in this case for any consequences that may follow from those acts which the legislature made it lawful for them to do in accomplishing a great public work, unless the statute gives them a right to claim compensation. I will only say at present, that I do not see in the clauses I have referred to, nor elsewhere in the act, any clear indication of the legislature intending to give compensation for consequential injuries to persons whose possessions have not been interfered with. But if the seventh or any other clause can be held to admit properly of being so extended, then the remedy is given by the act, and must be pursued. An arbitration must be applied for, and if declined, means can be taken, we take it for granted, to compel it, provided the claims be such as it was clearly intended by the legislature to afford compensation for. Nothing is said in either of the counts demurred to of any refusal by the company to arbitrate.

Judgment for defendants on demurrer.

During this term the following gentlemen were called to the bar, and sworn in:—JOHN O'CONNOR, Junr, CALEB PLATT SIMPSON, THOMAS A. HUDSPETH, THOMAS APPLEBY LAZIER, A. R. DOUGALL, AUGUSTUS GEORGE BOSWELL, JOHN CHARLES RYKERT, EDWARD WILLIAM HARRIS.

EASTER TERM, 1854..

Present :—THE HON. JOHN BEVERLEY ROBINSON, C. J.
"   WILLIAM HENRY DRAPER, J.
"   ROBERT EASTON BURNS, J.

SHORT V. RUTTAN.

Assignment—Construction of, as to goods acquired after its execution—Registration—12 Vic. ch. 74.

The plaintiff and W. entered into an agreement, by which the plaintiff was to make advances upon certain conditions to W.. to enable him to draw out, and to make and get to market, a quantity of timber. It was agreed that the timber then made, and all that might thereafter be made, should be delivered to the plaintiff as security, and in proof of such delivery should be marked as specified, and that it should be rafted to market under W.'s directions. The timber was seized under an execution by the defendant as sheriff, and the plaintiff, claiming under this deed, replevied.

Held, that W. could not be looked upon merely as the agent of the plaintiff, and the timber regarded as the plaintiff's from the first, for that would be inconsistent with the terms of the deed.

Held, also, that the statute requiring registration could apply only to that part of the timber in existence as timber, and owned by W. at the execution of the instrument, but that it clearly applied to that portion, and therefore for want of registration the deed must be held void altogether; but, at all events, it could have operated to pass only that part of the timber which was made and capable of delivery at the time of its execution, and such as being made afterwards was delivered to the plaintiff and marked for him.

This was an action of replevin against the sheriff of the united counties of Northumberland and Durham.

The declaration stated that the defendant took the goods and chattels—viz. a quantity of timber marked in a particular manner—and then unjustly detained the same from the plaintiff.

The pleas were—1st. *Non cepit;* 2ndly, That the property was not the plaintiff's; and 3rdly. That the property belonged to Thomas Waters. Issue on all.

At the trial, before *Burns, J.,* at the last autumn assizes, held at Cobourg, the facts appeared to be these:—In the fall of 1852 Waters was getting out timber in the township of Belmont, and he made application to the plaintiff for assistance to enable him to proceed with his work. On the 10th of January, 1853, they made an agreement under seal, as follows :

"Memorandum of an agreement made and entered into
this 10th day of January, 1853, by and between Thomas
Short, of the Township of Otonabee, in the county of Peterborough, merchant, of the first part, and Thomas Waters, of
the Township of Asphodel, in the said county, shoemaker,
of the second part, witnesseth, that the said Thomas Short
agrees to make certain advances to the said Thomas Waters,
to enable him to make and draw upon the ice of the River
Trent, or upon the bank of the said river, a quantity of
timber, as follows : say 400 pieces of rock elm, to average
45 feet or over ; 15 pieces of oak, 100 feet or over; 350
pieces of white pine, 70 feet or over ; also some red pine spars.
Such advances to be made as follows, that is to say, the
amount of £100 in goods, from the store of the said Thomas
Short, at the usual marked prices, such goods to be delivered
to the said Waters, or his order, after the completion of
this agreement ; the sum of £100 in cash, in the month of
January ; the sum of £75 currency, in the month of
February ; and the further sum of £75 in the month of
March; also a further sum to pay hewers in spring, not to
exceed £40. These advances to be made on condition that
the quantity of timber above mentioned is likely to be
drawn and delivered as above mentioned during the sleigh-
ing, but not otherwise. Any hay, grain, or chaff, that may
be advanced by the said Short to be counted out of the
cash advances as before mentioned. The said Thomas Short
further agrees to advance what money may be really necessary to meet the current expenses of the raft, from the
landing to Quebec, or wherever it may be sold, but no other
advances or payments until the timber is sold and the proceeds realized. Now it is hereby distinctly agreed between
the parties aforesaid, that the above advances are to be
made by the said Thomas Short on the following conditions,
which the said Thomas Waters hereby agrees to—viz. that
the said Thomas Short shall charge interest on the cash
advances from the time the money may be paid until the
timber is sold and the proceeds realized, and that for his
trouble and risk he shall be entitled to charge ten per cent.
on the sales of the timber whenever made ; that the timber
which is now ready and lying in the woods, or in course of
being drawn together, with the whole that may be hereafter made, shall be delivered over by the said Waters to
the said Short as soon as made, in security for the said
advances, and shall be held by the said Short, as hereinafter provided, until the whole is paid or satisfied, and in
proof of such delivery shall be all marked, in addition to
any other mark, with the diamond <a> with the racing iron

and also with Mr. Short's hammer-mark, as follows: ⟨⟩ HORT, as soon as it can be done. The said timber to be rafted by the men now employed upon it, with as many more as may be necessary for forwarding it to market, under the general directions of the said Waters, and the foreman employed by him, as long as they shall use all due diligence in forwarding it speedily and economically to market; but should they neglect or refuse to do so, then the said Short, or his heirs or assigns, or men in his or their employment, may and shall take charge of the same and forward it to market, paying all necessary expenses of so doing, also the advances and remuneration for trouble as above mentioned, when the balance, after paying men's wages, shall be paid over to the said Thomas Waters, his heirs or assigns. It is further hereby agreed and understood, that as collateral security for the goods already delivered, and for the advances to be made under this agreement, the said Waters shall make a mortgage in favor of the said Short upon his lands in Belmont, say the 22nd and 23rd lots in the 9th concession, and 22 and 23, in the 10th concession of the said township of Belmont, containing 800 acres more or less, for £200, which security Short hereby agrees to discharge on receiving payment in full as above mentioned."

This instrument was not registered according to the chattel mortgage or sales acts. On the 19th of January, 1853, a document was signed and sealed at Belmont, by Waters, as follows :—

" Whereas, by an agreement between Waters and Short, dated 10th of January, 1853, Waters agreed, under certain conditions, to deliver over to Short a certain quantity of oak, elm, and pine timber. This is therefore to certify, that I, the said Waters, have delivered over to the said Short, by his agent Mr. Richard White, 40 pieces of white pine, 311 pieces of elm, and 9 pieces of oak timber, in the name of the whole thereof, which timber has been by him marked, in accordance with the said agreement. And I hereby agree to have the remainder of the timber marked in the same manner as fast as made, and to retain and defend it for him, Short, in the manner provided for in the said agreement."

It was proved that when the first agreement was entered into, the timber then ready, and all that was manufactured afterwards, was marked with Waters's mark, T. W., and at the time of the delivery on the 19th of January it was all marked also with the plaintiff's mark, and so were some of

the pieces made after that time.   Shortly after the 14th of
February the plaintiff went to where the timber was being
manufactured, in order to see Waters.   They had some dispute about the amount of advances.   No delivery was then
made of any timber, but the plaintiff told Waters he was
ready with the money to pay the hewers as he had agreed,
but would not give the money to Waters without delivery
of the timber.   Waters's workmen grumbled about their
wages, and they would not let the timber be delivered to
the plaintiff.

A writ of *fi. fa.* against goods was placed in the hands of
the defendant, in a suit of James Waters v. Thomas Waters,
indorsed to levy £184 17*s.* 9*d.*, with interest from the 24th
of March, 1853, and 20*s.* for writ and sheriff's fees.   This
writ was placed in the sheriff's hands on the 18th of April,
1853, and thereupon the defendant made a warrant to W.
S. Conger, dated the same day, authorizing him to make
seizure.   Mr. Conger was sheriff of Peterborough, and also
had a writ against the goods of Waters.   This warrant was
given because it was doubtful whether the timber when
seized might be within the defendant's counties, or within the
county of Peterborough.   The timber was seized by James
Gallan, the deputy sheriff of Peterborough, on the 29th of
April, 1853, while in the possession of Thomas Waters, and he
held possession of it until it was replevied by the plaintiff.
Whether the timber was within the defendant's counties
when seized was not shewn.   Gallan had no authority from
the defendant to seize it; the warrant was to Conger, and
he never made any seizure, but Gallan stated that he acted
for Conger.   It was proved that the defendant advertized
the timber to be sold upon the execution of James Waters,
after the seizure of it, and before being replevied.

The defendant's counsel at the trial objected to the plaintiff's recovery.   1st. Because there was no proof that the
defendant ever seized the timber, or that it was seized by any
one authorized by him, and therefore under *non cepit* the
defendant should succeed.   2dly. That for want of registration
of the instrument under which the plaintiff claimed, he must
fail, unless he had the actual and continued possession, and as
to that, the evidence established that Waters always continued

in possession, and the agreement contemplated that he should do so, and therefore the plaintiff could not rely upon the possession being changed. 3rdly. That there should be a demand before replevin could be made, because the action for unjustly detaining is given in such cases only where trover would lie.

The learned judge, expressed his impression to be that the instrument under which the plaintiff claimed would require registration, inasmuch as it could not be said that it transferred the possession entirely to the plaintiff, and that afterwards Waters was merely his servant or agent in respect of the timber, it was agreed between the parties that a verdict should be entered for the plaintiff, with 1s. damages, subject to the opinion of the court. It was also agreed that the court should upon the evidence dispose of the case upon the issue on *non cepit*, it appearing to the judge that some difficulty might arise as to whether it was a material issue or not, in consequence of the declaration not alleging that the defendant *unjustly took*, but that he *took* the goods and *unjustly detained* them. It was agreed that the court might might alter the verdict, and direct one to be entered for the defendant.

Weller obtained a rule *nisi* to enter a verdict for the defendant according to the leave reserved.

Wilson, Q. C., shewed cause, citing Barratt v. Price, 9 Bing, 566; Gregory v. Slowman, 1 Ell. & Bl, 360; Waters et al. v. Ruddell et al., 11 U. C. R. 181; Galloway v. Bird, 4 Bing. 299.

Vankoughnet, Q. C., supported the rule, and cited Ballard v. Ransom, 1 O. S. 70.

ROBINSON, C. J., delivered the judgment of the court.

The only question upon the legal operation of the deed made to Short on the 10th of January, 1853, besides the objection taken on account of its not having been registered, is in regard to its effect upon the timber that was purchased and manufactured by Waters after the execution of that instrument.

Nothing can be more just than that Short should be paid the full amount of his advances out of the proceeds of that timber, bought and prepared for market with his money before any third party or creditor of Waters should be paid his debt out of those proceeds. As a general principle, we take it to be clear that an assignment of personal property whether absolute or by way of mortgage, can only operate upon such property as was in existence, and as the assignor had an interest in, at the time of executing the assignment. —Coote on Mor. 235.

No doubt an instrument might be so framed (and we do not say that the one before us is not) as to give power to the mortgagee to seize the future chattels of the grantor, as they shall be acquired by him ; but that does not by any means shew that they became his *ipso facto*, by virtue merely of the assignment, as soon as they are acquired.

It seems to have been contended at the trial that the court could look upon Waters as the mere agent of Short in getting out this timber so that the timber might be regarded as Short's from the first, and during the whole process of felling it and preparing it for market ; but that, we think, is a position inconsistent with the terms and nature of the instrument. It is that timber only which was made and capable of delivery at the time of the assignment that could pass under it, and such timber also, as being made afterwards, was delivered to Short or marked for him.

But we apprehend, however just the plaintiff's claim is, we are under the necessity of deciding against him, on account of the non-registry of the assignment.

We do not consider that our statute 12 Vic. ch. 74, could be held to apply in regard to any of the timber that was not in existence as timber, and not owned by Waters at the time of the execution of that instrument ; because the possession of that timber not being capable of being transferred to the mortgagee at the time, the mortgagor could not be said to be retaining or continuing in possession of it inconsistently with the purport of the deed, and there could be no ground in such a case for the inference of such a fraud as the statute was meant to repress : and, besides, in such a case there could be no legal registry of the instrument, because there could not be that affidavit of an existing debt due which is required by the amending act 13 & 14 Vic. ch. 62.

But these considerations apply to the assignment only so far as it effects a portion of the timber, though perhaps the larger portion. It is plain from the deed, and from the evidence, that when the assignment was executed there was a considerable quantity of the timber that is now in question that was owned by Waters, and was cut and lying in the woods and ready for delivery, and which nevertheless continued in the possession of Waters as before. If we might hold with respect to such timber, that the deed was "accompanied by an immediate delivery" of it, treating the marking as a delivery, yet still that delivery was not *"followed by an actual and continued change of possession of the thing mortgaged,"* and therefore the necessity for registering that assignment arose under the express words of 12 Vic. ch. 74.

Not being registered the statute makes it *absolutely void;* and we cannot, in our opinion, uphold it, as to that other part of the timber of which possession could not in the nature of things have been changed at the time of making the deed. For, in the first place, it is a statute that makes this deed void, and not merely a principle of the common law ; and it is a maxim that in such cases the deed must be taken to be altogether void, and not merely as to that part to which the objection of illegality applies. And, in the next place, it is also a maxim, that when a deed or instrument is objected to on the ground of fraud, if liable to be avoided at all it must be avoided altogether, and not allowed to stand good so far as regards any portion of it to which the objection of fraud may not apply *(a)*. And in truth it is not even necessary to enter into these questions; because upon the ground which we have already stated, the assignment could at any rate not operate so as to pass an interest in the after-acquired timber ; and the plaintiff's claim in this action resting wholly on the assignment, he fails altogether as regards the timber owned by Waters on the 10th of January, 1853, on account of the omission to register the grant ; and, as regards the other part, because the assignment could pass no interest in timber which Waters did not then own, but could at the most give a power to seize and dispose of it.

In our opinion, the rule must be made absolute for setting aside the verdict for the plaintiff, and entering a verdict for the defendant.

Rule absolute.

(a) See Taylor v. Whittemore, 10 U. C. R. 440.

In re Barclay and the Municipality of the Township of Darlington.

Sale of spirituous liquors in taverns—By-law to limit the number of taverns to one, held unreasonable—13 & 14 Vic. ch. 65, sec. 4—16 Vic. ch. 184, sec. 4.

The Municipality of the Township of Darlington passed a by-law, enacting
1. That the number of taverns which should receive license to sell wines and spirituous liquors in the municipality should not exceed one.
11. That the sum to be paid by any person who should obtain a license to keep such tavern should be £10 annually, above the duty imposed by the Imperial or Provincial statute for such license.
IV. That the person receiving such license should be subject to the following regulations, amongst others :
2. That no innkeeper shall sell or permit the drinking of any intoxicating liquors on the Sabbath Day, except in case of sickness, or to travellers.
4. That no innkeeper shall sell intoxicating drink to any apprentice or minor, without the permission of his legal protector ; nor shall he sell to any habitual drunkard, after being forbidden so to do by any relative or friend of such drunkard.
6. That no innkeeper shall be allowed to sell, give, loan, barter, or dispose of in any way, any intoxicating liquors after the hour of ten o'clock at night, or before five in the morning, travellers excepted.
By a subsequent by-law the fee to be paid for the license was increased to £25.
It appeared by the affidavits, that a by-law to prohibit absolutely the sale of spirituous liquors, &c., had been submitted to the electors, but not passed, as a sufficient number did not attend the meeting—that this by-law had not been so submitted—and that the township of Darlington contained a population of six thousand.
Held, that the first enactment was bad, as amounting in effect to a total prohibition, and being therefore in attempt to evade the provisions of 16 Vic. ch. 184, sec. 4, by which no such by-law can be passed without the assent of a majority of the electors :—
That the second enactment was also bad, being inseparably connected with the first.
That the second, fourth, and sixth regulations, were beyond the jurisdiction of the Municipality to impose.
Held, also, that the second by-law was bad, as the fee imposed exceeded £10, and no reference had been made to the electors.

On the 28th of January, 1854, the municipal council of the township of Darlington passed a by law, No. 58, intituled "A by-law for limiting the number of taverns, and for regulating the same," in which they recited, that it was necessary to limit the number of taverns in the township, and to make rules and regulations for the good government of the same ; and the by-law provided that after its passing the number of taverns which should receive licenses to sell wines and spirituous liquors in that Municipality should not exceed one in number.

2ndly. That the sum to be paid by any person who should obtain a license to keep such tavern should be £10 annually above the duty imposed by the imperial or provincial statute

for such license ; and that the license should expire on the
1st of February in each year while the by-law continued in
force.

3rdly. That the tavern to be licensed under the by-law
should possess certain accommodations, which were specified.

And the fourth section of the by-law provided, that the
person receiving the license should be subject to the regulations contained in that section—among which were these :

Regulation 2. That no innkeeper shall sell, or permit the
drinking of any intoxicating liquor on the Sabbath day, except in the case of sickness, or to travellers.

4. That no innkeeper shall sell intoxicating drink to
any apprentice or minor, without the permission of his legal
protector, nor shall he sell to any habitual drunkard, after
being forbidden so to do by any relative or friend of such
drunkard.

6. That no innkeeper shall be allowed to sell, give, loan,
barter, or dispose of in any way, any intoxicating liquors
after the hour of ten o'clock at night, or before 5 o'clock in
the morning, travellers excepted.

C. Robinson obtained a rule *nisi* calling upon the Municipality to shew cause why this by-law should not be quashed,
wholly or in part, with costs, on the following grounds :—

1st. As to the enactment contained in the first section of
it, which limits the number of the taverns in the township
to one, that it is unreasonable, illegal, and oppressive, and
inconsistent with the intent and object of the powers given
to the Municipality :—that it is in effect an attempt to prohibit absolutely the sale of wines and spirituous liquors in
taverns within the township of Darlington, and is beyond
the jurisdiction of the Municipality to ordain :—and that the
by-law was not adopted and approved by a majority of the
qualified electors of the Municipality before the final passing
thereof.

2ndly. As to the enactment in the second section of the
by-law, that it does not state with sufficient certainty what
sum is to be paid for the license:—that a sum exceeding £10
for the year is required to be paid for the license, and yet the
by-law was not adopted and approved by a majority of the
municipal electors of the Muncipality before its final passing.

3rdly. As to the 2nd, 4th, and 6th regulations prescribed by the 4th section of the by-law, that they are illegal, and beyond the power of the Municipality to impose or enforce.

On the 13th of February, 1854, another by-law (No. 63) was passed by the council of the same Municipality, for amending the by-law 58, by which it was enacted, that the words "ten pounds," inserted in the by-law 58, (as the sum to be paid for a license to keep a tavern,) should be erased, and the words "twenty-five pounds" inserted instead thereof.

A rule was also obtained upon the Municipality, to shew cause why this by-law should not be quashed, with costs, on the ground that it imposes a charge of more than £10 per annum for the license therein mentioned, and yet was not, before the final passing thereof, adopted and approved by a majority of the qualified municipal electors of the said Municipality.

Both applications were made on behalf of Lawrence Barclay, who swore that he was a resident freeholder of the township of Darlington ; that he was then keeping a tavern in the township, and had done so for five years past ; that neither of these by-laws was before the final passing thereof, adopted and approved by a majority of the qualified municipal electors of the said Municipality, nor was the same in any way submitted to the said electors for their consideration. He swore further that a by-law for preventing absolutely the sale of spirituous and intoxicating liquors by retail in the Municipality of Darlington and for other purposes mentioned in it was submitted to the electors for their approval on the 13th and 14th days of January last, in the different wards, and that at the close of the poll it was decided that there was not a sufficient number of votes polled to warrant the final passing of such by-law, and therefore they did not pass the same ; that in the township of Darlington, exclusive of the incorporated village of Bowmanville, there is a population of about six thousand inhabitants ; that there was no tavern within the said Municipality, or within seven miles of him, the deponent, licensed to sell wines or spirituous liquors by retail ; and that his tavern possessed the accommodation required by the by-law 58.

J. D. Armour shewed cause.

C. Robinson, in support of the rule as to the first section of the by-law, cited Peters v. The London Board of Police, 2 U. C. R. 545; Angell & Ames on Corp. 2d Ed. sec. 343; Grant on Corp. 92.

The statutes referred to are noticed in the judgment.

ROBINSON, C. J., delivered the judgment of the court.

In a case in which this same applicant complained of a by-law of the municipal council of Darlington (11 U. C. R. 470) we had occasion last term to consider the effect of the different legislative provisions to which reference has been made in the argument of this case. They are the statutes 13 & 14 Vic. ch. 65, 14 & 15 Vic. ch. 120, and 16 Vic. ch. 184.

The objection taken to the 1st clause of the by-law No. 58 (passed on the 28th of January, 1854,) is new, and must be decided on reason and principle. It is not probable that any by-law has been elsewhere passed upon which the same question could have been raised. The 13 & 14 Vic. ch. 65, sec. 4, gives power to the municipality of each township "to make by-laws for *limiting the number* of inns or houses of public entertainment in such township, for which license to retail spirituous liquors to be drunk therein shall be issued."

The 16 Vic. ch. 184 sec. 4, gives power to the municipality of any township to make by-laws for limiting the number of houses or places (other than houses or places of public entertainment) in which persons may be licensed to sell wine, brandy, or other spirituous liquors, or ale, beer, &c., by retail; or for preventing absolutely the sale of such liquors, or any of them, by retail, within the municipality.

This last enactment, it is plain has no reference to houses of public entertainment, whether we are to regard those words as including taverns, or as meaning something distinct from taverns because houses or place of public entertainment are expressly excepted.

The legislature considered, as it appears, that they had provided sufficiently for such houses or places by the statute 13 & 14 Vic. ch 65, except in one respect, for which they resolved in this act to make additional provision, which is contained in a proviso in the fourth clause of this last act, which I will recite entire, though part of it refers to other places for retailing liquors besides houses of public entertainment :—"Provided always that no by-law made under the authority of this act, which shall be intended absolutely to prevent the sale of wine, brandy, or other spirituous liquor, ale, or beer, within any municipality, at any place other than a house of public entertainment, or shall require the payment of a greater sum than £10 per annum for any license to sell the same, or to exercise any other calling, or do any other thing for which a license may be required under this act, *nor any by-law to be made* after the passing of this act under the authority of the act 13 & 14 Vic. ch. 65, for prohibiting the sale of wine or spirituous liquors, ale, or beer *in any house of public entertainment* in such municipality, shall have force or effect unless before the final passing thereof it shall have been *adopted and approved by a majority of the qualified municipal electors of the municipality,* (to be ascertained in such manner as shall be determined by a by-law to be previously passed for that purpose), after public notice," &c. &c. (prescribing the manner of giving such notice).

The by-law No. 58, which is now before us, provides, in its first section, that after its passing the number of taverns which shall receive license to sell wines and spirituous liquors in that municipality shall not exceed one in number.

It is objected, that to allow but one tavern to be licensed to sell wines and spirituous liquors in a township ten miles square, containing six thousand inhabitants, besides a large and populous village, and through which travellers must pass and repass in going to and from other parts of the province, is not a legitimate exercise of the power given by 13 & 14 Vic. ch. 65, sec. 4, *to limit the number* of inns or houses of public entertainment :—That it is in effect an exclusion or prohibition, when taken in reference to all but those portions of the township which are situated within a convenient distance of the one house proposed to be licensed ; and that, as regards such house, it establishes an unreasonable and unjust monopoly, for that it would give to it a preference over other taverns as regarded all that portion of the public who might desire the privilege of using wine or other liquors either moderately or immoderately ; and that viewing it, as it is just to view it, as a prohibitory law with respect to all parts of the township not within convenient distance of the single tavern to be licensed, it could not be legally passed without the previous approbation of a majority of the electors of the municipality, as required by the enactment I have last. cited.

We are of opinion that this by-law must be regarded as an intended evasion of the provision in the 4th clause of the provincial statute 16 Vic. ch. 184 ; and nothing can shew that more clearly than the fact which is sworn to and not denied—that two weeks before this by-law' had passed, a draft of a by-law for prohibiting absolutely the selling of spirituous liquors by retail within the municipality was proposed to the electors at a public meeting, and was not adopted or approved of.   Then a few days after the municipal council passed this by-law, prohibiting all licensed taverns but one, and no care was taken that this one should not be situated in a remote corner of the township.   We cannot look upon this as anything else than a contrivance by the municipal council to do that indirectly which they found they could not accomplish directly and in the manner required by the legislature.   It was not a *bonâ fide* exercise of the discretion of limiting the number of licensed taverns, with a view to the reasonable and convenient accommodation, and, so far as could be managed, the *equal* accommodation, of the inhabitants of the township.   It was in reality a prohibitory measure as to its general effect and tendency, and was intended to give the go-by to a legislative enactment which gave to the inhabitants of the township a direct voice upon the question of prohibition.

It may naturally be objected to this view, that the by-law complained of is literally nothing but a by-law limiting the number of taverns, and that is true; but taken with reference to the subject as it applies, and to the whole municipality, it is in its effect a prohibitory by-law, and we can have no doubt was passed in that spirit.   To desire to establish such a prohibition may be a laudable desire, prompted by good and wise motives, and it might be well, perhaps, for the township of Darlington. and for all other townships, if an absolute prohibition against selling intoxicating liquors in taverns or houses of public entertainment were established. That is a question upon which public opinion is divided, and which we are not in any manner called upon to decide. In deference to that known diversity of opinion, the provincial legislature has provided for an appeal to the people within each municipality, before any such measure of absolute prohibition shall obtain the force of law within its limits, and this provision must be carried out and submitted to in good faith. Whether politic or not to require such a previous approbation by the inhabitants, it is in itself reasonable and just.

It may be asked, if we hold that a by-law allowing but of one licensed tavern in a township be illegal, as not being a reasonable exercise of the discretion given to limit the number of such taverns, whether the municipal council could legally limit the number to twenty, or ten, or two, and where the line is to be drawn; and no doubt this is a pertinent and reasonable question, and one of such a nature as makes it a matter difficult and delicate to answer.

The best, and perhaps the only answer we can give, is that the tribunals of the country, to whom jurisdiction is given in this respect, must be relied upon for exercising a just and sound discretion. It will not often be found difficult to draw the line, and it may be safely assumed that wherever there is fair ground of doubt, which we think there is not in this case, the inclination will always be to let the by-law operate, and leave it to the legislature to interpose, if they see a necessity. It is quite plain that a superintending power of a judicial character is necessary to be exercised, in order to keep municipal bodies of this discription, as well as corporate bodies of all other kinds, within legal and reasonable limits in the exercise of their powers. There has always been such a power where English law has prevailed; without it great oppression might be exercised, and great confusion created. It is a discription of control which any court to whom it is committed would rather be relieved from.   In the nature of things the supreme legislature could not exercise such a control so as to meet the exigency of each case ; it is in their power,· however, to vest the authority where they think best ; and as the law stands, it is nowhere but in the superior common law courts, and these, while they retain it, must exercise it in each case under the same sense of responsibility as they discharge their other duties.

We think the first clause of this by law (No. 58) illegal, for the reason we have given—not because it did not receive the previous approbation of the electors, because, as the clause stands, such approbation could not in strict law be called for and obtained, the enactment not amounting in terms to an absolute prohibition ; but because that clause is an evasion of the enactment referred to, being in effect a prohibition, and intended to operate as such in the township generally, and to deprive most parts of it of an accommodation not contrary to law, which they have as good a right to as others, and which they have a right to in a convenient degree, until the electors within any municipality have by a vote of a majority approved of a measure imposing a prohibition, from which time the inhabitants of such municipality must submit to the restriction.

The first clause of the by-law being in our opinion illegal, the second must also be quashed, for it is inseparably connected with it and dependent on it.   It is founded on the assumption that there shall be but one tavern in the whole township, and applies only to such tavern.   If there were to be taverns licensed in different parts of the township, more or less populous, it could not be right to impose the same fee on every house.   We need not, therefore, go into the other objections to this clause.

And indeed it seems reasonable to take the same view of the second, fourth, and sixth regulations prescribed by the fourth section, though the remark does not apply with equal force.

But, as to the second regulation, it appears to go further than we think the municipal council had power to go.   They may clearly make such regulations as they please to prevent the bar-room being kept open on the Sabbath, and to prevent tippling on that day in the tavern. They did not, we think, mean to go further, for they made an exception in the case of travellers ; but that exception would not extend to people ordinarily lodging in the house, and not resorting to it merely to get liquor. Unless there is some statute of the province under which the municipal council can legally deprive such lodgers of the privilege of drinking at their rooms in the inn, anything in moderation with their meals, as other people may do in their houses, there is no right to impose the restriction, for certainly at common law a man may drink wine or beer with his meals, to make the assertion no stronger.

In the case of Baker v. The Municipal Council of Paris (10 U. C. R. 621) we had this subject before us. It escaped at that time, I believe, the attention of every one, that the statute of 13 & 14 Vic. ch. 27 had a direct bearing upon the question under consideration. Its title having no direct reference to municipalities or to licenses, it was, in the multiplicity of statutes, overlooked. Among a variety of provisions, some of them rather singular, there is, at the end of the 7th clause of that act, this enactment:—"And any person who shall be convicted of retailing intoxicating liquors without license, or of keeping a disorderly house, or of selling intoxicating liquors on Sundays and holidays, shall for every such offence incur a penalty of £10 currency."

The by-law in Baker's case provided that between Saturday night and Monday morning "no intoxicating liquors should be *sold or furnished* at a licensed tavern to any one." We think, so far as that by-law went to prohibit the landlord of an inn from putting liquor on the table of his lodgers with their meals, as he would on his own table, or as any private person might choose to do in his own house, it was not warranted by any sanction given to it by the statute just referred to, for that evidently means a distinct act of selling liquor on the Sabbath; and, besides, what that act prohibits, and what that or any other act authorizes municipal councils to prohibit, under such penalties as they may choose to impose, are altogether different questions. We think the second rule contained in the fourth section of this by-law, which enacts that

no innkeeper shall permit the drinking of any intoxicating
liquor on the Sabbath day in his house, is illegal, because
it is too unqualified and extends too far. It does except sick
persons and travellers ; but surely an ordinary lodger at an
inn has as good a right to drink a glass of beer at his meal,
until the legislature makes the very drinking it unlawful, as
a traveller can have, or as the landlord and his family can
have, or as any other person can have in his own house ; and
this by-law does not, like the provincial statute referred to,
merely prevent the innkeeper from selling it, but it prohibits
him from *permitting it to be drunk,* so that a lodger could
not quietly in his own room consume what he had bought
elsewhere, or what he had bought at the same inn before that
day.

The fourth rule or regulation is, that no innkeeper shall
sell intoxicating drink to any apprentice or minor, without
the permission of his legal protector ; nor shall he sell to
any habitual drunkard, after being forbidden so to do by any
relative or friend of such drunkard.

Any one under twenty one years of age is a minor, and
may be an apprentice. Whether he is one or the other may
be unknown to the innkeeper ; and if he comes to his inn as
a traveller, without his legal protector of whom the innkeeper may be equally ignorant, he ought not to be held
guilty of an offence in selling him a glass of liquor to drink,
under such circumstances as would justify him in selling to
others. It would be held, probably, that we must intend the
by-law to mean that it is only where the innkeeper knows the
facts that he shall be held to have offended; but laws creating
offences should be more precisely framed. The words *knowingly or wilfully* should have been inserted. It is not the
want of those words, however, which constitutes the only or
chief objection, though they ought to have been inserted. It
is that we think the municipal council have taken an incor-
rect view of their powers in selecting any particular class as
persons who shall be unable to obtain wine, or spirits, or beer,
at an inn, under any circumstances.

If the legislature should think it expedient to enable municipal councils to do whatever they like in respect to inns and

spirituous and intoxicating liquors, we could have no particular objection, and should be saved the necessity of pronouncing upon questions of this kind; but till the law has
been placed upon this footing, we are obliged to consider that
by the common law, though actual drunkenness is an offence
and an indecency, it is no more illegal to drink a glass of
liquor than to eat or drink any other article of diet, and that
any change of the law in this respect must be made either by
the legislature of the province, or by some other legislative
body to whom they have dedicated an authority to pass such
a law.   Now, all the authority which the municipal councils
have in this particular is to be found in 13 & 14 Vic. ch. 65;
for the additional power of absolute prohibition which is given
by 16 Vic. ch. 184, to be exercised under certain restrictions,
has nothing to do with such a rule as we are now discussing.
It is in the fourth clause of the first mentioned act that the
powers committed to them are defined; and the only words
in that clause which are applicable are those which give
authority to pass by-laws for "regulating inns and houses of
public entertainment."   Now that fairly means nothing more
than making general regulations respecting the conduct of
the house; it does not give power to enact that any one
class of persons shall not have the same meat and drink,
or other accommodation (all equally lawful till prohibited
by law, and all equally harmless till abused by excess),
as others are allowed to have.   There is no more power to
say that no person under twenty-one years of age, or no
apprentice, shall be able to procure liquor at an inn, than
to say that no woman, married or unmarried, shall have it,
or no soldier, or no aged person, or no laborer, or person
following some particular trade.

  The difficulty in the way of this law is, that power is not
given by law to municipal bodies to debar any class of the
community more than another from procuring such refresh-
ments at an inn as it has not yet been made unlawful to consume; and until that is the case, the power of merely
"regulating inns and houses of public entertainment" cannot, in our opinion, be carried that length.   This prohibition
regarding minors is unqualified, and if every municipality

were to exercise their discretion of regulating in the same way, and had a right to do it, then a minor or apprentice travelling alone through the province might be unable to procure, in the whole extent of his journey, what, whether wisely or not, is deemed a refreshment and taken as such, though anybody a year or a month older would not be prevented. He might be all the better for the prohibition, and by no means the worse ; but that is for the legislature to pronounce, and not, we think, for the municipal councils. In passing such a by-law they are not merely regulating inns but are regulating minors and apprentices. It is a regulation suggested, no doubt, by a proper feeling, but it is not framed with sufficient caution, even if it were admissible in its nature.

That part of the same rule (4th) which provides that the innkeeper shall not sell to any habitual drunkard, after being forbidden to do so by any relative or friend of his, appears to us exceptionable. An habitual drunkard may go into an inn perfectly sober, and call for something to drink, either with his meal or without : he may be wholly unknown to the landlord ; and because any person who chooses to call himself his relative or friend tells the landlord that he is an habitual drunkard, he must at his peril forbear selling to him ; so that the party, whether lodger or traveller, shall be unable to procure any intoxicating drink of any kind or in any quantity. That at once raises an issue to be tried, as to whether the man, who is then perfectly sober, is an habitual drunkard or not ; and how is this issue to be tried ? Some regulation of this kind, properly guarded, might be very beneficial. It might be made the duty of the landlord to refuse liquor to any person who had been already drinking, or was drinking to excess, and to compel him to leave his house ; and this regulation, as it stands, was no doubt dictated by a good feeling, but we do not think it a regulation which the municipal council had any authority to prescribe in such terms as they have framed it.

We have had more question respecting the legality of the sixth regulation—that no innkeeper shall sell, give, or in any way dispose of, any intoxicating liquors after ten at night or before five in the morning, except to travellers. We

have already held, in another case, that until the legislature
has made it illegal, the municipal councils have no authority
to debar a traveller from getting something to drink, when
he arrives at an inn, whatever may be the hour; and we do
not see that there is any more authority to make it an
offence to let a lodger, whose home is at the inn, have any
reasonable refreshment of that kind after ten o'clock, if he
is ill, or if, not being ill, he is sitting alone, or with a friend,
if the innkeeper chooses to take the trouble of supplying
him with a moderate quantity.

The municipal councils, by going through the requiste
form of obtaining the sanction of a majority of the electors,
may make a radical cure of what no doubt proves in the
great majority of cases to be a great evil, by prohibiting the
sale of intoxicating liquors at an inn, to any person, or at
any time, or under any circumstances; and it would perhaps be better to do so than to attempt to impose some
such regulations as have been suggested; but we think they
cannot, of their own authority, legislate against a class, or
create such offences as this by-law creates, under the general
authority given to them to regulate inns. We have more
doubt respecting the sixth regulation than the others, but
we think it a bad by-law, so long as the law which applies
to all other persons remains on its present footing.

Much might be done, within the scope of the power given
to the council, towards regulating inns, by preventing tippling on Sundays or at unseasonable hours, and many
regulations imposed for preventing the house being disorderly, or people drinking to excess; but these are regulations of a different character.

The by-law 63, it was admitted in argument, cannot be
upheld. It imposes a duty of £25 upon the only tavern
permitted to be licensed. The imposition of so high a duty
in any case, required (by the 4th section of 16 Vic. ch. 184)
a reference to the electors, at a meeting duly convened, and
there was none such.

Rule absolute.

IN RE McAVOY AND THE MUNICIPALITY OF SARNIA.

By-law to prohibit absolutely the sale of liquors, &c.—Approval of electors.

By-laws for prohibiting the sale of spirituous liquors, &c., which, under 16 Vic. ch. 184, sec. 4, require to be submitted to the electors, must be adopted and approved of by a majority of all the qualified municipal electors of the municipality, not merely by a majority of those who may attend at the meeting called to consider such by-law.

Where the by-law which provided for calling such meeting assumed that the approval of the majority of the voters present would be sufficient: *Held*, that it was nevertheless proper to move against the then proposed by-law, after it had been passed on such approval, and not against that which laid down the improper course of proceeding.

Vankoughnet, Q. C., obtained a rule *nisi* on the Municipality of the Township of Sarnia, to shew cause why a by-law passed by them, intituled " A By-law to repeal the first four sections and part of the fifth section of by-law No. 33, intituled, ' A By-law for the limitation and regulation of taverns and temperance hotels in the township of Sarnia, and for preventing absolutely the sale of wine and brandy, or other spirituous liquors, ale or beer, by retail, within the municipality of Sarnia,'" or the said by-law, with the exception of the first section, should not be quashed with costs, on the grounds that the municipal council had no jurisdiction to pass such a by-law, or any portion thereof, excepting the first section ; and that the said by-law, excepting the first section, is, on the face of it, illegal, and does not shew that it had been approved of by the majority of the electors ; and that it was not, before the final passing thereof, approved of and adopted ; and on grounds appearing on the face of the by-law, and on the affidavits and papers filed.

The by-law complained of was numbered 48, and was passed on the 8th of November, 1853.

It repealed certain clauses of a previous by-law, No. 33. The second section enacted "that there shall be no license issued for the sale of intoxicating liquors in any house of public entertainment, and that no wine or brandy, or other spirituous liquors, ale or beer, shall be sold by retail within the limits of the municipality of the township of Sarnia." The third section was, " that if any person shall sell any wine or brandy, or other spirituous liquors, ale or beer, by retail, within the said municipality, to any person, he shall forfeit and pay a fine of not less than one pound and not more than five pounds, for every such sale ; and in default of payment, or for want of sufficient distress, shall be imprisoned for a term not exceeding twenty days ;" and the fourth section directed " that the by-law shall come into force on the first of January, 1854, except as to licenses already granted, and not yet expired.

It appeared that there were 290 qualified electors in the municipality.

On the 6th of September, 1853, a by-law was passed for determining the manner of ascertaining the adoption and approval of a majority of the qualified municipal electors of the then proposed by-law (that now moved against) ; and this by-law provided that there should be a general meeting of the qualified municipal electors, to be held at a time and place named in it, at which meeting the reeve, or, in his absence, some member of the council, should preside : that the only question to be determined at such meeting should be, whether *the majority of the municipal electors present thereat* did or did not approve of the said by-law : and directions were given as to the mode of proceeding at the election : and it was enacted that, at the close of the poll, the person presiding should count the yeas and nays, and ascertain and certify to the council whether *the majority* was for the approval or disapproval of the by-law.

The meeting was held as directed by the by-law ; and the by-law No. 48, the one now complained of, was passed on the 8th of November, 1853, upon a certificate, dated the 7th of November, signed, not by the presiding officer, but by the clerk of the council, as secretary of the meeting, to the effect that the meeting was held as directed by the by-law for that purpose : that the reeve presided : that the draft of the by-law was read to the meeting, and the question of approval or disapproval put to them by the reeve, and that the reeve did then and there declare his opinion that *the majority of the municipal electors present thereat* was for the approval of the by-law ; which decision was not appealed from.

The by-law respecting the taking the vote had provided for the declaring the proposed by-law approved of, when no poll was demanded, as seemed to have been the case here.

It was sworn in affidavit made by the clerk, who gave this certificate, that he attended the meeting, and that there was less than twenty of the municipal electors of the township of Sarnia present thereat.

Leith shewed cause, and cited Rex v. Bower, 1 B. & C. 492; Rex v. Monday, 2 Cow. 531; Rex v. Varlo, 1 Cow. 248; Rex v. Grimes, 5 Burr. 2598; Rex v. Bellringer, 4 T. R. 823; Gosling v. Veley, 16 L. J. (Q. B.) 209, 211; Oldknow v. Wainwright, 1 W. Bl. 29; Regina v. Hirons, 7 A. & E. 962.

Vankoughnet, Q. C., contra, cited Pierce v. Bartram, 1 Cow. 269; Shaw v. Pope, 2 B. & Ad. 465; Eldwood v. Bullock, 6 Q. B. 383; Wooley v. Idle, 4 Burr. 1951; Rex. v. Devonshire, 1 B. & C. 610.

ROBINSON, C. J., delivered the judgment of the court.

Giving due weight to what has been decided in England in the cases cited by Mr. Leith, respecting the sufficiency, upon common law principles, of a majority of those present at a meeting to bind the whole body, we must in this, as in other similar cases, where there is a statutory provision upon the subject, determine what is the intention and proper construction of the language used by the legislature.

The question here arises under the statute 16 Vic. ch. 184, sec. 4, which provides for submitting to the electors of the municipality the question whether a by-law shall pass which is intended absolutely to prohibit the licensing of any inn or house of public entertainment to sell wine or spirituous liquors by retail, or to prohibit altogether the selling of wine, brandy, or other spirits, or ale or beer, by retail, within the municipality.

There are other statutes, such as 16 Vic. ch. 22, and ch. 181, secs. 6 & 7, which provide for a reference to the electors before any by-law for certain purposes shall pass. They are not closely alike in their provisions; ch. 22 making the result depend on the majority of votes of those present at the meeting to be convened; while the other statute, ch. 181, requires evidently that the proposition must be approved of by a majority of those residing within the municipality who are qualified to vote at elections, or it cannot be passed. We have no doubt that the legislature, having reference to the questions to be determined, did intend to make the difference which they have done in these two cases.

The provision in ch. 184, upon which we are now called to decide, is not so explicit in its terms in regard to what it demands, as either of the two other statutes which we have mentioned. But we have no hesitation in determining that it does make it necessary that a majority of the qualified electors of the municipality should concur, and that a vote of a majority of those present at the meeting, unless it amounts in numbers to a majority of the electors both present and absent, will not suffice.

The 4th clause of ch. 184, provides that no such by-law as is therein mentioned "shall have force or effect, unless before the final passing thereof, it shall have been adopted and approved by *a majority of the qualified municipal electors of the municipality* (to be ascertained in such manner as shall be determined by a by-law to be previously passed for that purpose)."

Where the legislature have meant as in ch. 22, that a majority of those present at the meeting shall decide the question they have said so in express words. Here they have not said so, but have required that there shall be the assent of "a majority of the qualified municipal electors of the municipality."

Judging from the words used in the clause before, we cannot say that the legislature meant to place it in the power of any meeting, however small, convened at a part of the township however remote from the bulk of the population, to determine whether, not merely all the other inhabitants of the township but all who might have occasion to sojourn in it or travel through it, should be able to buy a glass of beer. Such a meeting might be less numerous than the council itself, and the legislative body might in such a case be binding all their constituents under the sanction of a reference made to a number of voters less than the number of members of the council who concurred in passing the by-law. It is not likely that the legislature intended that; and the language they used certainly imports otherwise, and, as we think, very plainly.

It is true that the by-law under which the approbation of twenty electors was obtained out of the two hundred and ninety residing in the township, does assume that it will be sufficient to ascertain what is the opinion of the voters who attend the meeting, and the certificates which forms the foundation of this by-law does accordingly comport with the by-law in stating that the majority of the municipal electors present at the meeting was in favour of the proposed by-law, but the statute of the province says that the approval must come from the majority of the qualified municipal electors of the municipality..

Where the two provisions conflict, we must be governed by the statute. It was objected that even in this view of the case it was necessary to have moved, in the first instance, to quash the by-law which laid down the improper course of proceeding ; but that was passed only for the occasion of that meeting and is spent. It would be an idle act to move against it and being illegal on the face of it, it could never form a good legal foundation of the by-law afterwards passed. We make the rule absolute with costs.

Rule absolute.

FORWARD ET AL. V. WILLIAM THOMPSON & JOHN THOMPSON.

"£228 7s. 6d.   "Port Hope, December 8, 1853.
"Three months after date pay to the order of William Thompson, at Port Hope, the sum of two hundred and twenty eight pounds, seven shillings, and sixpence, currency, for value received,
(Signed)   "JOHN THOMPSON."
Held, not a promissory note.

Assumsit on an instrument in the following words :—

"Port Hope, December 8th, 1853.
"£228 7s. 6d.

"Three months after date, pay to the order of William Thompson, at Port Hope, the sum of two hundred and twenty-eight pounds, seven shillings, and six pence, currency, for value received.
(Signed)   "John Thompson."

This was declared upon as a promissory note, made by John Thompson in favor of the defendant William Thompson, who was stated to have endorsed to the defendant, John Thompson, who endorsed to the plaintiffs.

Pleas denying the making and endorsing, and other pleas not material to mention.

At the trial at Cobourg, before *McLean, J.*, it was objected that the instrument produced was not a promissory note. Several other objections were raised ; but it is only material to notice the one on which the judgment of the court proceeded.

Wilson, Q. C., shewed cause. This is in fact a bill of exchange not directed to anybody. For want of a drawee it cannot be treated as a bill, but it may be declared on as a promissory note. No precise form of words are essential— "I will pay" would be sufficient, so would "I pay," and the word *I* which is omitted here, may be supplied. It must mean *I pay,* for as it is not directed to any one, nothing else can be meant. [DRAPER, J. Suppose that it had been addressed to a person not *in esse*, would it have been a note ?] I think so. [DRAPER, J. If it would have been, then it ought equally to be so in this case.] It is in effect as if the words had been "I, the signer, pay to."—Davis v. Clarke, 6 Q. B. 16 ; Gray v. Milner, 8 Taunt. 739 ; Allan v. Mawson, 4 Camp. 115; Shuttleworth v. Stephens, 1 Camp. 407 ; Edis v. Bury, 6 B. & C. 433 ; Lloyd v. Oliver, S. C. 16 Jur. 833, 12 Eng. Rep. 424 ; Eddison v. Collingridge, 14 Jur. 869.

Richards, contra. There are many cases in which an instrument has been held capable of being treated either as a note or a bill, and the authorities cited on the other side are principally of that nature; but in all of them it will be found that the writing, though ambiguous, was perfect in itself. Here is nothing in fact but an incomplete bill of exchange, the drawee's name being omitted. In every other respect it is perfect as a bill, and this omission of an essential party will not make it a promissory note. Suppose the word "pay" struck out, there would then be no meaning at all, and the simple word "pay" means nothing when it is addressed to nobody.—Robinson v. Bland, 2 Burr. 1077 ; Dickenson v. Teague, 4 Tyr. 452 ; Block v. Bell, 1 Moo. & Rob. 149 ; Miller v. Thompson, 3 M. & G. 576 ; Rex v. Hunter, Russ & Ry. C. C. 511 ; Stoessiger v. South Eastern R. W. Co, 23 L. T. Rep. 65.

DRAPER, J., delivered the judgment of the court.

The first question to be decided is, whether the instrument, declared upon in point of law amounts to a promissory note.

The authorities cited (to which may be added Russell v. Powell, 14 M. & W. 418, and Peto v. Reynolds, 18 Jur. 472), establish clearly, as we think, that it could not have been treated and declared upon as a bill of exchange for want of a drawee; and if not, then those cases which have been decided on the ground that the instrument in question is made in terms so ambiguous as to make it doubtful whether it be a bill of exchange or promissory note, have no application. Then as a promissory note it wants the very essence of a promissory note, that which mainly distinguishes it from a bill of exchange, viz.: a promise in terms by the maker, which makes him primarily liable to pay the money. Here are the proper words used, and no others, for drawing a bill of exchange, and if there had been a drawee there would have been no room whatever for treating the instrument as anything but a bill of exchange. But for want of a drawee, it is incomplete as a bill of exchange; and for want of a promise, it appears to us incomplete as a note. It is quite true that no particular words are indispensable, but that any form of words from which the court can extract an expressed intention to promise to pay are sufficient ; but in this case we see nothing but an omission to complete, by adding a drawee's name, what in all other respects is a good bill of exchange, and we cannot find either reason or authority for holding that this is sufficient to convert it into a promissory note.

Rule absolute.

GREAT WESTERN RAILROAD COMPANY V. BABY ET AL.
Do.   V. HUNT.
Do.   V. DOUGALL.
Do.   V. DODDS.

GREAT WESTERN RAILROAD COMPANY V. BABY ET AL.

Award as to compensation for lands taken—Excessive valuation—9 Vic. ch. 81 sec. 26—Submission by married woman—Land owned by several devisees— Reservations or conditions in award—Form of such awards, and principles on which the court will interfere with them.

The court, in this and the succeeding cases, set aside the awards, made under 9 Vic. ch. 81, as to compensation to be paid to parties whose land was required for the Great Western Railway ; the sum awarded being so excessive as to show clearly that the arbitrators had disregarded the direction of the statute, to consider the benefit conferred on the property as well as the damage done.

The fact of one of the parties having an interest in the land being a married woman was held no objection to the award ; for it was known to the company when they agreed to the submission, and both she and her husband were willing to convey their interest in accordance with the award.

The following proviso was inserted in the award, "It being understood that the Great Western R. R. Co. shall construct and maintain a public water tank south of the railway, sufficient at all times to supply the inhabitants of the front of said lots 79 and 80 with water from the Detroit River, and shall keep open Ferry Street at its present width,"— *Held*, that the Company could not object to the award on this ground.

It was expressed in the award that the land should be subject to the reservation of the bordage road expressed in the patent to F. B. of the said land, and to any public or private right, excepting the right of the parties submitting to the arbitration, in respect of Water Street and River Street having been laid out on a certain plan.— *Held*, also, no objection.

Where the parties interested in the land were devisees under a will, it was held unnecessary to state in the award how much each was to receive ; for the money might be paid to the executors, and left to them to divide.

Semble, That as the submission to arbitration in matters of this description is in a measure compulsory, the court might interfere to prevent injustice where they would hesitate to do so in an ordinary case.

[For suggestions as to the proper form of award in these cases, see the conclusion of the judgment of the Chief Justice.]

[In this and the three following cases applications were made to set aside the awards of arbitrators appointed under the statute 9 Vic. ch. 81, to value lands taken for the Great Western Railway. The chief ground of complaint was the exhorbitant valuation set upon the property ; and as this applied throughout, the cases were all argued at the same time. It will be seen, however, that there were other exceptions taken, having reference particularly to each case,]

Galt obtained a rule *nisi* last term to shew cause why the award made between these parties should not be set aside, for the following causes :

1st. Because it appears, by the submission, rule, and award, that the parties in whose favour the award was made, James Baby and others, were jointly interested in the lands mentioned in the award, and that all the said parties executed the submission; whereas it appears in the face of the submission, and is recited in the award, that one of the parties, Emily Dewson, is a married woman, and consequently could not enter into the submission, and is not bound by, and could not be compelled to fulfil the award.

2ndly. Because the award was not *final*, the arbitrators not having decided finally on the matters submitted, but having taken into their consideration the rights of other parties than those who are parties to the submission; for their award contains this proviso—" It being understood that the Great Western Railway Company shall construct and maintain a public water tank south of the railway, sufficient at all times to supply the inhabitants of the front of the lots 79 and 80 with water from the Detroit river, and shall keep open Ferry Street, aforesaid, at its present width."

3rdly. Because the arbitrators have exceeded their authority in this, that they have awarded on the rights and claims of persons not parties to the submission; also, that they have awarded that the company shall keep open a street, which is a matter not submitted to them.

4thly. Because they have also exceeded their authority in this, that they have made their award subject to the reservation of the bordage road expressed in the patent for the lands, and to any public or private rights affecting lands mentioned in the award, other than the rights of the said James Baby and others.

5thly. Because the award is uncertain, in not stating what sum is to be paid to each of the parties, and it does not appear that they are entitled to equal portions of the money awarded.

6thly. Because the conduct of the arbitrators was corrupt, in awarding the exorbitant amount directed to be paid by the Great Western Railroad Company; and that the sum awarded is extravagant and excessive.

The submission recited that the company had located their

line of road so as to run across a portion of the lands of the
parties of the second part, and that disputes and differences
existed between them as to the value of the land required by
the company for the use of the road, and also the damage
which the parties of the second part might sustain thereby,
and it was stated to be agreed upon between the parties, that
all disputes and differences existing between them should be
referred to the arbitrators named, viz., Joseph Woods and
Francis Curran, Esquires, and of such other person as they
should appoint, according to the several acts of parliament
in that behalf, or a majority thereof.

This submission was signed and sealed by all the parties
named, some executing in their own persons and others by
attorney.   Archibald Young, Esq., was appointed the third
arbitrator.

On the back of this submission there was this indorsement : " It is understood that the Great Western Railway
Company shall construct and maintain a public water tank,
supplied at all times with water from the Detroit river,
sufficient to supply the inhabitants of 79 and 80, and to
keep open Ferry Street at its present width ; such tank to
be south of the railway."   This was signed by the solicitor
for the Great Western Railway Company.

On the 27th of January, 1854, an award was made by two
of the arbitrators, Curran and Young, in which they awarded
that "the heirs and devisees (meaning the parties submitting) have sustained damages by the location and appropriation of their lands for the said railway, to the amount of
£10,487 10s., and that the company shall pay that sum to
the said heirs and devisees, being in full for all damages
done, and also for the land required by the said company for
the uses of the said railway," which lands they described as
being composed of village lots, and parts of village lots,
numbered and laid down on a map or plan of the subdivision
of lots 79 and 80, in the first concession of the township of
Sandwich, made by Philip Donelly, deputy provincial surveyor, and filed in the registry office of the county of Essex.

The award contained a description of each of the small
tenements, and included certain buildings on the lots so

described, called the ferry house and the custom house, also the lands covered with water in front of some of the said lots, as far northward as the channel bank or navigable water of the river Detroit, subject however to the reservation of the bordage road expressed in the patent to François Baby of the said lands so covered with water, and to any public or private rights, excepting the rights of the said heirs and devisees, in respect of Water Street and River Street having been laid out in said plan. "All of which said lands," the award stated, "lie northward of the highway on the top of the southerly bank of the river Detroit, which crosses the front of said lots 79 and 80, and may be further described and known as laid down on a plan of the survey of the said railroad, as it runs through the said township of Sandwich, and as the line is marked on the said plan, which is to be deposited in the registry office of the county of Essex, and which lands are now represented by the said heirs and devisees of the said François Baby as being all the lands so designated in the said last mentioned plan, as required by the said company, on and out of the said lots 79 and 80, to which the said heirs and devisees claim title. *It being understood that the Great Western Railway Company shall construct and maintain a public water tank south of the railway, sufficient at all times to supply the inhabitants of the front of said lots 79 and 80 with water from the Detroit river, and shall keep open Ferry Street at its present width.*"

It appeared by the affidavits and papers, that the late François Baby, Esquire, was the owner of lots 79 and 80 in the first concession of the township of Sandwich, fronting on the river Detroit. (It was not stated whether these lots were each of the ordinary size of lots in the older townships—that is, 200 acres each— or whether they contained a less quantity of land. No doubt, however, they would embrace a large quantity of land subject to be affected, beneficially or otherwise, by the introduction of the railway.)

He was also the proprietor, under a patent issued to him in 1836, as the water lot in front of these lots, extending from the shore or edge of the river ten chains into the river, more or less, to ten feet water, on the edge of the navigable channel; with a condition inserted in his grant that he should not obstruct the road (or bordage) commonly used in winter along the margin of the said river Detroit.

On the 8th of October, 1840, Mr. Baby made his will, by which he devised to his children all his real and personal estate, to be equally divided between them, giving to the children of his deceased son Francis a share equally with his eight surviving children, making in all nine shares, "deducting from each portion the sum they may have received respectively."

He made his son James Baby, and his son-in-law James Dougall, his executors, giving them power to divide his real and personal property amongst his children; and if they should not agree among themselves, he directed his property to be sold to the highest bidder, "except the town lots, as far as it has been surveyed, shall be sold separately or divided among them, if they can possibly agree; if not, they must be sold."

Mr. Baby died in 1852.

The Great Western Railway Company, which had been chartered for some years for the purpose of constructing a railway from Hamilton to the river Detroit, at or near Windsor, required a small portion of the front of lots 79 and 80 for the track of their railway, and had surveyed and laid out in the usual manner the portions required. These portions consisted of several small pieces of land, some above the bank of the dry land, others covered with water, being small parts of the water lot granted to Mr. Baby in 1836. Mr. Baby had been selling small village lots in the village of Windsor, laid out upon the front of his lots 79 and 80, and these divided the small lots of lands still belonging to his estate, which the company required to occupy. In all, the dry land taken by the company was stated to amount only to forty-two hundreths of an acre, and the pieces covered with water to ninety-nine hundreths of an acre, making in the whole about one acre and a third.

There were also upon the land taken two buildings, called the ferry house and custom house.

Vankoughnet, Q. C., and *John Wilson*, shewed cause.

As to the legal objections in the case against the devisees of Mr. Baby, the first, is, that one of the devisees is a married woman.   This cannot prevail for several reasons, *first*, if she could not refer, neither could she agree to make the reference a rule of court, and the court cannot interfere : if the submission is bad as to part, it is bad altogether, and this application must fall to the ground.   *Secondly,* the company entered into the submission knowing her to be a married woman, and therefore they cannot move to set aside the award on that ground: they are estopped.—In re Warner et al., 2 D. & L. 148 ; Wrightson v. Bywater, 3M. & W. 199; Jones v. Powell, 6 Dowl. 483.   *Thirdly.* Under the Statute 9 Vic. ch. 81, sec. 30, it would seem that a married woman can refer.   In England it is considered doubtful whether a married woman cannot refer a matter in which she is directly interested.   In this country the case is a little different, for our acts enabling married women to convey their real property (1 Wm. IV. ch. 2, 2 Vic. ch. 6) shew that they must have the power of making a bargain for the disposal of it ; the power to make a conveyance presupposes that. Take the case of an infant, which is more analogous to the case of a married woman here, than is the case of a married woman in England : a bargain by him with an adult is binding upon the adult, although he cannot enforce it against the infant : 'so it is in this case : the married woman is not objecting, but the company, and if they cannot enforce it against her, she can against them, and she is willing to abide by the award.—Bendix v. Wateman, 12 M. & W. 97.   It may be argued that the same rules as are applied in England to property settled on a married woman should be applied here in all cases, for the act is in fact a statutory settlement.

The second, third, and fourth objections are of the same nature, and apply in all cases, though not to the same extent.   Not merely the value of the land is submitted, but all damages sustained by the rail road.   It was declared by the company before the arbitrators, with a view to reduce the damages, that they intended to allow a crossing ; surely they might shew that the damages would be less on this account ; and if so, the arbitrators might say that they had considered this in making their award.   The parties whose land is required come and claim large damages, because their whole communication will be cut off. The company's agent says, No! do not give damages on that footing, because we mean to allow a communication; and that being settled, the arbitration proceeds upon such understanding. It is always competent to both parties to settle certain points verbally before the arbitrators, as the bases of the award. In this case, the award merely says "it being understood :" it is not made a condition, and can at least do no harm : it is a protection to both parties. At all events, the company cannot complain of it; for it is a principle that no one can set aside an award on account of something in it to his own advantage. If this arrangement is not binding, so much the better for the company; it is the loss of the parties. It is clear, therefore, that there can be no interference on this ground; for if the reservation had not been inserted, the damages would certainly have been much greater.

As to the amount of damages allowed, the court will not interpose on the ground of excessive valuation, for these arbitrations would be useless if the value is afterwards to be decided by the court upon contradictory affidavits. It is purely a matter of discretion, and not one in which the court will interfere, The company are not obliged to run their road along the front of the town, but may go elsewhere if they choose.

Cameron, Q. C., and *Galt*, contra. These are statutory submissions, and under the statute the arbitrators have no right to award anything but compensation in money.—4 Wm. IV. ch. 29, sec. 3. They have no power to award any privilege whatever, but they must say as a matter of certainty what value they award for the land in money, and they must take nothing for granted, for that the statute does not allow.—Ware v. The Regent's Canal Co., 9 Ex. 395; S. C. 23 L. J. (Ex.) 145 ; Regina v. South Wales R. W. Co. 13 Q. B. 988; Skerratt v. The North Staffordshire R. W. Co. 5 R. W. Cas. 166 ; Gould v. The Staffordshire Potteries Waterworks Co., 6 R. W. Cas. 568. It is of no consequence whether they would have given more or less with or without the reservation; the Company are entitled to have the amount of compensation fixed in money.

As to the damages given, they are shewn by the affidavits to be clearly exorbitant. The arbitrators are directed by the act to take into consideration the benefit conferred on the property, as well as the damage done.—9 Vic. ch. 81, sec. 26. It is plain that they have entirely disregarded this direction, and have in fact allowed what they conceive will be the value of the land when the railroad is in full operation, and nothing in proportion to the worth at present, or what it would ever be without the benefits which are to be conferred by this very road. In such extreme cases the court will interfere.

ROBINSON, C. J.—If it were at all material towards determining upon the justice of this award that we should know how much could with reason be allowed to the devisees on account of the two buildings mentioned, supposing them to belong to the estate, we ought to have a more particular account of them; and so, also, if the award must have been taken to have been made up partly upon considerations connected with the ferry spoken of, it ought to have been shewn who holds now the interest in the ferry, and for how long a time, and whether it is or is not on the same footing as other ferries in the province, liable to be put up to public auction by the government at stated periods, and leased to the highest bidder.

But on a view of all the papers, it does not seem that much turns upon either of these points. The buildings must be small and of little worth, for they are spoken of as not of more value together than £250; and as to the ferry, it does not seem to have entered much into the consideration of the arbitrators, whose award appears to have been almost wholly confined to the estimate of the value of the land taken at so much per foot frontage.

Mr. Woods, one of the arbitrators, annexes to his affidavit memoranda of the different items of allowance, as the same were furnished to him by the two other arbitrators, who made the award from which he dissented; and these shew what I have just stated, that the £10,487 was given almost wholly as the value of the acre and one-third of land taken by the company, nearly two-thirds of which is covered with water.

If any of the legal objections taken to the award are such as we could hold to be entitled to prevail according to the principles which govern courts of justice, we should very willingly give effect to them ; for we have no hesitation in coming to the conclusion, that it is highly desirable that the value of the property in question should be submitted to another investigation and decision.

But as regards the first of these objections—grounded on Mrs. Dewson being a married woman, and therefore incapable of executing a submission—this objection, if it be one, was well known to the company, when they agreed to the reference. She and her husband have joined in the reference ; they avow themselves ready to convey their interest in the land; in pursuance of the award ; they are quite capable of doing so, and it will be easy to take measures which will insure the company against any imperfection in the title on that ground by authorizing them to withhold the money till the land is legally conveyed.

The second and third objections seem also to have been satisfactorily answered. It is not the devisees who are moving against the award, on the ground that some things are directed in their favor which cannot be enforced against the company ; it is the company who are complaining of the extravagance of the award. If they choose to object against the making and maintaining the tank spoken of, and to keeping open the ferry street, and can successfully resist both or either of them, that would only shew that, so far as the amount of the award can have been influenced by assuming that those things were to be done, the devisees may have reason to complain that they have been deluded by promises of advantages which cannot be secured to them and that the sum awarded as the value of their property should therefore have been larger, as they cannot reckon upon enjoying these benefits which the arbitrators may have taken into account as considerations in their favor, tending to diminish the sum to be awarded. Besides, these are not things which the arbitrators have taken upon themselves to direct. They seem rather to have inserted them as being things understood between the parties, and which they had therefore taken into consideration in estimating the damages.

It is stated, and not denied, and indeed the papers plainly shew it, that the mention of these things came rather from the company than from the devisees or the arbitrators. They desired, and properly too, that it should be plainly understood upon what footing the proprietors would stand after the award and took care to have it stated that they, the company, undertook to do the things spoken of; wishing, as we may suppose, which would also be very just and proper, that these burthens which they undertook to bear should be considered in making up the award. Any influence that consideration could have had must have been in diminution of the sum awarded ; and if the company can now decline to fulfil the expectation which they held out, that can surely be no reason why we should at their instance set aside the award. That we might do so, if, in the exercise of our discretion, on such an application, we saw good reason for it, I do not doubt, and cases might be cited which would seem fully to warrant us in giving way to that objection.

The fourth objection seems to us as little tenable. The award, where it alludes to the bordage road, evidently only makes mention of it by way of keeping in view an existing easement which the public had as against Mr. Baby and his successors in the title, by the very terms of the patent, and from which, as the arbitrators desired the company to understand, it was not in the power of them or of the devisees to relieve the land proposed to be taken, whatever other means the company might have of overcoming any inconvenience arising from it.

As to the fifth objection, so far as we can see from any thing before us, the devisees may take an equal interest in the lands. The provision that there is to be deducted from each portion the sum they may have received each respectively does no doubt throw an uncertainty about the division, because, for all we know, it may have the effect, according to circumstances of which nothing is shewn to us, of making the distribution very unequal.

We cannot doubt that Mr. Baby was aware that something had been done which would call that direction into effect, or he would hardly have said anything of the kind; but we do not see that the apprehension of an unequal distribution need create any difficulty. The sum awarded might properly be paid into the hands of the executors, leaving it to them to divide it under the responsibility thrown upon them by the will, as they may have to divide all the proceeds of all the real and personal estate in case of their finding it necessary to sell it for the reasons suggested by the testator. The case of McGill v. Proudfoot (4 U.C.R. 40) is against setting aside the award upon this objection.

It is not surprising that the company should have attempted to avail themselves of any and every apparent objection to the award, whether substantial or not, under the impression, which we cannot doubt they entertain, that the award is excessive, and, as they term it in their application, exorbitant. That is evidently their main objection; and if they did not feel that they had any just complaint to urge on that head, I dare say we should have heard nothing of the other objections which I have remarked upon.

As to the footing upon which our right of reversion rests, the general Railway Clauses Act does not apply to this company : we must look to the provisions in the statutes which specially concern them—namely, the original act constituting the charter of the company (4 Wm. IV. ch. 29), and the acts 8 Vic. ch. 86 and 9 Vic. ch. 81, amending it. The third clause of 4 Wm. IV. ch. 29, provides for the appointment by the parties of arbitrators, in case they cannot themselves agree, either upon the value of the lands and tenements, or private privileges proposed to be purchased, or upon the damages to be paid to them in consequence of the intended railroad being made upon their lands : and the statute enacts that the persons so chosen shall be arbitrators, to award, determine, adjudge, and order the sum of money which the company shall pay to the person entitled to receive the same : and that the award of a majority shall be final. It directs that they shall meet at a convenient place, after eight days notice, " then and there to arbitrate and award, adjudge and determine, *such matters and things as_shall be submitted to their consideration by the parties interested :* "and that they shall be sworn well and truly to assess the damages between the parties, according to the best of their judgment: and it provides, "that any award made under that act shall be subject to be set aside on application to the court of King's Bench, *in the same manner and on the same grounds as in ordinary cases of submission by the parties*," *in which case a* reference may be again made to arbitration as directed by that act.

In the statute 9 Vic. ch. 81, sec. 26, it is provided that, in all arbitrations under that or any other act relating to this railroad, " *the arbitrators shall take into consideration the benefit conferred on the property on which they are arbitrating as well as the damage done to any particular portion thereof*."

In considering in any cases of this description how far it may be proper for us to interpose upon the merits, on a complaint that the award is outrageously excessive, it seems to me to be a material consideration that the submission to arbitrate under this and similar statutes can hardly be said to be the voluntary act of the parties.   It is in a manner compulsory ; either party has it in his power to drive the other to arbitration.   The force therefore of the remark, that the arbitrators are judges of the parties' own choosing, is in such cases very much diminished.   Each party does indeed select his arbitrator, but the arbitrators select the third ; and if unwarily an inexpedient choice is made by the two, the party who suffers from it must submit, except so far as the courts of justice can afford him relief.   The same risk is run in voluntary submission between parties.   The difference is, that in such cases the parties, sensible of the risk, may avoid incurring it, as many do, and may prefer abiding by the judgment of a court and jury.   In these statutory cases there is no such option.   That is not a consideration which can warrant us, I think, in being governed by other principles in disposing of applications than those which usually govern us ; but to this event it should, I think, reasonably influence us— that wherever we would hesitate on a submission between parties, about setting aside an award upon the ground of its being manifestly outrageous in amount, or unjust otherwise if the same case had happened to be one under a statute of this kind, the consideration that the submission was in a measure compulsory should have a strong influence in turning the scale.

It is plain that, under the power given to us by the statute in question, we are bound by the same general principles, in acting with respect to awards under it, which govern us in other cases ; and, in the next place, that the ground of excessive damages is one upon which we could only act in extreme cases.   We do not, I think, differ on these points from any thing that was said by this court in the case of the Commissioners of Public Works v. Daly (6 U. C. R.40-43), or in Scobell v. Gilmor (5 U. C. R. 51).   To say that the courts can in no case of submission between party and party set aside an award, because it is so manifestly excessively in amount as to be outrageous, would clearly be wrong.   We can suppose many cases in which they would find themselves compelled to do it, and could not in conscience decline.   For instance, suppose a man, in driving his vehicle along a public highway, negligently or unskilfully drives against the gig or waggon of another person, and breaks it, he may acknowledge his fault, and be willing to make compensation, but not being able to agree with the owner of the carriage as to the amount of the injury, there would be nothing more reasonable and natural than that they should refer it to a third party to estimate the damages.   If in such a case the arbitrator should determine the carriage to be worth a thousand pounds, could we refuse to interfere ? Again, one neighbour may unintentionally trespass upon another, and cut a few feet over the boundary, supposing that he was clearing upon his own land ; suppose, that in such a case, upon the damage being referred to arbitration, the arbitrator should award a sum three times larger than any one would be willing to give for the whole farm trespassed upon—can we say that there should be no redress? I state extreme cases purposely, because it is only in what the court takes to be an extreme case that an interposition would be thought of, where there is no imputation of misconduct in the arbitrators; and because, if any such extreme case the court could not justifiable refuse to interfere, then it must be admitted that there is a duty incumbent upon the court which involves a responsibility which they are not at liberty to decline.   They must at least ask themselves whether the award is or is not manifestly and undeniably and outrageously excessive, or on any other ground unjust, where the party against whom the award is, complains of it upon such ground.

If we should be satisfied, on the facts shown to us, that an acre of land taken by this railway company anywhere along the line, could, before they began their work, have been bought for £5, and if the abitrators called to value that same acre, after they had taken it, should value it at £5000, I could not but look upon such an award as manifestly and outrageously excessive; and yet I should not think the inference clearer in such a case than it appears to me to be in the present.   If this railway had not come near Windsor, but had terminated at Sarnia or Amherstburg, without a prospect of the Baby property being more immediately benefited by it than any other land forty miles distant, I do not believe, from anything shown to us, or from anything that I know or have ever observed, that an acre and a third of land in the front of lots 79 and 80 would have been worth at this time £10,000, or anything beyond a small proportion of that sum.   I may be wrong in that, but it is at present my conviction.   In valuing it at £10,487 10s. it appears to me that the arbitrators must have disregarded entirely the express direction of the statute 9 Vic. ch. 81. sec. 26, and that they cannot have taken into consideration the benefit conferred on the property on which they are arbitrating; that is, on lots 79 and 80, or such parts of them as still belong to the devisees.

If the effect of the railway has been to make this minute portion of the land worth £10,000 and upwards, it must surely have added immensely to the value of the adjacent property.   If it has not added to the value of the rest of the land by any means in the same proportion (as indeed it obviously could not have done), yet surely it is manifest that it must have very greatly increased it; and it is equally obvious, I think, that if the acre and one-third of land in question is really now worth £10,000, it must have attained to that immense and almost incredible value in consequence of the railway; and if so, then the effect of such an award is to make the company pay a ruinous price to the proprietors, in consequence of the very advantages which the company has at its own expense created. It is very evident, I think, what is meant by the clause I have cited. We cannot expect it to be so literally and stringently carried into effect, as that the lands taken shall not in general be valued somewhat more highly than they would have been if there had been no railway, because it is hard to distinguish nicely how much of the general improvement in the price of lands may be attributed to that cause; but in this case before us, if not in all the four cases, the arbitrators seem to have thought it just to make the company pay according to a valuation which would have been altogether imaginary and fictitious if it were not for the effect of what the company have done or are doing on the particular piece of land taken, or in its immediate vicinity.

I think in all these cases there is so much reason to apprehend that the arbitrators have either misconceived the direction of the statute which I have just cited, or have failed to attend to or be governed by it, that we cannot properly forbear to set any of these awards aside, but must subject them to the consideration of other arbitrators; though, if the award in the case of Hunt stood alone, I do not think that we should have found ourselves called upon to interfere upon the ground of the damages being so manifestly outrageous as to afford ground for believing that the arbitrators had disregarded the injunction in the act of parliament to make allowance for the benefit conferred on the property by the railroad.

In this case, of the devisees of Mr. Baby, we think we are bound to make the rule absolute, for the reason that it appears to us that the valuation is so excessive as to make it plain that the arbitrators have not conformed to the statute in making their estimate, but have made the company pay, and apparently pay most extravagantly, for the expected advantage of an immense trade which the railway has brought or is expected to bring there, and for the effect of that trade in enhancing the value of the property.

It is on this ground that we make the rule absolute in this case; but, to avoid occasion for question upon any future award, we would suggest that it should be clearly expressed, in the first place, that the sum awarded is given for the value of the lands and tenements or private privileges proposed to be purchased, or for the amount of damages which the claimant is entitled to receive in consequence of the intended railroad in and upon his lands (as the case may be); and that the award should either be silent in regard to any other matter on which the statute gives no authority to the arbitrators to give a direction; or that, if the estimate has been influenced by anything which the company has engaged to do in order to lessen the inconvenience, it should be plainly expressed that the company have undertaken to do it; and the particular thing should be so defined as to leave no uncertainty, and no room for future litigation as to what is to be done or allowed by the company, and at what particular point in their work, and in what manner it is to be done.

It would be better, too, that an undertaking under the seal of the company, securing the advantage or privilege in precise terms, should be taken; and if they will not give such undertaking, there should be no allowance made for such proposed advantage or privilege in estimating the value or damages to be paid by the company.

In England care has been taken for guarding against litigation and injustice upon these points, by some provisions which have not yet been made in this province.

BURNS, J.—If the provisons respecting the keeping of a tank to supply the inhabitants of the fronts of certain lots, together with the keeping open of Ferry Street, were sufficient, as being apparent on the face of the award, to render it void, we need not then be called to upon to set aside, for it never could be enforced either by action or attachment.

The objections in other respects to this award bring up a question of great importance to public companies, and one not less interesting to the members of the community.   Can

an over value be made the means of attacking the award?
If the principles upon which the arbitrators proceed are
within the legal bounds of their jurisdiction,|then I feel clear
that an overvaluation on their part cannot *per se*—unless that
proceeds from corruption, partiality, or misconduct (or the
overvalue in itself is such as to afford intrinsic evidence of these
objections)—be made the means of attacking the award. The
question here is, when there are legal principles established
upon which a valuation shall be made, can the court review the
facts upon which the arbitrators have proceeded, in order to
accertain whether those principles have been followed? If
the arbitrators had stated that they were guided by such
principles in the conclusions they have arrived at, there
might be a difficulty in receiving evidence to contradict such
expressed determination on their part; but if they do not so
inform us, then are we at liberty to make the inquiry into
what the arbitrators did, in order to ascertain whether they
have proceeded upon legal principles? In Johnson v. Durant
(2 B. & Ad. 930) Lord Tenterden says, "Now, if an award,
made in pursuance of a judge's order drawn up by consent of
parties, proceeds upon a mistaken ground, the proper course
of relief is an application to the court to set aside the award."
See also, for the same principle, Broadhurst v. Darlington
(2 Dowl. 38), and Bartle v. Musgrave (1 Dowl. N.S. 325).

The statute 9 Vic. ch. 81, says that the arbitrators shall
take into consideration the benefit conferred on the property
on which they are arbitrating, as well as the damage done to
any particular portion thereof. Whether this provision be
considered obligatory or directory, it is certain the legislature
intended it should have attention on the part of the arbitrators;
and no doubt the legislature felt it right to impose such an
obligation on arbitrators, for the right to have a valuation
made by a jury, is not conferred, but arbitrators are substituted
in the place of a jury, and it is made compulsory upon parties
to proceed in that way, The questions are, whether in this
case the arbitrators have disregarded this principle of valuation; and if so, whether it be a sufficient ground to interfere
with the award. I have already shewn that were there are
principles which would legally govern, and it is shewn that

from mistake a wrong ground of decision is assumed by the arbitrators, that is a reason for interfering with the award. Many cases other than I have mentioned might be cited to establish this principle.   Then have the arbitrators here disregarded, or acted without reference to, the legal principle upon which the legislature says they shall be governed?   If this principle had been brought to their notice, and they had utterly disregarded it, and had passed their judgment upon the matters shewing that no intention was paid to this provision, I have no doubt the court would interfere, and would not allow an award to stand under such circumstances.   Then in a case where it is not shewn that such principle of valuation was brought to the notice of the arbitrators, but still the facts shew that the principle did not and could not possibly have been acted on by them, can the court interfere?   This may, I think, be solved by considering what is the jurisdiction of the arbitrators.   However the provision in the act of parliament may be viewed, yet still it is an ingredient to be considered, and forms part of their jurisdiction, and a legal principle to be acted upon.   If the arbitrators act without doing so upon a legal principle which should govern, it may be asked whether there is any distinction between such a case and a case where the arbitrators have disregarded that principle.   I do not think there is.   It then simply remains to ascertain whether this is a case in which the valuation of the damages has been made upon principles different from what should in law have governed the arbitrators.   It appears, to me impossible to view it in any other light.   The testator in 1852, appears to have been willing to have sold what was then considered sufficient for the road for £1,125. We must suppose he knew very well the value to himself of the increased value, by reason of the railway, of the remainder of his property, and also the injury he would sustain by the construction of the road.   It is difficult to conceive what could have occurred in the space of a year to raise the value of that portion added to some more land the company required, being a small addition, and also the injury to the owner, from £1,125 to £10,500.   It is imposssible to believe otherwise than that the arbitrators have estimated the damages without any reference to the benefit conferred on the property, if indeed they could with any truth be said, taking that also into consideration, to amount to so enormous a sum. The position of the property, as shewn by the affidavits, brings it within the provision of the act of parliament, that the construction of the road would confer a benefit as well as do an injury, and consequently both matters should have formed the basis of the award. From the evidence on the part of the parties supporting this award, it as clear to me that the basis of the award is upon one part of the proposition, that is, that it is confined to the value of the land taken and the damages, without regard to benefit the parties have gained. Strictly speaking, the words of the award are the words of the reference, but then the provision which is to govern the arbitrators with respect to estimating damages is a statutory one, and it would not be necessary to embody it in the reference, but the arbitrators by law must obey it.

Without meaning to impute actual corruption and partiality to the arbitrators in this case, it appears to me there is such a legal misconduct proceeding from a want of acting upon a legal and proper principle, which should have guided the arbitrators in assessing the damages, as compels me to say this award ought not be allowed to stand.

DRAPER, J., concurred.

Rule absolute.

GREAT WESTERN RAILROAD COMPANY V. HUNT.

Compensation for matters not within the submission—Reservation of right to cross the track.

In this case the arbitrators awarded a certain sum for the defendant's interest in the land as lessee, "and for the lumber taken by the said Company now piled upon that part of the wharf taken by the said Company." The award then proceeded to say, "we have taken it for granted, in making this award, that the said C. H. shall have the right to cross the railway track from one part of his property to another."

Held, That the arbitrators had no power to award compensation for the lumber ; and that the provision as to the right to cross was objectionable as not being sufficiently definite or certain.

The submission was in the same form as the others.

The award was made on the 21st of January, 1854, and determined that Charles Hunt had sustained damage by location of railway to £3,047, which the arbitrators directed to be paid to him in full, for all damages done to him by reason of said location, referring to the railway plan for a description of the ground occupied, which the award said was leased by Hunt from one Ouillette; and for his future interest as lessee in the lands so taken, and *for the lumber* taken by the said Company now piled upon that part of the wharf taken by the said Company.

"We have taken it for granted' (the award proceeded to say) "in making this award, that the said Charles Hunt shall have the right to cross the railway track from one part of his property to another."

The award was moved against on the grounds—1st. That the arbitrators have not decided in all matters submitted to them; in this, that they take it for granted that Charles Hunt shall have the right to cross the railway track, whereas the matter submitted to them was the amount of damages from the construction of the railway, and no authority was given to the arbitrators to make any reservation.

2ndly. That it was not final, because the said Charles Hunt might claim damages if the Company should prevent his crossing the track of the railway, whereas the arbitrators should have decided on all damages arising from the construction of the railway.

3rdly. For excess of authority in awarding on the price to be paid for lumber taken including it in the sum of £3,047, whereas all they had to determine was the damages arising from the location of the railway.

4thly. For misconduct of the arbitrators, in awarding an exorbitant and extravagant amount.

Mr. Woods, one of the arbitrators, swore that he refused to join in the award, because he considered the amount extravagant, and because the other arbitrators awarded £556 10s. for a quantity of lumber then on the premises taken by the Company.

It was sworn also that the land taken was fifteen-hundredths of an acre, covered with water of the Detroit River, and that it was in the possession of Charles Hunt, part of the premises taken being a wharf.

ROBINSON, C. J.—In this case the award is in one respect very unsatisfactory at least; it awards £3,047 to Hunt for his interest *as lessee* in less than one-sixth of an acre of land covered with water on one portion of which is a wharf, and for damages sustained by him as lessee. It is not explained in the award, and it is not shewn, for what time Mr. Hunt is tenant of that property. His right, for all that appears, may expire in a very short time. We should, perhaps, however assume in favor of the award that the arbitrators took care to ascertain the facts, and have acted according to them, though they have given no information on the subject. The having awarded for lumber taken, under this statutory submission, seems to have been irregular; and if the consent of the Company that such an item should be included could cure it, or should estop them from moving on that ground, we cannot say that we see evidence of that assent being given in such a manner as we could say bound them.

As to what is said as to Hunt having a right to cross the railway track *from one part of his property to another*, that, as in the case of Mr. Baby's devisees, is rather an expression of what the arbitrators have been given to understand was intended (but which is not shewn to have been in any way secured), than anything which the arbitrators have themselves directed. We should, perhaps, not have set aside the award on that ground, as it is not a direction, and if it were, could not be binding upon the company, and could have had no influence prejudicial to them in raising the amount of damages awarded, but rather the reverse. From its tendency, however, to produce litigation, as an attempt to describe an understanding which is too indefinite to be binding it is no doubt objectionable.

BURNS, J.—If the grounds upon which this award is attacked were such as that upon the face of it, we should be compelled to say that what the arbitrators have done was clearly contrary to the statute, then the decision must be, that as it could neither be enforced by action or attachment, so neither would the court interfere to set it aside.—In re The

North Staffordshire Railway Company and Landor, and also the same Company and Wood (2 Ex. 235 and 244).

There are two points, however, as it appears to me, upon which we should interfere to set the award aside, in order that the case may be reopened between the parties, and that there may be another arbitration between them, as the 3rd section of the charter 4 Wm. IV. ch. 29 says there may be.

1st. The submission in this case is of two distinct things —first, of the value of the land occupied by the track ; and secondly, the damage that Hunt has sustained by reason of the location of it on his lands The award is silent with respect to the value of the land, and only awards damages. It may be that it would be considered sufficient, inasmuch as it appears that he is but a lessee. The award is not objected to on that ground, but it is complained against as not being final; because the arbitrators have said they take it for granted, in making their award, that the said Hunt shall have the right to cross the railway track from one part of his property to another. This shews there must have been a severance of the property into portions by reason of the railway track. Now was it within the power of the arbitrators to consider that matter in estimating the damages, and might they do so with reference to a crossing to be provided from the one portion to the other of the property ? The charter granted to this company is very different in that respect from the provisions contained in the English acts. The ninth section of the act forbids the company to interfere with private rights without the permission of the owner first had and obtained, either by consent or by reference ; and the fourth section says the company shall have power to complete the work, doing as little damage as may be, and making satisfaction in the manner in the act mentioned, for all damages to be sustained by the owner. I incline to think that though there may be cases where the portions cut off from other portions of lands would be such that the company would not be bound to pay for in the way of damages, as being useless or worthless to the owner, and so there would be no necessity for a crossing ; yet, in other cases, where the property is severed, and the company would not be bound to take one portion, but *the doing as little damage as might be* would be complied with by a crossing or building of a bridge for the convenience of the proprietor, then the arbitrators would have authority to deal with the question of crossing the track in estimating the damages. It appears to me, however, this must be settled by the parties to the reference, or if they do not or cannot, then that the arbitrators must do it for them. The setting apart of the road track and occupation of it operates as a statutory conveyance of the land, and all that remains to be done is to value the land occupied, and estimate the damage sustained—Osler v. Cook (13 Q. B. 143.) If the proprietor is to retain the portion cut off from the other, it follows that he must be provided with some way to get at it. On the other hand, the whole road track is vested in the company, and the company is bound to fence it in. It may be a great inconvenience to the company to have the line of the track subject to private rights extending over the whole and undefined. The vice of this award, as I view it, is that it neither shews any definite understanding between the parties as to the right to cross, where it shall exist, nor does it define it by the award ; and therefore this matter may be a subject of future litigation between the parties. If it is to exist over every part of the the land occupied, or in such places as the proprietor may choose, it may entail very heavy expenses upon the company hereafter, if it be necessary to buy off that right ; or, on the other hand, if the company should desire to confine the proprietor to some particular place, then he may complain of that limitation. Now does the award mean that Hunt shall have the right to go over every part of the track ? If so, then it would seem inconsistent with the right of the company, because we can only understand their object to be to have the land to be used as a road or way. Each having a right of way over it might clash in the user. Which then is to have the primary right of using the way, if both rights are to exist to that extent ? These are matters which should be precisely defined either by the parties or by the award. In this case it is not pretended the parties have settled it, and the award most certainly does not. The sum awarded as damages does not, with any certainty that I can see, settle this difficulty ; and it may be that in the end, if the award is to be interpreted as meaning that the proprietor shall have a right to cross the track when and where he pleases, that the company may have to pay a further sum to settle such right, in the shape of damages ; and it may be that if the company seek to limit Hunt, it may be to his disadvantage. This right of crossing is, I think, a material ingredient in the amount of damages, and must affect them, and should therefore, as this case shews that the proprietor retained his several portions, have been clearly defined, so as not to leave the parties liable to future disputes; and therefore, large as the damages are which have been awarded, and that it may be said that if the crossing had not been conceded the damages would have been more, yet I think it renders the award uncertain and not final.

I think this position, and that this is a good ground of objection to the award, are fully borne out by the cases I have already mentioned, and the following :—In re Bradshaw's Arbitration 12 Q. B. 562), Regina v. South Wales Railway Co. 13 Jur. 1095 and 13 Q. B. 988), Manning v. Eastern Counties R. W. Co. (12 M. &. W. 237).

2ndly. The award is uncertain as to the amount of damages for the location of the track on the lands of Hunt, inasmuch as a sum therein included for a quantity of lumber, which it is said the company have taken, which belonged to Hunt, and the award does not tell us how much was awarded for the lumber. Taking the lumber into consideration was clearly outside the written submission, and Hunt admits such to be the case, but contends that. at the time of the arbitration being proceeded with, the solicitors of both parties agreed that the arbitrators should take the matter into consideration. That involves the question, whether a solicitor having no authority to defend a suit, so far as this case discloses, could bind a corporation by a mere verbal reference. It may be urged that Hunt would be estopped in any action he might bring against the company in respect of that lumber. Possibly he might ; but that is uncertain, inasmuch as the obligations should be mutual, and different opinions are entertained about it, and the company should, as contended, be bound also by such a reference. I take it to be clear that, in a matter not pending in a court, a solicitor would not have any authority to refer a matter to arbitration without the corporation seal. There is an inconsistency in this case upon the face of the award. The arbitrators first tell us that the sum of £3,047 is awarded as the amount of damages sustained by Hunt in respect of the location of the road, and then afterwards say that sum is also in full of the lumber piled upon the land taken by the company. Viewing this part of the award by itself, I should say the arbitrators had exceded their authority, because the reference in respect of the lumber was not mutually binding; but looking at it mixed up with the other, I do not think the company should be put to defend themselves against it, and take the chance of its being held whether Hunt would be estopped from recovering in an action, were he to bring one for the lumber. It would appear rather in the light of a trespass committed by the company, if the lumber were taken by their authority than a contract for purchase of it. However desirable it might be thought to settle all matters in one arbitration, yet the parties should stand upon an equal footing in being bound as well before as by the award; and I do not see they did, even supposing they might be a reference of such a matter with the other matter respecting the land. It does not appear that the corporate body were acting, so far as there is evidence in the matter, beyond the written submission; and the matter is too uncertain, I think, to hold that the company should be bound.

DRAPER, J., concurred.

Rule absolute.

GREAT WESTERN RAILROAD COMPANY V. DOUGALL.

Uncertainty—Excessive compensation.

The award in this case also was held bad for want of certainty and definiteness, in the provisions respecting the right to cross the track and the manner of doing so. It appeared, too, that the sum awarded was excessive.

The submission in this case, as in that between the company and the devisees of Mr. Baby, recited that disputes and differences existed between the company and him, Dougall, " as to the value of the land required by the company for the use of the road and also the damage which he, Dougall, may sustain thereby;" and it referred " all disputes and differences which exist between the parties to arbitration of the same arbitrators as in other case."

The award was, that Dougall had sustained damages by the location and appropriation of his lands for the railway, to £5,870, in full of damages done and for the land required, forty feet in width through his lands, and described particularly in the award and by reference to the registered plan.

And the award proceeded thus :—"And in making this our award, we have taken it for granted that the said James Dougall, his heirs and assigns, owning this wharf, *shall have a right of way at all times for ever, over the ferry lot, and north of the railway line. twenty feet in width, leading from Ferry Street to his wharf, in lieu of a right to cross the said railway track and line ; and that he shall have the right to bridge or arch over the said track at the points on his said lots, for at least twenty-five feet in width at each place, at the usual height of road crossings, which is seventeen feet in the clear.* But the plan, quality, material, and construction of the said arches or bridge, shall be subject to the approval of the engineer of the western section of the Great Western Railway Company, provided that his right of approval shall not be understood as enabling him to make objections so unreasonable as to prevent the construction thereof; and that the said James Dougall shall be at the expense thereof, and that the same shall be constructed in as substantial a manner as the railway work of a similar kind." This award, like the others, was signed by two only of the arbitrators.

It was moved against, on the grounds—

1st. That it is not final:—referring to the directions respecting the right of way, and the bridged or arched way to be constructed.

2ndly. That the arbitrators have awarded upon matters not submitted to them: referring to the same portion of the award.

3rdly. That the arbitrators have not decided on the description, quality, and construction of the arches and bridges, but have referred these to the engineer of the company, and they had no power so to delegate their authority.

4thly. And for misconduct in the arbitrators, in awarding an extravagant and excessive sum to be paid.

It was sworn that the land taken by the company was in quantity sixteen-hundredths of an acre—about one sixth.

ROBINSON, C. J.—Mr. Dougall makes an affidavit, that he values the land taken at £4,000, and his other damages at £4,950; in which case, if I understand his affidavit, he considers that the award does not give him half as much as he should have had.

For reasons given in the case of the award made by the same arbitrators upon the claim of the devisees of the late Mr. Baby, we think we cannot refuse to give the company the relief which they have applied for from this award, in order that an award may be made, after giving, as the arbitrators are bound to do, reasonable effect to the directions of the legislature in 9 Vic. ch. 81, sec. 26. But, independently of this consideration, we should have found it difficult, we think, to uphold this award, on account of the directions contained in it respecting the arching and bridges, which we think very objectionable, being in their nature vague and undefined as to the points of crossing, and assuming to bind the company in matters in which the arbitrators had no jurisdiction, and leaving open very important points, in which they declare the judgment of the company's engineer shall only govern when it is not unreasonable; while at the same time no means are provided, or could possible be provided, by the arbitrators, for determining what may or may not be unreasonable.—See Stonehewer v. Farrar (6 Q. B. 730).—

There is also the circumstance that it encourages Mr. Dougall to think that he may go to work himself and make the bridges or archways, which could hardly fail to bring him at once into conflict with the company.

BURNS, J.—Independent of any objection to the validity of the award on the ground of excessive value it appears to me it cannot be supported on account of the indefiniteness of the provision respecting the crossing and arches to be built ; providing the proprietor shall do it, if the award confers on him that right The loose and indefinite manner in which the provisions may be carried out, very likely will lead to further litigation between the parties, and therefore it appears to me the award cannot be said finally to dispose of the matters between them.

DRAPER, J., concurred.

Rule absolute.

_____

GREAT WESTERN RAILROAD COMPANY v. DODDS.

Sum awarded excessive—Reservation of right to cross.

This award also was objectionable for the excessive compensation given. It contained the following reservation :—"Reserving to Dodds the right to cross the said railroad line from one portion of his land to the other."

Held, That the arbitrators had no right to make an absolute reservation as this assumed to be, and that even if they had, so indefinite a provision would have been a void exercise of their authority.

But *semble*, that such reservation, being unauthorized and void, would not necessarily invalidate the whole award.

The submission in this was like that in the other cases. The award was made on the 27th of January, 1854—that the company should pay to John Dodds £690, in full for all damages done, and land required by the company for the uses of the railway, being forty feet in width along the track, and described as in the said railway company's plan—"reserving to Dodds the right to cross the said railroad line from one portion of his said land to the other."

This award was moved against on the grounds : 1st Excess of authority in reserving to Dodds a right of way across the track of the railway company, when they had no authority to grant or reserve such right, but only to determine the damages sustained from the construction of the railway.

2ndly. That it was not final, because Dodds might claim damages if the company should prevent his crossing the track, whereas the arbitrators should have decided on all damages arising to Dodds by reason of the construction of the railway.

3rdly. For misconduct of the arbitrators, in awarding an extravagant and exorbitant amount.

The land taken was seven-hundredths of an acre, covered with water of the river Detroit.

ROBINSON, C. J.—In this case the fourteenth part of an acre of land, covered with water has been valued at £690. It is sworn to be worth no more than £200. Whether, valuing it at that sum allowance has been made for the additional value given to it by the railway, when otherwise it might have been worth even less than £200, we do not know.

In this, as in two, I think of the three other cases, the claimants are not shewn to be proprietors of other lands adjacent, which, being raised in value by the railway, might compensate them for being deprived of the small portions of land taken by the company ; but even supposing they had no other land than that taken, it is evidently the intention of the legislature, and not an unjust intention, that if the small piece of land taken has received its present value chiefly from the operations of the company in constructing the railway there, it is not such increased value that should be awarded against them, but only fair or rather liberal compensation for any thing that they can be said to have suffered from the company : in other words, that they shall at least be as well off as if the company had not brought the railway there, and had not required any of their land.

It is because we think that these four awards, all made by the same arbitrators, present manifest evidence to our minds that they have not so applied the statute, that we think it not just or safe to assume that they have in any one of the instances done so, especially where the valuation strikes us as being very high.—In this case, it would be at the rate of £9000, and upwards for an acre, which I do not imagine was understood to be a common value for land on the southern bank of the river Detroit, before there was any expectation of a railway coming there.

If two, or three, or four times what we might see to have been the fair value had been given, and in a case where the sum would not be large, we should perhaps not have felt ourselves bound to interfere, and it is probable we should not have been asked to do so ; but these do not appear to us to be cases of that description.

In this case the objection is raised that the award assumes *absolutely to reserve* to Dodds the right to cross the railroad form one portion of his land to the other, which certainly they had no authority to do, and which, if they could have done it, would have been a void exercise of their authority from the indefinite nature of the reservation, not pointing out at what point, or under what restrictions or precaution such a right to cross should be used.

Strictly speaking, I apprehend, without having had an opportunity to look as fully into that point as I should wish to do in any case that turned wholly upon it, such a reservation, when the arbitrators had no authority to make it, would not necessary invalidate the whole award, because the company might disregard it. It could not be enforced if ever so definite, and therefore its being indefinite would seem of little consequence, though if the want of certainty occurred in a direction which they had a right to give, it would be otherwise.

For the other reasons already given, we make the rule absolute in this case also.

BURNS, J.—The observations I have made in Hunt's case in respect to the crossing apply in this case, and I need add no more.

DRAPER, J., concurred.

Rule absolute.

IN RE JOHNSON AND THE MUNICIPALITY OF GLOUCESTER.

Award under 16 Vic. ch. 183, sec. 33—No notice of meeting given to municipality.

The court set aside an award, made in pursuance of 16 Vic. ch. 181, sec. 33, as to to the damages to be paid to a party through whose land the municipality had opened a road, where it appeared that no notice had been given to the municipality of the meeting of the arbitrators, and that no one had attended on their behalf.

Richards obtained, in Hilary term last, a rule on Johnson, to shew cause why the award made on the 6th of December, 1853, between these parties should not be set aside, on the grounds—

1st. That the arbitrators made their award without giving the municipality an opportunity of being heard, or being present through their attorney or agent, or with their witnesses, at any of the sittings or meetings of the arbitrators; and without giving notice of any meeting, or of their intention to proceed.

2ndly. That the award was made without having heard the said municipality, or any one on their behalf, or any of their witnesses.

3rdly. That the award is extravagant an unjust.

4thly. On other grounds disclosed in affidavits filed.

On the 26th of September, 1853, the municipality of Gloucester passed a by-law establishing a road therein described, and Johnson was, on the same day, personally served with a copy of it, as being a party interested. On the 10th of November, 1853, Johnson gave notice of his appointment of an arbitrator on his part to award on the damages to be paid to him in consequence of the road passing through his land.

On the 6th of December, 1853, the arbitrators, three in number, made an award, in which they recited that they had been attended by the parties and their witnesses, and had heard and considered the allegations and proofs of the respective parties, and had viewed the lands, and in making their award had regarded, not only the value of the interest of the said James Johnson in the said lands taken for the road, but also the damage to be sustained by him in consequence of the road dividing his land, and the cost and charge of making and keeping up fences along each side of the road; and had considered on the other hand any benefit which he would ordinarily derive by opening up the road. And they awarded, that there was due to him the sum of £236, as the purchase money and compensation for his interest in the land intended to be taken for the road, and for all damages as aforesaid, which sum they awarded to him " over and above any advantage which he may derive from the opening out of the said road," and they directed the money to be paid on or before the 2nd of January, 1854. The award was signed by all the arbitrators.

Many affidavits were filed on both sides. The arbitrators

gave particular details of the grounds on which they allowed the sum which they had done, but none of the affidavits filed on the part of Johnson repelled or took any notice of statements made on the part of the municipality which served to shew the sum awarded to be extremely unreasonable in amount.

The road ran across two lots of Johnson, 23 and 25, and also across the intervening lot 24, which was owned by another party. Across this intervening lot, it was stated, and not denied, that there was no road before, and that the new road would be a positive benefit instead of an injury to Johnson, as it would give him the means of convenient access from one of his farms to the other. Then it was stated that Johnson's lots had been rated at the last assessment, one of them at £1 5s. an acre only, and the other at £1 2s. 6d.; that the whole quantity of land taken was between four and five acres; that the large sum awarded was attempted to be justified on the ground that Johnson would have to make and maintain a fence on both sides of the new road, but that in fact this new road, where it crossed his lots, was only a substitute for a public road which already crossed the same lots, and had existed for many years, making it straighter and shorter, and in many parts following the old line, so that he would have no additional charge imposed upon him in respect to fences.

Eccles shewed cause.

Richards, contra, cited Dobson v. Groves, 6 Q. B. 637; Anon. 2 Ch. Rep. 44.

ROBINSON, C. J. delivered the judgment of the court.

While the statements on the part of the municipality are unrepelled, it really does seem that the award is most unreasonable; but, independently of any consideration of that kind, there is the objection that the arbitrators admit that they gave no notice whatever of their time and place of meeting, not being aware that it was necessary to do so; that they took no evidence, and were not attended by any one on the part of the municipality.

One of the township councillors, living on the adjoining

lot to Johnson, was present, it seems, when they examined the line of road, but he swears that he was attending only casually, not by any direction of the council, nor in any manner authorized to represent them.

The provision in the statute 16 Vic. ch. 181, sec. 33, under which this award took place, is, that the arbitrators, or a majority of them, shall have power to determine upon and award the amount of damages, if any, to be paid to the person through whose property the new road shall be laid out, and their award is to be binding if made in writing within thirty days—"provided *that every such submission and award* shall be subject to the jurisdiction of Her Majesty's superior courts of common law *in the same manner and to the same extent, for all purposes whatsoever,* as if there had been a submission of the matters in difference by bond between the parties containing an agreement that such submission should be made a rule of court."

It is true that the arbitrators, by inspecting the farm, and with the aid of their own local knowledge as to value of lands, might have been able to come to a reasonable and just conclusion without examining witnesses, or hearing the parties; and it is also true that in the statute there is no express direction that the arbitrators shall give to the parties notice of their meeting, and an apportunity of being heard; but this we take to be essential, at least to this extent, that, whether there has been a formal notice of meeting or not, it must appear that the parties at least had knowledge of the meeting and an opportunity of being heard, and of producing evidence before the arbitrators. There might be considerations on either side which a mere view of the premises might fail to suggest to disinterested parties, and, as was remarked by Lord Ellenborough, in the case referred to in the argument (2 Ch. Rep. 44) "though the premises might almost tell their own tale, yet there might be other facts which should be inquired into." The arbitrators should not have assumed that the corporation had no desire to be heard.

Rule absolute.

IN RE BAXTER V. HESSON ET AL.

Inspectors of Licenses—Jurisdiction of—Mandamus.

The court refused to interfere by mandamus to compel the inspectors of licenses to examine a certain house fitted up by the applicant as a saloon, and to grant him the proper certificate, if he should be found to have complied with the by-law of the municipality in that behalf.

Miller moved for a mandamus to the inspectors of licenses for the village of Stratford, commanding them to inspect the house fitted up by William Baxter in that village as a saloon, and if he should be found to be entitled to a certificate of his having complied with the by-law of the Municipality of Stratford relating to the licensing of saloons, to grant him the proper certificate to that effect.

Cur. adv. vult.

ROBINSON, C. J., delivered the judgment of the court.

The inspectors of licenses derive their power under the statute 13 & 14 Vic. ch. 65, and under the by-law to which this motion refers ; and the by-law, as amended, requires that before any person can obtain a license the inspectors should certify that he is a person of sober habits and well fitted to conduct such an establishment. The statute law of the province says nothing of saloons, and we do not pretend to know judicially what qualifications they are which fit a person to conduct them well. We are, therefore, not entitled to insist upon our discretion overruling that of inspectors who are by the Legislature made judges of these matters.

In Rex v. The Licensing Justices of the Ward of Farringdon Without (4. D. & R. 735) a mandamus was applied for to compel the licensing alderman of the ward to hear the application of A. B. for a license for Joe's coffee-house, suggesting by affidavit that the alderman had refused to hear the application. It was shown for cause that the application had been heard and refused, on the ground that under the circumstances, there was no authority to grant a license. It was admitted that the application had been heard, but *refused under a mistaken view of the statute,* and the object was to have the application reconsidered upon more mature deliberation. But the court said—"It being conceded that the magistrates have heard and determined upon this application for a license, which is a matter peculiarly for their considèration, we cannot grant a mandamus to them to re-hear what they have already determined"—and the rule was discharged but without costs.

Now in this case the applicant assumes that because the municipal council have not yet passed a by-law limiting the number of saloons or other houses of public entertainment, therefore every inhabitant of the village of Stratford who is in fact of sober habits, and well fitted to conduct a saloon, has a right to insist upon a certificate which will enable him to obtain a license.   We cannot accede to this view of the law; and, moreover, we can no more command the justices to certify that any man is of sober habits, and fitted to keep a saloon, than we can command a jury to find a fact of which they are by law the proper judges.

Rule refused.

In re Burns v. Butterfield.

County Court—Mandamus.

A mandamus will lie to the judge of the County Court, commanding him to hear and determine a matter, but not to correct his judgment when given.

Miller moved for a mandamus to the judge of the County Court of Oxford, requiring him peremptorily to set aside the judgment entered in his court in the suit of Morgan Burns v. David Butterfield, and all proceedings had thereon.

Butterfield had been arrested on mesne process from the County Court for £17 10s., and upon the trial Burns received a verdict for £11 5s. only.—

In the following term in that court, Burns obtained a rule that the defendant should be allowed his costs under the statute 49 Geo. III. ch. 4, as for a vexatious arrest.   The defendant's costs were taxed at £13 and upwards.

The plaintiff's attorney afterwards, without notice to the defendant, proceeded, nothwithstanding the rule, to tax his costs to the amount of about £10, and entered judgment for his verdict and such costs, deducting from the aggregate amount the defendant's costs taxed, and he issued execution for the balance.

The defendant had obtained a rule to shew cause, not merely why the defendant should not be allowed his costs, but also why the plaintiff should not be disabled fron taking out execution for the sum recovered by him unless it should exceed the defendant's costs; but for some reason not explained the rule absolute was not drawn up in that shape, but was merely a rule allowing the defendant his costs.

After the execution had issued against him, the defendant obtained a rule to shew cause why the judgment and execution, and the taxation of the plaintiff's costs in the cause should not be set aside for irregularity, with costs, on the ground that the plaintiff's costs were taxed and judgment entered, and execution issued contrary to the statute and to the terms of the rule of court made in the cause, and contrary to the practice of the court; and why the defendant should not have leave to enter a suggestion on the roll, or to enter judgment, according to the practice of the court, and issue execution in favor of the defendant for the balance of his costs above the plaintiff's verdict.

The learned judge of the County Court having heard the parties, discharged the rule, giving as the reason for his judgment that the defendant having drawn up a rule without inserting anything disabling the plaintiff from entering judgment for his verdict or taxed costs, could not consistently with the practice come afterwards to the court with an application to that effect.

Cur. adv. vult.

ROBINSON, C. J., delivered the judgment of the court.

The decision of the learned judge was probably in accordance with the practice of the court before which the application was pending, but it seems at variance with the language of the statute which only requires that the judge shall, where he thinks the case justifies it, make an order that *the defendant shall be allowed his costs*—in other words, just such an order as was made in this case; and the statute itself declares that, upon *such an order being made*, the other consequence is to follow—namely, that the plaintiff shall be disabled from taking out execution for his verdict ; and the decisions of the courts in England upon a statute precisely similar have established that it shall follow as a further consequence that no costs can in such case be taxed for the plaintiff.

Mr. Miller was therefore probably right in contending that the order which he had obtained was sufficient to prevent the plaintiff from taking execution as he has done. Still it does appear by the case cited by the learned judge, of Clarke v. Fisher, 1 Smith 428), that it has been thought right, in acting on this provision, to include in the rule an order restraining the plaintiff from entering judgment for his verdict. And whether the judge determined the case which had been argued before him upon his knowledge of the practice of his court or upon his view of the intention and effect of the act, we cannot correct the judgment which he deliverd by issuing a mandamus commanding him to reverse his judgment. That is not the purpose to which the remedy by mandamus is applied. If he had refused to hear and adjudge upon the application made to him under the statute, the defendant might have applied for this writ to compel him to act in the matter. Besides the case Ex. parte Morgan (2 Ch. Rep. 250), to which Mr. Miller candidly referred us, the Court of King's Bench in England, in Rex v. The Justices of Monmouthshire (4 B. & C. 849), in language equally clear, disclaimed the right so to interfere. It appeared in that case that the Court of Quarter Sessions had given their judgment. "This court," Lord Tenterden observed, "is not a court of error from that court ; it may compel the Court of Quarter Sessions by mandamus to proceed to hear and decide the appeal ; but when they have determined it, this court cannot compel them to correct their judgment if it appears to be erroneous."

The learned judge of the County Court may yet be asked, we suppose, to grant an order to set off the defendant's costs against the verdict ; but whatever course may be taken there, we find no authority that would justify us in making such an application of the remedy by mandamus as is desired in this case.

Rule refused.

BONGARD v. McWHIRTER.

Order for trial of Division Court suit under 16 *Vic., ch.* 177, *sec..* 9—
Prohibition.

On an application for a writ of prohibition the question was, by whom the order referred to in 16 Vic., ch. 177, sec. 9, should be granted, whether by the judge who would ordinarily have cognizance of the suit, or by the judge in whose court it is desired to sue under such order.

The court considered the point to be doubtful, and the writ was therefore refused, and the applicant ordered to declare in prohibition.

Paterson moved for a writ of prohibition, directed to the judge of the Eighth Division Court of the County of Prince Edward, and to the plaintiff Bongard, on the grounds that McWhirter, the defendant, at the time of entering the said suit, and of the service of process therein, and at the time of rendering judgment, resided out of the jurisdiction of the said Division Court, and was not legally served with any process requiring him to appear in the said suit ; and that judgment was rendered against McWhirter without his having appeared in the suit, or pleaded thereto. The facts were :—

1st. That the cause of action arose in the eighth division of the county of Prince Edward.

2nd. The defendant resided out of that division, and out of the county of Prince Edward, viz., in an adjoining division of the county of Lennox.

3rd. the plaintiff resided in the eighth division and obtained an order from the judge of the eighth division Court to try the suit in the eighth division.

4th. The summons was issued from the eighth Division Court of Prince Edward, upon that order and was served on the defendant in the county of Lennox.

5th. The defendant's attorney attended at the eighth Division Court on the 29th of April, 1854, and objected to the summoning of the defendant under the circumstances stated. The judge over-ruled his objections. McWhirter did not appear to defend the suit, and judgment was given him by default, for £25 and costs.

It was contended on the part of McWhirter, the defendant in the Division Court, that this was not a case in which an order could be made under the statute 16 Vic. ch. 177, sec.

9, transferring the cognizance of the cause to another division than that in which the defendant lived, for the reason, that the cause of action having arisen in the eighth division of Prince Edward, the jurisdiction belonged to that division of right, under the statute 13 & 14 Vic., ch. 53, sec. 25, except for the circumstances that the defendant, living in another county could not be compelled to attend there ; and that, at any rate, if an order in such a case was proper, and could be effectual, the order should have been made by the judge of the Division Court in which the cause was of right ordinarily triable, and not by the judge of the other court, to which it was desired to remove it.

Leith shewed cause.

ROBINSON, C. J., delivered the judgment of the court.

I have read again and again the 25th clause of 13 & 14 Vic., ch. 53, and the 8th and 9th clauses of 16 Vic., ch. 177, and I confess I am not by any means confident that I apprehend the real intention of them.

It is only in a perfectly clear case that the court directs a writ of prohibition to issue upon motion, or rather upon a suggestion of record. Where they see any room for doubt, the common course is to leave the party to declare in prohibition, and then the question comes before the court in a formal manner upon pleadings, with the advantage of a writ of error, if either party is dissatisfied with the judgment. The application in this case, besides not being, as we apprehend, in the usual form, comes after judgment in the Inferior Court which, though in general an objection, is not always so.

If the court in this case, in assuming jurisdiction as they did, have plainly violated the provisions of the statute, we think there would be no difficulty in granting a prohibition ; but there should, we suppose, have been a suggestion, and an affidavit of the truth of it, as the objection to the jurisdiction does not appear on the face of the proceedings.

But we cannot say that we find this to be by any means a clear case ; we mean, as to what it is that the statute really means in the 8th and 9th clauses, which relate to the transferring causes by order of a judge from the division to which the cognizance of them would belong according to the general practice under the statute.

It is so far from being plain in our apprehension, that, after a great deal of consideration, we came each of us to a different conclusion as to the intention and effect of those clauses; and are all now, I believe, inclined to adopt a construction which did not at first occur to any of us.

The 8th clause of 16 Vic., ch. 177, provided, that all suits cognizable in a division court may be entered and tried in the court holden for the division in which the cause of action arose, or in the court holden for the division in which the defendant shall dwell or carry on his business at the time of the action brought, "or by leave of the judge, according to the provisions contained in the next section, in the court holden for any division (whether in the same or in adjoining county) adjacent to the division in which the defendant is resident.'

Then the 9th clause recites, that in certain divisions the places fixed for holding the sittings of the courts, and the offices of the clerks thereof may be situated at an inconvenient distance fron the place of residence of *certain parties* residing in such divisions, while a division court is held in the same or in an adjoining county more convenient for such parties, and it is desirable that procedure in the said division courts should be made as easy and inexpensive as may be to the suitors; and it enacts "that any suit cognizable in a division court may, by leave of the judge of the court in which such suit is to be brought, be entered and tried in any court (whether holden for a division for the county in which the defendant resides, or holden for a division in an adjoining county) in which the said judge shall specially order such suit to be entered and tried." I do not think it material to cite the remainder of the clause.

When both parties live in the same county, whether in the same or different divisions, I suppose the option is with the plaintiff to bring his action either where the cause of action arose or where the defendant resides . But where the defendant lives in a different county, the plaintiff, before this act was passed, must have entered his suit in the proper division

court of the county in which the defendant is residing,
although the cause of action may have arisen in the same
county in which the plaintiff is resident because he could not
have summoned the defendant to come from another county
into his.

This last act was intended to make a change in this respect,
but I do not see clearly the effect of it, or by what steps the
change is to be effected. The 9th clause speaks of the convenience of *parties,* but does not explain whether of either or
both the parties, or who is to apply, or whether the opposite
party is to have any notice of the application.

The defendant's counsel, Mr. Paterson, objects that this
was no case for an order, because the cause of action having
arisen in the eighth division, the case might have been entered
there without any order under the law as it formerly stood;
and so no doubt it might if the defendant had been living in
the same county, but not otherwise, as we lately decided (*In
re* Dulmage, *ante* page 32), so that without an order
it could not have been entered, as it was, in the eighth
division of Prince Edward.

But we do not see why the circumstance of that being the
division in which the cause of action arose, and in which, but
for the defendant's residence in another county, it might have
been tried, should prevent an order being made to try it
there as well as in any other division, if the case could, consistently with the statute, be transferred thither.

Mr. Leith, however, has objected that if any order in
this case was necessary, and could be had, for entering
the case in the eighth division of Prince Edward such
order could only be regularly made by the judge of the
division in the county of Lennox in which the defendant
was living, whereas in this case it was by the judge of the
Division Court in Prince Edward.

The order, it appears, was so made under the impression
that the act authorised and required the order to be made by
such judge. The words are, "may by leave of the judge of
the court *in which such suit is to brought,*"—and according
to the natural import of the words, that has been taken to
mean the suit of the court in which the suit shall in fact be

brought under the order which is to be obtained. At present I doubt whether that can have been meant, because then the words would more naturally have been "in which such suit is desired to be brought,"—and the direction would have been that the case should, by order of the judge, be entered and tried in any court in his county that he should appoint. But this is not what the statute provides. It enacts that the judge of the court in which *such suit is to be brought*, may direct to be brought in any court for a division in the county in which the defendant resides, or *holden for a divi-ion in an adjoining county.* I do not see how the plain-tiff can go to the judge of the court *in which the suit is to be brought* for his order, if that means the court to which it is to be transferred, because it does not depend upon the plaintiff to select the place of trial, and it cannot be known where it will be tried, till the judge has made his order,— for it is clear, by the words of the clause, that whatever judge is meant, he is to have a discretion to allow the case to be entered in his own or in an adjoining county.

I believe the meaning of the words, "by leave of the judge of the court *in which the suit is to be brought*," is rather that leave is to be asked of the judge of the court in which the suit is to be brought, according to the general provision of the law, and supposing no order were made ; which is what Mr. Paterson contends for. There are several considerations of convenience in favour of such a construction, and some perhaps against it.

I have some doubt whether, as my brother Burns has suggested, the word "parties," as used in the recital of the ninth clause, does not refer to the· inhabitants of certain localities situated as described in that clause, rather than to the parties in any suit, and I am not sure that any thing more was meant than this :—that when both parties live in a part of a division more convenient to the place of sitting of the court for another division than of the court holden for their own division, application may be made to the judge having ordinarily cognizance of the cause; to allow it to be brought in the more convenient division, whether it be in the same or an adjoining country.

But it is too doubtful, we think, which construction should prevail, to make it right that we should send the writ at once.

If a proper suggestion has been filed, the party must declare in prohibition, and then the question will be properly brought before us.

Defendant ordered to declare in prohibition.

THOMAS, SHERIFF, &C. V. COTTON.

Sheriff's right to poundage.

Where the sheriff, under a writ of *fi. fa.*, seized goods sufficient to cover the claim, and afterwards withdrew from the possession, in obedience to a judge's order founded upon an undertaking of the defendant to give credit for the amount of the levy on an execution which he held against the plaintiff ;

Held, that the sheriff was entitled to poundage.

This was an action of debt to recover sheriff's fees and poundage. The defendant pleaded *nunquam indebitatus.*

At the trial, at the last assizes held at Hamilton before *Burns, J.*, the facts appeared as follows :—A writ of *fi. fa.* at the suit of the present defendant was sued out against James Russell, on the 30th of June, 1851, endorsed to levy in all the sum of £1859 16s., which writ was placed in the hands of the plaintiff, as sheriff of the united counties of Wentworth and Halton, on the 1st of July, 1851. A sheriff's officer was immediately sent to make a levy, and the defendant Cotton and his attorney accompanied the officers. It was found that there were much more goods on Russell's premises than sufficient to satisfy the amount endorsed on the writ. A judge's order was put in without date, but which in fact should have been dated, as it was made, on the 5th of July, 1851, in these words:

JAMES COTTON, *Plaintiff,*
      and
JAMES RUSSELL, *Defendant.*   }   IN THE QUEEN'S BENCH.

Upon reading the summons issued in this cause, and hearing both parties, I do order that all further proceedings be stayed on the judgment and execution issued in this cause, and that the sheriff of the united counties of Wentworth and Halton do withdraw from the possession of the defendant's goods on the levy made on the said execution—the defendant undertaking to give credit on his execution against James Roe in the hands of the sheriff of the county of York, to the amount agreed upon by the arbitrators between the parties.

(Signed)   WM. H. DRAPER, J.

On this evidence the jury were directed to find a verdict for the amount of sheriff's fees and poundage, amounting to £41 13s. 6d., and leave was reserved to the defendant to move against it.

George Duggan, for the defendant obtained a rule to shew cause why the verdict for the plaintiff should not be set aside, and a verdict entered for the defendant, pursuant to leave reserved, or why the verdict should not be reduced to the sum of £3 8s. 6d.; being the sheriff's fees without poundage, the verdict being contrary to law and evidence, and excessive, or why a new trial should not be had on such grounds.

The papers in chambers upon which the judge's order set out was made were referred to for the purpose of ascertaining whether they afforded any ground for saying that the sheriff ought not to be entitled to charge the defendant with his poundage, he having obeyed the order, and withdrawn from the possession of the goods. The following facts were disclosed by the papers so filed : It appeared that Russell had an action pending against the defendant in this action, which was referred to arbitration at the assizes at Hamilton on the 9th of April, 1851; on the 7th of June, 1851, the time for making the award was enlarged by consent of the parties, and on the 27th of June the parties and the arbitrators met. At that meeting the parties agreed upon the basis upon which the arbitrators should proceed, and that basis included the items which formed the demand in the suit in which Cotton had obtained judgment against Russell. The memorandum signed by Cotton and Russell respecting this was in these words :—" *Note, by this the arbitrators will dispose of the verdict against Russell ats. Cotton, by wiping out the debt, but the costs will form an item in Cotton's favour.*" The further meeting of the arbitrators to dispose of the matters was adjourned at Cotton's request until the 3rd of July, to to enable him to adduce evidence. ·In the meantime, Cotton on the 30th of June, sued out execution on his judgment, and caused the sheriff to levy on Russell's goods on the 1st of July; and, on the 3rd of July, Russell made an application in Chambers for a summons upon Cotton, to shew cause why all proceedings upon the judgment and execution shall not be stayed, which summons was made absolute, in the terms before mentioned, on the 4th of July, 1851.

Leith shewed cause, and cited Morris et al. v. Boulton, 2 Chamb. Rep. 60 ; Corbett v. McKenzie, 6 U. C. R. 605.

ROBINSON, C. J., delivered the judgment of the court.

The question turns upon the effect of the allowance of poundage to sheriffs made by authority of 2 Geo. IV. ch. 1, which authorizes the court to regulate costs. The tariff provides that poundage on executions and attachments in the nature of executions where the sum *levied and made* shall not exceed £100, shall be five per cent. : where it shall exceed £100, and be less than £1000, five per cent. on the first £100, and two and a-half per cent. for the residue (and so on, giving another scale where the sum is over £1000.)

The statute 7 Wm. IV. ch. 3, sec. 22, if it could otherwise, upon a fair construction, have affected this question, cannot now do so, being repealed by 9 Vic. ch. 56, and a provision substituted for it which seems expressly designed to leave the claim of sheriffs to poundage upon the footing on which it stood under the existing law, independently of the repealed clause of 7 Wm. IV.

The plaintiff we think, is entitled in this case to his poundage, for he was authorized by our statute 2 Geo. IV. ch. 1, sec. 19, to levy the poundage, and had done so, and he is not to be deprived of it, we think, (no statute interfering with his right) because he was directed to give up the goods in consequence of the plaintiff obtaining satisfaction, through the set-off which Russell agreed to make, under compulsion of the levy which had taken place.

Rule discharged.

TUBBS ET AL., EXECUTORS OF JOHN MORGAN, V. THOMAS MORGAN.

Share of crop sown in testator's life time, and reaped after his death.— Whether it goes to his executors, or to the devisee of the land.

M. in the spring of 1852, agreed by parol with A. to work his farm on shares, and put in a crop of rye. In December, 1852, A. entered into a written agreement with G. to rent the farm to him for three years ; and in January, 1853, A. died, leaving a will. M., in 1853, with the assent of G., reaped the crop which he had sown in the previous year.

Held, That the share of such crop to which A. would have been entitled, must go to the devisee of the land, and not to the executors.

This was an action of trover brought by the plaintiffs, as executors of one John Morgan, to recover from the defendant. the value of 155 bushels of rye. The defendant pleaded, first, the general issue; and, secondly, that the plaintiffs were not possessed.

At the trial, before *Burns, J.,* at the last fall assizes held at Picton, the plaintiffs' title to the rye in question was as follows :—John Mogan was the owner of and lived upon the west half of lot letter F, upon the west side of East Lake, in the township of Athol. By an agreement, dated 21st of December, 1852, entered into with one Thomas Gordon, John Morgan let the farm to him for three years. That agreement was in these words :

"This article of agreement, made by and between John Morgan, yeoman, and Thomas Gordon, labourer, both of the township of Athol, County of Prince Edward, Canada West. The aforesaid John Morgan doth hereby agree to allow the said Thomas Gordon his farm to work ; and also doth agree to furnish him with team and tools suitable for use for the said farm, and seed grain, and allow a house to live in, and also to allow him to keep two cows and six sheep for his own use, and wood in the woods ready to cut. And Thomas Gordon, of the second part, for his part, doth agree to do all the work required in the said place, fix fences, get wood, and fit it for the stove, for the aforesaid Morgan, also feed cattle and sheep, horses and hogs, and all things necessary in the place, also cut the hay and fat the pork, and agrees to do all work in good order and good season. And this agreement is understood that the said John Morgan is to have two-thirds of all raised on his place, and the said Thomas Gordon is to have the one-third of all he doth raise on the said place—

hay, apples, grain and pork ; grain to be divided in the half
bushels, pork when butchered.   And the said Gordon is to
make rails on the place if needed, and is to get pay for
making what is necessary.   This agreement is to be in full
force and virtue for the term of three years from date.   The
said Gordon is to have a horse and carriage to go to Picton
or other places, always using the horses well, and also is to
have a garden spot.   The said John Morgan doth agree to
pay one half the threshing done with a machine."

After this agreement was entered into, John Morgan, on
the 27th of December, 1852, made his will, and thereby
devised the farm to the defendant.   In his will was contained
this passage : "It is further my will that all my agreements
and contracts heretofore entered into shall be fulfiled."
The testator constituted the plaintiffs executors of his said
will.   A further clause in the will was, "that my personal
property shall be equally divided between my son Thomas,
and my daughters, Sally, Maria Eleanor, Elizabeth Brown,
and the heirs of my daughter Jane, deceased."

The testator had, in the spring of 1852, made a verbal
bargain with one John Mince to work the farm upon shares,
and the rye in question was sown by Mince in 1852, and
harvested by him in 1853.   The testator died in January,
1853.   When the rye was harvested by Mince, he sold his
share to Gordon, and the defendant came and took away the
share which would have belonged to the testator, contending
that as devisee of the land he was the person entitled to the
grain, as and for rent reserved in kind.

The plaintiffs at the trial contended, that, taking the agreement with the testator had entered into with Gordon, and
the will into consideration, with the fact of the agreement
existing with Mince under which he was still to harvest the
crop in 1853, an intention was evinced on the part of the
testator, that the crops should go to his executors, and not
the devisee ; and that the plaintiffs, as executors, were
entitled to take the share of the rye harvested by Mince
which would have gone to the testator.

The jury were directed to assess the value of the rye which
the defendant had taken, subject to the opinion of the court,
whether the plaintiffs, as such executors, were entitled in
law to the rye in question.

Richards, for the plaintiff, cited Lord Hatherton v. Bradburne, 13 Sim. 599 ; Platt on Leases II. 82-3 ; Haydon v. Crawford, 3 O. S. 583.

Paterson, contra, cited Crabb, R. P. sec. 150 ; Doe Bunnill v. Link, E. T. 7 W. IV.

ROBINSON, C. J.—The rye in question was not sown by John Morgan the owner of the land but by his tenant Mince, upon shares. A certain part of the rye was to go to John Morgan as his rent ; after it was sown, and while it was in the ground (viz : in January, 1853,) John Morgan died— Mince harvested it, and sold his own share to Gordon, who had in the meantime become tenant of John Morgan, and was living on the place ; and after John Morgan's death, this defendant, Thomas Morgan, his son and devisee, came and took the other share, which would have belonged to John Morgan if he had lived, claiming that it belonged to him as devisee of the land on which it grew.

The executors of John Morgan sue in this action, for the value of the rye so taken, contending that it forms part of his personal estate.

It does not appear from anything in the case that Mince (whose lease was verbal) did anything wrong or contrary to tho agreement, in entering and harvesting the rye in 1853, though before that Gordon had become tenant. On the contrary, Gordon buying his share from him assented to its being his. Then if it was his, all was his as it grew till the harvest, and till a division took place. When he separated his own part from the crop the remainder as it stood was rent due (not emblements), and the question is to whom should it be paid,—to the devisee, or to the executors of John Morgan. No doubt, if the accruing rent of Gordon goes to the devisee, the only question is whether this rent (for it is rent though payable in kind), goes to the executors or the devisees on the principal of its not being subject to apportionment. The rye was sown while Morgan lived, but reaped after his death. Mince had the farm by agreement with John Morgan from the spring of 1852. The rye, as we may suppose, was put in, in September, 1852. In January, 1853,

u—VOL. XII. Q. B.

John Morgan; the landlord died, but even then the devisee was not entitled to the possession of the profits of the land, for it was under lease made by John Morgan to Gordon. The circumstances make this a peculiar case, the rent being not a money rent but a share of a growing crop, that had begun to grow in the testator's lifetime, but did not mature till after his death, and the estate, while it was growing, being in the possession of the testator's lessee, whose term was continuing. But, as the facts appear, the fields on which the rye was growing in summer of 1853, were fields in respect of which Gordon could not be paying rent to the devisee, and I see nothing which should make this case an exception to the general rule, that where the rent falls due after the testator's death, (however short a time after), it all goes to his heir or devisee, and not to his executors.

DRAPER, J.—If the agreement with Mince is to be treated as a contract of hire of service to be rendered by him to the testator in working the farm, for which he was to be paid by a fixed share of the produce, then. the testator must be looked upon as cultivating his own farm by the labor of Mince, and no question of rent arises. And in such case the devisee would clearly be entitled to the crop.—Com. Dig. "Biens" G. 3; Cro. Eliz. 61; Dy. 316 a; Bull N. P. 34, and Vaisey v. Reynolds (5 Russ. 12. and notes.)

A legatee of the goods, stock, and movables on a farm, is entitled to growing corn in preference to the devisee of the land or the executors—6 East, 604, note; West v. Moore, (8 East 339, which is strongly to this point; but the words of the bequest of the personalty in the present case, do not extend far enough to fall within these authorities.

But if the agreement is to be construed as a demise for a year to Mince, he rendering a fixed share of the crops by way of rent, then as no rent became due until long after the death of the testator, it would become due to the devisee of the land.

BURNS, J., concurred.

Judgment for the defendant.

SAYERS V. FINDLAY, STAFFORD, AND PURDY.

Demand of perusal and copy of warrant, under 16 *Vic. ch.* 177, *sec* 14.

The provisions of 16 Vic. ch. 177, sec. 14, do not apply in an action against a bailiff acting under a warrant of attachment or execution from a division court where the wrong complained of is the misconduct of the defendant, and not anything illegal in the writ itself or in the act of granting it.

But in this case the defendants could not have availed themselves of the statute, for the general issue was not pleaded "by statute," and it did not appear on the plaintiff's case that the defendants were acting in the execution of any process.

TRESPASS.—The first count complained of the defendants for breaking a close of the plaintiff situate on the easterly half of lot 15, 11th concession of Dawn, destroying gates, locks, fences, &c., and taking away a horse of the plaintiff. The second count *de bonis asportatis.*

The defendants pleaded first not guilty, to the whole declaration. 2ndly. As to so much of the declaration as charged the taking and converting, &c., that the goods and chattels were not the palintiff's. 3rdly. The defendant Findlay pleaded a justification to the first count. 4thly. The defendant Purdy pleaded a justification to the first count. 5thly. The defendant Stafford pleaded a justification to the first count

The plaintiff took issue on the 1st and 2nd pleas, and replied *de injuriâ* to the 3rd, 4th, and 5th, on which issue was joined.

At the trial in April last, before *Draper*, J., at Chatham, the plaintiff. at the close of the case, gave up the first count. It appeared that in February, 1853, one Young sold the horse in question to Peter Windover, together with some furniture,—Young being a tenant of Windover, who was called as a witness for the plaintiff, and proved that he had previously sold this same horse to Young and bought him back again. Evidence was drawn from this and other witnesses called by the plaintiff to the effect that Young had been occasionally permitted to use the horse after the re-sale to Windover; that some of the other things sold to Windover had been afterwards seized and sold to satisfy an execution against Young, but Windover swore that he had paid both for the horse and the other things before he ever knew of the execution; and that, as to the horse, he had (knowing of a previous execution against Young) inquired of and been told by defendant Stafford that it was all clear. The sale to the plaintiff by Windover was clearly proved, and the payment of £20, the price of the horse ; and that it was removed from Wright's, a stable-keeper in Dresden, to the plaintiff's own place in the township of Dawn, where it had been a week or more, and was taken away from thence by the defendants Findlay and Purdy, and afterwards sold by the defendant Stafford at a sale conducted by him as a bailiff of a division court. A notice of action addressed to Findlay, "bailiff of the Fifth Division Court for the United Counties of Essex and Lambton," to Stafford, "bailiff of the Third-Division Court of the county of Kent," and to Purdy "of the Village of Dresden in the County of Kent, merchant," was proved to have been served a month before the commencement of the action. On the defence it appeared that on the 10th of February, 1853, an attachment was issued by the clerk of the Third Division Court of the county of Kent, directed to the defendant Stafford, against the personal effects of Young to secure the defendant Purdy, in £25. It was brought back to the defendant with a memorandum indorsed of this horse and other things being attached, but no property was ever delivered over to the clerk, nor any appraisement of, nor receipt or security for, the forthcoming of the property. On the 7th of April, 1853, the same clerk issued an execution against the goods of Young in favor of the defendant Purdy, directed to Stafford, to make £6 12s. 3d., a balance of a judgment recovered on the 26th of March preceding. Young had on that day paid part, and the balance for which the execution after was paid a few days after by Windover. The same clerk, on the 22nd of April, 1853, issued a second attachment, directed to Stafford, against the goods of Young, to secure Purdy £10, which was also returned with an indorsement of a seizure of a horse and other things, but no property or appraisement was ever brought to the clerk. The same clerk, on the 21st of May, 1853, issued an execution against the goods of Young, on a judgment recovered on the 21st of May, 1853, against him by William Findlay, directed to Stafford, to make £21 8s. 4d.; on which was returned that Stafford seized one horse (alleged on the defence to be the horse in question) and some other articles. And the same clerk, on the 22nd of May, 1853, issued another execution in favour of the defendant Purdy, on a judgment recovered on the 21st of May, 1853, against Young, directed to Stafford, to make £12 12s. 4d; this was returned "no goods." The same clerk, on the 7th of April, 1853, issued an execution in favour of William Vanallan against the goods of Young and Purdy, reciting a judgment recovered against them on the 24th of May, 1852, for 18s. 11¼d., directed to Stafford, to levy 9s. 8¾d. He admitted that Purdy (one of the defendants in that writ) had previously paid him the whole amount; but that at Purdy's request he had issued this execution in order to levy half the sum from Young's goods, as Young and Purdy were joint defendants in the writ. It was on this writ that Stafford took the horse out of the possession of Findlay and Purdy, who, it appeared, had seized him at the plaintiff's on a writ of attachment issued out of the Fifth Division Court of the Counties of Essex and Lampton, dated the 5th of May, 1853, against the goods of John Young, to secure the defendant Purdy £10, directed to the defendant Findlay, and which attachment Findlay returned with a memorandum of the seizure, but neither the property nor any appraisement were returned to the clerk.

At the close of the case it was objected for the defendants that there had been no demand made of perusal and copy of the warrants under which the bailiffs, and Purdy in aid of them, had acted, under 16 Vic. ch. 177, sec. 14, and 13 & 14 Vic. ch. 53, sec. 97. Leave was reserved to the defendants to move to enter a nonsuit on this objection. The plaintiff then elected to proceed on the second count of the declaration only, and the jury found for the plaintiff, and £22 10s. damages.

McCrea obtained a rule *nisi* to enter an nonsuit on the leave reserved.

J. Wilson shewed cause.

ROBINSON, C. J., delivered the judgment of the court.

By 16 Vic. ch. 177, sec. 14, it is enacted that no action

shall be brought against a bailiff of a division court, or any person acting by his order or in his aid, *for anything done in obedience to any warrant* under the hand of the clerk of the court, and the seal of the court, until demand has been made of the bailiff of the perusal and copy of such warrant, and the same has been refused or neglected for six days after the demand; and if, after the demand has been complied with, by the bailiff shewing the warrant and permitting a copy to be taken, any action shall be brought against the bailiff, &c., for *any such cause as aforesaid,* without making the clerk who signed the warrant defendant, then, on producing or proving the warrant at the trial, the jury shall give their verdict for the defendant, notwithstanding any defect of jurisdiction or other irregularity *in or appearing by the said warrant*; and in any action to be brought as aforesaid, the defendant may plead the general issue and give the special matter in evidence.

By the general Division Court Act, 13 & 14 Vic. ch. 53, sec. 107, the usual protection is given to persons sued for anything done in persuance of that act, which seems however to be repealed by the general statute on that subject, 14 & 15 Vic. ch. 54; and this latter act having made similar provisions in regard to notice of action, limitation as to time of suing, and pleading the general issue and giving the special matter in evidence, it is of no consequence which of them is to govern.

Upon the facts and pleadings we think the nonsuit cannot be granted, but that the plaintiff is entitled to his verdict. There is no room for doubt, we think, that the statute 16 Vic. ch, 177; sec. 14, does extend to the case of a bailiff of a division court who has acted either under a warrant of execution or warrant of attachment. But this provision only applies were the action is for something for which the clerk would be liable as having issued an illegal process, so that the burden can be shifted to his shoulders, and the plaintiff compelled to take his remedy against him and not against the bailiff, were the latter has only acted in execution of the duty enjoined upon him by the warrant. Where the wrong complained of is the misconduct of the bailiff, and not anything illegal in the writ itself or in the act of granting it, then we take it to be settled that this enactment does not apply; and this, we took it to be conceded upon the argument, is a case of that kind.

But there is besides, this fatal objection, that the general issue is not pleaded "by statute" as our rule of court requires, and the defendant was not therefore entitled to give this special matter in evidence. On the plaintiff's case, it did not appear that the defendants were acting in the execution of any process.—Brown v. Shea (5 U. C. R. 141); Spooner v. Juddow, (5 Moo. P. C. Rep. 282).

Rule for nonsuit discharged.

CAMERON V. CAMPBELL.

13 & 14 Vic. ch. 53, *sec.* 78,—*Set off of defendant's cost against plaintiff's verdict.*

The 13 & 14 Vic. ch. 53. sec. 78—enacts, that in any suit which might have been brought in a Division Court, unless the judge shall certify as therein mentioned, so much of the defendant's costs as shall exceed the costs which would have been incurred by him in the Division Court shall be set off by the master, in entering judgment, *against the plaintiff's costs* and the defendant shall be entitled to execution against the plaintiff when the costs so set off shall exceed the plaintiff's verdict and Division Court costs.

Held, That under this provision the defendant might set off the excess of his costs of defence above his own and the plaintiff's Division Court costs, against the plaintiff's verdict—Draper, J. dissenting.

Held, also, That the plaintiff's attorney, having advanced to the plaintiff the amount of the verdict, could have no lien so as to deprive the defendant of the benefit of the statute.

Wilson, Q. C., moved that the defendant should have leave to set off the amount of his costs upon the judgment in this cause, against so much of the verdict of the plaintiff as would be sufficient to discharge the defendant's costs, and that it be referred to the master to reduce the verdict accordingly.

The action was assumpsit. The plaintiff at the assizes recovered £12 10s., which sum being within the jurisdiction of the division court, the learned judge was asked by the plaintiff to certify, under the 78th clause of 13 & 14 Vic. ch. 53; but he saw no ground for it, and declined. The plaintiff being in consequence confined to division court costs entered judgment for £12 10s. damages, and £1 8s. costs, in all £13 18s.

The defendant had his costs of defence taxed, and the excess of them above divisions court costs amounted to £6 5s. 9d., which he now moved to be allowed to be set off against the plaintiff's verdict, or rather so much of such sum as might exceed division court costs.

Read shewed cause. He objected chiefly on behalf of the plaintiff's attorney, who swore that he had from time to time advanced to the plaintiff the amount of the verdict, trusting that he would receive it under the judgment.

Wilson, Q. C., contra, cited, as against the attorney's lien, George v. Elston, 1 Bing. N. C., 513 ; Dunn v. West, 10 C. B. 420 ; Stephens v. Weston, 3 B. & C. 535.

ROBINSON, C. J.—It has been contended that the defendant has not under the 78th clause of the statute, the right of set off now claimed, because under the words of that clause the defendant has only a right to recover the excess of his costs above the plaintiff's costs, when such excess amounts to more than the verdict as it may do in some cases, so as to entitle him to the benefit of the execution which the clause allows to him against the plaintiff for any excess *above the verdict.* The clause is—"And be it further enacted, that in case any action shall be prosecuted after the commencement of this act, in any county or superior court of record, for any cause which might have been entered in a division court under this act, and the plaintiff shall obtain judgment for a sum not exceeding the respective sums to which the jurisdiction of a division court is by this act limited, no more costs shall be taxed against the defendant than would have been incurred in the division court in carrying on the same action, unless the judge who presides at the trial of such action shall certify in open court, immediately after the verdict is recorded, that it was a fit cause to be withdrawn from the division court, and to be commenced in such county or superior court; provided also that so much of the costs of the defendant to be taxed as between attorney and client, in any such suit, wherein the judge shall not certify as aforesaid, as shall exceed the costs of defence taxable, and which would have been incurred in the division court in defending the same action, shall be set off and allowed by the taxing officer, in entering judgment, against the costs to be taxed for the plaintiff and recovered from the defendant, *who shall be entitled to execution, with the costs thereof, against the plaintiff when the amount of the costs so set off shall exceed the plaiutiff's verdict and taxable costs:* And provided also, that no execution on such suit shall issue against lands, unless the amount of such judgment shall equal the sum for which execution against lands is authorized by this act."

It is true that this clause is inaccurately framed, no express provision being made in it for those cases in which it may happen that the excess of the costs of defence above division court costs exceeds the plaintiff's taxed costs against the defendant, and yet does not also exceed the whole amount of his verdict. Still the intention is palpable, that the defendant should receive from the plaintiff any excess above the plaintiff's costs, whether such excess shall cover a part or the whole of the plaintiff's verdict, or more. And here the plaintiff is urging an execution against the defendant for the amount of his verdict and fees of execution, while the defendant has, as it seems to me, a clear right to receive from him the excess of his costs above the plaintiff's taxed costs.

It is sworn that the defendant would be unable, from the plaintiff's circumstances, to collect the amount from him upon an execution; and if he could do so, still it would be absurd not to allow it to be set off against the plaintiff's verdict as being the most ready and just way of adjusting their respective claims, and one clearly within the spirit and intention of the statute, if not otherwise within the discretion of the court to order.

I do not think there is any ground in this case for the objection that was taken in Taylor v. Blair (3 T. R. 452), or Anster v. Lilly (1 M. & Ry. 764, Jackman v. Cother (5 M. & W. 147), where the defendant was held to have lost the benefit of the statute because he had not pleaded it in bar of the action. The provision here is of a different kind. We could not say to this defendant, as was said by Lord Tenterden, in Anster v. Lilly, "you chose to resist the action, and ought to pay the costs;" because under our Division Court act, the fact of the plaintiff having sued in the higher court for a sum which he could have recovered in the inferior court is not made a defence to the action, and could not therefore be pleaded. He sues in the higher court in peril only of losing costs, and having costs to pay to the defendant; and the nature of the pleadings, taken in connection with the verdict, shews, without anything to be done or moved on his part, what the rights of the defendant are when no certificate has been obtained by this plaintiff.

The first, and it seems to me the only question is, whether, under the statute, the defendant is in this case entitled to recover from the plaintiff the whole excess of his taxed costs of defence, above the costs that would have been taxed against him in the Division Court, or only so much of such excess as shall not exceed the costs to be taxed for the plaintiff.

It is quite evident that the legislature did not mean the latter, because they provide for the defendant a remedy by execution against the successful plaintiff, so that he may recover such excess to the full extent, even when it amounts to more than the plaintiff's verdict and costs, taken together. Upon the principle that *omne majus continet in se minus*, we are compelled, I think, to hold that the legislature meant that the defendant should receive his whole excess of costs, when it comes to less than the plaintiff's verdict and costs, though they omitted very naturally to give him any remedy in such a case by execution against the plaintiff, because it could not be necessary.

We must suppose, I think, that they intended us in such a case to exercise a discretion very commonly exercised in practice without any legislative authority, of setting off what the defendant was entitled to receive from the plaintiff against what he was bound to pay him, especially in the same action.

Assuming the defendant's right to the excess of costs in such a case to be clear, there can be no disadvantage or injustice whatever to the plaintiff in compelling him to give credit for the sum which he is bound to pay. The master could hardly have taken upon himself to set off the excess against the verdict in entering the judgment, because the statute does not say so. If, therefore, the statute gives the defendant his excess of costs, as I think it does, it remains for the court to give the defendant the advantage of such allowance, as we should in any other case, by the convenient practice of ordering it to be set off, as is common with regard to cross demands for costs in the same action, or even with regard to cross demands under judgments in different actions.

As to the objection raised on behalf of the plaintiff's attorney, we cannot allow any claim or arrangement of that kind to deprive the defendant of the benefit of the statute, and to prevent us from ordering, not a set off of one judgment against another, but an adjustment of debt and costs in the same cause, according to the provision of the statute.

It is no part of an attorney's duty to advance to his client the amount he has recovered a verdict for against the defendant, and by doing so he never could have prevented the defendant from obtaining an execution under the statute, if his costs had happened to exceed the verdict. The only difference between such a case and the present is, that here there is no necessity for giving the defendant an execution, as he can obtain all he is entitled to by the simple process of deduction from the verdict, leaving the plaintiff still a right to enforce his execution for some amount, if the balance be not paid to him, which makes the attorney's position so much better than it would have been, if the whole verdict had been absorbed.

DRAPER, J.—I regret my inability to concur in the judgment just delivered, and I may without affectation add that it is not from want of every effort on my part to arrive at the same conclusion with the rest of the court. I have no doubt that had the question been suggested, the act would have been so framed as to leave no room for question; and this being so, I feel it to be more than probable that the right construction has been arrived at by the rest of the court.

All turns upon the proviso, "that so much of the costs of the defendant to be taxed as between attorney and client in any such suit, wherein the judge shall not certify as aforesaid, as shall exceed the costs of defence taxable, and which would have been incurred in the Division Court in defending the same action, shall be *set off* and *allowed* by the taxing officer on entering judgment." If it had gone no further, I should have felt no doubt that the intention was that the defendant was to set off his costs against whatever sum—debt and costs—the plaintiff might otherwise have entered judgment for; but the proviso goes on thus, "*against the costs* to be taxed for the plaintiff and recoverable from the defendant." Now if the maxim, *expressio unius est exclusio alterius,* has any application in this case, we have here the clear expression of that against which the defendant has conferred upon him the right to set off the costs of defence, viz. " the costs to be taxed for the plaintiff and recoverable from the defendant"— limiting the right of set off, as appears to me, in express terms to the costs, and giving no authority, at all events to the taxing officer, to set them off against the amount of the plaintiff's verdict. Nor do I see how the court can permit it without assuming the functions of the legislature. The statute of Gloucester gives the plaintiff a right to costs, unless he is restrained by some statutory enactment, and it does not appear to me that the court can impose that restraint by implication from the words above set forth. The residue of the proviso declares that the defendant " shall be entitled to execution with the costs thereof against the plaintiff, when the amount of *costs so set off* shall exceed the plaintiff's *verdict and taxable costs.*" The right to have execution is as plainly limited to one state of facts as language can express it; and I have been unable to satisfy myself, that because the defendant is entitled to have execution for the excess of his costs, which he is by the preceding words authorized to have set off against the plaintiff's taxed costs, if such excess exceeds in amount the sum of the plaintiff's verdict and costs, the defendant not being entitled to execution, can claim from the court to have their interposition to set them off. To do this appears to me to be rather supplying an omission in the act, than giving a construction to its provisions; and I feel the greater difficulty in doing this, for the purpose of restraining by the loss of his own costs and the payment of the defendant's, the right of a plaintiff to sue in the superior courts. It is a case, as appears to me, overlooked, if it was ever in contemplation to provide for it, or otherwise designedly omitted; and therefore, in my humble judgment, the court should not interfere.

BURNS, J.—I have already given a decision in Chambers in this case, agreeing with the view taken by the Chief Justice, and I still adhere to that opinion.

Rule absolute—DRAPER, J., dissenting.

ROYS v. CRAMER.

Trespass—Pleading.

Trespass—The plaintiff charged the defendant with *cutting down* and carrying away trees. It appeared the plaintiff had leased the land to the defendant's brother, making no reservation or mention of the trees.

Held, that on this declaration the plaintiff could not recover.

TRESPASS—*qu. cl. fr.*

First count, for breaking and entering into the plaintiff's close, being lot 37 in the 3rd concession of Osnabruck, and cutting down and destroying the trees (specifying the description of trees), and taking away the wood and underwood therefrom arising, and converting them to the plaintiff's use.

Second count—That the defendant on, &c., and on divers other days, &c., with force and arms, felled, cut down, prostrated and destroyed the trees, viz., 300 cedar trees, &c., of the plaintiff, then growing and being on lands of the plaintiff, to wit, lot 37, in the 3rd concession of Osnabruck, and took and carried away the same, and converted and disposed thereof to his own use.

The defendant pleaded—1st, not guilty; 2ndly, to the first count, that the close was not, nor were the trees, timber, &c., nor any of them, the close or property of the plaintiff; 3rdly, to the second count, that the lands in which, &c., were not, nor were the said trees, or any of them, the property of the plaintiff.

At the trial at Cornwall, before *Richards*, J., it appeared that the plaintiff had leased to the brother of the defendant the whole lot for two years, making no special reservation or mention of the growing timber. The defendant's counsel objected on the trial, that there being no special reservation of the timber, trespass by the plaintiff would not lie. The learned judge held that it might upon the second count, and the jury found for the plaintiff, and £5 damages.

McLean moved for a new trial, on the law and evidence, and for misdirection. He cited Wheeler v. Montefiore, 11 L. J. (Q. B.) 36.

Brough shewed cause, and cited Ward v. Andrews, 2 Ch. Rep. 636; Saund. 322, note 5; Gordon v. Harper, 7 T. R. 13; 2 Saund. Pl. & Ev. 1114.

ROBINSON, C. J., delivered the judgment of the Court.

We think the verdict cannot be supported, under the circumstances, upon the second count, as it has been attempted to be. That count is not confined to the taking away the timber as a distinct trespass. The injury complained of is the forcibly cutting down and prostrating the trees and carrying them away, as if it were all one continued trespass. In Ward v. Andrews (2 Ch. Rep. 636), to which Mr. *Brough* referred, the recovery under similar circumstances, was supported wholly on the third count, which was a common count in trespass for taking goods— not upon the second count, which exactly resembled this.

It is to be regretted that the objection must prevail, for the verdict is small, and the plaintiff entitled to recover if he had sued in trover, or in trespass, simply for taking the timber that had been cut. But the objections were insisted on at the trial.

Rule absolute, without costs.

IN RE WOODS V. RENNETT.

County Court—Mandamus.

A mandamus will not lie to the judge of the county court to reverse his decision on a point of practice.

Miller moved for mandamus to the judge of the County Court of the county of Perth, directing him to enter an exoneretur on the bail-piece in the suit of Woods v. Rennett.

On the 26th of December, 1853, the sheriff of the county of Oxford certified that on that day, the defendant, Maria Rennett, (a married woman), being resident and found within the county of Oxford, was duly rendered in discharge of her bail; and that, at the time of the render, a copy of the bail-piece filed in the county of Perth, and duly certified by the clerk of the County Court of that county, was produced to him by the bail. Bail for the limits was given by the defendant on the same day. On the 5th of January, 1854, the defendant's attorney (Mr. Gray) served a notice upon the plaintiff's attorney, that the defendant had been that day rendered in discharge of her bail, to her custody of the sheriff of the county of Oxford.

The *Ca. Sa.* had issued against Mrs. Rennett on the 28th of November, 1853, directed to the sheriff of the county of Perth, and was returned *non est inventa.*

On or before the 7th of January, 1854, a summons issued out of the County Court of Perth, against Lee, *one of the bail to the action* against Woods the plaintiff.

On the 7th of January, 1854, a judge's summons was taken out and served on the plaintiff's attorney to shew cause why an exoneretur should not be entered on the bail-piece, and proceedings against the bail stayed. This summons was discharged, without costs. It was not shewn on what ground.

Cur. adv. vult.

ROBINSON, C. J., delivered the judgment of the court.

When the judge of a County Court has heard and decided an application on a point of practice, in a cause depending in his court, we have no right to interpose by mandamus, and direct him to reverse his decision. As the court said, in

Ex Parte Morgan (2 Ch. Rep. 250), "We can command the judge of an inferior court to give judgment in a matter proper for his cognizance, but we cannot in this manner review his proceedings, or try upon affidavit any alleged irregularity in his judgment. If there is an erroneous judgment given, a writ of error will rectify it, if error lies; but we cannot tell the judge what he is to do. We can command him to give judgment, but we cannot interfere to regulate the practice of an inferior court."

Rule refused. (a)

REYNOLDS v. CRAWFORD.

Agreement for sale of land—Conveyance by vendor to railway after agreement— Rescision of contract—Money had and received.

The plaintiff purchased from defendant, who held a bond for a deed from one C., his right to certain land. Before the purchase money was paid up by the plaintiff, and after the defendant had obtained his deed from C., he conveyed to the Great Western Railway Company a small part of the lot for their road. It appeared that the railway had been surveyed before the sale to the plaintiff; that the plaintiff has taken and for some time held possession of the land under his agreement: and the defendant declared that he was ready to convey to the plaintiff, on receiving what was due, giving him credit on account for the sum paid by the railway company.
Held that under these circumstances, the plaintiff could not treat the contract as rescinded. and recover the amount paid by him, with interest, in an action for money had and received.

The declaration in this case was, on the common counts, for money received for the plaintiff's use, money paid, and for interest, and upon an account stated. The defendant pleaded non asumpsit and set off.

The case was tried at the last spring assizes held at Wood-stock, before *Burns*, J., and the facts established were these :

In the year 1850, the defendant was the equitable owner of the east half of lot 14, in the 3rd concession of North Oxford, 100 acres, holding a bond for a deed from David Carroll. In the month of March of that year, he bargained with the plaintiff to sell him 50 of the 100 acres, upon which the plaintiff paid £37 10s., a receipt for which was given and proved in these words :

"Received from Doctor Reynolds thirty-seven pounds ten shillings, to apply on purchase money of fifty acres of the farm fronting the river which I now occupy.

"6th March, 1850.   J. AUGUSTUS CRAWFORD."

(a) See Burns v. Butterfield, *ante* p. 140.

Another payment was made to the defendant on the 8th of August, 1850, for which the defendant gave a receipt, as follows :

"Received from Doctor Reynolds the sum of eighteen pounds ten shillings and sixpence currency, to apply on the purchase of fifty acres of my farm which I had sold him.

"Ingersoll, 8th August, 1850.

"J. AUGUSTUS CRAWFORD."

The plaintiff made other payments, amounting in all to the sum of £76. In the latter part of the year 1851 the defendant made a conveyance of a small part of the 50 acres to the Great Western Railway Company for the purpose of the railway, for which the company paid him £12, and they also paid him £18 on his agreeing to dispense with a crossing. The line of the railway passed through the 50 acres, leaving a portion on each side of the road.

Under these circumstances the plaintiff considered that the contract was rescinded on the part of the defendant, and he therefore brought this action to recover back the money he had paid on account of the purchase.

The plaintiff at the trial did not produce the original memorandum or writing between the parties respecting the sale, nor account for it. He proved the receipts mentioned; and it was also proved that the defendant had assigned the bond to the plaintiff which he held from Carroll; and that paper embraced the terms of the contract. A witness proved that in February, 1851, he was called on to prepare a deed of conveyance from the defendant to the plaintiff, and a mortgage to secure the residue of the purchase money, which he did. The witness stated that he knew nothing of the original terms of the contract; but having prepared the conveyance and mortgage which were proved, he read over both to the defendant who admitted them to be correct, except that the mortgage should have stated the interest to be payable from the time he, the defendant, was in a situation to convey to the plaintiff. The instruments were not executed.

Upon this evidence, which was all the plaintiff then proposed the defendant contended he was entitled to a nonsuit, because the original contract was not produced or its terms

shewn in any way. On the part of the plaintiff it was contended that the arrangement to give a conveyance and take
a mortgage, waived the production of the original agreement.
The learned judge thought that such evidence did not dispense with the original agreement, because it appeared that
the defendant objected to the terms of the mortgage as
respected the interest, and it might be that the terms of the
original contract well warranted him in so doing. The
plaintiff then called the defendant as a witness, which he
was allowed to do. The defendant stated that the agreement
was that he was to sell the 50 acres for £175, and at that
time the Great Western Railway Company had run the road
over the land, but there was no reservation of that in the
agreement. The agreement was, that he was to convey to
the plaintiff, so soon as he was in a situation to do so by having Carroll's conveyance of the whole. The plaintiff paid on
account £37 10s.; and Carroll's bond was assigned to the
plaintiff to secure him in the conveyance, and to make him
secure as to that payment. The plaintiff gave a memorandum to the defendant, to shew the terms upon which the
plaintiff held the assignment of that bond. The defendant
further stated, that when he was in a situation to procure his
conveyance from Carroll, he applied to the plaintiff for the
bond, and it was given up with the assignment, and the defendant returned the paper he held. He also applied to the
plaintiff for the residue of the purchase money but the plaintiff wanted time until September following, to which the
defendant assented, if the plaintiff would pay interest. The
defendant completed his arrangement with Carroll, and
obtained his conveyance on the 6th of July, 1850; and it was
on the 8th of August after that the plaintiff paid the £18
10s. 6d. The defendant further stated that he applied again
to the plaintiff for the residue of the money, but he said he
was not prepared to pay; and then the defendant agreed he
would take a mortgage, if the plaintiff paid interest from the
time he was prepared to execute the conveyance. When the
instruments were prepared, the defendant objected on account
of the terms of the interest. The defendant then, being
questioned by his counsel on his own part, stated that the

railway had been surveyed before he sold to the plaintiff; that he had never wished to keep the amount he received from the company on his own account, but had always desired to give the plaintiff credit for it on account; that he had always been, and was still ready to convey to the plaintiff on receiving what was due, and did not desire to rescind the contract; that he did not convey willingly to the company, but was informed that he was obliged to do so, as he had the legal estate, and the company had a right by their charter to take the land, and could compel him to convey. The plaintiff had previously left the country, and neither the company nor the defendant could readily communicate with him on the subject. Nothing was mentioned in the conveyance to the company about dispensing with a crossing, or in any writing in any way.

Evidence was then gone into on the part of the defence, to shew that the plaintiff knew when he purchased that the road was surveyed, and to shew that the plaintiff had himself in fact abandoned the contract, alleging that the place was unhealthy, and he had left the country, having sold the materials which he had collected for building a house. It was proved that the defendant had gone to the plaintiff, and informed him that he was then ready to procure his conveyance from Carroll, and wished the plaintiff to pay the residue of the purchase money. The witness advised, that, as the plaintiff said he should be prepared to pay in September, it was scarcely worth while to draw a mortgage for so short a period, and that both parties had better let it remain till September, when the plaintiff could pay the residue, and the defendant make a conveyance, which was agreed to. The solicitor of the Great Western Railway Company stated that when he applied in November or December, 1851, to the defendant, respecting the land the company wished that the defendant should have his position as respects the plaintiff explained to him, and that he did not wish to prejudice the plaintiff; and he, the solicitor, explained to him the powers of the company. If the defendant had not assented to dispensing with a crossing, the company would have taken more land, but there was a crossing near by on a side line, which was considered as sufficient.

The defendant's counsel then renewed his objection, that the original agreement should be produced or accounted for. The learned judge thought at the time it was not, after what was stated by the defendant indispensable ; and then it was agreed by the parties that a verdict should be entered for the defendant subject to the opinion of the court on this point, and also whether upon the evidence the contract should be treated as rescinded, so as to give the plaintiff a right to recover back the amount so paid.   If the plaintiff should be found entitled to recover, then the verdict to be entered for him for the £76, and for £12 15s. interest upon it, if the plaintiff was entitled to the interest.

In Easter term last, *Hagarty*, Q. C., obtained a rule to enter a verdict for the plaintiff according to the leave reserved.   He cited 4 W. IV. ch. 29, sec. 3 ; 9 Vic. ch. 81, sec. 26 ; Strother v. Barr, 5 Bing. 136 ; Seage v. Deane, 4 Bing. 459 ; Goss v. Lord Nugent, 5 B. & Ad. 65 ; Tay. Ev. secs. 751-5.

In Trinity term *McMichael* shewed cause, and cited Sweet v. Lee, 4 Scott, N. R. 77 ; Cæsar v. Norton, 9 U. C. R. 100 ; Vincent v. Cole, Moo. & Mal. 257 ; 14 & 15 Vic. ch. 51, sec. 11

ROBINSON, C. J., delivered the judgment of the court.

This case was argued before us in Trinity term last, and we reserved it for consideration till the next term, suggesting that in the meantime the parties should refer to arbitrators to determine whether in the opinion of disinterested parties, the sum which had been paid by the railway company to the defendant for the small portion of land taken by them is or is not a reasonable compensation for the land.   If it be, then the plaintiff can be clearly entitled to nothing more in justice than to receive the money which the defendant, it seems, has always considered himself as holding for the plaintiff's use, being willing to pay it to him, and to convey to him the remainder of the land.

If it were shewn that this sum is much less in value than the land, then it might be insisted by the plaintiff with some reason, that he should be at liberty to reject it, for that it was not the defendant who should have taken upon him to accept the offer made by the company for land which he had sold to the plaintiff, making him in fact the equitable owner. It may be argued that the defendant, in the plaintiff's absence, should have left the company to act at their peril, so that the plaintiff, if he were not satisfied, might have had the benefit of the arbitration clauses in the railway act, and might have shewn himself entitled to a larger sum. We do not say, however, that we are prepared to hold that the defendant has clearly done anything wrong in acting as he has done. There are severel provisions in the railway acts that must receive attention before we come to that conclusion; and we are still less prepared to pronounce that, whatever it may be right to hold in that respect, the plaintiff could be entitled to recover back the £76 paid by him on his purchase, either with or without interest.

That must depend on his right to treat the contract of sale between himself and the defendant as wholly rescinded, by reason of the railway company having taken possession (which they had a right to do) of enough land for their track. Before we could hold that to be so, we should have to consider the effect in law of the plaintiff being well aware, when he made the purchase, that the railway company had laid out their track through the land which he was buying. We should require also to see the written agreement, or to have a more particular account of its contents (if its non-production can be accounted for), than is now before us, for we ought to be quite certain that no exception or allowance for the land taken by the company was made in the agreement. Then, again, we must know whether the parties could be placed *in statu quo* upon a rescision of the contract; for, if not, we could not hold that there was that entire failure of consideration which could entitle the plaintiff to reclaim the purchase money, but should find it right to leave the plaintiff to his action upon the agreement, in which the jury might give such damages as the case may justly call for.

The defendant could not help the land being taken by the railway company. A court of equity would compel the plaintiff to accept and pay for the land, upon receiving proper compensation for the part taken by the company. This action for money had and received is an equitable action, and before the plaintiff can, by means of it, force out of the defendant's hands the money he has paid him, he must shew that *ex æquo et bono* the defendant should not retain it.

The justice of the case, and, as we apprehend, the principles which regulate this description of action, do not point to that conclusion. The case, we thought, was one very proper to be arranged by an amicable compromise, the real justice of the thing being, that the plaintiff should take the conveyance of the land, receiving also the money which the defendant got from the company, or anything beyond it which disinterested parties may consider to be the value of the land taken. When we say this, it is not because we suppose that what the company has paid is probably not the full value, for they generally are made to pay as much as there is a pretence for asking; and it may be, that in this case the plaintiff, if he took the money, would be receiving considerably more than the value of the railway track, according to the price which he himself was to give the defendant per acre for the whole. He appears to be unreasonable in desiring to make what has occurred a ground for annulling the contract; and we trusted that the parties would make such arrangement between themselves, as might do more complete justice, and at less expense, than might be obtained in this action, if we should be driven to dispose of it upon strict legal principles. We therefore kept the matter under consideration till next term, there being an intimation that the plaintiff's attorney had communicated with his client, and might perhaps find himself in a situation to accede to the suggestions of the court.

It appears, however, that any expectation of that kind has failed, and we are now asked to give judgment upon the plaintiff's application to be allowed to enter a verdict in his favor for the £76, which he has paid to the defendant in part payment of the land, with interest upon it: in other words, he seeks to recover back his money, as if there was a total failure of consideration.

In our opinion, the plaintiff can neither in reason nor law succeed in his action. He is not entitled to treat the agreement as rescinded, neither has there been a total failure of consideration for the money which he advanced. He obtained possession of the place, and retained it as long as suited his convenience and inclination to do so. The defendant seems upon the evidence to have acted fairly and justly; the plaintiff, on the other hand, appears to have become, for some reason or other, anxious to get rid of his purchase, perhaps rather because he had made up his mind to leave the country, than for any other reason, and he claims the right to treat his bargain as cancelled, because the railway company have exercised an authority which the law gives to them, and which neither the defendant nor he could prevent. If the defendant has in any point failed, which we do not see, the plaintiff has his remedy upon the agreement ; but we cannot hold that by anything that was proved the contract was rescinded.

Rule discharged.

SHENSTON V. BAKER.

14 & 15 *Vic. ch.* 5, *sec.* 12—*Sheriff of Oxford, sale by, of lands in Oakland after 1st of January,* 1852.

Under a *fi. fa.* issued upon judgment entered in November, 1851, the sheriff of the county of Oxford in 1853 conveyed certain lands in the township of Brant, reciting in the deed that they had been seised in December, 1851. By 14 & 15 Vic. ch. 5, which came into force on the 1st of January, 1852, the township of Oakland was annexed to the county of Brant, but by the 12th clause it was enacted that all proceedings in any court at the time when the Act should come into effect, might be continued to trial and judgment in such court, and such judgment might be executed as if the Act had not been passed :
Held, that under this provision the sheriff was authorized to convey as he had done.

EJECTMENT for part of lot 6, in the 2nd concession of Oakland, specially described ; verdict for 1s. damages.

M. C. Cameron moved that a nonsuit be entered, pursuant to leave reserved.

Read shewed cause.

The only question upon this rule was, whether a sheriff's deed, under which the plaintiff made title, was valid under the circumstances.

Absalom Baker was seised of the premises ; one Nelson Phillips recovered a judgment against him for a debt in the Queen's Bench, in November, 1851, and issued a *fi. fa.* against goods, which was returned *nulla bona.* A *fi. fa.* issued on the 18th of December, 1851, against the defendant's lands, returnable on the 1st of Hilary Term, 1853.

This was directed to the sheriff of the county of Oxford,

who received the writ on the 20th of December, 1851, and returned that he had taken of the lands and tenements of the defendant to the value of £25, which remained unsold for want of buyers, and that the defendant had no more lands in his county, &c.

On the 21st of March, 1853, a *ven. ex.* issued, directed to the sheriff of the county of Oxford, commanding him to sell the lands, &c., returnable on the 1st of Easter term following, with a *fi. fa.* for residue. This writ was delivered to the sheriff on the 28th of March, 1853.

On the 16th of May, 1853, the sheriff of the county of Oxford made a deed under his seal of office, in which he recited the writ of *ven. ex.* in full, and that he did, on the 10th of May, 1853, after due notice, publicly expose to sale the lands in the said deed described, (which were the premises now in question), and sold the same to William Lapenotiere and William Gray (being the two highest bidders) for £40 : —that under the writ of *fi. fa.* issued from this court against the lands of Absalom Baker, and directed to him the said sheriff, he had seised and taken the said lands on the 20th of December, 1851, and after duly advertising the same for sale, and not being able to sell the said land so seized by him, he then returned the writ as already stated, on which return the said writ of *ven. ex.* was afterwards issued directed to him.

And then, by his deed under his seal of office, he granted, bargained, and sold to Lapenotiere and Gray all the right, estate and interest of Absalom Baker in the land, as fully and absolutely as he could grant, bargain, and sell the same, as such sheriff, by force of the statute in that case made and provided, and of the said writs of *ven. ex.* and *fi. fa.* for residue, or otherwise howsoever.

On the 28th of October, 1853, Messrs Lapenotiere and Gray, by deed of bargain and sale, conveyed this land to the plaintiff.

The objection taken to the title was, that by the statute 14 & 15 Vic. ch. 5 sec. 12, the township of Oakland, in which this land was, was annexed to the county of Brant, and on the 1st of January, 1852, ceased to form part of the county of Oxford, and the defendant denied that the sheriff of Oxford under the circumstances, had any legal authority to sell and convey the lands as he did, when it no longer formed part of his county.

It was not shewn, further than by the return in the *fi. fa.* against lands and the sheriff's recitals in his deed, that any thing had been done by him by way of inception of the execution of the writ against lands before the township of Oakland ceased to form part of his county.

The same officer (Mr. Carroll) was sheriff of Oxford during the whole of the proceedings.

ROBINSON, C. J., delivered the judgment of the court.

There is nothing in the evidence to shew whether the sheriff of Oxford sold the land within his own county, or whether, under his assumed inception of the execution, he proceeded to sell it in the county of Brant, though that was no longer within his bailiwick.

I do not imagine, however, that anything could turn upon that, because the authority which the law recognizes as continuing in the late officer, even after his tenure of office has ceased, to perfect an execution which he has begun while in office, rests upon the principle that all has reference back to the commencement of the execution of the writ. Whatever is done under it is regarded all as one act. At the time when Mr. Carroll seized under this writ (if upon the evidence we can say that a seizure is shewn *prima facie* by the recital in the deed), the county of Brant formed part of his baili_ wick, and he could have sold the land then in one part of it as well as another.

But we have come to the conclusion that no proof of seizure before the separation of the counties is required in this case, nor any application of the doctrine of relation, for that the statute 14 & 15 Vic. ch. 5, sec. 12, provides for just such a case as this, when it enacts, as it does, that actions pending when it was passed may be continued to trial and judgment, and *such judgment* may be executed as if the act had not been passed, although the local jurisdiction of such court may be changed as to other matters. If we have the dates correctly, this action was not literally pending when the act passed, but that makes the case stronger in favor of the method of proceeding in execution of the judgment remaining undisturbed and unchanged by the act. If the legislature did not desire any change to take place, even in cases which had not yet been tried, *à fortiori* those cases in which judgment had been entered and execution issued were not to be affected by the change, but might be carried on as they otherwise would have been.

Rule discharged.

CLARK v. THE HAMILTON AND GORE MECHANICS' INSTITUTE.

Corporation—Necessity for contract under corporate seal.

Where work done for a corporation is such as was evidently contemplated by their charter, and they have accepted and availed themseves of it, they cannot refuse to pay on the ground that there was no contract under seal. *Held*, therefore, that the Hamilton and Gore Mechanics' Institute were liable to the defendant for services rendered by him as an architect upon a verbal agreement, in preparing plans and superintending the erection of a hall for their accommodation.

Draper, J., dissenting, on the ground that—as there was nothing in the defendants' charter to bind them by any particular form of contract, and the claim was not one for small or ordinary services which might constantly be required—the case could not be held within any of the recognized exceptions to the general rule, which requires a contract under the corporate seal.

This was an action of assumpsit upon the common counts, for work done and materials found.

The defendants pleaded—1st, Non-assumpsit to all except as to £95; 2ndly, As to £45, parcel of the £95, payment before action brought; 3dly, As to £50, residue of the £95 payment into court.

The case was tried before *Burns, J.*, at the last assizes at Hamilton, and it appeared that the plaintiff had been employed by the defendants to prepare plans for building a hall for the defendants, and as an architect to superintend the erection of the building. No contract under seal was shewn, or anything beyond the verbal directions to the plaintiff, whose plans had been adopted, that he was to superintend the erection of the building according to his plans. It was admitted that the building cost £3,000, and it was proved that the usual charge for an architect superintending the building according to his plans, if adopted, was five per cent. on the cost. A mistake had been made in the correct level of the walls, and in consequence the great hall of the building presented an unsightly appearance in the inside, and this caused a dispute between the defendants and the plaintiff, and the defendants refused to pay him anything more than the £95, contending that they had sufficiently compensated him for his services. The jury disposed of that question upon the evidence by finding for the plaintiff, with twenty-two pounds damages.

The defendants contended that, as they were a corporation, the plaintiff, though the work was done and the defendants in possession of it, could not compel them to pay any more than had been already paid, as no contract was proved under the corporate seal, and leave was reserved to move for a nonsuit on this ground.

Vankoughnet, Q. C., obtained a rule *nisi*, according to the leave reserved. *Eccles* shewed cause.

It was argued for the plaintiff, that the objection taken at the trial could not be made after a plea of payment into court; and on this point Dearle v. Barret, 2 A. &. E. 83; Fischer v. Aide, 3 M. & W. 486; Tyr. on Pl. 222, 231-2; Story v. Finnis, 6 Ex. 123; Booth v. Howard, 5 Dowl. 438; Steavenson v. Berwick, 1 Q. B. 153; Dilk v. Keighley, 2 Esp. 181, note, were cited. This question was not decided by the court. The other authorities referred to are fully noticed in the judgments.

ROBINSON, C. J.—Upon the merits at the trial, the plaintiff, it appears to me, stood in an unfavorable position, and had a very weak case to stand upon, and the jury, in giving him the small sum which they did as a balance yet due to him of the value of his services rendered for and accepted by the defendants, dealt rather hardly, I think, by the defendants, for it would really appear that the plaintiff had been already overpaid for his services. He sued on the common counts, not on any alleged special agreement, and the jury in valuing the services which he had rendered, were certainly extremely indulgent, for either he or his clerk, for whose skill and attention he was of course responsible, must have failed greatly in superintending the building which he had under his charge, or such defects could not have been found in it as were proved on the trial to exist.

Still the defendants have resolved, and perhaps judiciously, to waive contesting the suit further upon the merits and they confine their objection to the plaintiff's recovery entirely to the point which they raised at the trial—viz. : that the defendants, being a corporate body, cannot be made liable to pay, even for goods or labor furnished to them in the proper course of their business, and which they have accepted and availed themselves of, unless it can be shewn that they have contracted under their seal to pay for such goods or labor.

On that point, I agree fully in the opinion which has been formed by my brother Burns, and his arguments in support of it, which I take to be in accordance with all former judgments of this court, so far as they affect this precise point (a), and with the current of authorities in England from a very early time.

Some later decisions in the Court of Exchequer, which seem to militate against it, are not deemed satisfactory by the other courts in England, and they have been produced by an anxiety on the part of that court to avoid the dangerous and inconvenient consequences which, it appeared to them, must follow from the new doctrine advanced by the Queen's Bench, in Church v. The Imperial Gas Light and Coke Company (6 A. & E. 846,) that it was impossible to maintain the distinction formerly acted upon between executory and executed contracts as governing the liability of corporations.

Instead of rejecting the innovation — not chargeable against the judgment in that case, but intimated in the language of the court—and adhering to the principles which had been long well established, the Court of Exchequer seem rather to have suffered themselves to be driven by it to depart even more widely from former authority than the Queen's Bench had done, and to have made up their minds that, if there was to be no distinction between executed and executory contracts, it must follow, as a consequence, that even upon executed contracts there can be no recovery allowed against a corporation, unless in very trivial matters, except upon their contract under seal.

(a) See Hamilton v. Niagara Harbour and Dock Company, E. T. 5 Vic. ; Raines v. Credit Harbour Company, 1 U. C. R. 174 ; Lyman v. Bank of Upper Canada, 8 U. C. R. 354.

I think this change in our law, attempted to be introduced without legislative authority, is by no means yet established in England, but that the weight of authority, if we look at the decisions of all the courts, is very much against it down to the present moment and before I could bring myself to concur in holding against the decisions of courts for a series of five hundred years (for the principle I now refer to, can be traced as far back), that a corporate body can avail themselves of the property or labor of others, and accept and apply it to their own legitimate purposes within the scope of their charter, and yet refuse to pay for what they are enjoying because they never bound themselves under their seal to pay for it, I must see either an act of parliament abolishing what certainly till lately was undisputed law, or must feel myself bound by a decision to that effect by some higher tribunal, whose judgments have by the constitution a direct authority overruling us.

In any case where a plaintiff is endeavouring to recover against a corporation upon an executory agreement, either as to time or mode of payment, or containing conditions of any kind, such as, if he were proceeding against an individual would require him to give evidence upon the trial of an actual express contract such as alleged, because it is of a description such as the law never would of itself imply,—there I have no doubt the plaintiff must prove a contract under the seal of the corporation unless the cause of action should be of that trivial kind, and so constantly recurrring in the course of their business that it would be absurd and intolerably inconvenient to exact such a formal undertaking.

But when as regards the plaintiff, the contract has been executed, and the corporation has received and used the goods, or benefited by the labor and that in the course of business within the scope of their charter, I think the law saves the corporation the trouble of undertaking by their seal to pay for what they have consumed by applying a promise and of course a binding promise, as it does in the case of an individual, who would, under the same circumstances, be held liable to pay, though he had never actually promised to do so, and had even done all that was possible to evade it.

DRAPER, J.—The general rule established by the old authorities appears to be fully maintained in the very latest; namely that a corporation aggregate is not bound unless by contract under its corporate seal.

There are some exceptions as old as the rule, and which as is said in one case form a rule as much as the rule itself. These are acts of daily necessity, or of a very insignificant character, or where the corporation had a head who might give commands without the sanction of the corporate seal, or where acts to be done must be done immediately.

The cases establishing the rule, and these older exceptions, are to be found in every digest and text book, as well as in the modern cases where the principle has been discussed.

The next exception recognized, was the drawing and accepting of bills, and the making of notes, by trading corporations incorporated for purposes which made such acts indispensable, or the corporation could not fulfil the purposes for which it was brought into existence.—Horn v. Ivy (1 Ventr. 47).

It was also held at an early period that assumpsit would lie by a corporation—as for scavage by custom, without a special promise—Mayor of London v. Gorry (2 Lev. 174) ; for money forfeited under a by-law—Barber Surgeons of London v. Pelson (2 Lev. 252) ; and in a later case, for use and occupation—Mayor of Stafford v. Till (4 Bing. 78, which was rested on the footing of a *condition executed,* where the law implies a promise by the party benefited— East London Waterworks Company v. Bailey (4 Bing. 287).

But as late as the year 1832, the question was put from the bench, in Dunston v. The Imperial Gas Light Company (3 B. & Ad. 125), "Is there any case where their contract, without seal, has been held a sufficient ground for an action ?" And the answer of the council is, that it would be so in the case put in some of the books of hiring a cook or butler, shewing that it was only supported when it came within the exception above stated. Another exception is the liability of a corporation in tort for the tortious act of its agent, though that agent was not proved to have been appointed under seal—Yarborough v. the Bank of England (16 East 6) ; Tilson v. The Warwick Gas Light Company (4 B. & C.

962); Smith v. Birmingham Gas Company (1 A. & E. 526) —Eastern Counties Railway Company v. Broom, in Error (15 Jur. 297).

The exceptions of matters of daily occurrence and of insignificant character, have received an extension in their application in modern cases. The leading case, and I apprehend the first which *unequivocally* decided that assumpsit will lie against à corporation aggregate on an executed contract not under the corporate seal, is that of Beverley v. The Lincoln Gas Light and Coke Company (6 A. & E. 829). The arguments in that case, indeed the whole reasoning of the judgment, almost induce one to suppose that the court felt an inclination to lay down that in respect to corporations of that character assumpsit would lie upon an executed consideration without restriction as to amount; but the concluding words of the judgment repel such a supposition, or at least prevent the case being quoted as an authority to that extent, for they bring the decision within the reason and principle of the established exceptions—" It seems clear that for a matter *of such constant requirement* to a gas company as gas-meters, *and to so small an amount* as £15, the company, whether with or without a head, might contract without affixing the common seal. " (page 845).

Immediately after came the case of Church v. The Imperial Gas Light Company (6 A. & E. 846), which was decided by the Court of Queen's Bench sitting in Error, and decided the right of the plaintiffs, a corporation aggregate, to maintain assumpsit upon an executory contract; and the reasoning in the judgment on that case seems at first sight calculated to lead to a conclusion far beyond what the case expressly determines. But that case, also, at the end, confines the application of the previous language—" We cannot be ignorant " (says Lord Denman) "that such contracts must be of frequent and almost daily occurrence, and to hold that for every one of them, of the same or less amount (for where the sum is so small, a diminution of half could not vary the principle) it was necessary to affix the common seal, would be so seriously to impede the corporation in fulfilling the very purpose for which it was created, that we think *we are bound to hold the case fairly brought within the principle of the established exceptions. Leaving, therefore, the ancient rule still unbroken* in all the instances to which it is fairly appli-cable, we are of opinion the present action was well brought."

Notwithstanding this last case, I find no English decision in which assumpsit has been held maintainable against a corporation aggregate on an executory contract, and the language of *Lord Campbell*, C. J., in The Governor and Company of Copper Miners v. Fox (15 Jur. 703), intimates a doubt whether that case has placed executed and executory contracts on the same footing as respects actions by such corporations, and he upholds the general principle in his concluding words—" We regret very much that any techni-cality should interfere with the enforcement of a fair contract, but the law under which a corporation is not bound unless by contract under seal can only be altered by the legislature."

These two cases were observed upon in The Mayor of Ludlow v. Charlton (6 M. & W. 815), and they were approved, espe-cially the former, as having no such meaning or intention as to explode the old rule of law and in place of it to decide that in all cases of executed contracts corporations were to be con-sidered bound in the same manner as individuals. The Court of Exchequer refer to the exceptions to the general rule in clear language, and their decision shews not the slightest disposition to extend them. This judgment is of the more importance, because in subsequent cases in the same court it is again and again referred to as containing a sound and accurate exposition of the law, and its authority is recognized by the other courts when brought under their consideration.

Tindal, C. J., recognizes the rule and the limited character of the exception, in Gibson v. The East India Company (5 Bing. N. C. 262), and after intimating an opinion that a trading corporation may " in matters of frequent require-ment and small amount," be liable on an executory contract, winds up with re-asserting the ancient principle, " that a corporation aggregate cannot be sued upon a contract not being under their common seal."

Similar views are expressed by the same eminent judge in Arnold v. The Mayor of Poole (4 M. & G. 860), which case is cited and approved of in 6 Q.B. 443. He takes occasion to

refer to another class of cases, such as The Dean of Rochester v. Pierce (1 Camp. 466), from which it had been argued
that all contracts to be binding must be mutual, and that
therefore where corporations may sue upon simple contracts,
it followed that they must also be liable to be sued.   He
treats that proposition as too broadly stated, and says it
must be confined to those cases where the want of mutuality
would leave one party without a valid or available consideration for his promise.

This latter question underwent further discussions in The
Fishmongers' Company v. Robertson (5 M. & G. 131), where
it was held that a contract not under the corporate seal
having been executed on the part of the corporation, and
the defendants having received the full consideration, the
latter were bound by the contract, and the corporation could
maintain an action thereon.   There are some observations
in this judgment as to the effect of the corporation thus
setting up a contract not under their seal as valid; and it is
thrown out that in a cross action they might be estopped
from asserting that such contract was not binding on them.
This can hardly be considered as settled law; and in regard
thereto I refer to the observations of Lord Campbell, in The
Copper Miners' Company v. Fox, already cited.

But the Court of Queen's Bench, in Hall v. The Mayor of
Swansea (5 Q. B. 526), comment upon the decisions reported
in 6 A. & E., in connection with those in the Mayor of
Ludlow v. Charlton and Arnold v. The Mayor of Poole, and
they support their own judgments in these two cases on the
footing of necessity.   Where the transaction is of small
amount, and of daily occurrence, where the supposed contract is for things of small moment, the occasion for which
frequently occurs, for trivial matters frequently occurring
and essential to the business of the corporation; in all these
cases it is matter of necessity that the corporation should
be bound without an engagement under seal.   This decision
effectually restrains the application of the previous cases,
and shews a harmony of sentiment on the question between
all the courts.   And in Paine v. The Strand Union (8 Q. B.
326) the Court of Queen's Bench again reiterate their

approval of the decision of the Exchequer in The Mayor of
Ludlow v. Charlton.

Lamprell v. the Billericay Union (3 Ex. 283) upholds the
same doctrine. The plaintiff claimed for work done under
a sealed contract, and also for work done beyond what was
expressed in the contract, though upon the subject matter
of the contract, and, admitting that he had no remedy on
the deed, insisted that the defendants had accepted the
additional work, and so had the full benefit of it, and the
plaintiff had a right to be paid on a *quantum meruit*. But
the court held otherwise.

The same principle is upheld in Cope v. The Thames Haven
Dock and Railway Company (18 L. J. Ex. 345), and again
most forcibly in a subsequent case of Diggle v. the Blackwall
Railway Company (14 Jur. 937), in which the Chief Baron
specially alludes to the two cases in 6 A. & E., and observes
that "those were cases of urgent necessity, within the exception, which is a rule as much as the rule itself."

Homersham v. the Wolverhampton Waterworks Company
(20 L. J. Ex. 193, 6 Ex. 137) is also a very strong case upholding the rule, and the limited nature of the established
exceptions, clearly and forcibly.

Indeed there are only two cases which I have seen that
are *even apparently* at variance with the tenor of these
later authorities. The first is Doe Pennington v. Taniere
(13 Jur. 119, 12 Q. B. 998), where the court held that the
presumption arising from the payment and receipt of rent
is the same in the case of a corporation as of other persons.
But in giving judgment Lord Denham says, "This is by no
means inconsistent with the rule that in general a corporation can only contract by deed. It is merely by raising a
presumption against them from their acts, that they have
contracted in such a manner as to be binding upon them
whether by deed or otherwise."

The other case is Sanders v. St. Neot's Union (8 Q. B.
810), which was assumpsit for iron gates supplied by the
plaintiff to defendants, which had been erected at the Union
Workhouse, the only order given by the defendants being
a verbal one to one of their own officers (since dead), who

gave the order to the plaintiff.   The court, on motion for a
nonsuit for want of proof of a contract under the corporate
seal, upheld the action, Lord Denman saying. "We think
they could not be permitted to take the objection, inasmuch
as the work in question, after it was done and completed,
was adopted by them for purposes connected with the corporation."   And certainly, if this case is rightly reported and
rightly decided, it is a strong authority for the plaintiff, and
conflicts with what has been held in the case already referred
to.   But in Lamprell v. The Billericay Union, *Rolfe*, B.,
says, "It is fit we should refer to the case of Sanders v. The
St. Neot's Union, merely for the purpose of saying that the
Court of Queen's Bench certainly did not mean to overrule
their former decision.   The objection there was perhaps
rather an objection on the record, than to the ruling of the
judge at Nisi Prius; or, if this was not so, the court only
meant to say that the goods there ordered and supplied were
such as brought the case within the exceptions referred to in
the former authorities."   In the subsequent case of Diggle
v. The Blackwall Railway Company, when Sanders v. The
St. Neot's Union was cited, *Rolfe*, B., remarked " My
brother Parke told me that there was an error in the report
of that case, and that the real point was not on the record."
After this it would be unsafe to act upon this case as an
authority establishing anything averse to or inconsistent
with the other authorities.

Subsequently comes the case of Clark v. The Guardians of the Cuckfield Union (16 Jur. 686), decided in the
bail court by *Wightman*, J., in which Lamprell v. The
Billericay Union is questioned, and this general doctrine is
laid down as the result of the cases decided before Lamprell
v. The Billericay Union, that "wherever a corporation is
created for *particular purposes,* which involves the necessity
of *frequently entering* into contracts for goods or work
essentially necessary for carrying the purposes for which the
corporation is created into execution, a demand in respect of
goods or work which have been actually supplied to and
accepted by the corporation, and of which they have had
the full benefit, may be enforced by action of assumpsit, and

the corporation will be liable, though the contract was by parol only, and not by deed." The learned judge suggests also a distinction between such a corporation as the guardians of a poor law union and municipal corporations, and others of a similar character; and that contracts under seal may not be necessary in the former case where they would be in the latter. In giving judgment the learned judge expresses his regret at the state of the law on the subject, adding, "It would perhaps have been better, and have avoided the uncertainty which now exists, if the old rule had never been relaxed; but being as it is, the question is, whether the demand in question comes within any of the recognized exceptions to the general rule"—thus, as I take it, implying no intention to go beyond the exceptions referred to.

The case of Finlay v. The Bristol and Exeter Railway Company (7 Ex. 409) was decided a short time before this case, but was not adverted to in it. It was an action of assumpsit against the defendants, a corporation, for use and occupation, and the plaintiff sought to recover for three-fourths of a year during which the defendants had not in fact occupied, because they had quitted the premises without giving six months' notice, and only paid an additional quarter's rent. The court held the plaintiff could not recover, because the occupation was only constructive, which could only arise from contract. In giving judgment *Parke,* B., observes, "The cases in which corporations can bind themselves without seal are reduced to these: First, where there is a parliamentary charter, shewing an intention that the corporation should be bound by contracts of a particular description, though not under seal." The other cases are the ancient common-law exceptions, which are simply confined to orders given by a corporation with a head, such as the appointment of a servant, and small matters of that description, upon which an action lay for wages although the appointment was not under seal. No case has gone the length of saying that a corporation may bind itself by a contract not under seal, which does not range within either the small services excepted by the common law, or contracts authorized by parliamentary charter."

Lowe v. London and Northwestern Railway Company (17 Jur. 375) was also an action for use and occupation. The foregoing case was referred to, and as to the maintenance of the action approved, though some expressions by Lord Campbell might lead to the inference that they are not fully prepared to go as far as the Court of Exchequer in maintaining the exemption of the corporation from the action of assumpsit.

I do not see in the parliamentary charter of the defendants (12 Vic. ch. 110) anything to bring them within the first exception pointed out by *Parke, B.*, in Finlay v. The Bristol and Exeter Railway Company; and the employment of the plaintiff as an architect does not, to my apprehension, fall within the class of "the ancient common-law exceptions," —nor in my humble judgment is it within the principle of Mr. *Justice Wightman's* judgment "that wherever a corporation is created for particular purposes which involve the necessity of frequently entering into contracts for goods or works essentially necessary for carrying the purposes for which the corporation is created into execution" such an action may be maintained. It is to be hoped, and I think may without any great presumption be assumed, that these defendants will not be very frequently under the necessity of erecting a hall for their accommodation, and as a consequence will not have a perpetually recurring occasion to contract for the services of an architect. It is true the plaintiff claims to recover on an alleged excuted consideration, but I am not prepared to hold, that in all cases where the plaintiff makes that the foundation of his action, and a jury find for him, that the court must hold that a contract under the corporate seal can be dispensed with. It appears to me, therefore, that the concurrent authority of the three common law courts in England is against the plaintiff in this case, and that, without overruling their decisions, we cannot hold that he is entitled to recover. We may regret, as Lord Campbell expressed himself, the necessity for our conclusion, but the law can only be altered by the Legislature. While it remains on its present footing we can but repeat the warning given in Williams v. The Chester and Holyhead Railway Company (15 Jur. 828) : " Persons dealing with these companies should always bear in mind that such companies are a corporation—a body essentially different from an ordinary partnership or firm, for all purposes of contracts, and especially in respect of evidence against them on legal trials—and should insist upon these contracts being by deed under the seal of the company, or signed by directors in the manner prescribed by the act of Parliament. There is no safety or security for any one dealing with such a body upon any other footing. The same observation also applies in respect of any variation or alteration in a contract which has been made,"

In my opinion the weight of authority is against the plaintiff, and I therefore think the rule should be made absolute.

BURNS, J.—The question now presented to the court was raised, and underwent considerable investigation in this court, in Cotton v. The Port Hope Harbour Company; but in consequence of the settlement of the action the court was never called upon to give judgment. I was at some pains in comparing the decisions of the different courts up to' that time ; and it appeared to me that, contrasting the cases of Sanders v. The Guardians of the St. Noet's Union (8 Q. B. 810), Doe Pennington v. Taniere (12 Q. B. 998), and the Governor and Company of the Copper Miners of England v. Fox (16 Q. B. 229), with the cases of Lamprell v. The Billericay Union (3 Ex. 283), Diggle v. The London and Blackwall Railway Company (5 Ex. 442), Homersham v. The Wolverhampton Waterworks Company (6 Ex. 137), and Williams v. The Chester and Holyhead Railway Company (15 Jur. 828), there was certainly a conflict of opinion between the judges of the Court of Queen's Bench and the barons of the Exchequer upon this subject. I was then prepared to express my opinion that I agreed with the position taken by the Queen's Bench, that a corporation could not take the benefit of work done for and accepted by them, or of goods furnished to and kept by the corporation, when the work done and goods furnished were in the course of business, or for the very purposes for which the corporation was created, and afterwards say the company was not bound to pay, because there was no contract under seal.

Since the consideration of the case of Cotton v. The Port Hope Harbour Company, several decisions have been published from the English courts, and the opinions therein expressed relieve me from entering into any disquisition upon the previous cases. Clark v. The Guardians of the Cuckfield Union (16 Jur. 686, 11 Eng. Rep. 442) was carefully considered by *Mr. Justice Wightman,* as he says, and as is apparent from the time he took to deliberate upon the case, and the pains he bestowed in reviewing the subject. That case is undistinguishable from the one before us, and the fact that in this case the work was performed in fulfilling and carrying out the very objects for which the company was incorporated renders every word of *Mr. Justice Wightman's* reasoning applicable. This decision was given on the 12th of June, 1852, subsequent to the case of Finlay v. The Bristol and Exeter Railway Company (7 Ex. 409) in which the Court of Exchequer adhere to their former decisions, and also subsequent to Lowe v. The London and North Western Railway Company (21 L. J. Q. B. 361), in which the case in the Exchequer is mentioned. As *Mr. Justice Wightman* says, it is greatly to be regretted that such is the present state of the law upon a subject so important and whenever a case now occurs in which the facts form an exception to the rule, that a corporation can only be bound by its seal—that is, such a case as comes within the category of any of those cases already decided—it merely remains for a judge to say whether he will decide similarly in a similar case to what has been held before, or whether he will, as Mr. Justice Erle says of the Court of Exchequer strictly maintain the exemption of corporations.

Until the question shall be set at rest by a decision of a court of the last resort, I think it more reasonable—in cases where the things furnished to, or work done for the corporation be of a character which is for the existence of, and to carry out the very thing for which the corporation was created, after an acceptance by the company and an acting thereupon as if there were a binding contract—to hold that the law implies a contract on the company; that is, a request and promise as strong as if the same were proved under the corporate seal, and that a company should not be permitted to dispute its liability in such cases for want of a contract under seal.

Rule discharged—DRAPER, J., dissenting.

ABEL v. LEONARD.

Assumpsit—Pleading—Plea not answering whole breach.

Assumpsit on a contract to make and furnish a steam engine and boiler, and that the said boiler should be made of good and sufficient materials, and should be reasonably fit and proper for the said engine, and the reasonable and proper working and use thereof. *Breach*, that the boiler furnished was not made of good and sufficient materials, and was not reasonably fit and proper for the said engine, and the reasonable and proper working and use thereof.
Plea, that the said boiler was made of good and sufficient materials.
Held, on demurrer, plea bad, as not answering the whole breach.

ASSUMPSIT.—The declaration set forth a contract, by which the defendant promised to manufacture and furnish to the plaintiff a steam engine and " boiler for the same, and promised that the said boiler should be made of good and sufficient materials, and should be reasonably fit and proper for the said engine, and the reasonable and proper working and use thereof." The plaintiff then averred payment to the defendant, and that the defendant did furnish a steam engine and boiler, as and for one which was in accordance with the terms of his promise. The breach was, that the " boiler so supplied and furnished by the defendant to the plaintiff as aforesaid was not made of good and sufficient materials, and was not reasonably fit and proper for the said engine and the reasonable and proper working and use therof; but, on the contrary thereof, was made of bad and insufficient materials, and was wholly unfit and improper for the said engine, and for the reasonable and proper working and use thereof."

To this the defendant pleaded " that the said boiler was made of good and sufficient materials : concluding to the country.

The plaintiff demurred to the plea, as not containing an

answer to the whole declaration, but traversing only one part of the breach assigned.

Connor, Q.C., for the demurrer. *John Wilson*, contra.

ROBINSON, C. J.—The plea cannot, as I think, be supported. It answers only part of the breach assigned, though it is pleaded as an answer to the whole cause of action.

The boiler being of bad materials is one thing, and its being, as it might be, of perfectly good materials, but yet unfit and improper for the engine, and for the reasonable and proper working and use thereof, is another and totally distinct thing ; and both are expressly complained of in the declaration, and should therefore have been answered.

Mr. Wilson argued that we must understand the plaintiff to mean that the boiler, being made of bad materials, was *on that account* and no other unfit for the engine, and that when the defendant asserts that it was made of good and sufficient materials, he does in effect answer all that is complained of. But we are not at liberty so to narrow the effect of the language used by the plaintiff. He may well mean that the boiler had both defects, and we cannot know that he does not mean that.

DRAPER, J.—I think the declaration must be treated either as containing two breaches,—one, that the boiler was not made of good and sufficient materials ; the other, that the boiler was unfit and improper for the engine, and for the reasonable and proper working and use thereof—or else it contains one entire but divisible breach, the proof of either part of which would entitle the plaintiff to recover. In either view the plea is bad ; for on the first assumption it answers only one breach ; on the second, it answers only one part of a divisible breach, while it is pleaded as an answer to the action. The plaintiff should therefore have judgment on the demurrer.

BURNS, J., concurred.

Judgment for plaintiff on demurrer.

FORWARD ET AL. V. JOHN THOMPSON AND WM. THOMPSON.

Promissory note—Presentment—Pleading.

Assumpsit against the maker and endorser of a promissory note. The first count alleged that the maker had absconded, and was absent from Canada when the note fell due. The second count averred, as an excuse for presentment, the absence of the maker, and the plaintiff's inability to find him.

Pleas, to the first count, 1st, That the note was not duly presented for payment. 2nd, That it was not duly presented at the maker's last place of abode. To the second count, that the maker's last place of abode was well known to the plaintiffs when the note fell due.

Held, on demurrer, pleas bad.

ASSUMPSIT, on a promissory note made by one John Thompson, payable at Port Hope to the defendant William Thompson, or order, who endorsed to the defendant John Thompson, who endorsed to the plaintiffs.

In the first count it was averred that the maker of the note, John Thompson, had absconded and was absent from the province when the note fell due, but that one Almon Harris, of the said town of Port Hope, was his agent, and that the said note was duly presented to the said Harris in Port Hope, as such agent.

The second count excused the want of presentment by averring the absence of the maker from the province, and the plaintiff's inability to find him.

The defendants pleaded, 5thly, to the first count, That the note was not duly presented.

8thly, That the said note was not duly presented at the last place of abode of the said John Thompson for payment thereof, as it should, and might, and ought to have been.

16thly, To the second count, That the last place of abode of the said John Thompson was, when the note became due, well known to the said plaintiffs.

The plaintiffs demurred to each of these pleas. The causes of demurrer sufficiently appear in the judgment.

Richards for the demurrer.   *Wilson*, Q.C., contra.

ROBINSON, C. J., delivered the judgment of the court.

The fifth plea is no doubt bad. It is not at all supported by the case cited of the Bank of Upper Canada v. Sherwood (8 U.C.R.116). The defendants in this plea take no notice of the alleged presentment to the agent, and so leave it uncertain whether they mean to deny that any such presentment was in fact made, or to deny the legal sufficiency of a presentment to an agent under the circumstances pleaded,— or whether they may not mean that there was something in the time or manner of the presentment to the agent which made it insufficient.

The eighth plea was, I believe, given up on the argument. It denies what the plaintiffs have not alleged. If the defendants mean that, whether presented to an agent or not, it was necessary that the note should be presented at John Thompson's last place of abode, they should have demurred to the declaration, because it contained no averment of such presentment.

The sixteenth plea is also, we think, manifestly insufficient. The defendants do not demur on the ground that a formal presentment was not in such case indispensable, and that the note might have been presented at the last place of abode of J. Thompson, but they plead merely that the last place of abode of J. Thompson was at the time of the note maturing well known to the plaintiffs, not saying whether they mean the last place of abode in this province or out of it, and not averring any such circumstances as might make a presentment at the last place of abode sufficient. For all that is stated in the plea, the last place of Thompson's abode in this province may have been deserted, or no one may have been living there who had any connection or privity with him.

Judgment for plaintiffs on demurrer.

BEATTIE V. HATCH.

Account stated—Pleading.

Assumpsit on account stated for £1200. Plea. That after the cause of action accrued, and before the commencement of the suit, the plaintiff and defendant accounted together of and concerning the causes of action in the declaration mentioned, and of and concerning certain other demands of the plaintiff against the defendant and of the defendant against the plaintiff, and on such accounting the defendant was found indebted to the plaintiff in £800, and no more, which sum the defendant promised, and hath been, and is ready to pay.
Held, on demurrer, plea good.

ASSUMPSIT.—The last count was on an account stated, by which it appeared that the defendant was indebted to the plaintiff in £1200.

The declaration also contained other counts, for the good-will of a trade, goods sold and delivered, &c.

The defendant pleaded—1st, Non assumpsit; and 2ndly, to the last count, that after the accruing of the cause of action in that count, and *before the commencement of this suit,* the plaintiff and defendant accounted together of and concerning the causes of action in that count mentioned, and of and concerning certain other demands of the plaintiff against the defendant, and of and concerning certain other demands of the defendant against the plaintiff; and on such accounting the defendant was found indebted to the plaintiff in £800 and no more, which the defendant promised to pay, and which he had always been and still is willing to pay.   Verification.

Demurrer, assigning for causes—1st, That no tender of the £800 is shewn, or that the plaintiff refused it.   2ndly, That the plea attempts to put an immaterial point in issue, and that the averment that the defendant was willing to pay the £800 is not issuable.   3rdly, That the plea shews "no satis-faction" or discharge of the claim therein said to be accounted upon.   4thly, That it amounts to the general issue, setting up a different accounting from that set forth in the declaration.

Connor, Q. C., for the demurrer.   *Eccles,* contra.   In addition to the authorities cited in the judgment, Hanscombe v. Macdonald, 4 C. P. 190, was referred to.

ROBINSON, C. J.—I think it was in the case of Melville et al. v. Carpenter, lately decided in this court (11 U. C. R. 133), that the kind of plea which is now before us on demurrer first came under our consideration.   I confess it appeared to me upon the argument that it could not be a sufficient defence, that plea, like the present, containing no allegation that the sum found due upon the accounting had been satisfied.

In that case the defendant pleaded to a count for work and labor and materials found that after the accruing of the cause of action therein mentioned, and before the commence-ment of the suit the plaintiffs and the defendant accounted together concerning the causes of action declared upon in that count, and concerning other demands of the plaintiffs against the defendant, and of the defendant against the plaintiffs, and that upon that counting £50 was found to be due from the defendant to the plaintiffs, which he then promised to pay to the plaintiffs, and which he had always been and still was willing to pay.

The case of Smith et al. v. Page (15 M & W. 683) fully sustained that plea, as it appeared to us, though the judgment of the court was against the plea there pleaded, on account of the defect in it noticed by *Baron Parke* in his judgment, from which defect this plea is free—namely, that there was there no allegation of any other claims of the plaintiffs on the defendant than those declared on, nor of any cross demand of the defendant against the plaintiffs, which had been settled on the alleged accounting; so that in effect the plea, as it stood on that record, amounted to nothing more than an attempt to make the payment of the smaller sum found due on the second accounting a satisfaction of the larger, by way of payment, which has been always held inadmissible.

"In order to make the plea good" (his Lordship said) "*as resting on the defendant's new promise merely*, it should have alleged that after the accruing of the causes of action laid in the declaration, and before the commencement of the suit, an account was stated between the plaintiffs and the defendant, of and concerning the said causes of action, and of and concerning other demands of the plaintiffs against the defendant, and a certain other demand of the defendant against the plaintiffs."

Now the plea before us, like that in Melville v. Carpenter, fully and exactly complies with what *Baron Parke* in that judgment stated was necessary to make such a defence a good plea, and the dictum of *Baron Parke*, in Smith v. Page, seems to have received confirmation in Callander v. Howard (10 C. B. 302), in which the court treated such a plea as amounting to an extinguishment by way of payment of the sums allowed in the former accounting, leaving the sum found due upon the last accounting to be the only existing debt.

We therefore hold this plea good. The plaintiff, I apprehend, might have new assigned that he brought his action not for the moneys found to be due upon the first accounting mentioned in the plea, but for the moneys found to be due on the last accounting.

DRAPER, J.—Either the plea is true or false—*i. e.*, there were two accountings or only one; if only one accounting, on which the plaintiff has declared, he might traverse the second plea, and must succeed on the first, as no subsequent accounting could be shewn. If there were two accountings, why could not the plaintiff new assign that he brought his action not for the accounting (or as well for the accounting) in the introductory part of the plea, but (or as) for the accounting stated in the plea, and inasmuch as the defendant has not answered, but, on the contrary, has admitted it, pray judgment as a matter of course?

BURNS, J., concurred.

Judgment for defendant on demurrer.

NOURSE V. GOODEVE ET AL.

*Usury—Pleading—*16 *Vic. ch.* 80*—Meaning of "legal interest."*

Debt on bond. Plea—That the defendants owed the plaintiff £800, and gave their notes for that sum, payable by instalments, *with legal interest*; that it was agreed that the defendants should pay certain sums, by way of bonus and usurious interest, in addition to *the said legal interest*; and that the bond sued on was given to secure such payments.

Held on demurrer plea good; for the court would intend that by the words "legal interest" six per cent. was meant, and therefore the bond was shewn to be wholly void.

Debt on bond, conditioned for payment of the following sums: £40 on the 1st of January, 1854, £30 on the 1st of July, 1854, on 1st of January, 1855, £20 on 1st July, 1855, and 1st of January, 1856, and £20 on 1st of July, 1856, and 1st of January, 1857.

Plea—That before and at the time of making said bond the defendants were indebted to the plaintiff in the sum of £800, which was then due and payable to the plaintiff; and that before the making of the said writing obligatory—to wit, on the 30th of July, 1853—it was corruptly, and against the form of the statute, &c., agreed by and between the plaintiff and the defendants that the plaintiff should forbear and give days of payment of the said sum of £800 in manner following —that is to say, that the defendant should on the 4th of

March, 1854, pay to the plaintiff the sum of £200, parcel of
the said sum of £800, together with legal interest thereon;
that they should on the 4th of March, 1855, pay to the plaintiff the further sum of £200, other parcel, &c., together with
legal interest thereon; that they should on the 4th of March,
1856, pay the plaintiff the further sum of £200, other parcel,
&c., together with legal interest thereon; and that they
should on the 4th of March, 1857, pay to the plaintiff the
further sum of £200, residue of the said sum of £800,
together with legal interest thereon; and that, to secure such
several payments to the plaintiff, they (the defendants) should
give to the plaintiff their four several promissory notes for
the payments of the respective sums aforesaid, with interest
as aforesaid, at the respective times aforesaid, and that the
defendants should for such forbearance and giving days of
payment as aforesaid, by way of bonus and usurious and illegal interest, beyond and in addition to the said legal interest
so secured as aforesaid, pay to the plaintiff the sum of £40
on the 1st of January, 1854, and the further sum of £30 on
the 1st of July, 1854, &c. (setting out the payments as mentioned in the condition of the bond sued on); and that, to
secure to the plaintiff the payment of the said several lastly
mentioned sums, they (the defendants) should make their
certain bond or writing obligatory in a certain penal sum,
with a condition to become void upon payment by them of
the said lastly mentioned sums of money in manner and at
the respective times aforesaid; and that, after the making
of the said corrupt and unlawful agreement, to wit, on the
said 30th of July, 1853, in pursuance of the said agreement,
and for the purpose of securing unto the plaintiff the said
usurious and illegal interest, they (the defendants) did, contrary to the statute aforesaid, make, sign, and seal and execute the said writing obligatory in the declaration mentioned;
and, further, that the said sums of money in the said condition mentioned, and so agreed to be taken as aforesaid, in
addition to and together with the legal interest so secured
as aforesaid, exceeds the rate of £6 for the forbearance of
£100 for a year, contrary to the form of the statute aforesaid; and this the defendants are ready to verify, &c.

   Demurrer--That the defendants profess to allege the whole

of the moneys in the condition of the writing obligatory mentioned to be due for illegal and usurious interest, yet they do not shew how that can be, or that it is so in fact : that the said plea professes to answer the whole of the moneys in the said condition mentioned, while it shews no answer to any part thereof, or, if to any part thereof, to any definite part thereof : that the defendants have not shewn in and by the said plea with sufficient certainty that the said sums of money in the said plea alleged to exceed the rate of six per centum per annum, do in fact exceed that rate : that the defendants have not stated or alleged by how much the said moneys in the said plea alleged to exceed the rate of six per centum per annum do in fact, if they do at all, exceed that rate

Wilson, Q. C., for the demurrer.   *Eccles*, contra.

ROBINSON, C. J.—We must consider this plea in connection with the late statute 16 Vic. ch. 80, modifying the usury laws, which, while it abolishes all penalties for charging an excessive rate of interest, and saves contracts and securities from being held void by reason of any rate of interest, however exorbitant, being stipulated for between the parties, does yet provide in the 3d section "that every such contract, and every security for the same, shall be void, so far and so far only as relates to any excess of interest thereby made payable above the rate of six pounds for the forbearance of one hundred pounds for a year."

Now here it is plain, upon the facts stated in the plea and admitted by the demurrer, that the whole original debt of £800 was secured by the notes of the defendant to be paid on certain days, *with legal interest*, which we must now understand to mean such interest as the law makes payable when the parties are silent, and such interest alone as the law can lend its aid to enforce.

And the defence pleaded is, that after the debt and *legal interest*—which, used in this sense, we are bound to know can only mean six per cent., as no less or other rate is named,—had been thus secured, the defendant, by agreement with the plaintiff, gave the bond sued on, for the purpose of securing to him the further sum of £160, payable as a *bonus* for the forbearance granted on the occasion of taking the notes for the £800. The bond, therefore, according to this statement, must inevitably have been given to secure a sum of which every farthing was interest that had been exacted beyond six per cent., for forbearance.

We should not be giving effect to what the legislature plainly meant by the late statute, if we were to give judgment for enforcing the payment of this bond; and as, by the words of the act, we are bound to hold it void *so far* as it relates to the payment of interest above six per cent. for the forbearance of money, we must treat it as altogether void, for the objection lies to the whole sum. The bond was wholly given for interest above six per cent. We see no defect or informality in the plea.

DRAPER, J.—The argument to support the demurrer turns upon the use of the phrase "*legal* interest."

The plea in substance is this : that the defendant owed the plaintiff £800, payable by certain instalments with *legal* interest, and that the bond was given to secure more than legal interest, and cannot therefore be enforced.

The statute 16 Vic. ch. 80, repeals the 51st Geo. III. ch. 9, which limited the rate of interest to six per cent., made void all contracts, &c., for securing a higher rate of interest, and subjected parties taking a higher rate of interest to penalties. But while it enacts that no contract for a higher rate of interest than six per cent., nor any payment in pursuance of such contract, shall subject the party to any loss or penalty for usury, it also provides that such contract, &c., shall be void only so far as relates to any excess of interest above six per cent., which rate of six per cent. interest, or such lower rate of interest as may have been agreed upon, shall be recoverable in all cases where it is the agreement of the parties that interest shall be paid.

The plaintiff's counsel argues, that the court will not intend that by the phrase "legal interest" the rate of six per cent. is meant—that it may as well mean one per cent., or any other rate less than six, &c. ; and therefore, that it is not shewn that this bond is wholly void, even if it be partially so, and if not wholly void the plea is bad. The plea, after

2 *c*—VOL. XII. Q.B.

shewing that the several instalments of the debt of £800 were secured by promissory notes payable with "legal interest" thereon, avers that the defendant, for such forbearance, &c., agreed, by way of bonus and usurious interest beyond and in addition to the said legal interest, that they should pay the several sums stated in the bond sued upon, and to secure such payment should give this bond; and that the defendant, in pursuance of the agreement, and to secure to the plaintiff the said usurious and illegal interest, gave this bond; and that the sums of money in the condition mentioned and agreed to be taken "in addition to the legal interest so secured as aforesaid, exceeds the rate of £6 for the forbearance, &c."

There is no doubt that the plaintiff would be entitled to recover on the several promissory notes given interest at the rate of six per cent. Such would be the plain effect of the statute as applied to the terms in which the notes are stated to have been given. The meaning of the phrase "legal interest" is, I think, on the facts pleaded, a matter of inevitable construction, and, applied to the transaction as set forth in the plea, it imports six per cent. If this be conceded, then the bond is given to secure something more than six per cent., and being so it is void, and though subjecting the plaintiff to no penalty or loss, cannot be enforced in any court.

BURNS, J., concurred.

Judgment for defendant on demurrer.

JONES v. RUTTAN.

False return to fi. fa. of goods on hand for want of buyers—Pleading—Nul tiel record.

Case for falsely returning to a *fi. fa.* goods on hand for want of buyers, when the defendant might have levied the amount.

Pleas—1. That no such writ of *fi. fa.* was duly sued out, as in the declaration alleged.

5. That the defendant did take goods out of which he could have levied the sum directed to be levied, which goods remained and still remain in his hands for want of buyers.

Held, on demurrer, both pleas bad.

When *nul tiel* record is pleaded the issue is complete, and no replication or entry on the record is necessary, but the court may give day of trial by the record.

This was an action on the case against the sheriff of Northumberland and Durham, for a false return to a *fi. fa.*

issued out of the County Court. The declaration after setting out the judgment and the suing out of the writ charged that although there were goods out of which the defendant could have made the moneys endorsed on the writ, yet that he did not nor would, before the return of the writ, levy the same or any part thereof, but returned that he had caused to be levied of goods and chattels of the defendants in the *fi. fa.* the sum of money as directed in the writ which said goods and chattels remained in his hands for want of buyers.

The defendant pleaded—2. That no such writ of *fi. fa.* was duly sued out upon the said judgment, as in the declaration alleged.

3. *Nul tiel* record of the judgment.

5. That he did take goods and chattels of the defendants in the *fi. fa.*, to the value of the damages mentioned in the said writ, and by the endorsement thereon directed to be levied out of which he could have levied the said damages; which said goods and chattels remained, at the time of the return of the said writ, and still remain in his, the defendant's, hands, for want of buyers.

The plaintiff demurred to the second and fifth pleas. The grounds of demurrer sufficiently appear in the judgment.

The third plea, of *nul tiel* record concluded with the ordinary prayer of judgment, and nothing was added to the record by way of entry in respect to this defence. The defendant objected that there was no proper issue upon it, and that judgment could not be given for the plaintiff.

Cameron, Q. C., for the plaintiff, cited Drewe v. Lainson, 11 A. & E. 529; Mullet v. Challis et al., 16 Q. B. 239.

Weller, contra, cited Grantham v. Jarvis, 6 U. C. R, 511; Keightley v. Birch, 3 Camp, 521; Pitcher v. King, 5 Q. B. 758; and as to the plea of *nul tiel* record, Aylward v. Garrett, 15 Jur. 155; Ch. Arch. Prac. 838.

ROBINSON, C. J., delivered the judgment of the court.

The second plea is in our opinion bad, for the reasons given in Grantham v. Jarvis (6 U. C. R. 511), and not the less so because the writ was issued by the County Court. If there could be anything so illegal or irregular in the manner of suing out the writ that although the writ itself was good upon the face of it, yet it would have afforded no justification to the sheriff for anything done under it, the defendant, should have shewn what that illegality consisted in, so that the fact on which the inference of illegality was founded might have been traversed.

The 5th plea is also in our opinion insufficient. The charge against the defendant is, that although there were goods out of which he could have made the money yet that he did not, nor would before the return of the writ, levy the money, or any part thereof. The defence pleaded is, that the defen- dant did take goods and chattels of the execution debtor to the value of the damages, *out of which he could have levied* the said damages; which goods remained at the time of the return of the writ, and still remain, in the *defendant's hands for want of buyers*. It is true, as was contended by the plaintiff in the argument, that this plea fully confesses the breach of duty charged; for the defendant says that he did take goods out of which he could have levied the whole amount. It is evident that we must take him to mean by the word levied, as used here, something more than the mere *taking* the goods, for he says that *out of the goods which he had taken* he could have *levied* the money.

Then why did he not? That they remain in his hands when he might have levied the money for them is *primâ facie* a breach of duty. It is consistent with what is stated in this plea that the defendant may have let the time go by when he could have sold the goods, and that they now remain in his hands unsold in consequence of that neglect. The declaration has been excepted to, but it appears to us to be good, and to be fully borne out by the case of Mallet v. Challis et al. (16 Q. B. 239).

As to the plea of *nul tiel* record, it appears from the cases cited in Grantham v. Jarvis in this court (6 U. C. R. 513), that the issue is complete when the defendant, as in this case denies the record, and concludes with a prayer of judgment, and this whether the record is of the same court or of another court. There seems to be no necessity for the plaintiff to reply, reasserting the existence of the record, though it is often done. Then, the issue being complete, the court may give day of trial by the record. Regularly, I suppose, an entry of that kind should have been made on the record, but that can be done at any time.

> Judgment for plaintiff on demurrer,
> and on plea of *nul tiel* record.

RUTLEDGE v. McLEAN.

Agreement to admit deeds, a waiver of objections—Estoppel—Registry laws.

Where the defendant's attorney had agreed, in an action of ejectment, to admit deeds by the production of memorials without accounting for the deeds, and to admit the execution of such deeds as the plaintiff might produce, without proof by a subscribing witness—

Held, that it could not be objected at the trial that a memorial signed by the grantee was no evidence of the deed.

The plaintiff proved a deed to himself from D., dated 3rd of July, 1851, registered on the 7th of the same month. The defendant put in an instrument under seal, dated 3rd of June, 1847, between one M. and D., reciting that differences had arisen between them, and that M. had brought ejectment to recover possession of this lot "belonging to the said M." and in consideration of M. withdrawing the record, D. agreed that the lot should be valued by certain parties, and covenanted to pay to M. or secure by mortgage on the land whatever that value might be." No valuation was made.

Held, this agreement being unregistered, that the recital in it could not affect the plaintiff's title.

This was an action of ejectment, tried at Cobourg before *McLean, J.,* in which the plaintiff sought to recover the north half of No. 3, 7th concession of Darlington. The patent granting these premises to Eliakim Weller, dated 1st of May, 1802, was put in. The plaintiff then put in an agreement signed by the defendant's attorney, and dated 13th April, 1854, to admit deeds by the production of memorials, without accounting for the deeds, and to admit the execution of such deeds as the plaintiff might produce, without proof by a subscribing witness. The registrar of the county of Durham then produced, 1st, a memorial of a deed from Eliakim Weller to Richard Smith for the premises; the date of the deed as stated in the memorial was 4th of April, 1815, the memorial was registered 29th of April, 1815, on the oath of Benjamin Fairfield. 2ndly, a memorial of a deed from Sidney Smith, as heir-at-law of Richard Smith, to James Preston, for the premises; the date of the deed, as

stated in the memorial, was 9th of June, 1834. The memorial was registered on the 6th of August, 1835, and was
executed by the grantee ; and it was objected by the defendant's counsel, that a memorial executed by the grantee was
not evidence of the deed ; that the due execution of a deed ʲ
from Sidney Smith to James Preston could not be proved by
the production of a memorial signed by the latter. For the
plaintiff, it was insisted that the agreement of the defendant's
attorney precluded this objection being taken. The learned
judge held the memorial was admissible, so far as it proved
a deed.—3rdly, A memorial of a deed from James Preston
to Francis Phelps and Charles Thompson for the premises,
dated 8th of December, 1834, and registered on the 12th of
December, 1834. This memorial was executed by the grantor.
A deed was put in from Henry Phelps, as heir-at-law of
Francis Phelps, to Thomas Dennis, for the premises, dated
31st of December, 1845, and registered 10th of January,
1846. The registrar then produced a memorial of a deed
from Charles Thompson to Thomas Dennis, the grantee, of
the premises, dated 27th of February, 1845, registered 14th
of July, 1845. This memorial was executed by Dennis the
grantee, and the same objection was taken to it as to the
memorial of the deed to James Preston. Then the plaintiff
put in a deed from Thomas Dennis to himself, for the premises, dated 3rd of July, 1851, consideration £562 10s., registered 7th July, 1851. Evidence was given to shew that
Sidney Smith was heir-at-law of Richard Smith, and that
Henry Phelps was heir-at-law to Francis Phelps. It was also
proved by Thomas Dennis, that when he purchased, the land
was wild; that he cleared about eighty acres and planted
an orchard, and continued in possession until he sold to the
plaintiff. Leave was reserved to the defendant to move for
a nonsuit on the objection above noted.

For the defendant was proved an instrument under seal,
dated the 3rd of June, 1847, made between Allan Neil
McLean of the first part, and Thomas Dennis of the second
part, reciting that differences had arisen between the parties,
and that an action of ejectment had been commenced by
McLean to recover possession of the lot " belonging to the

said Allan McLean," and stating that in consideration of McLean withdrawing the record, Dennis agreed that the lot should be valued by Henry Adams, Matthew Jones, and Samuel Wilmot, or any two of them, and Dennis covenanted to pay or secure by mortgage on the lot whatever that value might be. The subscribing witness to this instrument stated that he understood McLean claimed under a sheriff's deed; which was put in, not registered. No valuation was made, Jones refusing to act; Adams went to Dennis and told him he was prepared to value the land, but he replied he had changed his mind, and did not think McLean had any title.

The charge of the learned judge was in favor of the defendant, on the ground of the estoppel against Dennis, created by the recital of defendant's right to the land in the instrument of the 3rd of June, 1847. But the jury found for the plaintiff.

A. McLean moved for a nonsuit on the leave reserved,— or for a new trial on the law and evidence.

J. D. Armour shewed cause, and cited Doe Ubele v. Kilner, 2 C. & P. 289; Collins v. Maule, 8 C. & P. 502; Com. Dig. "Estoppel" F.; Lynnett v. Parkinson, 1. C. P. 145; Warburton v. Loveland dem. Ivie, 2 Dow. & Cl. 480.

DRAPER, J., delivered the judgment of the court.

There are two points made for the defendant. The first is, the insufficiency of the evidence of the plaintiff's title; the other, the estoppel.

As to the first, it appears to us that the language of the admission put in was such as to render the production of the memorials evidence of the deeds, no matter by whom the memorials were executed. It seems to have been understood that the calling of subscribing witnesses was dispensed with, as no objection was raised on account of their absence. Now, as the memorial could only have been registered on the oath of a witness to the execution of both deed and memorial, to dispense with calling the witness who could prove these facts ought to be considered as equivalent to an admision of them; and whether the memorial was executed by grantor or grantee would then be perfectly indifferent. The memorial proved by a witness to the deed would be good secondary evidence of the contents of the deed.

As to the estoppel, if the objections raised were tenable, it would destroy the benefit and defeat the object of the registry laws, for the result would be, that although a deed duly executed and conveying an estate in fee simple, being unregistered, would be fraudulent and void against a registered deed subsequently executed, yet a bond to refer disputes to arbitration, which happened to recite the title, being earliest, would prevail by way of estoppel against the subsequently executed but duly registered conveyance. This would be an estoppel against the express terms as well as against the policy of an act of the legislature. A more complete *reductio ad absurdum* could scarcely be stated. Independently of this, I am not satisfied that this recital would estop the present plaintiff, a purchaser for value from Dennis, and for all that appears without notice. He does not derive title in any way through or by means of the instrument containing the recital relied upon to estop him; and though the instrument does in relation to this land recite that it is land "belonging to the said Allan McLean," yet when we find in the operative part of it a covenant on the part of Dennis to mortgage to the defendant, and it is proved that Dennis had at time a title derived from the grantee of the Crown duly registered, it might be fairly questioned whether Dennis himself would be estopped from shewing the truth and denying the right of the defendant. We are of opinion the rule should be discharged.

Rule discharged.

LINES ET AL. V. GRANGE.

Sale by sheriff—Estoppel on claimants.

When the sheriff under a *fi. fa.* seized and sold certain goods claimed by the plaintiffs,

Held, that the fact of one of the plaintiffs having attended and bid at the sale did not estop them from complaining of the seizure of the goods as their own.

This was an action of trespass against the defendant, for seizing, and taking away and converting a steam engine and boiler of the plaintiffs. The defendant pleaded—1st, Not guilty; 2nd, That the goods were not the plaintiffs'.

At the trial before *Burns*, J., at the last assizes held in Toronto, the facts appeared to be these. Mr. Paterson, of Toronto, as assignee of one Becket, sold the steam engine in question, on the 23rd of May, 1853, to the plaintiffs for £175, and took their promissory notes in payment. The plaintiffs employed one Isaac May to remove the engine from the township of Bentinck, where it had been used in a saw-mill by one Parkins, to the Saugeen river, where the plaintiffs intended putting it up in a sawmill they were erecting; and when May had removed a part of the engine into the County of Bruce, and was engaged removing the residue, all having been removed from Parkins's mill, a bailiff of the defendant, who was sheriff of the county of Wellington, in which county the engine then was, made a seizure of it. This occurred in the latter part of May or beginning of June, 1853, and the seizure was made upon the sheriff's warrant upon a writ of *fi. fa.* against Parkins *ats.* Jarvis. May, the person engaged in removing the engine, swore that while he was so engaged, the sheriff's officer came and seized, and asked him if he would give a bond for the due forthcoming of the goods. May refused to give any bond, and told the officer that the engine was the plaintiffs', and asked if he intended to detain it, to which the officer replied he did not, and then he completed the removal to Saugeen of all except some small portions which had been taken to some neighbours' houses, and which the officer afterwards took and sold. The sheriff's officer followed the engine to Saugeen some ten days after it

2 *d*—VOL. XII. Q. B.

arrived there, and after it had been placed in the plaintiffs'
possession, and he took possession, and at the same time
served Lines, one of the plaintiffs, with a notice that the
sheriff claimed the property as seized by him, and that if
the plaintiffs did not restore the same to the possession of
the sheriff he would take steps to recover it.   The officer
advertised the engine, and sold it on the 23rd of June, 1853,
for £102, and the witness May became the purchaser, and
afterwards sold the same to the plaintiffs for a small advance
on what he had paid.   The sheriff's officer proved that when
he served Lines with the notice, and about the time he made
his seizure at Saugeen, he had a good deal of conversation
with him.   Lines complained that he had much trouble with
it, removing it, &c., and that they could have got an engine
much cheaper elsewhere.   He further stated that *Lines
finally said he would not have anything to do with it, and
he (the officer) might take it.*   He then, he said, advertised
it for sale, but would not have done so if Lines had not said
he would have nothing more to do with it.   In eight days
after, the officer returned, and sold the engine.   Lines was
not present at the sale, but the other plaintiff was, and he did
not forbid the sale, but on the contrary bid upon it himself.
May stated that he was present at the conversations of the
officer with Lines, and that the result of those conversations
was, that Lines said to the officer that he would take the
engine, if he did take it, on his own responsibility.   It
appeared also there had been a doubt at first whether the
plaintiffs had taken possession of the engine so as to constitute a delivery by Paterson, and Paterson had commenced
an action against the defendant, and in answer to an application on their part the defendant wrote a letter as follows :

" Sheriff's Office, Guelph, June 22, 1853.

" Jarvis v. Parkins and others.

"I have duly received your letter herein of yesterday.
In reply I beg to state that it is my intention, on the return
of my bailiff, to apply to the court under the Interpleader
Act.   You claiming for the assignees of Becket, who calls
himself, I suppose, assignee of the defendants, and the plaintiff having ruled me to return the writ, the court must decide

to whom the property seized really belongs. It is too late for me to stop the sale, so if the money is made I shall hold it for both parties."

Upon this evidence the learned judge left it to the jury to say upon the plea denying the plaintiff's property in the engine, whether the fact as stated by the sheriff's officer, if it were a fact, but of which they must decide between what he said and what the other witness, May, stated, and the fact of one of the plaintiffs being present at the sale and not forbidding it, but in fact bidding himself, destroyed the plaintiffs' position of having purchased from one who, so far as appeared, was the owner, and had a right to confer title, the plaintiffs being responsible for the purchase money, and also having incurred considerable expenses in removing the engine, and the same being in their actual custody at the time of seizure. If the jury credited May's account of the conversation of the officer with Lines, then there only remained the fact of the other plaintiff being present at the sale, and to contrast what he did with the other facts. The jury were told that the plaintiffs could only recover on the strength of the facts in their favour convincing them of the plaintiffs being the actual owners, and not upon any weakness of title in any one else, or because the sheriff had not, attempted to shew title in any one else.

The defendant's counsel objected to the charge, and contended that the jury should have been told that the conduct of the plaintiffs constituted an estoppel upon them against the defendant's right to sell the property. Other points were made at the trial, and other objections made to the charge which are not called in question now.

The jury found for the plaintiffs, with damages £110.

Wilson, Q.C., obtained a rule to shew cause why the verdict should not be set aside, and a new trial had between the parties, the verdict being contrary to law and evidence, and for misdirection, and upon the discovery of new evidence.

Two affidavits were filed. One of Mr. Paterson, the holder of the notes which were given in payment for the engine. This affidavit simply verified a letter received from the plaintiffs, which was in these words :

"Southampton, Saugeen, 23rd June, 1853.

" Messrs. Thomas Clarkson and David Paterson.

" Gentlemen,—We advised you of the seizure and sale of part of the engine sold us by you in May last. We have now to advise sale here yesterday of remaing portion with boiler. The lot was sold at the price of £102 cy. to Isaac May, of Durham. We trust to-morrow to hear from you in answer to ours, as also that you intend without any demur to cancel your sale to us, as well as refund us expenses incurred.

"We are, yours truly,

"LINES & HAMILTON."

The other affidavit was from the sheriff's officer who conducted the proceedings on the *fi. fa.*, and who was examined as a witness at the trial. His affidavit was a mere reiteration of what he proved at the trial.

M. Vankoughnet shewed cause.

Wilson, Q. C., contra, cited Pickett v. Sears, 6 A. & E. 469 ; Howard v. Hudson, 17 Jur. 855 ; Freeman v. Cooke, 2 Ex. 654.

The only point argued was whether the plaintiff was not estopped by his conduct from disputing the legality and propriety of what the sheriff did.

ROBINSON, C. J., delivered the judgment of the court.

The case cited by Mr. Vankoughnet, of Freeman v. Cooke (2 Ex. 654), is very material, and when we compare the facts of that case with the present, and consider also that in this case there is no plea of leave and license upon the record, as there was in Freeman v. Cooke, we cannot feel any doubt that the plaintiffs should retain their verdict.

There was evidence that one of the plaintiffs told the sheriff's officer if he seized the engine he must do so upon his own responsibility. It was left to the jury to say whether they gave credit to the witness May, who made that statement, or to the sheriff's bailiff, who represented the plaintiff as rather assenting without objection to his seizing and selling the engine. If the jury gave credit to May's statement, then the fact of one of the plaintiffs bidding at the sale made by the officer would surely not constitute such an estoppel as would preclude him from complaining of that sale as wrong.

Doe dem. Harley v. McManus (1 U. C. R. 141) was cited as supporting the existence of an estoppel in this case, but there the sale objected against took place at the instance of Harley, whose son afterwards complained of it. It was to suit his purpose, and he received the surplus of money produced by it. If it were true that the plaintiffs objected to the sale, and asserted their right to the property, and told the officer that he must act on his responsipility if he took it, we could never look upon the mere act of one of the plaintiffs purchasing at such sale, either directly or through another, as an act that would destroy his remedy, if the property were in truth his and had been seized illegally.

It may happen in some cases that the sheriff under a writ against the goods of A. may seize the goods of B., and beleiving that he is right in treating them as the goods of A. upon a statement made to him, he may persist in selling them notwithstanding his notice of B.'s claim. It would be hard if in every such case B. were compelled, for fear of estopping himself from afterwards complaining of the sale, to allow his property to be sacrificed, and to get into the hands of strangers, though the things seized may be articles upon which for certain reasons he placed a particular value, and which could never be replaced.

There seems to me to be a further difficulty in the defendant's way in this case. The engine seems to have been taken at last out of the actual possession of the plaintiffs; that possession was sufficient to prove the second plea in their favor; and the sheriff, if he meant to dispute their right to the possession, should have pleaded his authority to seize under the *fi. fa.* the goods of Parkins, to whom he contended they belonged.

The damages seem not to be unreasonable, and we are all of opinion that the rule should be discharged.

Rule discharged.

JONES ET AL. v. McDOWELL.

Too small damages.—New trial, costs to abide the event.

Where the damages given were complained of as being too small, a new trial
was granted with costs to abide the event—viz., the event of the plaintiffs
recovering more than the amount of the first verdict.

The plaintiffs in this case had recovered a verdict for
£50, and they moved for a new trial, complaining that the
verdict was manifestly unjust, as being too small, for that
they had actually paid the defendant £68 15s. in advance on
a contract to deliver timber, which he had wholly failed
to fulfil, leaving the plaintiffs to bear not only all the
damage arising from the defendant's non-fulfilment, but also
the loss of a considerable portion of their advances.

Richards, for the plaintiff.

Paterson, for the defendant.

ROBINSON, C. J., delivered the judgment of the court.

We are of opinion that there should be a new trial, with
costs to abide the event, as was ordered in a case similarly
situated—Hudson v. Marjoribanks (1 Bing. 393); which
will mean the event of the plaintiffs recovering more than
they recovered in the former action.

Rule absolute.

REGINA v. WHITTIER.

Indictment.—Certiorari.

After an acquittal in a criminal case, the court refused a *certiorari* to remove
the indictment with a view of applying for a new trial; or to stay the
entry of judgment, so that a new indictment might be preferred and tried
without prejudice.

The defendant had been indicted and tried at the last court
of Oyer and Terminer, holden at Belleville, for a nuisance
in obstructing a highway, by placing a building on a portion
of it. It was a question of disputed boundary; and the jury
acquitted him.

Wallbridge moved for a writ of *certiorari* to remove the
record of the indictment and trial with this court, with a
view of applying for a new trial.

He moved this on the part of the Crown, and with the
assent, as he declared, of the Attorney General. And he
urged that if the court should hold themselves unable to grant

a new trial after an accquittal in a criminal case, they might pursue the course which was taken in the case of Rex. v. Sutton, 5 B. & Ad. 52, where the court, following a precedent set in Rex v. The Inhabitants of Wandsworth, 1 B. & Al. 63, stayed the entry of judgment upon the verdict, that a new indictment might be preferred and tried without prejudice.

ROBINSON, C. J., delivered the judgment of the court.

We take it that both the cases referred to in applying for this rule were cases in which the trials took place upon the Nisi Prius side of the court, upon records sent down from the Queen's Bench, and were not cases removed by *certiorari* after verdict of acquittal upon an indictment tried by a court of oyer and terminer. They were besides not indictments for nuisances, properly speaking, but for not repairing a highway, in which the obligation to repair formed the question, and where the acquittal of the defendant threw the burthen of repairing upon another party contrary, as it was contended, to the plain merits of the case.

We are convinced that no instance can be shewn of such a course being taken as we are asked to adopt in this case ; that is, to remove a case by a *certiorari* after verdict in order to deprive the defendant of the benefit of his acquittal.

Rule refused.

LYMAN ET AL. v. MILLER.

Guarantee—Appropriation of payments.

In April, 1850, R. became security to the plaintiffs for S. to the extent of £100, and S. thereupon received goods from them to the amount of £151. In April S. desired to make a further purchase. R. wrote to the plaintiffs becoming security to the extent of £75, and in his letter he said, "I understand from S. that he has paid you £75 on account of the £100." The plaintiffs sent no answer, but supplied the goods required. The £75 had been paid by S., and, in his letter enclosing it he said, "I send you £75 on account of goods bought by me, being one-half of the whole."

Held, that R. was entitled to have the whole of this payment credited against the £151 secured by his first guarantee, and that the plaintiffs could not appropriate it to any part of the debt of S. for which R. was not liable.

This was an action of assumpsit brought by the plaintiffs to recover from the defendant the balance of an account for goods sold and delivered to one Samuel Miller, and for which

the plaintiffs contended that the defendant was liable upon
the guarantees hereinafter set out.

A special case was agreed upon, of which the following
are the material facts :—

In the month of August, 1850, the said Samuel Miller was
desirious of purchasing goods from the plaintiffs, and as the
plaintiffs desired security before they would sell to him, the
defendant wrote the letter following :

"Toronto, 15th August, 1850.

" Messrs. Lyman, Kneeshaw & Co., Toronto.

" Gentlemen,—My brother Samuel being about to commence business at Galt, proposes to purchase from you stock
to an amount not exceeding one hundred pounds; and in
consideration of your furnishing him with the said goods, I
do hereby undertake and agree to become responsible for the
payment of that amount to you on the following terms,.
namely, one-half at the expiration of six, and the remainder
at twelve months from this date.

" Yours, &c.,

(Sd.)   " RICHARD MILLER."

Upon receipt of this letter the plaintiffs sold and delivered
to said Samuel Miller goods amounting to the sum of
£151 0s. 9d., ; and the plaintiffs continued to furnish small
orders for Samuel Miller until the 28th of April following,
when he desired to make a further purchase. The plaintiffs
required security, and the defendant wrote to them the
letter following :

"St. Catharines, April 28th, 1851.

" Messrs. Lyman, Kneeshaw & Co., Toronto.

" Gentlemen,—My brother, Mr. Samuel Miller, of Galt,
informs me that.he has left with you an order for drugs, &c.,
amounting to £75. In consideration of your forwarding
these goods to him at Galt without delay, I do ·hereby
guarantee the payment of that sum to you on the same terms
as contained in my former guarantee for one hundred. I
understand from my brother that he has paid you on account
of the £100 the sum of £75.

" I remain your obedient.,

(Sd.)   " RICHD. MILLER."

The plaintiffs gave no answer to this letter, but upon
receipt of it they forwarded to Samuel Miller, on the 5th of

May, 1851, goods to the amount of £60 11s. 10d., and on subsequent days other goods.

On the 8th of October following, the said Samuel Miller requiring more goods, and the plaintiffs requiring security therefor, the defendant wrote the letter following :

"St. Catharines, Oct. 8th, 1851.

"Messrs. Lyman, Kneeshaw & Co., Druggists, Toronto.

"Whatever amount of goods my brother, Mr. Samuel Miller, of Galt, may require of you, I hereby guarantee the payment of the same to you to an amount not exceeding two hundred pounds.

"Yours, &c.,

(Sd.)   "RICHARD MILLER."

Upon receipt of this note the plaintiffs furnished further orders, making the total amount of goods furnished by them to the said Samuel Miller £223 3s. 7d., upon which amount the said Samuel Miller had paid on the 17th of March, 1851, £75, accompanied by the following note :

"Galt, March 15, 1851.

"Messrs. Lyman, Kneeshaw & Co., Toronto.

"Gentlemen,—Enclosed I send you £75 cy. on account of goods bought by me, being the one-half of the whole amount purchased, the receipt of which please acknowlege.

"I am, Gent., yours most obtly.,

(Sd.)   "S. MILLER."

Which sum of £75 the plaintiffs contended they had a right to apply as follows—first, to pay off the sum of fifty-one pounds, being the amount due to the plaintiffs, and not secured by the defendant's guarantee ; and the balance, twenty-four pounds, to the defendant's first guarantee of £100, which would leave due on the defendant's first guarantee the sum of £76.

On the 14th of July, 1852, Samuel Miller gave the plaintiffs his note for £50, and on the 27th of October one for £25, and another for £25, all which sums the plaintiffs applied to the general account then outstanding and in part secured by the defendant's guarantee, leaving due to the plaintiffs by the said Samuel Miller, and secured, as they contended, by the defendant on his said guarantees, the sum of £127 19s. 7d., which the plaintiffs claimed to hold the

defendant liable for as follows—viz., on the first guarantee,
£76 ; on subsequent guarantees, £51 19s. 7d. — making
£127 19s. 7d.; against which the defendant contended he
had a right to have the first payment of £75 applied to the
guarantee of 1850 entire, which if correct would reduce the
plaintiff's claim to the sum of £61 19s. 7d. cy., which sum
the defendant paid into court.

Bell, for the plaintiffs, cited Mills v. Fowkes, 7 Scott, 444 ;
Williams v. Griffith, 5 M. & W. 300.

Vankoughnet, Q.C., contra, cited Marryatts v. White, 2
Stark, 101 ; Goddard v. Cox, 2 Stra. 1194.

ROBINSON, C. J., delivered the judgment of the court.

We think the defendant is right in what he contends for,
and that the £75 paid in March, 1851, should be applied
on account of the first purchase to the amount of £151,
discharging that as far as it goes.

Mr. Samuel Miller, the principal debtor, shews that he
meant that when he remitted the money, for he says in his
letter, " I send it on account of goods bought by me, being
one-half of the whole." We should suppose by this that
he had not at that time bought anything more than the first
goods, which came to £151, though on that point the statement is obscure. The case would have been much plainer if
the accounts had been set out, as they were furnished, with
the dates of the several purchases. Moreover, he says he
sends it as one-half of the whole amount purchased, which
seems to shew that he had the £150 alone in his mind, and
wished at all events to have the money applied, as far as it
would go, in discharging what he then owed.

Then, when the defendant, in his letter of the 28th of
April, 1851, in which he assents to assume a further liability,
tells the plaintiffs that his brother had informed him that
he had paid them on account of the £100 the sum of £75 ;
and when the plaintiffs, not contradicting that statement or
claiming to have made, or to have a right to make, any other
appropriation of the £75, tacitly acquiesce in what the
defendant tells them, and being satisfied with his letter, act
upon it by making a further advance to his brother, which

they had declined doing till he should give such a guarantee, they place the matter, we think, beyond all doubt; for they could not, after knowingly allowing him to guarantee a further advance under the impression that £75 of the former had been paid, turn round upon him afterwards and claim a right to make a different appropriation of the £75, which would leave him in a worse situation than they allowed him to suppose he was in when he agreed to the further liability.

The postea, in our opinion, should go to the defendant, as he has paid into court all for which he was liable.

Judgment for defendant.

NICKERSON V. GARDNER.

Agreement—Construction—Necessity of request—Issue on defendant's readiness to perform.

The defendant made the following agreement in writing :

"Within three months, and when desired by him, I promise to pay Moses C. Nickerson," (the plaintiff) "or bearer, £50 currency, in such stone and marble-work as he may want, at cash price, delivered at Port Dover, value received, with interest."

Held, That the plaintiff was bound to prove a notice to the defendant of the kind of stone or marble work required and when it was to be delivered, and that until such request there could be no default.

Quære, Whether a plea, that after the making of the agreement, and within three years from the date thereof, the plaintiff was and still is ready and willing to perform the agreement, would raise a material issue.

Semble, That the defendant on a proper demand, would have been bound to carry out the agreement, even after the expiration of the three years.

On the 19th of June, 1850, the defendant made the following promise and agreement in writing :—"Within three years, and when desired by him, I promise to pay Moses C. Nickerson" (the plaintiff)," or bearer fifty pounds, currency, in such stone and marble work as he may want, at cash price, delivered at Port Dover, value received, with interest."

The plaintiff sued upon this agreement as made upon a consideration of land sold by the plaintiff to the defendant, setting it out truly, and averring that although he had always been ready and willing to receive the said stone and marble work at the rate aforesaid, according to the terms of this agreement of which the defendant afterwards—to wit, on the 19th of June, 1853—had notice, and was then requested to deliver certain stone and marble work, according to the terms of the said agreement, yet that the defendant did not within the time aforesaid, or at any time afterwards, deliver the said stone and marble work as required, or any part thereof, to and for the plaintiff at Port Dover, or otherwise, although a reasonable time for such delivery had elapsed before the commencement of this suit ; but wholly neglected, and still neglects and refuses so to do.

In another count the plaintiff averred that £50 was due from the defendant to the plaintiff upon an account, stated and that this agreement setting it out as in the first count was made upon consideration of forbearance and giving time for the said debt.

The defendant pleaded—1st, Non-assumpsit ; 2ndly, that after the making of the agreement and within three years from the date thereof, he was ready and willing, and from thence hitherto hath been and still is ready and willing, to pay the amount of the said agreement to the plaintiff, or bearer, in manner and form, &c. ; 3dly, that after the making of the said agreement he had not notice, nor was he then requested, nor hath he ever been requested, to pay the amount of the said agreement, in manner and form, &c. : concluding to the country.

The plaintiff replied to the second plea, that after the making of the agreement, and within three years from the date thereof, the defendant was not "ready and willing, nor hath he from thence hitherto been "ready and willing to pay the amount of the said agreement to the plaintiff, or bearer in manner and form, &c." —concluding to the country ; and to the third plea, "that the defendant *had notice, and was then requested* to pay the amount of the said agreement, in manner and form as in the declaration alleged": concluding to the country.

Upon the trial no evidence was given by the plaintiff of any request made by him of stone or marble work ; and it was objected, on the part of the defendant, that there ought to have been proof given of a specific request to deliver, at Port Dover, marble or stone work of some particular description.

The learned Chief Justice of the Common Pleas ruled at the trial that the plaintiff was entitled to recover on the issue of non-assumpsit, and also on the second issue; because the stone being yet undelivered, though the three years had elapsed, was in itself proof that he was not always ready, if that be a material issue, which was not to be determined at the trial. Upon the third plea, as there was no proof of any request, he directed the jury to find for the defendant.

A verdict was given for the plaintiff on the 1st and 2nd issues for £59, and for the defendant on the last issue or 3rd plea.

McMichael obtained a rule to shew cause why judgment should not be entered for the plaintiff on the issue raised on the third plea, notwithstanding the verdict; and why the verdict should not be set aside, and a new trial had between the parties, on the ground of misdirection, and on the law and evidence. He cited Staley v. Long, 3 Bing. N. C. 781; Empson v. Fairfax, 3 N. & P. 385;

Read shewed cause and cited Armitage v. Insole, 14 Jur. 619.

ROBINSON, C. J., delivered the judgment of the court.

The difference between this case and Teal v. Clarkson in this court (4 O. S. 372) is, that the promise sued upon therein was to pay a certain sum of money, "*in work, in twelve months from the date,*" nothing being said about a request to be made by the plaintiff. Here the contract is to pay, "within three years, *and when desired by the plaintiff,* £50 currency, *in such stone and marble work* as he may want, at cost price, delivered at Port Dover, for value received." There is a clear difference in the undertaking to pay a certain sum in work at a certain time, and to pay a sum, *when desired* by the plaintiff, within a certain time, *in such stone and marble work* as the plaintiff may want. Upon such an agreement as the latter there can be no default until the person to whom the stone or marble work is to be furnished gives notice of what stone or marble work he requires, and when he requires it to be delivered.

The case of Armitage v. Insole (14 Jur. 619) is a strong authority to that effect, and the law would be very un-

reasonable if it were otherwise.   The second plea of the
defendant could not be necessary to be pleaded; as a defence
if the declaration would have been defective without stating a special request, as we think it would have been, and
as the plaintiff has assumed, for he has stated a special
request.   If it was indispensable to state it, it was as necessary to prove it; and therefore the defendant, if no request
had ever been made upon him, need only have traversed
that request.   It is an immaterial issue, perhaps, standing by
itself; though an averment of readiness of the defendant
often forms part of a plea in which he denies that any
request was made upon him.

But it is of little moment to consider this, for we are of
opinion clearly that the third plea, which denies that any
request was made, is a complete bar to the action.   It was
incumbent on the plaintiff upon that issue to shew a request
and he gave no evidence whatever that he had ever given
notice to the defendant to deliver to him worked stone or
marble of any kind; wherefore the defendant rightly received
a verdict on that issue.   The plaintiff only could know what
he wanted and would accept; the defendant could not be
expected to prepare stone or marble work of any kind without a requisition, for it would be all liable to be rejected.   It
is impossible that we can treat the third plea as immaterial,
and allow judgment to be entered for the plaintiff *non obstante*.
We have no reason to suppose that the plaintiff is in a condition to prove a request, or that he ever made one; so that,
for all that appears, he would be no better off as regards
this action if he had the opportunity of another trial.

He has not lost his preëxisting debt by omitting to demand stone work within three years; but he has not gained
a right by that omission of his own to compel the defendant
to pay in money instead of stone.   If he had at any time
before action brought, demanded some particular kind of
stone or marble work to be furnished according to the
agreement, and the defendant had failed after a reasonable
time to deliver it, I apprehend the plaintiff could then have
sued for damages for breach of the agreement; for I take
the construction of the writing to be such as to admit of a
demand after the three years.

Under the circumstances we think we shall do well to take such a course as was taken in Lee v. Shore (2 D. & R. 196, 1 B. & C. 94), and order a nonsuit, for otherwise the plaintiff may be concluded by this verdict and lose his debt.

> The court ordered the rule to be made absolute for a nonsuit; but if the plaintiff should refuse to accept it, or should not declare his intention before next term, then the rule to be discharged.

HAVILL v. FREEMAN.

Agreement—Rescision of Contract—Right to sue on the common counts.

In March, 1852, the plaintiff and defendant made an agreement in writing, by which the plaintiff was to build a cottage for the defendant, and to complete it by the 1st of November, for £212 10s., of which part was to be paid on the completion of the building, and the remainder at the times specified in the agreement. The defendant requested the plaintiff to postpone the work, and it was in consequence not commenced until August, 1853, and finished in March, 1854. It was not shewn that any new agreement had peen made; but it appeared that, as wages and materials had increased in price, the plaintiff, when asked to proceed with the work in 1853, objected to being bound by the old agreement, and the defendant then promised to pay £100 at the completion of the building, and the whole sum if he could, saying he would probably pay the whole.
Held, That the first contract was clearly at an end, and that the plaintiff was not bound to declare specially on the subsequent promise, but might sue upon the common counts.

The plaintiff sued on the common counts, for work and labour and materials, goods sold and delivered, money lent, money paid, money had and received, and on an account stated.

Pleas—Non-assumpsit, payment, and set off.

At the trial at Brantford, before *Macaulay,* C. J., it appeared that on the 15th of March, 1852 the plaintiff and defendant agreed by writing, not under seal, that the plaintiff should furnish all materials for a cottage to be built for the defendant, and should build, paint, and complete it, except mason work, lathing and plastering. A detailed description of the cottage was given in the agreement. It was to be built in a good, workmanlike manner, and with good materials, and to be completed by the 1st of November, 1852. The plaintiff was to take such materials as the defendant had on hand, at a fair market value, and to board with the defendant while employed on the job, at 7s. 6d. a week. The sum to be paid by the defendant was £212 10s., to be paid as follows :—"£37 10s., at the completion of the work, £25 in three months and 15 days thereafter, and the balance, after deducting for materials and board provided by the defendant, in annual payments of £50, half of the £50 to be paid on or before the 1st of February following the two first payments, and the other half on or before the 1st of June in each year until the sum of £212 10s. be paid." (a).

Instead of the cottage being finished by the 1st of November, 1852, according to the agreement, it was not begun till August, 1853, and not finished till March, 1854 ; not from any fault of the plaintiff, but because the defendant was not prepared, as he said, to go on, and he requested the plaintiff to postpone it for his convenience.

There was a claim made in this action for extra work done, and the defendant on his part objected to many parts of the work as insufficient. These matters were fully gone into and considered, and in the opinion of the learned judge the jury adjusted the balance fairly.

The main question argued upon this rule was the objection taken at the trial by the defendant, that the plaintiff should have declared especially upon the agreement, and that he, the defendant, was entitled to the credit stipulated for in the agreement in regard to the terms of payment.

There was no distinct evidence of any new agreement made between the parties, but only that wages and prices of materials having materially increased in 1853, the plaintiff objected at first to being bound by the old agreement, when he was asked by the defendant to proceed with the building, in answer to which objection the defendant, it seemed, promised to pay £100 as soon as the building was finished, and the whole if he could, saying it was likely he would pay the whole.

As the work proceeded the defendant made small payments,

(a) The times and manner of payment were so stated in the agreement.

one on the 25th of August, 1853, of £12 10s.; and another on the 12th of December, 1853, of £25; for which receipts were taken, which were written as well as signed by the defendant; and in the first of these receipts it was expressed that the money was " to apply on the first payment of the house;" in the second, " to be applied to the payment on his house;" and at the foot of the latter receipt the plaintiff wrote and signed, "I hereby promise to have the rest of the work to be done on Mr. Freeman's house in three weeks from the 16th of December, 1853.

The action was brought on the 23rd of March, 1854, soon after the whole work was done.

The learned Chief Justice left it to the jury to find whether the agreement had been abandoned or not as regarded the time of payment; telling them that he apprehended in strictness the plaintiff was only entitled to recover for the extra work. or, at all events, only for the extra work and the £100 spoken of as agreed to be paid on completion, and that the residue should be postponed, and the set off proved be allowed to stand against it.

The jury found for the plaintiff, and £125 10s. damages; and this verdict was intended by them to close and settle the whole transaction.

Connor, Q. C., for the defendant, obtained a rule nisi for a new trial on the law and evidence, and for misdirection.

M. C. Cameron shewed cause, and cited McMahon v. Coffee, 1 U. C. R. 110.

ROBINSON, C. J., delivered the judgment of the court.

It seems to us impossible that the first agreement can be held to be in force as regarded the time of payment, if it be true, as was sworn by the plaintiff's witness, that the defendant, when he certainly had lost the benefit of the agreement, and when the plaintiff was entitled if he pleased to treat it as rescinded, agreed, if the plaintiff would go on with the house, that he would pay him £100 when it was finished, if not the whole. Such an agreement could not co-exist with the original agreement. But it was objected that, at any rate, if the first agreement was superseded by the second alleged agreement, then such latter agreement should have been specially declared on, instead of attempting to recover on the common counts. The jury probably did not look upon what was said by the defendant respecting the £100 as a precise agreement, made on the one part and assented to on the other; they rather considered, perhaps, that in the conversation proved the defendant admitted the right of the plaintiff to treat the first agreement as at an end; and that anything said about paying £100 when the house was finished, and. the whole sum if he could, was not so properly a contract as an assurance of what the defendant expected he would be able to do; in other words, that by his own conduct and admissions the defendant had lost any advantage of the first contract, and could not be said to have entered into any other special contract, but rather to have done the work without an express understanding as to payment, in which case he could sue as for a debt presently due under the common counts. The jury made a very just settlement of the count in the opinion of the Chief Justice, and the defendant has apparently on the whole nothing to complain of.

Rule discharged.

PROUDFOOT v. TROTTER ET AL. EXECUTORS OF JOHN M'GILL.

Covenant for not rebuilding after fire—Plea of former recovery of prospective damages for the whole term—Award between plaintiff and third party.

COVENANT against the executors of a lessor for not rebuilding after loss by fire.

2nd *plea*,—That after the said fire, the defendants, as executors, were sued in a former action by the plaintiff on the covenant; that the plaintiff at the trial claimed to recover prospective damages for the whole term in the lease; that the defendants not intending to rebuild, assented to this; that the jury were therefore directed to give and did give damages accordingly; and that the defendants, in consequence of the understanding at the trial, made no attempt to disturb the verdict, but allowed judgment to be entered, and considering that full damages had been given did not rebuild; that the damages then given far exceeded all damages sustained up to the time of that action—and that, in consequence of the matters above mentioned, this action is prosecuted fraudulently and wrongfully against the defendants.

The third plea set up an award as to the damages sought to be recovered, between the plaintiff and one G. M., who, it was averred, was assignee of the premises under the will of the plaintiff's lessor for a term in the said will mentioned; but it was not averred that the plaintiff had obtained satisfaction through this award.

Held, on demurrer, second plea bad, at least in point of form: third plea bad as shewing no defence.

This was an action by a lessee for a term of nine years against the executors of his lessor, on a covenant in the lease to insure, and to rebuild the premises within a reasonable time after any loss by fire. The declaration averred that the insurance had been effected ; that the premises were burnt down; and that the defendants as executors, would not rebuild.

The second plea set up in substance as a defence, that the mill having been burnt down on the 10th of February, 1840, more than five years before the expiration of the term, and after the death of the lessor, John McGill, they, the defendants, as executors, were called upon to rebuild, and that not having done so, they were sued upon their covenant ; that at the trial of the action the plaintiff claimed a right to recover all the damage that it would be to him to be deprived of the mill during the remainder of the term that is, to May, 1845, and not merely such damages as he had sustained up to the time of bringing his action in 1841 ; that the defendants, not intending to rebuild, did not resist his right to recover for his whole damages prospectively, but assented to it ; that the jury were thereupon directed to give damages accordingly and did, upon such direction, give £500 damages to the plaintiff ; that the defendants, in consequence of the understanding and direction upon which the case went to the jury, made no attempt afterwards to set aside the verdict, but suffered judgment to be entered upon it, and conceiving that full damages had been recovered in that action for the breach of the covenant, as applied to the whole term, did not afterwards rebuild the mill ; that the sum of £500 far exceeds all the damages suffered by the plaintiff up to the time of his bringing the said first action ; and without saying that the defendants had satisfied the sum recovered by the judgment, the plea concluded by averring that this suit is, for the reasons and upon the matters in the plea appearing, prosecuted fraudulently and wrongfully against the defendants.

The third plea alleged, that after the expiration of the term, one George McGill, was assignee of the premises, under and by virtue of the last will and testament of the plaintiff's lessor, John McGill, whereby the said J. M. had demised to the said G. M. the said premises for a certain term in the

said will stated, and still unexpired ; that the said G. M. by
the death of the said J. M., became possessed of the reversion in the premises for the term so to him granted ; and
being so possessed, and as such assignee liable to the plaintiff
for all damages sustained by the breach of covenant declared
on, and such damages being matter of dispute between them,
among other matters, bonds were executed by which all differences were referred to the award of certain arbitrators named:
that an award was made in pursuance of such reference, in
respect of the said damages, as well as of other matters, by
which award it was directed that the plaintiff should pay to
the said G. M. a certain sum mentioned : that the plaintiff,
after the making of the said award, assented thereto; that the
same remains in full force ; and that the plaintiff made his
election to settle with the said G. M., his claim to damages
for the breach of covenant assigned in the declaration.

Demurrer to the second plea—That it is doubtful whether
the defendants intend to plead a judgment recovered, or an
agreement in bar of the action, and that the alleged agreement is no defence to the action.

To third plea, that the bonds of submission are not made
profert of, and that the said plea offers no defence.

Cameron, Q. C., for the demurrer.

Vankoughnet, Q.C., contra, cited 1 Saund. 237 ; Luxmore
v. Robson, 1 B., Al. 584; Platt on Leases I. 731, II. 184.

ROBINSON, C. J., delivered the judgment of the court.

We are of opinion that we cannot uphold the second plea
as sufficient in point of form but must hold it bad, for the
reasons assigned. It rests the defence upon the allegations
of what was understood, and believed, and intended and
considered by the judge and jury, and the plaintiff and
the defendant and draws from all these alleged understandings and intentions the inference that the plaintiff is
acting fraudulently in bringing this action. Independently of the fact that much of what the plea sets up
as leading to the inference of fraud is not matter
ssuable or traversable—as, for instance, what the judge
or jury intended or considered, or what the defendants.

intended or conceived—there is the objection, good in point of form, that we are left uncertain by the plea whether the defendants intended to rely upon the strictly legal effect of the prior recovery upon the same covenant, or upon an estoppel upon the plaintiff by reason of his conduct upon the trial of the former action, or upon an actual fraud as disabling him from making this claim. No doubt, if all be true that is set out in the plea, and if the mere former recovery constitutes no legal defence, stripped of all the alleged understandings and intentions of the parties and of the court, it would be most unjust and unconscientious in the plaintiff to be at this late day, or at any time, bringing a claim to future damages; and the defendants would seem to have had, if not still to have, a clear ground for appealing to the equitable jurisdiction of this court to stay proceedings in this action, or to invoke the aid of a court of equity. But we are only called upon to dispose of the plea upon special demurrer, and for the reasons given, we take it to be insufficient.

We do not, however, determine that the former recovery might not have been properly pleaded in bar, either with or without any special statement of circumstances.

The defendants seem to have assumed that damages could not as of right be given in the first action in regard to the whole term, and that the covenant in question is one upon which actions could be brought and damages recovered *toties quoties*, as for successive breaches, in the same manner as upon general covenants to repair or to pay rent; and therefore, that without something special having occurred, such as this plea sets out, the former recovery would be no bar to another action at the end of the term, or to any number of actions during the term, for the continuing damage arising from the mill not having been built within a reasonable time.

They should consider whether they are right in this view. We give them leave to move within a month to amend their pleadings upon affidavit of the truth of this defence.

As to the third plea, which is also demurred to, we have no doubt that it is bad in substance, and that it sets up matter which is no defence. It does not show satisfaction through the alleged award, but it rests upon the assumed conclusive

effect of the award between the parties. It is clear, however, that an award between the plaintiff and a third party,
giving to the plaintiff a right to recover against such third
party, does not estop the plaintiff from recovering against the
executors of the covenantor, so long as he has not actual
satisfaction for the damages sustained from the breach of the
covenant. The award can only interfere with an action by
the plaintiff against George McGill or his representatives,
who, for all that appears, may have been assignee only as
termor for a year or two, and in that case he would not be
liable on a covenant, as running with the land.

Judgment for plaintiff, on demurrer.

In this term the following gentlemen were called to the
bar:—

J. JERMY MACAULAY,
EDWARD TREVOR BOULTON,
DONALD CAMPBELL,
HECTOR CAMERON,
HENRY MACDERMOTT,
JOHN B. READ, and
JOHN BLEVINS, Esquires.

TRINITY TERM, 1854.

Present :—THE HON. JOHN BEVERLEY ROBINSON, C.J.
  "   "   WILLIAM HENRY DRAPER, J.
  "   "   ROBERT EASTON BURNS, J.

THORNHILL V. JONES.

Inchoate right to dower, no breach of covenants for seizin or quiet enjoyment—
Variance between bond as pleaded and as set out on oyer.

The plaintiff declared on the covenants for seizin and quiet enjoyment contained in an ordinary conveyance of land, alleging as a breach the prospective claim for dower of the defendant's wife.

The defendant pleaded, that at the making of the said indenture, it was agreed between the plaintiff and defendant that the plaintiff should convey certain lands to the defendant in exchange for the lands by the said indenture conveyed, and that the prospective claims to dower of their respective wives should be wholly provided for by a separate instrument, to be taken as part of the said indenture, and to form a distinct provision between the plaintiff and defendant as to the said respective contingent claims to dower, including the claim of the defendant's wife, and thereby excluding it from the operation of the covenants declared on: that thereupon the plaintiff, by his certain writing obligatory, after reciting the said respective conveyances in exchange as aforesaid *and the said agreement*, agreed with the defendant that the said prospective claims to dower, including the claim in the declaration mentioned, should be exclusively and completely provided for as a separate matter, not included in the covenants declared on; and that, as soon as the defendant's wife should bar her dower in the lands conveyed by the said indenture, the plaintiff's wife should release her dower in the lands conveyed in exchange as aforesaid: and the defendant averred that the claim in this action was covered and provided for by the said writing obligatory, and excluded from the covenants in the declaration.

The plaintiff craved oyer, and the instrument as set out appeared to be a bond in £100 given by the plaintiff to defendant, reciting the conveyances in exchange mentioned in the plea, and that it had been agreed that the plaintiff's wife should bar her dower as soon as the defendant's wife had released hers; and conditioned to be void if this was done; but nothing was said of any further agreement that such dower should be excepted from the covenants in the deed executed by the defendant, as stated in the plea.

Held on demurrer, plea bad, for not describing the bond correctly as regards the recital, or setting it out according to its legal effect; but the court gave judgment for the defendant, on the ground that a prospective claim to dower is no breach either of the covenant for seizin or quiet enjoyment.

Quære, however, whether the intention of the parties did not sufficiently appear from the bond, to enable the court to stay proceedings in this action as being against good faith, unless the plaintiff would swear that the agreement was not such as alleged by the defendant.

Quære, also, whether, taking the bond and award together as one instrument, the covenant might not be read as containing an exception of the claim for dower.

COVENANT.—The plaintiff in his declaration set forth, in substance, that the defendant, in an indenture whereby he

conveyed certain land to the plaintiff situated in the township of Bertie, covenanted with the plaintiff that he was
lawfully seised of a good, sure, perfect, absolute, and indefeasible estate of inheritance in fee simple of and in the
premises conveyed, without any manner of reservation,
limitation, proviso, or condition, or any other matter or thing
to alter, charge, change, encumber, or defeat the same; and
further, that it should be lawful for the plaintiff, his heirs
and assigns, peaceably to enter into, hold, possess, and enjoy
the said lands, without interruption or denial of the defendant, his heirs or assigns, or any other person or persons,
acquitted and discharged of and from all manner of incumbrances whatsoever.

And the plaintiff assigned as a breach of the first covenant,
that the defendant " was not at the time of making the said
indenture lawfully seised of a good, sure, perfect, absolute,
and indefeasible estate of inheritance of and in the said lands,
without any reservation, limitation, proviso, or condition, or
any other matter to alter, charge, change, incumber, or defeat the same;" and further, that the plaintiff could not
peaceably enter into, hold, possess, and enjoy, the said lands,
free and clear, and freely and clearly acquitted, exonerated
and discharged, of and from all incumbrances whatsoever;
but that, on the contrary, there was at the time of the sealing
and delivery of the said indenture, and from thence hitherto
hath been, and still is an incumbrance existing on the said
lands, &c., contrary to the tenor and effect, true intent and
meaning of the said indenture, and of the defendant's covenant in that behalf, " that is to say, the prospective claim
for dower of Mary Jones, the wife of the said defendant,
in, to, and out of the said lands," &c., and the plaintiff
averred that, by reason of the existence of this claim for
dower, he had suffered and still suffers great damage, inasmuch as he had been unable to perform certain agreements
made by him with divers persons for the sale of the said
lands, and the securing a good and clear title to the same,
and has been, and is unable to dispose of the said lands at as
good a price as he could have done if they had been free from
all incumbrances, and from the said claim for dower as the

defendant covenanted that they were ; and so, the plaintiff avers, the defendant hath broken his said covenant.

The defendant did not demur to this declaration, but he pleaded the following plea :—

That upon the treaty for the making of the said indenture in the declaration mentioned, and forming part and parcel of the said treaty, it was agreed by and between the plaintiff and the defendant that the plaintiff, on the appointment and by the direction of the defendant, and contemporaneously. with the making of the said indenture, should convey certain lands in the city of Toronto to Jane Jones the sister of the defendant, in exchange for the lands in and by the said indenture conveyed by the defendant to the plaintiff; and that the prospective and contingent claims for dower which might thereafter possibly affect the title to the said respective parcels of land so to be conveyed in exchauge as aforesaid by reason of any claim to dower therein respectively by the respective wives of the plaintiff and defendant, should be wholly provided for and completely disposed of in and by a separate instrument in writing, under the seal of the plaintiff, and made between the plaintiff and defendant contemporaneously with the said indenture and to be taken as part and parcel thereof, and to form a distinct and complete provision and satisfaction between the said plaintiff and defendant in respect of the said respective contingent claims for dower, including therein the prospective claim for dower of Mary Jones in the said declaration mentioned, and thereby excluding and excepting the said prospective claim for dower of the said Mary Jones from the operation and purview of the covenants in the said declaration set forth; and thereupon, and contemporaneously with the making of the said indenture, and forming part and parcel thereof, the said plaintiff by his certain writing obligatory sealed with his seal, and now shewn to the court here, bearing date the 30th of January, 1845, after reciting the said respective conveyances in exchange as aforesaid and the said agreement hereinbefore set forth, agreed with the defendant that the said prospective and contingent claims for dower, including the prospective claim for dower in the said declaration mentioned, should be wholly, exclusively, and

2 *g*—VOL XII Q.B.

completely provided for and disposed of between the plaintiff
and defendant as a distinct and separate matter, not covered
by or comprehended within the covenants in the said declaration mentioned and set-forth; and that if and as soon as
Mary, the wife of the said defendant, should bar her dower
in the said lands in the said indenture described and thereby
conveyed, then immediately thereafter Elizabeth Bellesaigne,
wife of the plaintiff, should release her dower in the said
lands in the city of Toronto conveyed in exchange as aforesaid; and the defendant in fact said that in and by the said
writing obligatory the said prospective claim for dower in the
said declaration mentioned is covered by, comprehended
within and provided for by the provisions in the said writing
obligatory contained, and excepted out of and from the
covenants in the said declaration set forth.

The plaintiff claimed oyer of the alleged writing obligatory
and the condition thereof.   The obligatory part was in the
ordinary form, in £100.   The remainder of the instrument
was set out as follows :—

"Whereas the said Charles Jones hath this day conveyed
to the said Richard Hull Thornhill part of lot number five,
in the first and second concessions of Bertie in the Niagara
district of said Province, and the said Richard Hull Thornhill
hath likewise conveyed unto Jane Jones, (sister of the said
Charles Jones, of the said city, widow, one acre of land in
the city of Toronto aforesaid, the same being known as lot
number three in Lot street, now Queen street, of the said
city; and whereas the wives of the said Charles Jones
and Richard Hull Thornhill, have not barred their
dowers in the said conveyed lands; and whereas it is
agreed by the said Richard Hull Thornhill, that as soon as
Mary, the wife of the said Charles Jones shall bar her dower
in the said lands in the Niagara district so conveyed to the
said Richard Hull Thornhill, that Elizabeth Bellesaigne, wife
of the said Richard Hull Thornhill, shall also release her
dower in the said lot number three in Lot street, now Queen
street of said city of Toronto, immediately thereafter.   Now
the condition of this bond is such that if the above bounden
Richard Hull Thornhill, his heirs, executors, administrators,
or any of them, immediately after Mary, the wife of the said
Charles Jones, shall have executed a release of her dower in
the said lands in the Niagara district, shall and will procure

and deliver unto the said Charles Jones, his executors or administrators, a good and sufficient release from Elizabeth Bellesaigne, wife of the said Richard Hull Thornhill, of all her dower in the said lot number three in Lot Street, now Queen Street, in the said city of Toronto, then this obligation to be void and of no effect, or still to remain in full force and virtue.

(Signed)   " R. H. THORNHILL.
" Witness,
   (Signed)   " E. G. O'BRIEN,
                  " CHARLES S. MADFORD."

The plaintiff demurred to this plea, objecting, among other things that the bond does not shew such an agreement as is alleged in the plea, and that the defence pleaded, is material and argumentative, and does not deny or confess, or avoid the breaches of covenants complained of.

The defendant joined in demurrer, and gave notice of exception to the declaration, that no cause of action was shewn.

Cameron, Q. C., and *Hector Cameron,* for the demurrer, confined themselves principally to the declaration as the court intimated an opinion that the plea, could not be supported. The precise point in this case is new here, and almost so in England. The only two cases in which the question has arisen in this court are Bower v. Bass, E. T. 5 Vic., and Hoyt v. Widderfield, 5 U. C. R. 180; and in both of these the action seems to have been brought on the covenant for further assurance, whereas here it is on the covenant for seizin and quiet enjoyment. The question is much discussed in an American work, Rawle on Covenants for Title ; the only authorities quoted as against the right of action are at page 137-8 and they do not bear out his conclusion. In Soule v. Fleming, decided by our Court of Common Pleas last term, it was held that a sum paid to get rid of a right of dower might be recovered under the covenant, for quiet enjoyment. In the American Edition of Cruise's Digest, by Greenleaf, vol. ii., page 463, it is stated in a note, " No inchoate title to dower is an incumbrance ;" and in the same page, "Every right to or interest in the land granted to the diminution of the value of the land, but consistent with the passing of the fee of it by the conveyance, must be deemed in law an incumbrance." King v. Standish, 1 Keb. 927, is

very much in point in favor of the action, and so is Andrews
v. Tanner, 1 Keb. 937. The result of an examination of the
cases is, that there is no distinct authority against the action,
and some, though nothing decisive, in favor of it. This being
so, on principle and in reason the action should be supported,
and more particularly under the circumstances of this country.
Land here is much more an article of commerce, and more
constantly changes hands than in England, and therefore it
is right to consider anything as an incumbrance which will
depreciate its marketable value. Now in practice, there is
no doubt that a possible or contingent claim to dower is a
serious injury to title, and impedes a sale almost as effectually
as an absolute right. Moreover, it is well known that when
a vendor desires to evade a contract for sale, it is very
common to allege that his wife refuses to bar her dower ;
and a decision against this action will encourage such frauds.

Connor, Q. C., and *McDonald*, contra.—The fact that land
is treated more like goods and chattels here than in England,
will not influence the judgment to be given, for the action
is unsupported by authority, and when the nature of the
covenants is considered, it will be seen that it cannot
be sustained. The covenant for seizin means a seizin, notwithstanding anything *at that moment* existing, and a dower
is nothing existing which can alter or change the seizin then
delivered. The cases refered to in our own court were not
on these covenants, but in Hoyt v. Widderfield it is expressly
said that a dower is no incumbrance until the wife's death.
[ROBINSON, C. J.—It seems to me that the decision in Bower
v. Bass must involve the opinion of the court on this question,
and I do not see the distinction to be drawn between the
action being on the covenants for seizin and quiet enjoyment,
and for further assurance. DRAPER, J.—These covenants are
substitutes for the old warranties ; could, then, a man
conveying have been obliged to charge other lands, on the
supposition that his wife might survive him ? BURNS, J.—
Could a vendor, having agreed to convey free from all
incumbrances, oblige the vendee to except the title without a
release of dower? *Cameron*, Q. C.—Not in America, according to the cases cited by Mr. Rawle. *Vankoughnet*, Q. C.,

amicus curiæ.—The Court of Chancery here have intimated that they would not oblige acceptance of such a title. ROBINSON, C. J.—If we pay proper attention to precision of language, the covenant for seizin merely is, that *the husband* is seised, without anything, &c.; and this is true; no claim of the wife can affect his title; after he sells, it may become a claim against the vendor, but never against him. The covenant is not broken according to its literal import.] The question is in fact decided by the cases in this court; and at all events the verdict must be nominal only, for it would be absurd to give substantial damages when it is quite possible that the wife may die first, and then the claim would never arise.

ROBINSON, C. J., delivered the judgment of the court.

The defendant, in support of his plea, relies upon the principle that a deed or instrument in writing need not be set out *verbatim,* but may be pleaded according to its legal effect, which no doubt is true; but the question now is, whether the defendant is not endeavouring to push that principle too far. It appears to us that he is; for there is nothing in the bond or condition set out on oyer to support the allegation in the plea, " that by such bond or undertaking the plaintiff agreed with the defendant that the prospective claim for dower should be provided for in that writing as a separate matter, not covered by or comprehended within the covenants; and that in this same writing obligatory the prospective claim for dower in the declaration mentioned is covered by, comprehended in, and provided for, by the provisions in the said writing obligatory contained, and excepted out of and from the covenants in the declaration set forth."

Averments so precise and direct as these entitle us, we think, to expect to find in the writing referred to something expressed to the effect of what the plea mentions in this respect—not indeed in the very words used in the plea, but at least something equivalent, and in substance the same. But the fact is, as we see, that nothing whatever is said, either in the bond or condition, about the dower on both sides being distinctly and expressly provided for in this separate instrument, and excepted out of the covenants in the indenture, and we think we can hardly hold that such is the legal effect, though I have really no doubt that it was in fact the intention of the parties. We are not entitled, we think, to say conclusively that the bond may not have been executed in a different spirit, and upon a different understanding

The plaintiff, for all that we see on this record, may have given in his conveyance no such covenants as could by possibility be held to protect the defendant against the claim of the plaintiff's wife to dower : he may purposely have omitted it, or may have expressed in his deed that he gave no such assurance or protection. And under such circum- stances, it may still have been natural and reasonable for the defendant to require, and for the plaintiff to assent, that he, the plaintiff, should give a bond to the effect of the one set out in these pleadings, binding himself to have his wife's dower barred in case the defendant should procure his own wife to bar her dower in the land taken in exchange.

We can suppose the plaintiff saying in such a case : " I have, it is true, your covenant in the usual terms against in- cumbrances, under which I assume that I can hold you liable in damages, if your wife should refuse to bar her dower ; but I will not, in consideration of that, give you a bond in abso- lute terms to have my wife's right of dower extinguished. I will do this, however—I will willingly give you my bond, that if you should actually obtain a release of your own wife's right of dower in the land conveyed to me, I will see that my wife's dower shall be actually barred in the land which I am giving in exchange." In such a case, if the defendant should never succeed in obtaining a release by his own wife of her claim to dower, the plaintiff might nevertheless be in a con- dition to sue upon his covenant, and bring up the question whether it did or did not entitle him to recover damages for the contingent claim to dower as for an incumbrance.

And if this may have been the understanding and the spirit in which the plaintiff gave the bond, we are not entitled to hold it to be a legal inference inevitably arising upon the face of the bond, that the parties did certainly intend that the covenant in the indenture should not touch the claim of dower although the words of the covenant might in the absence of such a bond, have such an effect.

I cannot say that I have any doubt as to what the parties did mean. On the contrary, it is my conviction that the defendant (whatever may be the legal effect of the covenant which is contained in the conveyance signed by him) did not mean to engage that his wife would release her dower, and that the plaintiff did not consider him as covenanting to that effect, but that the defendant thought it nevertheless reasonable, as it would be, to exact what the plaintiff could not in reason refuse to undertake—namely, that if he, the defendant, should succeed in procuring his own wife to execute a release of dower, then that the plaintiff would see that the land which he was conveying should be in like manner discharged from his wife's claim to dower. The writings do not entitle us, we think, to hold as an undeniable inference of law from what is contained in them that this certainly was so ; but they do, in our opinion, furnish so good reasons for believing it, that if the defendant were before a court of equity seeking to restrain the plaintiff from proceeding in this action, or if this court had been applied to, to stay proceedings, on the allegation that the action was brought against good faith the defendant would find, we think, a strong inclination to interpose for his relief, unless the plaintiff should distinctly deny that the understanding upon which the deed and bond were executed was such as the defendant alleged it to be.

This however, is a very different question from the strict one which this demurrer presents ; for though we do believe the intention and understanding to have been such as I have stated, yet we cannot say that we read in the bond anything which certainly amounts to that. And there is, besides, we think, another ground on which the plea cannot be supported. It avers distinctly, that in the writing obligatory the alleged agreement that the claim for dower should be excluded from the covenant, and should be provided for by a separate instrument, is recited. Now that averment is clearly a matter of description : the defendant is bound to produce a bond containing a recital to that effect, in some form of words, but in the oyer which he has given there is actually no recital of the kind.

The plea cannot therefore be supported ; and we have to consider whether the defendant is entitled to succeed upon the substantial objections which he has urged against the plaintiff's declaration.

This brings up two questions : first, the general one, whether an inchoate claim for dower constitutes a breach of a covenant for title given in the terms in which the covenant was given in this case. And secondly, if it would give in general a right of action, though for nominal damages only, whether it would, under the circumstances which appear upon the record in this case, that is, taking into view the bond set out in the plea. If it were necessary to go into the second of these questions, it might be difficult to shew that it involved any consideration different from those which I have already stated and disposed of in my observations upon this plea, though the question might not perhaps be found to the full extent identical. The objection to the plea is strictly on the ground of variance ; the defendant having rested his defence on a bond, which he alleges contained a particular recital and certain express provisions, whereas the bond which he produces on oyer contains no such recital nor any such provisions ; and in regard to the latter, it cannot, in our opinion, be said that they are to be certainly and necessarily implied from anything which the bond contains. But it seems to me that there exists a question distinct from this one of variance upon the sufficiency of the plaintiff's case, taking the declaration in connection with the bond set out on oyer, for it does now appear on the record that at the time the covenant was made the plaintiff knew that the defendant's wife was living, and that she had a claim for dower which had not been barred ; and if there were no other point in the case, it would, we think, deserve consideration, whether, if we are to look upon the bond executed at the same time with the conveyance as incorporated with it, a court of law even might not hold that whatever might be the case generally upon such a covenant for title, yet that, under the circumstances appearing in this case, the wife's contingent claim for dower did not form an incumbrance.—Rawle on Covenants, 149, 154 ; Lutw. 317 ; Sugden on Vendors, vol. ii., 449, 10th Ed. ; Platt on

Covenants, 387.) We have no doubt that the mere fact of the alleged incumbrance being known to the purchaser from any information derived *aliunde* has not the effect of excepting it from the covenant, where nothing relating to it appears in the deed; but a different question is presented where the deed itself takes notice of the particular incumbrance, and makes some special provision respecting it. In other words, the question that might be raised here is; whether the bond does not reflect upon the deed as one passage of an instrument does upon another, so as to authorize us to read the covenant as if it contained an exception of the claim for dower in respect of which a special provision had been made in the contemporaneous writing.

This question, however, is after all of no importance, further than as regards the costs of the action, for in reason and acccording to abundance of authority, until the right to dower has attached, and while it is uncertain whether the purchaser can ever be disturbed by such a claim (which it must be so long as the husband lives) nominal damages only can be recovered in any action brought upon the covenant for title. The main objection upon the defendant's part is, that no such action will lie during the husband's lifetime, and that there can be no recovery, even of nominal damages, for that the possibility of the wife surviving the husband, and being able at some future day to make good a claim for dower, does not form, in contemplation of law, an actual present incumbrance while the husband is still living.

There are two cases at least in this court in which that question has come up. We refer to Bower v. Bass, decided in Easter Term, 1841, and Hoyt v. Widderfield (5 U. C. R., 180), in both of which it was assumed by a majority of the Court, and in the former case expressly determined, that the contingent and uncertain claim for dower did not constitute a present incumbrance within the words of such a covenant for unincumbered title as was given in the present case. The judges, however, were not unanimous in that opinion upon either occasion, and therefore it may be considered to be a point fairly open to further discussion, and perhaps even in this court, though the common course is to abide by repeated

2 *h*—VOL. XII. Q. B.

decisions in cases of real property which have been long
acquiesced in, because many titles may have been acquired
in the meantime by persons relying upon such decisions.
They must at all times be liable to be overruled by higher
tribunals, though they may reasonably be expected to be
adhered to by the court which pronounced them, until they
shall have been so overruled, or the law altered by the
Legislature.

The best opinion which I could form was expressed in the
cases referred to, and the reasons were given at some length
in Bower v. Bass. It appeared to me that the possible claim
of the wife to dower, dependent upon the contingency of her
surviving her husband, did not form an actual present incumbrance so long as her husband lived ; and therefore that
the husband's covenant that he was seised of a good estate
in fee simple, free from incumbrances, was not broken as
soon as he gave it, which it must be held to have been if
the plaintiff in such a case as this is entitled to recover.

I found little or nothing bearing expressly upon the point
in English authorities. All that I did find I cited, and it
led me to the conclusion I came to ; but I cannot say I was
free from doubt. In Bower v. Bass, the covenant for title
very closely resembled the covenant in this case in its
language, and it appeared to me then, as it does now, that
when the vendor covenanted that he was seised of a good,
perfect, absolute, and indefeasible estate of inheritance in
the land which he was conveying, without anything to alter
change, charge, incumber, or defeat the same, he asserted
only what was strictly true, for he had such an estate.
There was no claim for dower that then affected him, or that
ever could affect him, for in his hands his wife's claim for
dower could never by possibility affect the estate. What
he held thus unincumbered, he was transferring as he had
held it to the vendee. He was not covenanting that there
was or could be nothing which in the time of his vendee
might take the shape of an incumbrance, but that he was
then himself seised of an estate not incumbered, and not
liable (that is, his estate) to be charged or defeated by any
incumbrance then existing.

The distinction may seem too refined to be relied upon : but our inclination should be, we think, to lay stress upon a distinction which has the effect of repressing idle and useless litigation ; for it is satisfactory to be able to hold upon any intelligible ground that an action will not lie, rather than be forced to admit that it does lie in form, but not for any substantial purpose, and that the damges can only be nominal. That they could only be nominal in such a case seems undisputed—Vane v. Lord Barnard (Gilp. Eq. Rep. 7), Rawle on Covenants for Title, 155, note 1.

Some additional light has been thrown upon the question by the valuable work on covenants for title lately puplished by an American author, Mr. Rawle, from which several passages were cited in the argument. He treats this point expressly in several pages of his book (2d Ed. pp. 134-140), but is compelled to examine it with very little aid from English authorites. He is more fortunate in being able to cite some American decisions bearing directly upon the point, but they are not all consistent. The late Mr. Justice Story, in a case before him, refused to admit " that the covenant against incumbrances is broken by the mere existence of a possible incumbrance ;" and he held that " a possibility of dower is not, within the meaning of the covenant, an incumbrance, which means," he says,"a settled fixed incumbrance." Mr. Rawle cites cases which have been decided in Massachusetts and Ohio in accordance with Mr. Justice Storey's view and others which have been determined both in Massachusetts, and in other States, and in which it has been held that an inchoate or contingent right of dower is an existing incumbrance amounting to a breach of the covenant for title; while there are cases also of a middle class, in which the courts have held that whether under all the circumstances an inchoate right of dower when husband and wife are both living shall be deemed an incumbrance, is a question which must depend upon the contract and the circumstances ; that no general rule can be laid down to determine absolutely whether such an inchoate right of dower is an incumbrance, and that it must depend upon many and various circumstances and considerations. The learned author draws from his investigation of the subject the conclusion, that where the covenant is that the purchaser shall enjoy free from all incumbrance, the covenant is not broken by the mere existence of a right of dower, whether inchoate or otherwise; but that where the form of the covenant is *in presenti*, that the premises are free from all incumbrances (whlch are not exactly the words of this covenant), then the covenant is broken by the existence at that time of a right of dower, though it may be inchoate and contingent : but that if the purchaser then sue upon the covenant, his damages must be but nominal.   With the view that Mr. Rawle gives us of the question as it stands upon American authorites, and with no decisions of English courts directly bearing upon it, we adhere to the judgments already given in this court upon the point, and are of the opinion, upon this demurrer, that the plea, for the reasons we have stated, is bad, but that our judgment should nevertheless, be in favour of the defendant upon the demurrer, upon the ground that the declaration shews no breach of the covenant for quiet enjoyment, and that the covenant that the defendant was seized at the time of the conveyance of a good title, free from incumbrances, was not broken by the mere existence of the wife's inchoate and contingent claim to dower, which may never ripen into a title so as to enable her to give any molestation to the vendee or his assigns.

DRAPER, J.—I should have felt bound by the judgments in the two cases already decided in this court, even if I had not concurred in them ; but I agree with the Chief Justice that they are fully borne out by the authorites.

BURNS, J., concurred.

Judgment for defendant.

PHELPS V. THE GRAND RIVER NAVIGATION. COMPANY.

Grand River Navigation Company—2 Wm IV, chap. 13—Liability for obstructions to navigation.

The Grand River Navigation Company are liable under their charter for injuries caused by obstructions in any part of the natural channel, and not merely for such as occur in the artificial channels or works constructed by them.

This was an action on the case against the defendants, a company incorporated by 2 Wm. IV. chap 13.

The declaration alleged that the defendants, having completed and improved the navigation of the river according to their charter, on the 25th of April, 1853, had been and were accustomed to take and receive rates, duties, and tolls, in respect of boats and vessels passing on the river :—that the plaintiff then was owner of a scow of such size as the locks would commodiously admit, and was therewith accustomed to pass and repass along the navigation with goods and freight belonging to the plaintiff and others, paying the defendants such rates and duties as were required by them; that at the time of the accident the scow was loaded with 5000 bushels of wheat, of the value of £1250, belonging to the plaintiff for the purpose of being carried from Brantford to the feeder of the Welland Canal, and from thence to St. Catharines :—that on the 1st of April, 1853, a large tree, stump, or snag, drifting or being carried down the river, became grounded and imbedded in the bed of the river, in the channel, in the navigation between the feeder and Brantford along which channel and part of the navigation the plaintiff had of right and necessity to pass with the scow and the freight for the purpose aforesaid ; which tree, stump, or snag, at the time of the accident, was out of view and sunk below the surface of the water, and obstructed the navigation, so that boats and vessels passing and repassing could not without difficulty avoid or pass the obstruction, and were in danger of running foul of and striking against the same ; and that such obstruction so remained and continued from the 1st of April until the happening of the injury to the plaintiff's scow, of which the defendants had notice and knowledge. The declaration then alleged that it became and was the duty of the defendants, by their servants and agents, within a reasonable time after such notice and knowledge, to draw up the said tree, stump, or snag, and remove the obstruction, or cause the same to be removed from the said channel, as they might and ought to have done before the damage occurred; and that they might, and could, and ought in the meantime, and until such obstruction should be removed, to have placed or caused to be put or placed, a buoy, signal, mark, or other thing in the immediate vicinity of the obstruction, to denote the obstruction being there, so as to enable persons steering or guiding boats or vessels in that direction to avoid the same, or to have given due notice to the plaintiff of the fact of the same being there, and also the position thereof; yet the defendants, neglecting their duty in that behalf, did not, nor would, within a reasonable time after such notice and knowledge draw up or remove the same from the channel, although before the happening of the accident and injury a reasonable time had elapsed; and they did not place any buoy, signal, mark, or other thing to denote that the channel was obstructed, nor did they give notice to the plaintiff of the fact of such obstruction; by means whereof the plaintiff's scow, lawfully and rightfully passing along the river in the proper channel, for the usual tolls,—and the persons in charge of the scow being unable to see the obstruction, and having no knowledge thereof,—on the 27th day of April, 1853, ran foul of and struck against the tree, stump, or snag, in the channel through which the scow with the freight was passing, and by means thereof the scow was sunk, broken, damaged, and spoiled, and the wheat was spoiled, damaged, and rendered of no use, and thereby the plaintiff was put to expenses, &c.

The defendants pleaded, *first*, not guilty by statute; and *secondly*, that the plaintiff was not possessed of the scow.

At the trial at the last assizes at Cayuga, before *Burns, J.*, it was proved to the satisfaction of the jury that the defendants did know, through their engineers and persons engaged as servants and in charge of the navigation, that there was an obstruction in the channel, and that they had three or four days before the accident attempted to remove it, but had failed for want of applying the proper means. It was also established to the satisfaction of the jury that the plaintiff's servants were in no way to blame, and that the defendants were in fault in case there was a duty cast upon them by law to remove the obstruction in a reasonable time after notice of it, or to give notice in some way that there was an obstruction existing in the channel. It was contended on the part of the defendants that under the charter, 2 Wm. IV. chap. 13, no obligation existed upon the defendants, further than to keep free the locks and such parts of the navigation as consisted of canals or cuts to shorten the distance, or such works as the campany actually made for the purpose of navigation; and that, as the obstruction in the present case was in the channel of the river, about a quarter of a mile distant from the works put up by the defendants, they were not responsible for the obstructions remaining in the channel. The learned judge told the jury, that in his opinion the whole river belonged to the defendants, and that no one, except within the exceptions mentioned in the act, had a right to use it without paying the defendants the tolls imposed by the company, and no one had a right to interfere with the company in the mode in which they might choose to complete the navigation; and he overruled the defendants' objection. A further objection was made, that the defendants were bound to furnish only a channel of *three* feet water, but this was abandoned. Leave was reserved to the defendants to move to enter verdict for them if they were not in law liable to remove the obstruction under the facts.

Connor, Q. C., obtained a rule accordingly. He cited Harris v. Baker, 4 M. & S. 27; Rex. v. The Commissioners of Sewers for Essex, 1 B. & C. 477; Henry v. The Mayor of Lyme, 5 Bing. 91; S. C. In Error, 3 B. & Ad. 77; 8 Bligh N. C. 690; Makinnon v. Penson, 18 Eng. Rep. 509, 22 L. J. M. C. 57; Ferguson v. Earl of Kinnoull, 9 Cl. & Fin. 251; 16 Vic. ch. 256.

W. Eccles shewed cause, and cited Parnaby v. the Lancaster Canal Co., 11 A. & E. 223; 2 W. IV., ch. 13, secs. 1, 2, 11; 3 W. IV., ch. 21, sec. 2.

ROBINSON, C. J., delivered the judgment of the court.

This is a case of some consequence to the defendants, for the verdict against them is for a considerable sum, though

apparently not by any means excessive, if the plaintiff's
right of action is well founded; and if the recovery in this
action be finally confirmed it will shew the defendants to
be subject to a liability which it is possible neither they
nor others have thought much upon hitherto. We do not
see upon what ground the liability can be disputed under
'such facts as are stated in this record. All that can be
necessary for shewing a neglect or omission of the duty
assumed to be incumbent upon the defendants is carefully
averred in the declaration—notice of the obstruction to
the navigation—the lapse of a reasonable time for removing
it—and the failure to remove it, though the defendants
could have done it, are all alleged, and were all, in the
opinion of the learned judge who tried the cause, satisfac-
factorily proved. The defendants have pleaded not guilty,
which denies, not the duty to keep the channel clear, but
the breach of that duty. If it was intended to dispute that
any such duty as is alleged was incumbent upon the defendants, the course would have been to demur to the declaration, or to move after verdict to arrest the judgment; at
least we take that at present to be so, though in the case
of Parnaby et al v. The Lancaster Canal Co. (11 A. & E. 223),
it seems to have been tacitly conceded by the court that
the duty was in issue upon the plea of not guilty. However
that may be, that same case is, in our opinion, a very clear
and conclusive authority that in the present case it was the
duty of the company to take all reasonable care for securing to the public a safe and commodious channel.

This case is quite undistinguishable, we think, from that
referred to, and in many other cases the same principle is as
clearly affirmed. In Henley v. The Mayor of Lyme (5 Bing.
108), the duty as arising from the fact of reward being paid
is stated in strong terms in the elaborate judgment of Lord
Chief Justice Best.

Indeed it seemed to be scarcely denied in the argument of
this case on the part of the defendants that such duty would
in general arise; and it was rather attempted to contend
against the right to recover in this case, upon the particular
ground that it was only the artificial channels created by the

company which they were bound to keep clear; and that the natural channel of the river, on which it seems this stump or snag was grounded, was not so exclusively under the charge of the defendants as to raise the same duty in respect to such natural channel.

We are clear that we can recognize no such distinction. It is plain, on a perusal of the statute 2 Wm. IV., ch. 13, that the whole channel of the Grand River within the limits assigned is made subject to the control of the company, as regards the making, repairing, and maintaining, and even the using of the navigable channel, except when a privilege is reserved to individuals to be exercised with certain limitations. The toll is allowed to be imposed in respect of the whole course, and the company have so completely the control of the river that no one could presume to interfere with them in any manner, for deepening or otherwise improving the channel, or removing obstacles.

We cannot doubt that the company themselves have always understood this to be their own position, and they must take the burthen with the privilege. It is easy to perceive the difference between a navigation of this nature on a small inland stream to be formed by a succession of dams and cuts, which make it in a manner an artificial navigation in the whole or the greater part of its course, and the case of a great river like the St. Lawrence, where at certain points only it may be necessary to deviate from the river in order to avoid rapids. If a private company had been empowered to construct canals and locks at such points on the St. Lawrence as were necessary, and to charge tolls as a compensation, they would have no duty incumbent upon them in regard to the river generally, because they would have no authority or privilege except in respect to the points where there were obstacles to overcome. But the Grand River Navigation is a description of canal, and has been placed as such wholly under the charge of the defendants; who have undertaken to form and maintain upon it throughout a navigable channel, which they could not have engaged to do unless they had the exclusive right to manage the whole in their own way.

We are of opinion that the rule for entering a verdict for defendants must be discharged.

Rule discharged.

REGINA V. GREAT WESTERN RAILROAD COMPANY.

G. W. R. R. Co.— Width of bridges to be erected when highways crossed.

A railway company by their charter were bound to restore any highway intersected by their track " to its former state, or in a sufficient manner not to impair its usefulness." They constructed their road across a street in the city of Hamilton, which was sixty-six feet wide, and connected the street again by a bridge across the track forty feet two inches in width : *Held*, that the jury might with propriety find this to be a sufficient compliance with the act, and that the defendants were not necessarily guilty of a nuisance because the bridge was not of equal width with the street crossed.

This was an action for nuisance, in obstructing a highway.

The jury specially found the following facts, and found the defendants guilty if there be an obstruction in law, there being no obstruction in fact :

The defendants by their act of incorporation are empowered, whenever it may be necessary for the construction of their road to intersect or cross any road or highway, to construct their line of road across or upon the same, provided that they shall restore the road or highway thus intersected to its former state, or in a sufficient manner not to impair its usefulness.

The defendants in the construction of their road have occasion to intersect several streets in the city of Hamilton, and have in the exercise of their powers excavated for the railway several feet below the level of the streets, and have erected bridges over the railway to connect the streets so intersected, in lieu of the old street or road.

The width of each of the streets so intersected is, and was at the time of such excavation, sixty-six feet ; and until the excavation for the railway there was a raised footway or sidewalks extending the full length of James Street, one of the streets so intersected, on the west side thereof.

The defendants have erected the said bridges over the said railway in no part thereof exceeding forty feet two inches in width, inclusive of the sidewalks on each side, of four feet six and a half inches each in with, leaving a carriage way of thirty-one feet one inch wide.

Although the width is diminished, as stated in the case, the usefulness of the roads is in no manner impaired or obstructed otherwise.

Frequent applications have been made to the defendants, by the corporation of the city of Hamilton, on behalf of the inhabitants of the said city, to cause a bridge or bridges to be erected over the railway at the points so intersected of the full width of the street intersected, with which the defendants have refused to comply.

Vankoughnet, Q. C., for the Crown, cited Regina v. The London and Birmingham R. W. Co., 1 R. W. Cas. 317.

Cameron, Q. C., and *Connor*, Q. C., contra, cited Regina v. Betts, 16 Q. B., 1022; Abraham v. The Great Northern R. W. Co., Ib. 586; Regina v. Eastern Counties R. W. Co. 3 R. W. Cas. 33; The Manchester and Leeds R. W. Co. v. The Queen, Ib. 634; Priestley v. Manchester and Leeds R. W. Co. 2 R. W. Cas., 134; Regina v. Sharpe, 3 R. W. Cas., 22; Her Majesty's Attorney General v. The London and Southampon R. W. Co. 1 R. W. Cas. 302, S. C. 9 Sim. 78.

ROBINSON, C.J.—The first and last counts of the indictment are neither counts as for a nuisance at common law, nor do they charge any offence to have been committed contrary to the statute referred to. The only question I think, is whether the evidence supports a conviction under the second count as for a nuisance at common law, on the ground taken in the Queen v. Scott et al. (3 Q. B., 543), that what the defendants have done in digging away the old road was only made legal upon condition of their doing what they have not done, and that so they may be properly convicted of nuisance in obstructing the old road. It is hardly possible to doubt that the manner in which the original street has been and is interfered with by the railway track, must constitute such an obstruction as amounts to a nuisance, though nothing can dispense with the necessity of the jury pronouncing expressly upon that point, for the question of nuisance or no nuisance is always to be disposed of by the jury, and cannot be reduced to a dry question of law independent of the consideration whether the obstruction complained of is or is not in truth inconvenient and injurious to the public. I refer particulary to the case of the Queen v. Betts et al. (16 Q. B. 1022.) We should have great difficulty, then, under any view which we might take of this case, in directing a judgment to be given for the crown upon what the jury have in this case found, which seems to amount to this, that they cannot deny that the bridge which now forms a substitute for the street is of less width than the street was, but that they cannot and will not take upon themselves to say that the usefulness of the road is in any manner impaired or obstructed by its being less wide. Now that was precisely what it rested with them to pronounce, for they are to be the judges of that, and not we. We are desired to determine, not as a question of fact, but as a question of law, that the bare fact of making the street narrower is necessarily a nuisance. That is directly at variance with what has been repeatedly held by the courts in England in the cases to which I have referred, and in others. If the passage being narrowed must of necessity constitute a nuisance, then we should have to apply such a principle without discrimination, for we would have as judges no discretion to exercise, but must go by the rule, and the bridge being a foot or an inch narrower than the street must be held to be inevitably fatal; and the consequence would be that as a part of the judgment in all such cases must be that the nuisance be abated, every bridge by which the former highway has been carried above the railway must be pulled down, and that not merely in the case of this line of railway, but of many others, for there are many railway acts in which the very same words are used in relation to bridges as in the one now in question, as in the Montreal and Kingston R. W. Co., 10 Vic. ch. 107; Peterborough and Port Hope R. W. Co., 10 Vic. ch. 109 ; Hamilton and Toronto Railroad Co., 10 Vic. 110 ; and the Railway Clauses Consolidation Act, 14 & 15 Vic. ch. 51, sec. 9, gives room for the same question that has been raised here, for it directs that in such cases the highway shall be restored to its former state, "or to such state as not to have impaired its usefulness."

If we read the various canal acts, in which, as in some of

the railway acts the proviso is merely that the company shall erect a "sufficient bridge," or a "commodious" bridge, or that they shall by a bridge carry the road over, we must be satisfied that as the consideration of the public convenience must be the same in all these cases, so the same thing must have been meant, and the Legislature never could have been so unreasonable as to intend to insist that every bridge built across a road that is sixty-six feet wide must itself be sixty-six feet wide.   In truth, the public could not in such case have the full use of sixty-six feet, as a passage way for the side timbers and railing of the bridge must occupy some portion of the space.

What is contended for by the prosecution in this case might compel the company in some cases (as, for instance, if they had to cross the main street in Hamilton) to construct such a bridge as is nowhere else to be found in the world, one, two, or three hundred feet wide.   Westminster bridge is but forty-four feet wide, and Blackfriars bridge, one of the greatest thoroughfares in the world, is forty-two feet wide.   The bridge complained of which leads across one of the streets of Hamilton, in Upper Canada, is wider than Blackfriars bridge by two inches.   I do not wonder that the jury should rather have thrown it upon the judges to pronounce it a nuisance, than have found such a verdict themselves.   The Legislature, and the justices, and municipal councils, and private individuals and public companies, have been building bridges in this province for sixty years and more, and it ought to be tolerably good evidence of public opinion as to what is necessary in such matters, that no bridge, as I believe, has yet been built in Upper Canada of the width of sixty-six feet. This may at least serve to shew that public convenience may, according to the universal understanding of mankind, have been sufficiently consulted in this instance, although the bridge is narrower than the highway commonly is, unless there is something peculiar in James street, in Hamilton, which renders something more necessary than is to be found anywhere else.

No evidence is given of any such peculiarity; but it has been contended that we are bound to say what the jury has declined saying—that the bridge must of necessity be a nuisance, from the bare fact that it is of less width than the street at either end, or rather of less width than the former street over which it runs. It was an argument no doubt to use with the jury, that they had no business to consider whether the public convenience was reasonably or sufficiently answered, but simply whether the forty-two feet was as great a width as sixty-six; and if the jury had felt themselves driven to look at the question of nuisance or no nuisance in that point of view, then a verdict of guilty might have been forced from them contrary though it must have been to their conviction of what the Legislature must have intended. It is not until the jury, in such a case have been brought to take that view, and give that verdict, that a judgment of guilty can be entered. It cannot be the opinion of the judges, but the verdict of the jury, that must establish the fact of nuisance. We cannot say that a bridge of forty-two feet wide may not be as useful to the public as one of sixty-six feet. It seems to be so regarded in this and all other countries, and if the bare fact of its being narrower than the former street makes it of necessity less useful, and in consequence a nuisance, then the same comparison of the new means of transit with the old would make every bridge a nuisance, for there must be more or less of an ascent in the approach to it, and it might with more reason be held that the necessity for such ascent is a nuisance, since undoubtedly so large a load could not be drawn up it by the same force as on level ground. It may be answered that the Legislature must be taken to have contemplated and allowed this, when they allowed the bridge to be substituted for the road, and so, I think, did they contemplate and allow that the bridges to be erected by the company should be what bridges usually are.

It seems singular, while unexplained, that the prosecutors in this case should be insisting upon that which, for all that appears, can be no more just and reasonable in this case than in others, and which if it could be carried into effect in all other cases would probably not leave a bridge standing in the province.

DRAPER J.—I think the connection between the intersected portions of the highway might be formed by a bridge. The company were not bound to make a tunnel for their railway, over which tunnel the highway might have been continued in its original state. I do not think, as a mere proposition of law, that a bridge of the dimensions stated in the case must be considered as insufficient, or as inevitable impairing the usefulness of the highway. In the Railway Clauses Consolidation Act, 14 & 15 Vic. ch. 51, sec. 12, a less width is declared by the Legislature as sufficient for the width of the highway to be left between the arches of a bridge on which the railway is carried over such highway.

But if it is not clearly a question of law, but it is on the contrary a question of fact, which the jury have determined in favor of the defendants, there is nothing for the court to decide upon, except whether on the evidence the jury were bound to convict the defendants ; and I cannot see any ground for holding the evidence to be so conclusive as to lead to such a result. What they have found is in my opinion in reality an acquittal, and is in accordance with the evidence submitted to them.

BURNS J., concurred.

Judgment for defendants.

BUTLER AND McNEIL v. DONALDSON.

Statute of Limitations, 3 & 4 W. IV., c.   —*Discontinuance—Land in question forfeited for plaintiff's treason.*

EJECTMENT.—The plaintiff in 1814, being charged with high treason, fled from the province, leaving his family on the property in question, and they afterwards joined him in the enemy's country.

Held, that the circumstances of his leaving should have been considered by the jury as conclusive of an intention to abandon the possession : and that it could not be said that leaving his family in possession was the same as remaining himself, that the discontinuance commenced when they left, and that being abroad then the plaintiff was entitled to the benefit of the disability.

It was shewn by affidavits, in moving for a new trial, that the plaintiff had in fact been attainted for treason, and the land in question forfeited to the crown, and on this ground the court granted the defendent a new trial on payment of costs.

EJECTMENT—on the several demises of the plaintiffs, to recover lot 14 in the 5th concession of the township of Grantham.

At the trial before *Burns, J.*, at the last spring assizes held at Niagara, the facts appeared as follows:—It was admitted that the land in question had been granted by patent from the Crown in 1798 to Andrew Butler, who died intestate, leaving Joseph Walter Butler, one of the plaintiffs, his heir-at-law. The case did not turn upon this, and it was admitted that the verdict rendered against the plaintiff Butler was correct. A deed of bargain and sale from Lockwood Street to the plaintiff Luther McNeil, dated 29th May, 1808, was proved. It was proved that Street lived upon and was in possession previously to the plaintiff, and after Street left the possession then the plaintiff took possession. Street had been in possession from 1803 or 1804 until he sold to the plaintiff McNeil. A person of the name of Wilson had been in possession before Street's time; and Street had purchased from him his good will, as it was termed. A witness named James Secord, eldest son of David Secord, then proved that his father, David Secord, who died many years ago, had sold this land in 1803 or 1804 to Street, that he recollected seeing a deed from Andrew Butler, who died about the year 1806, to David Secord, which he had no doubt was for the land in question, though he had not read it or heard it read, but heard it spoken of as being the deed from Butler to his father for the land. This deed, he said, was taken from his father's posesssion by one Goring or one Harris—he was not sure which of the two—for the purpose of preparing a deed from his father to Street for the land in question. Mr. Goring and Mr. Harris were both in the habit of preparing conveyances for the people in the country, and they have been dead for many years. The witness proved that after the sale by David Secord, Street went into possession of the land. The witness then further proved that he had again seen the deed from Butler to his father, in his father's possession, shortly previous to the war of 1812, but why it had come back to his possession he could not say, but suggested that it might be because Street had not fully paid him for the land, for he said his father claimed that, at the time of the breaking out of the war, Street still owed him, though he had conveyed the land to Street, and, at the same time, he confirmed that

McNeil should be living on the land, he, Secord, not being paid for it. It was proved that David Secord's house and many of his papers were destroyed by the enemy during the war, and that search had been made with his executors and different members of his family for the deed in question, but it could not be found. Lockwood Street died also many years ago, and it was proved that searches had been made among his papers, which his sons had got, but no deeds or papers relating to the land in question could be found. The plaintiff's papers were searched by his son, but no deed could be found.

The plaintiff, Luther McNeil, remained in possession of the land till the year 1813 or 1814; there was a discrepancy between the witnesses as to the exact time. Some of the witnesses said he left the country very soon after the battle of Stoney Creek, which was on the 5th of June, 1813, and others that he left in 1814. He left the country voluntarily, having, as appeared by the evidence, rendered himself amenable to the law for having in some way connected himself with the enemy, and he never returned to this province. At the time plaintiff left this country his family remained behind, living upon the land. It was said the Sheriff of the district went to the family after McNeil left, and told them they could not remain in the country, but must join the plaintiff in the United States. Be that as it may, the plaintiff's family, a few months after he left, did join him in the United States, and remained there ever since. The plaintiff became a citizen of the United States, and his sons held offices under that Government, and it was quite understood that the plaintiff and his family had removed from this province, without any intention on his part of returning here, and with the intention of making the United States their permanent place of residence. It was proved that one Samuel Cassidy shortly after the destruction of the town of Niagara, went into possession of the land, under some kind of permission from Sir Gordon Drummond, then Administrator of the Government of Upper Canada, and he remained in possession from 1814 until he died, some three or four years ago. Cassidy had gone to the land before the family of

McNeil left, though he did not take possession till after they had left. The defendant claimed through him. It was proved that one of the plaintiff's sons came to this province at his request, in the year 1820, to make enquiries respecting the land. He went to the place, and found one Ransier upon it, but did nothing towards asserting title in any way. Another son of the plaintiff came twice to this country, as he stated, to look after the land ; first in 1818, and again in 1836. On the first occasion, he said that he called upon Colonel Clench, in the town of Niagara, who was then Clerk of the Peace, and on consulting him he said that Colonel Clench advised him to let matters remain, because the feeling against those who were supposed to have connected themselves with the enemy had not died away.

This action was commenced on the 3rd of March, 1853, within the period of forty years from the plaintiff's leaving this province.

The learned judge left it to the jury upon the question of discontinuance remarking to them that the case afforded a strong presumption of an abandonment of the property altogether, without any intention, when the plaintiff left this country, of resuming possession ; that such intention would operate upon the plaintiff's mind, if it had any operation at all, while he yet was in the province, and consequently the statute of limitations would have begun to run. The jury were told that if the plaintiff had originally discontinued the possession without any intention of resuming it, or preserving his right to the land, then he must fail. The question of discontinuance was left upon the facts proved, however, in the hands of the jury. Both parties objected to this charge. On the part of the plaintiff it was contended that the question of discontinuance of possession did not arise, for that when the plaintiff left this country the family were left in possession, and their possession was his, and they did not leave the country till some months after the plaintiff had left, and the inquiries in subsequent years on his part proved the reverse of any abandonment by him. On the part of the defendant it was contended that the simple fact of the plaintiff leaving the land, and another going into possession adversely, and remaining for more than twenty years in adverse possession, destroyed any claim the plaintiff might have had.

The jury found for the plaintiff McNeil.

Cameron, Q. C., obtained a rule nisi for a new trial on the law and evidence, and for misdirection, and upon affidavits disclosing that the Commissioners in whom the estates of those attainted of high treason had vested, returned the land in question as forfeited to the crown. This return was made under the 58 Geo. III c. 12, and shewed that the treason for which the forfeiture took place, was "searching for and plundering public property, and aiding and assisting the enemy.

Vankoughnet, Q. C., shewed cause.—It is quite clear that whatever may be McNeil's rights the defendant has none, and deserves no consideration. The land was bought by him for a trifle, and the court will not willingly interfere in favour of a mere speculator. If there is any question of right it must be as between McNeil and the Crown, and the Crown can assert this right, but if they do not choose to interpose the court should allow the matter to rest. As to the question of discontinuance, McNeil going away as he did, leaving his family, was the same as continuing in possession; he was not obliged to live on his own land; the fact of leaving his family shews that he did not leave with any intention of abandonment. They were in fact turned out, and this makes it not a case of discontinuance but of dispossession. While he was away he constantly made inquires as to his right to recover, thus shewing not only that he did not leave with an intention to abandon, but that he never had any such intention while away. In Rimington v. Cannon, 12 C. B. 18, the question of discontinuance was considered. Doe. Taylor v. Proudfoot (9 U. C. R. 503) was a clear case of discontinuance, and therefore wholly different from this, for McNeil was in fact frightened out of the country. Suppose a person commits some offence against good morals and finds it necessary to go away— [ROBINSON, C. J.—Suppose you own a place on Lake Huron and once occupy it after the patent has issued by building a fishing hut there, and then leave it—can you, after twenty-five years, recover against a stranger who has occupied it only for two years, or can he say " You were in possession, you discontinued and remained away for twenty years, and now you are precluded?" This is an important question, though it may not apply in this case.] Here there was a dispossession, not a discontinuance. In a late case of Smith v. Lloyd, 22 L. T. Rep. 289, it has been decided that forty years of want of actual possession by the plaintiff is no bar, but that the statute applies only where there has been both absence of possession by the person who has the right, and actual possession by another.

· *Cameron*, Q. C., and *Eccles*, supported the rule.—The learned Judge at the trial thought the case turned on a question of forty years' posssession, while the defendant contended, as he contends now, that it was a question of twenty years. The fact of a man going away and another taking possession ·constitutes a discontinuance and a taking of possession, and that makes the period of twenty years a bar. [ROBINSON, C. J.—The first question is, when is the discontinuance to be dated from, when McNeil went or when Cassidy came ? DRAPER, J.—If it is a discontinuance at all it must date from the going.] Certainly. Under the circumstances the discontinuance of one and the possession of another made twenty years a bar. There was no dispossession of the family, for the dispossession meant by the statute is, that there shall be an actual dispossession and taking possession *by the party who goes in.* The simple fact of McNeil going out and Cassidy coming in, if simultaneous, were clearly a bar after twenty years, and no question of forty years arose. The jury should have been asked if the discontinuance and taking possession were simultaneous, and if so, then twenty years would preclude the plaintiff. [ROBINSON, C. J.—Take the case of an agent ; if an owner leaves the country and an agent behind him, he would not have discontinued so long as he receives rent ; the discontinuance would date from the cesser of rent, and then, being abroad, would he come within the exception?—I suppose he would. DRAPER, J.—Then you argue that the fact of the family remaining had no bearing on the case ?] Yes. The sole question is, whether the discontinuance and taking possession were simultaneous acts, and that should have been left to the jury. As to the defendant being a mere squatter or speculator, if he is not entitled to consideration the plaintiff is less so, for his claim has passed into other hands. Cassidy, through whom the defendant claims, went into possession under a license from Sir Gordon Drummond, not wrongfully.

ROBINSON, C. J.—Upon the argument of this rule several matters were freely discussed on both sides, of which regular evidence had not been given at *Nisi Prius,* but which being notorious and capable of being easily proved, the usual formal proof of them seems not to have been insisted on.

Upon consideration of the case, I am of opinion that it is incumbent on us to grant a new trial, for two reasons:—first as regards the discontinuance of possession by McNeil in 1814, it would have been proper, I think, to have submitted that to the jury in terms more strongly in favour of the defendant than seems to have been done at the trial, and I think the jury should have been led very clearly by the evidence to a different conclusion from that which they came to. It was proved to them that the plaintiff, McNeil, being charged in 1814 with acts of high treason in a time of public war, fled from the province, abandonding his property, and betook himself to the country of the enemy with whom his sovereign was at war; and fron that time to the present, more than forty years, he has never returned to Upper Canada, though living within a short distance of it, and has never asserted his right to this property until he brought this action at the end thirty-nine years, and within the very verge of that period of limitation which would have inevitably barred him. They could, I think, have had little doubt that he left his property with no idea of returning to it unless indeed the enemy should succeed in conquering the country which they had invaded. It would have been proper, it appears to me, in such a case to conclude that his mind was made up when he was still in this province, and that his discontinuance of possession was with no view of ever resuming it. His family, it is true, continued a short time upon the place after he left, but that was for their own convenience. It is not reasonable to infer that they were holding possession under such circumstances either for him or under him. It seems to me to do violence to the plain sense of the thing, upon such facts, to regard McNeil as having first discontinued the possession after his faimly had gained the enemy's country, and that by that means to hold him entitled to the benefit of the exception in the statute of limitations, so that, on account of his absence, time could not run against him until he should return to the province from which he had fled, and so that at the end of thirty-eight or thirty-nine years he is in a situation to dispossess persons who had lived openly upon the land, and cultivated and improved it during that whole period.

Then on the second ground on which a new trial was moved, it was stated in the argument, and was not and cannot be denied, that while the plaintiff McNeil is endeavoring to get into possession of this property by a judgment of this court, or rather a person who it appears has bought as a speculation the right at this distance of time to use his name in this action, the title to the land is in fact in the Crown, having been finally returned by inquisition many years ago as forfeited upon McNeil's attainder by judgment of outlawry on an indictment of high treason. We could not but take notice that, if this was so, the title of the Crown must appear of record in this court, and we have felt it to be our duty, under the oath of office which we have taken, to inspect the record of the attainder and inquisition, which shows the truth to be so. This fact was indeed suggested after the first trial, and it is not explained why advantage was not taken of the last trial to produce evidence of it. Surely it should not be left to the judges alone to guard the Queen's rights, though their oath of office has strong words to bind their conscience in this respect.

It has been for many years a striking defect in the administration of justice in Upper Canada that the Crown is but seldom represented in the Queen's courts, while they are sitting in banc, by either the Attorney or Solicitor General. If it had been otherwise we must suppose that means would have been taken to guard the interests of the Crown in this instance. For all that appears to us, the defendant in this

cause might be shewn to be holding in privity with the Crown,
and yet in case of a recovery in this action it might happen
that the circumstances are such that at the end of forty years
which have elapsed while this action is pending even the
Crown would be barred and lose its interest in this land;
and if there be no reason to apprehend this, it would still be
to no purpose to allow the plaintiff in this cause to recover
and dispossess the defendant if he is liable to be at once dispossessed by a proper proceeding on the part of the crown.
Having called attention to the facts of the case, which we
hope may engage attention in the proper quarter, we grant
a new trial, on payment of costs, in order that the real
facts in regard to the attainder and inquisition may be
made to appear.   If there be any ground on which the
Queen's title can be held to have ceased or not to have
attached, they can and ought to be proved.

BURNS, J.—There are three matters to be considered in
this case in order to determine correctly the rights of the
parties, and what should be done upon the present application.

First, then, was the charge of direction which was given to
the jury correct in point of law upon the evidence ?   After
giving the question the fullest consideration in my power, I
still retain the opinion expressed at *Nisi Prius.*   Cassidy,
through and under whom the defendant claimed, had been
in possession of the premises adversely for more than twenty
years, but not for forty years, after the time that McNeil
left the province and before the bringing of the action.   Is
the mere fact of the owner leaving the possession and another
coming in adversely after the lapse of twenty years in all
cases a bar to the claimant's right ?   It is a bar if the claimant at the time of adverse possession taken labors under
no disability   If a disability exists, then adverse possession
of itself will be no bar, if the action be brought within
the time allowed by the act.   At the time Cassidy took
possession the plaintiff was not in this province, and he has
never been in it since that time.   Assuming that the act of
Cassidy's taking possession was the first occasion of the
plaintiff's right being invaded or disturbed, and that the

plaintiff should be considered as constructively in possession up to that time, and that such act was done while the plaintiff was out of this province, then it appears to me that the action, being brought within forty years is in time. This case does not depend upon the act of Cassidy, but must be decided upon the acts and conduct of the plaintiff. That involves the question whether his acts and conduct establish a discontinuance of possession within what the legislature meant by that expression in the seventeenth section of the act. The rule of law has always been that a person having a title to real estate need not be in the actual possession, but he will be held to be constructively in possession so long as no one is in possession adversely to him ; in other words, the possession if not actual yet constructively follows the title, unless there be disturbance of the possession. Is the meaning of the statute such, that when a person who has at one time been in the actual possession shall afterwards have ceased to be so, from the moment of the actual possession ceasing there is a discontinuance of possession which then at once reduces the owner's right to a mere right of entry ? I cannot bring my mind to that view. I agree with a good deal of what has been said by the late Mr. Justice Sullivan in Doe Cuthbertson v. McGillis (2 C. P. 124). The right of entry is something distinguished from the possession ; and so long as the owner is in possession the right of entry is merged in that. It would be absurd to say, while the owner was in actual possession that he had only a right of entry. In Partridge v. Strange (Plow. 88) *Montague, C. J.*, says, "If one has a right or title to land, and afterwards he comes to the possession of the same land his right or title is extinct or suspended in the land; for during the time he has the land it is not *in esse ergo* during that time it cannot be termed a right or title." If the owner has never been in the actual possession, but is held to be constructively so by reason of the possession accompanying the title, then it is equally absurd to say that the owner has only a right of entry. Then may the true owner leave or abandon the actual possession and yet retain a constructive possession ? I think he may, and I can see no reason or authority against that position.

When the actual possession is left by the true owner the question of constructive possession then becomes one to be dealt with according to the circumstances of the case; and the fact whether a constructive possession remains, or whether the owner's right is at once, upon actual possession ceasing, reduced to a right of entry, depends upon the acts and conduct of the owner and all the facts of the case. I view the seventeenth section as providing for two classes : first, where the owner has been dispossessed, which supposes the acts of other parties interfering with the owner; and secondly, where the owner has discontinued the possession, an act proceeding from himself. Being dispossessed is an unequivocal act, and discontinuing may also be unequivocal; as, for instance, if some other than the true owner be in possession adversely, or he should leave the possession for another to take it. If the property is left vacant by the true owner merely because it is his pleasure to do so, not intending to abandon his right to it, but he supposes and believes that he may return whenever it suits his convenience to do so, it appears to me he is constructively in possession, and that his right is not reduced to a mere right of entry until that constructive possession is disturbed. In this case the plaintiff had been in the actual possession; he left with his family and abandoned the premises, not to allow some other person to assume it, but another person did assume the possession afterwards. With what motives or intentions did the plaintiff so abandon the possession, and was such abandonment a discontinuance of possession? This being a case which depends not upon some unequivocal act done, which leaves no other alternative than some inevitable consequence as the result, but upon motives and intentions proceeding from the person creating the discontinuance, which requires the intervention of the jury to determine what those motives and intentions establish as a conclusion of fact, I consider in a case like the present that the question whether there be a discontinuance is a mixed question of law and fact, so inseparably blended together that it is impossible to separate the one from the other so as to withdraw the consideration of any part of the question from the jury, and it must remain for the consideration of the court to say whether the jury has exercised a sound judgment upon the facts.

The second consideration is with respect to the evidence, and whether the verdict be contrary to that. The weight of evidence, as it appeared to me at the trial, did establish that the plaintiff had discontinued the possession of the premises at the time he abandoned the land, and that leaving his family upon the place was merely for a temporary purpose until they could be removed, and their subsequent removal was for the purpose of carrying out his own intentions. Suppose, however, that the part of the family remaining after he had himself left is to be construed as a possession by the plaintiff, yet the discontinuance at the time the family left would still be his own act, and according to my view of the statute if the limitation is to be determined from the act of the owner himself and he allows twenty years to elapse from the time of that act done before asserting his rights he is barred. The plaintiff leaving the province with an intention of permanently abandoning the property (supposing that, for the sake of the argument, to be established), but leaving his family behind him for a short time upon the premises, would not in my opinion preserve to him the right of saying that the discontinuance commenced only from the time the family left the premises. He had formed the determination himself previously, and as far as he himself was concerned, had carried out his determination. The leaving of his family was merely for convenience. I do not see that the fact of the family remaining there for a short period with the object in view of removal preserved to the plaintiff a right to say that on their removal the discontinuance commenced, and as that commenced while he was absent from the province he was therefore under a disability and might bring his action within forty years. Some stress was placed upon the circumstance of the family being told, as it was said, that they must leave the province. I think that a matter of no moment because the family of the plaintiff could not be involved in his offence, if offence the plaintiff had committed, and they could not legally be sent out of the province. In the case of Doe ex dem. Corbyn v. Bramston (3 A. & E 63), Lord Denman says : "The departure of the former possessors to a distance, without appearing to have received any rent or made any demand, is the strongest evidence of their intending to abandon at once all occupation and all claim of ownership." In our case, if the evidence had shewn that the plaintiff had abandoned the province for some offence which worked a forfeiture of his property, then the inevitable result, I think, would be drawn that there was an intention also to abandon the property. The evidence, however, left the matter whether the plaintiff had been guilty of anything which rendered him liable to the laws of the province merely to be surmised, but it certainly did appear to me to be very cogent to establish that the plaintiff had abandoned the property in question at the time he left the province. It is possible he may have thought in after years that he might succeed in obtaining it ; but then he should have made the attempt within twenty years, or within the time allowed by the statute of 1834, and sending his sons to make enquiries on the subject did not preserve his right for the period of forty years. The act of abandonment of the property must have been conceived and acted upon before any disability by reason of being absent from the province could arise. As this case is one of actual possession, and not merely constructive, there is the less difficulty about it. There is no question but that the plaintiff did in fact leave the property : did he leave it with the intention of abandoning it ? I must say the jury took a different view of the question from that which appeared to me to be the correct one. If the case rested entirely upon this it might perhaps be difficult satisfactorily, with a due and proper respect for the opinion of those in whom the law rests the disposition of the facts of a case, to disturb the verdict, but it remains to consider the case further upon another branch of the application.

The third matter for consideration is, how to deal with the case upon the disclosures made in the affidavits. If the object were merely to set up the title of the crown in order to defeat the plaintiff I should be disposed to adopt the views urged by Mr Vankoughnet, but I look upon the evidence

which it is said can now be produced quite in another point
of view. The question in disbute between these parties is
whether the plaintiff has rendered himself subject to be
defeated by the operation of the Statute of Limitations, not
through negligence in asserting his rights, but from an act
proceeding from himself, namely, having voluntarily abandoned the property and producing the result that his right is
entirely extinguished. He asserts that he never did abandon
it. The affidavits shew that the species of treason for which
the lot in question was forfeited was aiding and assisting the
enemy. If it had been established to the jury that such
inquisition was made, and that the plaintiff had never traversed
it or taken any means to procure a reversal of it, but apparently seemed to have acquiesced for nearly forty years, I
should have said that it incontestably established that the
plaintiff had abandoned all ownership to the premises in
question and there would be no fact of intention for the jury
to decide. When the owner of real property has committed
such an offence as is here charged, and which has the effect of
forfeiting the property, and he abandons the country and
remains away to avoid personal consequences, I think the
conclusion irrisistible that he abandoned the property to its
fate as well as the country. Should the defendant have
another trial to enable him to shew that to be so ? The
evidence was not a matter over which the defendant could in
any way have or exercise a control, and it could only be
known by search made upon some suggestion that it existed.
So far as the evidence produced at the trial went, it rather
tended to shew that the plaintiff had been acquitted, if tried,
or discharged from any prosecution; and to avoid any further
arrest or charges being substantiated he abandoned the
country, and, as contended for on the part of the defendant,
he so abandoned and discontinued the possession of the property. The value of the evidence proposed to be adduced
may be tested in this way. Suppose the present plaintiff
succeeds and the possession be changed, the defendant, if
under the new ejectment act he is not barred, might bring his
ejectment upon the twenty years previous possession of himself and those through whom he claims, and so the contest

in such suit would be whether the plaintiff had discontinued the possession at the time alleged ; for if he had, then, the time having expired within which to bring an action, that fact is not only a bar to the remedy but under the twenty-seventh section of the act the right is extinguished, and if that were proved the defendant would then succeed in his action.   Whether a recovery since the new ejectment act be a bar to another action has been agitated several times, but never yet formally determined (*a*).   If it should operate as a bar then it affords a strong reason why the defendant should now have the opportunity of establishing that the plaintiff's right is relinquished, and if it should not operate as a bar then it is better that the question of extinguishment of title should be determined before there be a change of possession.   If the bar set up in defence of an action be a bar of the particular remedy the court will not interfere with a verdict unless upon clear grounds of or some strong reason to suppose there may be an injustice to the person against whom the verdict stands ; but if the bar be of a character which extinguishes the right and that extinguishment proceeds from the plaintiff's own *active acts* as distinguished from being merely a passive party, then, I think, the fullest investigation of the case ought to be had before the change of possession takes place.   I view this case in that light, and I think that the evidence proposed to be adduced has the tendency to establish that the plaintiff voluntarily abandoned the property in question in 1813 or 1814, thereby determining himself to discontinue the possession.   For these reasons I think there should be a new trial on payment of costs.

DRAPER, J., concurred.

Rule absolute, on payment of costs.

(*a*) See Clubine v. McMullen, 11 Ul C. R. 250.

SMITH v. McGowan.

Declaration under·5 & 6 Wm. IV., ch. 62.

In support of a claim for work and labor, in an action of assumpsit, the plaintiff produced declarations of witnesses, taken under the Imperial acts 5 & 6 Wm. IV. ch. 62, purporting to be taken before one Alexander Dick, a justice of the peace in Glasgow, and annexed to each declaration was his certificate to that effect, under his hand and seal, The signature of the justice was not authenticated in any way, nor was it proved that he held the office, or that the plaintiff at the time of the declaration made. was a resident of Great Britain or Ireland. These declarations were not transmitted under the seal of the justice, but brought into court by the plaintiff's attorney.

Held that such evidence could not be received.

The court remarked upon the great want of caution apparent in the provi-sions of the statute above mentioned.

ASSUMPSIT for work and labor, and on other common counts.

Pleas, non-assumpsit, payment, and set off.

The report of this case, when before the court on a former occasion, will be found in 11 U. C. R. 399. The court then granted a new-trial on the ground of surprise, in order to enable the defendant to take out a commission, if he should desire to do so. The defendant did not take advantage of this opportunity, and the case went to trial a second time on the same evidence as before. The plaintiff again obtained a verdict, the defendant renewing his objections to the sufficiency of the evidence, and leave was reserved to move for a non-suit.

Read obtained a rule nisi accordingly. He cited Moises v. Thornton, 8 T. R. 307; Collins v. Carnegie, 1 A. & E. 695; Walmsley v. Abbott, 3 B. & C. 218; Barret Navigation Co. v. Shower, 8 Dowl. P. C. 193; Tay. Ev. 9, 1068.

Eccles shewed cause.

The statutes referred to are fully noticed in the judgment.

The application against this verdict turned upon the admissibility of the only evidence which was offered by the plaintiff in support of his demand, which consisted of three papers brought into court by the plaintiff's counsel, not returned close under what purported to be the signature or seal of any official or other person, but brought before the court open, as any documents would be of an ordinary kind in the course of a trial and advanced by the plaintiff's counsel in proof of his demand, without any proof given, other than what was stated on the face of the papers themselves, in regard to the occasion or manner of the declaration contained in each paper respectively being made, or in regard to the fact of its being made, or the identity and official character of the person by whose signature the declaration was verified as having been made before him by the declarant.

These papers were all entitled—

" In the Queen's Bench,
         Between Daniel Smith, Plaintiff,
                 and
         Quentin McGowan, Defendant,"

without any mention of Canada, or any county in Canada, or anything on the face of the paper to denote that the "Queen's Bench" referred to, was a court in Canada, or that the paper had any connection with, or reference to, any cause or matter depending in any court in Canada.

They purported respectively to be the declarations merely (not on oath) of Thomas Smith, William Manford and Edward Buchanan—that of Thomas Smith beginning, like the others, as follows :—"I, Thomas Smith, of the city of Glasgow, in that part of the United Kingdom of Great Britain and Ireland called Scotland, plasterer, do solemnly and sincerely declare that I was in the employment of the above named plaintiff when he executed certain work for the above named defendant," &c., and then proceeding to state what the declarant knew revelant to a demand of the plaintiff against the defendant for work done for the defendant upon a certain house in the city of Glasgow.

The parties making these several declarations, all stated in them their places of residence in Scotland at the time of the transactions which they spoke of, and also at the time of their making the declarations ; and each stated also his proper addition.

They shewed also by the statements contained in them that the plaintiff and defendant were both in Glasgow at the time of the transactions spoken of, which was in the year 1847, but it was not stated where either party was resident at the time of making the declaration. Each declarant concluded his declaration in the following words :—" And I make this

solemn declaration conscientiously believing the same to be
true, and by virtue of the provisions of an act made and
passed in the sixth year of the reign of his late Majesty,
King William the Fourth, entitled ·an act to repeal an act
of the present session of parliament, entitled, an act for the
more effectual abolition of oaths and affirmations taken and
made in various departments of the state, and to substitute
declarations in lieu thereof, and for the more entire suppres-
sion of voluntary and extra-judicial oaths and affidavits, and to
make other provision for the abolition of unnecessary oaths."

In the place ordinarily occupied by the *jurat* of an affidavit the following words were written :

· "Solemnly declared and subscribed by the said Thomas
Smith, at the city of Glasgow, in the county of Lanark, in
Great Britain aforesaid, this twelfth day of May, one
thousand eight hundred and fifty-three, before me.
                        (Signed)   "ALEX. DICK, J. P."

And annexed to each declaration was the following certificate :

Glasgow, to wit : . } To all to whom these presents shall
come, I, Alexander Dick, Esquire, one
of her Majesty's Justices of the Peace for the county of
Lanark and city of Glasgow, in that part of the United Kingdom of Great Britain and Ireland called Scotland, *send
greeting*, and in pursuance of an act of Parliament, &c.,
(reciting the act by its title), do hereby certify and make
known, that on the day of the date hereof personally came
before me Thomas Smith, of the city of Glasgow aforesaid,
plasterer, a person well known and worthy of credit, and did,
by solemn declaration which he made before me, solemnly
declare to be true the several matters and things related to
and contained in the declaration hereto annexed.

In faith and testimony whereof, I have hereunto set my
hand and seal at Glasgow aforesaid, this 12th day of May,
1853.
                        (Signed)
[L.S.]   ALEX. DICK, J. P."

Each declaration was subscribed by the declarant.

ROBINSON, J.—The British statute 5 Geo. II., ch. 7, to
which the late act 5 & 6 Wm. IV. ch. 62 refers, contained a
provision (sec. 1) to this effect—that in any action or suit in

any court of law or equity in any of the British plantations in America, *for or relating to any debt or account,* wherein any person residing in Great Britain shall be a party, it shall be lawful for the plaintiff or defendant, and for any witness to be examined in such action or suit, to give his evidence *by affidavit in writing upon oath,* or by affirmation, if a Quaker, made before the *mayor or other chief magistrate of the city, borough, or town corporate, in Great Britain,* in or near which the person so making affidavit or affirmation shall reside, *and certified and transmitted under the common seal* of such city, borough, or town, or *the seal of office* of such mayor or other chief magistrate. And that every affidavit or affirmation so made, *certified and transmitted,* should in all actions and suits be of the same force or effect as if the person making the same had appeared and sworn or affirmed the same matter *vivâ voce* in open court, or upon a commission issued for the examination of witnesses, or of any party, in any such action or suit.

It was provided that the addition of the party making such affidavit, &c., and the particular place of his abode, should be set forth in the affidavit.

And any person making wilful or false statements in any such affidavit, &c., was made liable to the same punishment as persons convicted for perjury.

This statute had continued in force more than a hundred years unaltered, until its provisions were extended by the 5 & 6 Wm. IV. ch. 62; and British creditors had availed themselves in some cases, not in many, of the facilities which it afforded for recovering their debts in the courts of Upper Canada. It will be observed—

1st. That this method of proof was confined by that statute to actions brought for or relating to any *debt or account.*

2ndly. That the evidence was to be given on oath, or in the case of Quakers upon their affirmation.

3rdly. That the oath or affirmation must have been made before the mayor or chief magistrate of some city or corporate town in Great Britain, in or near which the party making the affidavit resided.

4thly. And that affidavit, &c., must have been certified and transmitted under the common seal of office of such Mayor or other chief magistrate.

In 5 & 6 Wm. IV. (1835) an act was passed in England (chap. 62) providing for the abolition of unnecessary oaths, and there is strong evidence upon the fact of the act (sec. 7), that as it was originally framed it was not meant to extend to evidence to be given in the course of any judicial proceeding in any court of justice. It passed, however, with the following clauses :—

Sec. 15. "And whereas an act was passed in the fifth year of the reign of His late Majesty King George the Second, intituled &c., (5 Geo. II., chap. 7,) and whereas it is expedient that in future a declaration should be substituted in lieu of the affidavit on oath authorised and required by the said recited act : be it therefore enacted, that from and after the commencement of this act, in any action or suit then depending, or thereafter to be brought, or intended to be brought in any court of law or equity, within any of the territories, plantations, colonies, or dependencies, abroad, being within any part of His Majesty's dominions, for or relating to any debt or account, wherein any person residing in Great Britain and Ireland shall be a party, *or for or relating to any lands, tenements, or hereditaments, or other property, situate, lying, and being in the said places respectively,* it shall and may be lawful to and for the plaintiff or defendant, and also to and for any witness to be examined or made use of in such action or suit, to verify or prove any matter or thing relating thereto, *by solemn declaration or declarations in writing,* in the form in the schedule hereunto annexed, *made before any justice of the peace,* notary public, or other officer now by law authorised to administer an oath, and certfied and transmitted under the signature and seal of *any such justice* or notary public duly admitted and practising, or other officer : which declaration, and every declaration relative to such matter or thing as aforesaid, *in any foreign kingdom or state,* or to the voyage of any ship or vessel, every such justice of the peace, notary public or other officer, shall be and he is hereby authorized and empowered to administer or receive."

"And every declaration so made, *certified and transmitted,* shall in all such actions and suits be allowed to be of the same force and effect as if the person or persons making the same had appeared and sworn or affirmed the matters contained in such declaration *vivâ voce* in open court or upon a commission issued for the examination of witnesses, or of any party in such action or suit respectively ; provided that in every such declaration there shall be expressed the addition of the party making such declaration, and the particular place of his or her abode."

The 17th clause extends the privilege (as 5 Geo. II, ch. 7, had done) to cases in which the Crown shall sue in the colonies for any debt, &c.

The 20th clause enacts that in all cases where a declaration in lieu of an oath shall have been substituted by this act, or by virtue of any power or authority hereby given, such declaration shall be in the form prescribed in the schedule hereto annexed, which form runs thus, " I, A. B. do solemnly and sincerely declare that ————; and I make this solemn declaration conscientiously believing the same to be true, and by virtue of the provisions of an act made and passed in the &c., intituled" &c.

The 21st clause is : "And be it further enacted, that in any case where a declaration is substituted for an oath under the authority of this act, or by virtue of any power or authority hereby given, any person who shall wilfully and corruptly make and subscribe any such declaration, knowing the same to be untrue in any material particular, shall be deemed guilty of a misdemeanor."

At the time of passing the statute 5 Geo. II, chap. 7, it must have seemed a strong measure for the Legislature to take in favor of the British creditor to allow him to prove his debt in a colonial court by an affidavit taken in Great Britain, without notice to the defendant of the intention to take such an affidavit—without any opportunity for him to be present and cross-examine the witness or party, and without any precaution being taken to secure to him by the statute an opportunity of procuring the testimony of witnesses on his behalf, either upon affidavit in the same manner, or upon commission, before the cause of action should be finally established against him by judgment of the court; but strong reasons could be urged in favor of some such measure, from the delay and expense, and even danger, which at that time attended the intercourse by sea between Great Britain and the American colonies.

. Now, however, when circumstances are in this respect so totally changed, that by the aid of steam the intercourse between these colonies and Great Britain is carried on with much more ease, regularity, and safety, and even with more expedition than used to attend the intercourse between one colony and another in America, or even between portions of the same colony that were distant from each other, it does seem remarkable that it could have been thought necessary or prudent to carry the facilities afforded by the 5 Geo. II. so much further; in other words, to sanction so much wider a departure from what has been always hitherto considered the only safe course of administering justice. I feel myself compelled to add an expression of surprise that it could have been thought just to do so.

When I refer to the ordinary course of administering justice as that which had been hitherto considered the only safe one— namely, the establishing facts by evidence on oath given in presence of the party against whom it is to be used, or his attorney, with fair opportunity to cross-examine the witness— I do not mean to say that there is on the face of the new statute any appearance of Parliament having changed its opinion in regard to the propriety in general, of that course; on the contrary, in the 7th section of this same statute it is expressly enacted, "that nothing in that act contained shall extend or apply to any oath, solemn affirmation or affidavit which now is, or hereafter may be made or taken, or be required to be made or taken, in any judicial proceeding in any court of justice, or in any proceeding for or by way of summary conviction before any justice or justices of the peace, but all such oaths, affirmations and affidavits, *shall continue to be required,* and to be administered, taken and made as well and in the same manner as if this act had not been passed." But notwithstanding this ' section of the statute, the provision has been made respecting the colonies which I have recited, sanctioning the reception of evidence there which has not been given under the solemnity of an oath, or indeed any such solemn obligation as there is reason to believe the person giving the evidence would feel to be equivalent to an oath, and it is further remarkable that the effect of this statute is not confined to the substituting a mere declaration of a witness instead of an oath in those cases in which under the 5 Geo. II., chap. 7, the affidavit of a party or a witness was admissible—namely, in proceedings for the collection of debts, due to British creditors; but the same declaration of a witness not on oath is made admissible as evidence in any action or suit brought or intended to be brought in any colonial court of law or equity for or relating to any lands, tenements, or hereditaments, or other property situated in such colony, so that a man's title to real estate in this colony, of the greatest value is liable to be determined upon evidence not given under the obligation of an oath. It is even left subject to some doubt by the language used in this part of the statute whether the admission of evidence of this unsatisfactory description is confined, in suits which regard lands *or other real property*, to those cases in which any person residing in Great Britain *or* Ireland (or, as the statute is inaccurately expressed, in Great Britain *and* Ireland) shall be a party.

I do not know what may have moved the Imperial Legislatnre to so great an extension of the enactments contained in the 5 Geo. II., granting this facility now for the first time in all actions for or relating to any lands or tenements; and indeed I am not sure that we could confine the construction to suits respecting real property, for the words are, "*or other property* situate and being in the said places pespectively," which are large enough to embrace actions respecting personal property of every description. It may be doubted whether the statute was intended to be so comprehensive and yet we may suppose that if the Parliament were willing to subject the right to real estate to be adjudicated upon evidence not given under oath, they would very probably not hesitate to deal in the same manner with rights to personal property.

Whatever may have been intended in this respect, the statute bears marks of these provisions not having been very carefully and deliberately framed; and when we consider this double relaxation from former law and practice, of admitting, in the first place, in an additional and most important class of cases, the reception of evidence which has been given not *vivâ voce* in open court, but *ex parte* in the absence of the party against whom it is to be used, and without his having an opportunity to cross-examine; and in the next place, of admitting as evidence in all the cases to which the 5 Geo. II., ch 7, or this new statute extends, the mere statements of parties, not delivered under the solemnity of an oath, it does seem singular that so much wider a departure from the law of evidence should have been for the first time permitted after the improved intercourse between Great Britain and her colonies has rendered the obtaining of evidence in Great Britain or Ireland upon interrogarities administered in the regular manner under a commission, so easy a proceeding that it is constantly resorted to and even in cases where the parties might, if they had pleased, have availed themselves of the course open to them under the 5 Geo. II., chap. 7.

That there was no very pressing necessity for such a measure whatever may have been represented at the time, seems very strongly proved by the fact, that though it is nineteen years since the act was passed, this is the first time we have known it to have been made use of in any suit in Upper Canada; but at the same time we must consider, that whenever the provisions of this act are made use of as, in the present case, the suitor whose rights are attempted to be affected by testimony not given under the obligation of an oath, and by a witness whom he has had no opportunity to cross-examine, will not be reconciled to an enactment which must appear to him to be unprecedented and unjust, by being told that it has been resorted to in so very few instances.

This may seem to shew that the enactment might without

difficulty be dispensed with, but it does not mitigate its effect in any instance in which it may come to be applied.

When I speak of the provision in question as one that must appear to be imprudent and unjust, I must remark, in the first place, that the Legislature it which passed seems in a measure to have admitted this by the very careful manner in which they have excluded the operation of the change from any judicial proceedings in Great Britain or Ireland, leaving it to apply, under the 15th clause, to the colonies only—

And, in the next place, upon the reason of the thing it must be plain to every man that the dispensing with evidence on oath in judicial proceedings is an imprudent measure, and one that may operate very unjustly. The statute, as I have already remarked, appears, from the terms in which it stands at present, to have been at first introduced chiefly if not entirely with a view of abrogating oaths of office, and some other oaths not affecting judicial proceedings, such as what are commonly called custom house oaths. In regard to oaths of the latter class, it can hardly be said that there were of no value, as a general rule, though no doubt in many cases they afforded no security in truth. People who were long in the habit of taking them repeatedly might in time become so hardened as to be indifferent to their obligation, at least many might, but certainly not all; and in regard to persons not so hackneyed in their use, we cannot doubt that as a general rule they would be found more scrupulous in regard to facts which they were solemnly swearing to, than they might be in regard to statements not made on oath. In every case where this would be the case something has been lost by dispensing with the oath. But this is a consideration which affects only the interests of the community at large; no private individual has his rights and property endangered by it; and though the revenue may suffer, yet that is an inconvenience which Parliament may well be allowed to judge of, and if they are content to incur the risk of it nothing need be said. With regard to mere oaths of office, it is probable that they never formed any important security, and that little or nothing has been lost by abolishing them; for after a time the impression which such an oath may have made at first is commonly effaced; the oath is forgotten, and the officer is influenced in the discharge of his duty, not by an oath of office which he took years before, but by his character and habits, or by the sense of the legal liability which he must incur by malversation or neglect.

But in regard to the evidence to a jury who are to determine between one man's claim and another's it is surely most important that all possible means should be taken for getting at the truth; and I think any man who has had much experience of what passes in courts of justice must have looked round him to very little purpose, if he believes of men in general that they would take a false oath with as little scruple as they would make an untrue statement without oath. The obligation of an oath administered at the time the statement is given, is unquestionably a very great security.

It is not the proper business of courts of justice to find fault with what the Legislature has done, though we often find them expressing themselves strongly upon the incautiousness of particular enactments.

I have two reasons for saying what I have said in regard to those now in question. In the first place, it seems desirable that attention should be called to the propriety of interceding for a reconsideration of the provision contained in the 15th clause, for it is very certain that there will be indisposition found in Parliament to remove any impediment to the due course of justice which they may have unintentionally sanctioned; and in the next place, I have this reason for speaking of the operation of this statute—that the more hardly and unjustly it may operate, the more it must be felt to the incumbent upon us to observe all due caution for protecting suitors in the manner of carrying its provisions into effect.

When this case was before us after the first trial (11 U. C. R. 399) the defendant's counsel made objections to the reception of the declarations purporting to be taken in Scotland, which formed upon that trial, as they did upon the last, all the evidence in support of the plaintiff's demand, except that upon the first trial the declaration of the plaintiff himself, taken in the same manner, was given to the jury, which was not done upon the last trial.

Without determining then, whether the exceptions taken were entitled to prevail, we thought it right at least to accede to the plaintiff's application for a new trial on the ground of surprise (reserving the question of costs until the final result,) in order that the defendant might have the opportunity of examining the plaintiff's witnesses in Scotland upon oath, under a commission, if he desired to do so, and also of examining in like manner, and upon due notice to the plaintiff, any witness whom he might choose to call in his defence.

The defendant, being referred to by his attorney, has made no use of this opportunity, but has declined suing out any commission, and the plaintiff upon the production of the statements of his witness in court, not otherwise authenticated than they were upon the first trial, has obtained a verdict for the amount of his claim £118, 4s. 9d., subject to our opinion upon the objections taken to the reception of his evidence.

The defendant's declining to sue out any commission may probably be owing to his consciousness that the debt is justly due by him, and is incapable of being disproved. We had no impression to the contrary when the case was last before us, but our judgment upon the legal questions raised cannot be influenced one way or the other by any thing that we may believe on that point; and whatever we determine in this case will lay down a rule binding upon ourselves at least in other cases, so that we can only attend to the legal considerations which the questions present.

It has been objected, 1st, that the statute 5 & 6 Wm. IV., chap. 62, cannot be admitted to have any force in this province.

2ndly. That if it can, yet the declarations were inadmissible, because they were not authenticated as the law requires.

3rdly. That it was indispensable, at any rate to the admission of the declarations, that it should be proved by evidence given to the court *aliunde* that the plaintiff was at the time of the declarations taken resident in Scotland, and so was a person entitled to use the privilege given by this act.

Upon the first point we see no ground for argument, for the objection goes the length of denying the power of the Imperial Parliament to bind the colonies by a measure of this description. The statute in question is a late statute, passed long after the power was given to us to legislate for ourselves, and it cannot therefore be contended with respect to it, as it has been, though I think without ground, in respect to the 5 Geo. II. chap. 7, that it was virtually repealed by the 31 Geo. III. chap. 31, giving a Legislature to Upper Canada with power to make laws for the good government and welfare of the province, and by the course of legislation which has taken place under this latter statute.

As to the second point, that the declarations given in evidence were not so authenticated as to make them admissible, it is quite true that they were in fact not authenticated at all. As we observed when this case was last before us, there was no proof given that there is or was such a gentleman in existence as Mr. Alexander Dick, whose name is subscribed to them as the name of the person before whom they were made, or that he was a justice of the peace, or had power to administer an oath, without which he could have no authority under the statute to receive such a declaration, or that the signature was his, or the seal. There was in fact nothing to give the court any assurance that the papers were not all written in this province the day before they were produced in court.

Whether they could be so received is the question. We have always allowed that the protest by a foreign notary of a bill or note, under his hand and seal of office, proves itself; that is, that we may recognize the seal without proof of its authenticity. There is abundant authority for that; courts in England have done so from the earliest time, and for the reason given by Lord Holt (12 Mod. 345,) that to require proof that there was a notary, and that the seal produced was his seal, "would destroy commerce and public transactions of this nature."

In the case of witnesses examined in causes in our courts upon interrogatories under a commission, we have been always in the habit of receiving the depositions without proof of the signature of the deponent or of the commissioner certifying the examinations: and this although our statute contains no such provision as there is in the English statute 1 Wm. IV., chap. 22, sec. 10, "that the deposition certified under the hand of the commissioners may, without proof of the signature to such certificate, be received and read in evidence saving all just exceptions." Our statute 2 Geo. IV., chap. 1, sec. 18, requires that the commission, with the examinations taken under it, shall be returned to the court with an affidavit of the due taking annexed, sworn before and certified by the mayor or chief magistrate of the city or place where the same shall be taken close under the hands and seals of the commissioners; and that, being so returned, it shall be taken *prima facie* to have been duly executed and returned, and shall be received as evidence in the cause, provided that it cannot be received in evidence if the deponent shall be living within the jurisdiction of the court at the time and be of sound mind; and provided it be made to appear to the court that the examinations have not been duly taken.

Under this enactment we have received the depositions without other proof than the production of the certificate purporting to be under the seal of the mayor or chief magistrate. I refer to the case of Doe dem. Lemoine v. Raymond 5 O. S. 337); though indeed the practice had become established long before our time, under the King's Bench Act of 1794. Reason is in favour of such a course; for otherwise, after great trouble and expense in executing a commission, and upon due notice of it by both parties, all the trouble and expense might be thrown away in consequence of exceptions raised to the proof of authenticity, and this by a party who had either been concurring in taking the evidence or had declined doing so. It would in most cases be found impossible when the commission had been executed in a distant country to produce a witness in court who could speak from his own knowledge of the genuineness of the seal of a corporate town, or of the signature of its chief magistrate.

The Legislature by requiring such a seal seem to have intended, and indeed I have no doubt they did, that it should prove itself upon production, and be accepted as evidence of the office and signature of the person whose name is subscribed to the certificate; and the provision in the statute (2 Geo. IV. chap. 1, sec. 18,) that the depositions shall not be received, if it shall be made appear to the court that they have not been duly taken, seems to import that the certificate is to be deemed authenticated till it has been discredited.

At any rate whether any or all of these arguments in favor of the practice be satisfactory or not, we have gladly conformed to it as we found it established, being satisfied that it was safe as well as convenient; and it only places the reception of evidence so taken on the footing that it has been thought not imprudent to place it on by express statute in England.

What comes nearer, however, to the present case is the practice in regard to affidavits which have been sent from England and used in courts under the authority of 5 Geo. II., chap. 7, for there has been in such cases as in this case, no previous commission, and in general no suit previously pending, no notice to the opposite party, and no opportunity to cross-examine. Yet no doubt it has been the course here to receive the affidavit when certified as that act directs; that is, when certified and *transmitted* under the seal of the city, borough or town corporate, or the *seal of office* of the mayor or chief magistrate, which seal we have received as genuine without its being verified by proof given in court. It has not been required that the party producing the affidavit should be prepared with the evidence of a witness to be examined *vivâ voce*, who could prove the seal to be in fact what it purported to be. So far undoubtedly the practice has been carried, and I am not aware that the course has been at any time disapproved of by the court.

But now we are desired to go a step farther and to recognize the signature and seal, or at least the seal of a justice of the peace—that is, his private seal, for we have no ground for supposing that he has any official seal; and to treat a paper brought into court purporting to be signed by an individual of whom we know nothing, as being actually signed and sealed and transmitted by him. We are desired also to assume, without any proof whatever of the fact, that the plaintiff on whose behalf the declarations are offered in evidence, was at the time of their being taken resident in Great Britain or Ireland, or, as the statute says, in Great Britain *and* Ireland, for the total absence of evidence to that effect constitutes the third objection which has been taken to the reception of the evidence.

The statute itself, 5 & 6 Wm. IV., chap. 62, contains no provision whatever on the subject of the proof that shall be given, or that may be dispensed with, in regard to the fact of the declaration having been made before a person legally authorized to take it, and under such circumstances as would entitle the party to avail himself of the act. Our late statute 13 & 14 Vic., chap. 19, for facilitating the admission of evidence of foreign judgments, and certain official and other documents, contains nothing that can apply to this case; neither in the late Imperial act, called the "Documentary Evidence Act," 8 & 9 Vic. chap. 113, is the relaxation carried far enough to meet this case, if its provisions were in force here, for this is no public official document remaining in charge of any officer whose certificate is required for proving a copy. The plaintiff's attorney comes into court, and produces a paper having no corporate or official seal of any kind annexed to it, and not being transmitted under any such seal, and requires us to assume that there is such a person in existence as Alexander Dick, that he is a justice of the peace in Glasgow, and that what the attorney shews us is his signature and seal; that he took the declaration to which his name is attached as verifying it, and that when he took it the plaintiff, Smith, was resident in Scotland or somewhere in Great Britain or Ireland.

All this we are asked, without any legislative warrant, to take for granted without any evidence whatever, merely because the party who is directly interested in recovering upon such declarations as evidence brings into court by his attorney papers containing the name *"Alexander Dick,* J.P.," subscribed to them.

We are of opinion that we cannot, in the absence of any thing but what appears on the face of a document not even purporting to be *transmitted* under any corporate or public seal, assume all these things, or any of them.

We may adhere to all that has been determined or practised in regard to affidavits transmitted under the 5 Geo. II., chap. 7, but the authority of such decisions or practice does not go the length of warranting us in receiving without proof such documents as these; and we think we should do wrong if we were to go one step beyond what express authority or a long course of practice has warranted, in order to admit a declaration not on oath as evidence to bind the rights of parties by establishing the cause of action sued upon.

If we should admit such evidence in this case, we must on the same principle do so in all others coming within the act and a man may be deprived of his estate by the mere production of a declaration not on oath respecting the execution of a deed or will, or a descent in cases of intestacy, without opportunity of cross examination, and without its being shewn that if there is such a person as the plaintiff in existence he was resident in Great Britain or Ireland, and while the whole writing from first to last may have been fabricated, signatures and all, a few hours before it was advanced in evidence. We think parties are entitled by law to be better protected against fraud and injustice than they would be by such a course.

I do not recollect whether in cases where affidavits were produced in court for proving a declaration under 5 Geo. II., chap. 7, (which cases have occurred very seldom and at distant intervals) it has been proved by evidence *aliunde* that the party in whose behalf the affidavit was taken was at the time a resident in Great Britain, or whether the question of the necessity of such proof has been ever raised.

There is, however,, this difference between these cases and the present, that in the former the fact of such residence would be stated on oath on the face of the affidavit, and so would appear to have been sworn to according to the certificate of a public officer, attested by such a seal as we may suppose the legislature intended we should recognize; whereas in the present case, even if we should recognize the justice's seal without proof, it is very clear on the face of the document that the residence of this. plaintiff in Scotland has never been sworn to at all, but is only stated in a declaration not on oath, which declaration we are at the most only permitted to receive as evidence of any matter or thing relating to " *the action or suit.*"

It is worthy of remark, as shewing the hasty manner in which the fifteenth clause seems to have been framed, that it does not, as the 5 Geo. II. did, require the witness to go before the proper public authority of the city or town in or near which he shall be residing; but, for all that is said in the statute, he may be living in any part of Great Britain or Ireland, and may go before any justice or other person authorized to administer an oath in any other part of Great Britain or Ireland : and the latter part of the clause in which the words "in any foreign kingdom or state" are used, seem to me to be quite unintelligible.

DRAPER, J.—I entirely concur in the judgment just pro-anounced ; nor do I desire to weaken by further observations the effect of the temperate but clear and decided manner in which the objections to the statute have been pointed out. One is almost driven to suppose that some theorist who wished to abolish all oaths in all proceedings, finding no support for the application of his ideas in the mother country, (for the statute most carefully guards against their introduction into any of the courts of justice at home,) had obtained their concurrence to try the effect in the colonies, quoting, no doubt, *"Fiat experimentum in corpore vili."* Or, if we can imagine such influence ever to creep into and effect so august a body as the House of Commons, it might be imagined that some attorney, being or desiring to become an agent for colonial suits, had devised this scheme of getting up his cases without requiring any sworn evidence, and without subjecting his witness to cross-examination. In any point of view, the enactment is at variance with the rights of self-government possessed by the North American provinces, and I sincerely hope may be repealed.

BURNS, J., concurred.   Rule absolute.

IN RE HENDERSON V. MCMAHON.

Plaintiff's name used without authority—Attorney ordered to pay costs.

Where an attorney had made use of the plaintiff's name in a suit without his consent, he was ordered to repay to such plaintiff the costs which he had been obliged to pay to the defendant on failure of the suit.

Nanton moved that James Boulton, Esquire, an attorney of this court, be ordered to pay £17 1s. 8d., being the amount of costs paid by the said J. Henderson (the plaintiff), and taxed to the defendant, and which the said J. Henderson had been obliged to pay—the said attorney having commenced and carried on this suit without the authority, knowledge, or consent of the said James Henderson.

This application was founded on an affiadavit of James Henderson (whose name was used in this action as plaintiff) to the effect that this suit had been carried on without his knowledge or consent by Mr. Boulton, the attorney :—that before the process had issued, as he believed, Mr. Boulton applied to him for permission to use his name, in order to put on record a will of the late Edward McMahon (under which the defendant claimed) representing to the deponent, that he, the deponent, was a trustee under the will for the property for which this action had been brought :—that the deponent thereupon informed Mr. Boulton that his name had been inserted in the will without his consent, and that he had refused to have anything to do with the will, and would not claim or assert any right under the same :—that he heard no more of the will or the property, until he was informed, to his surprise, that a suit brought in his name by Mr. Boulton as attorney, but for the benefit of some person unknown to the deponent, had been decided against the plaintiff :—that some time after the trial he was informed by the sheriff that he had in his hands an execution against the dependent's goods :—that he thereupon applied to an attorney to take steps to protect him against the demand, and was told that £25 had been paid on account of the said costs, and that it was believed the balance would soon be paid :—that he was nevertheless required afterwards to pay the sum remaining due on the execution, and did so on the 16th of August last, being £17 1s. 8d.

On shewing cause, Mr. Boulton filed an affidavit made by himself that he was employed by the legatees of Edward McMahon to prosecute this action which had to be done in the name of the trustees or one of them, under the will, of whom the plaintiff Henderson was one :—that before bringing the action he called on Henderson to sign a memorial for getting the will registered, but he declined doing so, or acting in any way under the will :—that he did not request Henderson's consent to bring this action, but told him that it must be brought in his name, or that of the other trustees, and that he had instructions to do so :—that he proceeded with the action in good faith, under instructions from a Dr. McMahon, (an uncle of the defendant) one of the legatees in the will:— that the action was brought for the last autumn assizes, but on account of the absence of a witness the trial was postponed:— that the costs of the day were moved for in Hilary Term, and were paid by Dr. McMahon :—that if any demand had been made (by Henderson) on Dr. McMahon for security, it would have been given, but no such demand being made, and the plaintiff (Henderson) knowing as he did that the suit was going on in his name, he, Mr. Boulton, supposed he did not intend to object to it :—that Dr. McMahon, who lives in this province, is perfectly responsible, as he believes, to the amount of this balance of costs, and that he, Mr. Boulton, expected him to pay it this term.

M. C. Cameron shewed cause.

Nanton, in support of the rule, cited Doe dem. Thwaites v. Roe, 3 D. & R. 226 ; Doe dem. Davies v. Eyton, 3 B. & Ad. 785 ; Hubbart v. Phillips, 13 M. & W. 702.

ROBINSON C. J.—If there were any doubts as to the facts of the case it would be proper to leave the plaintiff to his action against the attorney, who had used his name, as he swears, without his authority ; but taking the case upon the attorney's own statement, and looking at the smallness of the sum in question, we think we shall best exercise our discretion in making the order desired, having no doubt of our authority to do so in a perfectly plain case.

Mr. Henderson swears positively that he knew nothing of

the proceeding, till he heard that a suit brought in his name had been decided against the plaintiff.

Mr. Boulton does not assert or pretend that after he had received a distinct refusal from Mr. Henderson to take any part in the matter he ever even asked him to consent to become plaintiff or informed him that he would take or had taken the liberty to make him a plaintiff without his consent, but admits that he used his name when he had every reason to be satisfied that Mr. Henderson would not have consented. All that can be said is, that when Mr. Henderson learned the fact after the trial, he might have applied to stay further proceedings, but that was after all the expense of the action had been incurred, and Mr. Boulton has no ground of complaint that he did not apply sooner.

DRAPER, J., referred to Hambidge v. De La Crouee, 3 C. B. 742 ; Hoskins v. Phillips. 16 L. J., Q. B,, 339.

Order granted.

STEPHENSON V. GREEN.

Bankruptcy and Insolvent Debtors' Acts, 7 Vic., ch. 10 ; 8 Vic., ch. 48—Con-stuction of.

Quœre—Whether a person having failed before the passing of the Bankruptcy Act, but continuing a trader, and unable to meet his engagements, after that act had come into force, and being therefore in a position to avail himself of its provisions, could, notwithstanding, take advantage of the Insolvent Debtors' Act. *Semble*, Per *Draper* and *Burns, JJ.*, that he could not. Per *Robinson, C.J.*, that he could :

But *held*, that a final order obtained under the above circumstances was conclusive and not to be questioned in an action brought for a debt barred by it.

This case was before the court on demurrer in Michaelmas term last, and a report of the decision then given will be found in 11 U. C. R. 452.

The pleas of the defendant had since been amended by inserting what was determined upon that occasion to be a necessary averment—namely, that the debts upon which the defendant is sued in this action were included in the scedule annexed to the defendant's petition, presented under the Insolvent Debtors Act, 8 Vic., ch. 48.

The plaintiff replied in the same terms to each of the pleas, setting up, as an answer to the defence under the final order, that though it is true, as the pleas assert, that the defendant had failed in business as a trader before the Bankrupt Act (7 Vic., ch. 10) was passed, yet that after the passing of that act, and while it was in force, and before the defendant had presented his petition, he had been and was a trader (to wit, a merchant), within the meaning of that act, which was still in force when he presented his petition, and when the order thereon was made ; that he owed debts to a larger amount than £100 when he presented his petition, and was then, and at the time of making the final order, entitled as a trader to the benefit and protection of the statute so in force relating to bankrupts, and was not in any manner excluded therefrom.

The defendant demurred.·

Richards for the demurrer. *Kirkpatrick*, Q. C., contra. Leaf v. Robson, 13 M. & W. 651 ; March v. Alexander, 10 U. C. R. 435 ; were referred to. See also the cases cited on the former argument.

ROBINSON, C. J.—These replications bring up two questions :—

1st. Was the defendant, upon what is shewn in the replication, in a condition to avail himself of the bankrupt law when he petitioned to have the benefit of the insolvent act.

2ndly. If he was, is that sufficient, under the terms of the insolvent act, to shew that he could not legally have the benefit of the insolvent act, although the defendant had shewn by his pleas that he came expressly within one of the classes of persons to whom the benefit of the insolvent act as in terms extended by the first clause of that statute.

And there is yet a third question, I think, which calls for consideration ; and that is, whether the final order pleaded must not be allowed in this action to be a bar, so long as it has not been rescinded by the tribunal which granted it.

It happens that one of my learned brothers presiding in this court was concerned in passing the two acts upon which this demurrer turns, and that the other of my learned brothers has had some years' experience in administering their provisions in the bankruptcy and insolvency courts, and they both, I believe, concur in the opinion, that what the plaintiff has set forth in his replication does clearly shew, that the defendant was not in fact in a position to take the benefit of the act for the relief of insolvent debtors, because at the time he made his application and obtained his certificate, he was in a condition to avail himself of the bankruptcy act then in force. If my brothers are of that opinion, and should also think that we can on that account refuse to give effect to the final order, their opinion will of course dispose to the demurrer in this plaintiff's favor, and I dare say rightly, though I confess I have not been able to take the same view of the effect of the statutes.

If the legislature had given particular attention to the question, whether any person 'who could, under the 15th clause of 7 Vic., ch. 10, bring himself within the provisions of that statute by filing a declaration of insolvency, should be allowed to take the benefit of the insolvency act instead, I think it probable they would have resolved that he should not, and that they would have so framed the latter act as to shew that to be their intention. But what they have done is this:—In the next year after they had passed the bankruptcy act, and while that was in force, they passed the other act, 8 Vic., ch. 48, for the relief of insolvent debtors, and in the first clause they declare what descriptions of persons may take the benefit of this latter act, viz :—

1st. Any person not being a trader within the meaning of the bankruptcy act.

2nd. Or not having been such trader before the passing of that act.

3rd. Or any person having been a trader before the passing of that act, but excluded from the operation thereof.

4th. Or being such trader, but owing debts amounting in the whole to less than £100.

This defendant, according to the facts set forth in the replication, and not denied, could only have been entitled to take the benefit of the insolvency act as coming under the third head—namely, as having been a trader before the passing of the bankruptcy act, *but excluded from the operation of it.*

By the bankrupt act (sec. 2) all acts called acts of bank-ruptcy, and by reason which a person may under that statute be made a bankrupt, must be such as have taken place *after* the passing of that statute. And the legislature, bearing this in mind, in passing the insolvency act (8 Vic., ch. 48) have treated all traders as *excluded* from the opera-tion of the bankrupt act, *who had, before the passing thereof failed in their business.* The 5th section of the act and the schedules A. 2 and 4, shew this.

The plaintiff avers in his replication that the defendant petitioned upon that footing, and he admits that the defendant's statement of his case in his petition was true so far as he did state it, but he alleges that the defendant did not state his whole case, and he contends, with a strong appearance of reason that if the defendant had done so, he would have shewn that he was not a proper object of the insolvency act, from which he draws the inference that, although he has obtained from the insolvency court a final order of protection, it cannot avail him. It is true, he says, that the defendant, being a trader within the meaning of the bankrupt laws, *had failed before the bankrupt act was passed,* but he avers that he continued to be a trader after that act was passed and while it was in force ; that he owed debts to a larger amount than £100 ; and that, at the time that he petitioned as an insolvent, and obtained his order of protection, he was enti-tled to the benefit of the statute of bankruptcy and was not *excluded fron its operation.* The plaintiff does not pretend that the defendant could have been made a bankrupt on the ground of anything he had done or omitted before the bank-rupt act had passed, nor does he allege that the defendant had committed any act of bankruptcy since ; but I suppose he means to contend, that as he was a trader, and has in his petition admitted himself to be insolvent while the bankrupt act was still in force, it is plain that he could have been made a bankrupt by any creditor proceeding against him under what are called the summoning clauses of the act (7 Vic., ch. 10), or that he could have been made a bankrupt by his filing declaration of insolvency, according to the 15th clause.

We must take that upon the pleadings to have been the

defendant's position and that he was not in fact excluded from the operation of the bankruptcy law, but might have been made a bankrupt under it.

Yet the judge of bankruptcy seems to have considered that he might nevertheless receive protection under the insolvency law, coming literally, as he does, under the explanation given in the act itself of what the legislature meant should exclude a trader from the operation of the bankrupt act because he had *failed before the act was passed*, as his petition stated ; which, according to the 5th clause of the act, and the forms of petition and final order given in the statute, made him a trader entitled to petition under the insolvent act. The judge saw only what appeared in the papers before him no late act of bankruptcy was imputed to the defendant, or is even now imputed to him. The defendant could not compel any creditor to proceed against him under the summoning clauses, and his own petition under the insolvent act was not, as I take it, *ipso facto* any act of bankruptcy with us, though it has been made such in England by an express clause in the statute 1 & 2 Vic., ch. 110, sec. 39.

The judge, therefore, had before him a man, of whom all that he saw was, that he was a trader, but *had failed before the passing* of the bankrupt act, and so came literally under the 5th clause of the act, and was one of the classes of persons prescribed in the forms of petition and the protection order given in the statute 8 Vic., ch. 48. He saw nothing of any act of bankruptcy imputed to him since the bankruptcy act was passed, if that would have disabled him from applying as an insolvent, notwithstanding his having "failed before," and he saw no step taking against him under the bankruptcy act by any creditor We must assume that all things were regularly done which this act directs to be done for giving notice of the defendant's petition; and, for all that appears, no opposition was made to his application for the benefit of the act.

That may not have been known to the judge in bankruptcy, which the plaintiff in his replication has now pleaded in this action—namely, that the defendant continued to be a trader after the bankruptcy act, and while it was in force. If that should have been held fatal to the defendant's application, we should assume it was not disclosed; for till the contrary is shewn we are to presume that the judge made an order which was legal upon the facts that appeared before him, and nothing to the contrary is averred.

But it is now shown to us, in this action, by the plaintiff's replication, that the defendant's position at the time he applied as an insolvent was in fact such as I have stated; that is, he was a trader at that time, not having, for all that even now appears, committed any act of bankruptcy *since the passing of the bankruptcy act,* but nevertheless unable 'to meet his engagements, and so capable of being made a bankrupt if any creditor should chose to take the proper proceeding against him, which would necessarily drive him to an act of bankruptcy.

My brothers, I believe, consider it to be quite clear, that if the judge in bankruptcy had known the defendant's real position, as stated now by this plaintiff, he ought not to have granted him the protection of the insolvent act, but should have left him to abide by the bankrupt act, as the one suited to his case. And that probably is so, though I have had some doubts; for it is true that a defendant proceeding as this defendant has, according to the plaintiff's statement of the case, has obtained an unfair advantage, by being placed, under the fifth clause, is as good a situation as if he had been made a bankrupt in consequence of the effect given to his certificate, and this upon the ground of his being supposed to be excluded from the operation of the bankrupt laws, although a trader, by reason of his failure—that is, his only failure—having taken placed before the statute of bankruptcy was passed, which would prevent him from obtaining the benefit of that act.

Admitting that my brothers are right on this point, still it is to be considered that the defendant has, upon a proper petition, obtained his final order, under the insolvent act, and that the 24th clause of the act provides in positive terms that "if any suit or action be brought against any petitioner for or in respect of any debt contracted before the date of filing his petition, it shall be a sufficient plea in bar of the said suit or action, that such petition was duly presented, and a final order

for protection and distribution made *by a judge or commis-*
sioner duly authorized, whereof the production of the order
signed by the judge, or commissioner, with proof of his
hand-writing, shall be sufficient evidence."

The plaintiff's replication assumes that, notwithstanding
this clause, the final order will be no bar to the action, if
there were facts, although not known to the judge or commissioner, which, being proved in this action, brought against
him to recover a debt that would otherwise be barred by the
final order, would show that the defendant was not in reality
a person entitled to petition as an insolvent debtor.

I do not concur in this. The final order has been granted
by a judge duly authorized to make such an order in cases
under the statute, and it has not been rescinded. In general
such final orders can be rescinded by the judge under the
twenty-sixth clause of the act, but only, perhaps, in case of
such a fraud being shown as is mentioned in that clause; from
whence I draw the conclusion that, except upon proof of such
fraud, the final order must be allowed to stand, which I suppose the legislature considered to be both reasonable and
expedient—considering, on the one hand, the ample provision
made in the act of notice to creditors, and for enabling them
to resist the application, if on any ground they desire to do
so; and considering also, on the other hand, the strange and
most inconvenient state of things that must be produced, if,
after the surrender of all the petitioner's effects, and even
after distribution, and after the rights and interests of other
parties have become involved in the proceeding, as may be
the case under various clauses of the act, the whole could be
unsettled by rescinding the final order. Not, indeed, that
the rescinding it would in itself do more than deprive the
insolvent of that advantage which was the consideration
moving him to the voluntary disclosure and surrender of all his
effects; but if the final order could be rescinded upon the
ground that the judge decided erroneously upon what was
before him, or had decided in ignorance of grounds of objection which no creditor had taken the trouble to raise—in
short, if it could be rescinded upon any other ground than
the fraudulent imposition specified in the twenty-sixth
clause of the statute—then it must be so rescinded upon the

principle that the foundation of the judge's jurisdiction was wanting, and such an objection would go to the whole proceeding. All must be taken upon the same principle to be void, as having been *coram non judice*, and that confusion must follow which I have spoken of. The legislature therefore, have, as I apprehend, determined and directed that the final order shall be final, so far as any authority of the judge in bankruptcy to rescind it is concerned, except in the single case of fraud such as the act specifies.

The final order granted to this defendant, it is true, could not be rescinded under the twenty sixth clause, even on that ground, on account of the exception contained in that clause— namely, that this rescinding power shall not extend to final orders granted to persons who are described in the fifth clause (namely, traders), who could not take advantage of the bankrupt act, only because they had failed before it was passed.

Why they were thus excepted I do not quite understand, except that, as they might have been traders to a large amount, and were intended to be placed on as good a footing as if they had not been excluded from the operation of the bankrupt laws, it seems to have been intended not to leave them at the discretion of the judge of bankruptcy, as regarded their protection, but to place them on as secure a footing, as respects their certificate of discharge, as bankrupts would be under the other act; and in their case, the judge in bankruptcy seems to loose all control over the certificate, after it has been confirmed by the Court of Review. But then I do not see clearly that, in regard to such final order as came under the fifth section, there was any provision for subjecting them to the control of the Court of Review, and if not, they would seem to be absolutely final, except we can allow what the plaintiff in the case before us contends for, that the protection order can be indirectly rescinded by being disallowed in any particular case, when it is pleaded in bar, upon the ground that such a petitioner as the defendant may be shewn to be in that action, even by facts then brought forward for the first time; ought never to have obtained a final order for protection, and therefore that when called immediately in question in a superior court of common law, it must be held void.

2 *p*—VOL. XII. Q. B.

If there were in the Insolvency Act any clauses declaring that, under certain circumstances, the final order should be void, as was enacted in the sixtieth section of our bankruptcy act with respect to certificates of discharge, and as is provided in certain cases in the English bankrupt laws, then I have no doubt the certificate, when set up as a defence to an action in a court of law, would fail of its effect, because otherwise the express enactment that it shall be *void* would be contravened.—Hughes v. Morley (1 B & Al. 22); Wilson v. Kemp (2 M. & S. 549); Archbold's Bankrupt Law, 345. Hughes v. Morley is a case of that kind; but I find no clause in our statute 8 Vic. ch. 48 which provides that the final order shall be *void* under any circumstances, but merely that it may, upon proof of certain frauds, be rescinded by the tribunal which granted it.

These bankruptcy courts are not, like certain inferior jurisdictions, subordinate to the superior common law courts; They have a special jurisdiction to deal with certain subjects; and I conceive, when they have found those facts to exist which gave them jurisdiction, and have adjudicated upon them, they must be taken to have disposed of such cases finally; and we cannot in affect rescind their certificates and final orders by determining incidentally in an action that they are void, because those facts did not exist which they had reason to find did exist, or because facts are for the first time shewn to us in a civil action, which were never shewn to them. In short, upon this point I adhere, after all the consideration I can give to this case, to the opinion expressed by me, when the demurrer to the former plea was before us, which has been since amended (11 U. C. R. 452). I think the Case of Cook v. Henson (1 C. B. 914) fully establishes that we must treat the final order as a bar, notwithstanding what has been set up in this replication.

The 12th clause of the English insolvency act, 5 & 6 Vic. ch. 116, is exactly the same as the 24th clause of our act, giving the commissioner power to rescind his certificate; but only for such fraud as is specified in both the clauses, the kinds of fraud being the same in both. Lord Chief Justice Tindale, therefore, had no more reason to say what he said in that case than we have to say the same in this—namely, that "power is given to the commissioner, in the earlier sections of the act to inquire into the matters of the petition and adjudicate upon them, and make a final order for protection and distribution if he thinks fit to do so ; and it seems to us," his Lordship said, " that it was the intention of the Legislature to make his decision final, and not capable of being controverted in an action ; especially as by the 12th section any creditor or assignee is enabled to petition the commissioner to rescind his final order."

It would be one striking inconvenient effect of allowing the final order to be thus incidentally annulled in a civil action, that the effect could only be partial, and it would remain in force as to other debts, only being liable to be questioned indirectly in each individual case.

It has been urged that the defendant could have no right to protection under the insolvency act, unless he came within some one of the classes of persons who are embraced in the act which no doubt is correct ; and from thence it is argued that if the matters stated in this replication are true, which in arguing this demurrer, we must assume, the defendant rested his claim by his petition solely on the ground of his having been a trader, but *excluded from the operation of the bankrupt act* ; so that the whole foundation of the jurisdiction in his case rested upon the truth of that allegation ; and that when the plaintiff in his replication avers that the defendant was not in fact *excluded from the bankrupt law*, for that he was a trader while the act was in force, he. offers to shew that which strikes at the very root of the jurisdiction exercised in this case by the judge of bankruptcy, and which established to the satisfaction of a jury, must necessarily shew the final order to be void.

But in Cook v. Henson the court drew no distinction between objections which, if substantiated, would shew a want of jurisdiction, and others that might be raised. *Chief Justice Tindal* says the commissioner has power given him to inquire into the matters of the petition and make a final order for protection if he thinks fit. No doubt, as regards the exercise of authority by a limited jurisdiction there is that general principle which is contended for, that unless the judge keeps himself within his jurisdiction, his acts are *coram non judice.* But the broad ground of holding the final order and the certificate in bankruptcy to be final until rescinded, is clearly stated by the court. . It seemed to them, they said, that the Legislature meant to make the judge's decision final and not capable of being controverted in an action. If we see this to be the intention of the Legislature, then of course that ground is strong enough to sustain the final order against the objection raised. I do not indeed see how such a system could be carried out with any convenience or certainty, except in this manner; for if the want of jurisdiction could be shewn by facts first brought forward in a collateral proceeding in another tribunal, and at any distance of time after the insolvent's effects have been surrendered and vested in assignees, the property sold and proceeds distributed, everything would be thrown into confusion.

Let us suppose that in the present case the defendant had petitioned solely on the last ground mentioned in the first clause of the statute—namely the limited amount of debts due by him; and that, instead of stating that he owed debts amounting in the whole to less than £100, he had stated in his petition that he owed debts amounting to £200, and no more, and that, upon that petition and no other, he had obtained an order of protection : there the want of jurisdiction, which ought to have been fatal, would have appeared on the face of the proceeding ; and if, after due notice, no one opposed the proceeding on that ground or any other, and he obtained the order, the question whether, in an action by a creditor against the insolvent debtor, we could hold his protection order void, is one scarcely worth our while to consider, because such a case is never likely to happen. It is almost impossible that any one framing a petition under the statute would make so absurd a blunder, or that, if he did, it would escape the attention of tne judge in the whole course of the proceeding.

But let us suppose that the petitioner had made his statement agree with the act, and had alleged that he owed debts amounting in all to less than £100, then the case would come more nearly to the point before us. After a final order had been duly granted in such a petition, without opposition on the part of any creditor, or without opposition from any quarter on that ground, could we hold the protection void in this court, in an action by a creditor, upon his proving to us that in fact the insolvent owned debts to the amount of £150 ? Or, if this defendant had petitioned on the first ground— namely, that he was not a trader within the bankrupt act; or upon the second ground—which I do not, I must say, understand the reason or meaning of—that he had not been a trader before the passing of the act, and had succeeeded in obtaining his order; could we reverse in effect all that had been done, by holding the final order void upon the ground that it was proved to us, in an action by a creditor, that the petitioner was in fact not entitled to represent what he had represented? I think clearly not, and I cannot distinguish any such case from the present ; for, in all such cases, the creditor would be resisting the effect of the final order in an action upon ground which shewed that in fact the case was not one within the act. We are bound, I think, to say to the plaintiff in any such action, that if facts existed which would have shewn the petitioner to stand on different ground from that which he had represented to the judge in bankruptcy, they should have been brought forward in proper time and before the proper tribunal; that the object of the notice and various provisions in the act was to give to all concerned ample opportunity of disputing the petitioner's case, and to call upon them to do so at the proper time and, in the proper manner; and that, if that has been omitted the judge's order was warranted, and any opposition comes too late.

Upon reflection, too, there is in the present case no strong reason for holding parties concluded by the final order, granted by the proper authority and not rescinded; for, if this defendant had gone into bankruptcy, as the plaintiff insists he should have done, he could have got a certificate having the same operation as is given to the final order by the fifth clause of this act.

In my opinion the defendant is entitled to judgment on this demurrer; his plea being sufficient, and the replication being, as I think, no answer to it; because, under the 24th

clause of the statute, the final order is a legal bar, notwithstanding what is stated in the replication.

DRAPER, J.—I have not very readily arrived at the conclusion just now expressed by his Lordship the Chief Justice.

I have felt two great difficulties in the way. First, that
upon the facts which stand admitted on the demurrer, the
defendant has, I think, clearly obtained a final order in a
character in which he was not entitled to it. Second, that in
the character in which he has so obtained it, he is not subject
to the power conferred by the twenty-sixth section of the act
on the judge to rescind the final order. I must add to these
the further objection, that his obtaining the final order seems
to me, in the first instance at least, the result of his not disclosing his true position as a trader when he petitioned : in
other words, a *suppressio veri* in his petition, though, on the
other hand, this plaintiff, as a creditor named in his schedule,
might have successfully resisted the petition by making the
truth appear.

I must confess that until a very recent period I had been
induced on these grounds to a conclusion in the plaintiff's
favor. And it is only when endeavoring to distinguish this
case on satisfactory grounds from the decision of Cook v.
Henson, and from the operation of the principle on which
that case proceeds—namely, that the decision in matters of
fact of the tribunal having jurisdiction of the question and
power to hear and determine it, must, as long as it is unre-
versed by some competent authority, be final, at all events in
a suit instituted by parties who might have contested it before
the primary jurisdiction—that I have felt this difficulty to be
more insuperable than those which operate to bring about the
conclusion above suggested, and consequently acquiesce in the
conclusion that the defendant must have judgment on this
demurrer.

BURNS, J.—The facts stated in the replications to the
defendant's two pleas raise this question—whether, in any
case where a person has obtained a final order under 8 Vic.,
ch. 48, that order can be attacked otherwise than by an

application to the county judge in a case wherein the jurisdiction to rescind is conferred upon him ; or perhaps, more properly speaking, whether in a case where a debt is sued for, which would be barred by the effect of the order according to its terms, can any extraneous facts be inquired into to shew that in truth the matter of the petition is not true in fact, and thus dispute the jurisdiction of the county judge. I have no doubt, if the facts shew that the matters of the petition were within the jurisdiction of the county judge to grant or refuse the order, then the effect of the statute is to render the final order a complete bar to an action. What is contended for in this case is, that the facts shew the county judge never ought to have had jurisdiction, and consequently that the order made is outside of the judge's authority, and cannot bind this plaintiff.

The twenty-sixth section of the act expressly takes away all jurisdiction from the county judge over an order which he has once made in a case coming under the 5th section. The facts stated on the defendant's petition clearly bring his case under the 5th section, and so far the plaintiff admits the truth of that statement ; but he contends that, because subsequently to the bankrupt act being in operation the defendant was again a trader, and therefore liable or subject to be made a bankrupt, he was not then in a position to take the benefit of the insolvent law, or to fall back upon his position before subsequently again becoming a trader, to enable him to do so. I take it to be clear that the facts as admitted shew that the defendant might have been made a bankrupt, notwithstanding a failure in business previous to the existence of the bankrupt law. The subsequent trading rendered him liable for the time being tô its operation. If he was subject or liable to be made a bankrupt, then could he at the same time present a petition to the insolvent court, and proceed under the provisions of 8 Vic., ch. 48 ? The effect of this statute, I take it, is that of providing for three classes of persons : 1. Persons not *being* traders within the meaning of the bankrupt law, or not having been so before that was passed. 2. Persons having been traders before the bankrupt law was passed, excluded from its operation. And 3. Persons who were traders but owing debts less than £100. This classification leaves persons subject to the bankrupt laws untouched. I do not see that the legislature intended the bankrupt law and the insolvent law to be concurrent remedies; for if they were, there would have been no necessity for the distinctions evidently made. This view is, I think, borne out by the subsequent act, 14 & 15 Vic., ch. 116, wherein the legislature recognizes that traders are not entitled to the privileges of 8 Vic., ch. 48, and makes provision for a certain class of traders to take the benefit of the insolvent law. If this be the correct interpretation of the act, then does the fact that the defendant, though a trader after the bankrupt law was in operation yet having failed in business before the bankrupt law, alter the case? I do not think it does. The language of the fifth section, speaking of the person having failed, is, that he did so under such circumstances as in the event of such failure having taken place after the passing of the bankrupt law would have enabled him to avail himself of that law. This, I think, shews that the legislature contemplated the cases under the second class existing at the time of the insolvent law being passed, and if the *status* of the person was altered so that he became a trader again subsequently, that *status* could not be regained. So far then I agree with the argument for the plaintiff, that the defendant has obtained the final order in a case which did not warrant him in obtaining it, but the question remains, whether having obtained it, and pleaded it in proper form, it concludes the plaintiff in this action. I have entertained doubts whether the plaintiff may not be right in contending that he can shew in an action for his debt, that the proceeding before the insolvent court was *coram non judice*, and therefore that the final order is no bar. The best opinion that I can form, however, is that the defendant must, upon this demurrer, succeed; and my reasons for that opinion are these:—The effect of the twenty-fourth section is, that the order may be pleaded in bar, and under the twenty-ninth section it is a bar against such debts as are named in the schedule to the petition. Then, operating against the plaintiff in that way, the question is, whether it was not his duty to have opposed the granting of the order when it was applied for before the county judge. Turning back to the fourth section of the act, we see that the judge, before he can grant|the final order, must have before him the petitioner, and notice of the sitting must have been given to the creditors, and they must have an opportunity of being heard; and then the clause says, *if it shall appear to the judge that the allegations in the petition and the matters in the schedule are true,* and also various other matters, then it shall be lawful for the judge to cause notice to be given that on a certain day he will make the final order if no cause be shewn. In this case the facts on the face of the petition shew that the judge had jurisdiction. Was it not then incumbent upon the plaintiff to appear before the judge and shew him that the allegations in the petitions were not true ? The facts as stated were true, but there were other facts which, if established, displaced the truth in law of those stated ; and should they not have been advanced, to prevent the order being obtained, rather than now be presented to attempt to avoid its effect ? I do not say what the effect might be if it were now shewn that such matters were made known to the judge, and yet that he notwithstanding had made the order. There would be little use in making the judge the tribunal to try the truth of the allegations contained in the petition, if every creditor could, in an action to recover his debt, dispute the truth of those matters after the judge's adjudication. There is no confirmation of the judge's decision required, and no power is given to him to review his decision, except in certain cases, within which this case does not come ; but all this was a matter to be provided for by the legislature, and it may be that they thought the rights of parties were sufficiently guarded by vesting the power in the county judge to examine and try the truth of the allegations contained in the petition. Either the judge has adjudicated the point upon hearing the parties, or it has been allowed to be taken by default. Whether this court can possibly review the decision of the county judge I do not say ; it will be sufficient to pronounce upon that when the question may be presented ; but it appears to me that we should not do right by throwing open the door to every plaintiff to dispute the truth of the allegations of a petition for the first time here, which would be the case if

these replications were sustained.   I have come to the conclusion that the legislature most certainly has vested the power in
the county judge of inquiring into the truth of the allegations
of the petition ; and if the final order is an adjudication on
that petition, which it seems to be, then I think we cannot
go behind it on a simple allegation that the matters of the
petitions are not true, for that in effect is the substance of
these replications.

I think, therefore, that judgment should be for the
defendant.

Judgment for defendant for demurrer.

BISHOPRICK AND WIFE V. PEARCE.

Dower—13 & 14 *Vic.*, ch. 58—*Offer to assign*—*Plea of tout temps prist, effect
of, as to damages and costs.*

Dower—The tenant pleaded *tout temps prist.*   The plaintiff replied, denying
the readiness of the demandant to assign, and averring a demand under
the 13 & 14 Vic. ch. 58 and a refusal.   The tenant traversed the refusal.
It appeared that after receiving the demand, the tenant gave a written notice
to the demandant that he was willing to assign her dower.   In pursuance
of this notice the tenant and the demandant's husband met on the ground,
and the tenant then offered what he considered a third and put up
pickets to mark the boundary.   The husband, however, refused this, and
would not say what particular portion the demandant wanted or would
take.   The parties then separated and this action was brought.
Held—that the offer proved was sufficient, and that a verdict was therefore
rightly found for the tenant.
Draper, J., considered that the late statute was not intended to interfere with
any right to costs existing under the old practice or to render necessary
a demand in cases where the demandant would before have been entitled
to costs without it: that the plea of *tout temps prist* admitted a right to
damages from the commencement of the suit to the issuing, if not to the
execution of the writ of inquiry without any suggestion that the husband
died seised—and that on these pleadings therefore the demandant might
strictly have recovered such damages, and consequently the costs; but
as this was not insisted on at the trial, and the verdict was just, he concurred in refusing to interfere.
As to to the practice and pleadings in dower under the late act, see the judgments of *Draper* and *Burns, JJ.*

This was an action for dower on the third part of the westerly half of lot 6, in the fifth concession of Marlborough.

The declaration contained no averment that the husband
died seised.

Plea—that from the death of the husband of the demandant to the time of her, the demandant's, marriage with the
plaintiff Bishoprick, defendant has always been ready to

render to the demandant, and since her marriage to her and her now husband, the dower, &c., and rendereth the same here in court to the demandant—concluding with a verification.

The replication traversed the readiness of the defendant to render dower, and averred that after the demandant's marriage to her present husband, and more than one month and less than one year before the commencement of this suit, viz., on the 18th of March, 1853, the demandant demanded from the tenant her dower, &c., but the said tenant did not render dower to the demandant, but wholly neglected and refused so to do,—concluding with a verification and prayer of dower, and also of damages for the detention of the same.

The tenant rejoined, traversing the alleged refusal to render dower, and the demandants joined issue.

At the trial, before *Richards, J.*, at the last assizes held at Bytown, the evidence appeared as follows : On the 18th of March, 1853, a written demand of the wife's dower was made upon the tenant. On the 2nd of April, 1853, the tenant served on the demandant a notice in these words :—

" I, William John Pearce, of &c., do hereby give you notice that I am ready and willing, and hereby offer, to give, set off and assign to you the dower to which, as widow af the late David Harrison, deceased, you, the said Martha Bishoprick, are entitled of and in the westerly half of lot No. 6, in the fifth concession of the township of Marlborough, and that I will attend for that purpose on the land, on Tuesday the 5th of April instant, or on such other day as you may appoint."

The husband of the demandant and the tenant did accordingly meet upon the land on the 5th of April. The tenant offered to the husband of the demandant what he considered to be a third part of the premises, and pickets were put up to designate a boundary. The husband refused to take it, and then the tenant offered to give a third part in any place he wished, with one-third of the buildings, &c., and offered to measure or have it measured off. The only answer which the demandant's husband gave to the tenant's offer was, "I will send the sheriff." No specific land was measured off or set apart as the dower of the wife, or to designate a third bart distinctly from the remainder, further than by one line of pickets.

It appeared rather to be the object of the husband to obtain a settlement by compromise for a sum of money for the wife's dower, than to obtain the dower in the land. He would not name any portion of the land the demandant would take, and refused to take what the tenant offered: and he appeared to cast the whole responsibility on the tenant to set off and designate the third part for dower, and would do nothing more than say generally, he wanted a third part of the cleared land, a third part of the wood land, and a third part of the improvements: and to this the tenant replied, if they would not take what he offered, then to say what they would take. Nothing more was done, and this action was brought.

The learned judge told the jury that he did not consider the tenant's offer sufficient; that it was his duty, in assigning dower, to designate something specific which the demandant might identify, and might take possession of without the necessity of an action being brought to ascertain what she should have; and that a mere statement of the tenant that he would give a third part, either in one place or in another, was not sufficient.

The jury, however, found a verdict for the tenant.

Wilson, Q. C., obtained a rule to shew cause why the verdict should not be set aside and a new trial had, on the ground that the verdict is contrary to law and evidence.

Riarhcds shewed cause. In addition to the authorities cited in the judgments, Empey v. Loucks, 8 U. C. R. 374; Hawkshaw v. Hodgins, 11 U. C. R. 71; Park Dower on 301, 303, were referred to.

ROBINSON, C. J.—The issue is upon the refusal of the tenant to assign dower, and that issue has evidently been raised with a view, on the plaintiff's part, to make the defendant liable for costs, under our statute 13 & 14 Vic., ch. 58, sec. 5. If the legislature meant, by the provision which they there made, that the plaintiff should not have his costs where it appeared that he had harassed the defendant with an action without necessity, I do not understand how a case could be presented to a jury that would shew the defendant more clearly entitled to be exempt from costs under this statute.

It is not surprising to me that the jury found themselves unable to say upon their oaths that the tenant had refused to assign dower, when it was plainly shewn to them that before this action was brought he had in writing offered to assign dower, and appointed a day when he would attend for that purpose, on which day he did attend, and when it appeared further that the only reason the demandant did not obtain her dower *de rationabile parte* on that occasion was, that she, or her second husband, who acted for her, would concur in nothing, and would accept nothing, when full liberty of choice was given by the tenant, but disappointed the tenant's wish to make an amicable adjustment, evidently under the impression that by being unaccommodating and impracticable, they could force him to compound by paying a large sum in money.

The tenant's plea to the action which the demandant chose to bring without necessity, was such as fully admitted the right of dower, and enabled them to take judgment at once, Any further proceeding on their part could only have been with a view to obtain judgment for costs also, to which they were neither entitled, as I think, in justice or law, under the facts proved.

It appears to me that what the legislature meant by the provisions referred to was that the demandant in dower should not have costs from the tenant except where the tenant had denied the right to dower, or at least had declined, or omitted, upon written demand made, to acknowlege it. If the tenant admits the right, but will not or cannot come to an amicable arrangement with the demandant in regard to the part which is to be taken, it is always in the power of the demandant to have the dower admeasured by the sheriff; but the costs of proceeding with that view should not be at the charge of the tenant, and would not have been at common law, upon a record like the present. The legislature, I think intended that the tenant should not have costs to pay, if he throws no impediment in the way of the demandant's recovering judgment for her dower, and by his conduct shows that there is no necessity for an action in order to establish her right.

There was certainly no misdirection here, of which the demandant has any right to complain, The verdict is perfectly just and in accordance with the evidence; and the rule, in my opinion, must be discharged—which only decides that the jury cannot be held by us to have given a wrong verdict upon the only question of fact submitted to them.

If the demandants mean to contend that they were still entitled to costs on the record, they must contend for that before the master on taxation.

DRAPER, J.—By *Magna Charter*, cap. 7, a widow "for her dower shall be assigned to her the third part of all the lands of her husband which were his during coverture."—(1 Inst. 37.)

Then by the Statute of Mertbn (20 H. III. ch. 1), it was provided that persons convict of the wrongful deforcement of widows of their dowers of the land whereof their husbands died seised, "shall yield damages to the same widows ; that is to say, the value of the whole dower to them belonging, from the time of the death of their husbands unto the day that the said widows, by judgment of our court, have recovered seizin of their dower, &c., and shall be in mercy.—(1 Inst. sec. 36 ; Co. Lit. 32 *b.*)

In the olden times, whether on a writ of right of dower, or of dower *unde nihil habet*, the demandant was obliged to produce her warrantor—*i. e.* the hair of her husband ; it being a rule that no one should answer a woman concerning her dower, unless she brought her warrantor to shew what right he had to the other two parts; and again, that no woman should answer without her warrantor. The assignee of the fee being in *loco hæredis*, dower might be claimed against him.—(Reeve Hist. C. L. I. 144 ; Bract. 297 *b*, 299 *b*, 300).

Nothing can be more explicit than the language of the Statute of Merton, to show that damages are only recoverable for the detention of dower out of land whereof the husbands died seised. This statute extends only to the action of dower *unde nihil habet*, and not to the writ of right of dower; the former being in the nature of a possessory action, in which damages for the detention of that possession are sought ; the latter being brought where the right itself is questionable.— (Co. Lit. 32 ; Dy. 284, Pl. 33 ; 2 Inst. 80.)

This distinction is therefore to be observed. The widow is entitled to dower out of all lands whereof her husband was seized at any time during the coverture ; she is entitled to damages for the detention of her dower only as to those lands whereof her husband died seised.

The measure of damages to which the dowress may be entitled differs apparently in some particulars in an action against the heir or against the feoffee of her husband. As against the heir she is entitled according to the value of the land at the time of the assignment of her dower, though the heir have improved the land by drainage, &c., or hath erected buildings. But against the feoffee, it is said, dower shall be as it was in the seizin of the husband ;. for the heir is not bound to warrant, except according to the value as it was at the time of the feoffment, and so the widow would recover more against the feoffee than he would recover in value, which is not reasonable.—(1 Inst. 32 *a* ; Ib. note 193).

The right to dower and the right to damages being perfectly distinct, the widow may recover the former, though she cannot make good her claim to the latter; therefore the judgment *quoad* the land may be affirmed on writ of error, and the judgment for damages be reversed, because they are several in their nature, and error lies after judgment for seizin and before judgment for damages.—(1 Inst. 32 *b*, note 198.

The pleadings in bar of *damages* in dower, pleadings in fact arising only since and by reason of the Statute of Merton, are given under a separate head in the *Doctr. Plac.*, 152 ; and the plea of *tout temps prist et encore est de render dower*, is given as a good bar to damages by the heir ; and, unless the widow has demanded it, she shall lose the mesne profits or value, and the damages for detaining.

The reason given by Lord Coke is, because the heir holdeth by title, and doth no wrong until demand be made ; and in a note on this passage it is said—if the *tenant* comes the first day and acknowledges the action and avers *tout temps prist*, the demandant may take judgment of seizin immediately, *et nihil de misâ (a)*. If she would have damages, she may aver that she requested her dower, and the tenant

_____

(a) The word *misâ* is only an abbreviation for *misericordiâ*. See Jones v. Jones, 2 Cr. & J., 606.

did not endow her, and then the judgment for damages and value shall wait till the issue be tried.—(1 Inst. 33 *a.*)

I apprehend that the word " tenant" in the foregoing note should be read "heir," or (since the statute of wills) "devisee," for the husband must have died seised of the freehold and inheritance, so that the possession immediately devolved upon the heir or devisee.

As the right to damages depends on the husband dying seised, the widow cannot recover them *a morte viri* from the alienee of the husband. It would therefore be an absurdity in him to plead *tout temps prist,* for that would be admitting a right which the demandant, as against him did not possess. Jones v. Jones (2 Cr. & J. 601).

Neither can the feoffee of the heir plead *tout temps prist,* because he had not the land all the time since the death of the ancestor ; and therefore the widow shall recover the mesne value and damages for the detention from him.

If the demandant admit the plea, and has judgment, she is entitled to mesne profits and damages from the commencement of her suit to the award of the writ of enquiry. For though by the plea of *tout temps prist* her right to dower is admitted, she must get a writ of seizin ; and have dower assigned, in order to enable her to enter or bring ejectment, and she is delayed from the time she began her suit until this writ is awarded, or perhaps executed. Or she may take issue on the plea of *tout temps prist,* or reply a demand or refusal ; and if found for her she shall recover damages *de morte viri.* The writ of enquiry of damages in such cases, therefore, usually is coupled with the writ of seizin ; and upon this, when it is established that the husband died seised, the jury should find the annual value, the damages for the detention, and as a consequence of her right to these damages, the costs. A plea of *assignment* of dower is a bar to the action, and must not be confounded with *tout temps prist,* though that concludes with " and rendereth her dower," &c.,—2 Wms. Saund. 44, *e* note ; Dobson v. Dobson (Cas. Temp. Hardw. 19) ; and see Kent v. Kent (2 Stra. 971).

I gather from the foregoing, that as against the alienee or feoffee of the husband the demandant in dower can have no judgment for costs; because, as her husband did not die seised, she can recover no damages, but only seizin. But as against the heir or his feoffee she would have a right to damages, and, as a consequence, to costs, whenever her dower had not been assigned to her and set out, and this, though the heir had pleaded *tout temps prist ;* for she would have a right to the mesne value and damages from the commencement of her suit until the obtaining the writ of enquiry.—Bac. Abr. "Dower" D. 2.

Assuming this to be a correct statement of the law as it stood at the passing of our statute 13 & 14 Vic. ch. 58, it remains only to examine what change that statute has made as to costs. Section 5 enacts that costs shall be allowed to the *demandant* in all cases, in the same manner as costs are now allowed to a plaintiff or *defendant* in personal actions, provided it shall be made to appear on the trial that a demand in writing had been made of the dower claimed from the tenant one month before action brought—the action to be brought within a year from demand as aforesaid. Provided, also, that the tenant shall not make it appear on the trial that he or she offered to assign the dower demanded before action brought.

Although the words of this statute only give costs to the *demandant* in express words, yet, I apprehend, if the defendant succeeds, he would be entitled to costs, under the statute 23 Hen. VIII. ch. 15, and 4 Jac. I. ch. 3,—a construction strengthened by the words immediately following—" in the same manner as costs are now allowed to a plaintiff or defendant in personal actions."

In an action against the alienee of her husband, the widow would be entitled to costs on any issue found in her favour going to the right of action, as upon *ne unques accouple,* or *ne unques seizie,* always supposing she proves a demand in writing, according to the act; and in neither of those cases, nor indeed of any other plea in bar of the *right to dower,* can it be supposed that the tenant would make it appear that he offered to assign dower; and the demandant would be liable to costs if she failed on any such issue.

The case would stand on the same footing with regard to the heir of the husband, on the alienee of such heir, as to all pleas going in bar of the right.

So as to pleas in abatement—such as non-tenure of the whole or part—she will be entitled or be liable to costs, according to the finding on the issues.

But the statute gives no new right as to costs where damages are recoverable; for there, without the aid of this statute, she would recover costs, and the question there would rather appear to be whether any condition not existing before—*ex. gr.*, making a demand in writing a month before bringing her action—is imposed on her as necessary to enable her to recover costs where she is already entitled to damages.

According to English authority, damages must be after demand of dower; still, unless the heir plead *tout temps prist,* he cannot object to the want of such demand, nor is it necessary that it should be in writing, and it may be made of an infant heir; and "though he did not refuse to do it, but was prevented by his guardian," the non-assignment was held to be a refusal in law. And even if *tout temps prist* be pleaded, yet, according to Sellon's Practice, the demandant shall recover damages from the teste of the original to the execution of the writ of enquiry; though, if the heir had *assigned* dower, and she had accepted it, she would have lost her claim to damages.—" The request in *pais est bon."*—Corsellis v. Corsellis (Bull. N. P. 117).; 2 Sell. Pr. 210, Doctr. Plac. 152.

I do not read our statute as diminishing any previous right of the demandant to costs, or as any otherwise intended than to *give* a right to costs, subject to the provisoes in cases where that right did not previously exist.

Upon any issue, therefore, merely affecting the right to damages, where costs would follow independently of this statute, it seems to me the statute has no operation. Where *tout temps prist* is pleaded, according to English precedent, and a demand is replied, I apprehend that, inasmuch as dower is not assigned, the demandant would, although the issues were found against her, only be barred of her damages up to the commencement of the action, but would be entitled to them from that period to the issuing, if not to the execution, of the writ of enquiry; and if so, costs would follow as a matter of course. I do not at present think that our statute can be held to affect her right to these damages, nor to take away the right to costs in such a case, unless she proves a demand in writing. Such a construction would make the statute operate against, instead of in favour of, the demandant, which I think was its obvious intention. It would so far be a disabling, though its language is that of an enabling, statute.

I do not think it can in any case be necessary for the tenant to plead, for the mere purpose of preventing the demandant obtaining costs. It will be necessary for her to make a demand of her dower in writing, according to the terms of the Act, and she must prove this in all cases when, not being entitled to damages, she would not, but for this enactment, be entitled to costs. But this necessity is little, if anything, more than what is stated by Lord Coke : " It is necessary for the wife, after the decease of her husband, as soon as she can, to demand her dower before good testimony; for otherwise she may, by her own default, lose the value after the decease of her husband, and her damages for detaining her dower "—to which may now be added, and her costs in cases in which this statute would entitle her to them.

If, however, the tenant should neither plead to the right nor to the damages, but altogether make default, then, if the demandant claims mesne value and damages, she will enter the usual suggestion of her husband dying seized, and obtain the writ of inquiry, on the execution whereof she will get damages and, as a consequence, costs. See Watson v. Quilter (11 M. & W. 760), and the cases there cited.

But if she cannot claim damages, then she may, I think, enter a suggestion of a demand in writing, made according to the provisions of our Act, to which the tenant may plead an offer to assign dower, and on this the parties may go down to trial. If the tenant either confesses the suggestion, or does not plead such an offer on his part, or set up any other answer, I do not see any necessity for the intervention of a jury to enable her to recover costs. I think the statute will be satisfied, if on the trial of any issue affecting the right to dower, besides the proof in support of that issue, a

demand according to the statute is also proved, to entitle
the demandant to costs; but if there be no such issue to be
tried, nor any other question arising out of a suggestion for
costs, but the fact be admitted which gives the right to
costs, whether by confession or default, judgment for costs
may be rendered. If a trial, in the strict sense of the
word, were necessary in order to give the demandant a
right to costs, then a tenant who would not deny anything
alleged against him, or assert anything in his own favour,
might always defeat the claim to costs, when there was no
claim to damages; in which case the demandant, I have
endeavoured to establish, has a right to costs without the
aid of our statute, if she recovers any damages.

In the present case the right to dower is not denied. *Tout
temps prist* is pleaded, unnecessarily as it seems, perhaps
untruly. The replication sets forth a demand, in the terms
of our Act, adding (what the statute does not contain) that
the tenant neglected and refused ; and the tenant rejoins
traversing his refusal, but not asserting in the terms of the
statute any offer to assign. If pleading according to the
statute were necessary, either to give the demandant the
right to costs, or to enable the tenant to resist it by shewing
an offer to assign, then this tenant has not pleaded such offer.
I have already stated my opinion that no such pleading is
necessary. But the demandant at the trial gave evidence
only on the issue joined on demand and refusal, not offering
to prove anything on which a computation of damages could
be made, nor insisting that the plea of *tout temps prist* admitted that the case was of that character that she might
claim at least nominal damages. The tenant on his part met
her evidence by his proof of an offer to assign. His right to
do this was not contested, and I think he gave proof sufficient
to warrant a verdict in his favour ; for though I think a mere
verbal declaration of "You may take your dower wherever
you please," or the like, wholly insufficient, the evidence
in this case went much further,   Limits, as I understand,
were pointed out, within which she might have entered, but
would not, desiring to enforce pecuniary compensation. On
the proof given, I think there was enough to warrant the

verdict; and the new trial is sought, apparently, to regain the opportunity of doing what was previously overlooked, and of harassing the defendant by resting the claim to costs on a footing which I think he could not, at least as the pleadings stand, successfully resist. I therefore concur in discharging this rule, the granting a new trial being a matter in the discretion of the court, and the ends of justice not calling for our interposition; though I still think, with every respect for contrary opinion, that on the plea of *tout temps prist* a suggestion that the husband died seised was unnecessary, for, unless that were the case, such a plea is absurd, for it is a plea in bar of damages, the right to which would not exist unless the husband did die seised; and, if that fact is admitted, then the demandant would have a right to some damages, however small, which would carry costs without the aid of our statute. If, instead of pleading *tout temps prist*, the tenant had pleaded an offer to assign dower, he would have brought his case within the express terms of our statute, without any implied admission of the husband having died seised; and, if it be necessary for him to have pleaded at all, under the circumstances of this case, before there was a suggestion to entitle the demandant to costs, such, at present appears to me, was his proper course.

BURNS, J.—The demandants might have had judgment of seizin immediately upon the plea of the tenant, and may yet have the same judgment. It does not appear that the wife's former husband died seised; and according to Jones v. Jones (2 Cr. & J. 601), though *dicta* appear in some of the books to the contrary, in a case where the husband did not die seised the widow is not entitled to mesne profits and damages. It is only under the Statute of Merton that she was entitled to damages; and if there were no damages, then she was not entitled to costs, for the Statute of Gloucester only gave costs when damages were recovered. The plea of *tout temps prist* is merely to save the tenant pleading it from damages and costs; and if the demandant is only entitled to damages in cases where the husband dies seised, it follows that the plea is proper only as against damages by the tenant who

becomes tenant of the freehold upon the husband's death.
If the demandant admits the tenant's plea, she takes judgment of seizin immediately, without any judgment for
damages or costs; but if she disputes the truth of the plea
and claims damages, besides seizin of her dower, by reason
of having demanded her dower from the tenant, and he has
not complied with the demand, then to entitle her to
damages from the death of her husband, given her by the
Statute of Merton, she must reply that demand: and upon
that there is a trial, and if she succeeds, then she is entitled
to a second judgment for damages and costs. But if, as
before remarked, her husband did not die seised, there
could be no damages or costs; and consequently, the tenant
not becoming tenant of the freehold by reason of the death
of the husband, could not properly say he was ready to
render her dower in order to save himself against a claim
for damages. Our statute to alter the practice in actions of
dower has made no alteration in the law as respects the
demandant's right to damages; that stands as yet according
to the Statute of Merton. The alteration is as respects costs,
which are now to be allowed in all cases, whether damages
be recoverable or not, provided it be made to appear on the
trial that a demand in writing had been made of the dower
one month before action brought, and the action be brought
within a year after the demand made; and provided that the
tenant shall not make it appear on the trial that he offered to
assign the dower before action brought. In this case, for aught
that appears, the tenant had no occasion to plead *tout temps
prist* in order to save himself against a claim for damages,
for as to such, as before stated, it would not be proper. Had
he then, it may be asked, any occasion to plead such a plea
to save himself against a claim for costs given now by our
statute? That question can best be answered by an inquiry
whether, in a case where the demandant had made her demand
in writing, according to the statute, and the tenant had refused
compliance, so that a suit became necessary, and in that suit
the tenant had made no answer, but suffered a default, the
demandant could recover her costs, or whether she is confined
in the recovery of costs to cases where there is a trial of some

matter to be tried independent of the question of costs ? I have no doubt the Legislature intended—when the language was used, *that in all cases,* whether damages were recoverable or not, costs should be allowed as in personal actions— that the demandant should have costs where the written demand had been served; and that such right was not confined to cases merely where there might be a trial of some issue involving the right to dower or to damages. Then, it may be asked, how is the demandant to obtain them where there should be a default of the tenant, and there is nothing to try? The answer to that, I think, consists in this, that the very *right* to costs depends upon a matter of fact, which fact the statute has not empowered the court to dispose of, and which must therefore be disposed of by a jury. The right to costs depends upon the fact whether the demandant had made a demand in writing within the time mentioned, and is subject to be defeated by the tenant proving that he offered to assign the dower before action brought. These are matters which neither the court in banc, nor the judge at Nisi Prius are called upon to determine, but which must be pronounced upon by a jury. I have no doubt the Legislature so intended, and that was the trial which is meant by the act. If that be not so, then in all cases where there was no trial upon a contested right to dower or to damages, the demandant could have no costs, though she had taken the precaution to make a demand, and yet was driven to bring her action by reason of the non-compliance of the tenant. Take the case where there is a default, and the demandant claims damages—after she has obtained judgment of seizin she must suggest that her husband died seised, upon which there is a writ of inquiry ; and the jury must find, before she is entitled to damages and costs, that her husband did die seised ; the jury failing to find that fact, she would be entitled to neither. If she succeeds in proving that fact, then such finding of the jury entitles her to costs as well as damages, and that forms the second judgment. Our statute entitles the demandant to a second judgment for costs, even though she may not be entitled to damages; but I apprehend, before she is entitled to the costs, there must be a finding of the jury of the fact upon which the right depends. In a case where default was made, she would, I apprehend, be obliged to enter a suggestion the truth of which the tenant may dispute, or answer in the manner the statute authorizes him to do, and which must then be determined by a jury. It appears to me the points upon which the right to costs is to depend or be disputed must appear upon the record, and each must have an opportunity of answering. And though there may be an issue raised independent of the right to costs, yet still the demandant would be obliged to enter a suggestion if she claims them, because the costs are not given merely by reason of her recovery upon the issue, but only in the event of having given notice according to the statute, which certainly the tenant has a right to reply to. If no claim to costs were made to which the tenant would have a right to answer, he may very fairly suppose the demandant intends to rest her claim upon ordinary grounds. As to this right and the course to be pursued, I refer to Bartlett v. Pentland (1 B. & Ad. 710), and Watson v. Quilter (11 M. & W. 760), where all the cases are fully collected.

Then, has the tenant in this case prejudiced himself in any way by pleading before he was called upon to say whether he admitted or denied the demandant's right to costs and will the plea he has put in be a sufficient answer, or be the basis of an answer, to excuse him costs in case such demand after the plea be made? If the tenant in this case were, such as he might be, liable for damages, then the plea is in proper form to excuse him from damages, and if from damages, consequently also from costs. Then why should not the same plea have the limited operation when applied to the costs alone, for the demandant by the replication treats it as applicable to the costs of the suit only? I confess I can see no reason why it should not. The tenant says, "I have always been ready to render you the dower; you had no occasion to sue me." The demandant replies to that the written demand, made obligatory on her to give before she is entitled to have costs, and says the tenant refused to comply with it, which refusal the tenant in his turn denies. This seems to me to bring up the very matter to be tried upon which the right to costs depends; and if found in the demandant's favour would be the second judgment for costs, and if found against her would entitle the tenant to costs.

If the parties be before the court upon a proper issue to determine the right to costs, then is the finding of the jury correct upon the evidence ?   That mainly depends upon what the legislature meant should be sufficient on the part of the tenant to be excused when a written demand shall be served upon him.   The expression is, *if the tenant shall not make it appear on the trial that he offered to assign the dower.*   We must bear in mind that the expression merely relates to something to be done which will excuse the tenant from costs.   If the demandant did not make a written demand, her right to costs would be dealt with according to the law, irrespective of our statute.   She is made an actor in the matter as well as the tenant, and the question is, whether, after such written demand made upon him, the tenant is bound, in making his offer to assign the dower, to do so in such a way that she may at once enter upon the portion he sets off ?   I must say I think he should do so.   The question in this case is, whether the tenant did do enough to enable the demandant to enter and take possession.   An assignment of dower need not be by deed, but a parol assignment is good.   Now, in this case pickets were put to designate a boundary, and the tenant offered the dower on either side of the line, or, if that were objected to, then for the demandant to say where it should be ; but the offer was refused, and the only answer given in return was that the sherriff should be sent.   If the offer made by the tenant was not sufficient, then that fact should have been replied ; that is, if the offer he did make was one made in sincerity, and not merely for the purpose of a sham offer.   If the offer made was for the purpose of putting off the demandant and avoiding a proper assignment, the demandant would be right in treating the demand as being refused. In this case there is no reason whatever to doubt that the tenant was acting with a view of settling the claim ; and therefore, if there were any complaint that the tenant did not offer as much as he ought, or that he did not offer it in a proper manner, and such as by law the demandant was entitled to, that should have been replied to by the demand-

2*s*—VOL. XII. Q.B.

ant, and then it would become a question under the statute whether what the tenant had done was sufficient to excuse him from costs. Here, however, the demandant replies that the tenant refused to comply with her demand. Now it is evident he did not, but on the contrary was anxious to have the matter arranged between them, and the conduct of the demandant prevented it. The tenant did offer on the land to the demandant who was also on the land, that of which he, for himself and wife, might have entered into the immediate possession. The tenant was not bound to fence it off for them, for they would by the common law be bound to fence against each other, and under our statute would be bound to contribute to division fences, but that is a question independent of the assignment of dower. The question here is, whether the tenant did offer something for dower, which the demandant might have taken possession of, and I must say I think he did, and therefore did offer to assign dower. When a line was designated, on one side of which the tenant pointed that he assigned the dower, that was something specific of which the demandant might have entered into possession, Because he declined to take that or to take any other portion, that fact did not the less make what the tenant did an offer to assign, and the demandant was not in a position to say the tenant refused to assign dower. He may not have offered enough, or may not have offered it in such a way as the demandant had a right by law to claim it, but that is not made a question by the pleadings. I think the statute meant, in dealing with the question of costs to make both parties actors in the matter and to throw the costs upon the one who should be to blame for the suit being brought. What is sought in this case is, to place the whole responsibility of coming up to what the law would require the sheriff to do in assigning dower upon the tenant at once upon a written demand being made upon him. Now, when we consider that the parties between themselves might agree upon an assignment differing very materially from what the law would make if compelled through a court to do so, and that even where the assignment was without the intervention of the demandant, but she has accepted what was offered, the law has adjudged such to be binding and not revocable, I think the statute did not cast upon the tenant in making his offer the duty which the law casts upon the sheriff. The statute conferred a benefit upon demandants in enabling them to recover costs in cases where before they were not entitled to them, but in so doing did not in my opinion cast upon tenants the responsibility which the law casts upon its own officers. It left to the parties to arrange, if they could, upon such footing as they law stood with regard to assignments of dower, as they could agree among themselves without resort to law. If they come to law, however, I apprehend that the tenant must shew that his offer is of something that the demandant might enter at once, into possession of, for the demandant has no legal right to enter until the tenant assigns and in doing that he had made a legal offer. In this case a legal offer is, I think proved ; and no question by the pleadings has been made as to the sufficiency of the offer.

I think, therefore, the verdict is right according to the law, as I understand it, and the evidence well warrants the finding.

Rule discharged.

QUIN V. MCKIBBIN.

Dower—13 & 14 *Vic. ch.* 58—*Damages—Costs.*

DOWER.—There was no suggestion in the declaration that the husband died seised an l no claim for damages. The tenant pleaded *tout temps prist.*

Replication—a demand and refusal. *Rejoinder,* taking issue on the refusal. It was proved that after demand served on the tenant, under 13 & 14 Vic. ch. 58, section 5, he went to the demandant's attorney, and said that she was ready and willing to assign dower whenever she would come for it, to which the attorney replied that the tenant must take his own course. The jury found for demandant and 1s. damages ; and a rule having been obtained for a new trial—*Held,* per *Draper, J.,* and *Burns, J.,* that such rule should be discharged.

Per Draper, J.—That by pleading *tout temps prist* the tenant had admitted a right to damages, at least from the bringing of the action, which would carry costs.

Per Burns, J.—That the offer proved was insufficient, and in effect amounted to a refusal, and the demandant should therefore have costs ; but that there could be no damages, as the husband was now proved to have died seised.

Robinson C. J., dissenting, on the ground that the evidence shewed no such refusal as could do away with the effect of the offer proved, and that the offer was sufficient under the statute to exempt the tenant from costs.

The demandant, Ann Quin, sued as widow of Owen Quin, deceased, demanding the third part of 200 acres of land, being

the south-east part of lot 7, in the 10th concession of Paken-
ham,—not alleging that her husband died seised, and not
claiming damages.

The tenant pleaded—1st. That from the death of her
husband he had always been ready, and still was ready to
render to this demandant her dower of the said tenements
and premises, with the appurtenances, and rendereth the
same here in court to the said Ann Quinn, &c.

2nd. That from the death of her husband he had always
been ready to render to the demandant her dower of the said
tenements, &c., and that before the commencement of this
suit, viz., on the 1st of June, 1853, he tendered and offered
to the demandant her dower, &c., to receive which she
wholly refused ; and that he is still ready and willing to
render to the demandant her dower of the said tenements,
&c., and rendereth the same to her here in court, &c.

The demandant replied to the first plea that the tenant was
not always from the death of the husband, ready to render,
&c., as in the said plea alleged ; "for that, after the accruing
of her right of dower, and more than one month and less than
than one year before the commencement of this suit, to wit,
on the 24th of February, 1853, she demanded of defendant her
dower, but that he did not then, nor at any time before the
commencement of this suit render to the demandant her
dower, but wholly neglected and refused to do so ;" concluding with a verification and prayer for her dower.

And to the second plea, traversing the readiness to render
as averred in the plea, "for that after the accruing of the
right to dower, and before the tenant did offer and tender her
dower, as in the plea mentioned, and more than one month
and less than one year before the commencement of this suit,
viz., on the 24th of February, 1853, she demanded from the
tenant her dower, but he did not then, nor at any time before
the commencement of this suit, render to the demandant her
dower, &c., but then and there neglected and refused so to
do ;" concluding with a verification and prayer for dower.

The tenant rejoined to the first replication, *traversing the
refusal alleged;* and in the same manner to the second replication.

Upon the trial, at Perth, before *Richards, J.*, it was admitted that a notice, such as the late statute 13 & 14 Vic. ch. 58, section 5, provides for, was served on the tenant, more than a month and less than a year before the action.

And on the part of the tenant a witness was called, who proved that he was present with the tenant, in March last, in the office of the attorney for the demandant, where the tenant said that he was ready and willing to assign dower to the demandant or her agent at any time that she would come for .it or send an agent : that the demandant's attorney replied that the property was in a good situation, and they could procure a tenant ; and that the tenant must decide for himself as to the course he should pursue.

This witness swore that he thought the tenant was sincere in the offer he made, and that he would have assigned the dower if it had been applied for ; that he did not say he had actually assigned the dower nor mention any time when he would do so, but said that he would assign it whenever the other party should give him notice.

The learned judge inclined to think that the tenant did not shew such an offer to assign dower as complied with the intention of the statute 13 & 14 Vic. ch. 58, section 5, and directed a verdict for the demandant ; but reserved leave to the tenant to move to have the verdict rendered in his favor if the court should think he was entitled to it upon the pleadings and evidence. A verdict was accordingly found for demandant and 1s. damages.

Crawford obtained a rule *nisi* to enter a verdict for the tenant on the leave reserved, or for a new trial on the law and evidence, and for misdirection ; or that a re-pleader be ordered, or the demandant restrained from taxing her costs against the defendant.—he cited Rowe v. Power, 2 N.R. 34 ; Park on Dower, under the head of "Assignment of Dower."

Wilson, Q. C., contra, cited Bac. Abr. "Dower," D. 2 ; Isherwood v. Whitmore, 10 M. & W. 757 ; Startup v. Macdonald, 6 M & G. 593 ; Doe dem. Sturges v. Ward, 2 Dowl. N. S. 706.

ROBINSON, C. J.—The clause referred to enacts that costs shall be allowed to the demandant in all cases, whether damages be recoverable or not, in the same manner as costs are now allowed to a plaintiff or defendant in personal actions ; *provided it shall be made appear on the trial that a demand in writing had been made of the dower claimed from the tenant one month before action brought, the action to be brought within a year from demand as aforesaid; provided also that the tenant shall not make it appear on the trial that he or she offered to assign the dower demanded before action brought.*

If such pleas as these had been pleaded before the late dower act, 13 & 14 Vic. ch. 58, was passed, the demandant would have had nothing to do but take judgmennt for her dower,—there being no damages recoverable in such a case under the Statute of Merton, for want of an allegation on the record that the husband died seised, nor any such finding by the jury, and the fact of the case being otherwise. No damages being recoverable, there should be no costs, according to the Statute of Gloucester; and there could therefore have been no object, before our late statute, in replying as this demandant has done.   The form of the replication as well as the reason of the thing, shews clearly that it was with a view to establish her rights to costs under our statute that the demandant replied, charging the tenant with having refused on a certain day, which was more than a month and less than a year before action brought, to render to the demandant her dower.

. The pleadings rest the issue upon an alleged refusal was tenant to render dower, not upon the offer alleged to have been made by him.

How can it be said that on this evidence a refusal was proved, after the tenant's admitted offer and before this action brought; that is, such a refusal as should cancel the admitted offer?

I cannot say that I see any evidence whatever of a refusal. All the proof that was given seems to relate to the alleged offer to render dower, which is not denied.

The case of Corsellis v. Corsellis, cited in Buller's N. P. 117, from Finch 200, was referred to as shewing that what was proved to have passed here, instead of being an offer, was in fact a refusal, inasmuch as it did not amount to an actual assignment of dower, but left the defendant as she was before. That case, however, is not parallel with the present, for there the infant expressed his own willingness to do what he ought, but alleged that he could not assign dower because he was prevented by his guardian. Now that did amount in effect to a refusal, for the infant was apologising for his inability to render dower, and was thereby admitting a refusal in effect, though he alleged such refusal to be by compulsion. It made no difference to the demandant that the infant's refusal arose from his erroneous impression in regard to his own authority to assign dower, and the legal right of his guardian to restrain him; the fact was that he declined doing it, thinking himself incapable without his guardian's assent. Here on the other hand all that we see is that the tenant went to the demandant's attorney, as I understand it, after demand of dower had been served upon him and before action brought and declared "that he was ready and willing to assign dower to the demandant or her agent at any time that she would come for it or send an agent," Now, as that is all that is shewn or alleged to have taken place between the parties, I have no doubt it was the offer to render dower which the tenant has pleaded, and which the demandant in one of her replications admits; and it would be strange to hold the same words as amounting also to a refusal, because they were followed by no act.

It is explained in the evidence why no assignment took place. The discretion to mete out to the demandant any particular portion could not rest with the tenant ; the demandant must have a voice in it and if they could not agree then other measures must be taken ; but the demandant, it seems by the answer of her attorney, was not disposed to facilitate an amicable adjustment ; he said the property was in a good situation and she could get a tenant, seeming desirous of forcing the tenant to some kind of terms.

The question then is, whether any refusal was shewn here in evidence, such as would neutralize the effect of the offer to assign dower which was proved.

I think not and that there should have been no verdict for damages, for none were demanded, but a verdict for the tenant on the issues of refusal; taking the refusal pleaded by demandant to mean such a positive actual refusal as would either disprove, or cancel, or revoke the offer to assign, which, as it was proved, was, I think sufficient under the statute to exempt from costs though there may be a doubt whether it would have entitled the tenant to succeed on a plea of *tout temps prist* after refusal replied.

DRAPER, J.—On these pleadings the demandant has a right to her judgment for dower. The right to damages is all that is in issue on the first plea, and I do not see any substantial distinction between the two pleas in this respect. If true, they afford reasons why she should not recover the mesne value and damages for detaining. In my opinion neither of the pleas are sustained by proof, because they assert a readiness ever since the death of the husband, and no such readiness is in fact shewn, nor any readiness or attempted proof of readiness until demand made, as I understand the case. But the issue raised at last on these pleadings, is, whether the tenant refused on demand made,—the demand being by the rejoinder admitted. The proof shewed a demand in writing. The tenant afterwards went to the office of the demandant's attorney, and said he was ready and willing to assign her dower whenever she would come or send an agent for it.

It appears to me that the right to damages is admitted, for unless demandant's husband died seised the tenant should not have pleaded *tout temps prist,* or a tender. He does not appear to be the heir, who would not be bound to assign dower until requested. He must therefore, if the husband died seised, stand in the light of feoffee of the heir; and then, even if his plea bars the damages until the bringing of the action the widow is entitled to them from that time, for even yet she has no assignment of dower : and if entitled to any damages the right to costs follows—2 Wms. Saund. 44, *e* note.—I therefore think the verdict for damages should not be disturbed. I have so fully explained my views as to the effect of our statute in the case of Bishoprick v Pearce (*ante* 306), that I need not now repeat them.

BURNS, J.—According to my view of what constitutes a legal offer to assign dower, it is not merely saying the tenant was ready to do it when the demandant would come for it. I have no doubt that the statute contemplated the demandant was to be an actor as well as the tenant, in order if possible to prevent a suit. After the tenant had received the written notice, if he then appointed time and place when and where he would assign dower, or request the demandant to do so, and that he would attend for the purpose of assigning it, that would be a sufficient offer. A parol assignment is good, and it requires no deed to make it legal and binding, but the dowress cannot by law enter till the assignment be made. If, therefore, it is done by parol, it can only be done by the parties themselves, or their authorized agents, attending to agree upon the specific portion to be designated, upon which the dowress thereafter may enter. If the tenant takes this course, then I think he makes a legal offer, which will have the effect of excusing him from costs. The tenant may, however, assign dower by himself setting off what he thinks equivalent to it, and so designating it by a description that the dowress can go and make entry without the tenant's presence, when she is apprised what it consists of. That also would be a legal offer. If any dispute should arise between the parties as to the sufficiency or the legality of the manner in which it is offered, then such question should he made by the pleadings; but when the tenant makes an offer which if accepted would be a legal assignment of dower, and prevent any other claim being made, I think he complies with the statute; that is, when the question to be determined is merely whether he has offered to assign dower. In this case the proof is that he merely said he was ready to give her the dower when she or her agent came for it. Resting upon that is in effect making the doweress the active and the tenant the passive party. If the tenant be the heir of the husband, and the husband die seised, then, inasmuch as he comes into the title by operation of law, he is not a wrongdoer until demand made upon him ; but if the tenant comes in by purchase, he is in a different position. Our statute applies to all cases, and to excuse the tenant from costs after a demand made he must prove that

2 t—VOL. XII. Q. B.

he was an active party; and the offer meant, I think was of something which would be a legal assignment of dower if accepted; and his remaining passive and saying "I am ready to give you your dower when you come for it," is not an offer of it, and in effect amounts to a refusal.

The verdict for the plaintiff is therefore right, but it should not be entered for even the shilling damages, for as the husband is not proved to have died seised, there can be no damages whatever, and the determination of the issue in favor of the plaintiff only gives her the costs.

Rule discharged.—ROBINSON, C. J., dissenting.

CUMMING V, ALGUIRE.

Dower—Non tenuit—Ne unques seisie.

W. C. died seised in fee of the land in question, having devised the same to his wife for life, and after her death to his son, the demandant's husband in fee. The testator's widow, the devisee for life, died before the demandant's husband, and during her life his interest was sold under a *fi. fa.* against lands, and conveyed to one J., who having recovered possession, sold to the tenant, who mortagaged back again to J., but continued in possession. It was not shown whether all the mortgage money had been paid or not; but the time for payment of several of the instalments had not arrived.

Held, that the demandant should not succeed, for the tenant was not tenant of the freehold, but the mortgagee; nor was the husband ever so seised as to entitle his widow to dower, for his reversionary interest was sold during his life time.

Mary Cumming sued, as widow of William Cumming, for her dower in the west half of lot No. 3, in the 3rd concession, of Cornwall. The declaration contained no averment that the husband died seised, and no damages were claimed.

Pleas—1. *Ne unques seisie due dower.*

2. *Ne unques accouple,* &c.

3. That the said Daniel Alguire is not, nor was on the day of filing the plaint, nor at any time since has been, tenant of the said land, &c., or of any part thereof: concluding to the country.

On the trial at Cornwall, before *Richards, J.,* these facts were admitted:—William Cumming, senr., father of the demandant's husband, died before 1825, seized in fee of the west half of this lot, having devised the same to his wife Anne Cumming (see Doe Jarvis v. Cumming, 4 U. C. R. 390), for her life, and after her decease to his son William, the demandant's husband, in fee, "provided that he will pay all such demands as may be against the said William Cumming (the testator) by his having signed any promissory note or notes with his said son William, or any other sums of money that he might be owing on account of his said son. And if his said son should make default in paying all such demands as aforesaid, or if any part thereof should be collected from any divisee in this will mentioned, then he devised his said land to his daughter Margery, her heirs and assigns for ever": —that this will was made during the coverture of the demandant: that the testator's widow (the devisee for life) died before the son William, who had since died, leaving the demandant, his widow, surviving him: that the estate and interest of the demandant's husband was sold under a *fi.fa.* against lands, and conveyed by the sheriff to George S. Jarvis, Esquire, before the death of the testator's widow— the judgment and execution were admitted to be regular: that before the commencement of this suit, Mr. Jarvis brought ejectment against Margery Cumming, one of the devisees, and recovered judgment, and received possession under a writ of *hab. fac.*, during the life-time of demandant's husband, who was never in actual possession of the land : that Jarvis afterwards conveyed in fee to the tenant Alguire, who entered, and had been always since in possession : that notice of this claim of dower was given in due time, under the late statute 13 & 14 Vic., ch. 58, sec. 5 : that the tenant, Alguire, mortgaged the premises in fee, to Jarvis, but was still in possession; and whether the mortgage money had or had not been paid was not shewn.

It was objected on the part of the tenant, what it was necessary for the demandant to shew that Alguire was tenant of the freehold; in other words, that he had not made default in paying the mortgaged money.

The mortgagor was present at the trial, but neither party called him to prove how the fact was.

It was provided in the mortgage, which was dated 3rd of July, 1851, that the deed should be void on payment by the mortgagor, his heirs, &c., of £120 with interest, as follows— viz: £20 with interest on the £120, on the first of May, 1852; £20 with interest on £100, on the 1st of May, 1853;

£20 with interest on £80, on 1st of May, 1854, and so on, providing for annual payment on the 1st of May in each successive year, till the whole should be paid up, with interest on the sum due at the time of paying each instalment.

Alguire covenanted to pay the money according to the condition. Nothing was said in the mortgage in regard to the possession before or after default.

A verdict was directed to be given for the demandant, with leave reserved to move for a non-suit, or verdict for the tenant, if the court should think she was not entitled to recover. The jury accordingly found for the demandant and 1s. damages.

Vankoughnet, Q. C., obtained a rule *nisi* to enter a verdict for a tenant.

A. McLean shewed cause, insisting that, the judgment in Doe Jarvs v. Cumming having determined that William Cumming, the younger, took the remainder in fee, subject to a conditional limitation, which estate, during the life of the tenant for life, was held liable to sale under execution for his debts, it followed that his wife was dowable out of it; and he contended that the defendant, having purchased in fee from the purchaser at sheriff's sale, must be considered as tenant of the freehold, though he had reconveyed the land to secure part of the purchased money, inasmuch as no default was shewn.

Vankoughnet, Q. C., contra, cited Doe Dem Roylance v. Lightfoot, 8 M. & W. 553, to shew that Jarvis took the estate on the execution of the mortgage. He also cited 2 Saund. 43,44, note *b*. See also Doe Parsley v. Day, 2 Q.B. 147.

ROBINSON, C. J.—I take it to be clear that in this case the mortgage was tenant of the freehold, and not the mortgagor, for we can regard only the legal estate, and dower is a strictly legal right, except so far as the Statute 4 Wm. IV. ch. 1, sec. 13, has altered the law in that respect, but that provision can only receive effect through a court of equity, and has made no difference in the right at law, or in the proceeding in a court of law to recover dower.

The mortgage in this case, made by the defendant Alguire to Mr. Jarvis, was a mortgage in fee, not for years; and the legal estate which it vested in the mortgage, could not, by reason of anything appearing upon the trial, have become revested in the mortgagor, for there was not only no re-conveyance shewn, but there was no ground for imagining even that the mortgage might have become void under the terms of the proviso by payment at the day, for the period for paying the greater part of the money has not even yet arrived.

Unless therefore the plea of *non tenuit*, which has been pleaded by the tenant in this case, is to be treated as meaning something different since our dower act, 13 & 14 Vic. ch. 58, from what it imported before that statute was passed, there can be no doubt that the tenant was entitled to succeed at the trial upon that issue, for undoubtedly he did not appear upon the evidence to be tenant of the freehold.

But whether the plea of *non tenuit* ought, upon the evidence to have been found in favour of the tenant or not, we need not determine, for besides pleading *non tenuit*, which is a plea in abatement, and not pleaded as to a part only of the premises, but as to the whole, the tenant has pleaded, as a plea in bar, that the husband of the demandant was never so seised during her coverture as that she could be endowed. We are not to determine upon this application whether a plea in abatement and a plea in bar could properly be pleaded together to the whole action but only to determine whether, upon the issues which the jury were sworn to try, the verdict should have been for the demandant or the tenant; and it is perfectly plain, upon many authorities, that considering the footing upon which the law of dower still continues in this province, not changed by any such enactment as the English statute 3 & 4 Wm. IV. ch. 105, the husband was not so seised as to entitle his widow to dower, for he had only a reversion expectant upon the life estate devised to the testator's widow.

That life estate was an intermediate estate of freehold, during the existence of which the immediate freehold could not vest in the husband as it would have done if the testator had devised an estate for years only to his widow instead of the estate for life. In the life time of the widow the reversionary interest of William Cumming the son, husband of the demandant was sold in execution so that the immediate seizin of the freehold never in fact came to him, and on that account his widow has no legal claim to dower (a).

DRAPER, J.—The writ of dower *unde nihil habet* would lie only against such tenant as could render the demandant her dower, which he in reversion or remainder/expectant on the determination of an estate for life cannot do; otherwise if the intermediate estate were for years for he might render the demandant a third of the rent pending the tenancy and a third of the land on its determination, It was for this reason that the tenant by receipt could not plead detention of charters even though he was the heir of the demandant's husband, for being only tenant by receipt, he could not render the demandant her demand, and the plea of detention must aver readiness to render, &c.—9 Rep. 19.

BURNS, J. concurred.

Rule absolute.

DACK v. CURRIE.

Dower—Inchoate right to, no breach of covenant for seizin.

A. executed to B. two deeds in fee of certain lands, containing the usual. covenants for seizin. The wife of M., from whom A. had purchased, afterwards brought an action of dower against B., and B., having compounded with her, and obtained a release, sued A. on the covenant for seizin contained in his deeds. This action was brought more than twenty years after the execution of one of the deeds.

Held, confirming Thornhill v. Jones, ante page 231 that the claim for dower, being inchoate at the execution of the deeds, constituted no breach of the covenant for *seizin*; and on that ground it would have been proper to arrest judgment but a verdict having been found for the plaintiff on a plea of the Statute of Limitations, contrary to the evidence, a new trial was granted.

This was an action of covenant against the defendant and his wife, who was the executrix of the last will and testament of William Dack, deceased.

The first count of the declaration set out an indenture between William Dack and the plaintiff, dated 16th of October, 1834, whereby Dack conveyed to the plaintiff the south-easterly half of Lot No. 20 in the fourth concession of the township of Kitley. In the indenture Dack covenanted that he was then lawfully and rightfully seised in his own right of a good, sure, perfect, absolute, and indefeasible estate of inheritance in fee simple in the land, without any condition, limita-

---

(a) See Ld. Raym. 326; Crabbe R. P. Secs. 1124, 1129, 1168, 1170; Bac. Abr. "Dower" B. 3; 1 Inst. 32 *a*; 1 Roll. Abr. 676, 677; 3 Co. 27 *a*.

tion of use or uses, or any other matter or thing to alter,
charge, change, incumber, or defeat the same. Upon this
covenant the breach alleged was that Dack was not so seised,
because a certain part of the premises—namely, the south
half thereof, being the south quarter of the lot—was then
liable to be charged and incumbered, and did afterwards
become charged and incumbered with a claim for dower—
namely one Elizabeth McLean, the wife of one Alexander
McLean, now deceased, who formerly and during his intermarriage with Elizabeth McLean, was seised in fee of the
south quarter of the lot, and while Elizabeth was his wife,
conveyed it to Willim Dack. The count then stated, that
after the death of William Dack, on the 1st January, 1851,
Alexander McLean died, leaving Elizabeth surviving whereby
she became entitled to dower, and thereupon did claim and
demand dower of and from the plaintiff, and on the 24th of
March, 1851, brought her action of dower against the plaintiff as tenant of the fee ; and so the plaintiff said the premises
thereby became charged and incumbered with the claim for
dower, contrary to the form and effect of the covenant: that the
plaintiff then, to remove the charge and incumbrance, compromised and compounded with Elizabeth McLean for a
release of her dower, for £15, and upon conditions that the
plaintiff should pay costs in the suit incurred: that the plaintiff paid those costs, and was put to expenses in negotiating
for and obtaining a settlement.

The second count set out another indenture, dated 20th of
June, 1827, between William Dack and the plaintiff whereby
he conveyed to the plaintiff the west half of lot No. 19 in
the 4th concession of the township of Kitley. A similar
covenant and breach were stated as in the first count. This
land was obtained by Dack from Alexander McLean also, and
Elizabeth claimed and obtained dower in this as well; and to
compromise the suit brought by her the plaintiff paid £15,
besides costs and other expenses, &c.

Pleas.—1. To the first count, *non est factum.* 2. To the
first count that the deed was obtained by fraud. 3. To the
first count that the deed was made and executed by William
Dack to the plaintiff as a gratuity. 4. To the first count, that

William Dack was lawfully and rightfully seised without any condition, &c.—without this, that the estate was ever charged or encumbered, or liable to be charged or encumbered by reason of the claim for dower. 5. To second count *non est factum.* 6. To second count that the deed was executed as a gratuity. 7. To second count, same as fourth to first count; that Dack was seised, &c. 8. To second count, Statute of Limitations. 9. To the whole declaration, *plene administravit,* by the defendant Anne, as executrix of William Dack, deceased.

The plaintiff took issue on all except the ninth plea; and to that replied that William Dack had lands, &c.

At the trial before *Richards, J.,* at the last assizes held at Brockville, the title of Alexander McLean was admitted; and the conveyances from William Dack to the plaintiff, as stated in the declaration, and containing such covenants as declared upon, were also admitted. The suit by Elizabeth McLean for her dower was proved and that it was compromised by the plaintiff paying her £12 10s., and obtaining a release of her dower by deed bearing date the 10th of April, 1851. The plaintiff also paid the costs.

At the close of the plaintiff's case the defendant's counsel moved for a non-suit, on three several grounds, the first of which only is material to consider ; and that was, that the breach of covenant assigned is that Dack was not seised of an unincumbered estate, because Mrs. McLean's claim for dower was not discharged ; whereas the claim of a married woman for dower while her husband is alive is no breach of the covenant: her claim is inchoate and contingent, and may never attach, and if the covenant is not broken as soon as executed, it cannot be broken by anything occurring afterwards.

The learned judge declined to nonsuit the plaintiff, on the ground that if the objection were well founded the defendant should have demurred to the declaration, and should not have pleaded a greater variety of pleas, which must be tried and disposed of by a jury.

The defendants then went into evidence to prove that the deeds were given and executed as gratuities. It is not material to consider this question.

The learned judge directed the jury to find for the plaintiff on the first, second, fifth, eight, and ninth issues. He left the third issue to be disposed of by the jury, remarking that, if the evidence satisfied them, that the plaintiff was to support William Dack, then the deed could not be considered as given by way of gratuity. Upon the fourth and seventh issues, involving the same question, namely, whether William Dack was seised without the claim for dower being an incumbrance—he left it to the jury to find for the plaintiff if they were satisfied McLean conveyed the land to William Dack after his intermarriage with Elizabeth. Upon the sixth issue he left it to the jury to say whether the evidence satisfied them that William Dack had given the land in the second count mentioned to the plaintiff to enable him to vote at an election, and if so it was a gratuity, and in that case to find for the defendant.

The jury found for the plaintiff on all the issues except the sixth, and £15 damages, and upon the sixth issue they found for the defendant.

Freeland, in Easter Term, obtained a rule nisi for a new trial on the law and evidence, and for misdirection, or to arrest the judgment.

In the present term, *Mr. Freeland* was heard in support of his rule, but no one appeared to shew cause.

ROBINSON, C. J.—This rule has not been opposed for some reason ; perhaps the case may have been settled.

According to our decisions in Bass v. Bower (E. T. 5 Vic.), Hoyt v. Widderfield (5 U. C. R. 180), and Thornhill v. Jones (*ante* page 231), judgment should be arrested.

Besides the point there decided—that an inchoate claim to dower, which may never become an incumbrance, is not in fact an incumbrance, and so that the covenant of seizin was not broken at the moment of its being executed, which it must have been if an action can lie upon it at all—there is in this case the further objection to the declaration, that it charges it as a breach of the covenant that the premises were, at the time of giving the deed, *liable to be* charged and incumbered, and that they were afterwards charged and incumbered. . Their being afterwards charged and incumbered is certainly no breach of the covenant *in præsenti*, though it would be a breach of the covenant to indemnify against incumbrances, and might lead to a breach of the covenant for quiet enjoyment; and as to the premises being *liable to be* incumbered, that surely is no breach of the covenant for title, which is a covenant *in præsenti*.

The grantor did not covenant that the land was *not liable to be incumbered*, for that it always must be; but that it was *then* unincumbered, or rather that *he* was seised of a good legal estate *in his own right*, without any thing to alter, charge, change, incumber, or defeat the *same*—that is, to incumber, or defeat *his estate*, which he was selling, and which was in fact unincumbered, for all that then appeared or might ever happen.

I am not clear that the defendant was entitled to succeed on the fourth and seventh pleas, for he traverses that "the estate was *ever* charged or incumbered, or liable to be charged or incumbered, by reason of the alleged claim of dower," which denial is contrary to the fact, for it was liable to be incumbered, and did become incumbered after McLean's death.

On the eighth plea, of the Statute of Limitations, however, it seems clear that the defendant should have succeeded and on that account I concur in the new trial; otherwise I should have thought that our proper course would have been to arrest the judgment.

BURNS, J.—The question presented in this case is nearly similar to the case of Thornhill v. Jones, decided in this present term, the only difference being that it is not the wife of the grantor in the conveyance to the tenant of the land who claims dower, but the wife of the proprietor preceding the grantor, who made the claim; and the question is, whether the covenant of the grantor for seizin of an indefeasible estate of inheritance, without any matter or thing to alter, charge, change, incumber, or defeat the same, is broken by the claim made for dower. There is a great distinction between a covenant of that kind and one to indemnify against incumbrances. It is the latter covenant which is used in English conveyances, and may be brought into existence at some future period, subsequent to the making of the convey-ance. This is shewn, and the distinction between such a covenant and the covenant *in præsenti*, in Platt on Cove-nants, ch. 11, sec. 4th. The covenants in both deeds in this case are covenants *in præsenti*, the consequence of which is that, if the wife's claim for dower be an incumbrance on the estate of inheritance, these covenants must have been broken immediately upon the execution of the indentures. A right of action accrued, if it ever did accrue, to the plaintiff at once upon the execution thereof. In the case of the inden-ture in the second count, the twenty years had expired from the date of the deed before the death of Alex. McLean, the deed being dated the 20th of June, 1827, and McLean dying, as proved, on the 9th of October, 1850. The wife could not advance her claim for dower until her title to it became com-plete; and if the covenant was broken as soon as executed, and a right of action immediately accrued, the Statute of Limitations must have begun to run from that time; and then the result must be that an injustice, in case of the lapse of twenty years from the time the covenant executed before the wife's title be completed, must be sustained by the tenant of the freehold. If he had brought his action during the life-time of the husband, it is not pretended that he would be entitled to recover more than nominal damages; and if the twenty years have expired before her title to dower is com-pleted, then the tenant is barred of his action. The statute 7 Wm. IV. ch. 3, sec. 3, gave ten years to bring an action of covenant after the passing of that act, or twenty years from the cause of action. The declaration in this case charges that the covenant was broken as soon as executed, by reason of the dower being an incumbrance; and goes on to shew what damages the plaintiff sustained by reason of its being en-forced against him when the title of the dowress was com-pleted. Whatever may be said in case the claim is made by the wife of the grantor, that it is not an incumbrance until the death of the husband, and so operates from that time only as a breach of the covenant, it is obvious that in this case the

claim being by the wife of a former proprietor, the grantor's
covenants were broken as soon as made.   These considerations establish either that there is a defect in the law, or that
it cannot be the case that a claim for dower comes within
the operation of the present covenant.   When I use the expression *claim for dower*, I mean an inchoate contingent
right.   It appears to me, however, that such a claim is not
within the meaning of the covenants declared upon in this
case.   The dower is not a condition or limitation of use, and
therefore, if it affects the covenant, must come under the
expression *other matter or thing*; and let us see what the
other matter or thing is required to do.   It must alter,
charge, change, incumber, or defeat the estate of inheritance.
Possibly it may incumber the estate at some future period;
but then the covenant is not against what may happen subsequently, but against a present matter which incumbers.
I do not see how that as to which no one can tell whether
it ever will happen to be an incumbrance or not, can be said
to be an incumbrance before the event does happen. What
is in existence undoubtedly is ; but how what possibly may
be in existence at some future time, and it is quite uncertain whether it ever will, can be pronounced to exist, I cannot understand. The claim for dower may all the time exist
but that claim cannot incumber ; it is only when the claim
becomes a title that it incumbers.   It wants the ingredient
which other demands present that may be said to be *debitum
in præsenti solvendum in futuro*, that of certainty of existence as an incumbrance ; the title may never come into
existence.   I think the covenant means something that at
the time is in existence as a certainty. The claim for dower
may be protected against by covenants to indemnify against
future incumbrances, or for quiet enjoyment of the estate.

    In this case the defendants have moved to arrest the
judgment, as well as for a new trial, and if the defence by
plea did not appear upon record, it might be a question
whether to arrest the judgment or grant a new trial.   In this
case the fourth and seventh pleas would raise precisely the
question which the defendant's counsel took at the trial, if no
special traverse had been inserted.   The eighth plea, of the

Statute of Limitations, should have been found in the defendant's favour ; and on the defence as to one count the defendants are entitled to have a judgment of record in their favour, notwithstanding that the declaration would not be sustained. The proper course is therefore to grant a new trial, with costs to abide the event.

DRAPER, J., concurred.

Rule absolute for new trial.

In re CÆSAR AND THE MUNICIPALITY OF THE TOWNSHIP OF CARTWRIGHT.

Resolutions of Municipal Corporations.

The Court has no jurisdiction over resolutions of municipal corporations, to set them aside summarily in the same manner as by-laws.

C. Robinson moved for a rule on the Municipality of Cartwright, to shew cause why the resolution passed by them on the 29th of December last, respecting the pay of the councillors for the said township, should not be quashed with costs, on the ground that they have exceeded their jurisdiction and powers in passing such resolution, and that the same is illegal.

This resolution was authenticated in the same manner as by-laws are under the statute 12 Vic. ch. 81, when they are intended to be moved against.

The paper transmitted was in these words :—

" A by-law was brought in by Dr. Howe to empower the council to receive pay for their services for the present year and in future, and to receive the sum of six shillings and three pence per day."

A copy of a resolution passed in council the 29th day of December, 1853.

" Moved by Howe, seconded by Taylor, that the clause referred to in the resolution or by-law respecting the councillors' pay, where it says six shillings and three-pence per day, shall be repealed, and to only be five shillings per day, which was carried."

The clerk certified the above to be a true copy taken from the journal of the Municipal Council of the township of Cartwright ; and that there had been no other by-law signed in relation to the above proceedings; and he added, at the foot of this, a certificate that there never was any by-law written; but that it was merely mentioned by Howe, and entered in the council book as above stated.

This was all certified under date of the 7th of September, 1854.

Daniels v. The Municipality of Burford, 10 U. C. R. 478, Grant on Corporations 378, were cited in support of the application.

Cur. adv. vult.

ROBINSON, C. J., delivered the judgment of the court.

The questions are:—

1. Is this resolution *properly* before us as to its mode of being verified?

2. If so, can we notice it, as there is no authority to bring resolutions before us, as in the case of by-laws; or should the motion be for a *certiorari*, in the first place?

3. Does a *certiorari* lie to a municipal council to return their resolutions appropriating money, or are they merely void acts, not being by by-law?

4. Have we authority to quash such resolutions when illegal?

Without going further into these points than is necessary for disposing of this application, we are of opinion that we cannot grant the rule nisi to quash the resolution. It is not before us so that we can notice it. Nothing is said in the municipal acts of this court quashing resolutions of the councils, but only their by-laws. If they pass illegal resolutions, such acts of theirs are simply void, and we doubt not they incur a liability by so transgressing their authority. The English statute respecting municipal corporations. 7 Wm. IV. and 1 Vic., ch. 78, sec. 44, makes provision for removing resolutions or orders of municipal corporations appropriating moneys, in order that, if they are illegal, a convenient remedy may be promptly obtained. We find no such provision in our statutes, and we have no common law jurisdiction over them, to set them summarily aside. They are not like the orders of justices in sessions, which are judicial acts of a court of record.   Rule refused.

FARREL v. The Mayor and Town Council of the Town
of London.

Corporation—Liability of, for injuries caused by construction of sewer — Corporate seal—Misnomer—Pleading.

Held, that a municipal corporation were liable for injuries committed in the construction of a sewer under the superintendance of their engineer, the work having been accepted by them, though no authority or contract was shewn under the corporate seal.

Held also, that an inaccuracy in the corporate name was immaterial after verdict, the identity of the corporate body being clear.

Held also, that the injury complained of was sufficiently alleged in the declaration to be a wrongful act.

CASE by the plaintiff, for injury to his reversionary interest in a messuage and premises in the possession of one Norris, as tenant, in the town of London. *First count*—that the defendant, contriving, &c., wrongfully and unjustly dug up, &c., large quantities of earth, &c., from a sewer then being constructed by the defendants in the said town, into and upon the street and the sidewalk adjoining the plaintiff's messuage, and permitted the earth so to remain and continue, by reason whereof, and of the rain and snow falling, and running down therefrom, mud and water flowed into and upon the plaintiff's messuage, and injured the doors, walls, floors, &c., &c., permanently. *Second count*—Similar injury to a house in the occupation of one Birs. *Third count* —Similar injury to a house in the occupation of one Soper. *Fourth count*—Similar injury to a house in the occupation of one Fraser.

Pleas 1.—Not guilty, "by statute." 2. That the water or mud did not flow, &c., into the houses in the 1st, 2nd, and 3rd counts mentioned—3. To so much of the 1st, 2nd, and 3rd counts as relates to digging up, and throwing earth, &c., out of the sewer then being made upon the street and side walk, justification under a by-law of the town council. The plaintiff took issue on first and second pleas, and replied *de injuriâ* to the last.

The case was tried at London, in May, 1854, before *Draper, J.*—It was sufficiently proved that the construction of the sewer was under the control and superintendance of the defendant's surveyor and engineer, and that they had in common council adopted resolutions for the undertaking this work, for the preparation of plans and specifications for it by

their engineer, and for accepting the tender of the person by
whom it was done; but no contract, or any authority under
the seal of the corporation, was given in evidence respecting
the performance of this work, or the employment of the
engineer who superintended it on their behalf. A good deal
of evidence on both sides was given to shew that the plaintiff's
premises were damaged by the mud and water being caused
to flow thereon, owing to the earth being thrown up out of
the excavation in the centre of the street on to the road and
side walk opposite the plaintiff's houses and being left there
some months while the sewer was being constructed ; and
that such damage was an injury not merely temporary, but
affecting the reversion. It was objected at the trial that the
evidence was legally insufficient to connect the defendants
with the work and the consequent injury. This was overruled,
leave being reserved to renew it on motion for nonsuit.—
Also, that defendants were discharging a public duty—
viz.: draining the town, and therefore were not liable. This
was overruled, as, though the act was lawful, yet it might
be so done as to injure third parties, who would have a right
to redress.—3rdly. That the case came within the 35th sec.
of 16 Vic. ch. 181. This was not however pressed, as on
reference to the statute the objection appeared untenable;
and the jury were left to say whether on the evidence they
were satisfied the work was done under the authority of
the defendants, and whether the plaintiff had sustained any
damage to his reversionary interest. They found for the
plaintiff, damages £5.

In Easter Term M. C. Cameron obtained a rule nisi to
enter a nonsuit on the leave reserved, also for a new trial
on the law and evidence.

In this term, Connor, Q. C., shewed cause, citing Eastern
Counties R. W. Co., v. Broom, 6 Ex., 314; Smith v. Bir-
mingham Gas Co., 1 A. & E. 526, 3 N. & M. 771, S. C.;
Maund v. Monmouthshire Canal Co., 4 M. & Gr. 452 ; Roe
v. Pierce, 2 Camp. 96 ; Regina v. Mayor of Stamford, 6 Q.
B. 433 ; Com. Dig. " Pleaded," B. 2.

Cameron, in reply, did not strongly press the point reserved
at the trial, but urged that the declaration was not sustained

by the evidence, for the charge was a wrongful digging up and throwing out of the earth from the drain or sewer, whereas that act was rightful. The wrong really urged at the trial was either leaving the earth there unnecessarily long, or without proper care to prevent injury to plaintiff—admitting that the digging and throwing up was rightful.—Mayor of Ludlow v. Charlton, 6 M. & W. 815. He also objected that the defendants were wrongly named *The Mayor and Town Council*, instead of *The Town Council.*—12 Vic. ch 81, sec. 61.

ROBINSON, C. J., delivered the judgment of the court.

We are of opinion that, upon the authorites cited in the argument, there is no doubt whatever that the defendants are liable in trespass on the case for the injury complained of, notwithstanding there was no proof of an authority given by them under their corporate seal for the commission of the injury complained of. It was left to the jury to say, whether they were satisfied of the fact, that the sewer was made for the use of the defendants and at their instance, and adopted by them as a work done under their authority ; and they found that this was so, which there could not be the least doubt of, upon the evidence given. This was the principipal point in the case.

As to any inaccuracy in the corporate name by which the defendants are sued, the only question now is, as to the identity of the corporate body, which is clear enough on the face of the record and on the evidence.

I agree, also, that the third objection, now first made, that the injury did not in fact arise from the cause mentioned in the declaration—namely, the digging and making the sewer—but from the suffering the earth to continue so long on the side of the road without being removed, should not be considered as open to the party now, not having been taken at the trial. But in truth the declaration does complain of the earth being permitted to lie for a long time near the plaintiff's house. Though the word *wrongfully* is not prefixed to the charge of permitting, yet, as used in the sentence, it applies, I think, to the continuing as well as to the digging up the earth; besides, if upon this new objection we were to grant a new trial, we could hardly refuse leave to the plaintiff to amend his declaration.

The damages are very moderate, and the rule, we think, should be discharged.

It seems not to have been noticed that in strictness the defendant was entitled to succeed upon the pleas to which *de injuriâ* was replied, as the leaving the earth unnecessarily for a great length of time near the plaintiff's house was not charged as access in answer to this plea.

Rule discharged.

REGINA v. BABY.

Indictment—No new trial under 14 & 15 *vic. ch.* 13—*Indictment under* 13 & 14 *Vic. ch.* 74, *for purchasing land from Indians without the consent of government —To what lands the Act extends—Scienter— Variance between indictment and proof, as to lands purchased—Meaning and object of the statute.*

The court has no power to order a new trial in a criminal case reserved under 14 & 15 Vic., ch. 13 ; but only to decide upon any legal exceptions raised, and whether there was legal evidence to sustain the indictment, taking it in a strong sense against the defendant as it will bear, and supposing the jury to have given credit to it to its full extent.

The 13 & 14 Vic., ch. 74, prohibits the buying or contracting to buy from Indians, not merely any lands of which they are in actual possession, but any lands held by the government for their use or benefit ;—but

Quœre, whether the clauses of the act relating to trespasses on Indain lands extend to any lands not actually possessed by them.

Held, that the indictment in this case, after verdict, sufficiently averred the lands purchased by defendant to be Indian lands—*i. e,* lands held by the crown for them ; and *Quœre,* whether the act extends only to lands so held, or as well to lands purchased by Indians from individuals.

A guilty knowledge on defendant's part sufficiently averred in the indictment.

Held, also, that no varlance was shown between the land described in the indictment and that which the defendant was proved to have contracted for.

Held, also, no objection that the purchase was alleged to have been from certain Indians named, whereas it was in fact from the tribe through their council.

Held, also, that the evidence in this case was sufficient to sustain the conviction.

Semble, that the meaning of the statute is, that no one shall attempt to bargain with the Indians for the purchase of their lands, until he has first obtained the consent of government ; and that it is therefore contrary to the act to make even a conditional agreement, subject to their approval. The proposal should be made to government in the first instance.

SPECIAL CASE, reserved under 14 & 15 Vic. ch. 13.

The defendant was indicted under the statute 13 & 14 Vic., ch. 74, for making a contract with certain Indains, concerning the sale and purchase of certain lands, and of the interest of the said Indians therein.

The indictment charged that Joseph White and two other persons, who were named in the indictment, were and are

Indians of and residing in Upper Canada—to wit, in the township of Anderdon, in the county of Essex—and as such Indians were, on the twenty-first day of June, in the sixteenth year of the reign of her present Majesty, entitled to and claimed certain lands situate in the town of Sandwich, in the said county of Essex (which were particularly described in the indictment); and that the defendant who was described as an attorney-at-law, well knowing the premises, and that the three persons named were such Indians in Upper Canada as aforesaid, on, &c., at, &c., without the authority or consent of her Majesty the now Queen unlawfully did make a contract with the said three persons, so being such Indians of Upper Canada as aforesaid, for and concerning the sale and purchase of the said lands, and of the interest of the said three persons, as such Indians, therein—against the form of the statute and against the peace, &c.

At the trial at Sandwich before *Draper, J.*, the following evidence was adduced on the part of the Crown :—

George Jessup, sworn—I married a daughter of the late Mr. Mears. I know a piece of land at the east and northerly end of the town (Sandwich), described by the boundaries in the indictment. I knew the late Mr. Mears twenty years ago. He was then in possession of this land. The Indians near Amherstburgh claim this land. I knew Alexander Clark and Joseph White; both Indians, part of those Indians who claim this land.

Cross-examined.—I only speak of the land between the road and river as being claimed by the Indians.

Alexander Clark sworn—I claim to be an Indian by usage. I am recognized as such. I know the land spoken of. The Indians claim this land where Mrs. Hand's house is and the steam-mill. I am fifty-four years old. Mears had one part of this land and Mr. Hands one, as long as I can recollect. It was decided by the Indians in our council here, the Indians named in the indictment being parties to the decision, that we did not want this land, and we resolved to take possession first and then to sell. We were prevented taking possession of the vacant spot. We then consulted Mr. Baby, the defendant. We could get no satisfaction from our agent to whom we applied to sell it. We negotiated with defendant for the vacant lot, which we valued at £250, and he agreed to take it from us at £250, and to run all risks and bear all expenses. I joined with other Indians in making this contract.

Cross-examined.—We tried to take possession before we consulted defendant, but Col. Prince opposed us. We were then only contending for the piece near the river, not for the whole block. We heard of an old lease called the Walker lease. The contract was written down by defendant. It was early in June. We all signed the paper, and afterwards signed another paper (looks at a paper). This is one of the papers, dated 28th of June, 1852; it is executed by me and the other chiefs, at the school house in council, (read). It is a power of attorney only, from the Indians to defendant. The defendant said it would not be lawful to purchase, except through the government. He drew petitions to the government, which we signed. The result was that, because the defendant was not the recognized agent for the Indians, Colonel Bruce, the chief superintendent, would not recognize him or the petition, a certified copy of the petition, put in by consent of *Prince, Q. C.*). The defendant prepared this petition for us, and sent it in. Our first desire was to have the whole sold in a lump, and to get the money to be used at our village for improvements. Afterwards we were willing to sell to the several parties in possession, The defendant told us this was the wish of the government, and we refer to this in the petition just read. The defendant was requested by us to attend our councils on the matter. He was acting for our interests, as we employed him.

Re-examined.—Before signing the power of attorney we sold to defendant for £250 this land, provided the government consented to it—*i. e.*, the upper piece. I don't think this first agreement was in writing. We sold to defendant on condition the government would sanction it. Then we found our rights extended to much more land than this piece, and therefore we rescinded the agreement to sell to defendant.

Dominique Langlois sworn—I am 57 or 58 years old. This property was in a great part occupied by old Williams for forty years and Hands occupied another part. I was present when a negotiation took place to sell this land, or an interest in it, or part of it, to defendant. He was to give $1000 or $1100. This was two years ago last June. I had a paper given to me by Mr. Baby, the defendant, but on search, I could not find it.

Cross-examined.—I went with the Indians to defendant, and know that they employed defendant. I previously employed him for myself. He told me, in presence of the Indians that there could be no purchase or lease from the Indians without the consent of the government. The last witness was there and some other chiefs. Joseph White was there. This was at the same time as the bargain about the sale to defendant. At first the Indians only thought they had a right to a part, but on seeing the old lease defendant said to the Indians they had a right to more. Defendant said "I will give you $1000,"—*i. e.*, to the Indians—"if the government will sanction the sale to me." Except the government did, he would not pay them anything at all.

Thomas King sworn.—At one of the Indian councils, where defendant was, I was present. There was a dispute among the Indins as to the value of these lands. At first they thought they had only two acres, then they found they had more, and they said they should get more. The defendant produced a paper which he said they had signed, and they admitted it. He said it was an agreement made for some land in the town of Sandwich for $1000, but that was to be kept secret. It was said, however, amongst them, that it had become null and void, in consequence of something, but what I cannot tell It might have happened at a council held in February, 1853. The conversation referred to an agreement made in June, 1852.

Louis J. Fluette sworn—I have heard of this dispute. I have been for ten years in possession of a part of the land. I saw the Indians coming to put up fences, and felt apprehensive of difficulty in consequence of something I heard. I went to defendant and asked if we were to be ousted of our property. He said it was too true; we had no title, and the Indians would oust us. I asked him what would become of my improvements? He said, you will have to purchase again to get a title. I said I would give anything to make good my title, and he asked me what I had paid? I said $150. He said, "if you and the rest will put your heads together, I will make, or I can make, your title good." He asked $150 to do this. From what defendant said, I understood he had the management of the whole concern in his hands. He said he had been to Toronto to see about it to the government, and the business was in a fair way.

William Clark sworn.—I am an Indian. I know this land. Our people claim it as part of their property.

The defendant's counsel admitted service of a notice to produce the contract spoken of.

DEEENCE.

Pierre H. Morin sworn.—The power of attorney put in was witnessed by me—I wrote it, read it to the Indians, and saw them execute it. The defendant was present. A petition to the government was signed at the same time. Nothing was said at that time about any contract between the parties.

Thomas Woodbridge sworn.—I am in possession of part of this land. I have no fear of what government will do.

The jury were out all night, and on the following morning returned a general verdict of guilty.

Mr. *Cooper* made the following objections in arrest of judgment.

1. The evidence is not sufficient in law to establish the offence created by the statute.

2. If evidence of a contract, it was only for a small piece of ground, parcel of the described in the indictment, wherefore the indictment, describing it as one piece by metes and bounds, is not sustained.

3. The evidence not only did not establish anything contrary to the statute, but it did prove an understanding consistent with the statute.

4. The indictment does not charge an attempt to purchase such lands—*i.e.*, lands *de facto* in possession of the Indians—as the statute refers to.

5. The allegation in the indictment is of a purchase from

certain of the Indians (named), whereas the purchase proved was from the body or tribe of Indians represented in their council.

6. There is no proof that these particular Indians named in the indictment had any interest to sell.

Prince, Q. C., for the crown, had previously agreed that any objections that might be raised to the legality of the conviction should be reserved for the opinion of the court; and as the learned judge entertained some doubt as to the sufficiency, in point of form, of the indictment, though no other objections than those above noted were taken, he reserved the case, without passing sentence, the defendant giving security to appear at the next assizes, for the opinion of the Court of Queen's Bench.

[The statute 13 & 14 Vic. ch. 74, is intituled "An act for the protection of the Indians in Upper Canada from imposition, and the property occupied and enjoyed by them from trespass and injury."

It recites that "It is expedient to make provision for the protection of the Indians in Upper Canada, who, in their intercourse with the other inhabitants thereof, are exposed to be imposed upon by the designing and unprincipled, as well as to provide more summary and effectual means for the protection of such Indians *in the unmolested possession and enjoyment* of the lands and *other property in their use or occupation.*

And it enacts "That no purchase or contract for the sale of lands in Upper Canada which may be made of or with the Indians, or any of them, shall be valid, unless made under the authority and with the consent of her Majesty, her heirs or successors, attested by an instrument under the great seal of the province, or under the privy seal of the governor thereof for the time being."

And (sec. 2) "That if any person, without such authority and consent, shall in *any manner or form,* or upon any terms whatsoever, purchase or lease any lands within Upper Canada of or from the said Indians, or any of them, or *make any contract* with such Indians, or *any of them,* for or concerning the sale of any lands therein, or shall in any manner give, sell, demise, convey or otherwise dispose of any such lands, or any interest therein, or offer so to do, or shall enter on, or take possession of, or settle on any such lands, by pretext or color of any right or interest in the same, in consequence of any purchase or contract made or to be made with such Indians, or any of them, unless with such authority and consent as aforesaid, every such person shall in every such case be deemed guilty of a misdemeanor, and shall, on conviction thereof before any court of competent jurisdiction, forfeit and pay to her Majesty, her heirs or successors, the sum of £200 and be further punished by fine and imprisonment, at the discretion of the court.]

Before the trial a notice was served upon the defendant that he would be required to produce a certain bond, agreement, and paper in writing, made or purporting to be made between him and others, and certain Indians of the township of Anderdon, in the county of Essex, and a certain person or certain persons on behalf of such Indians, for the purchase, sale, or transfer of the whole or part of the interest claimed by the said Indians in certain lands and premises in the town of Sandwich aforesaid, occupied by, &c. (naming the occupants), and which said bond, agreement, or writing was entered into by him, the defendant and others, the parties thereto, within the last twelve months or thereabouts.

And also a certain power of attorney from the said Indians or some of them, or their agent, to the defendant, relating to the said lands or to their interest therein; and also all other deeds, bonds, agreements, contracts, and writings made and entered into by the defendant with the said Indians, or any of them, or any agent of theirs, relating to the same lands.

Richards for the crown.

Cooper, contra, cited—Beasley v. Cahill, 2 U. C. R. 320; Rex v. Robinson, Holt N. P. C. 595; Rex v. Deeley, 4 C & P. 579; Regina v. Jones, 1 Cox 105; Regina v. Taunton 1 Moo. C. Ca. 118; Rex v. Great Canfield, 6 Esp. 136; Rex v. Upton-on-Severn, 6 C. & P. 133; Tay. Ev. 1. 190; Rosc. C. L. 111–112; Rex v. Philpotts, I C. & K. 112.

ROBINSON, C. J., delivered the judgment of the court

It is scarcely necessary to say that the statute 14 & 15 Vic. ch. 13. under which cases are submitted to us from the criminal courts gives us no authority to order a new trial, or to prevent a verdict of guilty from going into effect because we may think that the jury would have exercised a sounder judgment if they had acquitted. We may consider the evidence for the prosecution to be weak; we may find it to be conflicting, and may have a strong impression that, if we ourselves had formed part of the jury we might not have been satisfied with it. But it is not in that point of view that we are at liberty to look at any case referred to us under the statute : we have only to pronounce judgment upon any particular legal exceptions which have been or may be raised either upon the pleadings or the *evidence*, or upon the general question, which is strictly one of law, whether there was legal evidence given at the trial sufficient to sustain the prosecution, taking it in as strong a sense against the defendant as it will bear, and supposing the jury to have given credit to it to its full extent.

Now, as to the particular legal objections raised by *Mr. Cooper* in this case, the statute does we think, prohibit the buying from Indians, or contracting to buy from them, without the consent of the Crown, not merely any lands of which they are actually in possession, but any lands held by the government for their use and benefit, whether actually used and possessed by them or not. The consideration of policy which led to the enactment would apply in the latter case as well as in the former, and there is nothing in the language of the clauses relating to this prohibition which would warrant us in giving to it so limited a construction as that contended for. In those parts of the act which relate to the punishment of trespassers on Indian lands, there is some evidence of an intention to confine such provisions to lands actually possessed and enjoyed by Indians, though it is unnecessary now to determine whether they can or cannot be extended further.

Another objection taken to the indictment is, that it does not shew that the land contracted for by the defendant was what is called Indian land—that is, public lands yet vested in the Crown, and held by the Queen for the use and benefit of the Indians.

It is contended that the prohibition against purchasing without the consent of the government relates to such lands only, and not to any lands which an Indian or Indians may have acquired by purchase from individuals, or may hold like any other person by grant from the Crown ; and the objection is that for all that appears in the indictment, the land now in question may have been held under a title of the latter description.

We think the answer which must be given to this objection is, that the first and second clauses of the statute are as general in their language as the indictment is ; and that, by the 47th clause of our statute 4 & 5 Vic. ch. 24, it is provided that where an offence is created by any statute the indictment or information shall,after verdict,be held sufficient if it describe the offence in the words of the statute creating the offence.

Whether if it had appeared upon the trial that the Indians named were only contracting to sell to the defendant some land which they held by an ordinary title in fee simple, it would have been proper to hold such contract to be within the act, is another question, and one which at present seems to us rather doubtful upon a view of the whole statute. But we cannot doubt from the evidence that the land in question was in fact what we ordinarily understand by Indian lands ; and indeed the indictment does contain the averment that White and the others named where, *"as such Indians,* entitled to the land mentioned. We are of opinion,therefore, that we cannot give way to this objection.

It has been urged also that the indictment is deficient in not clearly enough averring a guilty knowledge on the part of the defendant. As to that it must be considered that the clauses of the statute on which it is framed contain nothing in express terms that calls for the introduction of a *scienter ;* and, in the next place, that the indictment does nevertheless contain the allegation that the defendant well knew that White and the others named were, as Indians, entitled to these lands. We cannot therefore see that there is any room for this objection.

Another fault found with the indictment,and intended,we think, to be strongly insisted upon, was that there was a fatal variance between the proof and the statement, in this, that the indictment charges that the defendant contracted to buy certain lands particularly described, being a certain messuage and lands in the town of Sandwhich occupied by one George Jessop, and a certain other messuage and lands occupied by one Hannah Easter Mears, widow, which said messuages and lands adjoin each other, and are bounded on the north by a certain run of water near the church line which there empties itself into the river Detroit, on the south by a messuage and premises belonging to Alexander Chewett, Esquire, on the east by the Queen's public highway leading from the town of Sandwich aforesaid to the village of Windsor, and on the west by the river Detroit aforesaid; whereas it is contended that all that can be said to have been proved was, that the defendant contracted to buy the small pieces of land between the public highway and the river, and not the land described in the indictment. We understood this to be the nature of Mr. Cooper's objection relating to the variance, but it appears to be founded on a misconception of the description in the indictment, for that comprises in reality only the small tract of land between the road and river, and the defendant is not charged with having contracted to buy more than that. There is some ground offered in the evidence for supposing that the written agreement spoken of by the witness King did in fact embrace more land than this, or at least that the defendant, after he had taken it, claimed that it included more.

If the defendant had produced the writing upon the notice given to him, we should have been able to see exactly what it did include. If it were found only to include the pieces of land between the road and the river—in other words, west of the road—then there would be no ground for the objection of variance, for the indictment and the writing would correspond. If it were found to contain that land as described in the indictment and other lands besides, that would be no variance, for the charge in the indictment would in that case be strictly proved, and it would only appear that the charge might have been carried further. But in the absence of the deed, which for all that appears, it was in the power of the defendant to have produced, we could not hold that any

variance was shewn. The exact purport of the deed is left
in some degree in doubt upon the evidence, and we cannot
tell what conclusion the jury came to in regard to the precise
land which it contained. All that can be said is, that they
could scarcely have doubted that it did include the land in
front of the road, if nothing more, which was all that was
necessary to support the indictment in that respect.

We do not think that there is anything in the objections
taken at the trial, that the indictment alleges that the defendant made a purchase from certain Indians named; whereas
the purchase, so far as it was proved, was from the body or
tribe of Indians through their council; and also that it was
not proved that the particular Indians named in the indictment had any interest to dispose of.

The statute is very general in its terms. It provides that
no contract made with the *Indians, or any of them,* for the
sale of land in Upper Canada shall be valid; and that if a
person shall make *any contract* with the Indians in Upper
Canada, *or any of them,* for or concerning the sale *of any
lands therein,* without the authority and consent of her
Majesty, he shall be deemed guilty of a misdemeanor.

The evidence given upon the trial tended to prove that the
defendant did make a contract with certain Indians in Upper
Canada for and concerning the sale of lands therein. The
persons named were proved to be three of the Indians interested in the land in question, or claiming to be so ; and it
was proved that they contracted to sell to the defendant for
£250 the land named. He knew they had not the legal title,
which was vested in the Crown, and not in a tribe of Indians;
but what they contracted to sell was the interest of the
Indians in it, including their own interest, which is what
the indictment charges, and is within the letter and the
spirit of the act.

If there appeared to us to be a clear objection to the conviction on any ground, however technical, we should have no
disinclination to give effect to it ; for we have received the
impression from the evidence that the defendant very probably either made his contract or commenced his treaty with
the Indians in ignorance of the prohibition contained in the

act of parliament and of the heavy penalty which it imposes; or that, if he was aware of these, it is doubtful whether he ever anticipated making a bargain otherwise than subject to the condition understood between him and the Indians that it should receive the sanction of the government. And, whatever effect this could be allowed to have in saving him from the penalties of the statute, it would go very far to relieve the defendant from the charge of criminal intention, if we could see clearly and certainly that such had been his conduct.

Being of the opinion however that none of the legal exceptions taken are fatal to the conviction, we have to consider the case as it stands upon the evidence, and to determine whether, upon the broad ground on which it was mainly argued, the defendant has been lawfully convicted of an offence within the statute. In determining this point, the impression which we have just intimated, that the defendant was perhaps ignorant of the terms of this statute on which he has been prosecuted, can have no influence upon our decision. He was bound, as others are, to know the law and to observe it, and we cannot be satisfied that he did not know it.

Upon what point it was that the jury had difficulty in coming to a conclusion does not appear, but it seems they were out a whole night; and I confess that, as a juror, I should have had some difficulty, merely upon consideration of what was safe and reasonable in convicting the defendant upon the account that was given of his conduct. The statute gives no power to mitigate the penalty according to the apparent degree of criminality, and every scruple would therefore be felt to apply with greater force.

But, upon an anxious consideration of the evidence, we cannot pronounce that in our opinion it does not in point of law sustain the conviction, and that the jury have given an illegal verdict.

It was desirable certainly that it should have been made plainer and more certain what was the precise nature of the contract into which the defendant entered. There was evidence on his own admission, and some evidence otherwise, of a contract in writing for the sale to him of this Indian land. That writing must be assumed to be in his possession, and he had notice to produce it. He did not attempt to contradict the evidence that there was a written contract in fact, nor give any reason for his not producing it. It is just therefore, under such circumstances, to take the account that was given of the purport of that contract most strongly against the defendant since, for all that appears, he had it in his power to shew the jury the real particulars of his contract by producing the writing which he had taken and, it is reasonable to suppose he would have done so if that would have disproved or weakened the charge against him.

It stands uncertain upon the evidence whether the defendant in the first instance fairly told the Indians that he could not and would not make any bargain with them except subject to the consent of the government, or whether, after he had made his bargain and had offended against the statute, whether in ignorance of it or not, and perhaps after his own conduct had been complained of by some of the parties interested, he made the Indians aware that he could not insist upon his bargain unless the government would sanction it.

It does not appear either, whether in the writing any reference is made to the consent of the government as a necessary condition of the contract.

That the defendant had not in fact the consent or authority of the government seems clear upon the correspondence produced.

We can easily believe it posssible that this defendant or any other person wishing to buy lands from the Indians, might be under the impression that if he entered into the contract only conditionally and openly and avowedly made his agreement subject to the consent and approbation of the government, he would not be offending against the act; and we can believe that if the jury in this case had been satisfied upon the evidence that the defendant had acted openly in that spirit and upon that understanding and no other from the first, they would probably not have found the defendant guilty. The learned judge who tried the cause is under the impression that, from the observations with which he gave the case to the jury, they would have acquitted the defendant if they had taken that view of his conduct on the evidence. It may be that the difficulty which the jury had in coming to a conclusion arose from the necessity of their considering very carefully the bearing of the evidence in that respect. But upon that point two considerations arise—first, if the jury had acquitted the defendant expressly upon the ground that he had only made his agreement subject to the approval of the government, would that have been taking a correct view of the intention and spirit of the statute? At present we will only say that we look upon that as very doubtful; for there is much force and reason in Mr. Richards's argument, that the considerations of policy which gave rise to the statute, and, as we must suppose the intention of the legislature, are at variance with that construction.

The meaning probably, is that no one shall attempt to traffic with the Indians for the purchase of their lands, till he has first obtained the authority and consent of the government for entering into a contract with them. The Indians would not seem to be adequately protected against the evils recited in the statute if persons were allowed first to enter into a treaty with them, and after the Indians had compromised themselves as to price and terms of payment, to apply then for the confirmation of the crown. It would appear to be a more effectual protection if no one were allowed to enter into a conditional bargain with them for their land without obtaining previously the authority of the government to make such bargain; for if the government were appealed to before any specific proposal were made to the Indians, the course which we may suppose would be taken would be such as would leave not merely the Indians but the government in a position to act much more freely than by the other course, where, by declining to confirm, the government would in fact be annulling a bargain already made. The government, if applied to before any treaty as to price or terms had been entered into, would first have to consider whether it would be proper to allow the Indians to sell, and if so, they could take care that before any of the Indians had committed themselves to a bargain from which they might think it dishonorable to retract, the proposal to purchase should be opened and discussed at a council fairly representing the tribe, and in the presence of some public officer, who might see that everything was duly considered and understood, and fully agreed to. If we look at the letter of the statute, we think it can hardly be denied that a person who without authority of the government makes a bargain with the Indians to buy certain lands from them for a certain sum of money, *provided the government will give its consent,* does without authority of the government make a contract with the Indians concerning the sale of their lands; and we would recommend all persons who are inclined to bargain with the Indians for their lands, to go in the first place to the government and make the proposal to them, for we think that is what the legislature intended.

But it is really not necessary that we should pronounce upon this question, because we are not warranted in assuming that the jury were satisfied that the defendant openly and avowedly, and from the first, dealt with the Indians named upon the express understanding that the bargain was to go for nothing unless the government approved of it.

The evidence tends a great deal the other way though it was sworn that the defendant did state that everything must depend upon the consent and approval of the government, and that may have been at the time that the contract of purchase was made; but there was no proof that anything to that effect was inserted in the writing. The defendant seems to have taken a writing which the Indians understood and intended was only to relate to the small piece of land in front of the highway, though he afterwards, according to some of the testimony, asserted under it an interest in the larger tract on the east side of the road; and although he was long afterwards in communication with the Indian department of the government, endeavouring to procure permission to the Indians to make sale of their land, he does not seem in any of his letters or, in the documents, sent to the government, to have conveyed the intelligence that he had himself concluded on his own account any purchase, conditional or otherwise; but held himself out as interceding for the Indians, as their agent, merely, and without any intimidation, so far as appears that he had a personal interest in soliciting the consent for which he applied. This coupled with the defendant neither producing the writing, nor giving any reason for not producing it, left his conduct subject to any construction which the evidence would warrant ; and we cannot on any clear ground hold that he was illegally found to have offended against the statute in the manner charged in the indictment. If by referring to any points that were proved, and others that were omitted to be proved upon the trial, the defendant can shew his conduct to be entitled to be viewed in a different light from that in which we must suppose the jury to have viewed it, he must submit himself to the consideration of the executive government. We consider the conviction legal upon the indictment and evidence.

Conviction affirmed.

BECKETT V. FOY.

Will, construction of—Term vested in executors—Descent under 14 & 15 *Vic., ch.* 6.

R. died in 1847, having devised to T., the defendant's son, the land in question. He also devised to one B. another lot of land not quite paid for, declaring it as his wish that the land devised to T. should remain in the hands of his executors until a deed should be obtained for the lot left to B., and the executors were to make the necessary payments from the rents of his real and personal estate.—It was proved that the land devised to B. had been paid for, but the deed had not been obtained as there were rival claimants, and the vendor required indemnity.

Held, that the land devised to T. would vest on payment of the money for B.'s lot, though the deed had not been executed.

Both plaintiff and defendant claimed by deed from T.'s sister the plaintiff having the first conveyance. It was not distinctly proved at the trial when T. died, nor was it left to the jury to find whether he died before or after the 1st of January, 1852 when the 14 & 15 Vic., ch. 6, came into force —this point having escaped attention. If he died before, then the defendant would be entitled as claiming under his sister, who would be his heiress—if after, the defendant would be entitled as his mother, in preference to his sister.

A new trial was therefore ordered, with costs to abide the event, in order to give the plaintiff an opportunity of establishing his case on this point.

EJECTMENT for part of lot 6 in the 1st concession of Thurlow. The cause was tried in May, 1854, at Belleville, before *McLean, J.* It was admitted that one George Reid, deceased, had lived upon the premises in question. He died soon after the 22nd February, 1847, having made a will duly executed.

dated on that day, devising to his sister, the defendant, the
north half of these premises, and to the defendant's son John
the south half of them, to be divided as pointed out in the
will. He also devised to one Bridget Gerrity another lot,
which he had purchased from E. Murney, Esq., but which was
not fully paid for. In the will the testator declared it to be
his wish that the lands devised should remain in the hands of
his executors until Mr. Murney was paid, and a deed obtained
from him. The executors were to make the payment from
the rents, &c., of his real and personal estate. Mr. Murney
had been paid in full by defendant, who took the sole management of the testator's estate but he had made no deed, as
more than one party claimed, and he required to be indemnified. The defendant's son John was a blind boy, and left
the province not long after the death of George Reid. About
two years before the trial, the defendant went to the United
States in search of him, and on her return stated that
a boy, whom she believed from the account and description of him to be her son John, had, as she was informed
and as was stated in a writing she brought back with
her, died in Bellevue Hospital. No other evidence than
the defendant's statement was given of his death, nor was the
time of such death more particularly stated, but the plaintiff
shewed that the defendant, who was in possession, had
obtained from her daughter and only other child, Bridget
Foy, a deed, dated 23rd of June, 1853, conveying, for a consideration of £5, to defendant, in fee, all the right and title
she had in her own right, or as the representative or heiress
of any other person, in and to both the south and north
halves of the lot in question. The plaintiff further proved a
deed, dated the 25th of May, 1853, from Bridget Foy to himself, for an expressed consideration of £12 10s., for the
premises sued for. At the time of giving this deed, Bridget
Foy was an inmate of a house of ill-fame, in which she executed the deed, and received £10 on account of the consideration money. The person who procured the deed, and who
was one of the subscribing witnesses to it, stated it was
understood between him and the plaintiff that he was to get a
share of the land. The other subscribing witness was called,
and both swore she knew what she was about, and seemed

perfectly satisfied. The whole premises were proved to be worth £250 or £300.

On this evidence the jury found for the plaintiff, the defendant's counsel objecting to the want of any evidence that John Foy died without issue.

In Easter Term *Richards* obtained a *rule nisi* for a new trial on the law and evidence, and for misdirection as to the point of proof that John Foy died without issue. He cited Stark Ev. II. 832; Doe dem. Sullivan v. Read, 3 U. C. R. 293; Doe dem. Magher v. Chisholm, Dra. Rep. 227; Doe dem. Place v. Skae, 4 U. C. R. 369; Doe dem. Banning v. Griffin, 15 East 293; 3 Rep. 19.

In this term *Wilson, Q. C.*, shewed cause.

ROBINSON, C. J., delivered the judgment of the court.

We do not think that this will, under the circumstances proved, creates any difficulty in the way of the estate vesting in the devisee, for it was proved that Mr. Murney had been paid long ago for his lot nine, which was devised to Bridget Gerrity; and that, we think, satisfies the desire of the testator, in regard to the direction that the other lands shall remain in the possession of the executors till this lot is paid for, and a title obtained.

He could not have meant that if Murney, being paid for his land, should refuse or neglect to convey, his executors were on that account to withhold from the other devisees the land he had devised to them. All he meant was, that the executors should keep his other lands, in order that from their profits, if in no other way, this lot nine might be paid for, so as to entitle the estate to call for a deed.

Then John Foy taking the land under the will, the jury were satisfied, as I infer, of his death, and that he died intestate.

The plaintiff claims under a conveyance from his sister, Bridget Foy, assuming her to be his heir.

She would be his heir if he died without issue, as both parties, by taking a deed from his sister, seem to have assumed—and if he died before the statute 14 & 15 Vic. ch. 6, came into force—that is, before the first of January, 1852.

If he died after that time, his father being dead, his mother would succeed before the sister, (his collateral relative), but could only hold for her life.

The right of the sister to be preferred to the mother depends entirely, therefore, on the time of John Foy's death, which it was for the plaintiff, who claims through her, to establish to the satisfaction of the jury.

This point seems not to have received attention at the trial, though the right entirely turns upon it, and it ought to have been submitted to and found by the jury.

There must therefore be a new trial, with costs to abide the event.

CLOSTER V. HEADLEY.

Chattel mortgage—Second mortgage by mortgagor without first mortgagee's consent—Entry by first mortgagee thereupon—Trespass.

The plaintiff mortgaged certain goods to defendant, with a proviso for redemption on payment of £125 on the 20th of October, and an agreement that the plaintiff should account to defendant for the price of the goods or any part thereof, sold by him in the course of business before the day of payment of the mortgage money; and that in case of default, or in case plaintiff should attempt to sell or dispose of the goods without defendant's consent first had in writing, it should be lawful for defendant to enter and take said goods.

On the same day the defendant gave the plaintiff a writing, authorizing him to proceed to sell the goods that day mortgaged to him, " and to continue selling the same until further notice in writing, subject nevertheless to the proviso of the said bill of sale in other respects."

The plaintiff, on the 17th of October, mortgaged the same goods to one C. to secure a debt.

Held, a violation of the agreement between the plaintiff and defendant, and that the defendant was entitled to enter and take possession of the goods.

First count, for assault and battery of the plaintiff.

Second count, trespass *quare domum fregit,* and taking plaintiff's goods and chattels, to wit, the books of account in which the plaintiff kept accounts of sales, and also taking other articles on the 20th of October, 1853, and converting and disposing of them to his own use.

Third count, trespass to a shop or store of the plaintiff, on the 20th of October, 1853, and expelling him, whereby the plaintiff was prevented from the use and enjoyment of his goods and merchandize therein.

Pleas—1. General issue to the whole declaration.

2. To the second and third counts denial of the plaintiff's property in the house and shop.

3. To the second and third counts, that on the 20th of

July, 1853, by an indenture between the plaintiff and defendant, the plaintiff bargained, sold, and assigned to the defendant certain goods and chattels, to wit, the goods and chattels in the second count mentioned, subject to a proviso that if the plaintiff should pay or cause to be paid to the defendant on or before the 20th of October, 1853, the sum of £125, with interest, the indenture should be void. And it was agreed that in case default should be made in payment, it should be lawful for the defendant, at any time during the day to enter upon any lands, tenements, houses, and premises, wheresoever the goods might be, for the purpose of taking possession and removing the same. The plea averred that the plaintiff did not pay the £125, and after default the defendant entered the dwelling house and shop for the purpose of taking the goods, and continued there a reasonable time, and did remove the goods, as he lawfully might, which are the same trespasses complained of.

4. To the second and third counts, that by the same indenture it was further agreed that in case the plaintiff should attempt to sell or dispose of the goods and chattels in the indenture mentioned, or any of them, without the consent of the defendant to such sale or disposal thereof first had in writing, it should be lawful for the defendant, at any time during the day, to enter into and upon any lands, tenements, houses and premises, wheresoever the goods might be, for the purpose of taking possession of and removing the same ; that on the 7th of October, 1853, the plaintiff did attempt to sell and dispose of the goods without such consent of the defendant in writing, to one Joel Carpenter, contrary to the indenture, and the defendent then entered the dwelling-house and shop for the purpose of taking the goods, and did take them —which are the trespasses complained of.

5. To the second and third counts, leave and license of the plaintiff; and

6. To the seizing and taking the goods and chattels in the second count, that they were not the plaintiff's property.

The replication took issue on the first, second, and last pleas. To the third plea, admitting the indenture, *de injuriâ* to the residue. To the fourth plea, the same. To the fifth plea, *de injuriâ*

At the trial, before *Burns, J.,* at the last assizes held at
Cayuga, the facts appeared as follow :—The mortgage from
the plaintiff to the defendant was produced, and the proviso
for payment of the money was in these words : "Provided
always, &c., that if the plaintiff should pay the full sum of
£125, and legal interest for the same from the date thereof,
on or before the 20th of October next ensuing the date
hereof, on the understanding that the said Closter shall
account to the said Headley, and pay over to him, or any
person by him authorized, at any time that he the said
Headley shall demand the same, the price or purchase money
of the said goods and chattels, or any part thereof, by him
the said Closter sold in the course of business between the
date hereof and the said 20th of October, or charged in said
Closter's books on which this shall be a lien, then these
presents," &c.   Then followed a covenant for payment of
the money, and also a covenant such as set forth in the
third and fourth pleas. On the same day that the mortgage
was executed the defendant gave a paper writing, signed by
him, to the plaintiff, in these words :

"I hereby authorize you to proceed to sell the goods,
merchandize and chattels, this day mortgaged by you to me
in a bill of sale thereof, and to continue selling the same
until further notice in writing, subject nevertheles to the
proviso of the said bill of sale in other respects.

(Signed)   "JAMES H. HEADLEY."

"To Christopher O. Closter.

"Cayuga, July 20, 1853."

On the 17th of October, 1853 the plaintiff made a bill of
sale of the same goods and chattels, with others, to one Joel
Carpenter, subject to redemption by payment of £160 10s.
by the 17th of January, 1854.

No part of the £125 was paid to the defendant, and on the
20th of October he entered, as it was proved, first into the
dwelling-house, where the books of account were kept, and
obtained them, and afterwards into the shop, which he
fastened up, and took possession of the key. This was done
on the 20th of October, the day that the £125 became due.
When the defendant first went to the premises he demanded
from the plaintiff the goods and the books of account, or that

the plaintiff should make out the accounts of sales that had been made since the 20th of July. The reason why the defendant took this course was, that he had heard of the mortgage to Carpenter, and when he went to see the plaintiff that matter was spoken of between them. The plaintiff and defendant had a scramble together for the possession of the books, but the defendant got them and took them away. It was in respect to this the count for assult and battery was inserted. The defendant locked up the shop with the goods, and the plaintiff sued out a writ of replevir., and after five days got possession again of the goods.

The learned judge directed a verdict for defendant on the first count, as there was no evidence to support it ; and then it was agreed between the parties that the jury should assess the damages, in case the plaintiff should be entitled in law to a verdict on the other two counts, leaving the court to judge whether upon the legal effect of the instrument produced, and upon the pleadings, the plaintiff was legally entitled to a verdict ; and if not, then a verdict to be entered for the defendant generally, or upon such of the issues as the court might think he was entitled to. The jury assessed the damages on the second count at 1s., and on the third count at £20.

Connor, Q. C., for the defendant, in Easter Term, obtained a rule to enter a verdict for the defendant, pursuant to the leave reserved. He cited Short v. Ruttan, 12 U. C. R. 79 ; Taylor v. Cole, 1 H. Bl. 555 ; Hartley v. Moxham, 3 Q. B. 701 ; Lunn v. Turner et al. 4 U. C. R. 282.

Eccles shewed cause.

BURNS, J., delivered the judgment of the court.

On the first and second pleas of not guilty, and that the house and shop were not the plaintiff's property, the verdict for the plaintiff should stand without damages. On the third plea, the verdict should stand for the plaintiff without damages. The plaintiff had the whole of the 20th of October in which to pay the defendant the £125, and therefore on that day the plaintiff could not be in fault. The defendant for that reason entered too soon, and his justification fails. The fourth plea is the defence which brings up the true question between the parties. The mortgage to the defendant

gives him permission to enter wheresoever the goods might be
in case the plaintiff attempted to sell or dispose of the goods
without the consent of the defendant in writing first had for
that purpose.   The question is, whether there was such a
violation of the agreement between the parties as gave the
defendant a right to enter.   One cannot but say the permission given by the defendant to the plaintiff, at the time the
mortgage was executed, to sell the goods, did confer a legal
authority upon the plaintiff to sell the whole of the goods in
one sale, as well as disposing of them by retail from time to
time.   In all probability the latter is what both parties contemplated; but then the rights of third parties must not be
jeopardized by what may have possibly been intended.   If
Carpenter had desired to purchase the whole stock in trade,
and to have taken a transfer, he would, on looking at the permission given, see that no restriction was contained therein as
to quantity at any one sale.   No question has been raised by
the pleadings, or upon the evidence at the trial, as to the *bona
fides* of the transfer to Carpenter ; but it was not an absolute
sale : it was a mortgage redeemable by the plaintiff on the first
of January, 1854.   A mortgage is a sale in a strictly legal
sense, and there are cases in equity to shew that where a power
of sale is given for the purpose of raising a sum of money for
certain objects, it is considered the power to mortgage is
included.   If Carpenter, when he took his mortgage, did not
know of the defendant's mortgage, then he is not prejudiced
by anything the defendant has done; and if he did not know of
it, and the terms upon which the plaintiff might sell—viz :
subject to the terms of the defendant's bill of sale—then he
must have seen that the defendant had a right to demand the
price or purchase money of the goods which might be sold
before the 20th of October.   Carpenter was not to pay any
price or purchase money for the goods; on the contrary, the
plaintiff was to pay him by the first of January, 1854, to redeem the goods.   The authority which the defendant gave the
plaintiff to sell and dispose of the goods cannot be understood
to be a power by which the plaintiff could charge the goods
with a debt he owed, or to enable him to borrow a sum of
money upon them, and to compel the defendant to discharge
the debt or repay the money, in order to get the goods.   The

authority given clearly meant that in case of sale *bonâ fide*, the price or purchase money should be in the place of the goods for the defendant. It is clear from the evidence that the defendant did enter in consequence of the mortgage executed to Carpenter. Every actual sale must include an attempt to sell, and if the mortgage to Carpenter be held to be a legal sale though conditional, then legally speaking an attempt to sell would be proved ; and if the permission given by the defendant to sell is to be understood in the popular sense, then the fact of mortgaging the goods to render them subject to a charge as against the defendant was a disposing of them requiring his permission first in writing, because the plaintiff was taking no price or purchase money that we see, which could be rendered to the defendant in lieu of the goods.

The defendant was justified in entering the dwelling house and shop, and he is entitled to succeed on the fourth plea. The fifth plea should also be determined in the defendant's favour, for the mortgage also gives the defendant a right to enter in case the plaintiff violates the stipulations agreed upon. The defendant is also entitled to a verdict on the sixth plea as to the ownership of the goods. Whether the defendant or Carpenter has the legal title to the goods is of no consequence in this action, for it is clear the plaintiff has no title to them.

The result is, that the defendant should succeed generally upon the merits ; and the plaintiff should have a verdict upon the first, second, and third pleas, to the second and third counts.

Robinson, C. J.—I agree in the opinion that the verdict should be entered for the plaintiff on the first, second, and third pleas, to the second and third counts; and for the defendant on the other issues.

I am clear, also, that the permission given by the defendant to the plaintiff "to proceed to sell the goods mortgaged," (in other words, to go on selling them), "and to continue selling the same till further notice in writing, subject to the bill of sale in other respects," was not such an authority as could warrant the mortgaging the whole bodily to Carpenter. That was no continuing to sell them—it was not selling them at all. The writing is only in accordance with the deed between the plaintiff and defendant, and contemplates nothing more than that the plaintiff might go on retailing the goods till forbidden, provided he paid over the proceeds to defendant.

The assignment to Carpenter was wholly unauthorized by the defendant, and the defendant was in a situation to assert his rights as first assignee. His mortgage, I think, by the express terms of it, gave him a right to enter and take possession of the goods, because the plaintiff had without his permission *disposed of* them to Carpenter, though in a qualified manner, yet in such a manner as gave Carpenter the right of possession at any moment he might choose to demand it, which clearly was a violation of the understanding between the plaintiff and defendant.

DRAPER. J., concurred.

Judgment for defendant.

IN RE SMITH & LOGAN v. GEORGE & LYND.

Award—Motion to set aside, while action pending.

Where an action was pending on an award the court refused to set it aside on grounds which could be urged as a defence under the pleas in such action.

Semble, that an objection that two of the arbitrators made the award without notice to the third, could be taken advantage of in the action.

The application to set aside an award under such circumstances should be made to the court in which the action is pending.

Wilson, Q. C., moved to set aside an award made between these parties. Several objections were taken, which are not material to mention, as they were not decided upon. The first was, that the award was made by two only of the three arbitrators, without notice to George Davidson, the third arbitrator, who was ready and willing to have acted in the matter.

M. C. Cameron shewed cause.

ROBINSON, C. J., delivered the judgment of the court.

We were told on the argument that an action between these parties on this same award is at this moment pending in the Court of Common Pleas, and we felt it necessary to call for the record in that action, in order that it might be seen what offence had been set up against the award, since it would be manifestly improper in us to decide upon a summary application points that have been formally raised between the same parties in an action upon the same award, giving to the parties the advantage of an appeal. It would be most embarrasing, also, to have conflicting decisions between the parties on the same award in the different courts.

We find that George and Lynd have sued Smith and Logan upon the award, laying as a breach of the submission the not having given endorsed notes for the £173 18s. 6d. according to the award. The defendants have pleaded many pleas, and among them "No award," to which there is a demurrer upon a point of form.

There are other pleas bringing up some of the other objections on which the defendants are moving in this court to set aside the award, as that one of the arbitrators was induced to execute the award by a fraudulent misrepresentation that Davidson had concurred in it; also that the award is not final on account of not disposing of the claim founded on an alleged guarantee. The Court of Common Pleas, it seems, have suspended judgment upon the demurrer, to give the plaintiffs an opportunity to apply to amend their declaration. They notice this application pending in this court to set aside the award, and it appears to have been agreed between the parties that the application to amend may be deferred till the result of this application to us is known.

We cannot but observe on this, that the application to set aside the award should surely have been made in the same court in which the action was pending, for the course that has been taken might lead to confusion.

We have always a discretion to decline setting aside an award upon motion, on grounds which, if fatal, could be taken advantage of by way of defence against an action on the award or in resisting a motion for attachment.

We should only, in our opinion, under the circumstances which we have mentioned, go into such of these objections as could not have been set up as a defence to the action. Whatever is open to the defendant upon his pleas, and whatever he could have set up as a defence by pleading, should not, we think, be acted upon by us as grounds for setting aside the award upon motion.

We therefore are of opinion that the fourth, fifth, seventh, and eighth objections should be left by us to abide the result of the action being all open to the judgment of the court in the action pending.

The first, second, and third objections all turn on the same ground of complaint, which does not impute partiality or corruption to the arbitrators, or misconduct in not hearing evidence or allowing the parties a fair opportunity of making out their case, but rather that the award has not been legally executed, and so is not an award, being made by two only without notice to the third, and without the third having either agreed or disagreed.

We incline to think that such an objection might have been taken advantage of in an action. What is said by the court in Stalworth v. Inns (13 M. & W. 470) confirms that view; and at any rate, after reading Mr. Davidson's letter which is in evidence, and the affidavits filed in answer, made by the other arbitrators, we do not think we ought to set aside the award on the ground that Mr. Davidson was not a freely consenting party.

Rule discharged.

PERRY V. MAURICE PIQUOTT.

Ejectment on Sheriff's deed—Proof of judgment—Disseisin.

Where ejectment is brought on a sheriff's deed against a stranger to the execution debtor, it is necessary to prove the judgment on which the execution issued:—but.

Quære—per *Draper, J.*—Where the judgment debtor is the tenant in possession, and a stranger to the judgment and to the tenant comes in to defend—whether any more need be proved against such defendant than would have been required against the actual tenant; or whether an application must be made under 14 & 15 Vic., ch. 114, sec. 2.

It was contended on the argument that a mortgage under which plaintiff claimed part of the premises could vest no interest, defendant being then in adverse possession; but *held*, that this objection should have been taken at the trial, and the fact of disseisin left to the jury; and *semble* that the evidence was against such exception.

EJECTMENT for lot four in the eleventh concession of Emily. The trial took place in April, 1854, at Peterborough, before *McLean, J.* It was shewn that the west half of this lot was granted on the 27th August, 1840, to Bartholemew Piquott, called Piggott in the patent; and the east half on the 26th of August, 1834, to Daniel Piquott, called Peggott in the patent.

It was next proved that Daniel Piquott died in April, 1846, unmarried, leaving his brother Bartholomow his heir-at-law.

The plaintiff then put in three writs of execution against lands. The first against the lands of Bartholomew Piquott, tested 9th June, 1849, in which Armour & McPhail, executors, were plaintiffs. The second against the lands of Bartholomew Pickot, tested 8th December, 1849 ; the exectors of Armour were plaintiffs. The third against the lands of Bartholomew Piquott, tested the 8th June, 1850, in which Ebenezer Perry and George Perry were plaintiffs. All were issued out of the County Court at Peterborough. The sheriff stated that he seized under the first writ, but sold this lot number five to satisfy all. The deed from the sheriff to the plaintiff was put in, dated 7th May, 1851, reciting the first writ against the lands of Bartholomew Piquott, and conveying this lot in question to the plaintiff, in fee, for £90 5s. The plaintiff was the person principally interested, and undertook to satisfy the two first executions. Bartholomew Piquott was examined. He swore that he had long ago conveyed the west half to his brother Daniel, but had subsequently occupied it by his permission : that the defendant Maurice had a tenant living on the east quarter for seven or eight years before the trial. He said his name was spelled Piggott and Piquott. He proved (as subscribing witness) an instrument, under the hand and seal of Daniel Piquott, dated 11th July, 1842 (see it set out at length in Doe Piquotte v. Piquotte, 4 U. C. R., 102). He had lived for several years on the west half of the lot, and was still living there. One McCarthy was living on the east half of the lot, as tenant to defendant, who had been a tenant in possession of it for seven or eight years. He sold the west half to his brother Daniel fifteen or twenty years ago.

No conveyance was put in or proved by Bartholomew Piquott to his deceased brother Daniel, and the instrument of the 11th of July, 1842, had never been registered.

A mortgage dated the 28th of October, 1848, was proved from Bartholomew Piggott, described as heir-at-law of Daniel

Piquotte, to one James Scott (registered 18th Nov. 1848) in fee, of the east half of the lot, to secure payment of £25, with interest, in three months from date. This mortgage was assigned by Scott to the plaintiff on the 8th of April, 1853, registered 25th of April, 1853.

For the defendant it was objected, that it was not shewn the execution was a year in the sheriff's hands before the sale; and that there was no proof of advertisement of the sale; that the execution on which the sheriff's deed was professedly made was against Bartholomew *Piquott,* while the second execution calls him *Pickett,* and the third *Piquotte :*

That the instrument of the 11th July, 1842, was a good conveyance, at all events for the east half of the lot :

That the plaintiff could not recover under the mortgage from Bartholomew Piquott to Scott, as Bartholomew's title was defeated by the assignment of Daniel Piquott to defendant.

That no judgment was shewn on which any of the executions were founded, and no levy shewn.

Leave was reserved to the defendant to renew any of the foregoing objections in term, and if the court upheld any of them a verdict for defendant or a nonsuit might be entered

In Easter Term *Phillpotts* obtained a rule *nisi* to set aside the verdict as contrary to law and evidence, and for misdirection ; or for a nonsuit on the leave reserved, or to enter the verdict for the defendant; or why the verdict should not stand for only one-half of the lot in question, and the defendant be held entitled to the other half.

In this Term *Wilson, Q. C.,* shewed cause, and cited Doe dem. Batten v. Murless, 6 M. & S. 110; Boulton v. Shand, 10 U. C. R. 351. He conceded that the sheriff's sale and conveyance could not be supported for want of proof of the judgment against Bartholomew Piquott.

Robinson, C. J., delivered the judgment of the court.

The plaintiff's right to recover this west half upon the evidence given at the trial, was, I believe, given up on the argument of this rule. His only title to that portion of the lot was under the sheriff's deed, given upon a sale under a *fi. fa.* against Bartholomew Piquott ; and this action being against a person who was not the defendant in that judgment, nor claiming under such defendant through any deed made since the judgment or holding possession under him, the production and proof of the judgment on which the execution issued was indispensable. No evidence was given of it upon the trial, and the want of it was objected to. The only question then is, whether the plaintiff shewed a legal right to recover for the east half of the lot.

That half was granted by patent to Daniel Piquott (or Piggott) in 1834. He died about 1846, unmarried and intestate, leaving his brother Bartholemew his heir.

On the 24th of October, 1848, Bartholomew Piquott mortgaged this land to James Scott in fee for £25, to be paid in three months. This mortgage was assigned on the 8th of April, 1853, by Scott to this plaintiff for £32 10s. ; registered on the 25th of April, 1853.

There appears to be no objection to this chain of title, unless we can see that a right was proved in the defendant, or some one else than the plaintiff, which we do not see. The defendant pretended no claim, except under a writing under seal given to him in 1842 by one Daniel Piquott, which was under consideration in this court in the case of Doe dem. Maurice Piquott v. Bartholomew Piquott (4 U. C. R. 101), and was there decided not to be an actual conveyance of any interest, but an executory agreement merely.

But it has been contended that the mortgage given to Scott could vest no interest in him, on account of this defendant, Maurice Piquott being in adverse possession, as it is alleged, at the time. No such objection, however, was raised at the trial ; it is founded on a supposed disseizin, which could only be found by the jury ; and it was therefore necessary that the defendant if he desired to avail himself of it, should have taken the exception at the proper time, when, for all we can tell, the plaintiff might have given such evidence as would have removed the difficulty ; and, indeed, we can see upon the evidence that was given that there was no ground for such an exception—at least so it appears to us at present. The transactions between the three brothers respecting this

lot seem strangely irregular. According to the case that
was before us in 4 U. C. R. 101, Daniel took upon himself
to bargain away to Maurice the half of the lot which had
been granted to Maurice, as well as his own. This east half
he was apparently in a condition to sell when he executed
the writing in 1842. The west half he had taken a deed for,
which there seemed every reason to apprehend was not *bonâ
fide ;* but however that might be, we considered that the
writing given in 1842 by Daniel to this defendant could not
operate as a conveyance, the parties having evidently in view
the execution of a transfer deed at another time, and this
writing seeming to be mere evidence of a bargain to that
effect secured by a penalty.

We think the plaintiff should have a verdict for the east
half of the lot and therefore discharge the defendant's rule
for a nonsuit or a new trial, unless the plaintiff is willing that
there should be a new trial in order to give him the opportunity of producing evidence of the judgment, in which case
we would make absolute the rule for a new trial, with costs
to abide the event.

DRAPER, J., observed on the fact that Bartholomew
Piquott's possession, apparently not under the defendant,
seemed to have been overlooked as to the effect it might have
on the necessity of proving a judgment; though as against
the present defendant a stranger to that judgment, it would
be necessary. He observed that it appeared the action was
originally brought against the parties in possession and that
the defendant had intervened to defend ; and suggested
whether in such a case, any more need be proved against
him than against the actual tenant in possession, or whether
an application should not have been made under the proviso
in the second section of the Ejectment Act, 14 & 15 Vic.
ch. 114, to strike out his defence to the west half, as it
would seem there was no privity whatever between him and
the tenant; and that, as no such application had been made,
the case must be proved against the defendant as a stranger
to Bartholomew.

BURNS, J., concurred.

ORR V .LAWRENCE RANNEY, THOMAS RUNDLE, AND WILLIAM BEATTIE.

Authority of School Trustees—18 *Vic. ch.* 185, *sec.* 6.

Two of the trustees of a school section are not competent to act in all cases without consulting the third; nor can the whole body, without any reference to the freeholders, determine upon the site for the school-house, and purchase it, and impose a rate to meet the expense.

This was an action of trespass for taking the plaintiff's property.

The defendants pleaded that the plaintiff and the defendants, Lawrence Ranney and Thomas Rundle, before the said time when, &c.—to wit, during 1853—were and now are resident householders in school section No. 15 of the township of Westminster, and were during the said year liable to be rated and assessed for the school purposes of said section : that before and after the said time when, &c.—to wit, during the said year—one Isaac Campbell and the said Lawrence Ranney and Thomas Rundle were and now are trustees of the said school section No. 15 of the said township; and that, there being no suitable school-house in or belonging to the said school section, they, the said ˙Lawrence Ranney and Thomas Rundle, being a majority of the said trustees of the said school section, on the 14th day of March in the said year, purchased and acquired a site within the said section for the common school therein : that afterwards, and before the said time when, &c.—to wit, on, &c.—the said Lawrence Ranney and Thomas Rundle, being the majority of the said trustees of the said section, judged it expedient to build a school-house in and for the said section on the said site; and thereupon, immediately afterwards, did cause to be built on the said site so required as aforesaid a suitable school-house for the said section : that in order to pay for the said site and for the building of the said school-house and the incidental expenses attending the same, they, as such trustees, assessed an equal rate upon the assessable property of the said section : and thereupon made out a list of the names of all the persons rated by them for the said school purposes of such section, and the amount rated upon and payable by each person in the said section : that they did, on the 7th day of November in the year aforesaid, duly annex to the said list a

warrant, under the corporate seal of the said trustees of the
said section, directed to the said William Beattie, who was
then the collector of the said section, by which said warrant
they authorized and required the said William Beattie, after
ten days from the date thereof, to collect from the several
individuals in the rate-bill thereto annexed mentioned the
sum of money set opposite the respective names of the said
parties mentioned in the said list, and to pay within thirty
days from the date thereof the amount so collected, after
retaining his own fees, to the secretary-treasurer, whose discharge should be his acquittance for the sum so paid; and in
default of payment on demand by any person so rated, he
was thereby authorized and required to levy the amount by
distress and sale of the goods and chattels of the person or
persons making default : that the said plaintiff, being a resident householder in the said section, was assessed and rated
on the said list attached to the said warrant for £9 16s. 8d. :
that the said William Beattie, by virture of the said warrant
on, &c., did demand of the said plaintiff the said sum of £9
16s. 8d., being the sum for which he was so rated and assessed, which the plaintiff neglected and refused to pay ; and
thereupon the said William Beattie, at the said time when,
&c., seized and took the said goods and chattels in the said
declaration mentioned, and sold and disposed thereof, as he
lawfully might, for the cause aforesaid—which are the
trespasses in the said declaration mentioned.   Verification.

Demurrer.—The causes assigned sufficiently appear in the
judgment.

Eccles for the demurrer.   *Cameron, Q. C.,* contra.

ROBINSON, C. J., delivered the judgment of the court.

The plaintiff is entitled to judgment on the demurrer,
which, we believe, was conceded by the defendants on the
argument.   Whether the plea is to be determined upon with
reference to the last school act, 16 Vic. ch. 185, sec. 6, or the
former act, 13 & 14 Vic. ch. 48, as governing the trustees in
the matters set forth in the plea, it would in either case be
impossible to sustain the plea.   The defendants have assumed
that two only of the three trustees could, as the majority, do

any act, however important, without consulting with the third, or giving him any notice or opportunity of uniting with or opposing them. That is clearly not so. Then under either of the two acts (and it appears to us the 16 Vic. ch. 185, sec. 6 was the statute in force at the time, and which required to be observed in this matter) the whole body of trustees were not competent without any reference to the freeholders, to determine upon the site of the school-house and purchase it, and impose the rate for raising the money to meet these charges ; and yet the plea proceeds on the assumption that the trustees and even a majority of them, could, without any formality do all that they judged it desirable to do.

Judgment for plaintiff on demurrer.

FERRIER v. MOODIE.

Boundary—Right by possession according to division line agreed on—Extent of such right.

If two parties owning respective halves of a lot agree to a division line which is not the true boundary, and one party clears a portion of land according to such line, and obtains a right by possession to such portion, this will not give him any right by constructive possession to the whole as if this line were carried out.

The jury having found a general verdict for the plaintiff, though the defendant was in fact entitled to the part he had cleared :

Held, that this was not ground for a new trial, but for an application to restrain the plaintiff from taking possession of such part.

EJECTMENT for the west half of lot No. seven in the tenth concession of the township of North Burgess.

The defendant did not limit his defence, but defended generally for the whole of the half lot.

The plaintiff gave notice that he claimed damages as mesne profits, &c.

At the trial, before *Richards, J.,* at the last spring assizes, held at Perth, it appeared that the plaintiff was, by patent dated 10th of April 1824, the owner of the west half of the lot in question and the defendant claimed the north east half of the lot by deed from the grantee of the Crown for that portion which was granted to one Alexander McMillan on the first of March, 1824. The dispute between the parties was as the boundary between the respective portions of the lot. The plaintiff gave a good deal of evidence to estab-

lish the bearing of the side lines of the lot as they should be
run according to the course of the town line of the township.
The weight of evidence appeared to establish this course, as
also the front angle of the lot in question upon the tenth
concession to the satisfaction of the jury. The defendant
gave no evidence to controvert or to cast any doubt upon
this part of the plaintiff's case, and no question was made
on the argument of this rule upon the correctness of the
view the learned judge took of that in submitting the case to
the jury. The plaintiff proved by a surveyor that he ran the
division line between the plaintiff's and defendant's land
according to the data so established, and found that the
defendant had in possession within his fences five and a half
acres belonging to the plaintiff. The land through which the
division line ran was not cleared from the front to the rear
of the lot, and the five and a half acres was the quantity
cleared which the defendant had included within his fences.
The remainder of the land was still in a state of nature, not
fenced in by either party. A portion of the land included
within the defendant's fences was cleared and fenced by him
more than twenty years before the commencement of the
action, and a portion of it had been cleared and fenced within
that time.

The defendant relied upon establishing that in the year
1825 the plaintiff and he had agreed that a surveyor should
run a division line, and that such a line was run between
their possessions accordingly from front to rear of the lot,
and marked by trees being blazed, and that the land cleared
and fenced in by the defendant was according to that line,
both as respects what was cleared more than twenty years
ago, and what been cleared within that period.

The plaintiff gave evidence to shew that he had assented
(by a verbal arrangement as must be supposed, for nothing
in writing was produced or alluded to in any way) to a line
being run between the respective halves of the lot, but that
the surveyor employed used only a compass for the purpose—
each party was to pay half of the expense :—that after the
surveyor had run half through the concession something went
wrong with his compass and the line was never completed ;

and because it was not completed the plaintiff would not pay any part of the expenses, but said he would do so if the survey should be completed, but which in fact he contended had never been done. The defendant in 1849 assented to a line being run, because he said that if he lost land on the plaintiff's side of his lot he should gain upon the other side ; but subsequently he receded from this, and stated he could rely upon his length of possession.

The learned judge left it to the jury to say what portion of the west half of the lot had been in possession of the defendant for twenty years before the commencement of this action, and as to such portion he told them the defendant was entitled to succeed. Then they were directed to ascertain what portion of the west half of the lot the defendant had included within his fences, and of which he had not had the actual possession for twenty years ; and as to such portion the plaintiff was entitled to recover, and the jury should assess · such damages per acre for six years past as they thought reasonable for the profits. The learned judge expressed to the jury his opinion that the plaintiff was not to be deprived of such portions of the west half of the lot as might be upon the defendant's side of the conventional line spoken of, by any constructive possession which might be supposed to arise from a protraction of that line from the land of which the defendant was in the actual possession, to the front and rear of the lot.

The jury gave a general verdict for the plaintiff and assessed damages for two and a half acres of the land in possession of the defendant at £7 10s.

Phillpotts obtained a rule to shew cause why the verdict should not be set aside and a new trial granted, on the ground that the verdict was contrary to law and evidence, and for misdirection. He cited Doe dem Hill v. Gander, 1 U.C.R. 3; Doe dem. Cuthbertson v. McGillis, 2 C.P. 124.

Richards shewed cause, and cited Doe. dem. Taylor v. Proudfoot, 9 U.C.R. 503.

BURNS, J., delivered the judgment of the court.

The defendant's council contends that the learned judge misdirected the jury in telling them there must be an actual possession on the part of the defendant, and that there could not be a constructive possession to deprive the plaintiff of the land up to the conventional line spoken of. It is contended that the agreement between the parties to run such a line, and their subsequently holding according to that line in such portions of the land as were actually cleared and fenced more than twenty years ago, in law and in fact establishes the line, and the possession of the parties respectively will be determined according to such line. If any agreement in writing had been shewn between the parties, which would in law and in fact amount to a transfer and conveyance of the land according to a line to be run under an agreement to that effect, then it might perhaps be argued that a constructive possession might exist and follow such an agreement. Constructive possession will only be inferred where nothing militates against it in favour of the true title, and will not be inferred against the true owner in favour of one who shews no shadow or claim of title. Without examining the merits of the case upon the question whether there was in truth a parol agreement established that the parties should hold by a particular line—and upon which the jury, it would seem, have arrived at a proper conclusion,—there can be no question the learned judge stated the law correctly. The defendant could not rely upon the agreement alone, if there were in fact one established to run a line between the parties, and that such a line was designated more than twenty years ago, without also shewing some visible occupation or possession of the land. The mere agreement and designating the line would not of themselves establish an actual possession of the land. Would they be sufficient to establish a constructive possession? I do not think they would. The kind of possession required successfully to defend an action of ejectment must be such as would enable an action to be brought. If the plaintiff, after such an agreement made and the line designated, had nevertheless ascertained the true line and cleared and fenced up to it, the defendant could not, on any idea that the effect of the agreement and designating the line transferred to him a constructive possession, maintain an action of ejectment against the plaintiff. Then does the fact that the defendant has taken possession of a part, and kept it for twenty years, establish a conventional line throughout the lot between the parties? No case can be cited to establish such a proposition; and it appears contrary to reason to say that twenty years' actual possession of a part is necessary to confer title, and yet that constructive possession of another part will be sufficient. The only way which the defendant can possibly argue the proposition is, that the actual possession of part carries with it the constructive possession of the whole. The answer to that is, that such presumption is never made except in favour of one claiming under colour of title; and, further, it is a proposition inapplicable to a question of boundary, in which case the possession ought to be unequivocally indicated, and according to law must have so remained for the space of twenty years before the commencement of the suit.

The verdict for the plaintiff is quite right according to the legal effect of the evidence. The defendant, however, contends further that the jury should have found a verdict in favour of the defendant for such portions as he had cleared and fenced for twenty years before the commencement of the action, because he says, as it now stands upon the verdict, the plaintiff may take possession of all the land proved to be part of the west half of the lot, as there is no restriction in the verdict, and the judgment and execution would be according to that finding. The eighth section of the new Ejectment Act, 14 & 15 Vic. ch. 114, declares that upon a finding for the claimant, judgment may be signed and execution issued as at present in the action of ejectment, "and the said judgment having the same, and no other effect than at present." According to the law as it then stood, in an action of ejectment, if the plaintiff proved himself entitled to any part of the premises mentioned in the declaration he was entitled to judgment generally. The judgment in ejectment determined nothing as to the *quantum* of land; and if the declaration mentioned more than the plaintiff proved title to, the course of the defendant was to apply to the court for relief.—See Doe dem. Drapers' Company v. Wilson (2 Stark

N. P. C. 477); Roe dem. Saul v. Dawson (3 Wils. 49) Fausset v. Carpenter (5 Bligh N. S. 75).

The defendant's rule must therefore be discharged (a).

WAFER V. BURNS.

When two new trials have been granted in order to dispose of the question on its merits, the court will not be disposed at the last trial to consider technical bbjections taken as grounds of nonsuit.

This was an action of ejectment, involving a question of disputed boundary, of which the particulars are not material to be reported. The case had been three times tried, the evidence being unsatisfactory and conflicting as to the original posts. At the last trial certain objections were taken as grounds of non-suit ; and these were renewed, and a third new trial moved for upon the evidence.

The cases was argued by *Smith, Q. C.,* for the plaintiff, and *Kirkpatrick, Q. C.,* and *Richards* for defendant.

The court refused to interfere again upon the evidence, upon which they commented at length.

As to the points argued as grounds of nonsuit, ROBINSON, C. J., said :—it was surely too late to raise upon the last trial any technical difficulty as to the sufficient proof of Mary Crawford's title. Both parties are evidently claiming through the patent to her for lot D., and both have reasoned again and again upon the effect of the description contained in that patent. It would be harassing both parties to open the cause upon any attempt at denying now what has been again and again assumed and admitted, and what we must all see to be capable of being readily and incontestibly proved.

Then as to the points raised of estoppel upon the plaintiff against disputing the line run by McDonald, as the dividing line between the two halves of the lot D., and as to the objection that the plaintiff could take nothing, under the convey-

---

(a) *Note.* The above decision is not intended to touch the question whether under the new rules the general issue in ejectment is distributable.

If there are different portions sought to be recovered which depend upon different titles, or one portion is clearly severable from the other, then the rule adopted and decided in Doe. d. Bowman v. Lewis (13 M. & W. 241) would apply.

ance made to him at least as regards the piece of land now claimed, because at the time of its execution the grantor in that deed was disseised by a possession adversely held against him; these are both objections which were taken and over-ruled on former trials, on grounds which were then stated, and to which we most certainly should not give effect now, after a new trial granted avowedly upon the conflicting testimony as to the true boundary, and upon that ground only.

DRAPER, J., (after remarking upon the objections raised, which he considered untenable),—Above all, when it is remembered that these objections are raised at a third trial granted in order that the question of boundary might be disposed of on its merits; that on former trials these objections were either not taken or were waived; that at one at least the patent to Mary Crawford was admitted;—they should not now be received with any favor.

BURNS. J., concurred.

Rule discharged.

AULT v. ARMSTRONG.

In an action for enforcing a judgment in itself regular, but which has been satisfied, malice and want of probable cause must be alleged in the declaration.

CASE for suing out an *Alias* and *Pluries Fi. Fa.* and selling the plaintiff's goods upon a judgment entered on confession, but which judgment had been satisfied after the sheriff had returned the first writ *nulla bona.* The declaration alleged that these writs were issued wrongfully and unjustly, but did not charge malice, or that the defendant had acted without probable cause.

The question for the jury was, whether the judgment had been in fact paid, and they found it had not, and rendered a verdict for defendant.

Smith, Q. C., obtained a rule *nisi* for a new trial, to which *Richards* shewed cause.

BURNS, J. delivered the judgment of the court.

(The learned judge stated the evidence, which it is unnecessary to report and which was held sufficient to sustain the verdict.)—Independent of the facts of the case, according to De Medina v. Grove (10 Q. B. 152), the frame of the declaration in this case would preclude the plaintiff from recovering upon it. There is no allegation that the defendant acted maliciously in suing out the subsequent executions, or that they were sued out not having any reasonable or probable cause to do so. The declaration in this case shews that the judgment was an unsatisfied judgment, and, from the the case cited the law is well settled, that where the process of the court is *primâ facie* correct the improper use of it must be stated to be malicious and without probable cause. There is no complaint against the judgment, and the execution of the judgment is in law *primâ facie* right.

Rule discharged.

SHIELDS v. DeBLAQUIERE.

Action for prosecuting false claim to land—Heir and devisee commission, false affidavit used before.

An action will not lie for knowingly prosecuting a false claim before the heir and devisee commission, to the plaintiff's injury and with knowledge of his claim.

One M., in 1839, having a right of purchase of a lot from the Crown, mortgaged to DeB. to secure payment of a sum by instalments, the last of which would fall due in 1849. Soon after this mortgage M. gave to B. a bond for a deed on certain conditions to be fulfilled by B., who took posession. In 1850 the plaintiff went in under an agreement for purchase from B., who had not fulfilled the conditions of his bond. In 1851 the defendant took an assignment of DeB.'s mortgage, and in the same year he claimed before the heir and devisee commission, making the usual affidavit of ignorance of any adverse claim, and obtained a patent.

The plaintiff thereupon brought an action on the case, alleging, in the first and second counts of his declaration, that the defendant, maliciously contriving and intending to injure him, represented himself as assignee of the original nominee of the Crown, and claimed as such before the heir and devisee commission ; and in order to defraud the plaintiff, and not having himself any well founded claim, and knowing the plaintiff's claim made affidavit that he was not aware of any adverse claim, and procured his own claim to be allowed—whereby, &c.

The third and fourth counts, founded on the Statute 32 Henry VIII. ch. 9, were for buying M.'s pretended right, the defendant being in possession claiming title.

Held, that on the evidence the allegations were not supported ; and that, admitting them all to be true, no ground of action would be shewn.

The first and second counts of the declaration in substance charged—that the plaintiff was in possession of lot two in the fifth concession of Zorra, for which lot no letters patent from the crown had issued ; that the plaintiff claimed the said land as deriving a title or claim under and through the *original nominee of the crown,* of which the defendant had notice:— that the defendant, maliciously contriving and intending to injure the plaintiff, represented and pretended himself to be assignee of the original nominee of the crown, and claimed in that capacity before the heir and devisee commission; and in order to defraud the plaintiff, and to prevent the plaintiff having notice of defendant's claiming, or claiming for himself (the plaintiff), or resisting the defendant's claim, *and not having any well founded claim to the land,* and being aware of the plaintiff's claim, made an affidavit that his (defendant's) claim was just and well founded, and that he was not aware of any adverse claim : and produced and used such affidavit before the heir and devisee commissioners, and procured his claim to be allowed, and by virtue of such allowance obtained letters patent to himself for the lot—whereby, &c.

The third and fourth counts in substance charged—that the plaintiff had been in possession of the same lot more than a year, claiming right and title thereto; that the defendant purchased the pretended right of one Reuben Martin to this lot, although neither Martin nor any one under whom he claimed had been in possession of the premises, or of the remainder or reversion, nor had taken the rents or profits thereof for a year next before such purchase, nor had the defendant been in lawful possession by taking the yearly farm rents. The third count went on to state that through the purchase from Martin the defendant obtained letters patent from the crown for the lot, and ejected the plaintiff. The fourth omitted the getting the letters patent, but stated that the plaintiff had been disquieted, &c., in the possession.

The defendant pleaded not guilty.

The cause was tried at Woodstock, in May last, before *Macaulay,* C. J.

The lot number two in the fifth concession of Zorra, a clergy reserve, appeared to have been sold on the 17th of January, 1835, by the commissioner of crown lands, to one Thomas Pearson.

At some time, when not appearing, he assigned, according to the notice for the heir and devisee commission put up and advanced by the defendant, to one Charles Griffith, deceased, who, according to the same notice, devised to certain parties in trust, who assigned to Reuben Martin, who assigned to defendant, who thereupon in July 1851 claimed, was allowed, and got a patent in fee for this lot, making the usual affidavit of ignorance of any adverse claim.

But the title set up in this notice (and which, must be taken to be correct, as the claim was allowed) seems at variance with documents put in evidence at the trial. The first document in point of date (*i. e.* 1st January, 1839) was a mortgage from Reuben Martin to the Hon. Peter B. DeBlaquiere, reciting that Martin was desirous of borrowing £91 11s. 10½d., and that Mr. DeBlaquiere had agreed to advance it on getting security by mortgage of his interest in this lot, and then witnessing that, in pursuance, &c., and in consideration of £91 11s. 10d½. Martin bargains, sells, assigns, transfers, and sets over to De Blaquiere this lot number two, together with, &c., *habendum* to DeBlaquiere, his heirs and assigns, for and during all the estate and interest of him (Martin) therein,—subject to a proviso for redemption on payment of £91 11s. 10½d., with interest, in five instalments of £18 6s. 4¼d. each, payable on the 1st of January, 1845, 1846, 1847, 1848, 1849, with covenants by Martin for payment according to the proviso; for right to convey for the estate and in manner aforesaid; that on default DeBlaquiere, his heirs and assigns, might enter; and for further assurance to DeBlaquiere, subject to the aforesaid proviso; and that if Martin, his heirs or assigns, should take out the patent deed from the crown for this lot before the last instalment was paid, he or they should mortgage the fee simple of the lot to DeBlaquiere to secure whatever might be due of the £91 11s. 10½d., and interest; that Martin should pay the instalments to government as they fell due, and on his default DeBlaquiere might pay them, and the land should be chargeable with all sums so paid, and interest; provided that until default, Martin, his heirs and assigns, might occupy, enjoy, &c., without interruption by the said Martin. This mortgage was registered on the 19th of May, 1841.

On the 7th of June, 1851, by indenture of that date, P. B. DeBlaquiere assigned this mortgage, the debt, and the land, to the defendant in fee, in consideration of £28 9s. 3d., subject to the equity of redemption in the mortgage, with a covenant that the said P. B. DeBlaquiere had not made, done, committed, &c., any act, &c., by means whereof " the said principal sum and interest, security and premises hereby assigned," " or the said piece or parcel or tract of land, hereditaments, and premises hereby released or intended so to be, or any of them, or any part thereof, are, is, can, or shall, or may be in anywise impeached, charged, assigned, discharged, affected or incumbered"—meaning, among other things, that the whole debt and interest is unpaid.

No claim was derived to the land through these two deeds in the defendant's notice before the heir and devisee commission.

By deed-poll, dated 5th of December, 1850, Martin, in consideration of 5s., assigned, transferred, and set over to defendant all his right, title, and interest in the lot, authorizing the defendant to pay government such sums as remain due, and to take such steps as may be required for getting the crown patent to himself in fee.

It seemed that, on the 27th of December, 1849, the defendant paid £28 9s. 3d., being the third instalment and interest due on the sale by government to Pearson. This payment appeared to have been made on some apprehension that the sale would be forfeited for non-payment of anything for so many years. On the 23rd of July, 1852, the defendant paid £215 5s. to the commissioner of crown lands, being the balance of the purchase money.

On the 13th of August, 1839, Martin gave his bond to the Rev. W. Bettridge in a penalty of £600, the condition being, that if Bettridge should pay whatever was due to government on the same lot, and pay to the Hon. P. B. DeBlaquiere £91 10s. 11½d., secured by a mortgage of Martin's interest in this lot, with interest, as the same should become due, and should also pay to P. B. DeBlaquiere five joint and several notes of hand, dated the 12th of September, 1838, drawn by Martin and his knowledge of Bettridge's interest. The bond from Martin endorsed by Abraham Carroll, for £18 6s. 4½d. each, and payable the 1st of January, 1840–1–2–3 and 4, together with all rates and taxes on the lot, and pay Martin £50, one-half down and one-half on the 13th of September, 1839 ; then if Martin should, on request of Bettridge, execute a good and effectual conveyance in fee simple of the said lot to Bettridge in fee, free from incumbrances, and in the meantime, and until default be made in some of the instalments and interest, permit Bettridge peacably to enjoy, &c.—then the obligation should be void.

Martin gave up possession to Bettridge at or soon after the date of the bond, and had never had possession since. The defendant never had any possession. Bettridge, by his tenants, occupied until the sale by Bettridge to the plaintiff, making large and valuable improvements. According to the evidence, the plaintiff entered into possession about August, 1850. Bettridge gave him a receipt, dated the 17th of June, 1851, for £50, being part of amount of purchase. According to Bettridge's evidence, given on a commission, the plaintiff entered as tenant to make such improvements as he should think advantageous to himself or landlord, until they could make an arrangement as to the purchase. But he said he had verbally agreed to sell to the plaintiff for £400, out of which all incumbrances on the lot were to be paid, including defendant's £40. The payment to Bettridge of £50 was made by giving him credit on an account he owed him. The plaintiff also promised to pay £50 at the expiration of ten years, and there was a writing under seal. He swore he paid the five notes of Martin and Carroll to DeBlaquiere.

Mr. Richardson proved he drew the assignment from Bettridge to plaintiff in April, 1852. After making the statement a paper was shewn him by the plaintiff's counsel in cross-examination, and he said that was the paper he referred to ; it was of the 3rd of May, 1852, but this paper was not put in.

Some evidence was given, extremely slight, from which it might be inferred that defendant may have known the plaintiff was in possession of these premises about two years before the trial—i.e., May, 1852. There was more evidence to shew to Bettridge was produced by him, and the payment of the notes of hand by Bettridge to the Hon. P. B. DeBlaquiere might have been known to him ; though at the same time it must be remembered that the notes themselves were not proved to have been in any way connected with the purchase or mortgage of this lot by Martin. They were not secured on it to DeBlaquiere, though the payment of them was undertaken by Bettridge.

It was left to the jury to enquire whether the defendant knew that the plaintiff or Bettridge were possessed of the land, claiming it on some ground or other :—whether the defendant had reasonable or probable cause to assert his own claim, and deny adverse claim as he did:—was the defendant's affidavit *bona fide*, or was there *suppressio veri* or *suggestio falsi* ?—were the commissioners imposed upon ?—were they informed of all the material facts the defendant knew, and of which he ought to have informed them ? The question of malice was left to them as a fact, and they found for the plaintiff—damages £350.

Freeman obtained a rule *nisi* for a new trial on the law and evidence, for misdirection, and for the reception of improper evidence, or to arrest judgment.

H. Eccles and *D. B. Read* shewed cause :—The plaintiff asserts that Martin's right was a mere pretended right. It is true the declaration shews the legal estate to be in the crown ; but the 8th Vic. ch. 8, sec. 5, establishes a sort of equitable right in a party having made payments, and constitutes him in effect the owner in fee as against all other parties. The plaintiff claims under the nominee of the crown, and therefore comes under this provision. It will be argued that no legal damages can be recovered because the title is merely equitable ; but this is not so : if an equitable title is interfered with, there is a remedy at law.

It is contended on the other side that the plaintiff is tied down to his rights under the statute of 32 H. VIII. ch. 9 ; but he may if he chooses bring his action on the case. The statute has made no alteration. It only declares what the law was and what it should continue to be, and annexes a penalty to any breach of it as thus laid down ; but a plaintiff is not limited to his action for the penalty ; that is only an additional remedy, and concurrent with that which existed before—Com. Dig. " Action upon Statute," C.

The main question, however, is whether a sufficient ground of action is shewn. Supposing all the facts noted by the learned judge left to the jury and found in the affirmative, would they support an action ? The authorities shew that they · would. In Pasley · v. Freeman, 3 T. R. 51, *Lord Kenyon* quotes from Com. Dig. " Action upon the case for a deceit," A. I., " An action upon the case for a deceit lies where a man does any deceit to the damage of another ·' and he then ¯ goes on to consider and approve of this opinion. It is of no consequence whether the deceitful representation complained of is made to the plaintiff himself or to a third party, provided the result be the same. It is in fact stronger when it is made to a third party, because the plaintiff then has no opportunity of making inquiries to satisfy himself. Green v. Button, 1 Gale 349, 2 Cr. M. & R. 707, 1 Týr. & Gran. 118, is more in point than the last case. There the cause of action was that the defendant represented himself to the sellers as having a lien on certain wood which the plaintiff had purchased, and the seller in consequence refused for some time to deliver it. That case is analogous to the present in this respect, that the representation was made to a third party. Foster v. Charles, 6 Bing. 396 shews that a person recommending an agent by statements which he knows to be false, is responsible, though no malicious motive or pecuniary interest is shewn : this case is much stronger, for the defendant had a clear personal interest—a wish to get the patent for himself. These cases, and Ley v. Madill, 1 U. C. R. 546, and Tennery v. Stiles, 5 U. C. R. 254, are suffi- cient to shew that in law the action is sustainable.

The non-production of the mortgage tells also against the defendant. Knowing that his father had the mortgage, he founded no claim on it, but claimed as assignee of Martin. The mortgage never was before the commissioners, and the defendant seems to have got an assignment of it merely for a nominal consideration and in order to patch up his case afterwards.

Vankoughnet, Q. C., and *Freeman* supported the rule. Here no legal title is outstanding in anybody, and the court has decided that when the crown grants land, the possession and right of possession are transferred to the grantee, notwithstanding there may be a squatter upon the lot.—Doe Fitzgerald v. Finn, 1 U. C. R. 70. The statute 14 & 15 Vic. ch. 7, sec. 5, allows the purchase of a right of entry, and therefore in effect repeals the 32 H. VIII.; but, admitting that act to be still in force, no case can be cited where an action has been brought under it for buying a pretended title, when that title is purely equitable. Besides, in the present case it is absurd to talk of a pretended title. When the defendant took the title from Martin he was buying the very title the plaintiff wished and intended to get, and therefore all relating to this charge is disposed of. The third and fourth counts are bad, because they shew clearly that the whole contest is about equitable titles only, and there is no precedent for an action with reference to such claims. Neither the statute nor common law were ever made to apply to such estates. As to the defendant's buying the mortgage, he had already an interest, and was only perfecting his own title. That is allowable, and has never been held as purchasing a pretended title. Where land has been twice sold, a court of equity in fact encourage a race for the legal estate, and whoever gets it first will prevail. Ross qui tam v. Meyers, 9 U. C. R. 284, and McKenzie qui tam v. Miller, M. T. 6 Vic., shew that a person may buy an outstanding title to protect himself.

As to the main question, there is no precedent for such an action as this; it is purely speculative, and if encouraged will introduce a new and numerous class of cases: for any step taken in a suit contrary to good faith, good practice, or the duty of a party to the court, must be held to form as good a right to sue as is stated here. If, however, the action could be sustained, the declaration is much too loose. It does not allege that the plaintiff had any right from the nominee of the crown, or any title, but only that he claimed to have it. There is no direct averment that the plaintiff really had any *bona fide* claim or any interest. His complaint in effect is

3 *d*—VOL. XII. Q.B.

" Because I said I had a claim, therefore you should have given me notice, and whether my claim was good or bad makes no difference. Now notice is quite immaterial unless the declaration shews some interest which the court would have protected. He may have been merely a squatter for all that is alleged. The authorities shew that in actions like those referred to on the other side, it must be averred clearly what the interest is. [ROBINSON, C. J.—Does the declaration mean more than; For that whereas the plaintiff professed to own ?] No, that is the precise meaning. An action cannot be brought for depriving a man of property to which he alleges no title. Cotterell v, Jones, 11 C. B. 713, shews that no action will lie unless damage is sustained, and therefore it is necessary to shew exactly what the interest was in order to estimate the damages. This action fails too on the principle of Davis v. Minor, 2 U: C. R. 464 ; for, if the interest amounts to anything, the plaintiff could have enforced his rights in equity by making defendant his trustee. Suppose the power of granting a patent in this case had remained in the crown instead of being vested in the heir and devisee commission, and a similar deceit had been practised on the crown, would any one imagine that an action could lie ? If the plaintiff has a clear equitable right he must go to a court of equity ; and if he has no such right, then there is clearly no right of action at law.—Cotterell v. Jones, 11 C. B. 713.

As to the omission to give the notice required by the 8 Vic. ch. 8, sec. 5, that is no ground of action, for there is nothing as between the plaintiff and defendant to make it obligatory, though the commissioners may insist upon it if they choose. The defendant might have made his claim as well as the plaintiff, and the plaintiff did nothing to prevent him. This action is in fact brought simply because the plaintiff neglected to supply the court with evidence of defendant's claim, and if that is actionable the suborning a witness by either party to a suit would be more so. [ROBINSON, C. J.—Suppose a plaintiff brings ejectment as on a vacant possession, concealing a lease which he has made, and turns the defendant out and drives him to his ejectment ; or suppose a plaintiff sues on a promissory note, concealing the fact of payment, and serves the process on an agent who is ignorant of such payment.] The charge is merely that by false evidence the defendant induced the court to arrive at a wrong conclusion. Take a case where payment is denied on oath, and a receipt afterwards found; even if the plaintiff had sworn on motion for new trial that no payment was made, no action would lie. The case may be adjudicated upon when the receipt is found, but that is the only remedy. Then, as to the heir and devisee commission : the applications to them are all published ; every one knows of the claim being preferred. [ROBINSON, C. J.—Is there any allegation that Shields did not know of DeBlaquiere's proceeding ?] No, nothing of the sort. Purton v. Honnor, 1 B. & P. 205, and Longmeid v. Holliday, 6 Ex. 761, shew that the action cannot be rested on the ground of deceit, but it must be on the ground that defendant had a right to notice :- there can be clearly no action for deceiving the court. Saville v. Roberts, 2 Salk. 15 ; Johnson v. Sutton, 1 T. R, 544; Hollis v. Goldfinch, 1 B. & C. 205 ; Graham v. Sandinelli, 10 Jur. 1061 ; De Medina v. Grove, 10 Q. B. 152 ; Roret v. Lewis, 5 D. C. L. 371 ; Francis v. Brown, 11 U. C. R. 558 ; and Williams v. Mostyn, 4 M. & W. 145 ; are also cases which tend to shew that the action cannot be maintained.

As to the evidence, it does not shew clear notice to defendant of the plaintiff's claim. The fact of the plaintiff being on the land and defendant knowing it, would not shew a claim ; and there is really no evidence that he knew of the plaintiff being in possession, but only that some one was. That is no proof of an adverse claim. There may have been enough to put the plaintiff on enquiry, but that is not sufficient to ground an action like this, of an almost criminal character.

DRAPER, J., delivered the judgment of the court.

We do not perceive any solid-distinction between the defendant and the mortgagee from whom he derived title at first.

The right and interest of Martin stand admitted, as both plaintiff and defendant derived their claims under him, treating him as entitled as a purchaser from the crown.

Then Martin makes a mortgage on the 1st of January, 1839, to secure a sum of money with interest by instalments, the last of which becomes payable on the 1st of January, 1849. On the 5th of December, 1850, the mortgagee having been paid nothing, either principal or interest, the defendant obtains a release from the mortgagor of all his interest in the mortgaged premises. The mortgagor had in the meantime given a bond with a penalty, to make a (legal) title to a third party on being paid a certain sum of money, and on this party also satisfying this very mortgage, neither of which conditions this third part had fulfilled, nor had he taken any steps to do so, though notified, as Martin swears, that he was about to make an absolute conveyance to the mortgagor, and though he had in the meantime made valuable improvements.

Now if the estate of Martin had been a legal estate, and the foregoing had been the true state of the transaction, even with the addition of a disputed fact, that the mortgagee had the fullest notice of the bond, and of the entry and possession under it, would the obligee on being evicted, have any cause of action against the mortgagee?

Then, does the fact that the defendant is assignee of the mortgagor make any difference? It is quite true that the release and conveyance from Martin to him is dated in December, 1850, and that the assignment of the mortgage is not made until the 7th of June, 1851. But we think there is no room for reasonable doubt that the defendant purchased from Martin with the privity and assent of his father, the mortgagee—very possibly for him. The defendant had paid £28 9s. 3d. to the agent of the commissioner of crown lands on the 27th of December, 1849, being for the third instalment on this lot; and the consideration for the assignment of this mortgage is that very sum of £28 9s. 3d., apparently connecting these two transactions, and giving to the obtaining the intervening conveyance from Martin, when coupled with the conversation which he proves took place with defendant respecting the mortgage money, a clear character of connection with the other two transactions; and therefore we look on the defendant as standing in every respect in the position of the original mortgagee.

In what view, then, can it be said that the getting this release from Martin, assuming notice of Bettridge's claim and possession, was a wrong, a malicious injury to the latter ? If Martin had been able, and had mortgaged the legal estate, and had given the selfsame bond to Bettridge, would not the mortgagee have had a complete right of entry to oust Bettridge from the possession ; and also, whether before or after, such ouster, to get a release of the equity of redemption from his mortgagor ?

Or, if he had filed a bill to foreclose, taking no notice whatever of Bettridge or· of his possession, and a decree of foreclosure were obtained—the court being kept in ignorance of Bettridge and his claim—would an action lie against the mortgagee by Bettridge for a malicious wrong ?

I can only say that as yet I have met with no authority which would enable me to answer the question affirmatively. Nor is it to be overlooked that Bettridge took no assignment from Martin, only a bond to convey when certain things were done by him, which are yet undone. If a wrong were done to Bettridge by the release of December, 1850, to defendant, who is apparently the principal wrong-doer —Martin or the defendant ? It would seem an anomaly that the defendant should through that release become liable to Bettridge, and that Martin should not. And yet I cannot see how an action could be brought against Martin by Bettridge, who has failed entirely in fulfilling the conditions of his purchase, for any act done after such failure, by which Bettridge lost the purchase; and if not against Martin, *a fortiori*, as would seem to me, not against the defendant.

Then the plaintiff's claim is derived under Bettridge, and this cannot, we apprehend, strenghten it. It is not clear *when* the plaintiff entered as a purchaser; but it is clear he acquired all his claims by his bargain with Bettridge, and equally clear that Bettridge could give him no higher or better claim than he had himself. There is evidence to shew that the plaintiff occupied in 1850 ; but it is, we think, very questionable if he entered as a purchaser. If there was a written assignment not made until 1852, it would go far to lead to the conclusion that the purchase was concluded on later than the time of his entry. If he purchased when he entered, he knew then that Bettridge had failed in the conditions which entitled him to call for a conveyance. He knew what payments Bettridge had to make and to whom, but he did no more than Bettridge had done towards fulfilling them.

But, assuming this in the plaintiff's favor, it should be made out, in order to sustain this action, that the injury complained of was a malicious wrong to the plaintiff; and to warrant the finding of malice in fact, there must be some evidence connecting the acts complained of with an intent to plaintiff's injury. The only evidence given for this purpose was—first, some vague generalities, that the witness or witnesses considered the claim was generally known; and, secondly, that the plaintiff's mother had seen defendant pass the place about two years before the trial, which would be about May, 1852. Now, all the matter charged as wrongful, and which led to the obtaining the patent, took place before or at the meeting of the heir and devisee commission of July, 1851. On what principle is it that the defendant's knowledge or notice of plaintiff's possession acquired in May, 1852, can reflect back upon and give a malicious character to defendant's actions on or before July, 1851 ?

We have hitherto taken no notice of a fact on which the plaintiff's counsel has placed the strongest reliance—viz., that the defendant made an affidavit, which was produced and used before the heir and devisee commissioners, that he believed his own claim to be just, and was not aware of any adverse claim. It was admitted this affidavit was made and used.

We have examined the case, without reference to this affidavit, to see if, apart from it, the action would be sustained, and cannot satisfy ourselves that it is. Without reference for the moment to the frame of the declaration, we do not think the facts disclose a cause of action. Does the affidavit make any difference, if untrue, and do the facts proved shew it to be untrue ?

Such an affidavit was indispensable to the allowance of the claim, but equally so is an affidavit of debt to the issuing of a *capias*. Actions for malicious arrest on such writs are

common enough ; but it is no part of the doctrine of the
courts that a declaration not setting forth such an affidavit,
or stating that it was made in order to procure the issuing
of the writ, would be bad, or that the action could not be
sustained without such an affidavit were proved. And we
do not see that the making the affidavit here complained of
has any greater or more direct bearing on the adjudication
of the commissioners than the affidavit of debt has on the
issue of the writ or the arrest made under its authority. The
affidavit is necessary, to enable the commissioners to proceed
—to give them, as it were, jurisdiction in the particular
case,—but it forms no part of the proof of the claim advanced,
nor aids in the disposal of it, so far as the actual facts and
intrinsic merits are concerned. So far as we can see at
present, if such an action be sustainable at all, it might, or
rather must, be by other facts independent of the affidavit,
but certainly not upon the affidavit, without proof of other
facts in themselves establishing the cause of action. The
statement in the affidavit that the deponent believes his
claim to be just and well founded, does not procure, nor as
evidence tend to prove, the decision of the commissioners
that his claim as alleged in his notice is sustained. It is
not the *per quod* the alleged injury was inflicted, though it
may be a step ancilliary to it. In our opinion the proving
such an affidavit, and proving it to be false, would not *per
se* sustain such an action as the present.

Then, is it proved to be untrue ? Take each member of it.
Is it untrue that the defendant believed his claim to be just and
well founded, when he was assignee of a mortgage long past
due, and the mortgagor had released all right to him expressly
because the mortgage was wholly unpaid, and after the mortgagor had referred to the person to whom he was bound to convey, without any result or action on his part ? Is it untrue that
defendant believed there was no other adverse claim ? Assume
that he was fully aware of the precise nature of Bettridge's
claim (which, as he produces Bettridge's bond from Martin,
should be assumed). He knew also that Martin had gone to
Bettridge before signing the release of 1850, and got no satisfaction. He knew that the condition on which Bettridge

would have had a right to call on Martin for a conveyance
had not been fulfilled, though the time for its fulfilment
expired on the 1st of January, 1849 ; and he knew that up
to the date of his making this affidavit (June,1851,) nothing
had been said or done implying that they meant to fulfil the
terms and pay the money. (unless holding the possession
acquired by Bettridge in 1839 could be deemed such an act).
May he not, even though erroneously, have assumed that this
long and continued default operated as an extinguishment of
the claim, which, in strictness, he might think never was a
claim on the land, but on the liability of Martin to the
penalty ? We are not prepared to say that upon all the
facts the defendant's affidavit must or ought to be considered
as made *mala fide.*

Then, looking at the frame of the first and second counts
(for if the plaintiff fails on these, he has, we think, no ground
to recover on the third and fourth), do they, coupled with the
proof, establish a right for the plaintiff to recover. We put all
considerations derived from any supposed analogy with the
statute of bracery out of the question ; and the facts of the
case negative the application of any such principle. The
possession of the mortgagor, or others holding under him, is
consistent with the right of the mortgagee ; for, whatever the
rights of subsequent holders, they must be subservient to the
prior incumbrance ; and therefore, as to any notice of plaintiff's title, as assignee of the nominee of the crown, which the
plaintiff's possession could give, we think it goes for nothing,
because we know the true state of the case. This possession,
and the notice inferrible from it, form the inducement.
Then the averment that the defendant, maliciously intending,
&c., represented and pretended himself to be, is, we suppose,
intended to mean a false representation and pretence—either
false because he had no claim whatever, or because his claim
was acquired under such circumstances that, as against the
plaintiff, he was disabled as setting it up as true. Can this
be said to be the truth, when it appears that the defendant
holds as assignee of a mortgage prior in existence to any
claim which the plaintiff has, and when the defendant obtained
a release from the mortgagor, as appears ? It may be even

admitted, as it seems to us, that the heir and devisee commission would not have allowed the plaintiff's claim had they known all the facts, or at least not without giving the plaintiff an opportunity of being heard ; and yet it would not follow that this action is sustainable, We have already remarked upon the materiality and effect of the affidavit of defendant. The remaining averments are, that he procured his claim to be allowed, and took out the patent in pursuance of such allowance, which, without what proceeds, would be immaterial. We do not see how it can be said that the defendant has procured the allowance of a claim, which had no foundation—a fraudulent or pretended claim, the assertion of which was a wrong, to the injury of the plaintiff. We are not prepared to determine that, with all parties before them, the heir and devisee commission ought not to, and therefore would not, have allowed the defendant's claim, leaving the plaintiff to such remedy as he might have, if any, against third parties. In July, 1851 there was due to the plaintiff, as assignee of the mortgage, about £160, about £30 for the third instalment paid by him in December, 1849 ; and, to get the patent out, some one must pay the seven remaining instalments and interest from 1835, a liability which in July, 1852, amounted to £215 5s. If Mr. Bettridge sold to the plaintiff for £400 in May, 1852, as seems the case from Mr. Richardson's evidence, the amount due to the defendant and to the crown on this lot exceeded the price which the plaintiff agreed to pay for it, with all its improvements up to the date of his agreement Upon what legal principle the defendant should pay the plaintiff a further sum of £350 we are unable to discover.

In this declaration there is not a word about want of reasonable or probable cause. That there was no want of such cause to prefer the claim, the decision of the heir and devisee commission allowing defendant's claim, and his subsequently obtaining the patent, must, we apprehend, be conclusive evidence. The only other point upon which there could be a suggestion of want of reasonable and probable cause is as to the statement in the affidavit, that the defendant was not aware of any adverse claim. We are not by any means clear that the declaration, as it is, can be sustained; and if we

have the whole facts before us, we do not see that, as a matter
of law, a judge could tell the jury that the plaintiff had not
reasonable or probable cause for making such an affidavit;
and even were it otherwise, the other objections on which
we have remarked must on these facts present difficulties
appeaently insuperable to the plaintiff's recovery. We
think there should be a new trial

Rule absolute.

<hr>

HARRIS V. FRASER.

*Case for obstruction of water-course—Argumentative traverse of plaintiff's
alleged right.*

The declaration stated that the plaintiff was lawfully possessed of a certain
saw-mill, &c., and enjoyed the benefit of a certain stream which ought to,
and, until the committing of the grievances complained of, did run from a
certain creek above the plaintiff's mill to the said mill, and thence to the
said creek below said mill, without being dammed back on said mill, by
which the water-wheel of the said mill was worked; and he complained
that the defendant wrongfully erected a dam across said creek below his
mill, and thereby penned back the water, &c.

The defendant pleaded, as to the erecting the dam, and thereby obstructing
and penning back the water, whereby, &c., that before the erection of
the plaintiff's mill, and the making the trench and comitting the
grievances above mentioned, one M. was the owner and occupier of the
land on each side of the creek, at the place where the said stream in the
declaration mentioned runs into said creek below the plaintiff's mill, and
for a long distance above such place, and to the premises of the defendant
hereinafter mentioned; that the said M., by deed, granted to C. & R.,
then the occupiers of the premises of the defendant hereinafter mentioned,
and their assigns, the easements and right of obstructing the water of the
creek, and of damming it back upon his said close whenever they should
require so to do; that the plaintiff, after the said deed, wrongfully and
without the leave of the said C. & R., or of the defendant, dug a mill race
from the said mill through the land of the said M, into the said creek
below the said mill, and within the close of the said M.; and in digging
the same lowered the sides of the creek at the place last aforesaid, which
said stream is the stream in the first count mentioned; that afterwards
the defendant became possessed of a certain grist-mill just below and
adjoining the land of the said M., and that it then became necessary, for
the purpose of working the said mill, to erect a dam across the said creek
and raise the water, and the defendant did then, with the consent of the
said M., erect and continue the dam, and thereby, in the enjoyment of the
easement so granted by the said M., who then was and still is in
possession and occupation of his said close and lands, and for the purpose
aforesaid, a little obstructed and diverted the said stream upon the land
of the said M., within the natural banks of the said creek, so that a small
quantity of the water of the creek so dammed back ran out of its usual
course through the said raceway, through the close of said M., upon the
plaintiff's mill, by reason of the said raceway being cut down through
the sides of the said creek as aforesaid, which water would have remained
within the creek, within the said close of said M., and would not have run
upon the mill of the plaintiff, if the plaintiff had not so lowered and cut
down the banks of the creek,—which are the said alleged grievances, and
which the plaintiff might lawfully do for the purpose aforesaid.

Held—Plea bad, as an argumentative traverse of the plaintiff's alleged right
to have the water flow unobstructed along the raceway.

CASE.—The first count of the declaration set out that the defendant was possessed of a saw-mill and premises in the township of Brantford, and enjoyed the benefit and advantage of a certain stream or water-course, which ought, and, until the committing of the grievances by the defendant as hereinafter mentioned, did run and flow from a certain creek called the Whiteman's Creek, above the said mill, to the said mill, and thence to the said Whiteman's Creek below the said mill whereby the water-wheel of the said mill was worked, without being flowed back or dammed back upon the said mill, or the wheel or apron thereof ; yet the defendant, well knowing, &c., but contriving, &c., wrongfully and injuriously erected a dam in and across the said creek below the plaintiff's said mill, and wrongfully and injuriously kept and continued the said dam so erected in and across the said creek, for a long time, to wit from thence hitherto, and thereby, during all the time aforesaid, wrongfully and injuriously obstructed and diverted the usual and proper course and natural flow of the water of the said creek, whereby the water of the said creek ran and flowed out of its usual course, and became and was dammed and penned back upon the said mill of the plaintiff, and the said wheel and apron thereof ; and the plaintiff, by reason of the said water being so dammed and penned back was deprived of the use of his said mill.

The defendant pleaded—as to the erecting of the dam in the first count mentioned, and continuing the same so erected as therein also mentioned, and thereby obstructing and diverting the usual and proper course and natural flow of the water of the said creek, whereby the water of the said creek ran and flowed out of its natural course, and became, and was dammed and penned back upon the said mill of the plaintiff, and the wheel and apron thereof as in the said first count alleged—that one Michael Force, for a long time before the said mill of the said plaintiff was erected, and before the digging and making the trench or mill race by the plaintiff as hereinafter mentioned, and before the committing the alleged grievances above in this plea mentioned, and before and at the time of making the deed hereinafter next mentioned, to wit, on the 15th of March, 1848, was, and

still is the owner and occupier of the land, sides, and banks
on each side of the said creek, and through and over which
the said creek then ran and flowed, and still ought to run
and flow, at the place where the said stream or water-course
in the said first count mentioned runs to and into the said
creek, below the mill of the said plaintiff; and then owned
and occupied, and still owns and occupies, the land on each
side of the said creek, and over which the same runs for a
long distance above the said last mentioned place, to wit,
forty rods above; and also then owned and occupied, and
still owns and occupies, the land from the said last mentioned
place, on each side of the said creek, and over which the said
creek runs, to the close and premises of the said defendant as.
hereinafter mentioned; and that the said Michael Force, on
the day and year last aforesaid, by a deed under his hand
and seal, gave and granted unto Henry Cope and Greaves
Robson, who were then the occupiers of the close and
premises of the defendant hereinafter mentioned, and their
assigns, the easement, right, and privilege of obstructing the
natural flow of the water of the said creek, and of raising and
damming the same back in and upon his said close and land,
at all times when they should require so to do (making
profert of the deed), of all which premises of the said plaintiff
then had notice : that the said plaintiff, after the said Michael
Force had granted the easement, right and privilege aforesaid, to wit, on, &c., wrongfully and unlawfully, and without
the leave or license of the said Henry Cope and Greaves
Robson, and without the leave or license of the defendant
dug and made a trench or mill-race from the said mill through
the said land of the said Michael Force into the said creek,
below the said mill, and within the said close of the said
Michael Force; and in digging and making the same, he, the
said plaintiff, cut down and lowered the banks and sides of
the said creek at the place last aforesaid, to wit, to the extent
of three feet, which said trench or mill-race is the stream or
water-course in the said first count mentioned as running
from the said creek to the said plaintiff's mill and thence to
the said creek, and not a different stream or water-course :
that afterwards, and before the committing of the said

supposed grievances in the introductory part of this plea mentioned, to wit, on the said first day of March, 1853, he, the said defendant, became and was lawfully possessed of a certain grist mill and premises situate upon the said creek, just below and adjoining the said land and close of the said Michael Force; and that it then became necessary, for the purpose of properly driving and working the last mentioned mill, to build, and erect, and maintain, and continue a dam upon and across the said creek, whereby to raise the water and obtain a sufficient head of water for the purpose aforesaid·; and that the said defendant did then, for such purpose, with the consent of the said Michael Force, erect, maintain and continue the dam in, upon, and across the said stream, upon the premises so in the possession of the defendant as aforesaid, and thereby, in the enjoyment of the easement so granted by the said Michael Force, who then was and still is in the possession and occupation of his said close and lands, and for the purpose aforesaid, and because the said defenant's mill could not otherwise be properly worked, then, and on the said divers other days and times between that day and the commencement of this suit, a little obstructed and diverted the usual course and natural flow of the water of the said creek, below and within, and upon the said close and land of the said Michael Force, within the natural banks of the said creek, so that a small quantity of the water of the said creek, raised and dammed back for the purpose aforesaid, ran and flowed out of its usual course and channel, through the said trench or raceway leading from the said mill of the plaintiff to the said creek, through the said close of the said Michael Force, upon the said mill of the said plaintiff, and the wheel and apron thereof, by reason of the said trench or mill-race being cut through the banks and sides of the said creek as aforesaid, and the said back and side thereof having been thereby lowered and cut away by the said plaintiff as aforesaid; which water would have remained within the banks and sides of the said creek, within the said close of the said Michael Force, and would not have run upon the mill of the plaintiff, or the wheel or apron thereof, if the said plaintiff had not lowered and cut down the banks of the said creek as aforesaid, which are the said alleged grievances, &c., and which the said defendant lawfully might do for the cause and purpose aforesaid, he the said defendant doing no unnecessary damage to the said plaintiff on the occasion aforesaid; and this the defendant is ready to verify, &c.

Demurrer.—The causes assigned sufficiently appear in the judgment.

Connor, Q. C., for the demurrer, cited Ward v. Robins, 15 M. & W. 237; Brind v. Dale, 7 M. & W. 775; Bridge v. Grand Junction R. W. Co., 3 M. & W. 244.

Freeman, contra.

ROBINSON, C. J., delivered the judgment of the court.

We think this plea is bad, not exactly as amounting to the general issue, because "not guilty" in an action of this kind only puts in issue the doing the act complained of; but as being an argumentative traverse of the plaintiff's alleged right to have the water flow along the raceway unobstructed from his mill into the river lower down.

We cannot distinguish this case from Ward v. Robins (15 M. & W. 237), so far as regards the application of the principle against an argumentative denial of what is essential to the plaintiff's action; for, though in that case the plea was held good, yet it was upon a ground peculiar to the case, and the court very clearly affirmed the general principle as applying to such cases, when there was nothing peculiar, as in that case there was, which could create an exception.

The declaration does not, in terms as precise as are generally used, aver the plaintiff's right to have the water flow unobstructed down the raceway. It says only, that it *ought* to have so run and flowed. But we may give such force to that expression as is necessary for supporting the action, and must take it to be intended as a positive assertion of a right. It follows then, if it is sufficiently averred to answer the plaintiff's purpose, that it may be traversed by the defendant for in truth it lies at the very foundation of the plaintiff's action. Then in this plea, instead of simply traversing the alleged right to the uninterrupted flow of water through the raceway, the defendant sets up certain facts tending to shew that the plaintiff could have no such right, and does not conclude with a special traverse of the right.

The obstruction complained of is the erecting of a dam across Whiteman's creek, below the plaintiff's mill and thereby obstructing the flow of the water of the creek whereby *the water of the creek*—that is, of Whiteman's creek— flowed out of its course, and was "dammed back upon the mill of the plaintiff, and upon the wheel apron thereof."

The plaintiff does not in express words tell us that the water was backed up the race to his mill, but his declaration shews that it must have been so, if his mill-wheel was obstructed. All therefore depends upon the plaintiff's right to have the water of the stream or raceway run from his mill unobstructed into Whiteman's creek, for if the plaintiff had not a right to have the water run into the creek by the raceway as freely as it was running when the defendant put up his dam, then no wrong has been done him.

The facts as they were pleaded, would, it appears to us, constitute a defence if substantiated in evidence, and if they had been well pleaded unless they could be repelled by new matter shewn by the plaintiff; but nothing turns upon this demurrer beyond the cost of the pleading, for there was upon the record another plea, simply traversing the plaintiff's right to the flow of water through the raceway. But the plaintiff, it seems succeeded upon that issue upon the trial. He has gone to the jury upon the same defence, which the defendant desired to set up in this plea.

Judgment for the plaintiff on demurrer.

During this term the following gentlemen were called to the bar :—E. B. WOOD, JONAS AP JONES, JAMES HENRY MORRIS, WILLIAM HENRY STANTON, MACDONALD BRIDGES, CHARLES ALFRED DURAND, GEORGE A. DREW, Esquires.

Present—The Hon. Sir JOHN BEVERLEY ROBINSON, Bart., C.J.
" WILLIAM HENRY DRAPER, J.
" ROBERT EASTON BURNS, J.

RENAUD V. THE GREAT WESTERN RAILWAY COMPANY.

G. W. R. R. Co.—Duty to erect fences.—Negligence in not slackening speed at crossings.

The Great Western Railway crosses a highway on a level, and one of their trains going *at its usual rate of speed* ran into and killed two cows, which were passing along the highway at their usual pace but without an attendant. The owner of the cows sued the company in an action on the case, founding his claim to damages solely on the ground of their neglect in not slackening speed at the crossing. It appeared in evidence that the track was not fenced.

Held, 1st.—That if the company were bound to fence in their road where the accident occurred, it was by their default the cows got upon the track, and therefore they could not object that the cows were not legally on the highway.

2ndly.—That if the company were not bound to fence, still they were guilty of negligence as charged in the declaration, and therefore as against them the cows were legally there.

Semble, that the effect of the 9th clause of 4 Wm. IV. ch. 29, is to oblige the company to erect fences, and to place gates where their road crosses highways, and to have such gates properly watched and attended.

Semble also, that this clause extends to all parts of the road, as well west as east of London.

This was an appeal from the County Court of the County of Essex.

The case is an important one, and the evidence and judgment in the court below are therefore given in full.

The plaintiff complained—For that whereas the defendants, &c., on the 17th of February, 1854, were by statute, 4 Wm. IV. ch. 29, the owners and occupiers of the Great Western Railway made by the defendants under the said act; which railway crosses a public highway in the township of Sandwich known as the Lozon Road leading from the second concession into the public highway along the river Detroit in the front of the township on a level and were possessed of locomotives, &c., propelled by steam, and used by the defendants for the conveyance of passengers, &c., upon the said railway, for hire; wherefore it was the duty of the said defendants in using said railway to propel their engines, &c., upon the said railway, towards, up to, upon and across the said high-

way, at a place where the highway is crossed by said
railway, with reasonable and proper care and caution, and
to use otherwise reasonable and proper care, precaution and
diligence, to avoid and prevent accident and injury by them
to persons and cattle, &c., lawfully being and passing in and
upon, and along said highway.

Yet the defendants, on, &c., regardless of their said duty
drove and propelled one of their said engines and several of
their said carriages and trucks attached thereto, in, upon and
along the said railway, towards, up to, upon and across the
said highway, where the said railway crosses said highway,
at such a rate of speed, and with such gross negligence, that
the same struck against and killed two of the plaintiff's
cows, of the value of £20, *then lawfully being and passing*
in and upon the said highway, so that *by the mere negligence
of the defendants and their servants in charge of the engine,
&c.*, the said cows were killed—damage £20.

The defendants pleaded not guilty, "By Statute."

The evidence given on the trial was as follows :—

M. Paquet.—The plaintiff lives on the Lozon Road, a public
highway from the Tecumseh Road, in the second concession,
to the River Road.   The Great Western Railway crosses it
at about five acres from the river, on a level with the public
road in Sandwich in a slanting direction.   The plaintiff lives
about five and a half acres from the crossing.   The country
is clear and open thereabouts, and a person on cars coming
on the railway can see all round half a mile from the railway,
which there is higher than the fences.   The Lozon Road is
pretty high.   Witness was coming from the plaintiff's house,
half a mile from the crossing ; saw the cars strike two cows
pushed one into the ditch the other on the ties.   The cows
belonged to the plaintiff.   They were both killed.   Witness
saw them before they were struck; knew they must be killed;
the cars were half a mile off when witness first heard the
whistle.   The cows came on the track.   It then blew three
or four times for an acre.   The cows ran against each other,
and obstructed each other, and were killed.   One might have
got off, but did not.   The cows first stopped and then walked
on.   The cars were going at their usual speed, pretty good

speed—speed was made no less before striking.   Witness
was about five and a half acres from the track at the time.

Cross-examined.—The cows came from the plaintiff's—
they had just been taken out of his stable into the road ;
the road is fenced up to the track.   It has a cattle guard on the
track.   It is a sort of a grating, laid edge-wise, to prevent
and terrify cattle from crossing and straying down the track.
Witness heard the whistle first—the cows stopped—the cars
were at three-quarters of an acre off—knows it is impossible
to stop cars at three quarters of an acre.   The plaintiff has
no cattle on the other side of the road.   The cattle were
turned out to water at a ditch, and have to cross the railway
to get at it.   The plaintiff has no land near or adjoining
either side of that railway.   The cattle had no other way to
cross except that.

Joseph St. Louis.—Was there when cattle were killed—
perhaps twelve rods off, on the opposite side of the road
from where last witness was.   The cars were going at their
usual rate of speed—did not slacken speed on coming to the
crossing.   The cows were coming from the plaintiff's, and
going to the other side of the railroad : heard the cars and
whistle : saw the cows try to turn.   They had not time to
turn.   They were on the road when witness heard the whistle
and were struck two or three seconds after whistle sounded.
They were at the crossing between the cattle guards on the
public road and on the railway at the same time.

The jury were charged, that the cattle having a right to
pass over the crossing, as well as the railway or the locomotives or trains, &c., if when struck the cattle were crossing without any unnecessary delay, the same as if they
had a careful attendant, they were lawfully there—and in
such case, if the locomotives, &c., were going on at a high
rate of speed without slackening or lessening their speed, with
proper precaution, in due time, the Railway Company, the
defendants, were liable for the damage, of the amount of
which evidence had been adduced.

That there was nothing in evidence to lead to the belief
that the cattle were unnecessarily delaying, or remaining on
and incumbering the crossing when struck.

That there was evidence that the locomotives, &c., were

going at the usual rate of speed, without slackening or lessening speed when the cattle were struck, which the learned judge thought should have been done in crossing a highway on a level, as the Railway Company were bound to pass or cross a highway (when permitted by statute) in some way so as not to do damage to cattle or persons, either by lessening speed when going over on a level, or by going over or under the highway by some or other of the methods now said to be known and used for such purposes.

O'Connor objected to that part of the charge relating to the attendant, as they were not bound to have one.

Albert Prince objected to that part of the charge which stated the necessity of either lessening speed or so constructing the crossing (other than on a level as it now is) that the accident could not have occurred ; that the only negligence charged was, running too fast.

The jury found for the plaintiff, and £15 damages.

Albert Prince obtained a rule in the county court to shew cause why the verdict should not be set aside, and a new trial had, on the ground of the verdict being contrary to law and evidence, and for misdirection.

O'Connor shewed cause. He contended that the 9th sec. of 4 Wm. IV. ch. 29, and 7 Wm. IV. ch. 61, under which the defendants made their railway, enable them to cross a road or highway on the route of their railway ; provided that the corporation shall restore it when thus intersected to its former state, or in a sufficient manner as not to impair its usefulness. He cited Fawcett v. York & North Midland R. W. Company, 2 Eng. Rep. 289, as shewing that when cattle are lawfully on the highway, or on a crossing over a highway, the company are liable for injury caused by carelessness or negligence, which he considered to be proved here.

Albert Prince contended that the case was not applicable as it was where cattle strayed on a railway through a defect of fences which the defendants were bound to keep up. And as to misdirection, the breach in the declaration was not sufficiently wide to let in the evidence that the defendants did not restore the highway to its former state of usefulness. It was that the engineers, &c. were going at such a high rate of speed as to cause the damage done ; and the restoring of the road, &c. did not come in question.   The question was not as to the rate of speed, but whether the cattle or the cars had the best right to be there, or whether either of them, at any rate, were not there each at their own peril, as the statute had legalized a dangerous trade for the public benefit.

Judgment in the court below was delivered by CHEWITT, J.

As to the exceptions taken at the trial regarding the attendant spoken of in the charge, that was only suggested as a means or precaution for the owner against cattle unnecessarily delaying on the crossing, thereby increasing the risk —not that it was in express words required by law, but that if they unnecessarily delayed on the crossing, and the injury happened while so delaying, they were there at the owner's risk, unless there was gross and culpable negligence on the part of the company's agents in charge. And so, as to that part of the charge referring to the going over or under, &c., it was stated to the jury as explaining some of the means used by railway companies to obviate the danger of passing or crossing a highway without materially lessening speed ; but that if none of these means were used, and they crossed on a level, as the act permitted, the locomotive owners must take such precautions as would prevent injury or danger to the public ; among which precautions slackening or lessening speed in due time was the principal—as blowing the whistle where required by the act (it is not so required in *these* acts, though it is in the General Railway Act,), could hardly be considered as notice to animals, though it might be to their attendant, if the law required that there should be one

As to the wording of the breach in the declaration, I conceive it is sufficient to let in the evidence offered of the injury, and the manner and cause of it.

With respect to the principal points raised, the best judgment that I can form on this new and difficult question is, that the legislature, in passing the acts which gave this particular railway company its charter, only intended to give the company a right of crossing the roads and highways on a level or in any other way, on a single or double track, &c., to be

made in such a way as not to impair the usefulness of the
road or highway, so as to exempt the company and the contractors of it from being proceeded against during its
construction, and afterwards, either for the works made
across the roads and highways on a level, or over or under
it, for the purpose of the railway, or for the future constant
crossing the same with their engines, tenders, tracks, cars,
or any length of train, which, from their noise ,smoke, sparks,
steam, extent and unusual appearance when crossing (or even
passing along, and parallel to and near) the roads or highways at all times, night or day, might otherwise subject them
to be considered as rendering cattle and persons on the roads
or highways liable to be frightened and endangered while
using the roads and highways there—Rex v. Pease (4 B. &
Ad. 30). Rex v. Gregory (5 B. & Ad. 555, 2 Nev. & Man. 478 2 Tyr.
201, S. C. in error)—and therefore, otherwise but for these
acts. a nuisance ; and so far only legalizing their operations,
as a dangerous (though very useful) enterprise, made across a
road or highway, which so far injured, by intercepting at
times its free passage, and rendering it less commodious to
the public.

But the legislature nowhere in the acts relating to the
Great Westeren Railway Company, it seems to me, gave or
intended to give the company a right, while passing or crossing a public road or highway on a level, to go at a rate of speed
so high as to be dangerous, more than any stage-coach or
other carriage drawn by horses has to go at a furious or
dangerous rate, either *along* a public road or highway, or
where two such roads or highways cross each other, otherwise
than at their own risk for any want of due care or caution;
and if either of them do so, and accidents happen to persons,
cattle, or goods lawfully on the roads or highway where they
cross each other, or where they are crossed by the railway,
they would equally be liable for the damages.—See *Baron
Parke's* observations in Sharrod v. London and N. W. R. W.
Co. (4 Eng. Rep. 405). where he says—"If the plaintiff's
cattle had a right to be on the railway" (here on the highway
and crossing of railway as well), "the plaintiff has a remedy
against the company for causing the engine to be driven in

such a way as to injure that right; for the defendants were bound to see that their carriages did not travel at such a speed as to make it impossible to avoid oth'er persons who had a right to be there. If the cattle were *altogether* wrong-doers, there has been no neglect or misconduct for which the defendants are responsible. If the cattle had an•excuse for being there, as if they had escaped through defect of fences which the company should have kept up, the cattle were not *wrong-doers*, though they had *no-right* to be there." In the present case the cattle required no *excuse.* They had a right to be there, unless unncessarily delaying *on,* and so *encumbering* the highway and crossing. And see the judgment of *Cresswell, J.,* in Rex v. East and West India Docks and Junction R. W. Co. (12 Eng. Rep. 525), which shews that legalizing a dangerous traffic will not cover negligence such as *Baron Parke* mentions, and which is the same as complained of in this case; and the case of Hewit v. Ontario, Simcoe & Huron R. R. Co. (11 U. C. R. 604), which shews the same thing, though not a case involving any question of rate of speed. I think the rule should be discharged.

· The defendants appealed from this judgment.

Cameron, Q. C. and *Connor, Q. C.,* for the appeal.—The learned judge below charged the jury that if the cows were crossing without unnecessary delay, as if they had been with a careful attendant, and the train was going at a high rate of speed, then the defendants would be liable. This was a misdirection; the cattle could not be lawfully upon the high way alone; they were straying, [ROBINSON, C. J.—Was anything shewn as to the township regulations on this point?] No. It is curious that nothing was said about this on the trial. [ROBINSON, C. J.—Then it must depend upon the common law.] Yes; and the defendants contend that no cattle can lawfully be out alone—Dovaston v. Payne, 2 H. Bl. 527. There was as much carelessness in the plaintiff allowing his cattle to be alone on the highway as in the defendant's going at a high rate of speed, if that can be considered negligence at all, which is an important question, and one of the first impression. Are the company bound to slacken speed at a crossing when all is clear ? If they are, it must be admitted their case here would certainly be much weakened. The 4 W. IV. ch. 29, sec. 9, expressly gives the right to cross highways, and no restriction whatever is imposed, nor anything said about slackening speed. It may be reasonable that they should do so, but it is not made their duty by statute, nor is it incumbent upon them by law, and only a legislative enactment can render it so. The language in Rex v. Pease, 4 B. & Ad. 30, is much to the point.

Then here there was nothing to induce the defendants to slacken speed—the track appeared to be clear—and even if if they had done so the accident could not have ben avoided, for the cows stepped upon the track when the train was only three-quarters of an acre off, and if they had been going more slowly than they were, it would have been impossible to stop in time.

The plaintiff was at least as much in fault as the defendants; and the question for the jury should have been whether there was sufficient negligence on the plaintiff's part to preclude him from recovering, as being equally to blame with the defendants. The facts shew that there was such negligence. The cattle had no right to be where they were ; and even admitting such right in general, the plaintiff here knew that they were going in the way of danger, and should have provided an attendant to look after them. Fawcett v. York & North Midland R. W. Co., 16 Q. B., 610 ; Ricketts v. East and West India Docks, &c. R. W., 12 C. B. 160, shew that cattle cannot be lawfully on a highway, unless in some pursuit or for some particular object—as in droves going to market, or in a waggon—otherwise they are there at their peril. [ROBINSON, C.J.—But although they are at their peril, would not the company be liable for any recklessness ?] Perhaps so ; but the jury should have been told that they were there at their peril, not that they were lawfully there. That was a clear misdirection. [ROBINSON, C. J.—If it is clear that they might venture at their usual speed as regards persons, then perhaps it would not be necessary to slacken because cattle might come in the way.] No person has a right at common law to turn his cattle out upon the highway for any purpose without an attendant, and the circumstances here shew strongly the propriety of the law.   If the plaintiff could do so because he lived close to the road, then where is the line to be drawn?   Why should not persons living five or ten miles away have the same right ?   The evidence shews, too, that the accident might have been prevented if a servant had been there with the cows.   It is true that they were crossing quietly, but they were confused by the noise of the engine, and stopped.   This might have been avoided by an attendant driving them on.   Hewitt v. Ontaró, Simcoe and Huron R. R. Co., 11 U. C. R, 604 : Thorogood v. Bryan, 8 C. B. 115 ; Greenland v. Chaplin, 5 Ex. 243 ; Clayards v. Dethick, 12 Q. B. 439 ; Sills v. Brown 9 C. & P. 605 ; Barnes v. Ward, 14 Jur. 334, are cases bearing upon the question of what the kind and degree of negligence must be to prevent a plaintiff from recovering.

Cooper and *O'Connor* contra.—The defendants were guilty of gross negligence in not slackening speed where the track crossed a public highway, and that was the cause of the accident, which would otherwise not have happened.   This is almost admitted by the fact that no one connected with the railroad—none of the firemen, nor the engineer—was examined at the trial.   They would have been called for the defendants to prove that proper precautions were taken, if that were the fact.   It is immaterial whether the cattle were straying or not, or whether they were delaying ; for even if there were some fault in them, if they were delaying a little the defendants would not be excused—Fawcett v. York and North Midland R. W. Co., 15 Jur. 173, 2 Eng Rep. 289 ; Sharrod v. London and N. W. R. W. Co., 20 L. J. Ex., 4 Eng. Rep. 401; and the language of the judgment in the last case, at page 405, quoted by the learned judge below is very applicable—Ricketts v. East and West India Dock & C. R. W. Co., 16 Jur. 1072, 12 Eng. Rep. 521.   The only warning the cows had here was some three or four seconds.   Suppose a team of three or four yoke of oxen had been crossing with a long stick of timber, they must have been run into, and without any fault on their part.   [ROBINSON, C. J.—There is no doubt that at a crossing it is incumbent on the company, as a matter of common prudence, to slacken speed, even in justice to their own passengers; but, granting that, the question is, are they liable in damages to a man whose cattle had no business there? What would you take to be the effect of this : suppose a man were to erect a booth on the track, and the train should run into it at full speed, could he sustain an action for damages?] The question for the jury would be, whether the obstruction was such as could have been removed if the defendants had behaved properly.   The plaintiff contends—*First,* that the cattle were using the road lawfully, and the absence of a driver is of no consequence if they were going just as they would have gone if he had been there. *Secondly,* even if there were evidence of some stopping on their part, still, if the jury find carelessness on the part of the company, the verdict is right.

ROBINSON, C. J., delivered the judgment of the court.

The Statute 4 Wm. IV., ch. 29, which incorporated this company, gives them the usual powers for entering upon property to construct a railway between London and Burlington Bay, and between London and the navigable waters of the Thames, and also between London and Lake Huron.   And this act provides, in the 9th clause, that whenever it shall be necessary for the construction of their railway to intersect or cross any road or highway, lying on the route of the said railway, *between the town of London and Lake Ontario,* it shall be lawful for them to construct their railway across or upon the same, provided that the corporation shall restore the road or highway thus intersected to its former state, or in a sufficient manner not to impair its usefulness ; and shall moreover erect and maintain, during the continuance of this corporation, sufficient fences upon the line of the route of their single or double railroad or way.

We have looked through the subsequent acts relating to this railway—viz., 7 Wm. IV. chaps 61, 62, and 63; 8 Vic. ch. 86 ; 9 Vic. ch. 81, and 10 Vic. ch. 110 ; and we do not find that there is anything in them which adds to, or expressly varies this provision.

The General Railway Clauses Consolidation Act does not apply in this case.

3 *g*—VOL. XII. Q.B.

The accident, if it be proper to call it such, occurred above London, in the township of Sandwich.

The 9th clause which we have cited, is confined by the language of it to the part of the road east of London, and indeed it was by a subsequent act that the power was given to this company to make the road from London to the river Detroit, on which line of road this casualty occurred. If it should be held that by a reasonable construction of all the acts taken together, the company were bound, whenever their track crossed a highway on the west side of London, as well as to the east to observe the directions on the 9th clause, then it would follow, as we understand that clause, that they were bound to fence in their railway track, where it crossed any such highway, in such a manner as to separate it from the highway on either side : though there is an obscurity in the act in this respect, and though it may be said that there is an apparent repugnance between such a construction of the clause and those words in it which direct that the company shall, in all such cases, restore the highway intersected by them to its former state, or *in a sufficient manner not to impair its usefulness.* It must be admitted, that to fence the highway from the railway, without providing for making and maintaining gates which shall open upon the railway and enable persons to cross it, would most materially impair the usefulness of the highway, and yet, as regards this railway, there is certainly no provision of the kind. In the English railway acts there are express directions respecting the making and maintaining gates at such crossings, and our statute 10 Vic., ch. 110, sec. 18, which incorporated a distinct company for making a railway from Hamilton to Toronto, intended to connect with the Great Western Railway, makes it obligatory on the new company to erect and maintain gates in the fences which are to separate the railway from the public road at every such crossing; but this provision has clearly no application to the Great Western Railway itself; and if the 9th clause of the first statute 4 Wm. IV., ch. 29, applies to the part of the Great Western Railway west of London, which is at least subject to doubt, it appears to be the only provision that can effect the question whether the company were obliged to fence their railway from the road at the crossing near which this accident occurred. And we think at present that the effect of that clause was to bind the company to place a fence between the railway and the highway, at the crossing, and to have a gate or opening in it on either side through which the public could cross the railway and continue to travel along the highway, which gate or opening it would be incumbent on them to have watched and attended in order that the highway might not be obstructed, or the railway trains exposed to accidents from persons or cattle getting unperceived upon the railway.

But if we are right in assuming that the company were bound to fence in their railway from the highway, and if the obligation clearly extended to this part of the line, still there is nothing in the pleadings or evidence to shew whether they had failed in that duty or not. The declaration rests the case altogether on the supposed culpable negligence of the defendants in crossing the highway at their ordinary speed, instead of taking the precaution to approach slowly, till they could observe whether there was anything upon or near the track at that point. No complaints made against the defendants for not maintaining a fence which would have kept the plaintiff's cattle away from the railway track. I did not clearly gather from the statements made upon the argument, whether in fact there was any fence at all on the sides of the railway track, where it crossed the highway, or whether there was a fence, but with open spaces merely, where in common prudence there ought to have been gates carefully attended.

The defendants counsel contended that the defendants' charter did not impose upon them the duty of erecting fences either with or without gates across the highway. If we admit this to be so, (though we have intimated an impression to the contrary), we shall be then taking the case most strongly in the defendants' favour, for it would follow that the cattle can not be said to have got upon the highway (or, which is the same thing upon the railway track, for they both at this point occupy the same ground) by any fault of the defendants.

They were upon a common public highway, and the plaintiff says they were lawfully there. What regulations were in force at the time within the township in regard to cattle running at large was not made to appear upon the trial. We must assume, therefore, that there was nothing to interfere in this respect with the principles of common law, and that being so, we take it that the cattle were either lawfully on the highway or not, according to the use they were making of it. We do not see how it can be held that the cows were not lawfully there; they were committing no trespass or nuisance, but, for all that appears, were passing along the road, across the track as they had a right to do in order to get to a place on the other side where there was water. We cannot say with certainty that if they had been driven by a person along the road instead of being turned into it to go to water the result would have been different. It might or might not have been possible to turn them back, or to stop them in time, if, according to the evidence, the train, when it was first seen, or when the whistle was first heard, was about half a mile off, and continued on its course, without slackening its speed. The manner in which the animals did in fact conduct themselves upon the highway running against each other in attempting to turn, and their unluckily going on, which brought them upon the track—all that arose from the confusion produced by the noise and hurry of the train coming upon them at its usual rapid rate, and without the conductor taking care to ascertain whether there might not be something upon the road at or near the crossing.

If the 9th clause of 4 Wm. IV., ch. 29, could be held to apply to the parts of the railway west of London, in the same manner as to the parts east of it, then, we repeat, our present impression is, that it would be the duty of the company to carry into effect, as well as the nature of the thing would permit, the two apparently inconsistent directions contained in that clause, that they shall restore the highway " in a sufficient manner, not to impair its usefulness;" and that "they shall moreover erect and maintain sufficient fences upon the line of their railway." Inserted, as both these directions are, in a clause expressly relating to the crossing of highways, we think it would be erroneous to hold that it does not require the railway to be fenced in at such crossings, especially when

it is evident that such a precaution is of manifest propriety;
and it appears to us that, as we must hold one of these directions to be literally complied with as soon as the company
have erected a sufficient fence across the road to inclose their
railway, so it would be right to hold that the other direction
in the clause about "restoring the highway in a sufficient
manner not to impair its usefulness," would be reasonably
complied with by the company taking care that their fence
shall form no greater obstruction to the use of the highway,
than is compatible with that use of the railway which the
legislature must be supposed to have contemplated.

To attain that object, it is indispensable that gates should
be erected at the crossings; and in the absence of any
particular enactment to the contrary, it seems to us that it
would rest with the company to have their gates so attended
as to facilitate the safe and convenient passage across the
railway of whatever had a right to pass along the highway.

If we could assume that to have been the position in
which the company stood in regard to that part of their line
where this casuality occurred, and if it appeared, as we understand from the papers and argument it did appear, that the
railway at this point was not fenced in where it traverses the
highway, then the case would be free from all ground of doubt,
because the company having left open and unenclosed their
railway, which they were bound by law to enclose, the plaintiff's cattle being on the highway, where it could not be said
they had no right to be, would be deemed to be lawfully there
as against the company, who had omitted by a proper fence to
guard from the danger of collision with their engines and carriages those who might upon any occasion be using the highway.   The case of Fawcett v. the York and North Midland
Railway Company, is an express authority on this point.

It is true that the plaintiff in this case does not found his
action on any allegation that the company were bound to
fence in their road, and had omitted to do so ; and therefore
a consideration of the question of their obligation to fence could
not be essential here as a part of the plaintiff's case, and it could
only come in question incidentally, if set up as we think it
might be, by the plaintiff upon the trial, as in answer to the ob-

jection on the part of the defendants, that the plaintiff's cows were not lawfully on the highway . He might, we think, say to the defendants, "You, having omitted to fence in your railway according to law, are in no situation to set yourselves up as the conservators of the highway, or of other persons' property from trespassers : my cattle were lawfully on the highway as to you." It is because cases of this kind are of great interest at this moment, and it is of much consequence that the duties and liabilites of the respective parties in such cases should as early as possible be discussed and understood, that I have said what I have upon this point ; and having considered the question, I have ventured to intimate my opinion, that if the 9th clause of 4 Wm. IV., ch. 29, can properly be held to extend to the whole line of railway as it is now constructed, leading from Hamilton to Windsor, (of which I have some doubt,) then the defendants were under an obligation to fence their road, and would have been clearly liable in this action on account of their non-performance of that duty.

But not thinking it clear that the case can be rested on that ground, on account of the absence of any express enactment extending the provisions of the 9th clause to any part of the line west of London, we must take up the case upon the other ground, of the negligence charged upon the defendants in the declaration—that is, their having driven the train at that rate of speed, and with that gross negligence, as they approached the highway, that by reason of their negligence and improper conduct the plaintiff's cows were run over and killed.

The learned judge of the County Court, confining himself to this view of the case, came, in our opinion, to a proper conclusion.

It cannot be said in this case, as was said by the court in Ricketts v. the East and West India Docks and Birmingham Railway Company, that there was no allegation in the declaration that the accident could be avoided, or that the Company had by themselves or their servants been guilty of any negligence ; on the contrary, the plaintiff here has founded his claim to recompence expressly on an imputation of gross negligence on the part of the defendants in conducting their business. The first question is, did he prove his complaint : and the second question is, if he did prove it, is there anything in the case which would exempt the defendants from answering to the plaintiff for the pecuniary damage which has suffered from their neglect.

As to the first point, the defendants called no witnesses upon the trial; they made no attempt to disprove what was shewn on the plaintiff's part. The plaintiff's witnesses did prove, we think, a case of most culpable negligence. The jury were right in the conclusion which they came to on that point, and the learned judge right in his observations, which had a tendency to lead them to that conclusion. We must remember that the defendants utterly deny that they were under any obligation to fence in their track from the highway. They have gone further in the argument, and insisted that they had no authority to do so, for that such an obstruction of the highway, by placing a fence across it, would have been a public nuisance. The statute, they insist, gave them no such power, and without it they could clearly not have the right to block up the road by a fence.

If they could not legally place a fence across the road, no one else could ; and it is plain, therefore, that when the conductor of their train approached this highway, he could have no reason for expecting that he would find anything placed there for the purpose of keeping people and cattle from getting upon the track. He knew well that there was no protection of the kind here. Now, if the collision with the plaintiff's cows had happened, as it might, to have thrown the engine or some of the cars off the track, producing such a deplorable casualty as has lately occurred on the same railway, would it be thought satisfactory to the mutilated passengers, or the relations of those who are killed, to be told by the conductor, that he took it for granted all the people or cattle that might be on the road on either side of the track would take care of themselves ; that every animal, rational and irrational, that might be upon the road for any purpose, would be fully aware of the approaching danger, able to calculate accurately both time and distance, certain to judge correctly of the course which they ought themselves to take, and to be careful in acting up to the exigency.

It would be reasonable, we think, to remonstrate with the conductor of the train, that he had no right to place the lives of hundreds of passengers at the mercy of all these contingencies; and, that if there was any force in the excuse, it would be an argument against the necessity of fencing in the line anywhere, for the danger of collision cannot be nearly as great at any other point as where the track crosses a public highway. Indeed, what we constantly find done upon railways, where the track crosses a public highway which is unenclosed, is a sufficient proof that caution is deemed to be necessary, for we usually see the speed slackened, and the train going at such a rate, that in case of anything unexpected being found to be upon the track, it could be stopped in time to prevent mischief. And it is surely the most reckless folly not to observe this caution; for how can it be known what people or animals may be wandering or loitering along a highway, which is accessible to everything? Or what assurance can be reasonably felt, that there may not be some animal lying by the side of the road, concealed from view, and so near to the crossing of the track, that when startled by the noise of the approaching train, it may rush upon the track, in time to produce a fatal collision?

If one or more persons were constantly watching at the crossing, so that it could be intimated by signal that all was clear, the case would be very different; but what has occurred in the present case shews that it is an unpardonable imprudence when no such precaution has been used, to proceed at an unchecked rate of speed, taking it for granted that all is right.

Then, if we must admit that in this case negligence was clearly shewn, as we think it was, the only other question is, whether there is any reason why the defendants should not compensate the plaintiff for the loss occasioned by their negligence.

Upon that point, such cases as Sills v. Brown (9 C. & P. 601) and Raisin v. Mitchell (Ibid 613, 618) are important to be considered; for these establish that the fault of the plaintiff, which will prevent his recovering, must be one directly tending to produce the injury ; and if in this case all that can be said is, that the plaintiff's cows were where they had no right to be at the time of the collision, still it would not necessarily follow that the defendants could not be held liable for damage done to them by their gross neglect. Upon that point Davies v. Mann (10 M. & W. 545) is an express authority; and also the case of Fawcett v. The North and York Midland Railway Company (16 Q. B. 610) where horses were run over by a railway train, and it was contended by the defendants that they were unlawfully on the highway, and that on that account the plaintiff could not recover—but the Court held otherwise. They found that in that case it was the duty of the company to keep the gate closed where the highway crossed the track, and that they had neglected to do so.   In consequence of this neglect on their part, they said it was not material to inquire whether the horses were straying or not, for that, whatever might be the case as against the owners of the soil in the highway, or the surveyors of the highway, the horses were lawfully there as against the railway company.

The case of Ricketts v. The East and West India Docks and Railway Company (12 C. B. 160) is to the same effect; for although there the defendants were held not to be liable upon the ground (which has been taken in the present case) that there was no obligation upon them to fence in their track, yet the court expressly took the distinction, that there was in the declaration no complaint that the accident could have been avoided, or that the defendants had in any respect conducted their business in a negligent manner.

The cases of Sharrod v. The London and North Western Railway Company (4 Ex. 581), Greenland v. Chaplin (5 Ex. 243), Skinner v. the London, Brighton and S. E. Railway (Ibid 786), were also referred to in the argument of this case, and have a material bearing.   The ground on which the defence was rested in the present case has a very extensive application, and if the defence could be upheld to the extent to which it has been urged the decision would lead to consequences which would tend very strongly to demonstrate its unsoundness.

If we are to assume that the cows in question had no right to run at large, by any particular public regulation, still they

had the same right to pass along this highway as other cows
would have to pass along any other highway. We know
that cattle have constantly occasion to pass along a highway
from the house or barn-yard of the owner to their pasture,
or in going to and returning home from any common or
waste land. It is common on such occasions to see them
passing along without a driver or attendant; but we do not
imagine that it has even been supposed by those driving carriages along the highway, that whenever they meet or over-
take cattle thus using the highway without a person attending them in order to keep them out of the way of
danger, they were therefore at liberty to drive over or
against them, without necessity, or at least were relieved
from the obligation to use the ordinary care to avoid it.

On the whole, we think, as to the obligation upon the
company to fence in their highway, it would be clearly their
duty, if the question had arisen in regard to any part of the
line specified in the 9th clause of the first act—*i.e.*, between
London and Lake Ontario. And when we consider that it is
in this clause only that any authority is expressly given to
cross a highway, it would seem unreasonable not to hold that
if the company can legally exercise under that clause the
right to cross any public highway, upon any part of their line as
contended, and not merely between London and Lake Ontario,
they must take the authority coupled with the conditions contained in that clause; and if they are bound to fence in their
track at any point along the line, they must do so at all points.

Then, if so, and they had no such fence here, they, the
defendants, were the persons first and most substantially in
fault; and it would be *primâ facie* by their breach of duty
that the plaintiff's cows got upon the track.

Although this is not complained of in the declaration as a
breach of duty on their part, yet it entitles the plaintiff to say
to them upon the evidence, that they have no right to resist
his claim upon the pretence that his cows were not lawfully
on the highway; for if they had kept their railway fenced in,
there would have been no need of any such inquiry, since the
cows could not have got upon the track in that part of the highway. Therefore, as to them, the cattle were legally where

they were at the time of the collision, because it was their duty to keep them off the track.

But if this should be held otherwise, and it should be determined that the defendants were not bound to keep up a fence at that point, still we are of opinion that the verdict is supported by the evidence given, on the ground that the defendants were guilty of the negligence charged upon them, in approaching the crossing, as they did, without precaution, and that, for the reasons we have already given, the learned judge was right in refusing a new trial.

We are of opinion this appeal should be dismissed with costs.

Appeal dismissed.

GILLIS V. GREAT WESTERN RAILWAY COMPANY.

G. W. R. W. Co.—Obligation to fence.

The declaration averred that it was defendants' duty to keep up sufficient fences along their line of railway, and that by the neglect of such duty the plaintiff's mare, which was lawfully depasturing on the adjoining land, got upon the track and was killed. No negligence was charged against defendants in the management of their train. It was proved that the mare had escaped from her stable on another farm, and was trespassing on the lot from which she got upon the railway.

Held, (confirming Dolney v. Ontario, Simcoe, and Huron R. R. Co. 11 U.C.R. 600) that the plaintiff could not recover ; the defendants being bound to fence only as against the owner of the adjoining lands.

CASE for driving defendants' locomotive engine over a mare belonging to the plaintiff and killing her. The declaration averred that it was the duty of defendants to keep sufficient fences upon the line of their railway, and that they neglected that duty, and by reason of such neglect the mare of the plaintiff, which was at the time " depasturing and lawfully being in and upon certain land situate in the township of Mosa, and adjoining and abutting upon the said railway of the defendants, and to and upon the land taken and found necessary for the uses and convenience thereof, strayed and escaped out of the said adjoining land upon the defendants' railway, and was killed, &c.

The defendants pleaded that the plaintiff's mare was wrongfully and unlawfully depasturing and being upon certain lands adjoining to the said lands of the defendants, and to the said railway, which lands were not the lands of the plaintiff, but of one Richard Roe, who had not given license for the said mare to be there ; that she strayed from them upon the defendants' land adjoining, and thence, at the said time when, &c., on the said railway, and then being so upon the said railway, was accidentally, without any design on the part of the defendants or their servants, killed, in manner and form, &c.

The plaintiff replied *de injuriâ*.

At the trial at London before *Macaulay, C. J. C. P.*, it was proved that the plaintiff's mare had been kept in a stable on the farm of the plaintiff's father, and that she escaped out of the stable on the 8th of February last, and got upon the railway through a gap in the fence, upon a farm two lots off from that from which she escaped.

The learned Chief Justice told the jury that if the mare was a trespasser on lot six from whence she got upon the track, she was then wrongfully there as alleged in the plaintiff's declaration, and that the evidence seemed to establish the facts set forth in the plea, and to entitle the defendants to a verdict. The jury found, nevertheless, for the plaintiff, and £20 damages.

Beecher moved for a new trial on the law and evidence, and because the verdict was perverse.

J. Duggan shewed cause.

The cases cited are noticed in the judgment.

ROBINSON, C. J., delivered the judgment of the court.

We are of opinion that we are bound in this case to grant a new trial without costs. We can draw no distinction between this case and that of Dolrey v. The Ontario, Simcoe & Huron Railway Company in this court, (11 U.C.R. 600,) which was decided in accordance with English authorities.

This declaration does not charge the defendants with causing the death of the plaintiff's mare by any negligence or want of skill in conducting their railway train, but rests the right to recover wholly on the defendants' breach of duty in not fencing in their track, in consequence of which the mare got on the track and was killed. That duty, it has been determined, or rather the breach of it, cannot give a right to recover to the owner of an animal which was at the time trespassing on the adjoining lands, the obligation being to fence in each case between the railway track and the adjoining close. The late case in the Court of Common Pleas in England, Wallis et al. v. The Manchester and Lancashire Railway (18 Jur. 268,) confirms the former decisions on this point. The defence is that the animal killed was not lawfully where she was at the time of the accident, but was wrongfully there; so that the allegation in that respect in the plaintiff's declaration was disproved, and that in the plea supported. And it follows, that when, as in this case, no negligence in the manner of using the railway track is charged upon the defendants, the action fails.

Rule absolute, without costs.

McGann v. Keyes.

16 *Vic. ch.* 19—*Verdict taken pro confesso—Rejection of evidence—Power of court to review judge's decision.*

A defendant having been notified (under 16 Vic. ch. 19) to attend as a witness for the plaintiff, did not appear, and the learned judge at the trial ordered a verdict *pro confesso* to be taken against him, declining to hear evidence tendered in support of the plea. The court afterwards refused to disturb the verdict, as it was not shewn clearly that any injustice had been done.

Quære, however, whether the evidence tendered should not have been received; and whether the court have power under this statute to review the decision of the judge at Nisi Prius.

This was an action of covenant, upon a mortgage for £100, payable by instalments of £25 each, on the 1st of November, 1851, and £25 a year thereafter. The breach was laid for non-payment of the first two instalments.

The only plea was that of non-payment.

At the trial before *Richards,* J., at the last assizes held at Kingston, it appeared that the plaintiff had given notice that he required the attendance of the defendant to give evidence; but the defendant was not present. It was admitted that the cause had been carried down for trial at a previous assize, at which the defendant was notified to attend and did attend, and then the suit was referred to an arbitrator. The arbitrator refused to act, and so the cause was brought down again, and the defendant again notified to attend by service of the notice upon his attorney. It was said the defendant was a seafaring man, and at the time of the trial his attorney did not know where he was.

The issue was upon the defendant to prove, but the learned judge refused to receive any evidence for the defendant under the circumstances of his non-attendance, and a verdict was entered for the plaintiff for the amount claimed.

Draper obtained a rule to shew cause why the verdict should not be set aside for misdirection, for improper rejection of evidence, and on grounds disclosed in affidavits. The affidavits shewed that the defendant was a mariner upon the lake; that about three weeks before the assizes the attorney told him that he would most likely be required at the court, but that notice of trial had not been served. The defendant swore that he sailed in the middle of September from Kingston for Oswego, and from thence to various ports on Lake Ontario, and had no information respecting what had been done until the 7th of November, when he returned to Kingston. He said he was not aware that his presence at the court was indispensable, or he would have attended, and that he did not absent himself to avoid being present. The affidavits of the defendant's former attorney and counsel stated that the defence on the plea of payment was that a receipt of £60 was to be offered in evidence, which was lost or mislaid by the attorney. The defendant did not state in his affidavit that he had paid the mortgage, or any part of it, but merely swore that he had a good defence on the merits. The defendant's present attorney swore that the defendant's witnesses were subpœnaed and in court, but the defendant's counsel was prevented from addressing the jury or going into evidence, in consequence of the non-attendance of the defendant himself.

Vankoughnet, Q. C., shewed cause, and filed affidavits in reply. The plaintiff denied that any more than £6 was paid upon the mortgage, for which credit was given at the trial, and that the £6 had been paid by the defendant's mother on his account. That a sum of £12 10s. and a mare had been taken in satisfaction of £25, but this £25 formed no part of the mortgage. The land for which the mortgage was given was sold for £125, of which £25 was paid in the manner stated, and the mortgage given for the residue, £100.

ROBINSON, C. J.—It is very difficult to interfere under such circumstances as have taken place at the trial of this case. The statute 16 Vic. ch. 19, sec. 2, provides, that whenever any party shall desire to call the opposite party as a witness, he shall either subpœna such party or give to him *or his attorney* at least eight days' notice of the intention to examine him as a witness in the cause; and if such party shall not attend on such notice or subpœna, *such non attend-·ance shall be taken as an admission pro confesso* against him in any such suit or action, *unless otherwise ordered* by the court or judge in which or before whom such examination is pending, and a general finding or judgment may be had against such party thereon, or the plaintiff may be nonsuited, or the proceedings in such action or suit may be postponed by such court or judge, on such terms as such court or judge may see fit to impose.

Where the party or his attorney has been duly notified, as was the case here, and the party does not attend, and no order to the contrary is made by the judge at Nisi Prius, the statute is imperative in imposing as a consequence that the case shall be taken *pro confesso* against him. No discretion is vested in the court in banc. to relieve from the consequence; and whether the judge at the trial will make such an order as shall prevent the consequence from attaching, is for his consideration. On general principles, the manner in which he exercises his discretion under a power so committed to him is not subject to revision. The effect is analogous to what takes place where a party loses his costs unless the judge will certify. The statutes there determine the right of the parties when the judge declines certifying, and so this statute settles the position of the parties here when the judge has not interposed to relieve against the operation of this clause. "The court or judge in which or before whom such examination is pending," can evidently mean only the judge or court before whom or in which the party would have been examined if he had attended, not the court in which the action is pending. The last two lines of the clause put that beyond doubt; and indeed a decision must be come to on the spot as to what shall be done under this provision, because it must depend upon whether any evidence shall be received to support the case of the party making default. This is an important point, to be carefully considered, for we may suppose a party meaning to attend, but prevented from attending for some cause which cannot be made appear to the court when the case is called on; or a party may really have been wholly ignorant of the notice having been served on his attorney, and this possibly without any fault of the attorney, who may have taken the usual and proper means of sending information to his client, which by some accident may have failed. If the judge, having all the facts before him, takes, as may be afterwards thought, too rigorous a course at the trial, or if he decides quite reasonably upon the facts as they appear before him, but something is afterwards shewn which would wholly excuse the non-attendance of the party, and would have led to a different course if it had been known, can the court in banc. in either or both of these cases, give relief by granting a new trial? We must pause, I think, before we should do it in the case first supposed, but may surely feel ourselves compelled to do it in the latter.

Now the present case stands thus: The defendant, we can have no doubt, knew what was the point to be cleared up on the trial, and that the genuineness of a receipt which he had advanced was to be pronounced upon. He had been notified to attend at a former assize, when the cause was not tried: he was told by his own attorney, three weeks before the last trial, that he would be required to attend and be examined; but he goes away, for all that appears, unnecessarily, though the time fixed for the assizes must have been well known to his attorney and himself, and he gives no reason for not coming back till some time after the trial had taken place. The amount involved is not very large, and the facts have a suspicious appearance as regards the defendant.

The plaintiff would perhaps be willing to allow a new trial on payment of costs, if the defendant will, in the mean time, pay the money into court to abide the event of the trial.

It is sworn by the plaintiff, in answer to this rule, that since the trial the defendant has offered to compromise with him, but we could not take that statement as the ground on which to dispose of this application, without affording to the defendant an opportunity of answering it.

Upon a view of the circumstances of this case, we are of opinion that we ought not to set aside the verdict; and therefore, unless the plaintiff chooses to consent to a new trial on the terms suggested, the rule will be discharged.

DRAPER, J.—I think that after a verdict taken *pro confesso*, it was incumbent on the defendant, who· seeks to be relieved, not simply to swear that he has a good defence on the merits, but to explain the whole transactions thoroughly in order that the court might clearly see that absolute injustice would be caused by suffering the verdict to stand. This he has not done, while the affidavits filed for the plaintiff are strong to shew that there is no ground for interference with the verdict, and I therefore agree this rule should be discharged.

At the same time I think it necessary to make a few observations as to some other questions which this case may be thought to involve.

I am not satisfied that where, as in the present case, the plaintiff's cause is of a specific determinate character, by the very nature· of the contract between the parties, and the defendant by his pleading admits the cause of action as stated, and only relies on proving it to be discharged and satisfied in the manner the plea states, that the plaintiff has a right to stop the defendant from entering into his evidence, and endeavouring to prove his plea. There can be no doubt that on this record the defendant had the right to begin.—Mercer v. Whall (5 Q. B. 447), Fowler v. Coster (M. & M. 241), Woodgate v. Potts (2 C. & K. 457). Now it does appear to me at-present that this was in effect ruling that the plaintiff on this record had the right to begin, while the contrary appears to me what should have been ruled. A mistake, however, in this respect, would not entitle the defendant to a new trial, unless such ruling shall have done him clear and manifest wrong.—Cannam v. Farmer (3 Ex. 700), Brandford v. Freeman (5 Ex. 734). It may be asked *cui bono* to allow the defendant to go into his defence, when, after it was con-

cluded, no matter how clear the proof the plaintiff would be
entitled to a verdict *pro confesso*, because the defendant did
not appear when called upon by the plaintiff to give evidence
on the plaintiff's case in reply.   Before admitting this objection to be insuperable, the second section of the Evidence Act
(15 Vic. ch. 19) must be carefully weighed.   It enacts that
after a party to a cause has been subpœnaed, or a specified
notice has been served for him to appear to be examined as
a witness for the other party, if he does not attend, " such
non-attendance shall be taken as an admission *pro confesso*
against him in any such suit or action, unless otherwise
ordered by the court or judge in which or before whom such
examination is pending; and a general finding or judgment
may be had against such party thereon, or the plaintiff may
be non-suited, or the proceedings in such action or suit may
be postponed by such court or judge, on such terms as such
court or judge shall see fit to impose."   The exercise of the
discretion given by the act might materially depend on
what might be proved under such circumstances.

It might be further objected, that this court has no power
to review the decision of the judge on such a matter, and
that when once a verdict has been taken *pro confesso* it is
conclusive for all purposes.   I shall content myself with
saying that it is not upon that ground that I concur in discharging this rule.   If, however, such should be the true
construction of the statute, it is very easy to suggest cases in
which it might work the grossest injustice, and might even
give success to the most palpable fraud, so that some legislative provision would be indispensable for the attainment of
justice, while, in the meantime the most scrupulous caution
would be requisite on the part of those with whom the discretion to allow a verdict to be taken *pro confesso* rests.

BURNS, J.—The affidavits respecting merits on the part of
the defendant are fully met by the plaintiff's affidavits. The
defence being that of payment, we should expect to see, after
a verdict for the plaintiff, how and in what manner the
defendant had paid the amount, to convince us that the
verdict is wrong.   Now, though the defendant's attorney

speaks of seeing a receipt of the plaintiff's for £60, yet surely the defendant could himself have given some account whether that receipt was genuine; and if he had paid so large a proportion of the whole debt, he could have given the day and time, or some approach to it, when it was paid After a trial, we should require something more than a general affidavit of merits.

With respect to the legal ground, the defendant claimed that, as the issue lay upon him, his counsel had a right in his absence to offer the evidence of his witnesses, and that the plaintiff could only claim the right he did claim when it became his turn to reply to the defendant's witnesses. The Statute 14 & 15 Vic. ch. 66, sec. 2, re-enacted in 16 Vic. ch. 19, sec. 2, enacts, that the non-attendance of the party required to attend shall be taken as an admission *pro confesso* against him in such suit or action, unless otherwise ordered by the court or judge in which or before whom such examination is pending, and a general finding or judgment may be had against such party thereon. It is impossible to state any general rule which will govern in all cases. The judge trying the cause must judge, upon hearing the parties, as to what he will order. The statute rests a discretionary power in the judge, and it should be shewn that in exercising that discretion injustice has been done. In this case the defence was payment. Now suppose, on the part of the defendant, it was alleged it could be proved that the plaintiff had signed a receipt for the debt, and on the part of the plaintiff it was alleged that no such payment had ever been been made, and that the receipt was a forgery: I do not imagine the judge would be bound in law to hear the evidence to prove the receipt, in order to exercise his discretion whether he would allow the case to be taken *pro confesso* against the defendant by reason of his non-attendance, but he might, on hearing from the counsel on each side what is proposed to be offered, decide whether he will allow the case to be taken *pro confesso*, or postpone the trial, upon such terms as he may think fit. Each case must depend upon its own particular facts and circumstances. The defendant does not shew that the course taken by the learned judge has caused him injustice.

FERRIS V. THE MUNICIPALITY OF THE TOWNSHIP OF KINGSTON.

Contract—Right of action.

A. contracted with the defendants to perform certain work, and B. entered into a bond as his surety. It appeared that B. was in fact the principal, and did the work, and that A. had tendered and taken the contract for him, and had executed a writing assigning to him all his interest in the proceeds.

Held, that B. could have no right of action against the defendants.

This was an action of assumpsit on the common counts, for goods sold and delivered, work done and materials found, money paid for the use of the defendants, interest due, and upon account stated.

Plea, non assumpsit.

At the trial before *Richards, J.*, at the last assizes held at Kingston, the facts appeared to be these :   On the 27th of March, 1854, the council of the township passed a resolution that tenders should be received to continue the plank walk from the terminus of Sparham's culvert, 25 rods, or more if required, the tenders to be opened, at the next meeting of the council.   In consequence of this the township clerk advertized for tenders on the 17th of April, to be handed in on the 24th of April.   On the 24th of April the Council met, and two tenders were received, one from Sparham at 16s. 3d. per rod, and one from Edward O'Reilly at 14s. per rod.   On the 8th of May the Council resolved that the treasurer be authorized to borrow £75 by such means as he might think proper, the same to be repaid as soon as possible out of the statute labour commutation arising from road divisions 12 and 13, for the purpose of continuing the plank walk from Waterloo towards Kingston, as far as the said sum will furnish the means as per the tender of Mr. O'Reilly.   On the 15th of May O'Reilly with the two sureties, the plaintiff and Edward Reilly, executed to the Municipality a bond reciting that O'Reilly had contracted with the municipality to complete the plank walk to the toll gate at 14s. per rod by the 1st of July 1854, and the parties bound themselves that the said O'Reilly should so complete it.   O'Reilly did no part of the work, but it was done by the plaintiff.   O'Reilly proved that the plaintiff asked him to tender for the work in his name and he complied with his request and it was understood between them that the plaintiff should do the work. On the 1st of July O'Reilly executed a paper, assigning all his claim, right or interest to the proceeds of the contract to the plaintiff.   On the 1st of August D. C. Smith gave a certificate that the work was completed. Mr. Smith was not an officer of or appointed by the Municipality, but was the superintendent of macadamized roads, and he gave the certificate, he said, because he was requested by the plaintiff and Dr. Yeomans, who was the township treasurer, to do so, and as such superintendent he gave directions about the construction of the plank walk.   Dr. Yeomans took a good deal of interest in the paving of the plank walk, and declared he would find the means to have it paid for, and carry on the debt or demand until the commutation for the statute labour would redeem it.   Dr. Yeomans is since dead.   On the 16th of August the Council met, and a minute was made that O'Reilly had assigned his interest to the plaintiff.   Mr. Smith's certificate was also read, and a minute made that he never having been appointed by the Council to examine the walk or report on the same, that matter was deferred for further action.   Smith stated that during the progress of the work he was requested by Dr. Yeomans to leave a certificate to advance some money to O'Reilly, say £20, and when he gave the final certificate he handed it to one of the councillors of the township, to be given to the plaintiff when he should remedy some defects which he, Smith, found in the walk.   Mr. Smith never had any authority from the Council to do what he did.   No money was ever raised by the Municipality under the resolution of the 8th of May.

It was objected to at the trial, on the part of the defendants—first, that the corporation could not be bound except under the corporate seal ; 2ndly, That no agreement was made with the plaintiff in any way ; but if there were a binding agreement, it was with O'Reilly ; 3rdly, That there was no evidence of any acceptance by the corporation of the work since it was done ; 4thly, That the plaintiff was prevented from saying that the contract was with him for the bond recites that it was with O'Reilly, and O'Reilly subsequently assigned the proceeds to the plaintiff.

The learned judge directed the jury that the plaintiff must fail upon the first point, but yet left it to them to say, first, whether the plaintiff did any work for the defendants at their request; 2ndly, Whether the defendants accepted the work after it was done.

The jury found for the plaintiff, damages £85 15s.

Hagarty, Q.C., obtained a rule *nisi* for a new trial, without costs, on the law and evidence, and for misdirection, and because the verdict was contrary to the judge's charge, and perverse. He cited Tully v. The Officers of Ordnance, 5 U. C. R. 6.

McMichael shewed cause, and cited Cooke v. Seeley, 2 Ex. 746 ; Cothay v. Fennell, 10 B. & C. 671.

ROBINSON, C. J., delivered the judgment of the court.

We can have no hesitation in granting a new trial in this case. The whole evidence shewed that the work was done by the plaintiff for O'Reilly, who was the tender for the work in his own name, which the defendants accepted; and not done for the defendants, who never employed him, and between whom and him there was no privity whatever. It was plain that this was perfectly well understood by the plaintiff himself, for he actually executed a sealed instrument as surety for O'Reilly that he would fulfil his contract.

The writing which O'Reilly gave to the plaintiff in July, if it could have the effect, which it clearly could not, of placing the plaintiff in his place so as to make the corporation his debtors to the plaintiff for the work done, and not debtors to him, whether they consented or not, still does not on the face of it appear to have been given for that purpose; for it only assigns to him, not the work or job itself, but the *proceeds* of the contract.

It is out of the question that after one man has taken a job of work upon a regular contract, putting forward another person as his surety for the due performance of it, the surety can, by any arrangement between the two, be intruded upon the other party as the principal in the transaction. He may do the work, no doubt, if the principal will employ him, and he may even be in fact the principal and the other the hired man, according to any understanding between themselves ; but such understanding can give him no legal claim upon the other party, as if he had been originally employed to do the work for such party.

The case of Young et al. v. Hunter et al. (4 Taunt 582) is in principle like the present.

The jury here gave the whole value of the work, as if the plaintiff and not O'Reilly had taken the job from the defendants, though they were rightly told by the learned judge at the trial that the law did not admit of it. To uphold the verdict, when the objection was distinctly taken and pressed at the trial, would be to open a door to claims that would confound all distinctions, and introduce much confusion and litigation.

Rule absolute, without costs.

SCHOFIELD V. TOWN.

AND

TOWN V. SCHOFIELD.

Agreement—Accidental fire—Rights of parties.

The defendant agreed with the plaintiff to saw for him at a certain price whatever logs should be delivered at the plaintiff's mill, the plaintiff to draw away the lumber as soon as possible after it was cut : the defendant also agreed to deliver at Port Perry, within a reasonable time, any lumber cut by him under the agreement after the first of March. Some lumber was cut before the first of March, and drawn away by the plaintiff ; some was also cut after the first of March, and this was destroyed at the mill by an accidental fire in June following. The jury found that of the latter portion the defendant might have delivered about 40,000 feet before the fire.

Held, that the plaintiff was entitled to recover the value of the lumber so destroyed and which might have been delivered, and that the defendant was entitled to be paid for sawing this lumber as well as that drawn away by the plaintiff.

ASSUMPSIT—The declaration was on a special agreement, that defendant should saw into lumber all the logs which J. M. and P.M., and other persons should deliver for the plaintiff at defendant's saw mill, the plaintiff to pay 15s. per 1000 feet for sawing; and should draw away the lumber from defendants mill as soon as possible after it was cut and the state of the roads would permit. And also that the defendant, within a reasonable time after the first day of March then next (1854), should convey and deliver by water by a scow, to Port Perry on Lake Scugog, all the lumber sawed by defendant (as above agreed), after the first of March, and which the plaintiff should not have drawn away from defendant's mill, to be paid for by the plaintiff. *Averment,* that before the first of March, 1854, 3000 saw-logs were delivered for plaintiff at defendant's saw-mill; that defendant proceeded to saw them, and the plaintiff drew away the lumber in the terms of the agreement; that after the first of March, 1854, the defendant sawed a large quantity of lumber, which the plaintiff had not drawn away, and which the defendant promised, within a reasonable time, to convey to and deliver at Port Perry. *Averment* of plaintiff's readiness, &c. *Breach,* that although a reasonable time had elapsed the defendant had not delivered the lumber and the same had become wholly lost to plaintiff.

The second count was founded on the same agreement, but varying the breech, which charged defendant's neglect to deliver after a reasonable time, and after request; and that, by and through the mere negligence, carelessness, and improper conduct of defendant, the lumber had been lost.

Pleas—1st. *Non assumpsit.* 2nd. To first count—denial that the quantity of lumber stated was sawed. 3rd. To first count, that before a reasonable time had elapsed for the conveying and delivery of the said lumber and before defendant had committed any default, the said lumber was accidentally destroyed by fire. 4th. To second count, denial that the quantity of lumber stated was sawed. 5th. To second count, traverse of the loss of the lumber by defendant's negligence *modo et forma.* 6th. To second count, similar to third plea.

The plaintiff joined issue on the 1st, 2nd, 4th, and 5th pleas, and replied *de injuria* to the 3rd and 6th.

The trial took place at Whitby, before *Draper, J.* It appeared that the plaintiff delivered a large quantity of saw logs at defendant's saw-mill of which the defendant sawed about 450, before the mill was burnt. The plaintiff drew away some of the lumber, but a large quantity remained. A good deal was sawed after, as well as before the first of March. The plaintiff had contracted with a man to draw 100,000 feet, and he swore he drew all he could get, upwards of

30,000 feet, keeping the mill clear. The mill was broken and lay idle some weeks during the winter. The navigation of Lake Scugog was open about the 21st of April, and the mill was destroyed by an accidental fire on the 5th of June, 1854. The evidence apparently shewed from 50,000 to 55,000 sawed after the 1st of March, worth from seven to eight dollars per thousand feet.

It was left to the jury to say what quantity of lumber sawed after the first of March the defendant could have delivered, and to give the plaintiff the value thereof. They were asked also to find what damages they would give the plaintiff for the non-delivery of the lumber if it were still lying for his use at the mill.

They gave a verdict for the plaintiff, and found that the defendant might have delivered 40,000 feet before the fire. They found the lumber was worth seven dollars per thousand feet at the mill, and valued the damages for the non-delivery only at £5. Leave was by consent reserved to the plaintiff to move to increase his verdict to £70.

Adam Crooks, obtained a rule accordingly, against which *Wilson*, Q. C., shewed cause.

The following cases were cited on the argument : Thirkell v. McPherson, 1 U. C. R. 318 ; Mondel v. Steel, 8 M. & W. 858 ; Skinner v. London and Brighton R. W. Co., 5 Ex. 787 ; 2 Saund. 421 *a*, note 2 ; Riley v. Horne, 5 Bing. 217 ; Leck v. Mæstar, 1 Camp. 138 ; Torrance v. Smith, 3 C. P. 411 ; Neal v. Ratcliffe, 15 Jur. 166 ; Friar v. Gray, 5 Ex. 584 ; Webb v. London and Portsmouth R. W. Co., 9 Hare 129.

TOWN V. SCHOFIELD.

This action was brought by the defendant in the preceding action, for the sawing the logs of the now defendant under the contract between them. The declaration contained a special count on the agreement, and common counts for work and materials, &c., &c. *Pleas.*—1st. Non assumpsit. 2nd. That the plaintiff did not saw defendant's logs into lumber. 3rd. That the defendant was ready to pay the plaintiff for the sawing, and to accept the lumber made from the said

3 *k*—VOL. XII. Q. B.

logs, yet the plaintiff did not nor would deliver the said lumber, but neglected and refused so to do—verification.   4th. Payment.   The plaintiff took issue on the 1st and 2nd pleas, replied *de injuriâ* to the third, and traversed the payment alleged in the fourth.

A verdict was taken by consent for the plaintiff, and £85 damages, subject to the opinion of the court, on the facts appearing in the last case, whether the plaintiff was entitled to recover for the sawing of the 40,000 feet, in regard to which the jury in the other case found that the plaintiff might have delivered that quantity to the now defendant —the verdict to be reduced by the sum of £30, if the court should decide this question against the plaintiff.

The two cases were argued together, and some of the authorities above cited bear only on the latter.

ROBINSON, C. J.—It appears very plain what are the rights of the respective parties in these cases.

The jury found, what the evidence seemed to establish, that Town had sawed about forty thousand feet of lumber from Schofield's logs after the first of March, which lumber he was bound by his agreement to have forwarded to Port Perry on Lake Scugog within a reasonable time, which of course must have reference to the opening of the navigation in the spring.

The lumber was unfortunately burned up at Town's mill on the 5th of June, he not having before that taken it down to the lake in scows, as it was intended he should do.   The jury considered that a reasonable time had elapsed before the fire for his removing down the lumber to Port Perry : and supposing that not to be a wrong conclusion from the evidence, which I think it was not, it then follows that the plaintiff's lumber having been destroyed on Town's premises where it ought not at the time to have been, and would not have been but for his default in not carrying out his agreement, he, Town, is liable to make good the loss to Schofield, for the legal consequence of his default was that the lumber was at his risk.   But then I am of opinion that the measure of damages which the plaintiff in the first action was entitled to recover was not the full value of the lumber which was sworn to be about seven dollars a thousand, but that value deducting the fifteen shillings per thousand which the defendant was to have for sawing, for it never was intended that the plaintiff was to have it sawed for nothing. If he had received the lumber he must have paid the fifteen shilings a thousand, and there can be no reason why he should gain anything from the defendant's misfortune. Justice is done to him if he is placed in as good a situation as he would have been in if this loss had not occurred.

In this action therefore I think the verdict should have been for £40, and not £70, as the value of the lumber, adding to it what the jury might think reasonable for his disappointment, which under such circumstances would hardly be otherwise than a moderate allowance—and I do not see why the whole should not have been settled in this one action.

Instead of that the defendant Town, knowing, perhaps, that the plaintiff intended, if possible, to make him pay the full price of the lumber which would include the necessary expenditure for sawing, brought a cross action against the plaintiff Schofield for the stipulated price for the sawing of all the lumber including the forty thousand feet that were burnt. If he is made to pay in the other action seven dollars a thousand for the forty thousand feet, he ought surely to be paid for his labor, which composed part of that value, and since it was not deducted in the other action it ought to be given to him in this. It happens that it comes to much the same thing as regards the costs, because, as he was clearly entitled to recover in this action for sawing the portion of the lumber which Schofield drove away, he must have got a verdict which would have given him the costs.

It follows I think, that £70 should be added to Schofield's verdict, and that the *rule nisi* for deducting £30 from Town's verdict should be discharged.

BURNS, J.—In this first action, which is brought for the value of the lumber by reason of non-delivery according to contract, the question turns upon the third and sixth pleas, setting up, by way of excuse of the defendant's breach of contract, that the lumber was destroyed by the unavoidable accident of a fire occurring before the defendant could deliver it. The logs from which the lumber was manufactured belonged to the plaintiff, but the contract on the part of the defendant was to saw them into lumber, and when converted into lumber his contract in respect of it was as follows: "All the lumber sawed after the 1st of March next, and which the said Schofield shall not draw away from the said mill, the said Town shall convey to Port Perry, on Lake Scugog, by a scow in good order and at such a price for freight and delivery as shall be current at the said Port Perry, say 3s. per thousand." The fire occurred on the 5th of June, 1854; and the jury found that the defendant might have delivered 40,000 feet of lumber which he had sawed from the plaintiff's logs. The rule laid down in Paradine v. Jane (Alleyn 27), is this, that "when the party by his own contract creates a duty or charge upon himself he is bound to make it good, if he may, notwithstanding any accident by inevitable necessity, because he might have provided against it by his contract." This position has been recognized in many cases since but that approaching nearest the present case is, The Company of Proprietors of the Brecknock and Abergavenny Canal Navigation v. Pritchard et al. (6 T. R. 750). In this latter case it was argued on the part of the defendants that they were not assurers of the bridge standing against extraordinary floods, but *Lord Kenyon,* in giving the judgment, says, "It is sufficient to say here, that the contract of the defendants extends to this case that they have not fulfilled it and therefore that they are answerable." In the case before us the jury has found the defendant in fault, and that he did not deliver what it was in his power to do. There can be no doubt the defendant has bound himself to deliver lumber, and it makes no difference that the same was manufactured from logs belonging to the plaintiff. The decisions on this subject are consistent with the rules of the civil law, which are thus stated in Domat, sec. 1587. "The failure in the performance of an engagement is also a fault which may give occasion to damages which the party who fails will be liable to. Thus, a seller who refuses to deliver what he has sold, a depository who delays to restore the thing deposited with him, an executor who detains the thing bequeathed, and all those who having in their possession a thing which they ought to deliver up, refuse or delay to do it, are liable not only for the damages which their delay shall have occasioned, but also for the value of the thing if it perishes after they shall have been in fault for not delivering it; even although the thing should perish by some accident; for that accident might not have happened to the thing if it had been in the hands of the owner, or he might have disposed of it before it perished."

I think the rule should be made absolute to add £70 to the verdict already entered of £5.

With respect to the second case, the question is whether the sum of £30 agreed to be paid for sawing the 40,000 feet of lumber, should be deducted from the amount now entered for the plaintiff. This depends upon the construction of the agreement. It is true the agreement says that Schofield shall, for the sawing of the lumber, and for fulfilling the covenants in the agreement contained, pay the sum of fifteen shillings per thousand feet. If there were no other words in the agreement respecting the matter than those, the inference to be drawn would be that the delivery was a condition precedent to the price being paid; and if that were so, then the defendant Schofield could claim a reduction. There are further words, however, which control the effect of the whole, and shew that the delivery was not intended to be a condition precedent. The payment for the sawing was to be made in the month of April. There is no time mentioned in which Town was to deliver the lumber, but the time being specified for the payment for sawing shews that the one was not dependent upon the other, for the payment for the sawing might become due before the delivery might take place, for it would be dependent upon the state of the weather and elements whether a reasonable time elapsed during the month of April to deliver the lumber by a scow upon the lake.

The defendant's rule to reduce the verdict should therefore be discharged.

DRAPER, J.—My impression at the trial was certainly contrary to the opinion now given as to the defendant's liability in the first action for the whole value of the lumber destroyed; and, though I do not dissent, I am not quite free from doubt on the question.

Rule absolute in Schofield v. Town.
Rule discharged in Town v. Schofield.

WILSON v. MCNAMARA.
"   v.   ".

Rent, when payable, quarterly or yearly—Inconsistent verdicts on same evidence.

Held, under the facts set out below, that it was properly left to the jury to say whether the rent was to be paid quarterly or yearly, and that they were supported by the evidence in finding it payable quarterly.

Different verdicts having been rendered in two cases on the same evidence, the court granted a new trial with costs to abide the event, in the case in which they considered the finding to be least supported.

REPLEVIN. Avowry, that the plaintiff held a dwelling house from the defendant, situated in the city of Toronto, at the yearly rent of £55, payable quarterly, on the 28th of February, 31st of May, 31st of August, and 30th of November, in each year by even and equal portions; and because £13 15s., for one quarter's rent, ending on the 28th of February, 1854, was in arrear and unpaid, the defendant distrained the plaintiff's goods.

Plea—*Non tenuit.*

At the trial before *Burns, J.,* at the last assizes held at Toronto, it appeared that the plaintiff was tenant to the defendant for the premises in question, for a year previous to the first of December, 1853, at a rent of £36 a year, and which was payable quarterly. The defendant was desirous of making some alterations in the house, and the plaintiff desired to take the house for a further term. The defendant could not make the alteration, so long as the plaintiff lived in the house, without his consent, and negociations were pending between them in respect to the matter. On the 9th of September, 1853, the plaintiff wrote a letter to the defendant, as follows:

" Toronto, 9th September, 1853.

"Mr. McNamara :

" Sir,—I will give you fifty-five pounds currency per year, for the term of five years from the 1st day of December next ensuing this date, for the double house now occupied by me, and owned by you, standing on Gould Street, provided you place a good foundation under the same, and finish it off in the manner and on the plan that I proposed to you."

The work had been agreed upon between the defendant and the builder who was to do it, but the plaintiff would not let the builder proceed with the work unless he had a lease of the house for a term of years ; and, at the plaintiff's request, the builder went to see the defendant, to endeavour to procure him to accept the terms mentioned in the letter. The builder did go to the defendant, who did not wish to let the plaintiff have the premises for more than one year, and the builder said to him it was of no use for him to tell the plaintiff so, for he would not consent to the alterations, if he were to have the premises for no longer period. On the interference of the defendant's daughter, the builder was directed to tell the plaintiff he could have the premises at £55 per year and the taxes. This the builder told to the plaintiff, who considered he held the premises for a period of five years, according to the terms of the letter ; but the defendant considered that the plaintiff held only for one year. This misunderstanding gave rise to the subsequent difficulty. Nothing was said on the part of the plaintiff or defendant as to how the yearly rent was to be paid. After the first quarter became due, on the 28th of February, 1854, the plaintiff sent his attorney to pay £13 5s. to the defendant. He wished the defendant to sign a receipt in a particular form, which the defendant would not do, but offered a receipt worded by himself, and which the attorney would not take. There was in truth no difference in effect between the two receipts, but each fancied that the other had worded his receipt in order to have a bearing upon the question, whether the plaintiff was a tenant for one year or for five years. The rent was not paid. The attorney said that when he tendered the quarter's rent, he informed the defendant that the plaintiff did not consider himself bound to pay quarterly, but that it was more convenient for him to pay in that way than at the end of the year, when he considered the rent would be due.

The contest at the trial was whether the rent was payable quarterly or not, and that question the learned judge left to the jury upon the circumstances of the case. During the progress of the charge, the plaintiff's counsel put it to the judge to tell the jury that, inasmuch as there was no legally binding lease for five years, the whole was void, and the plaintiff was a mere tenant at will, and so the defendant had no right to distrain. The learned judge declined so to put the question to the jury, because the plaintiff's counsel had not opened that to the jury as the ground upon which he contested the defendant's right to distrain, and had rested the case entirely upon the point whether the rent was payable quarterly or at the end of the year.

The jury found that the rent was payable quarterly, whereupon a verdict was entered for the defendant.

Leith obtained a rule nisi for a new trial on the law and evidence, and for misdirection. He contended, in addition to the point taken at the trial, that it should not have been left to the jury to decide how the rent was payable.

Hallinan shewed cause.

SECOND CASE.

This was replevin for the second quarter's rent, due 31st of May, 1854, for which the defendant had distrained. The same evidence was given in the case as the other.

The plaintiff's counsel did urge to the jury that the lease for five years was altogether void, and the plaintiff was merely a tenant at will. The learned judge declined to put the case in that way to the jury, considering that the plaintiff having been a yearly tenant previously, the defendant had acceded to another year certainly; and that the plaintiff was contending he had a right to be considered a tenant for five years, and having offered to pay a quarter's rent, the fair inference was, that, if there was no legal lease for five years, he should be treated as a yearly tenant rather than a tenant at will. If the plaintiff was to be treated as a yearly tenant, then the question was the same as in the other case, viz., whether the rent was payable quarterly; and that was the question he submitted to the jury.

The jury in this case found that the rent was payable yearly, whereupon a verdict was entered for the plaintiff for £25 damages.

Hallinan moved for a new trial on the law and evidence.
Leith shewed cause.

ROBINSON, C. J., delivered the judgment of the court.

We think the effect of what was proved upon the trial of this case to have taken place between the parties was to make the plaintiff tenant to the defendant by the year at a rent payable quarterly; or at least, that it was fairly open to the jury to consider that they were upon that footing. The rent had been so paid before; that is, it was a rent fixed at a yearly sum, but payable by the quarter. As the plaintiff had never left the house, and the negotiation between them was only about a proposed increase of the rent, and a desired extension of the time, it was natural to suppose, where nothing is shewn to have been stipulated to the contrary, that the tenant was to go on paying at the end of each quarter as before, but paying a larger sum, as the increased rent had been agreed to. Then when the jury found that at the end of the first quarter the plaintiff went with his rent, without being desired, and offered to pay it, that would naturally strengthen the inference that the plaintiff so understood it, and did not choose to run the risk of any measures which the defendant might take if he withheld his rent after the end of the quarter. It is true, he said, when he tendered it, that he was not bound to pay it then, but still he offered to pay it. If it rested with the judge. as has been contended, to determine the point upon this evidence, whether the rent was payable at the end of each quarter or of the year, that would be of no consequence, unless we should think that the jury have given a wrong conclusion. It gave the plaintiff a chance perhaps of a verdict in his favor, beyond what in strictness he was entitled to; but we think the point, con-

3 *l*—VOL. XII. Q. B.

sidering the nature of the evidence, was properly left to the jury, and that we cannot say that they have given a wrong verdict, though upon much the same evidence the jury who tried the next case took a different view.

In this case, in which the verdict was for the defendant, we think we have no good ground for setting that verdict aside.

As to the other case, it certainly is most undesirable that the event of legal trials should be so uncertain as that opposing verdicts should be given between the same parties, upon the same evidence, and upon the same question depending on that evidence, but we cannot help such things sometimes happening. Where the evidence respecting a transaction is conflicting, or does not amount to conclusive proof, but leaves ground for inferences one way or the other, it is not surprising if different juries come to different conclusions, after estimating the weight of evidence on both sides ; and the court cannot insist upon these different views being eventually reconciled ; nor would it be considerate towards the parties to keep up a litigation indefinitely upon a matter of small value, in the hope that on some occasion a verdict may be obtained in the one suit which will be consistent with that given in the order. It is not impossible that the jury in this case, who gave the last verdict, may have looked upon both parties as somewhat unreasonable in persevering in a contest about so small a matter, when they had taken so little pains to make the transaction between them clear ; and they may have been disposed on that account to place the matter upon such a footing, by the second verdict as would make neither party much the gainer by the contention.

We are not inclined to interfere with this verdict more than with the other ; but the action being one to try the right, and the goods held in pledge till it is determined, we think it will be better to allow the case to go before another jury, in order that the inconsistency be avoided of having contradictory decisions in actions of this nature upon the same evidence and in respect to the terms of the same tenancy. It may save future litigation between the parties to have the decision of a third jury upon the point where two have differed, and this verdict appears to be less in accordance with the weight of evidence than the verdict in the other case. But as we cannot hold that this verdict was absolutely and certainly wrong, we should make the costs of the last trial in this case abide the event of the new trial.

PERRY V. BUCK.

Purchase of growing timber—Right of purchaser to bring trespass qu. cl. fr.

The plaintiff had purchased from the Canada Company all the merchantable
  timber on a certain lot, and held a letter from them (set out below)
  authorizing him to enter upon the land and mark whatever trees he might
  choose, and afterwards to cut and carry them away.
Held, that he had not such a possession as would enable him to bring trespass *quare clausum fregit.*
Quære, what remedy he could have for trespasses on the land :—whether he
  could support an action on the case against the trespasser for interfering
  with his privilege: or would be compelled to look to the company,
  treating their letter as an agreement.

Trespass *qu. cl. fr.* to lot No. 11 in the seventh concession of the township of Emily, and there prostrating the trees and underwood—enumerating them. 2nd count, for seizing and taking a quantity of timber.

Pleas. 1st. Not guilty, to the whole declaration. 2nd. To the first count, that the trees and underwood mentioned were not the plaintiff's property. 3rd. To the last count, plaintiff not possessed.

At the trial before *Richards,* J., at the last assizes held at Peterborough, it appeared that the plaintiff claimed the right to the timber upon the lot under a letter from the Canada Company, as follows :

Canada Company's Office,
Toronto, 1st Dec., 1853.

SIR,—I hereby acknowledge the receipt, per letter of Samuel Strickland, Esquire, of the 18th ultimo, of sixty-five pounds, for the purchase of the merchantable timber and saw logs you may remove from lots twenty-one in the ninth concession, and eleven in the seventh concession of Emily, before the first day of November, 1855. You are now at liberty to enter upon the said lots, and also your agent and workmen, and cut the merchantable timber and saw logs thereon till the 1st of November, 1855, and carry away the same, but not after that date. In the meantime, should we dispose of the land, the purchasers or lessees shall have the right (which is hereby reserved specially) of clearing and improving, and using whatever unmarked timber they shall find necessary for fuel, fences, and buildings. Any dispute arising between you and him or them must be settled without reference to us. You are therefore requested to mark in a conspicuous manner such trees as you may wish to cut. This license is not transferable. Have the goodness to acknowledge the receipt of this letter."

(Addressed to the plaintiff.)

There was no doubt the defendant did cut a considerable number of trees upon lot No. 11, as ascertained by the surveyor, and it was proved that he offered the plaintiff to pay him $1 per tree for what he had cut.

The lot in question was treated by the agent of the Canada Company in the county of Victoria as belonging to the company, but their title was not proved. It was proved that the plaintiff's agent had gone upon the lot after obtaining the letter before mentioned from the Canada Company.

The learned judge left to the jury to determine whether the plaintiff was in actual occupation of the lot, and if not to find for the defendant.

The charge was objected to on the ground that in consequence of the plaintiff having the lines run by a surveyor, that was a taking of possession, and the judge should have so told the jury.

The jury found for the defendant.

Phillpotts obtained a rule to shew cause why the verdict should not be set aside on the ground that it was contrary to law and evidence, and for misdirection, and on the ground of surprise.

Eccles shewed cause.

The authorities referred to are cited in the judgment.

ROBINSON, C. J., delivered the judgment of the court.

We think, upon the evidence given, it cannot be held that the plaintiff was by his agreement with the Canada Company placed in exclusive possession of the land in question. He had only acquired a right to enter upon the land and mark whatever trees, fit (in his opinion) for making merchantable timber and saw logs he might choose to take. His entry for that purpose would be no trespass ; and he had acquired the further right of going afterwards upon the premises at any and all times up to the 1st of November, 1855, for the purpose of felling, and preparing, and carrying away the timber and saw logs which he had so indicated his determination to take.

The defendant in going upon the land was no trespasser as to him, for he might have many lawful occasions for going there, for purposes which would not interfere with the privilege which the plaintiff had acquired ; and if he had no such lawful occasion for going there, he would be a trespasser upon the owner of the land, not upon the plaintiff, who had only a limited and qualified right of entry. This applies to the alleged wrongful entry upon the premises.

Then as to the timber cut—whose property was it, as it lay on the ground after being cut ? Not, we think, the plaintiff's, for he had not yet made it his timber by marking it as timber which he elected to take. The agreement with the company required that he should do this, besides any legal question that might be raised as to the growing timber being capable of being transferred to the plaintiff otherwise than by deed.

The plaintiff, no doubt, ought to have a remedy for such a wrong as he complains of, and we do not see what should prevent his recovering in a special action on the case against the defendant for wrongfully cutting down and taking away the trees, whereby he was obstructed and prejudiced in the enjoyment of the privilege which he had purchased.

That might still depend, however, on whether the plaintiff had acquired the property in the trees, or whether he would not be compelled to look to the company, treating their letter as an agreement in writing sufficient to charge them under the Statute of Frauds.

These are points on which the plaintiff must act as he is advised. I refer to the case in this court of Ferguson v. Hill (11 U. C. R. 530), Scorell v. Boxall (1 Y. & J. 395), Ellis v. Grubb (3 O. S. 611), Teal v. Auty (2 B. & B. 99), besides the cases of Monahan v. Foley (4 U. C. R. 129), and

McLaren v. Rice (5 U. C. R. 151), which are expressly in point against the plaintiff's right to bring this action.

Rule discharged.

OTTY v. DAVIS.

16 *Vic. ch.* 228, *sec.* 1—*Limit between* 12 *&* 13, 1*st con. Monaghan— Birdsall's line.*

Held, that under 16 Vic. ch. 228, sec. 1, Birdsall's line, as laid out on the ground, must govern as the allowance for road between lots twelve and thirteen along their whole extent, and not merely up to park lot ten on lot thirteen; and that it was immaterial whether such line was correctly described in the statute.

EJECTMENT for part of lot No. 12 in the 12th concession of the township of Monaghan, described by metes and bounds.

Notice was given, on the part of the defendant, limiting his defence to so much of the land as is comprised in park lots Nos. 16 and 17 in lot No. 13, in the 12th concession of the said township, describing the same.

At the trial, before *Richards,* J., at the last assizes held at Peterborough, it appeared that the plaintiff was the owner of the whole of lot No. 12, by patent from the Crown dated the 6th of August, 1818. The question was, whether the land claimed comprised part of lot No. 12, or whether it formed part of park lots Nos. 16 and 17, which had been surveyed off of lot No. 13. Mr. Wilson surveyed the township of Monaghan in 1817; and it appeared that he ran the western boundary of the township, by which the division lines of the lots would be governed, No. 16° W. The lots number from west to east, and were surveyed with single fronts. The course of the side lines in the patents granted was N. 16°W. The surveyor called on the part of the plaintiff proved that, allowing for the variation, and taking the true boundary line of the township, the line now between 12 and 13 would be N. 17° 10′ W., both parties agreeing in the starting point at the S. E. corner of No. 12. This survey would shew that the defendant had a part of what, according to the patent, would comprise No. 12.

On the part of the defendant, the act of parliament 16 Vic. ch. 228, was referred to; and by the recital in that act it appears that Mr. Birdsall, deputy provincial surveyor, was employed by the government, in 1825, to survey certain park lots for the town of Peterborough, to be laid out of lot No. 13 ; and in doing so, instead of taking the line according to the boundary line of the township, N. 16° W., he commenced opposite the south-east corner of lot No. 12, making an allowance for road, and then ran N. 16° 30' W., so that, as the statute recites, the line diverges westerly and encroaches on lot No. 12. The present magnetic course of Birdsall's line is N. 14° 30' W., and· allowance being made for the variation according to time would prove Birdsall's line to have been an astronomical line of N. 16° 30' W. It was proved that the defendant's westerly fence was on the line on which Birdsall planted posts indicating the park lots which he surveyed off from No. 13, and that the allowance for road was upon the east of that line. The defendant, it would ,then appear, had enclosed the allowance for road ; but he would not have enclosed any part of lot No. 12, if Birdsall's line was to govern.

The jury found a verdict for the defendant, and found that the improvements he had made were worth £25, and the value of the land was £25 per acre. Leave was reserved to enter a verdict for the plaintiff, if the statute did not conclude him, and enable the defendant to hold the land as being part of park lots No. 16 and 17.

Leith obtained a rule to enter a verdict for plaintiff according to the leave reserved.

Adam Crooks shewed cause.

BURNS, J., delivered the judgment of the court.

It appears to us the statute is conclusive in the defendant's favour. It declares that the allowance for road laid out by Birdsall shall be the true and unalterable allowance for road between lots Nos. 12 and 13, and that the western limit of the said road allowance shall be deemed to be the eastern limit of lot No. 12, and the eastern limit of the road allowance shall be deeemed to be the rear boundary of the park lots, numbering from 1 to 10 inclusive, in the said 12th concesssion. Why the whole number of park lots were not included in the statute does not appear, but that can make no difference.   The question is, what comprises lot No. 12.; and the statute declares that it is to be bounded by the road allowance laid out by Birdsall.   The plaintiff can not come east of that road, whether the park lots 16 and 17 come up to it or not.   It appeared that the defendant contended he had enclosed no more than he had a right to do, and that the road allowance of Birdsall was west of his fence.   In that, however, he is not borne out by the testimony.; for the witness (surveyor) stated that Birdsall laid out the road allowance east of the defendant's fence.   The plaintiff, however, has no ground of complaint in this action that the defendant has fenced up the road allowance. It is quite clear, from the second section of the act, that the legislature was fully aware that the owners of the park lots would be the gainers, and the proprietors of lot 12 would be the losers by the confirmation of Birdsall's line for the provision for compensation only applies to the proprietors of lot 12.   The only question to be determined between the parties is where Birdsall's could be traced to exist on the ground. That seems to have been established to the satisfaction of the jury, and the plaintiff must resort to the remedy given him by the second section of the act for compensation. It is not important to consider whether the act did or not truly recite Birdsall's survey as to its course for the enacting part of the statute declares that the road as he laid it out shall be the unalterable boundary, and it was only* important to these parties to find where that road was upon the ground in order to determine their rights.

The rule must be discharged.

CONLEY V. LEE.

Ejectment—New trial on condition of receiving evidence from judge's notes.

Ejectment for a house and small lot of land adjoining.   It appeared that, as to the house, notice to quit had been given too late, but that the plaintiff was entitled to the land.   The jury found in his favor for all the premises.
Ordered, that unless the plaintiff would confine his judgment to the land, defendant should have a new trial ; but as one of the plaintiff's witnesses lived at a distance, it was imposed as a condition that his evidence, given at the last trial, should be read from the judge's notes.

EJECTMENT for land in the town of Dundas, tried at Hamilton, before *Draper, J.*

One Spencer, who afterwards sold to the plaintiff, rented to defendant a house on this land by the month, at five and a half dollars a month, on the understanding that he might have it for a year, if Spencer did not in the meantime sell it. He afterwards let him a small piece of vacant land on the same lot, at two shillings and sixpence a month, on condition that he must give it up at any time on demand made.

On the 20th of May, Spencer, being about to sell to plaintiff, required defendant to leave; and defendant refusing, he brought this ejectment on the 14th of June.

The learned judge told the jury, that, as to the house, the only question was as to the terms of the tenancy and the sufficiency of the notice. Was defendant a monthly tenant? from what date? and had he received a sufficient notice?

And that as to the vacant land, there was no question but that the plaintiff was entitled to recover.

The jury gave their verdict for the plaintiff generally, saying expressly for all the premises.

Robertson moved for a new trial on the law and evidence, and on an affidavit stating the discovery of new evidence.

Adam Crooks shewed cause, and filed an affidavit in reply.

ROBINSON, C. J., delivered the judgment of the court.

Strictly speaking, the plaintiff seems to have brought this action too soon as regards the house, for Spencer swore that he always considered defendant entitled to a month's notice to leave the house; then, as he also swore that it was on the 20th of May he first desired him to quit, and as this action was brought within the month, viz., on the 14th of June, it was too soon; but the only effect of that should be to restrain the plaintiff from taking possession of the house, or rather to entitle the defendant to a new trial, unless the plaintiff will agree that the verdict shall be confined to the vacant ground; and it would be proper, considering the difficulty and expense of obtaining Spencer's evidence upon another trial, in consequence of the remotenes of his present place of residence, in the State of Iowa, that it should be made a condition of the rule that his evidence given on the last trial should be read to the jury, on this, and considered as if given in court before them.

So that, if the plaintiff chooses to limit his verdict and judgment to the piece of land leased subsequently to the lease of the house, this rule should be discharged but without costs; and if he declines that, then the defendant may have a new trial, provided he consents that Spencer's evidence, given on the last trial, be received by transcript from the judge's notes, in case he is not present, and the plaintiff requires his testimony.

IN THE MATTER OF GREYSTOCK AND THE MUNICIPALITY OF OTONABEE.

By-law—Tavern licenses—Sale of spirituous liquors—Imprisonment on failure to pay fine.

The Municipality of Otonabee passed a by-law on the 25th of March 1854, enacting,

1. That there should be a license issued for one inn only where spirituous liquors should be sold, and that such inn should be in Peterborough East.
2. That persons applying for a license to keep such inn should produce a certificate from four municipal electors, residing in the locality where such house was to be kept of his honesty and good moral character, and a certificate from the township treasurer that he had deposited a bond with such treasurer, made in favour of the reeve and his successors, approved by the councillors of the ward in which such tavern should be situated binding him in £50, with two suffcient sureties in £25 each, to abide by all the by-laws of the township council for the regulation of such houses.
4. That all tavern keepers obtaining license under this by-law should shut up their bar and bar-room at 10 p.m., and keep it closed on Sunday, and should not give or sell liquor to any person in a state of intoxication.
6. That persons wilfully neglecting, refusing, or failing to comply with the provisions of the preceding clauses of this by-law, or selling by retail without license should be liable to a fine of £5, or *failing to pay the same*, to twenty days' imprisonment.
9. That there should be one shop license, and no more, granted within the said municipality, and that such license should be granted to one of the store keepers in the village of Keene.

The reeve of the township swore that the by-law was passed because 244 out of the 489 electors had expressed themselves in favor of limiting as much as possible the sale of spirituous liquors ; and that, at the last election three out of the five were returned on the understanding that they would support such a measure.

Held that these facts could not affect the question ; that the first and ninth sections of the by-law, and so much of the sixth as related to imprisonment of offenders fined on failure to pay, must be quashed : and that the second and fourth sections were good.

Eccles obtained a rule on the Municipal Council of the Township of Otonabee, to shew cause why the first, second, fourth, sixth, and ninth sections of the by-law No. 97

should not be set aside and rescinded, with costs to be paid by the municipality.

The by-law referred to was passed on the 25th of March, 1854. ˙ The first section provided, that after the passing of that by-law there should be license issued for one inn or house of public entertainment, in which spirituous and fermented liquors of any description should be sold, and no more ; and that the said house should be in Peterborough East, within the limits of lot 30, in the 13th concession of Otonabee, and that £10 should be paid for such license.

The second section provided, that the persons who might apply for a certificate to enable them to obtain a license for keeping such house of public entertainment, should produce a certificate from four municipal electors residing in the locality where such house was to be kept, of their honesty and good moral character, and a certificate from the township treasurer that they had deposited a bond with such treasurer, made in favor of the Reeve and his successors, approved by the councillors of the ward in which such tavern is situated, binding him in £50, with two sufficient sureties in £25 each to abide by all the by-laws of the township council for the regulations of such houses.

The fourth section provided that all tavern keepers obtaining license under this by-law should shut up their bar and bar-room at ten o'clock, P.M., and keep it closed on the Sabbath day, and should not give or sell any such liquors to a person in a state of intoxication.

The sixth section provided that persons wilfully neglecting, refusing, or failing to comply with all the requirements, or violating any of the provisions of the preceding clauses of this by-law ; or who should sell by retail without such license, directly or indirectly, any spirituous or fermented liquors ; should be liable, on conviction before any magistrate having jurisdiction within the municipality, on the oath of one competent witness other than the informer, to a fine of £5, or, failing to pay the same, to twenty days' imprisonment.

The ninth section provided that there should be one shop license, and no more, granted within the said municipality, and that such license should be granted to one of the store-keepers in the village of Keene, and that the payment for such license should be one pound.

It was sworn by the applicant that he was a resident freeholder of the township of Otonabee; that he was then keeping and had kept a tavern there for three years past; that this by-law was not in any manner submitted to the electors for their consideration; that in the township of Otonabee there were about four thousand inhabitants; that Peterborough East, mentioned in the by-law, is situated in the north-west corner of the township, at the distance of seven miles from his, the deponent's residence; and that his tavern possessed all the accommodation required by the by-law.

An affidavit was filed in answer to this application, made by the Reeve of the township, in which he swore that this by-law was passed by the municipality in consequence of two hundred and forty-four municipal electors, together with a large number of other resident inhabitants, having expressed themselves in favour of limiting or prohibiting the sale of spirituous liquors as much as possible; that the whole number of electors was four hundred and eighty-nine; that at the municipal electors for 1853, three out of the five councillors were returned upon the test of their being in favor of such prohibition, and with the understanding that they would support such a measure.

That under those circumstances the Council, in what they considered a reasonable exercise of the discretion vested in them, passed this by law, leaving one tavern to be licensed in Peterborough East, that being the most thickly populated and the most business part of the township; and limiting the shop license to one, in the village of Keene; there having been none, within the knowledge of the deponent, taken out for several years past for any other place in the township: and there were two temperance houses licensed in the village of Keene, and one in Peterborough East; and that the by-law now in question had been amended by one passed *on the 29th of September*, 1854, of which a copy duly verified was annexed to his affidavit.

This by-law provided that all fines imposed by the by-law now moved against, chap. 97, might, at the discretion and by the order of the convicting justice, be recovered by distress and sale of the goods to the offender.

Leith shewed cause.

The statutes referred to are noticed in the judgment.

ROBINSON, C. J., delivered the judgment of the court.

We are of opinion that, so far as regards the first section of this by-law, it is not essentially different from a similar provision, which we held to be illegal and bad in the case of Barclay v. The Municipal Council of Darlington (12 U. C. R. 86) ; and that the ninth section, which confines the power of licensing shops in the whole township of Otonabee, in which spirituous liquors may be retailed, to one shop in the village of Keene, is for the same reason illegal.   And I will only add to the reasons assigned for our judgment in that case, that we cannot allow our opinions to be influenced by such reasons as are given in support of this part of the by-law.   So long as the legislature has not made the retailing spirituous liquors in shops and taverns illegal, no municipality can accomplish the same end in any other manner than by such a proceeding as the legislature has prescribed.   They must see that they have the sanction properly given of a majority of the qualified municipal electors.   Upon the affidavit made by the reeve, it is evident that some informal attempt had been made to ascertain the opinion of the electors before this by-law was passed, which attempt did not shew that a majority were in favor of the prohibition, but the contrary.

No attention of course could be paid to the opinions of those, who, not being electors, would have no right to vote upon the question ; nor could any notice be properly taken by us of the alleged test by which the municipal elections were endeavoured to be influenced.

Of course it may be, and has been contended here, as it was in the case we have referred to, that the by-law does not impose an absolute prohibition, for it allows of one inn and one shop to be licensed in a township ten or twelve miles square, and containing four thousand inhabitants ; and that it can therefore be no objection to it, that no previous assent of the electors had been obtained, because no measure short of an absolute prohibition can be legally submitted to them. That is undoubtedly true ; but the real nature of the objection is, that such by-laws are in fact evasions of the statute, and it is plain in this case, as well as in the other referred to, that such was the intention. It is clear, from what has been stated in vindication of this by-law, that if the Municipal Council had felt satisfied that they could have obtained a vote of the majority of the electors in favor of the probihition, they would have put their by-law in that shape. As it is, they have endeavoured to establish a virtual prohibition, without that express sanction of the electors which the law renders necessary to an actual total prohibition literally imposed.

Until by some legislative measure properly passed it has been made illegal to obtain liquor by retail at an inn or a shop, we must regard the public as entitled to expect all reasonable accommodation in that respect, and the discretion given to limit the number of *inns* and *shops* in a township is not, as we think, legally exercised by making it impossible to obtain the accommodation except at one inn and one shop in sixty or seventy square miles of populous country.

That is not so much limiting the number of inns and shops as conferring an unfair monopoly upon one person of each class, who may, under such circumstances, without check, make the public pay what he pleases to extort. If the Law Society of Upper Canada, or the Medical Board, were authorized by statute to limit the number of practitioners in their respective professions, it would hardly be recognized as a reasonable exercise of such an authority if they were to allow but one lawyer and one doctor, and thus leave the whole community to the mercy of those two.

As regards the second section, we do not see why it may not stand consistently with the statutes 13 & 14 Vic. ch 65, and 16 Vic. ch, 184, which appear to be the enactments now regulating the licensing of inns.   Whether there might not be some difficulty in the way of enforcing the bond directed to be taken, we need not now consider.

The fourth section seems a reasonable and good enactment.

The sixth section is objected to on the ground that it

authorizes imprisonment upon failing to pay the fine that may be imposed without regard to the fact of the defendant having goods from which the fine may be made. And we are of opinion that the provision which authorizes imprisonment, not as a punishment, but only in default of payment of the fine imposed, without any attempt being first made to levy the money by distress, is illegal and void.

We think, therefore, that the first and ninth sections of this by law must be quashed, and so much of the sixth as relates to imprisonment of offenders fined on their failing to pay; and that the rule, as regards the remainder of the sixth section, and the second and fourth sections, must be discharged.

WILSON V. THE ONTARIO, SIMCOE, AND HURON RAILROAD UNION COMPANY.

12 *Vic. ch.* 196, *sec.* 18—*Obligation to fence—Request—Insufficient fence put up by plaintiff himself.*

The defendants, by their charter 12 Vic. ch. 196, sec. 18, are bound to fence off their railway from the adjoining lands, in case the owners of such lands shall at any time so desire.

The plaintiff, owning adjoining lands, made a verbal request on defendants' resident engineer to erect a fence, and as this was not done he put up a slashed fence for himself, and some bars in it being left down, his cows got on the track, and were killed.

Held, first, that the request made was sufficient.

Secondly, that the fact of the plaintiff having erected an insufficient fence for himself, and neglected to put up the bars, could not dispense with the duty imposed upon the company, or affect his right to compensation.

CASE.—The declaration stated, that after the passing of the act to incorporate the defendants, and at the time of the committing the grievances complained of, the plaintiff was proprietor of certain lands, and was using and farming the same, and had thereon a large stock of cows and other cattle grazing and running at large on said land; and that the defendants had commenced to construct their railroad through the plaintiff's land, and took a portion extending across the same from one side to the other, and prostrated and removed the fences at the ends thereof, and threw the said portion open, so that the cattle of the plaintiff could escape from the residue of the plaintiff's land and rove at large, and other cattle could enter on the same, and the plaintiff's cattle could cross and feed upon and about the track of the railroad ; that the part of the railroad crossing the plaintiff's land had long been and was finished and in operation, and locomotives and cars of defendants were running thereon : that afterwards, and before the committing, &c., the plaintiff required the defendants to separate and keep separated, by good and sufficient fences, the portion of land over which the railway ran from the remainder of the plaintiff's land and it became thereupon the defendants' duty within a reasonable time to make and construct such fence. Yet the defendants did not at any time construct, &c., but wrongfully neglected, &c., by means whereof the cows of the plaintiff escaped through the said portion of land so laid open and were lost.

Pleas—1st. Not guilty by statute. 2nd. Traverse of the request to fence.

At the trial at Barrie, in October, 1854, before *Draper, J.*, the plaintiff proved that he stated to the defendants' resident engineer, in the fall of 1853, or towards the winter, that he required a fence to be put up through his lot, which was nearly all in a state of nature. The engineer said he would see further into it and referred the plaintiff to the contractor. The trains had then been running two months. The engineer stated that he thought at that time there was no fence on the plaintiff's lot, not even round his clearing, which was only four or five acres then. It appeared that after this the plaintiff made a slashed fence upon his own land, on each side of the railway. There was no proof that the defendants did anything or that the fence made by the plaintiff, such as it was, was done in pursuance of any arrangement with the defendants. The engineer stated, that the slashing is usually done parallel to the track, the trees not being moved, but allowed to lie where they fall. The plaintiff's cows might, according to some of the evidence, have got through the slashing, but the plaintiff himself told the defendants' engineer that his cattle were browsing on his own land : that he had made an opening through the slashing to haul out cordwood off his land and put poles across the opening to keep his cattle in : that one evening he neglected to put these poles up, and on the following day two of his cows were killed on the track by the defendants' cars,—a fact which was proved by other witnesses.

It was objected for the defendants, that as the plaintiff had himself put up a fence the defendants were not bound to do it. This was overruled : and the jury were asked to decide whether there had been a request to defendants to fence, and if so, whether the defendants had, within a reasonable time, complied with such request, and put up a sufficient or indeed any fence; and if they found both these points for the plaintiff, they were told he would be entitled to a verdict, with nominal damages, for the defendants' breach of duty. With regard to the cows, the jury were directed to find whether they were killed by the defendants' cars in consequence of defendants not having fenced off their railway ; though if they thought the plaintiff had contributed to this loss by his own wilful or negligent act—as by removing a slash fence put up by defendants, and omitting to keep the opening so made secured—they were told he ought not to recover.   That in deciding whether a reasonable time had elapsed for the defendants to make the fence, they might take into account the season of the year at which the plaintiff required the fence, apparently in December or January, and the lapse of time until the cows were killed, which was in March following : or—if they only gave damages for the breach of duty, and not for the cows—until the 19th of April, when the writ was sued out.   And that a demand, though only verbal, on the resident engineer in charge, was evidence of a demand on defendants to make the fence.

They found for the plaintiff, and damages £15.

Phillpotts obtained a rule nisi for a new trial on the law and evidence, and for misdirection.

H. Eccles shewed cause.

Robinson, C.J., delivered the judgment of the court.

Upon the facts proved, we think the plaintiff's right to recover cannot be denied; and it is satisfactory that the damages are reasonable, for these occurrences are unfortunate in their effect upon the interests of a company whose exertions have conferred great benefit upon the community; and perhaps with the greatest care accidents will occasionally take place.

On the other hand, if the defendants have neglected a duty plainly incumbent upon them, especially by a positive statute, and an individual suffers loss in consequence, it is natural that he should seek recompence.

We think, as the learned judge did upon the trial, that the Company received sufficient notice of the plaintiff's desire to have the track fenced in, by the request made to the resident engineer.

The obligation of the company to fence in the track within a reasonable time after being requested by the adjoining proprietor, is imposed upon them in plain terms by the statute 12 Vic. ch. 196, sec. 18.

The jury considered that a reasonable time had elapsed after the request. And the obligation of the Company to put up a sufficient fence, such as the statute directs, was in no manner put an end to or suspended by the circumstance of the plaintiff having, in the absence of such fence, put up on his own land some kind of enclosure between him and the track; nor is his claim to compensation affected by that enclosure proving insufficient, or by his leaving open the bars which he had generally kept up in it as described. They had no right to expect him to keep up a fence there except for the preservation of his own crops, not for guarding against their railway cars, because that had been made the duty of the Company. We do not think that upon the facts of this case there was any room for a question about the right to nominal or substantial damages. The plaintiff, we think, was either entitled to recover for the loss he had suffered, or had no right to a verdict at all; for the mere neglect of their duty by the Company would give him no right of action unless he suffered damage in consequence of it, and such a damage as he sued for.

Rule discharged.

ROSS ET AL. v. HERON.

Pleading—Accord and satisfaction—Uncertainty—Demurrer.

Assumpsit on the common counts. *Plea*—That after the making of the promises, and before the commencement of this suit, it was agreed that defendant should sell to plaintiffs, and plaintiffs then and there bought of defendant, 20 shares of stock in a certain steamer ; and that defendant should hold such shares for plaintiffs' use, and transfer them to the plaintiffs when required ; and that the plaintiffs should then and there accept the said agreement of defendant, and the said shares so to be transferred, in full satisfaction and discharge of the said promises : that in pursuance of such agreement, and ever since the making thereof, defendant held and still holds such shares for the use of the plaintiffs, and hath always been and still is ready to transfer them when required. *Held*, on demurrer, plea bad, because it was not shewn whether the alleged agreement was before or after breach of the promise sued on.

ASSUMPSIT on the common counts. *Plea*—that after the making of the promises in the declaration mentioned, and before the commencement of this suit, to wit, on, &c., it was agreed by and between the plaintiffs and the defendant, that the defendant should bargain and sell to the plaintiffs, and the plaintiffs then and there bought of the defendant, twenty shares of stock in a certain steamer called the *Arabian,* which the defendant then held in his own name ; and that the defendant should hold such shares for the use of the plaintiffs, and transfer said shares to the plaintiffs when they the plaintiffs should thereafter require the same to be transferred to them the said plaintiffs ; and that they, the plaintiffs, should and would then and there accept the said agreement of the said defendant, and the said shares to be transferred, in *full satisfaction and discharge of the said promises* of the defendant in the said declaration mentioned : that in pursuance of the said agreement, and at all times since the making thereof, before the commencement of this suit, he, the defendant, hath held for the use of the plaintiffs the said shares, and still holds the same for the use of the plaintiffs, and hath always since the making of said agreement been ready and willing, and still is ready and willing to transfer the said shares to the palintiffs, when required so to do : verification.

Demurrer—That it is not sufficiently shewn by the said plea whether the matters therein set up as a defence took place before or after breach of the promises laid in the declaration : that if after the breach, it does not appear by the said plea that the damages which accrued upon the said breach were in any manner satisfied ; that the said plea does not state facts amounting to a good or complete accord and satisfaction : that there is no sufficient consideration shewn for the alleged promise of the plaintiffs of acceptance in satisfaction of the matters in that behalf in the said plea set forth, or that the plaintiffs did so accept, or that the said alleged transaction ever was completed.

Connor, Q. C., for the demurrer, cited Thomas v. Mallory 6 U. C. R. 521 ; Bayley v. Homan, 3 Bing. N. C. 919 ; De Wolf v. Bevan, 13 M. & W. 160 ; Francis v. Crywell, 5 B. & Al. 886 ; Balston v. Baxter, Cro. Eliz. 304 ; Finl. Lea. Ca 103 : Sibree v. Tripp, 15 M. & W. 23 ; Griffiths v. Owen, 13 M. & W. 58 ; Tyr. Plg. 327.

ROBINSON, C. J., delivered the judgment of the court.

We give judgment for the plaintiff on this demurrer, on the ground that it is not averred whether the alleged new agreement was before or after the breach of the promises sued on. If intended to be relied upon as a substituted agreement, it should appear distinctly that it was accepted before breach of the promises sued on. If intended to be advanced by way of accord and satisfaction, made after breach of the former promises, then it should be shewn that satisfaction had been actually received by the plaintiff ; a readiness to transfer the shares would not be sufficient.

The case of Francis v. Crywell (5 B. & Al. 886) is an express authority to shew that this plea is not a good bar to the action ; for although in that case it did appear in subsequent pleadings (which is not the case here) that the alleged satisfaction must have been after some damage had been incurred by reason of the non-performance of the first promise, and there is so far a difference between the two cases yet the alleged satisfaction there was by payment of a sum of money given and received. But here what is set up is not satisfaction actually received, but only an agreement to do a certain thing, which, unless it were accepted before breach, in discharge of the former promise, could be no defence.

The plea therefore does not contain all the averments which are necessary to make it a good bar.

Judgment for plaintiffs on demurrer,

HOLMES v. McDonell.

Pleading—Payment of a less sum in satisfaction, of a greater.

Plea of payment and acceptance of a less in satisfaction of a larger sum held bad.

Quære, whether a plea that the demand sued for was an of unliquidated nature, and was disputed either wholly or in part, and that it was agreed that plaintiff should receive a less sum in satisfaction of his alleged cause of action, could be supported.

ASSUMPSIT for goods sold and delivered, and on other common counts, claiming £100.

Plea—That after the making of the promises in the declaration mentioned, and before the commencement of this suit, to wit on, &c., the plaintiff made his bill of exchange in writing, and directed the same to the defendant, and thereby required the defendant, six days after sight thereof, to pay to the plaintiff's own order, at the office of the Bank of Upper Canada, Goderich, the sum of fifty pounds cy. (meaning currency), value received, in full satisfaction and discharge of the said promises in the said declaration mentioned ; which said bill of exchange when the same became due when payable, to wit, on, &c., was presented and shewn to the defendant for payment thereof, at the said office of the Bank of Upper Canada at Goderich ; and he, the defendant, then paid the said bill of exchange to the plaintiff, who accepted and received the same in full satisfaction and discharge of the said declaration mentioned and also of all damages sustained by the plaintiff by reason of the non-performance of such promises : verification.

Demurrer—Eccles for the demurrer ; *Becher* contra.

The causes of demurrer assigned, and the authorities cited, sufficiently appear in the judgment.

ROBINSON, C. J., delivered the judgment of the court.

It escaped my attention in considering this plea till it was pointed out to me by one of my learned brothers, that there can be no question here as to the sufficiency of a plea setting up the acceptance by the defendant of a negotiable bill drawn upon him by the plaintiff, and agreed by the defendant to be given and by the plaintiff to be taken in satisfaction of the causes of action declared on; because whether from any inadvertent admission in the plea, or because the facts could not be otherwise stated with truth, this plea does not aver that the defendant accepted the bill. There was therefore no negotiable security given by the defendant in satisfaction of the causes of action declared on, if the giving such security by the defendant for £50, without the added liability of any third party as indorsee, could be pleaded in satisfaction of £100, claimed on the common counts. The plea, in truth, resolves itself into this—that the defendant paid to the plaintiff £50 in satisfaction of his promise to pay him £100.' This we have no doubt is a bad plea. If the defendant had pleaded that the claim of the plaintiff sued upon in this action was of an unliquidated nature and was disputed either wholly or as to its amount, and that it was agreed between them that the plaintiff should receive £50 in full satisfaction of his alleged causes of action, then there are several recent cases, and among them that cited of Sipree v. Tripp (15 M. & W. 23), on which it might be attempted to support such a plea; but we do not imagine that any decision can be found which goes the length of supporting the present plea, because in it the defendant admits that he *promised to pay* the £100 for goods sold, and and being indebted to him in that amount, and that the plaintiff afterwards excepted from £50 in full discharge of that promise. In the case of Turner v. Collins (3 Eng. Rep. 363), decided in Hilary Term, 1851, Mr. Justice Coleridge held that verdict a plea of this kind would not be held to be insufficient to bar the action upon an application for judgment *non obstante veredicto,* and I gather from the conclusion of his judgment that on the principle on which he formed it, and which he deduced from the effect of the new rules of pleading, he would probably have considered the present plea sustainable on demurrer; but he does not say so expressly, and I find nothing elsewhere to support such a ruling.

The case of Down v. Hatcher (10 A. & E. 121) is quite decisive against this plea, for it was there held after verdict to be no defence. At the same time, I must acknowledge that, after tracing this point through the late English cases, I feel no confidence whatever as to what might be the decision there upon these pleadings, if it were to become a question in any of their courts, for the matter seems to rest there at present on a very unsettled footing ; a strong inclination being shewn in some cases to depart from what was clearly enough held to be the law formerly, while in other cases the obligation of the old rule of pleading is treated as in full force.

The rule itself is certainly not a very just or reasonable one, as has been of late frequently conceded ; for while the giving of the defendant's own negotiable note or acceptance for £50 would be allowed to be a good satisfaction of a promise to pay £100, if so accepted, the paying the same amount in money in satisfaction, though averred to have been accepted in discharge, would not bar the action—which certainly seems unreasonable.

We can only say that we find no adjudged case that has gone the length of sustaining this plea, while the books are full of cases against it ; and in the last edition of Saunders on Pleading (2 Saund. 137 *k*) it is treated as a clear point that payment of a smaller sum cannot be pleaded in satisfaction of a promise to pay a greater.

Judgment for plaintiff on demurrer.

DARLING V. MAGNAN AND BOUDREAU.

Partnership—Evidence of dissolution.

The plaintiff sued M. and B. upon upon a promissory note signed M. & Co., made by M., dated 10th October, 1853. For the defence, a deed of dissolution of partnership between M. and B. was proved, dated 25th May, and three *Canada Gazettes* giving notice of such dissolution, the first dated 25th June, 1853. It was not shewn that he plaintiff ever knew of B. being a partner, and the note was made at Port Hope, where M. and B. had carried on business, but B. lived in Montreal.
Held, that a verdict should have been found for defendants.
Quære, as to what is sufficient notice of a dissolution of partnership.

ASSUMPSIT.—1*st count*, upon a promissory note dated the 16th of May, 1853, payable to the plaintiff, or order, at the Bank of British North America in Montreal, for the sum of £93 8s. 11d. six months after date.

2*nd count*, upon a promissory note dated the 10th of October, 1853, for £154 1s. 10d., payable, as the other, in Montreal, six months after date.

Pleas by Boudreau—1st to the first count, that he and the defendant Magnan were copartners in trade under the firm of P. Z. Magnan & Co., and as such made the note therein mentioned for a debt due by them; that on the 25th of May, 1853, the partnership was dissolved, and the defendant Boudreau retired, and the other carried on business on his own account; and it was agreed that Magnan should assume the debts of the firm; and that the plaintiff assented to such arrangement, and discharged defendant Boudreau from the debt. 2ndly. To the first count, that the plaintiff drew his bill of exchange for the amount of the first note on Magnan, who accepted the same in discharge of the note. 3rdly. To the second count, that he (the defendant Bondreau) and Magnan did not make that note.

Replication—That the plaintiff did not discharge Boudreau from liability upon the first note, and that he did not take or receive the bill of exchange mentioned from Magnan in satisfaction of the first note. Issue taken on the plea to second count.

The defendant Magnan suffered judgment by default.

At the trial before *Burns*, J., at the last assizes held at Toronto, the defendant offered no sufficient evidence to sustain the defence to the first note. The contest turned upon the second note. The plaintiff called witnesses, all living at Port Hope, to prove that the business of the defendants was carried on there in the name of Magnan & Co., and that the defendant Boudreau was understood there to a partner with Magnan, and that no dissolution of the partnership was understood to have taken place till the spring of 1854, when Magnan failed, and Boudreau came to Port Hope for the purpose of settling the affairs. The plaintiff lived and carried on his business in Montreal; the defendant Boudreau also lived in Montreal, and his business in Montreal was carried on in the name of his wife, under the laws of Lower Canada. The wife's name was S. S. Boudreau. The defendant Magnan had nothing whatever to do with that business, except that the establishment at Port Hope was largely supplied with goods from S. S. Boudreau, but in the same way that they would have been purchased from any other house or establishment. On the part of the defendant was proved an examined copy of a deed of dissolution, made before a notary in Montreal, which took place on the 25th of May, 1853. It was proved by a witness, who was also present at the dissolution, that at the time of the dissolution the firm of Magnan & Co. was indebted to S. S. Boudreau in about £10,100. The business in Montreal was about the same time discontinued in the name of the wife, and it was taken up by Herrod (the witness) in conjunction with the defendant Boudreau. The firm in Montreal took up the outstanding business, and the winding-up of the accounts and affairs of S. S. Boudreau, and in that way they had large transactions in the way of bills of exchange with Magnan at Port Hope from May, 1853, until the failure, in endeavouring to wind up the outstanding debts due. In January, 1854, the defendant Boudreau took a judgment against Magnan for the balance then due, and it was upon this judgment that the concern was eventually shut up. The witness stated that after the dissolution of the Port Hope firm, notice thereof was given to various firms in Montreal; and he said it was notorious there that a dissolution had taken place. Three *Canada Gazettes* were put in containing notice of the dissolution of the firm in Port Hope, the first of which was dated the 25th of June, 1853. It was then proved, on the part of the defendants, that the cashier of the Commercial Bank at Port Hope— through which bank the firm at Port Hope was accustomed to do business—was aware of the dissolution of the partnership, having a copy of the deed of dissolution deposited with him in August, 1853. He said he could not say that it was notorious in Port Hope that there was a dissolution, but he had no doubt but that others knew of it as well as himself. Another witness stated that he knew of the dissolution in the summer of 1853, though he did not personally know the defendant Boudreau. Both notes were signed alike—*P. Z. Magnan & Co.* It was understood that the last note had been given for goods purchased when Magnan was in Montreal in the fall of 1853.

Upon this evidence the learned judge told the jury that it was a question of fact for them to determine, whether there was in truth a dissolution of the partnership on the 25th of May, 1853. That he saw no reason to question it upon the evidence, if the witness who proved the examined copy of the deed of dissolution, and who was present at it, told the truth, and the deed disposited in the notary's office, and publication in the *Gazette*, corroborated him in his statement. If there was a dissolution in fact, then upon this evidence the defendant was entitled to succeed as to the second note. *M. C. Cameron*, for the plaintiff, excepted to the charge, contending that the dissolution was secret from the plaintiff, and that a note given after the dissolution would bind the defendant Boudreau. The learned judge conceived that it could not be said that there was any secresy in the matter, and as respected the plaintiff, he did not shew that he had been deceived in any way in respect to the partnership.

The jury found a verdict for the plaintiff for the amount of both notes.

Richards obtained a rule to shew cause why there should not be a new trial, on the ground that the verdict was contrary to law and evidence, and against the judge's charge, and that the damages were excessive.

McMichael shewed cause, and conteuded that the learned judge took an erroneous view of the defendant's liability on the second note, and that it was a question for the jury upon the whole of the evidence to say whether the defendant Boudreau was liable to the plaintiff for the amount of that note; and though the jury had found against the judge's charge, yet the verdict was supported by the evidence, and the court should not disturb it.

In addition to the cases cited in the judgment, Farkin v. Carruthers, 3 Esp. 248; Fox v. Hanbury. Cowp. 449; Stables v. Eley, 1 C. & P. 614; 1 Stark. 375: Rooth v. Quin, 7 Price 193; Williams v. Keats, 2 Stark, 290, were referred to for the plaintiff; and Collyer on Partnership secs. 530–536, for the defendants.

ROBINSON, C. J., delivered the judgment of the court.

The only question, it seems, is upon the plaintiff's right to recover against the defendant Boudreau for the note declared

on in the second count. We think the learned judge took a
right view of the case in what he said to the jury, and that
upon the direction given there should have been a verdict for
the defendant upon the second count. The jury could not
arbitrarily assume, in the face of all the evidence that was
given of the dissolution, that it was a mere pretence, and that
the partnership in fact continued till October, 1853, when the
second note was given. The partners could dissolve their
association when they pleased, and for all that appears
they did so on the 25th of May, 1853, without any attempt
to conceal it, or to hold out an appearance contrary to the
fact.

The note was signed *P. Z. Magnan & Co.* The first
question is, had the person who wrote that signature any
authority in October, 1853, to bind the defendant Boudreau
as coming at that time under the terms of that signature ?
—in other words, was he then actually one of the firm in company with Magnan, who wrote the signature ? We think
the jury could not say otherwise upon the evidence than
that he was not ; for there was a formal act of dissolution
entered into before a notary, and the dissolution was openly
published in the provincial *Gazette*, and had become known
to several persons in Port Hope, though others seemed not
to have heard of it, and perhaps the plaintiff was one of
those to whom the fact was unknown. The case cited by
Mr. Richards in support of the rule—Carter v. Whalley et
al. (1 B. & Ad. 11)—is much in point ; we refer, also, to
Wrightson v. Pullan (1 Stark. 375), and to Gorham v.
Thompson (Peake's Ca. 60), and Graham v. Hope (Ibid, 208.)

After all the cases that have been decided, the question
of what shall be sufficient notice of a dissolution of partnership seems to be left on no very well defined ground.

In this case it seems that Darling (the plaintiff) lived in
Montreal, and carried on his business there, which made it
more likely that he would hear of the dissolution, which
had been regularly effected by a public notorial act there,
and perhaps more likely also that he would have seen or
heard of the notice in the *Gazette*.

Boudreau had only been formerly with Magnan in a trading

establishment at Port Hope--not in Montreal, where Boudreau lived. No proof was given at the trial that this note was given upon any purchase of goods which had been made for the use of the late firm before the dissolution, or that there was any attempt at concealment of the dissolution, or any artful contrivance to impose upon the plaintiff by inducing him to accept a note signed *Magnan & Co.*, which he would not have accepted if signed by Magnan alone.

It was not indeed proved that he knew who it was that would at any time have been bound, besides Magnan, by the signatnre *Magnan & Co.* There was only the fact that a note had been before given to him with the signature of Magnan & Co., and therefore that he had reason then to believe that somebody was associated in business with Magnan.

For all that appears, this note may have been given to him for a debt, or upon a consideration, to which he had never reason to regard Boudreau as a partner, and he may now be seeking to render Boudreau liable upon a subsequent discovery that he had before that time been a partner at Port Hope. It requires more, we think, than was shewn in this case to warrant us in holding Boudreau liable upon his note as coming under the designation of *Magnan & Co.*, seeing that he had five months before ceased to be a partner under a dissolution formally effected by a public act before a notary, and formally proclaimed many months before in the provincial *Gazette.*

The partnership appears to have been created in Montreal, where Darling lived, and also Boudreau, who was not associated then nor any time with Magnan, who lived at Port Hope; and it was not shewn that Darling had had any transactions with the firm at Port Hope.

We are of opinion that there should be a new trial, with costs to abide the event, unless the plaintiff consents to strike out the second note and interest from his verdict.

Rule accordingly (a).

(*a*) At the conclusion of this judgment, *M. C. Cameron*, for the plaintiff, asked that the defendants should be ordered to pay the amount of the first note into court, there being no question as to the plaintiff's right to recover on that. The court refused the application, saying that there was no pre-cedent for such a course.

WHITE ET AL. V. BROWNE.

Chattel mortgage—Estoppel—Saw logs mortgaged and afterwards made into lumber—New trial for discovery of new evidence.

A person advancing money belonging to others, but for which he himself is responsible, may legally take a chattel mortgage for it in his own name.

A bailee of goods is not estopped from disputing the bailor's title.

A mortgage on saw logs will bind the lumber into which they are sawn, but the mortgagee must prove that such lumber was made out of the logs mortgaged.

A new trial will not be granted for the discovery of new evidence, unless such evidence is specifically shewn in the affidavits.

CASE.—The first count of the declaration stated, that the defendant carried on the business of a wharfinger at a certain wharf, situate, &c., and that the plaintiffs, at defendant's request, caused to be delivered to defendant certain quantities of lumber, (specifying them) to be safely kept by defendant for reasonable wharfage and reward, and that the defendant received the said lumber for the purpose aforesaid : yet defendant did not safely keep the said lumber for the plaintiffs, but on the contrary, through the mere carelessness and negligence of the defendant, the same was wholly lost to the plaintiffs.

The second count stated a similar delivery of lumber to defendant, to be by defendant safely kept, and to redeliver the same for plaintiff upon request ; averment of request, and that the lumber, through the mere carelessness, &c., was lost. The third count was in trover.

Pleas.—1st. To the whole declaration, Not guilty. 2nd. To the first and second counts, denial of the delivery to and receipt by the defendant of the lumber *modo et forma.* 3rd. To the last count, plaintiffs not possessed. These pleas were pleaded on the 6th of October, 1853, and on the 6th of April, 1854, defendant, by a judge's order, added a plea to the first and second count, that plaintiffs were not possessed, &c.

The case was tried at Hamilton, before *Draper*, J. The plaintiffs put in a copy of an agreement between themselves and one George Hibbard, in the following words :

" Received of J. & J. White, January 25th, 1853, the sum of £50, and at various dates previous the sum of £194 12s. 6d. Cy., being in part payment for all the lumber now at my mill, in the yard, and at Browne's wharf, and on the way thereto, all of which I have sold to J. & J. White at and for the price or sum of £1 12s. 6d. per thousand feet, for good, sound, merchantable piece plank, and at the rate of £4 for clear, £2 10s. for fourth quality, and £1 15s for select box, according to the American inspection, said inspection to apply to the lumber sold as above and deliverable at Browne's wharf—the whole of said lumber, amounting to some 120,000 I have this day sold and delivered, and do permit J. & J. White to take possession of the same. (Signed) GEO. HIBBARD. Witness, THOMAS WHITE."

The subscribing witness said he was the plaintiffs' agent ; that he had occasion to consult the plaintiffs' attorney on this matter, and, as he believed, left the original with him, but that he had previously made this copy; that he had diligently searched for and could not find the original. And the plaintiffs' attorney swore that he had searched for and could not find the original, but that he had no recollection that he ever had it, though the other witness did leave some document with him. The copy was admitted in evidence. The plaintiffs' witness swore that directly after getting this paper he went to Hibbard's mill and received a delivery of the lumber which was there, and marked it in plaintiffs' name, and then took an order (not produced or accounted for) from Hibbard and went to defendant; that defendant pointed out Hibbard's lumber, and with the witness estimated it at 35,000 feet of piece plank, which the witness also marked in plaintiffs name, and this lumber the defendant undertook to hold subject to plaintiffs' order. Other lumber was afterwards' brought from Hibbard's mill to defendant's wharf, which this witness told defendant was plaintiffs' property, and he requested defendant to hold it for the plaintiffs, which the defendant refused, but agreed not to have it shipped unless in the witness's presence. At the opening of the navigation defendant shipped, without notice to this witness, 48,000 feet of the lumber which came from Hibbard's mill, including the 35,000 feet first spoken of, on account of other parties, having, as the witness understood, obtained an indemnity from them. On cross-examination, this witness said he estimated the lumber at Hibbard's mill, with the 35,000 feet at defendant's wharf, to amount to 120,000 feet; that he knew of no claim on this lumber, or on lumber or logs owned by Hibbard, but that on the 20th of February, 1853, he heard of a chattel mortgage made by Hibbard, and on search found one in the office of the clerk of the County Court, dated 19th February, 1852, in favour of one Abner Whitney, upon 4,000 saw logs, and filed in that office in the afternoon of that day. He said that on the 25th of January, 1853, £216 had been paid by the plaintiffs to Hibbard, and that he owed them - more, and agreed to make more lumber. Hibbard also gave the plaintiffs a cognovit, on which they entered judgment and issued execution, under which, on the 8th of March, 1854, the lumber at Hibbard's mill was sold. The witness said that in July, 1852, the plaintiffs made an arrangement with Hibbard to make advances to him, for which he was to make and deliver lumber to them at the prices stated in the agreement of the 25th of January, 1853. None of the lumber in dispute was sawed then. About 40,000 feet of lumber from Hibbard's mill was shipped in July, 1852. The plaintiffs claimed the value of the 48,000 feet admitted by defendant to have been shipped by him. They claimed also for a further quantity, which it is not now important to notice.

For the defence the principal witness was Abner Whitney, who described himself as agent for R. Ketchum and Sons, of Albany, in which character he entered into a contract, dated 3rd February, 1852, with Geo. Hibbard (put in) for the sale and delivery by him of 200,000 feet of white pine lumber, of specified quality and price; and on the faith of this contract he, on the 19th of February, 1852, advanced £125 to Hibbard, and to secure it took the chattel mortgage spoken of by plaintiffs' first witness, payable to himself; and he filed this mortgage with the usual affidavit of debt, made by himself as being Hibbard's creditor. He said it was money he drew from Ketchum and Sons, and for which he was accountable to them; but he took the mortgage to himself, to meet the requirements of the statute. Hibbard delivered a small quantity of lumber on this contract in May or June, 1852. The water failed during the summer, and Whitney agreed to wait. In November, 1852, Whitney went to Hibbard, and he made a formal delivery of the logs then lying in the mill yard, saying they were the identical logs mentioned in the mortgage. From November up to the 17th of February, Whitney swore he went repeatedly to Hibbard to see how he was getting on. On the latter day he found the lumber mostly sawed and piled up. Hibbard said he delivered that lumber to Whitney, and they two and one Wilson made an estimate of the quantity, and some short time after he, Whitney, made a contract with Hibbard to haul it down to defendant's wharf. About the 18th of February Whitney (as he swore) was at defendant's wharf, and found about 5,000 feet there, in the place from which the lumber was subsequently shipped. On the 7th of March he went again, and in the same place found a large quantity, over 50,000 feet, marked J. & J. White, which he swore was not there on the 18th of February. In the first week in March Whitney swore he met one of the plaintiffs, and having heard that they had an execution against Hibbard, and had levied on the lumber on the wharf, Whitney asked if the plaintiffs knew he had a chattel mortgage, to which the other replied to the effect that a mortgage on logs would not hold lumber. The witness said he was as sure as he could be that the lumber shipped (48,000 feet) was made of the logs mortgaged to him. He said there was a small pile hauled to defendant's from Hibbard's mill after the 17th of March, marked *J. J. White*, and that he erased the mark from a board of it. On cross-examination he admitted that there were not 4000 saw-logs at the mill when the mortgage was given. On the 26th of June he said there were 3,000 there. He said, after the 17th of February, 1853, he did not care, as enough had been sawed to cover his demand, and he let the rest go; that when he saw Hibbard at defendat's wharf on the 8th of March, Hibbard said plaintiffs had marked the lumber without his consent. On the 7th of March, 1853, he gave Hibbard a receipt (put in) for 2,727 pieces of piece plank " then lying on Alex. Browne's wharf, which is to apply on a note which I hold against him, which is secured by a mortgage dated February 19th, 1852." Other evidence was given to shew that after the 25th of January, 1853, the lumber at Hibbard's was sold under an execution at plaintiff's suit, and corroborating Whitney's statement, that the lumber in question, excepting about 5000 feet, was not delivered at defendant's wharf as late as on the 18th of February, contrary to the statement of Thomas White. In reply the plaintiff's gave some strong evidence to lead to the conclusion that the lumber in question was made out of logs brought into Hibbard's mill long after February, 1852.

The jury were told that the plaintiff's claim as to 35,000 feet rested on the proof of the agreement of the 25th of January, 1853, and the alleged undertaking of the defendant to hold that quantity, then being on the defendant's wharf, for the plaintiffs, and subject to their order as to which there was the evidence given by defendant's witnesses that no such quantity was there until after the 18th of February. And as to the additional 13,000 feet claimed, the plaintiffs' title rested on the same agreement, and the alleged delivery at Hibbard's mill, and the fact that so much of the lumber so delivered was hauled down to defendant's wharf. If there had been no evidence to contradict or rebut, the jury were told the plaintiff gave sufficient evidence of property that although it was contended that defendant, being a wharf-inger, could not be heard to deny the plaintiff's property in the lumber which defendant agreed to hold as theirs, still on the issues submitted it was the duty of the jury to determine the question whether the plaintiffs were possessed of the 48,000 feet of lumber in question as their property.

As to the defence, they were told that the sawing of the logs mortgaged was not inconsistent upon the evidence with the rights of the mortgagee, which were prior in point of date (February, 1852,) to the earliest arrangement between plaintiffs and Hibbard (July, 1852), and long prior to the written agreement made by Thos. White (January, 1853); but that this mortgage was not upon *any* logs which, to the number of 4000, might happen to be brought to Hibbard's mill, but could only affect and bind such as were specifically mentioned in it—*i.e.*, logs at the mill when the mortgage was executed and if the lumber, the 48,000 feet, was made from other logs the alleged delivery thereof at the mill to Whitney, made subsequent to the alleged sale and delivery to the plaintiff's could not prevail to deprive the plaintiffs of any right of property they had acquired.

The plaintiffs' counsel excepted to the direction that the defendant could not set up the chattel mortgage and the registry, because the debt thereby secured was not due to Whitney, the mortgagee, therein named ; that the defendant could not avail himself of the defence of "not possessed" to the first and second counts; and that a mortgage of *logs* will not cover lumber into which they may be sawed.

The jury, after an absence of about fifteen minutes, returned a verdict for the defendant.

Connor, Q. C., obtained a rule nisi for a new trial, on the ground of misdirection, the reception of improper evidence, the verdict being against law and evidence, and upon affidavits. He cited Storey on Bailments, 457, 582; Gosling v. Birnie, 7 Bing. 339 ; Kieran v. Sanders, 6 A. & E. 515 ; Gunn v. Gillespie, 2 U. C. R. 124 ; Brent v. Perry, 7 U. C. R. 25 ; Fallis v. Claus, 9 U. C. R. 273 ; Lee v. Rapelje, 2 U. C. R. 368; Short v. Ruttan, 12 U. C. R. 79 ; 1 Sm. Lea. Ca. 45, Am. notes.

S. Richards shewed cause, and cited Harrison v. Dixon, 12 M. & W. 142 ; Richards v. Symons, 8 Q. B. 90 ; Ashby v. Minnitt, 8 A. & E. 121 ; Jones v. Chapman, 2 Ex. 804.

BURNS, J., delivered the judgment of the court.

The first point to be considered is, whether there was any misdirection in the learned judge, in the reception of improper evidence or in the manner the case was left to the jury. It was stated by the witness for the defendant that he acted as the agent of a firm in Albany in contracting with Hibbard for the lumber to be made; but in making the advance of money which he did upon the saw logs he was responsible to the firm for it, and therefore took the mortgage in his own name. The objection taken that the witness could not properly make the affidavit required by our Chattel Mortgage Registry Act, and therefore could not take a security in this way, does not require much consideration in an action of this kind. Whether the witness were produced to prove property in himself or in another, he was competent for that purpose ;

and if it were true that he was personally responsible to his employers for the money he advanced, he might, we think, have legally taken a mortgage, by way of security for it, in his own name. If the affidavit had been special, setting forth the consideration just as the witness proved it to be, his mortgage would have been legal and his affidavit sufficient, as we already have held in Heward v. Mitchell (11 U. C. R. 625). In the present case the agent or trustee advances money instead of becoming liable by means of being security; and though that money was his principal's, yet if he were personally responsible for it, he may very well take a security for it in his own name. Then, as to the point raised at the trial, and again urged on the argument of the rule for a new trial—namely, that the defendant being a bailee of the lumber, having received possession from the plaintiffs, could not dispute their title, the cases are too strong to question the propriety of the learned judge's charge. If the right of property were in the firm at Albany, or the witness Whitney, though the defendant had received the possession from the plaintiffs, yet he would have been justified in delivering it to the rightful owner. Ogle v. Atkinson (5 Taunt. 759), Wilson v. Anderton (1 B. & Ad. 450), Cheesman v. Exall (6 Ex. 341), clearly establish this proposition. The defendant could therefore properly plead the plea of not possessed, and under it shew that the plaintiffs had no legal title to the property. With respect to the objection that the defendant could not establish title in some other than the plaintiffs, on the ground that Whitney's mortgage was upon saw logs, and the plaintiffs claimed no title to saw logs, but to lumber, we think the direction to the jury quite right. Of course, the burthen of the proof would lie on the defendant to establish that the lumber he admitted to hold for the plaintiffs was manufac-tured from the identical logs mortgaged to Whitney. The logs mortgaged were not intended to remain in that state, but were to be converted into lumber for Whitney or his principal. The sawing of them into lumber was consistent with the design and object of the parties, and did not destroy the distinctive character of title so that the mortgagee would lose his property. One way to test it is to ask whether, after the lumber had been manufactured, the mortgagee could have maintained an action of detinue against Hibbard in case he had refused to give it up, or could it have been replevied. I have no doubt the mortgagee could have done so. He might have applied to equity if he preferred having the specific lumber rather than damages. Mr. Wooddeson, in his Lectures, vol. iii. page 50, says, "If there be an apprehension of the specific chattel being defaced, as a curious piece of antiquity, or of its being transferred by sale, an injunction obtained in a court of equity is more expeditiously and effectually remedial than this action of detinue." Wood v. Rowcliffe (8 Jur. 771) shews that the remedy in equity is not confined to articles possessing any peculiar or intrinsic value. Our replevin statute gives that remedy in all cases where trover or trespass could be sustained. In the case before us the mortgagee of the logs had the legal title in them, and they were delivered to the mortgagor for the special purpose of being sawed. The mortgagor acquired no title, though, possibly he may have had a lien upon the lumber for the price of sawing it, but that would not entitle him to sell to the plaintiffs ; and though he did sell, it would not confer title.—See Baily v. Fermor (9 Price 262), Scott v. Newington (1 M. & Rob. 252). These positions imposed upon the defendant the burthen of proof that the lumber claimed by the plaintiffs was manufactured from the identical logs mortgaged, and upon this part of the case we do not feel satisfied with the verdict. We could not interfere, however, upon the affidavit of the plaintiffs' attorney that he can give better evidence that the lumber was in truth manufactured from other logs than those mortgaged. When a new trial is asked for upon the ground of newly discovered evidence, the evidence should be specifically shewn in order that the court may judge whether it may affect the verdict, and the opposite party may have an oppurtunity of replying to it. This case, however, upon the evidence given at the trial, renders it proper that it should receive the consideration of another jury ; for if it be true that the lumber in question was in fact manufactured from other logs than those mortgaged, then Hibbard has acted fairly enough to the plaintiffs, though his conduct has been dishonest as respects the other parties. There was considerable discrepancy between the witnesses as to the time when this quantity of lumber came to the defendant's possession, and the jury probably were guided a good deal by a view of the case resulting from what they considered to be the truth in that respect. We grant a new trial on payment of costs.

Rule absolute.

RUTTAN, SHERIFF, V. SHORT ET AL.

Repelvin under 14 & 15 Vic. ch. 64—Value of goods, how to be ascertained.

Goods seized under an execution in the hands of the debtor were replevied, under 14 & 15 Vic. ch. 64, by S. claiming under an assignment from such debtor. S failed in the action of replevin; and in this suit, brought by the sheriff on the replevin bond the defendants suffered judgment by default, and a verdict was rendered for the penalty. The jury having found at the trial the value of the goods, the court ordered proceedings to be stayed on payment of such value into court, together with the costs. *Quære*, as to the proper method of ascertaining the value.

This was an action upon a replevin bond. The defendants allowed judgment to go by default.

The declaration stated that on the 5th of May, 1853, the defendant Short sued out a writ of replevin, and thereupon Short, and Henry Fowlds and Thomas Scott, on the 5th of May, 1853, gave a bond jointly and severally with David Brodie, one of the coroners of the county, in the penalty of £1500, with a condition that if defendant Short should prosecute his suit against the plaintiff with effect for taking certain timber, then the bond should be void. It was alleged that the defendant Short did not prosecute his suit with effect, whereby the bond became forfeited, and the coroner Brodie assigned it to the plaintiff. Two of the parties, Short and Scott, were sued in this action without Fowlds.

Damages were assessed at the assizes held at Peterborough at £1500, the penalty of the bond.

In order to determine the amount for which the plaintiff would be entitled to obtain judgment, evidence was given to the jury of the value of the timber replevied, and also as to the amount of the debt due upon the execution which the plaintiff had in his hands.

The jury found that the value of the timber was £584 5s. 8d., and that the amount due upon the execution which the plaintiff had, to satisfy which the timber had been seized, was £277 10s. 5d.

Wilson, Q.C., obtained a rule to shew cause why the judgment should not be arrested, or why the assessment of damages should not be set aside, because no breaches had been suggested on the record, or because the actual damages were not assessed; or why the plaintiff should not be restrained from levying or proceeding for more than the actual damage sustained by the plaintiff, or why the damages should not be reduced to such sum as the court might direct, pursuant to the leave reserved.

Eccles shewed cause, and cited 1 Saund. 291 ; Mills v. McBride, 10 U. C. R. 145.

Armour supported the rule, citing Short v. Ruttan, 12 U. C. R. 79 ; Ward v. Henley, 1 Y. & J. 285 ; Hunt v. Round, 2 Dowl. 558.

ROBINSON, C.J., delivered the jndgment of the court.

We think this declaration should have more properly stated that the plaintiff in the original action did not make a return of the goods, as well as that he did not prosecute his action with effect, as in Chitty's Forms (Ch. Plg. II. 328 note *n*), but it is not necessary to assign default in both. There is no reason why we should arrest the judgment on that ground. The declaration is correct enough, and the judgment should be for the penalty. The defendants' course was (and is) to move to stay proceedings, on payment into court of the value of the goods and costs. The difficulty is, how that value is to be fixed.

We have no doubt that if this were an action on a replevin bond, taken after a distress for rent, the proceedings should be stayed on payment of the rent due, if the goods were of greater value, together with the costs of the action ; or on payment of the value of the goods according to the appraisement, when the rent exceeded it.

But we have to consider that this is not such a case, but one brought under our statute 14 & 15 Vic. ch. 64, in consequence of a dispute about the property in goods, seized by the defendant as sheriff, under a *Fi. Fa.,* at the suit of one James Waters, against one Thomas Waters, who—it was contended by this plaintiff Short—had before transferred the property in the same goods to him, on account of money advanced to him.

The case in this court of Short v. Ruttan (12 U. C. R. 79) states the circumstances of the seizure by the sheriff and the subsequent claim. The sum directed to be levied under the *Fi. Fa.* was £184 17s. 9d. Short's claim, and his interest in the goods, were of course limited to that; but the goods must have been of much greater value, we may suppose worth as much as £500, for our statute requires that the bond to be taken in cases under that act should be in a penalty to the amount of three times the value of the goods, and not double, as in cases after distress for rent. The difference between a replevin under ordinary circumstances, however, and the present case, is apparent. Here the goods were not taken out of a tenant's possession by a landlord, who could have no pretence for an objection against their being returned to him after the rent was satisfied; but they were taken out of the possession of Thomas Waters, the execution debtor, and Short claims them all as being his by title derived from Waters.

If they had been taken by the sheriff out of Short's possession, then when the execution against Waters should be satisfied, there could be no objection to the goods being restored to him, for then the object of the execution would have been attained; and as to all beyond that, matters would be left in the state in which the sheriff found them.

But here, Short, claiming a property in £500 worth of goods, as it seems, has had them all put in his possession by this legal proceeding. As between him and Thomas Waters, from whom they were taken, that may be perfectly just and legal, for the assignment or mortgage given to him by Thomas Waters, though void as against the judgment creditor, for the reasons given in the case of Short v. Ruttan, may have been binding, as between Short and Thomas Waters, to the full extent.

Still the event of the suit of Short v. Ruttan cannot be said to have settled that point, for Thomas Waters was no party to that action, and we must take care that he is not injured by the proceeding in the replevin.

It seems to us that we cannot, in such a case, relieve the obligors in the replevin bond upon any other terms than their restoring the goods or paying their appraised value to the sheriff, or rather, we should say, their value as sworn to by the plaintiff Short, for that seems to be the only test of value prescribed by the statute 14 & 15 Vic. ch. 64. And this, it must be confessed, rests the case upon an unsatisfactory footing, for the person from whom the goods were taken, ought not to be bound by the valuation of the person who claims them as his. What we should say rather, is, that there can be no propriety in stopping the action on the bond, unless that at least is done,—that is, all the goods restored, if they are forthcoming, or the value as sworn to by Short himself, if they are not forthcoming. And I confess I do not see how justice can be fully secured in such cases under our statute, otherwise than by allowing the case to go before a jury, to assess the value of the goods. If the bond had been assigned, and were sued in the name of the person from whom the goods were taken, then the recovery in such a case would put an end to the proceeding.

Where the sheriff sues on the bond, as in this case, he would hold the money recovered to the use of the execution debtor, from whom he had taken the goods. If there had been an appraisement, then we think we might stay proceedings, on paying such an appraised value.

What we have said is intended to apply to such cases generally. It seems that, in the present case, we are fortunately free from any difficulty as regards the value of the goods, for that has been found by the jury; and in order, we suppose, that we might take the value so found as the ground of any order which we might think it right to make. Upon paying that value into court, with the costs of this action, we think this action should be stayed, and a rule may issue to that effect (a).

As to the objection that the declaration is bad, as being against two only of three obligors jointly and severally liable, the case of The City of Toronto v. Coulter et al., 8 U. C. R. 133, is in point against that objection.

(a) See Gingell v. Turnbull, 3 Bing. N. C. 881 ; Miers v. Lockwood 9 Dowl. 975 ; Branscombe v. Scarbrough, 6 Q. B. 13.

GILDERSLEEVE V. BONTER ET AL.

Collision of steamers—Plaintiff not provided with lights, as required by 14 & 15. *Vic. ch.* 126, *sec.* 1—*Effect of such neglect under sec.* 11.

Case for injury caused by a collision. It appeared that the plaintiff's steamer had only one of the lights required by the statute, which was not seen by defendants, and that the defendants' steamer was properly provided with lights which were discerned in good time. The learned judge stated to the jury that he had no strong impression of the right on either side, and left it to them to say upon all the evidence, who was to blame for the accident. A verdict was found for the plaintiff.

Held, That sufficient weight had not been given to the fact that the plaintiff's boat was without the lights required by the statute; that the evidence tended to shew the accident to be in some degree attributable to such default; and that a new trial should be had to determine whether it was so or not, for if it were, the act would be conclusive against the plaintiff's recovery.

This was an action on the case for injuries done to the plaintiff's steamer the *Canadian,* by the defendants' steamer the *Novelty,* on the night of the 26th of April, 1854, in the Bay of Quinté.

At the trial before *Richards, J.,* at the last assizes held at Kingston, the facts appeared to be these :—The steamer *Canadian* was on her trip down the bay, loaded with freight and passengers, and the steamer *Novelty* was going up the bay with passengers. The night was dark and stormy, with rain at intervals, and the collision happened nearly half way between what is called Finkle's Point and the wharf at Fredericksburg. A great deal of conflicting evidence was adduced as to who was in fault. On the part of the plaintiff, it was alleged that the defendants' steamer must have crossed the bay from the south side to the north side, when the plaintiff's steamer was pursuing the usual channel down the bay, and not more than a hundred yards from the shore, and that the *Novelty* struck the *Canadian,* stem on, on the starboard side of the *Canadian,* about forty feet from the bow, coming towards her at right angles. The defendants asserted that the *Novelty* was navigated from Amherst Island across, as if intending to call at Bath, but the captain changing his mind as to calling there, then kept on in the usual course on the north shore; passing Finkle's point; and that the *Canadian,* instead of keeping to the right, crossed the track of the *Novelty,* and so caused the collision. Thus it appeared the *Canadian* was making towards Finkle's Point, which is a mile above Bath, in the usual course, if the plaintiff's witnesses were right; and the *Novelty* had already made Finkle's Point and passed it in the usual course upwards from Bath, if the defendants' witnesses were right. Each set of the witnesses, who were employed on the different boats, asserted that everything was rightly conducted and managed on the boat to which they respectively belonged. It is unnecessary to report this part of the evidence in full. The question on which the case turned on the argument was, whether either or both were to blame in respect of being properly provided with lights, in whose favor the weight of evidence was on this point, and what effect it should have in the consideration of the case.

It appeared very clearly that after the *Canadian* left Picton, lights were put up, but they went out. The lamp at the mast head went out from bad oil, and was taken down by the captain's orders. It was said that the lamp was lighted and placed on the deck of the vessel, but it did not appear whether it continued burning till the collision happened. A red light and a green light were carried. The red light went out also, and the captain said he put his hand lantern in its place about twenty minutes before the collision but no one stated whether it was burning at the time of the accident. No positive testimony was given as respected the green light, whether it went out or continued to burn, though the captain stated it was burning at the time of the collision. It was proved by several passengers who were on board of the *Canadian*, that they saw no lights on board the *Canadian* at the time of the collision. It was proved by those on board the *Novelty* that they saw no lights, and the first they knew of the approach of a steamer was hearing her paddle-wheels and seeing the sparks from the chimney. With regard to the *Novelty*, it was proved that her lights were put up, and those in the management of her stated that her lights continued in proper order all the time. It was also proved by passengers on the *Canadian*, that they saw the lights of the *Novelty* as she came up to the other boat, that is, at the time of the collision. Those in management of the *Canadian* said they did not see the *Novelty's* lights until it was too late to avoid a collision.

With respect to the management of the two boats, the evidence shewed these facts :—A few minutes after the *Canadian* left Fredericksburg, the captain perceived a light near Amherst Island, distant about four or five miles, which was taken for a schooner's light, not seeing any red or green light.   The *Canadian* was steered for it, intending to pass to the right, and ran, it was said, some seventy or eighty rods, when they thought, as it was a moving light, it must be a steamer or propellor going out at the upper gap, and consequently the *Canadian* altered her course and put back for the north shore.   The captain then went below, and was absent fifteen or twenty minutes, when he came on deck, and the collision happened immediately after.   The one defendant was captain of his own boat; and the other defendant was the mate ; but the evidence of others on board shewed that they left Kingston between eleven and twelve o'clock in the day, and were detained by fog, and also by the boiler springing a leak, which had to be repaired, so that it was late in the evening when the *Novelty* left Amherst Island.   When the boat left Amherst Island she was steered for Bath ; but when they crossed the bay they did not call at Bath, but went up, as they said, the usual track on the north shore.

The jury found for the plaintiff and £412 damages.

Richards (with whom was *O'Reilly*) obtained a rule to shew cause why the verdict should not be set aside, on the ground that it was contrary to law and evidence, and against the weight of evidence and the judge's charge.   Affidavits of both defendants were filed upon obtaining the rule.

Vankoughnet, Q. C., and *Draper,* shewed cause, and filed affidavits in reply.   They cited Wilson v. Stephenson, 2 Price, 282 ; Hankey v. Trotman, 1 W. Bl. 1 ; Lake v. Deer, 1 Jur. 983 ; Swain v. Hall, 3 Wills. 45 ; Deade v. Hancock, 13¾ Price, 226.

O'Reilly supported the rule.

ROBINSON, C. J.—I have gone very carefully, and more than once, over the whole of the evidence in this case.

In a very late case in the Court of Common Pleas in England, The General Steam Navigation Company v.

Morrison (13 C. B. 581), the consequence to the owner of a vessel not carrying the lights required by law, in rendering them liable to an action at the suit of the party injured by the collision, without proof that the accident happened from that particular cause, is a good deal discussed. The *case* was before the court upon a demurrer to the declaration, which sets out the admiralty direction issued under the authority of an Act of Parliament prescribing what lights should be carried, and acts out also the clause in the statute which provides that in case of default the master or other person having charge of any vessel, or the owner of such vessel, *if it appears* that he was in fault, shall, for each occasion upon which such regulations are infringed, forfeit and pay a sum not exceeding £20. The action was against the owner, not the master. The declaration then stated the position in which the respective vessels were, the plaintiff's vessel going down the river Thames at night, and the defendant's vessel lying at anchor in the roadstead or fair way; that it was the duty of the servants of the defendant to exhibit on their vessel such lights (specifying them as the admiralty regulations required; that not regarding that duty, they neglected to exhibit them, and that in consequence thereof the plaintiff's vessel, while she was proceeding down the roadstead or fair way, *by and through* the carelessness and neglect of the servants of the defendant in not exhibiting the night light at the masthead of the vessel, of the defendant, ran foul of and struck the vessel of the defendant, and was greatly broken and damaged, &c.

This was demurred to as stating no sufficient cause of action, and the court determined in favor of the defendant.

They said that it was an attempt to found an action against the owner upon the admiralty regulation, which imposed merely a penalty of £20 on the master as for an offence, or the owner, if it should appear that he was in fault, and they said that, for all that appeared in the declaration, the defendant's vessel might have been covered with lights, though she had not the particular light which the regulations required; and that it might have been great negligence on the plaintiff's part, and not the want of lights which occasioned the injury. I confess I am unable to perceive the reasonableness of this decision, which has at any rate, however, rather an indirect than a direct bearing upon the case before us. That declaration, it is true, did not set out that other regulation of the imperial statute which was cited in the argument, and is stated to be as follows : "That in case any damage to person or property be sustained in consequence of the non-observance of the said rules, the same should in all courts of justice be deemed, in the absence of proof to the contrary, to have been occasioned by the wilful default of the said *master*, or other person having the charge of such vessel : and such master or other person shall, unless it appears to the court before which the case is tried that the circumstances of the case were such as to justify a departure from the rule, be subject in all proceedings, whether civil or criminal, to the legal consequences of such default." There was probably no necessity for the plaintiffs to set out this provision of the statute in their declaration, for it was part of the public law applicable in all such cases, which the court would be bound judicially to notice ; and if there were circumstances (or could be) as regarded the regulation of carrying lights, which would justify a departure from the rule, it would seem that it might be left to the defendant to state them in a plea, or at least to show them upon the trial. But what I am unable to understand in that case is, that when the plaintiffs—having set out the duty incumbent upon the defendants' servants, for whom the defendant was responsible, *civiliter* at all events, and their disregard of that duty —complained *that through the carelessness and neglect* of the defendant's servants in not complying with the regulation, the collision took place, the court did not seem to think that they stated a sufficient cause of action.

The plea of not guilty to such a declaration would surely, as it seems to me, leave the onus of it upon the plaintiffs to prove what they had asserted—namely, that through the carelessness and neglect which they complained of the injury occurred ; for in every action of this kind, I take it, the plaintiff is bound to prove an injury of the nature he complains of, and occasioned by the breach of duty which he

charges upon the defendant. And I should have supposed
that on the trial of the case, upon such a declaration, with
the general issue pleaded, if it had been proved (as it very
possible might have been) that the collision did not happen
in consequence of the defendant not having the regulation
light, but from some gross negligence of the plaintiffs—as,
for instance, if it had been shewn, as the court suggest, that
the defendant's vessel, though it had not the proper lights,
was in fact covered with lights—then it would have been
for the jury to determine, as in all such cases, whether the
negligence complained of was the cause of the injury, and
they might probably, I should think, have found that it
was not.

But however this may be, the case between these parties
does not arise upon the sufficiency of the declaration upon
a demurrer, nor does the question of the consequence of not
exhibiting the proper light arise in the same manner. This
plaintiff does not found his action upon a breach of that
regulation, but upon the negligence of the defendant's
servants in running against his vessel. It is the defendant
that in this case objects to the plaintiff's right to recover,
upon the ground of his own negligence in not keeping up
lights having led to the collision, and that answer to the
action must be allowed to be always open to the parties
upon the general issue.

Then, again, our statute is in different terms from the
English statute, if the latter be correctly cited in the case
referred to, which I assume, it is, for it provides (14 & 15
Vic. ch. 126; sec. 11.) "That if any damage to any person or
property shall be sustained in consequence of the non-
observance of any of the provisions contained in this act, the
same shall in all courts of justice be deemed, in the absence
of proof to the contrary, to have been caused by the wilful
default of the master or other person having charge of such
steamboat, schooner, or other vessel as aforesaid ; and *the
owner* thereof in all *civil proceedings*, and such master or
other person in all proceedings, whether civil or criminal,
shall be subject to the legal consequences of such default."

Our enactment is express that the *owner* of the vessel in

default shall in all civil proceedings be subject to the legal consequences of the default; in other words, be subject to be held to have occasioned the collision by his wilful default unless he shews, the contrary; or, in the very words of the act, "in the absence of proof to the contrary;" by which I take it to be meant, unless it is shewn that the collision arose from other causes, which might more easily be the case in regard to the breach of some other regulations than of this.

I think it is clear that under our statute unless the defendant's vessel at the time of the collision was carrying the lights which under the circumstances she ought to have carried, the plaintiff shews a *primâ facie* case of negligence occasioning the collision, unless in the evidence given on one side or the other, it can be satisfactorily seen that the collision arose from some cause quite independent of the want of the proper lights; and that the same inference, subject to the same qualification, lies against a plaintiff where the default in not keeping up the proper lights is on his side. It will be such negligence as must prevent his recovery; by shewing that he was himself in fault, unless he has relieved himself from the difficulty by shewing that it could have had no influence in occasioning the collision.

The facts of this case having been particularly stated by my brother Burns from the notes of the trial, I will only say shortly that the evidence seemed to lead to this conclusion : that the boats were navigating the Bay of Quinté in a dark night, and where, the water being deep near the north shore, on which the touching ports lie, it is usual under such circumstances for boats going either up or down to keep near the land, in order that they may the better discern their proper course; that the defendants' vessel was coming up from Kingston to Picton, and the plaintiff's going down; and that it cannot be pronounced certainly from the evidence, because on that point the evidence was very conflicting, whether the defendants' vessel, which had touched as is usual, at Amherst Island had crossed over to the north shore so far as to be in the ordinary track or nearly so, of steam vessels bound up the bay which have passed Bath. If she were in that track, or nearly so, then, independently of any question about lights, the plaintiff must have been clearly wrong in the course he took for his own witnesses all state that his vessel kept as close to the main land, which was on his left, going down, as he dare do and perhaps within about three hundred feet of it; whereas if the vessels were approaching each other from opposite directions and so nearly in the same line that the rule ought to be observed which is given in our statute 7 Wm. IV. ch. 22, sec. 4, as to each vessel taking the right hand side of the channel, nothing could be more contrary to the rule than for the plaintiff to have hugged the north shore, for by that means he not only did not observe the rule himself, but made it impossible for the defendants to do so.

In regard to this point whether the position of the vessels as they were approaching each other was at any time such as to call for the observance of this rule—the evidence is perhaps too conflicting to admit of certainty one way or the other, though I confess I have been strongly impressed with some parts of the evidence which seem to make it improbable that the defendants' vessel in coming up the bay was so wholly out of the usual track—that is, out of the line of the other vessel's course—as to have made it safe and right to pay no attention to the rule about passing. The plaintiff maintains that the boats were not meeting each other; the defendants maintain that they were. Different people may well estimate the weight of evidence on this point differently, and where the testimony cannot be said to prove satisfactorily what the truth is, the jury must be left to settle the doubt as they best can. But I confess that what does seem to me to weaken the plaintiff's case a good deal upon this point is the fact, that after the master of his vessel saw the light of the other he changed his course for some time in order to pass on the outside as the rule under the circumstances required, but afterwards came in again and kept as near to the shore— that is, as far to *his left*—as he could.

It might be difficult for those navigating the other vessel in a dark night to know what to make of these uncertain movements. Of course, if it had been light, and they could see the land quite clearly so as to be able to judge of the distance the plaintiff's vessel was from it, and to see plainly and in time that there was no room for their vessel to pass up to the right of him, it would have been very reckless folly on the defendants' part to persist in attempting to pass between the plaintiff and the land. He would in such a case naturally keep out; though if he shewed in time, while he was approaching, that he intended to observe the rule, the defendants undoubtedly should have turned to the right, so as to have allowed him room to do so.

But instead of having daylight, they had a dark night in which to make their way, and that made it highly important that the proper lights should have been exhibited; because if the plaintiff's vessel had carried such lights they would undoubtedly have enabled the defendants' people to see in good time what was approaching, and to judge better of the course and movements of the plaintiff's boat.

Our statute requires (sec. 1) that each steamer should have had "a white light on the flagstaff aft, a bright white light on the foremast head, a green light on the starboard bow, and a red light on the port bow."

The evidence shewed that the plaintiff's boat had only one of these lights, while the defendants' boat, if it was not perfectly lighted according to the regulations came very much nearer to a full compliance with the rule, and that in fact the lights of his steamer were plainly discerned and in good time, and were such lights as the law required, and in their proper stations.

It appears to me that upon the evidence given no one could venture upon due consideration of such a case to say that the disaster was not attributable in any degree to the want of proper lights on the plaintiff's vessel; and if it was then the principle of the common law is opposed to his recovery, and the statute is in my opinion conclusive against it.

There ought, I think, to be a new trial with costs to abide the event; for it appears to me that the learned judge in expressing that he had no strong impression of the right one way or the other, failed to give sufficient weight to the fact, which appears to me to have been satisfactorily made out, that the plaintiff's boat was coming up the channel in a dark

3 r—VOL. XII. Q.B.

night without the lights required by the statute, and indeed very ill provided with lights that could have been relied on for giving notice of an approaching steamer.

It is to be borne in mind that since the law has required peculiar lights and peculiarly disposed to be kept up in steamers, when anything is seen on the water wholly wanting in lights of that description the conclusion would be naturally formed that it was not a steamer, and less activity and care would be used in keeping out of the way than there would have been if no such regulation had been established; and when two steamers approach each other at speed there is little time allowed to correct false impressions.

The late case of the *Aliwal,* before the Court of Admiralty in England (18 Jur. 296), and others that might be cited shew how decisive a degree of importance has been attached in the courts in England to the neglect to keep up the proper lights. My conviction is, that there would not be the slightest hesitation there in holding that under the circumstances established beyond contradiction in this case, the plaintiff could not recover.

BURNS, J.—The affidavits do not alter or throw any further light upon the facts disclosed at the trial. The learned judge reports that he had not any decided opinion in favour of either party, but left it to the jury to determine as a fact who was to blame on the occasion. The provision in our statute 14 & 15 Vic. ch. 126, sec. 11, is similar to that contained in the imperial act 14 & 15 Vic. ch. 79. Though it be true that the injured vessel would not be deprived of compensation simply because at the time of the accident she had been guilty of an infringement of the law provided that the absence of lights did not in any way contribute to the accident; yet the question here is, whether the weight of evidence does not shew that however well managed the plaintiff's steamer may have been, and though in her proper course, the accident was mainly attributable either to the want of lights upon the *Canadian* or to their own fault in not keeping a proper look out. See Morrison v. the General Steam Navigation Company (8 Ex. 733), the cross action of

The General Steam Navigation Company v. Morrison (22 L. J., C. P., 178, 13 C. B. 581, 20 Eng. Rep. 267, S. C. The Panther, 17 Jur. 1037, The Rob Roy (3 Rob. Ad. 191).

There is no doubt the defendants' vessel caused the injury complained of; and the only question is, whether under the circumstances the plaintiff's vessel was provided as the law requires; and if not, whether the accident is to be traced to that cause, and whether the plaintiff's vessel was so navigated that she did not contribute to the injury. The weight of evidence shews clearly that the *Canadian* was deficient in the lights required by law. It was the duty of the captain to see that his lights were properly trimmed and burning. Now it is admitted that the masthead light was taken down, and that the oil they were using was bad, and a difficulty was experienced in keeping the red light in. Were there then sufficient lights or other sufficient warnings to guard the *Novelty* against the approaching danger? Three considerations present themselves to the mind for discussion as to how far those in charge of the *Canadian* are blameless. 1st. The captain of the *Canadian* admits that shortly after leaving Fredericksburg he saw a light, which he supposed to be that of a steamer or propeller going out at the Upper Gap. That light when first seen was in the direction of Amherst Island, distant four or five miles. The captain did not wait on deck to see what that light ultimately proved to be, or what became of it. He went below, and was absent fifteen or twenty minutes, he says, and on returning to the deck the collision immediately occurred. Was that light which was seen the light of the *Novelty?* It would rather appear from the captain's examination he thought so, but he says he thought she was out of her course. If so, it proves that she was not in fault in respect of lights, and before the two vessels struck each other the *Novelty's* lights were seen from the *Canadian*. If the *Canadian* carried lights which could be seen, it would then go to prove that the *Novelty* might have been steered by those lights, but in that case it must be supposed that she mistook those lights for some other. This, however, is not pretended, for both steamers were above Findle's Point, where it is not pretended there were lights that might deceive, and both sides say they were well acquainted with the land. If the *Canadian's* lights could not be seen, then the accident might have occurred as suggested by the defendants. The evidence of the mate of the *Canadian* puts out of doubt whether the light seen was in truth that of the *Novelty*, for he says, after the *Canadian* had laid her course down the bay, on returning from her attempt to go to the right, he saw the *Novelty* haul her course up the bay straighter, and he watched her until he thought she would be clear of them. This proves that the *Novelty* was seen for some four or five miles before the collision happened. 2. It is admitted that on seeing the light before mentioned the *Canadian* altered her course, intending to pass to the right of the light, but supposing it was a steamer going out at the Upper Gap, after going a short distance she returned to the course she had been on before. When did this occur? The captain of the *Canadian* says it was about twenty minutes before the collision. If it were so long as that, one can scarcely imagine that such deviation would have produced the collision, and particularly if the light which was seen was on the south side of the bay. The time, however, is not accurately spoken of, but only guessed at. It was shewn also that the light was not lost sight of, though the *Canadian* turned back to the north shore, and the mate says that he thought the *Novelty*—that is, the vessel with the light so seen—would go clear of them. If the time were much shorter than spoken of, and that light was the *Novelty's* light, which it appears it was, then the fact of the *Canadian* attempting to go to the right, and afterwards altering her course and coming back to the land, supposing the time in doing this just about sufficient to bring the two vessels together, the accident would then have occurred in the way suggested by the defendants. 3rd. Admitting the *Canadian* not to have had such lights as the law required. did the accident arise from that cause, or did that contribute towards it if she had such lights as could be seen and were seen, as the *Novelty's* lights appear to have been, then, assuming that the *Canadian* was right in all respects, the collision could not have been the result of accident, but must have been wilful. If, however, she had not lights that could be distinguished, and wavered in her course, first attempting to go to the right and then changing her course to take the other side, if there was not time to accomplish this, and supposing the *Canadian* not visible from the *Novelty* in time, such alteration is likely to have produced the very result which did happen.

These points induce me to think that sufficient consideration has not been given by the jury to the question how far the plaintiff has contributed to his own loss, either by an omission to do what the law requires, by an act of commission in the navigation of the steamer; and I think it is proper the matter should undergo another investigation.

Rule absolute.

WOODRUFF V. WALLING.

*Proof of foreign judgment—*13 & 14 *Vic. ch.* 19, *sec.* 1.

To prove a judgment of the Supreme Court of the State of New York held at Watertown, in the county of Jefferson, a copy of the roll was produced certified by the *county clerk* under the seal *of the county*—*Held*, insufficient.

DEBT on a judgment of the Supreme Court of the State of New York, held at Watertown, in and for the county of Jefferson, on the 5th of November, 1853. 2nd count for interest.

Pleas—1st, That there is not any record of the supposed recovery remaining in the said Supreme Court of the State of New York. 2nd. Payment, to the first count; and 3rd, *nunquam indebitatus* to the last count.

Replication to the first plea, that there is a record remaining in the said Supreme Court of the State of New York. Issue taken on the other pleas.

At the trial, before *Richards, J.*, at the last assizes held at Bellevile, the proof of the judgment was by a copy, certified as follows :

" State of New York,
" Jefferson County Clerk's Office.

"I, John L. Marsh, clerk of said county, do hereby certify that, on examining the files of judgment rolls remaining in this office, I find a certain judgment roll under date of Nov.

5, 1853, at 2½ p. m., in the words, figures, and characters following, to wit (setting out what purports to be a judgment roll). And I further certify that I have compared the foregoing copy with the original judgment roll aforesaid, and that the same is a correct transcript therefrom of the whole of said original. In testimony whereof I have hereunto subscribed my name, and affixed the seal of the said county, this 6th day of April, in the year 1854.

(Signed)   " JNO. L. MARSH, Clerk."

It was objected that the judgment was not properly authenticated or proved according to our statute ; but the learned judge overruled the objection, and the plaintiff had a verdict.

Hagarty, Q. C., obtained a rule to shew cause why the verdict should not be set aside without costs, on the law and evidence, and for misdirection, and the reception of improper evidence.

Wilson, Q. C., shewed cause, and cited 13 & 14 Vic. ch. 19, sec. 1 ; Adamthwaite v. Synge, 4 Camp. 372.

BURNS, J., delivered the judgment of the court.

There can be no doubt that the defendant is entitled to succeed upon the objection taken. The statute 13 & 14 Vic. ch. 19, sec. 1, enacts, that any judgment in any court of record in the United States, or of any State of the United States of America, shall and may be proved in any suit, action or proceeding, either in law or equity in Upper Canada, in which proof of any such judgment shall be necessary, by an exemplification of the same under the seal of the said courts respectively, without any proof of the authenticity of such seal, or other proof whatever, in the same manner as any judgment of any of the superior courts of common law or equity in Upper Canada is proved by an exemplification thereof in any proceeding in the said last mentioned courts respectively.

In this case the copy is not authenticated under the seal of the court, but under the seal of the county. It may be that the seal of the county is by their law also the seal of the court, and it may be that the clerk of the county is also by virtue thereof the clerk of the Supreme Court. and properly has the custody of the records of the court. If the certificate had come from a person purporting to be the officer of the court, and under a seal purporting to be the seal of the court, then our statute makes that evidence without further proof. In this case, however, we must, in order to admit the judgment to be proved in the way offered, assume that the clerk of the county is the proper person to have the custody of the judgment rolls of the supreme court of the state for that county, and we must also assume that the county seal is the seal of the court. In the absence of proof as to how matters in respect of judicial proceedings are conducted and carried on in foreign states, we must assume them to be conducted similarly to our own. The statute says that such judgments are to be proved in the same manner as exemplifications from our own courts would be proved, and that would be under the seal of the court, certified by the officer of the court. Jefferson county may have a seal as a municipal corporation, similar to our own counties; and the clerk of the county may be similar to our own clerks of counties. We cannot assume, because he says he has the original judgment roll, that he has it legally in his custody; and if he had it legally, still we cannot assume that the county seal is properly the seal of the court. The clerk of the county may perhaps be properly entrusted with the custody of the judgment rolls of that county, and yet the court have its own seal. The presumption would rather be that it is so. The rule should be made absolute without costs.

Rule absolute.

McDONALD v. McHUGH AND WIFE, ADMINISTRATRIX
OF JOHN KELLY.

A new trial will not be granted for a misdirection as to the right to begin, unless it appears that injustice may have been occasioned by it.

ASSUMPSIT on common counts.

Pleas.—As to £21, part of the demand, payment, and set off; to the residue, non-assumpsit.

The plaintiff, by her particulars, claimed for wages due to her by the deceased, Kelly, £30, and gave credit for £9, claiming only a balance of £21. The defendants by their pleas set up payment of that amount, and the parties went to trial upon the issue of non-assumpsit as to the residue above £21 of the moneys claimed in the declaration (which was £25.) The defendants at the trial insisted that, as the plaintiff had, by her particulars delivered, narrowed her demand to £21, she could claim no more at the trial, and, consequently, that the only questions of fact to be tried were, whether the defendants' pleas, by which they had answered £21 of the demand, were true or not. They insisted therefore that they were entitled to begin at the trial. The learned judge ruled otherwise, and, a verdict having been found for the plaintiff, a new trial was moved for by *Hallinan* on account of that ruling.

ROBINSON, C. J., delivered the judgment of the court.

The courts in England have in several cases expressed regret that the ruling of the judge at Nisi Prius, in regard to which party had the right to begin, should ever have been made the ground of granting a new trial ; and after some fluctuation the practice seems to have settled down in this—that the court in banc. may and will take it as a ground if they find that the decision come to by the learned judge at the trial was certainly wrong, and if they can see that it may have had an important effect to the prejudice of the party against whom he decided. We have declined in this court in several cases to grant a new trial upon such an objection, and should at any rate not make a precedent in this case, where the amount of the verdict is small, and when we have no reason to suppose that any injustice has been occasioned by it.

Rule refused *(a)*.

(a) See Smart v. Rayner, 6 C. & P. 721 ; Thwaites v. Sainsbury, 5 C. & P. 69 ; Rex v. Yeates, 1 C & P. 323 ; Cooper v. Wakley, 3 C. & P. 474 ; Cotton v. James, 3 C. P. 505 ; Curtis v. Wheeler, 4 C. & P. 196 ; Williams v. Thomas, 4 C. & P. 234 ; Turberville v. Patrick, 4 C. & P. 557 ; Chapman v. Rawson, 8 Q. B. 673 ; Morris v. Lotan, 1 M. & Rob. 283 ; Ashby v. Bates, 15 M & W. 589 ; Doe dem. Bather v. Brayne. 5 C. B. 655 ; Bird v. Higginson, 2 A. & E. 160 ; Pontifex v. Jolly, 9 C. & P. 202 ; Aston v. Perkes, 9 C. & P. 231 ; Huckman v. Fernie, 3 M. & W. 505 ; Chapman v. Emden, 9 C. & P. 712 ; Doe Dem. Worcester Trustees v. Rowlands, 9 C. & P. 734—736, note a ; Burwell v. Nicholson, 1 M. & R. 304 ; Booth v. Millns, 15 M. & W. 669.

FORD V. M'GOEY.

Statute of Limitations—Writs not properly continued—12 Vic. ch. 63, sec. 25.

In an action on a promissory note, due 4th September, 1847, the original
writ issued on the 15th April, 1853, and was returned *non est inventus*, and
filed 3rd September, 1853. On the same day an alias writ was issued,
which was also returned *non est inventus*, but was not filed until the 12th
May, 1854 ; nor was any memorandum endorsed on it specifying the date
of the first writ. A pluries issued on 12th May, and was served on 31st
July. *Plea*, the Statute of Limitations.
Held, that the directions of the 12 Vic. ch. 63, sec. 25, not having been complied
with, the defendant was entitled to succeed.

ASSUMPSIT upon a promissory note.

Pleas 1st, *non fecit.* Then other pleas; and lastly, the
Statute of Limitations—that the cause of action did not
accrue at any time within six years next before the commencement of the suit.

Replication—that the action did accrue within six years.

The note was dated on the 1st of February, 1847, and
payable seven months after date.

The declaration stated that the defendant was summoned
by virtue of a writ issued on the 15th of April, 1853.

At the trial before *McLean, J.*, at the last assizes held at
Bytown, it was proved that the original writ of summons
issued on the 15th of April, 1853, and was returned *non est
inventus* by the Sheriff. The return of this writ was filed
in the Crown Office on the 3rd of September, 1853. On the
same day an *alias* writ of summons was issued, which was also
returned *non est inventus.* This writ was returned and filed
in the Crown Office on the 12th of May, 1854 ; and on the
same day a pluries writ was issued, which was served on the
defendant on the 31st of July.

The learned judge was of opinion that the action was
brought by the issuing of the first writ on the 15th of April,
1853, within six years from the accruing of the cause of
action, and therefore directed a verdict for the plaintiff with
leave for the defendant to move to enter a nonsuit or a verdict
for the defendant.

Wilson, Q. C., moved to enter a verdict for the defendant
on the plea of the Statute of Limitations, or a nonsuit, pur-

3 s—VOL. XII. Q. B.

suant to the leave reserved.   He cited Pratt v. Hawkins, 15
M. & W. 399 ; Higgs v. Mortimer 1 Ex. 711.

Helliwell shewed cause, and asked the court to modify the
rule, so that the plaintiff might amend his proceedings,
rather than that he should be barred.   He cited Higgins v.
Nichols, 7 Dowl, 551.

BURNS, J., delivered the judgment of the court.

The court cannot do anything which will assist the plaintiff
in any way.   The statute 12 Vic. ch. 63, sec. 25, enacts that
every writ of summons and capias may be continued by
alias and *pluries*, as the case may require, if any defendant
therein named may not have been served or arrested, "Provided always, that no first writ shall be available to prevent
the operation of any statute whereby the time for the commencement of any action may be limited, unless the defendant
shall be arrested thereon or served therewith ; unless such
writ, and every writ, if any, issued in continuation of a
preceding writ, shall be returned *non est inventus*, and
entered of record within one calendar month next after the
expiration thereof, including the day of such expiration and
unless every writ issued in continuation of a preceding writ
shall be issued within one calendar month after the expiration
of the preceding writ, and shall contain a memorandum
endorsed thereon, or subscribed thereto, specifying the day
of the date of the first writ."   Here the *alias* writ though
issued in time, is not indorsed as the statute directs, and
there is nothing upon it which shews the time of the issuing
of the first writ.   The *alias* writ was not returned within one
month after its expiration and the *pluries* writ was not issued
within one month after the expiration of the *alias* writ.
There is nothing upon the face of the *pluries*, or indorsed
thereon, to shew when the first writ issued.   It is incumbent
upon the plaintiff, on this issue, to shew that the suit was
regularly continued from the first process, otherwise the
commencement of the suit must be taken to be upon the
process upon which the defendant is served.   The words of our
statute are precisely similar to the English act, and the cases
cited for the defendant shew that, under the circumstances,

as shewn by the facts of this case, the plaintiff, must fail.
The rule should be made absolute to enter a verdict for the
defendant, upon the plea of the Statute of Limitations.

Rule absolute.

IN THE MATTER OF THE MUNICIPALITY OF THE TOWNSHIP
OF NORTH DUMFRIES AND THE MUNICIPAL COUNCIL OF
THE COUNTY OF WATERLOO.

*Township of North Dumfries—Exempted from debt for Guelph and Dundas
road—14 & 15 Vic. ch. 5, sec. 8.*

By the 14 & 15 Vic. ch. 5, the county of Waterloo is made to consist of
certain townships, including North Dumfries, which before formed part of
the county of Halton.   The 8th section provides that the townships
named, *in which North Dumfries is not included*, shall be responsible for
their share of the debt for building the Guelph and Dundas road.   This
debt had been incurred by the former district of Wellington, which embraced all the townships mentioned in sec. 8 except Dumfries.
Held, that the Municipal Council of Waterloo could not impose a rate on
Dumfries to pay such debt, the omission of that township in the 14 & 15
Vic, shewing clearly that it was not intended to be liable.

M. C. Cameron obtained a rule on the Municipal Council
of the county of Waterloo, to shew cause why a by-law,
number eight, passed by them on the 5th of October, 1853,
should not be quashed—

1st. Because it imposes upon all the municipalities compo-
sing the county of Waterloo, including the township of North
Dumfries, a rate for the payment of £3805, part of the debt
incurred by the former district of Wellington for the construction of the Guelph and Dundas road, being the amount awarded by the arbitrators appointed to determine the proportion
of the debt of the united counties of Wellington, Waterloo,
and Grey, on the separation of the county of Waterloo from
the union, to be paid by the county of Waterloo; whereas the
payment of the proportion of the debt for the construction
of the road to be borne by the county of Waterloo is
expressly imposed upon the townships of Waterloo, Wilmot,
Wellesley, and that part of the township of Woolwich not
included in the township of Pilkington, by the 8th section
of the provincial statute 14 & 15 Vic. ch. 5.

The by-law was passed "to provide for the debt due to the
united counties of Wellington and Grey, upon the disunion

therefrom." It recited that in contemplation of the separation of the county of Waterloo from the counties of Wellington and Grey it was, by an arbitration held under the 15th section of the act 12 Vic. ch. 78, on the 12th of January 1853, determined that the county of Waterloo, should in such separation be released from all debts then due by the united counties, except that portion of the debt incurred by the late district of Wellington for the construction of the Dundas and Guelph road, and imposed by the 8th section of 14 & 15 Vic. ch. 5, upon certain townships therein named, and forming a part of the county of Waterloo, in proportion to the respective assessments of the said townships for the year 1848, relatively to the corresponding assessments of other portions of the district of Wellington for that year, which was fixed by the arbitrators at £3809, to be paid by the county of Waterloo to the counties of Wellington and Grey, with interest to the time of the separation, as the debentures issued on account of the Guelph and Dundas road should mature, reciting the amounts and times for payment of the several debentures.

And in this by-law it was recited that it was desirable that a by-law should be passed to provide for the payment of the balance of the said £3809, in such sums as the same was required to be paid by the debentures, together with interest; and the sum which was to be paid in each year from 1854 to 1860 inclusive, was specified.

It then recited that the ratable property of the county of Waterloo for the year 1852 was £1,425,867, and imposed a special rate for each year, from 1854 to 1860 inclusive, for meeting the debt referred to as being imposed upon the county of Waterloo.

And it enacted that the by-law should take effect from the 15th of October, 1853; that there should be assessed *upon the whole ratable property within the county of Waterloo*, such special rate, over and above all other rates and taxes, to be applied in payment of the debt due by the county of Waterloo to the counties of Wellington and Grey.

McMichael shewed cause.   *Irving* supported the rule.
12 Vic. ch. 78, sec. 15; 14 & 15 Vic. ch. 5. secs, 6, 8;

12 Vic. ch, 81, sec. 41, subsec. 22, were referred to in the argument.

ROBINSON, C. J., delivered the judgment of the court.

By the Territorial Division Act, 14 & 15 Vic. ch. 5. the county of Waterloo is made to consist of the townships of North Dumfries, Waterloo, Wilmot, Woolwich, and Wellesley.

Before that act passed, the whole of the township of Dumfries formed part of the county of Halton ; and by the 8th section of that act it is provided "that the townships of Waterloo, Wilmot, Wellesley, and that portion of the present township of Woolwich not included in the new township of Pilkington, shall be responsible for their share of the debt incurred or to be incurred for the construction of the Guelph and Dundas road, in proportion to their respective assessments for 1848, relatively to the corresponding assessments of the other portions of the late district of Wellington for that year, and shall have a lien on the road for the amount of any payments they may be called on to make in consequence of such liability ; but any questions affecting the other debts of the said late district of Wellington, or the present county of Waterloo, or the new county of Wellington, shall be settled in the manner provided by this act and the said last recited acts in relation to similar cases."

The debt for the road had been incurred, by the district of Wellington as formerly constituted, which embraced Waterloo, Woolwich, Wilmot, and Wellesley, but not Dumfries, except for the single purpose of representation in the Assembly. Dumfries, therefore, was no party to that debt ; and the Legislature, by the clause which we have cited, evidently intended that it should not, by being made then for the first time to form a part of the county of Waterloo, be bound to contribute to this debt for which they were not before liable. They made therefore an express provision on the subject and upon the principle that *expressio unius, exclusio, est alterius,* we must understand that no liability was to attach to North Dumfries on account of this particular debt but only to the other townships named, which have all had a share in contracting the debt originally.

Then, the Legislature having made their intention clear, on what principle is it that such intention shall not prevail? North Dumfries, being now part of the county of Waterloo, is doubtless subject to the jurisdiction and action of the Municipal Council of Waterloo, for general purposes, as much as the other townships in that county ; but the Municipal Council cannot counteract, the provisions of the Provincial Parliament, and make this township subject to a burden from which Parliament has exempted it.   It may be truly said that the statute does not provide that North Dumfries shall be rated towards this debt, but only that the others shall.   It is clear, however, that the other townships were specified for the very purpose of shewing that North Dumfries was not to be charged.   And as to the argument that the Council could not impose a rate otherwise than upon every township, that no doubt is true as to rates imposed for general county purposes ; but the Legislature has made this an exception, and upon just grounds.   The townships named, and those only, are to bear their own share of the debt.

Rule absolute.

BROWN v. STUART.

Deed—Construction of—Condition void as repugnant to the premises.

The defendant claimed under a deed in fee, in which, after the habendum, was contained a proviso that the conveyance should be void and the estate revert to the grantor if the grantee should make default in performing the covenant thereinafter contained.   This covenant was, that the grantee should cultivate the land during the life of the grantor for his benefit.

Held, that the proviso was void as being inconsistent with the grant, and therefore that the defendant was entitled, notwithstanding the grantor's covenant had been broken.

Trespass *quare clausum fregit,* to part of the west half of lot No. 6 in the front concession of the township of Osnabruck, describing the lands by metes and bounds, containing 36 acres, 3 roods, and 8 perches, and charging the defendant with cutting trees thereon.

Pleas—1st. The general issue ; 2nd. That the close and the trees were not the plaintiff's property.

At the trial, before *McLean, J.,* at the last assizes held at Cornwall, it appeared that both plaintiff and defendant claimed title from John Reddick, who at one time was the owner of nearly the whole of the lot.

The plaintiff claimed from John Reddick, by virtue of two deeds—the first, for 14 acres, dated 16th of February, 1824, and the second, for 22 acres, 3 roods, and 8 perches, dated 14th of November, 1830.

The defendant claimed under a deed from John Reddick to his son Adam Reddick, in consideration of natural love and affection, dated 16th of February, 1824, which embraced the 22 acres, 3 roods, and 8 perches. The trespass complained of was committed on the last mentioned parcel of land. In this deed to Adam Reddick, the habendum was to Adam Reddick, his heirs and assigns, to the sole and proper use, benefit, and behoof of the said Adam Reddick, his heirs and assigns, for ever; "provided that the said presents are upon the express condition, that if the said Adam Reddick shall fail or made default in performing the covenant hereinafter contained on his part to be observed, then the said presents and everything therein contained shall cease and become utterly null and void and the lands and premises thereinbefore mentioned shall revert to and become vested in the said John Reddick as if the said presents had never been made." The covenant was as follows; "The said Adam Reddick, for himself, his heirs, executors and administrators, in consideration of the said grant thereinbefore mentioned, made to him by the said John Reddick, doth covenant, grant, promise and agree to and with the said John Reddick, in manner and form following—that is to say, that he the said Adam Reddick shall and will, from time to time, and at all times hereafter, during the natural life of the said John Reddick, and under his direction and control, work and labor in a farmerlike manner in and upon the said parcel of land therein granted, bargained and sold to him, or procure a good and able laborer, at his costs and charges, in like manner to work thereon for the benefit and advantage of the said John Reddick; that he the said Adam Reddick shall and will during the said period provide any necessary assistance to perform the necessary work of the farm, and that he will use every necessary and usual means to raise, produce, obtain, and save as good and sufficient crops from year to year as the season will admit of, without indolence, neglect, or inattention. It is known and understood between the parties to the said presents that any laborer employed by the said Adam Reddick shall be paid for out of the proceeds of any crops raised on the said premises, provided such laborer shall be employed thereon, and shall not be employed in the room, stead, or place of him the said Adam Reddick." Then followed a covenant on the part of John Reddick, thus—"That he, the said Adam Reddick, well and truly performing the said covenant by him to be observed and kept, shall and may, from and after the death of him the said John Reddick, have, hold, occupy, possess, and enjoy the said parcel or tract of land and premises thereinbefore granted and bargained, free and clear of all incumbrances, and without any let, suit, trouble, hindrance, molestation, interruption, or denial of any person or persons whatever, lawfully claiming the same."

A question was raised at the trial as to which of the parties was and had been in possession of the woodland were the trees were cut, since the deed to the plaintiff of the 14th of November, 1830. Each of them seemed to have cut and taken away wood and timber. For the plaintiff, Adam Reddick was called who proved that he had gone into possession of the 22 acres after the deed to him of the 16th of February, 1824, and that he remained from two to three years, and then failed to perform the stipulation contained in that deed. In consequence thereof, and to settle the matter with his father he left the premises, giving them up, and surrendering to him, not by any deed, but verbally, and retaining the deed executed to him. The whole bargain he said was considered at an end. He left the country, and returned after an absence of eighteen months; and then his father executed another deed to him, dated 12th of January, 1829, for 50 acres on the rear or north end of the west half of the said lot; and he gave his father security to perform the conditions, and his father gave him authority to cut timber. When he returned to the country again his father he said refused to permit him to occupy the premises under the previous conveyance, and they made the new arrangement.

The learned judge left the question of fact to the jury whether the defendant had committed a trespass upon any part of the 22 acres; telling them it was necessary that the plaintiff should either have an actual or constructive possession to enable him to maintain the action; and upon this the jury found for the plaintiff, with £3 damages. Whether the deed of the 16th February, 1824, under which the defendant claimed, was to be held as a conveyance upon condition, subject to be defeated by shewing the condition broken; or whether the stipulations contained therein were personal, and not so annexed to the estate as to render it an estate upon condition, the learned judge reserved for the consideration of the court. If the defendant should be found entitled to succeed upon the construction of the conveyance, then a nonsuit was to be entered, or a verdict for the defendant.

Richards obtained a rule nisi to enter a nonsuit or a verdict for the defendant, pursuant to the leave reserved, or to set aside the verdict, and for a new trial, on the law and evidence, and for misdirecton. He cited Doe dem. Meyers v. Marsh, 9 U. C. R. 242.

McLean shewed cause, and cited Co. Lit. 202 *a*.

ROBINSON, C. J., delivered the judgment of the court.

This case turns entirely upon the point whether the condition in the deed made by John Reddick to his son Adam was a valid or a void condition, If it were void, then the title under that deed could not be defeated by its non-performance; and it would follow that John Reddick, having divested himself of his estate by that indefeasible deed, could not afterwards make a title to the plaintiff by the deed which he executed in his favor in 1830.

The failure in Adam Reddick to perform the condition seems to have been very clearly proved.

One execption was indeed taken to the plaintiff's title, on the ground that when the deed to him was made in 1830, Adam Reddick was in adverse possession, and so the conveyance could not operate; but no such objection seems to have been raised at the trial, and it would therefore not be right to admit it now; for, if taken, the ground for it might perhaps have been removed by evidence which the plaintiff could have given; and at any rate the evidence that was given does not seem to afford foundation for the exception, but the contrary. ·

So there appears to be nothing to be considered but the one point—whether the condition of the deed made in February, 1824, by John Reddick to his son was a good condition in law, so that the making default in performing it would divest the estate.

We think the defendant should have leave to enter a nonsuit, for that the condition cannot stand with the grant, it is so utterly inconsistent with it. After the grantor had conveyed by the premises and habendum a title in fee simple, with right of immediate possession, he could not in the subsequent part of the same deed either postpone the grantee's right of enjoyment till after the grantor's death, or impose a condition that the grantee should cultivate it for the grantor's benefit while he lived. If the deed to Adam Reddick was in fact made upon no other consideration than natural love and affection, and if the deed to Brown was afterwards made to him as a *bona fide* purchaser for value, it might have been contended before the jury that the first deed was fraudulent and void·; but that must be found by a jury, not pronounced upon by the court of their own suggestion; and I do not say, having regard to all that was proved in this case, that if such an objection had been raised it could have prevailed; that would require to be carefully considered. Upon the whole, though there may be a case to go into equity with, if the plaintiff had notice of the facts as proved by Adam Reddick, we think the plaintiff must fail upon his title in a court of law, for that the deed made to Adam Reddick could not be defeated by the operation of a condition so repugnant to the grant as that contained in the deed of February, 1824.

Rule absolute.

MANNING V. MILLS.

Guarantee, construction of—Consideration—Acceptance—Defendant failing to attend as witness, effect of, on his affidavit filed in the term.

" MR. THOMAS MASON.

" " Dear Sir,—In answer to your favour of this day's date, I beg to say I will pay whatever sum you may agree upon to pay for an omnibus, if you should find one to suit you, so soon as the same is delivered to you in Hamilton ; and this may be considered as a guarantee to the party from whom you may purchase. I remain, yours very truly,

(Signed)   "SAMUEL MILLS.''

Held, that this, though addressed only to T. M., would attach at once as a guarantee in favor of any party who might furnish the omnibus ; and that no further proof of acceptance or of consideration was required.

The defendant having been notified, failed to·attend as a witness. *Held,* therefore, that no attention should be given to his affidavit impeaching the correctness of the verdict.

ASSUMPSIT.—The first count of the declaration stated that in consideration that the plaintiff, at defendant's request, would sell and deliver an omnibus to one Thomas Mason on credit, the defendant guaranteed and promised the plaintiff to be answerable for the due payment of the price : *Averment*—that the plaintiff did afterwards sell and deliver to the said T. M. on credit an omnibus, for the price of £62 10s. ; and although the credit and time for payment hath elapsed, and although the said T. M. was requested to pay the plaintiff, yet T. M. hath not paid, of all which the defendant had notice and was requested by the plaintiff to pay ; yet defendant hath not paid.

Common counts were added for goods sold and account stated.

Pleas.—1st. Non-assumpsit, 2nd. That the plaintiff did not sell and deliver the said omnibus to the said T. M on such credit *modo et formâ.* 3rd. That after the sale and delivery of the omnibus, and at the expiration of six months, being the credit mentioned, and whilst T. M. was indebted to the plaintiff for the same, it was agreed between plaintiff and T. M., without the consent of defendant, for a good consideration in that behalf to the defendant unknown, that plaintiff should give time to T. M. for three months for the payment of £62 10s., the same being a longer time than the credit that the plaintiff ought to have given according to the meaning of the said guarantee.

The plaintiffs joined issue on the first and second pleas and replied *de injuriâ* to the last.

The case was tried at Hamilton, in November last, before *Draper, J.* The plaintiff put in and proved the following letters in the handwriting of the defendant :—

"Hamilton, 9th August, 1853.

"Mr. Thomas Mason. Dear Sir,—In answer to your favor of this day's date, I beg to say I will pay whatever sum you may agree upon to pay for an omnibus, if you should find one to suit you, so soon as the same is delivered to you in Hamilton ; and this may be considered as a guarantee to the party from whom you may purchase. I remain yours very truly,   (Signed)   "SAML. MILLS."

And this :

"Hamilton, 20th July, 1854.

"Dear Sir,—With respect to the claim of Manning & Co., I beg to refer you to Mr. Footner, the assignee of Thos. Mason, or Mr. John F. Moore. I hold their bond of indemnity against this claim, and in case of your proceeding they will, I suppose, defend. They will no doubt inform you upon what ground they hold I am not liable. I would like the matter could be settled satisfactorily to Messrs. Manning & Co., as they no doubt ought to be paid by somebody."

This was addressed by defendant to the plaintiff's attorney. A letter from Mason was put in acknowledging the receipt of the omnibus, and other proof of its being in Mason's possession and of its value was given. Notice was given to defendant to appear at the trial to be examined as a witness for the plaintiff, but he made default.

For the defendant it was objected—1. That the guarantee put in, varied from the statement in the declaration, there being no reference to "credit." On application of the plaintiff's counsel the judge ordered the declaration to be amended by striking out all relating to the words "on credit." 2. That the guarantee was not addressed to any person excepting to Thos. Mason. 3. That there was no sufficient consideration for defendant's promise.

Leave was given to move to enter a nonsuit on the objection to the sufficiency of the guarantee ; subject to this the verdict was taken for the plaintiff, and £65 10s. 9d. damages *pro confesso* on account of defendant's failing to appear.

Proudfoot obtained a rule nisi to enter a nonsuit, pursuant to the leave reserved, or for a new trial on affidavits, and because the amendment was not authorized by the statute.

The affidavit stated that the defendant had furnished Mason with £75 to assist him in purchasing the omnibus, and that soon after its arrival he advanced Mason about £75 more to pay up the balance, after which he received a letter from the plaintiff stating that he had sold Mason an omnibus on which a balance of 225 dollars was due; that Mason wished a credit of six months, and referred them to defendant; and requesting a reference to some person in New York, or that the defendant would endorse his acceptance; that defendant did not answer this letter, in consequence of Mason's informing him he had obtained the omnibus on giving his note for the balance at six months, and that it was all right; that defendant never intended to guarantee the payment otherwise than as stated in his letter to Mason, that he should be apprised of his liability as soon as the omnibus reached Hamilton, in order that if called on to pay he might obtain security from Mason, who had absconded without giving defendant any security.

Connor, Q.C., objected, on shewing cause, that defendant having failed to appear at the trial, was not entitled to have his own affidavit read. He cited, as to the objections taken at the trial, Mozley v. Tinkler, 1 Cr. M. & R. 692; McIver v. Richardson, 1 M. & S. 557; Story on Contracts, sec. 864.

Start supported the rule.

ROBINSON, C.J., delivered the judgment of the court.

I see no clear ground for denying the plaintiff's right to recover. We ought not to be influenced by the statements which the defendant has made in his affidavit filed in support of this application, not only because he could not be examined as a witness in support of his own case if a new trial were granted, but also because, having been duly notified to attend and give evidence at the trial on the part of the plaintiff, who had a right to call him, he did not attend, and, for all that appears, without any reason being shewn to the court for his non-attendance. We could not in justice to the plaintiff, under such circumstances, give attention to his statements made since the trial, impeaching the correctness of the verdict.

Then upon what was shewn at the trial, the amount recovered is not objected to. The plaintiff seems to have a just claim to that sum, and the only question is as to the defendant's liability. There is no complaint of misdirection; an objection that was taken to an amendment made at the trial was not renewed on the argument, and the application is for a nonsuit on the points moved on the trial, which were, that the letter containing the alleged guarantee was not addressed to the defendant or to any person but Mason himself; and secondly, that there was no sufficient consideration for the defendant's promise.

In our opinion a letter so explicit as that written by the defendant required no other proof of acceptance than that which the plaintiff gave by furnishing the article to Mills, for the defendant there positively undertook that he would pay whatever sum Mason might agree to give for an omnibus, if he should find one to suit him, so soon as it should be delivered to him, Mason, in Hamilton, and that his letter might be considered as a guarantee to the party from whom he purchased. The cases of Morton v. Burn (7 A. & E. 23), Kennaway v. Treleavan (5 M. & W. 500), Mozley v. Tinkler (1 Cr. M. & R. 692), shew that in a case like this the guarantee attaches at once in favor of the party who furnishes the goods upon it.

There is no reason to doubt here, from the correspondence that took place, that the plaintiff relied on the defendant's liability when he furnished the omnibus, and in such a case there is no room for question about consideration, for that arises from the very transaction. The furnishing the omnibus to Mason on the faith of that letter was in itself the consideration. It is of no moment to the plaintiff what may have moved the defendant, as between him and Mason, to hold out this promise on Mason's behalf.

It does not appear that any exception was taken to the learned judge's ruling at the trial upon the effect of time being given to Mason in the manner shewn by the evidence;

and it appears to us that we cannot properly grant a new trial upon such objection raised now ; for it is shewn now on the defendant's own affidavit, that before the plaintiff gave the additional credit he wrote to the defendant apprising him of the application for indulgence which Mason had made, and it is admitted that the defendant made no reply to the letter. Upon the trial no proof seems to have been given in support of the defence that time was given to Mason.

It is not a case in which we should grant a new trial in the exercise of our equitable discretion, because it appears that after the defendant knew that Mason had obtained the omnibus he paid into his hands large sums, as he alleges, to enable him to pay for it, which sums he ought rather to have paid to the plaintiff, who had furnished the article upon the defendant's engagement to pay for it. It might, in truth, be a question whether the plaintiff might not have treated the omnibus as sold to the defendant considering the terms of the defendant's letter, although the word guarantee is used in it ; but both parties have treated the writing as nothing more than a guarantee, and not as a primary undertaking.

Rule discharged.

REGINA V. SPENCE ET AL.

Indictment—Right of jury to find general verdict of acquittal—Certiorari.

On an indictment for nuisance judgment had been arrested, and a second trial had, in order to take the opinion of the jury on a particular question which the court thought material. The jury upon the second trial found a general verdict of acquittal without answering such question, which was submitted to them by the judge. The indictment had not been removed by certiorari ; and

Held, therefore, that this court could not interfere by staying the entry of judgment until a new indictment could be preferred.

Semble, that the jury had a right to find generally, as they did.

Wilson, Q, C., moved for a rule on the defendants to shew cause why the entry of the judgment upon the indictment in this case, on which they had been tried and acquitted, should not be stayed till another indictment could be preferred and tried against the defendants, or such of them as it might be thought advisable to proceed against, for a nuisance to the alleged highway in the said indictment mentioned ; or why the entry of judgment should not be stayed till further order, and that in the meantime proceedings upon the said indictment be stayed.

This rule was moved upon an affidavit that the defendants were tried in May of the present year, at the court of oyer and terminer and general gaol delivery, upon on indictment found at that court for nuisance in fencing across a certain alleged public highway in the City of Toronto ; that the defendants pleaded not guilty, and upon the trial were acquitted : that the *said trial* was directed by this court, because upon a former trial of another indictment against the same defendants, or some or one of them, upon which a conviction took place, this court decided that judgment ought not to be given against the defendants convicted, but that another indictment should be preferred and another trial had, in order to determine whether, when the alleged highway was laid out by the proprietor of the soil, he did expressly reserve his right as proprietor in the soil over which it passed, or not (*a*) : that the jury on the last trial acquitted the defendants by a general verdict, and did not answer the above question, which was submitted to them by the Chief Justice, who tried the case : that the prosecutor desires to have the said question determined by the judgment of this court after the trial of the first indictment above mentioned, and which was not determined by [the jury upon the second trial.

ROBINSON, C. J., delivered the judgment of the court.

It is wholly out of our power to make any such order as is moved for in this case. The record is not of this court. If the indictment which was found at the assizes had been removed into this court by *certiorari*, as it might have been before verdict, and if the considerations applied which induced the Court of King's Bench in England to take the course which they did in the case of The King v. Sutton (5 B. & Ad. 53), we should possibly avail ourselves of that authority; though it will be found, in looking into the cases

(*a*) See 11 U. C. R. 31.

on this subject, that the court have had great reluctance in acceding to such applications. But here we have no control whatever over the record, in regard to which we are desired to interpose. The defendants are entitled to the full benefit of their acquittal before the court of oyer and terminer.

If the fact were otherwise in this respect, I believe it would be found that the right of the jury to find a general verdict in a criminal case, and to decline to find the facts specially, cannot be questioned, especially where their verdict is one of acquittal.

Rule refused.

GOODERHAM ET AL. V. GARDEN.

Declaration on promissory note—Special demurrer.

Endorsee against maker of a note. The declaration alleged that the defendant thereby promised to pay to certain persons trading under the name, style, and firm of W. B. Clark & Co., and that the said persons so trading, &c., by and under that name and style, *then* duly endorsed the said note to the plaintiffs.

Held, on special demurrer, that it sufficiently appeared when the note was endorsed, and that the endorsers were sufficiently described.

ASSUMPSIT on a promissory note by indorsee against the maker. The declaration stated that the defendant made the note, and thereby promised to pay to certain persons trading under the name and style of W. B. Clark & Co., or order, &c., and that the said persons so trading under the said name and style of W. B. Clark & Co., by and under that name and style *then* duly endorsed the said note to the plaintiffs.

Demurrer.—The causes assigned are sufficiently stated in the judgment.

Blevins for the demurrer ; *McMichael* contra.

The following cases were cited: 3 U. C. R. 325, 5 U. C. R. 509, 7 U. C. R. 88, Ib. 142, 5 B. & Al. 244, 14 M. & W. 154, 15 M. & W. 277, 16 M. & W. 51.

ROBINSON, C. J., delivered the judgment of the court.

We are of opinion that none of the causes of demurrer assigned are good exceptions.

The endorsement, as it is stated, can only have been made after the note, for it could not be at the same instant of time ; and the averment that the defendant made the note

by which he promised to pay to Clark & Company a certain
sum of money, and that Clark & Company *then* endorsed
it, is equivalent to saying that *after* the note was made they
endorsed it. *Then* is constantly used in that sense as
marking a succession of events, as if in this case the word
"thereafter" had been used. The forms given in the new
rules of pleading dispense with laying a particular day, and
expressly sanction this manner of declaring. As to the
objection which was mainly relied on, the not giving the
Christian and surnames of the endorsers, Clark & Company,
it is fully answered by the case cited in this court, City Bank
of Montreal v. Eccles (5 U. C. R, 509), and by Tigar et al.
v. Gordon et al. (9 M. & W. 347).

The other exceptions are all insufficient.

Judgment for plaintiffs on demurrer.

In re The Municipality of the Township of Augusta
and The Municipal Council of the United Counties
of Leeds and Grenville

12 Vic. ch. 81—Mandamus to M. C. to make road.

Semble that under the facts of this case there was clearly a duty incumbent
on the Municipal Council, under 12 Vic. ch 81, sec. 37, to make the road
which they were desired to make.

The court, however, granted only a mandamus nisi, in order that any
question raised upon the return might be disposed of formally.

Connor, Q. C., obtained a rule on defendants to shew cause
why a mandamus should not be issued to them commanding
them forthwith to plank, gravel, or macadamize the road
assumed by them between the village of Maitland and North
Augusta, in the said township of Augusta, being part of the
road known as the County Toll Road from Merrickville to
Maitland in the said united counties.

This rule was obtained upon an affidavit of the Reeve of
the township of Augusta, in which he stated that by a by-law
of the united counties of Leeds and Grenville, made on the
31st of January, 1850, it was enacted that debentures for
£16,000 should be divided equally into four parts, and one
fourth applied in making a macadamized, plank, or gravel
road from Merrickville to Maitland, in the the County of Gren-

ville; and commissioners were appointed for making the road, of whom he was one: that the commissioners under the by-law expended the money so appropriated in making that part of the road which lies between Merrickville and Bellamy's Mills, in North Augusta, which for some time had been macadamized and gravelled, and used as a county toll road, and tolls taken thereon: that all the means at the disposal of the commissioners were expended in making that portion of the road: that in another by-law of the County Council, made on the 7th of December, 1853, it was recited that the commissioners of the county toll road from Merrickville to Maitland had caused the part of the road between North Augusta and Maitland to be surveyed and reported to the council, which survey and report were set out, and the by-law enacted that the part of the said road so laid out shall be assumed, established, and opened as a county road for public use, subject to the payment of such tolls and the observance of such rules and regulations as are therein mentioned: and the reeve further swore that the portion of the road described and reported upon as aforesaid, and so assumed as a county road was wholly within the township of Augusta: that neither before nor since this by-law was passed had any portion of the road between Bellamy's Mills in North Augusta and Maitland been macadamized, planked, or gravelled, but the Municipal Council of Leeds and Grenville had neglected and refused to make the same, or to expend any money thereon.

It was shewn by by-laws produced, that the statements of the Reeve in regard to the acts of the County Council were correct, and that on the 14th of October, 1853, a draft of a by-law providing for the completion of the road in question was proposed in the council, and passed through committee, and further proceedings on it deferred till the 24th of January following, being directed to be published in the mean time, for the information of the rate-payers; and notice was also published of the day appointed for further considering this proposed by-law according to the statute 14 & 15 Vic. ch, 109, sec. 16: that upon the day appointed for proceeding further upon the said proposed by-law it was taken up in the County Council, and rejected by a vote of the majority of the council.

It was sworn by the Reeve that he had at the several sessions of the council, called upon them in behalf of the township of Augusta to make provision for completing this road, but that they had refused to do so, and had not done it.

On the 29th of January, 1853, the County Council passed a by-law appropriating all tolls levied and collected on each of the four county toll roads authorized to be constructed under the by-laws referred to, to be applied by the commissioners of each of the said roads to the purpose of completing them respectively, and enacting that any by-law making any other dispositions of the tolls should be repealed.

Hagarty, Q. C., supported the rule ; *Vankoughnet*, Q. C., contra.

ROBINSON, C. J., delivered the judgment of the court.

We do not at present see that there is not a duty plainly incumbent upon the united counties of Leeds and Grenville, under the statute 12 Vic. ch. 81, sec. 37, to make the road which they are desired to make. It may be that by reason of their having been a railway lately constructed in that section of the county the prospect of a remunerating revenue from such a road may have become impaired ; but that has not been set up as a reason, nor could, as we suppose, be accepted as a valid one. Neither is it shewn that for want of funds, or the legal authority to raise them, a compliance with the statute is impossible.

If the defendants should appear to be without any legal excuse for not proceeding with the road, then the case would be one of a duty imposed by act of Parliament remaining unperformed. And if there should appear to be nothing unreasonable insisting upon performance, why should it not be enforced ?

It could only be on acount of some difficulty in extending the remedy by mandamus to a municipal body, and in rendering it effectual. At present we do not see that there is such difficulty when there appears to be no other remedy. But we think it clearly proper that we should award only a mandamus nisi at present, in order that any question of law or fact that may be raised upon the return may be disposed of formally and subject to revision.

THE CHIEF SUPERINTENDENT OF COMMON SCHOOLS FOR UPPER CANADA, APPELLANT, IN A CAUSE OF THE TRUSTEES OF SCHOOL SECTION NO. 2, IN THE TOWNSHIP OF MOORE, v WILLIAM McRAE.

Alteraton of school section—Election of new trustees.

An alteration of the boundaries of a school section under 13 & 14 Vic. ch. 48, sec. 18, subsec. 4, does not make it necessary to call a school section meeting and appoint new trustees.

The trustees in this case proceeded to collect the rate by action instead of by warrant, as provided by 13 & 14 Vic. ch. 48, sec. 12, subsecs. 2, 7, 8 ; and *semble*, per *Draper, J.*, that the appeal might have been dismissed on this ground, but the objection was waived.

This was an appeal from the Division Court of the county of Lambton.

The action was brought by summons bearing date the 16th of May, 1854, issued out of the First Division Court of the county of Lambton, to recover £1 7s. 11d. for the causes stated in the plaintiff's statement of claim (which statement by the judgment returned appeared to have been for school assessments for 1851, 1852, 1853. The statement itself was among the papers, and was for 1851, for support of school, $1.52.; for 1852, for support of school, $1.12¼.; for 1853, for support of school, $1.47.; and for the same year 1853, for special assessment for building school house, $1.47.

It appeared that on the 11th of March, 1850, the Municipal council of the township of Moore passed a resolution that the following school sections were recommended by the Rev. Geo. Salter, and unanimously adopted by the council. Section No. 2, commencing at No. 19, front concession, running east to 19, 4th concession inclusive ; then north to 19, in the 6th concession inclusive; then west to the river St. Clair ; thence to the place of beginning.

On the 17th of June, 1851, a by-law was passed by the same municipality confirming the resolution of 11th March. 1850, and as to this section No. 2, enacting "Section 2nd to commence at No. 19, front concession, inclusive, running east to 19, 4th concession, inclusive ; thence north to 19, 6th con-

cession, inclusive; thence west to the river St. Clair; thence
south to the place of beginning."

The defendant was a resident in school section No. 2, as
defined by the resolution of 11th March, 1850, and the by-
law of 17th June, 1851.

The evidence of George Wright given in the court below,
as follows:

George Wright, sworn, says he was one of the trustees of
above section in 1850, '51, and '52. The section elected
trustees in 1851. Put the necessary notices up himself.
The regular annual school meetings were called on notices put
up for that purpose in '51 and '52 by himself. There were
only six or seven opposing these alterations. None made at
the meetings. There was but one meeting (annual) in 1850;
did not at any meeting see defendant there; does not recollect
receiving any notice of limits, &c., from the township clerk.
There was no change of number, but a part taken off the north
and parts added to the east and south sides. Read a written
notice of alteration from Mr. Salter, the township superintendent.

The defendant waived all objections as to the method of
proceeding, but objected, first, that the requisites of the 13
& 14 Vic., ch. 48, sec. 18, subsec. 4, had not been complied
with in passing the by law of 17th June, 1851; and secondly
that the section No. 2, as altered, constituted a new section,
and therefore new trustees should have been elected as provided by 13 & 14 Vic., ch. 48 secs. 4, 5, 6, which was not done.

As to the first objection, the learned judge, held that the
court below had no power to enquire whether the township
council proceeded legally in passing the by-law or not; but
that upon the second objection the defendant was entitled to
succeed, and on that ground a non-suit was ordered.

The Chief Superintendent appealed from this decision,
under the provisions of 16 Vic. 185, sec. 24.

ROBINSON, C. J.—The facts of this case are not stated with
any distinctness, but we are left to glean them from the evidence and documents as we can.

I infer from them that McRae lives in section 2, and that
he is sued in the Division Court for not paying school rates
imposed for that section. There is no paper annexed to the

summons shewing the claim, though such minute of claim is referred to as if annexed. The question which we are asked to adjudge upon is, whether an alteration made in school section 2, by taking a part from it, and adding to it what formed part of another section, *constitutes* the section No. 2 so altered, a *new section* within the meaning of the 18th clause of 13 & 14 Vic., ch. 48, subsec. 3, and made it necessary to call a school section meeting, and to proceed therein as in the 4th and 5th clauses of the act is directed, before any rates for such altered section could be imposed ; or whether, as the Chief Superintendent of Schools contends, the trustees chosen for the section before its alteration did not continue in office for that section in its altered state as before, and had power to impose rates without the necessity for a new election of trustees as at a first meeting for a new section.

I cannot say that I am certain I have succeeded in picking out the facts, but as I understand them, I think there was no necessity for any school section meeting or new appointment of trustees in the section 2, on account of the alteration that had been made in its limits and that the judgment of non-suit given in the Division Court should therefore be reversed, and judgment given for the plaintiffs in the cause.

I do not see on the face of the papers submitted why the trustees did not proceed to collect the rate in this case by warrant. I see no authority for proceeding by action except where the person rated resides out of the section. However, there is no appeal on this point, and what has done may be right in that respect, though the foundation of the proceeding is not explained.

DRAPER, J.—It is nowhere shewn what were the boundaries of school section No. 2, prior to the 11th of March, 1850, that a section No. 2, existed before the 11th of March, 1850, appears from the fact stated in the evidence of Geo. Wright that he was a trustee in 1850, in which year he says there was only one meeting (I presume for the election of school trustees) which was the annual meeting, and according to the 12 Vic. ch. 83, sec. 21, must have been on the second Tuesday in January of that year. Wright's evidence further goes on to state that the change made in 1850, was the taking off part from the north and adding a part to the east and south sides of section No. 2. Now it appears to me that this was the alteration of a school section, so far as the evidence shews. It is not shewn to have been a new division of the township into school sections: it certainly was not the union of two or more sections, and therefore only the third alternative provided for by the 18th section of 12 Vic., remains, namely, the alteration. If therefore we can assume that an alteration of the school section could be made by resolution, then this alteration made on the 11th of March, 1850, was expressly confirmed by the statute 13 & 14 Vic., ch. 48, and the appeal must be sustained. If it were necessary to rest the decision upon this point, however, I should require further consideration before concluding that the powers conferred for common school purposes on the Municipal Council do not require to be exercised by by-law. But it is not necessary to rest on that ground. In June, 1851, a by-law was passed almost in the words of the resolution of the preceding year, and the provisions of that act equally bring me to the conclusion that this is an alteration of a school section and no more, according to the evidence submitted. I think the learned judge held rightly in the court below that the regularity of the proceedings preparatory to that by-law were not a subject for his enquiry. He took it, and I think properly, as it stood before him. It was within the power of the township council by the 18th section, sub-sec. 4, of the 13 & 14 Vic., to make such an alteration, and they have done it in the way that is free from doubt as to the due execution of the power, *i.e.* by by-law. That an *alteration* involves a change of parties from being members of one school section by transferring them into another is quite clear from a part of the proviso to the 4th section of section 18, "that the inhabitants transferred from one school section to another shall be entitled, for the common school purposes of the section to which they are attached, to such a proportion of the proceeds of the disposal of the school house or other common school property as the assessed value of their property bears to that of the other inhabitants of the school section from which they shall have been separated."

This language expressly applies to the disposal of school property not required in consequence of the "alteration or union of school sections." In my opinion, therefore, confining attention to the statute 13 & 14 Vic., ch. 48—(the 16 Vic., ch. 185, does not effect the question)—the evidence in this case shews only an alteration of an existing school section, not the formation of a new one; and therefore, as there were three trustees in the section No. 2, elected according to law, before this by-law, they continued to be trustees after it. The judgment of nonsuit is therefore wrong. The plaintiffs should recover for the school rates for 1852 and 1853. As to those for 1851, treating the alterations to have been made by the by-law of June, 1851, sub-section 4 of section 18 of 13 & 14 Vic. ch. 48 provides "that any alteration in the boundaries of a school section shall not go into effect before the 25th day of December next after the time when it shall have been made." The rate bill is headed thus: "Rate bill of persons liable to school fees in section No. 2, in the township of Moore, for nine months, commencing 21st January, and ending the 30th November, 1851: and it is issued with a warrant to levy, addressed to the collector on 2nd September, 1851. Now, as I understand, the defendant only become a resident of school section No. 2, by force of the alteration. It seems to follow that he would not be liable for the rate imposed prior to the 25th of December, 1851, as the alteration made by the by-law of June in that year could not take effect earlier.

The judgment in this case was given in the court below on the 23rd of June, 1854. The notice of appeal was given as apears, on the 10th of July following. According to 16 Vic. ch. 185, section 25, the matter ought to have been set down for argument "in the *next term*," i. e. in Trinity. This seems to have been done, but too late for argument last term.

The only point I entertain any doubt upon is, whether this appeal might not have been dismissed upon the ground that the statute 13 & 14 Vic., ch. 48, section 12, sub-sections 2, 7, 8, provides specific means for collecting all school rates with the exception contained in sub-section 9, which in express terms authorizes the school trustees to sue for and recover by their name of office the amounts of school rates and subscriptions due from persons residing *without* the limits of their school section and making default in payment. This objection was not however taken on the argument.

BURNS, J.—I think the judge has taken quite a mistaken view of the effect of the 3rd and 4th subsections of section 18 of 13 & 14 Vic. ch. 48. The 3rd subsection gives the municipal council of the township power to form portions of the township, where no schools have been established into school sections, and in such case the proceeding to elect trustees is to take place under the provisions of the 4th section. This case does not come within that provision. Then under the 4th subsection the municipal council has power to do two things—first, to alter any school section already established; secondly, to unite two or more school sections. It is only in the case of two or more school sections being united that the provisions of the fourth section of the act is brought into operation. A mere alteration of the boundaries does not require a new election of trustees. A union of two or more sections might take place at any period of the year, and then it would be required to have a new election, which the fourth section of the act provides for. In the case of an alteration of the boundaries, the fourth subsection declares that such alteration in the boundaries shall not go into operation before the 25th of December next after the same shall have been made. This evidently contemplates that no new election is necessary upon a mere alteration of the boundaries. It was contended on the argument that there should have been evidence before the judge below that the people of the school section desired the alteration. I do not think such evidence required. So long as the by-law of the township council remained *de facto*, it was unnecessary for the trustees of the school to prove it to be correct *de jure*. In proceedings by the trustees of the school section it must be assumed that all preliminary matters were performed.

Appeal confirmed.

THE CHIEF SUPERINTENDENT OF SCHOOLS, APELLANT, IN RE
JOHN A. KELLY V. CHARLES HEDGES ET AL.

Under 13 & 14 Vic. ch. 48, school trustees are authorized to levy a rate for
the erection of a schoolhouse in their section.

Appeal from the Division Court of the county of Brant.

This was an action of trespass brought for seizing and selling the plaintiff's cow. It was admitted that the cow in question was seized and sold under a warrant of the defendants, as school trustees of Union Section No. 20 in Burford and No. 13 in Windham, to levy a rate imposed by the trustees for the purpose of building a schoolhouse in said section.

The only question to be decided was, whether the Common School Act of 1850, 13 & 14 Vic. ch: 48, authorizes school trustees to levy a rate to build the section schoolhouse.

The following is the judgment delivered in the court below :—

JONES, J.—The only clause of the act which shews for what purposes the trustees may levy a rate is the 7th clause of the 12th section. It is there enacted that it shall be the duty of the trustees "to provide for the salaries of the teachers, *and all other expenses of the school,* in such manner as may be desired by a majority of the freeholders or householders at the annual school meeting, and to employ all lawful means, as provided for by this act, to collect the sum or sums required for such salaries and *other expenses.*"

The 9th clause of the same section then goes on to shew how the trustees are to collect the "sums required for such salaries and other expenses," as follows : "To apply to the municipality of the township, or employ their own lawful authority, as they may judge expedient, for the raising and collecting *all sums* authorized *in the manner hereinbefore provided* to be collected from the freeholders of such section by rate," &c.

By these clauses it will be observed that the purposes for which the trustees are authorized *to levy a rate* " are to provide for the teacher's salary and the other *expenses* of the school." I take it that the word "expenses" here, in connection with "salary," means the necessary yearly outlay incidental to carrying on the school, and that it does not apply to the original cost of purchasing the site and erecting the schoolhouse. It will be seen by reference to the 1*st clause of the* 18*th section,* where township councils are empowered to levy moneys for school purposes, that the power conferred is much fuller than that given to trustees by the 7*th clause of the* 12*th section.* It enacts that they (the township councils) shall have the power to levy the required sum by assessment upon taxable property in any school section "for the purchase of a school site, the *erection,* &c., of a school house," and, in addition, gives them power to levy money for all the purposes that the trustees could under the 12th section. There seems to be that distinction between the power conferred on township councils and that given to trustees, that the latter are not authorized to levy a rate to purchase a school site, nor, as I think, for the reasons, stated, to erect a schoolhouse.

It will be observed that by the Supplementary School Act of 1863, 16 Vic. ch. 185, sec. 6, the power here contended for is expressly given to school trustees. It enacts " That the trustees of each school section shall have the same authority to assess and collect school rates, for the purpose of *purchasing school sites* and the *erection of schoolhouses,* as they are now invested with by law to collect rates *for other school purposes.*"

The Legislature, who should be the best interpreter of their own acts, clearly did not consider that the statute of 1850 gave trustees this power, else why the necessity for this enactment ?

It is agreed that the word "building," which occurs in the 4th clause of the 12th section, implies an authority to the trustees to levy a rate to erect a schoolhouse. I think this expression has reference merely to the trustees superintending the building of the schoolhouse and expending the money therefor, which they would require to do, though the rate were levied by the township council. I am therefore of opinion that, under the act of 1850, school trustees had no power to levy a rate for the erection of a schoolhouse, but that they should have applied to the township councils, as provided by the 18th section of that act.

The Chief Superintendent appealed from this judgment under the 16 Vic. ch. 185, sec. 24.

George Duggan for the appeal ; *VanNorman* contra.

The statutes and sections referred to, are cited in the judgment.

ROBINSON, C. J.—I cannot say that I am quite satisfied whether the Legislature did not mean by the statute 13 & 14 Vic. ch. 48 to give to school trustees the power to raise and collect the rates that may be required for building a new schoolhouse in their division.

If I confine myself to the consideration of what is to be found in that act without looking to any provision made before or afterwards upon that point I should have a strong impression that Mr. Jones's view of the question, which is clearly stated and precisely expressed, is the sound one ; but in tracing this subject through the three acts (12 Vic. ch. 83, 13 & 14 Vic. ch. 48, and 16 Vic. ch. 185), I find it no easy matter to form an opinion. Upon the first of these statutes, now no longer in force, there could be no room for doubt; for by the 30th clause of that act, it was provided in express terms, that no rate should be levied for the building of a schoolhouse otherwise than by a by-law of the municipal council of the township, &c., in which the section might be ; and it required that any such rate should be sanctioned by a majority of the landholders and householders ; and this restriction was inserted as a qualification of the former part of the same clause, by which the trustees were empowered to do whatever might be expedient with regard to *building,* repairing, &c. the schoolhouse of their section.

The inserting such a proviso affords a strong ground for argument that the Legislature assumed that without the proviso the power they had given in the beginning of the clause would have extended to the raising and collecting moneys to defray the expenses of building the schoolhouse.

Then, in 1850, the Legislature, after some experience of the measure, repeal this statute of 1849, and pass a new act providing for the whole subject of common schools. And when we find them in this case empowering the trustees, almost in the very words of the former act, to do whatever they might judge expedient for building schoolhouses, and at the same time dropping the proviso which had before restrained them from raising moneys for the purpose, one can hardly resist the conclusion that they did mean by the new act to allow the trustees to impose and collect the necessary rate.

Yet, as I have already said, if I were to place a construction upon the act of 1850, looking at its provisions alone, I think I should draw from the 4th, 7th, 8th, & 9th, subsections of the 12th section the same conclusions that the learned judge of the Division Court has formed upon them. Looking at the 13 & 14 Vic. in connection with the former statute which they were repealing, I should be inclined to think that the Legislature did intend by it to give the trustees the power in question, though they left their meaning obscure.

But the last act of the three increases the difficulty; for by the 6th section of that act (16 Vic. ch. 185) the legislature by express words, gave to the school trustees power to assess and collect rates for the erection of schoolhouses, and they give it in such terms as they would naturally use if they were conferring a new power : for they provide "that they shall have the same authority to collect those rates *as they are now, or may be* invested with by law to assess and collect rates for other school purposes." Any one must understand that the Legislature, when they used these words, were under the impression that they were giving power to trustees which they had not before.

The clause is not in the language of a declaratory law; it rather implies a consciousness that there was a restriction which it was expedient to remove.

Still, looking at all that has been done, and the footing on which the matter is now put, we think the authority of the trustees to impose the rate under the school law of 1850 may be vindicated. The words in the 4th subsection of the 12th clause of the 13 & 14 Vic. ch. 48—"to do whatever they may judge expedient with regard to the building, repairing, &c., the section schoolhouse"—are very comprehensive certainly, and when coupled with the other powers given to them, might not unreasonably be held to convey power to impose a rate for *building*, as well as for the other school purposes mentioned in the 7th subsection; though it might be objected that the enumeration of inferior objects, without giving specifically a power to raise a rate for this, creates a difficulty; and further, that a power to any public body to raise money should be given in express terms rather than be held to be included under a general authority to do whatever may be thought expedient.   But the fact that the Legislature, by the statute of 1849, seems to have looked upon these words as conveying the right to impose a rate, unless they had restrained their meaning, as they did in that statute, coupled with the fact that in 1850 they used the comprehensive words and dropped the restrictive; and in 1853 gave the power to raise the rate in express words which we may regard as done by way of removing all doubt merely—these considerations, I repeat, incline us to confirm the construction which we find has been hitherto put upon the act, and so avoid difficulty and confusion.

BURNS, J.—The question seems to me to turn upon the meaning and effect to be given to the 4th and 7th subsections of section 12 of 13 & 14 Vic. ch. 48.   The 4th subsection gives the trustees power in direct words to do whatever they may deem expedient with regard to the building the section schoolhouse.   Of course, they cannot build it without the means. Who, or what power then is authorized to raise the means ? It is said that because 16 Vic. ch. 185, sec. 6, gave the trustees the express power to assess and collect school rates for the purpose of building schoolhouses, therefore it must be inferred that they had no such power before.   The argument is entitled to great weight if there were no other acts or language of the Legislature to guide us in determining the matter When we turn to the 3rd subsection of section 30 of 12 Vic. ch. 83, which act was repealed by 13 & 14 Vic. ch. 48, we find the same language used as to building schoolhouses; but there is a proviso that no rate for the building of a schoolhouse, or purchasing a site for the schoolhouse, shall be levied otherwise than under a by-law of the municipal council. This 3rd subsection is divided in the act 13 & 14 Vic. ch. 48 between subsection 4 of the 12th section and the 1st subsection of section 18. In the statute of 1849 the power of the trustees is limited by the proviso; but in the statute of 1850 no limitation is attached to the power of the trustees, but what was formerly a limitation upon them is given to the municipal council, to be exercised upon the desire of the trustees. The removal of the limitation argues very forcibly that the trustees may build without asking the municipal council for the funds, provided the other parts of the act will enable them, from their own power and authority, to levy the means. Now when we look at the 5th subsection of the 30th section of 12 Vic. ch. 83 we see that all the trustees could levy on their own authority was the rate bill which was to be the amount the repective parties were liable for for instruction, for firewood, or for any charge necessarily incurred by such attendance. The 7th subsection of section 12 of 13 & 14 Vic. ch. 48, enabled trustees to provide for the salaries of teachers and all other expenses of the school. It will not be pretended but that this authority would enable the trustees to levy for the rent of a schoolhouse if they were obliged to rent, and which they have authority to do under the same fourth subsection. If they may do so to pay the rent of a schoolhouse, if there be no suitable one, or to pay the rent of a second schoolhouse if it be required, I cannot understand why they may not also do so to build one. The one seems to me to come under the denomination of expenses of the school as much as the other. This, I think, would be the construction of 13 & 14 Vic. ch. 48, if it stood by itself upon the repealed law.

Then it only remains to say what effect the provision contained in 16 Vic. ch. 185 has. Now we see by the sixth section that the legislature were conferring upon the trustees the same powers which formerly were vested in the municipal council, and the trustees were acquiring a power in respect of school sites which was altogether new to them, and in that power is also contained the other. I think it more reasonable to hold that the Legislature, in the last act, included the power to the trustees to levy rates to build school-houses *ex abundanti* than to reject the power to levy those rates from the former act, and yet say as we must, that an express power was given to them by the former act to build schoolhouses.

For these reasons I think the judgment of the judge of the Division Court should be reversed.

DRAPER, J., concurred.

Judgment for the appellant.

WELD V. SCOTT ET AL.

Trespass—Proof of possession—Erroneous survey.

Trespass *quare clausum fregit*, describing the *locus in quo* by metes and bounds, and as part of "what has heretofore been known as lot 15, 1st concession Delaware." The defendant gave no evidence of title. The plaintiff claimed by virtue of his possession, and it appeared that more than twenty years ago, relying on an erroneous survey, he had fenced in a part of the defendant's lot 14 in the broken front concession. This fence, if continued, would have included the part in question, but it had never been extended to any part of lot 14 in the 1st concession.
Held, that the plaintiff could not be considered as having any such possession of the *locus in quo* as would entitle him to recover.

TRESPASS *quare clausum fregit*, upon a close of the plaintiff in the township of Delaware, bounded on the north by a line run by Rosswell Mowat, on the west by the river Thames, on the east by the concession line between the 1st and 2nd concessions of Delaware, and on the south by the line run between one Sumner and the plaintiff; and being the northerly half of what has heretofore been known as lot number 15, in the 1st concession of the said township of Delaware. With a count for taking staves and timber of plaintiff's.

Pleas—1. Not guilty. 2. That neither the close nor the trees belonged to the plaintiff. 3. A similar plea. 4. That the close was the freehold of the defendants. 5. That it belonged to T. C. Street, Esq., by whose command defendants entered, &c. 6. Justification under Street's title, calling the *locus in quo* part of lot 14, and giving color. 7. Traverse of the plaintiff's property in the logs.

The plaintiff took issue on all the pleas.

At the trial at London, before Macaulay, C. J. C. P., a verdict was found for the plaintiff, and £60 damages.

Becher moved for a new trial on the law and evidence, and for misdirection, and on affidavits.

C. Robinson shewed cause.

The facts are stated in the judgment of the court, delivered by

ROBINSON, C. J.—The evidence shewed that the trees had been cut, not on 15, but on defendant's land, 14, in the 1st concession, though, according to an erroneous line which a surveyor had run more than twenty years ago, it was made out to be a part of 15.

The plaintiff claimed, however, by virtue of his actual possession, and the question was, whether he could be rightly held to have been in possession of the *locus in quo* in such a manner as was sufficient to confer title after twenty years, under the Statute of Limitations; or whether, as the defendants gave no evidence of title, he was not at least sufficiently in possession to enable him to maintain trespass against a wrong-doer, for cutting trees upon the close, as he had described it.

The affidavits were of the two defendants, stating that they purchased 14, in the 1st concession, in 1845, from T. C. Street, Esq., under whom they hold upon a written agreement, which entitled them to a deed when they should have made certain payments; that the trees in question were cut upon that lot, and that, supposing the boundary between 14 and 15 was to govern the question, they did not prepare themselves to prove Mr. Street's title. Mr. Street also made an affidavit that he had the title to the land in question, and had agreed to sell it to the defendants, as they had sworn.

There was no evidence here that the defendants, before they went on lot 14, had any knowledge that the plaintiff, or any one preceding him in the possession of 15, had encroached on 14, in the 1st concession; but no objection seems to have been taken at the trial upon that ground against the plaintiff claiming the benefit of the Statute of Limitations. It was indeed of no material consequence to agitate any question about the statute; for the defendants, for reasons which are explained in the affidavits, gave no evidence of any right on their part; and therefore, as it was not a question of conflict of titles, all that the plaintiff had to shew was that he was sufficiently in possession, at the time of the alleged trespass, to entitle him to recover for trees cut down and taken away from the tract described; which tract, it is to be noticed, he describes by certain metes and bounds, and does not venture to call it part of lot 15, but states only that it had been theretofore (that is, at some time theretofore) known as such.

Now as to the true state of the case, whether the trees had been cut on lot 15 or lot 14, there seems to be no doubt, when we examine the evidence. They were taken from lot 14, as a correct survey has established. Then these defendants had at least a right to put the plaintiff, as they did by their pleadings, to shew on what pretence of right he called the close his, and the timber his; and what right did he shew? He proved no title to any part of this lot 14, but relied wholly on an alleged possession. And what was that possession? He had never occupied, used or cultivated, any portion of the lot, but had enclosed wrongfully a part of the lot 14 in the broken front concession, coming to the river, and lying in front of the lot 14, in the first concession. He, or those preceding him in the title to 15, had by mistake, and relying upon an unauthorized and erroneous survey, fenced in a part of the lot 14 near the river, when they ought to have confined themselves to the limits of 15, and no doubt meant to do so: but that fence, created twenty years ago and more, did not even extend back to any part of the lot 14 in the 1st concession, which is now in question, and never has been carried back so far as the woodland on which these trees were felled.

So this is the case of a person not holding title, for any thing that appears, to any part of 14 in the first concession, and not visibly or actually occupying it, claiming nevertheless to be constructively in possession of all of it, because he has wrongfully and in error encroached on a part. The trees cut were clearly not his, nor the close his.

We think to allow the plaintiff to recover on the evidence that was given would be contrary to the legal principle constantly upheld and frequently made the ground of decision in this court—that a person wrongfully in possession of any land belonging to another, which is not covered by any title under which he can assume to hold it, gains no right under such possession to more than the land which his actual possession covers. He is confined to what has been called his pedal possession; and even occasional acts of trespass committed by him on other parts of the property will not be taken as extending his actual peaceable possession over such parts. The distinction between such an occupant and another, who either shews a right to the whole land in question, or is residing upon and cultivating part of a lot of land, to the whole of which he claims title under conveyances which, if they were valid, would cover the whole, is, that the latter classes of occupants are regarded as being constructively in possession of the whole lot covered by their deeds, while they are in possession of a part; but a mere trespasser's occupation is not to be extended in contemplation of law by any such construction.

We think there should be a new trial in this case without costs, for that the jury might have been properly told that the plaintiff was not entitled to recover.

———————

BEATY v. JARVIS.

Promissory notes—Special demurrer—Pleading.

Declaration on two promissory notes, including both in one count, and averring that the payee *afterwards duly endorsed the said notes respectively* to the plaintiff, and that defendant (the maker) did not pay the amount of the said notes, although they were duly presented for payment, &c. *Held*, on special demurrer, bad.

ASSUMPSIT by the indorsee against the maker of two promissory notes for £57 18s. 11d. each. The declaration was as follows:

The plaintiff alleged that whereas the defendant G. M. J., on, &c., made his promissory note in writing, and thereby promised to pay to one E. C., or order, at, &c., the sum of

£12, three months after the date thereof; which period had elapsed before the commencement of this suit.

And whereas also the said defendant did, on, &c., make his certain other promissory note in writing, and thereby promised to pay to the said E. C., or order, at, &c., the sum of &c., three months after the date thereof, which period had elapsed before the commencement of this suit.

And the said E. C. afterwards duly endorsed the said notes respectively, and delivered the said notes so endorsed to the plaintiff.

And the said G. M. J. did not pay the amount of the said notes, although they were duly presented on the days when they became due respectively, of all which the defendant had due notice; by reason whereof the said defendant became liable to pay to the said plaintiff the said respective sums of money in the said notes specified, and, being so liable, afterwards promised the said plaintiff to pay him the same :

Yet the said defendant hath not paid to the said plaintiff the amount of the said notes, or any part thereof, to the plaintiff's damage of £200; and thereof he brings suit.

Demurrer.—That there is no such date or time mentioned in the said declaration laid to the endorsement of the notes in the said declaration mentioned, as required by the rules of pleading, and the said declaration does not follow the form prescribed by the new rules; that the said declaration is composed of two counts, each upon a promissory note, and the breach of the promise laid in the said declaration is not sufficiently certain; that the breach charged is, that defendant did not pay the notes, and *non constat*, from all that is alleged in the said declaration, that he did not pay one of the notes.

McMichael for the demurrer. *Wilson*, Q. C., contra.

Cases cited—2 U. C. R. 426; 2 M & W. 91; 7 Bing 428; 4 M & W. 579; 1 Ld. Raym. 478; 13 M & W. 30; Chit. Plg. 332; 2 Stra. 232.

ROBINSON, C. J., delivered the judgment of the court.

This seems to be an experiment in pleading. It would have been better to have followed the beaten track, as nothing can well be more unnecessary than to supply occasion for a demurrer to a declaration upon a promissory note against the maker of it. The plaintiff, by suing for two notes in one count, has given rise to one or two objections. The case in this court, of Grant v. Eyre et al. (2 U. C. R. 427), is relied upon as supporting the exception to the statement of the endorsement. It does not apply strictly, because the declarations in the two cases are not similar, but it has some bearing in principle. We held there that the plaintiff should either allege formally a particular time of making the endorsement, or should adopt the substitute allowed by the rule of court, by using the word "*then.*"

Here he has, instead of this, taken the word from the forms given in our statutes, which permit the several parties liable in different capacities upon a note to be sued in one action. If he had made each note the subject of a separate count, as is usual, and after stating the making of the note, had alleged that the payee *afterwards* endorsed it, I should have thought that sufficient—as "afterwards," so used, would appear to mean the same as "then;" or rather "then," as used in the forms of the rules of court, could scarcely be taken to mean anything else than *afterwards*; but here the plaintiff has used the word "*afterwards,*" (*a*) in reference to two notes and two days of making, so that there is a want of precision, and strictly the averment does not import that the note latest made was endorsed after it was made.

As to the other objection, that the declaration avers only that defendant did not pay the *said notes*, without adding or either of them, it is sufficiently met by the case cited by Mr. Wilson, of Wood v. Peyton (13 M. & W. 30); and besides the plaintiff does aver at the end of his declaration, that the defendant has not paid "the amount of the said notes, or any *part thereof.*"

The objection on which we are inclined to hold that the special demurrer may be supported, is so unimportant that we give leave to the plaintiff to amend, paying five shillings costs.

(*a*) See Gooderham v. Gardner, ante page 521.

REGINA V. McDONALD.

Promissory note—Indictment—Forgery—10 & 11 *Vic. ch.* 9.

A forged paper purporting to be a bank note is a promissory note within the meaning of the statute, and it is equally so if there is no such bank as that named.

This was a criminal case reserved under 14 & 15 Vic. ch. 13.

The prisoner was tried at the session of Oyer and Terminer, held before *Richards, J.*, and his associates at Cobourg, and convicted of the crime of forgery, in uttering a forged promissory note for the payment of five dollars with intent to defraud John Kennedy.

The note was in the form of a bank note, the words being as follows :

" The President, Directors & Co., of the Montreal Bank, promise to pay Five Dollars, on demand, to W. Martin, or bearer. · Montreal, June 1st, 1853.

" A SIMPSON, Cashr.
" WM. GUNN, Pres."

At the trial it was objected, on behalf of the said prisoner,

1. That the instrument given in evidence and proved to have been uttered was not a promissory note for the payment of money within the meaning of the third section of the provincial statute 10 & 11 Vic. ch. 9—the evidence shewing that, so far as it was intended to be a forgery, it was of a bank note of the Bank of Montreal.

2. That if it be contended that the instrument is an imitation of a bank note, it is not a forged note of any existing incorporated institution, and does not carry on the face of it any semblance of any genuine note, nor does it contain any promise to pay by the person or persons whose names purport to be signed thereto.

3. That the instrument proven to be forged is neither a forged " bank note" nor a forged " promissory note."

In consequence of these objections the court, in its discretion, under the statute 14 & 15 Vic. ch. 13, reserved the questions arising on such objections.

The questions for consideration were—

First. Is the instrument produced at the trial and hereto

annexed such a promissory note for the payment of money, within the meaning of the statute, that the said Lemuel McDonald can be legally convicted of uttering it under this indictment.

Second. If it be an attempt to forge a note of "The Bank of Montreal," as proven at the trial, that corporation being erroneously mentioned therein as "The Montreal Bank," can the said Lemuel McDonald be legally convicted of forgery under this indictment for uttering a forged promissory note for the payment of money.

Third. If the instrument produced and given in evidence at the trial is not a forged "bank note," can it be considered as the forged promissory note for the payment of money of the person or persons whose names have been forged thereto, and can the said Lemuel McDonald be lawfully convicted under this indictment of forgery in uttering it, he then knowing it to be forged.

ROBINSON, C. J., delivered the judgment of the court.

We are of opinion that there is no force in the objections submitted to us in this case, and that the conviction was proper, and that judgment should be given against the prisoner.

The forged paper purports to be a promissory note of the President, Directors, and Company of the Montreal Bank, and it does not the less purport to be a promissory note for purporting to be a bank note, which is nothing more or less than the promissory note of a bank.

Then, if by reason of the slight variance in the corporate name used, it could not be held that a note so drawn purports to be the note of the Bank of Montreal, it is nevertheless a false and forged promissory note purporting to be the note of a non-existing bank, and would equally come within the statute, as has been decided in numerous cases.

CURRY V. McLEOD.

Government allowance for road not used—Trespass on—Justification—9 Vic.
c. 8—Misjoinder—Demurrer—Practice as to entering notice of exceptions.

The plaintiff complained of defendant for entering wrongfully into a close,
of which the plaintiff averred himself to be in possession, and pulling
down the fences, &c.; and a count for this cause of action was framed
in case, and joined with a second count in trover.

Held, a misjoinder, the first count being substantially for a trespass.

The defendant justified on the ground that the plaintiff had wrongfully
enclosed a government allowance for road, and that the grievances complained of were committed in removing the obstruction. It was alleged
in the declaration that this government allowance had never been used,
but had been in plaintiff's possession since 1816, another road parallel to
it having been travelled on instead.

Held, plea bad, as under 9 Vic. ch. 8 such government allowance could only
be opened by order of the municipal council.

Notice of exceptions to the declaration having been duly served by the
defendant, were omitted by the plaintiff in the demurrer books entered
by him. The court refused to give judgment in favor of defendant, as
allowed by the rule of court, the plea being clearly bad, but allowed the
exceptions to be argued.

Semble, that such cases will in future be struck out of the paper.

The declaration alleged that the plaintiff was, and still is,
seized in his demesne, as of fee, of a certain close, being
composed of the west three-fourths of lot No. 18, in the
second concession of Lancaster : that there was, and still is,
a certain government allowance for road in front of the said
second concession, and on which the said close of the plaintiff
abuts ; and there also was, and still is, a certain common
public highway, established by law, running through the
front half of the plaintiff's said close, and through divers
other closes, in the said second concession, parrallel to the
said government allowance for road in front of the said
second concession ; and the said last-mentioned highway so
running, &c., having been used and travelled upon by the
inhabitants of the said second concession for a long time—to
wit, since the 16th of January, 1816—and the same being
still used and travelled upon as aforesaid, that part of the
said government allowance for road in front of the said
second concession, and on which the said close of the plaintiff abuts, was never used or travelled upon to the eastward
of John Curry's nine-mile road, in the second concession of
said township of Lancaster, but remained in the possession
of the plaintiff and the occupiers of the said close for the
time being : that a certain portion—to wit, forty feet in

width—of the said government allowance for road in front
of the said second concession had been and was enclosed,
fenced in, and cultivated by the plaintiff and the occupants
of the said close for the time being, as part of the adjoining
close of the plaintiff so abutting thereon as aforesaid; and
the same portions of the said allowance for road, and the
said close of the plaintiff, were then under certain crops
thereon growing, consisting, to wit, of, &c. : yet the defendants, well knowing, &c., but contriving, &c., whilst the plaintiff was so possessed of the said close, and of the said portion
of the said government allowance for road as aforesaid; and
whilst the same respectively were under crop as aforesaid—
to wit, on, &c.—and on divers other days and times, wrongfully, unlawfully, unjustly, and injuriously removed, prostrated, destroyed, and carried away a portion of the plaintiff's
said fence enclosing the said government allowance for road
and the said close of the plaintiff on the south-west corner of
said close, and on that part of the said government allowance
for road abutting thereon as aforesaid; whereby, and by
reason of the removing, prostrating, destroying, and carrying
away of the said fence as aforesaid, divers cattle and other
animals—to wit, &c.—then running at large, strayed through
the opening caused by the removing, prostrating, destroying,
and carrying away of the said fence by the defendants as
aforesaid, into the said government allowance for road abutting on the plaintiff's said close as aforesaid, and from thence
into the plaintiff's said close, and then trod down, trampled
upon, eat up, depastured, consumed, and spoiled the said
crops of the plaintiff on said government allowance for road
abutting on said close as aforesaid, and on said close then
growing and being, the same being, to wit, of the value aforesaid; whereby the plaintiff was not only deprived of the use
and benefit of his said crops, and of all benefit to be derived
therefrom, but was also forced and obliged to pay out, incur,
and expend, and did pay out, incur, and expend divers large
sums of money, in the whole amounting to £40, in and about
the procuring timber for and setting up new fences to protect
the residue of his said crops on said close from further injury
by the said cattle, and in and about watching and protecting

the residue of his said crops from further injury until the said last-mentioned fence was set up and erected on said close.

A count in trover was added.

The defendant pleaded as to the removing, prostrating, and carrying away the said fence, &c., that before the said times when, &c., the plaintiff had wrongfully erected the said fence across the said government allowance for road abutting on the south-west corner of the said close of the plaintiff; and that the said government allowance for road is, and at the said several times when, &c., was a government allowance for road, and a public and common highway for all the liege subjects of her Majesty to pass and repass, &c.; and that all the liege subjects aforesaid, before and at the said times when, &c., of right ought to have passed and repassed, and still of right ought to pass and repass on foot, and on and along the said government allowance for road at all times of the year, at their free will and pleasure;—that they (the defendants), being liege subjects aforesaid, at the said several times when, &c., had occasion to use the said government allowance for road, and to pass on and along the same, and had passed on and along the same to the said part of the said government allowance for road in which, &c.; and because the said fence had before the said several times when, &c., been wrongfully erected, &c., and was then wrongfully standing and remaining in and upon the said part of the government allowance for road in which, &c., and obstructing the same, so that without removing, &c., the said fence, the said defendants could not then pass on and along the said allowance for road, as they ought to have done; and because the defendants could not then pass on and along the said part of the said government allowance for road in which, &c., the defendants, at the said several times when, &c., in order to remove the said obstruction on the said government allowance for road in which, &c., and in order to enable themselves to pass on and upon the said part of the said allowance for road in which, &c.,—removed, &c., the said fence and the materials thereof in the introductory part of this plea mentioned, and took and carried away the same to a small and convenient distance, and there left the

same for the use of the plaintiff, doing no unnecessary damage, as they lawfully might for the cause aforesaid, and
thereby caused an opening through which the said cattle in
the said first count mentioned strayed in and upon the said
government allowance and the said close in the said first
count mentioned, and a little tore down, &c., the said crops,
without the default of the defendant, or any or either of
them ; which are the same grievances, &c.

Demurrer—Because the defendants could not lawfully
remove the fence from the said government allowance for
road in said first count mentioned, and which had been so
long closed up, without an order of the county council authorizing them to do so, or under a by-law of the township
municipality in which said government allowance for road is
situate ; and because the said fourth plea, although it confesses the grievances complained of by the plaintiff against
the defendants in the said first count, yet does not sufficiently avoid the same in this, that, even admitting the
supposed right claimed by the defendants to remove the portion of the said fence on the said government allowance for
road, yet they had no right to throw open the plaintiff's close
in the said first count mentioned as they did, and thereby
allow cattle running at large to enter the plaintiff's said close
and consume his crops ; for if they removed the fence in the
government allowance for road, they were bound to protect
plaintiff's close from injury ; and the plea being pleaded to
the whole of the grievances complained of in the said first
count, and avoiding only part, is bad in part ; and being
bad in part, is bad in toto.

The defendant joined in demurrer, and served notice of
exceptions to the declaration, on the ground that there was a
misjoinder, the first count being substantially a count in trespass, which could not be joined with a count in trover.
These exceptions were not inserted in the demurrer books
delivered by the plaintiff, and on that ground it was objected that they could not be argued. The court, however,
allowed the plaintiff's counsel to support the exceptions.

Richards, for the plaintiff, cited in support of the demurrer
to the plea—9 Vic. ch. 8 ; Purdy v. Farley, 10 U. C. R. 545.

Christopher Robinson, contra, admitted the plea to be bad, but supported the exceptions to the declaration, citing Hudson v. Nicholson, 5 M & W. 437 ; Weeton v. Woodcock, 5 M. & W. 587 ; Hensworth v. Fowkes, 4 B. & Ad. 449.

ROBINSON, C. J., delivered the judgment of the court.

The plea is bad, we think, but most certainly not for the second reason assigned as cause of demurrer; for if the allowance for road referred to were at the time of the alleged injury a common public highway, along which all her Majesty's subjects had a right to pass and repass, and if the plaintiff had wrongfully enclosed and was wrongfully occupying it, then no doubt the defendant would be justified in abating the nuisance by simply pulling down the fence, and he would not be bound to take care of the plaintiff's crops by erecting a fence on the line on which the plaintiff ought to have erected it.

But the statute of 9 Vic. ch. 8, which is remarked upon in the case of Purdy v. Farley in this court (10 U. C. R. 545), having so far sanctioned and protected the possession on which the plaintiff has relied in this case, and which the plea does not traverse, as to forbid the opening of any such abandoned line until an order is made for that purpose by the municipal council, it follows that the fence in question cannot be held to have been wrongfully there at the time, as the plea asserts, and the defendants had no right to remove it without an order of the municipal council. They have therefore committed a wrong, which gave the plaintiff a right of action ; but the defendants, not being confident that they could maintain their plea, decided to take some exceptions to the declaration, of which it seems they gave due notice to the party demurring, who nevertheless omitted to enter them in the demurrer books which he delivered.

This authorizes us under our rule of court (29th) of Hilary Term, 13 Vic. (Draper's Rules 61), in our discretion, to give judgment in favor of the party who gave such notice of his intended objections ; but, as the effect of this would be to support a plea as a valid defence which is manifestly bad in substance, we forbear to take that course ; and we have not insisted, as we might have done, and as it will probably be better hereafter to do, upon striking the case out of the paper, leaving it to be again set down when what is required by the practice shall have been complied with.

The objections to the declaration have been discussed in fact on the argument, and it would be inconsistent with the spirit of the rule that the defendant, who has given notice of his exceptions, should suffer any disadvantage from the plaintiff not having noted them on the demurrer books delivered by him.

Then as to the sufficiency of the declaration, the plaintiff complains of the defendant for entering wrongfully upon a close of which the plaintiff avers he was in possession, and pulling down the fences which he had erected upon the close; and he treats that, not as a direct act of trespass, but as a wrongful act for which he may sue in case, claiming the consequential damage, and he joins with his statement of this cause of action a count in trover.

We do not see any ground on which we can distinguish this case from Weeton v. Woodcock (5 M. & W. 587). It has been always held that a misjoinder may be taken advantage of on writ of error or in arrest of judgment, and *a fortiori* on general demurrer.

JONES V. BAIN.

2 *Vic. ch.* 15, *sec.* 5—14 & 15 *Vic. ch.* 54. *sec.* 5.

An action against a Commissioner of Indian Affairs for seizing and selling lumber cut on Indian land, must be brought within six months from the seizure, not from the sale.

TRESPASS for seizing and carrying away the plaintiff's lumber, and converting and disposing of the same to defendant's own use.

A special case was stated, from which it appeared that defendant was one of the Commissioners of Indian Affairs, appointed under 2 Vic. ch. 15, and acted as such commissioner in making the seizure of the lumber, which was after-

wards sold under instructions from Colonel Bruce, the Superintendent General.

The seizure was made previous to the 12th September,
1853, and the sale took place on the 8th October following.
The writ issued on the 25th March, 1854.

The defendant claimed that he was entitled to the protection of the act 14 & 15 Vic. ch. 54, and objected that the
action was not commenced within six months after the trespass complained of.

There were other questions in the case, which were
discussed upon the argument, but they are omitted here as
the judgment does not proceed upon them.

Connor, Q. C., for the plaintiff. *Richards,* contra.

The cases referred to are cited in the judgment.

ROBINSON, C. J., delivered the judgment of the court.

The first question to be disposed of in this case is whether
the action was brought in time, for unless it was, there is no
occasion to consider whether the act of the defendant was
lawful or unlawful.

It is not disputed that the defendant is entitled to the
protection given to public officers by our statute 13 & 14 Vic.
ch. 54, which enacts (sec. 8) that no action shall be brought
against any public officer for anything done by him in the
performance of his public duty, "unless *commenced within
six calendar months after the act committed.*

This action was commenced on the 25th of March, 1854.
the seizure of the lumber by the defendant was made on the
12th of September, 1853, and it was sold on the 8th October
following. The action was therefore brought within six
calendar months of the sale of the lumber, but not within
six calendar months of the seizure.

We understand the act complained of was done under an
authority supposed to be given by the fifth clause of 2 Vic.
ch. 15, which directs that all timber and trees unlawfully cut
down upon Indian lands may be seised, detained, sold, and
disposed of as the government may direct ; and the proceeds
of the sale are by the act placed at the disposal of the
government ; and whether this timber was seized under that

act or any of the other acts which relate to trespassers upon public lands, it would equally have been seised as forfeited, and with the intention of depriving the person from whom it was taken of all beneficial interest in the timber.

This then appears to us to be one of that class of cases in which it has been held that the time allowed for bringing the action is to be reckoned from the time of the seisure, and begins to run before the subsequent sale, which in truth is not a distinct or additional wrong done, but a mere dealing with the timber subsequent to the seizure, by an act which gives no new or additional ground of complaint to the person from whom the timber was taken, because it inflicts upon him no additional injury, and the cause of action cannot therefore be treated as continuing.

I refer to Godin v. Ferris (2 H. Bl. 14), Saunders v. Saunders (2 East 254), Smith v. Wiltshire (2 B. & B. 619). On this ground we give judgment that a nonsuit be entered.

During this term the following gentlemen were called to the bar:—CHARLES SIDNEY COSENS, CHARLES FREDERICK ELIOT, J. D. BUELL, CHARLES HENRY POWELL, GEORGE L. W. MOWAT, JOHN CREASOR, Jr.

At a very numerous meeting of the Bar, in Osgoode
Hall, on Tuesday, the 21st of November, A.D. 1854, the
Hon. ROBERT BALDWIN in the Chair, and H. N. GWYNNE,
Esq., Secretary, the following resolutions were adopted
unanimously :

1st. *Resolved,* That the following Address to the Chief
Justice of Upper Canada be presented in open Court, by
the Bar, through the Chairman, the Treasurer of the Law
Society.

To THE HONORABLE SIR JOHN BEVERLEY ROBINSON, BART.,
CHIEF JUSTICE OF UPPER CANADA.

The Bar of Upper Canada desire to express to your
Lordship their warm congratulations on the testimony
recently borne by the Crown to your public and private
worth, in conferring upon you the title and dignity of the
Baronetage.

Presiding, as your Lordship has done, for more than a
quarter of a century over the Judiciary of Upper Canada,
your name has been associated with most that is worthy of
being rescued from oblivion in our brief legal history ; and
your influence and example have largely contributed to
uphold the character and conduct of the Courts in their
relations and intercourse with the Bar.

Some few of those who now address you can personally
testify to the whole of your Lordship's useful and distinguished career : to the memory of the majority belongs a
narrower retrospect.

All will, however, cordially bear grateful testimony to the
manly and becoming dignity, the patient attention, and the
considerate and gratifying courtesy which have invariably
characterized your presidency on the Bench and your intercourse with the Bar.

Believing, as we do, that the truest safeguards of rational
liberty lie in a Bench of unfettered independence and
unsullied purity, and in a Bar commanding the confidence
and respect of the public, we cannot be forgetful of the
important part your Lordship has borne in maintaining, by
influence and example, the high tone and dignity of the one,
and respecting on all occasions the position and privileges of
the other.   With the most earnest desire that a career in
which honor and distinction were so early won, and so long

and so worthily retained and increased, may be blessed with
a long, a peaceful, and a happy evening, the Bar again
repeat their congratulations to your Lordship on the acqui-
sition of an honor alike worthy of the gracious Sovereign
who has bestowed and the faithful subject who has received it.

2nd. *Resolved*, That the Bar request the Hon. Mr.
Baldwin, as their spokesman, to congratulate the Hon. Mr.
Justice DRAPER on his recent appointment to the Com-
panonship of the Order of the Bath.

3rd. *Resolved*, That Mr. Baldwin do leave the Chair, and
that Mr. Ridout do take the same.

Mr. RIDOUT having taken the Chair,

4th. *Resolved*, That the Bar also desire to offer to their
late excellent chairman, Mr. BALDWIN, their congratulations
on the honor recently conferred upon him by our Sovereign,
in nominating him to the Companionship of the Order of
the Bath, and to express to him their high respect for his
character as a man and a lawyer.

5th. *Resolved*, That the Chairman be requested to communicate the above resolutions, to the Law Society, for
insertion in their minutes.

The Bar having taken their places in Court, and the
Judges of the Courts of Chancery and Common Pleas being
also present, Mr. BALDWIN read the address to the Chief
Justice, and communicated the substance of the resolution
to Mr. Justice DRAPER.

THE CHIEF JUSTICE returned the following answer :—
Mr. Treasurer of the Law Society, and Gentlemen of the Bar:

I am wholly taken by surprise by this kind expression
of your warm congratulations upon the notice which Her
Majesty has been graciously pleased to take of my public
services, for I could not imagine that a compliment entirely
personal would have been regarded by your learned body
with so lively an interest. This is the more gratifying to me
from the circumstance that this proof of your friendly regard
comes after so long an intercourse between myself and the
Bar,—an intercourse which, I am happy to say, I can look
back upon without any recollection that can detract from
the pleasure which it gave to me while it was passing.

I should not do justice to the Bar of Upper Canada, or to
myself, if I did not take this suitable occasion of declaring
the gratification I have felt in observing the increasing claims
which the profession in Upper Canada are daily establishing
to the confidence and admiration of their fellow subjects.

Present—THE HON. WILLIAM HENRY DRAPER, J.
"   ROBERT EASTON BURNS, J.*

TOWSLEY v. SMITH.

Dower—Exchange—Evidence.

Dower—Plea, that the husband exchanged other lands with one F. for the lands in question, and that the demandant elected to be endowed of such other lands. To prove this exchange, an ordinary deed of bargain and sale of other lands was produced, executed by demandant's husband, for an expressed consideration of £600; and it was shewn clearly by parol evidence that the transaction between F. and the husband was in fact an exchange.

Held, that such evidence could not avail; that the exchange must be proved in proper technical form and by deed; and that the demandant was therefore entitled to succeed.

The count claimed dower in lands in West Oxford, on the seizin, of Alanson Towsley, demandant's late husband.

The plea admitted the seisin, but avoided the claim of dower by asserting that the husband, during the coverture, was also seised in fee of lands in Zorra, and that he *exchanged* these lands with one Fairbush for the lands wherein the demandant claimed dower, whereby the demandant became entitled to dower in either of the lands at her election. The plea then asserted that she elected to be endowed of the lands in Zorra, and released her dower therein in consideration of £50.

The replication was, that demandant's husband did not exchange the lands in Zorra for those in West Oxford *modo et formâ*.

At the trial at Woodstock, before *Robinson*, C.J., evidence was given that demandant's husband located the land in Zorra, and occupied it on or before 1819 ; that Fairbush, claiming, and no doubt being entitled, as owner in fee, occupied the land in West Oxford ; that the two exchanged their repective possessions; and that in November, 1823, demandant's husband conveyed the Oxford lands to one King, under whom the defendant derived title. No title to Fairbush was

---

*The Chief Justice was absent during this term in England.

put in, nor any deed from Fairbush to the demandant's husband. It was sworn that demandant's husband gave a bond for a deed of the Zorra lands to Fairbush, which bond Fairbush assigned to one Dodge, to whom demandant's husband gave a power of attorney to take out the crown patent. The patent was sworn to have issued in the name of demandant's husband, but it was not produced. A deed, bearing date 29th of May, 1832, from demandant's husband to Dodge for the Zorra land was proved, being a bargain and sale for an expressed consideration of £600. These lands became, by a chain of regular conveyance, vested in one Jones, to whom the demandant, by a deed poll dated 29th of April, 1854, in consideration of £50, released all claim to dower in the Zorra lands. Two witnesses distinctly swore that demandant's husband and Fairbush, on several occasions, said that they had exchanged lands.

The admissibility of any parol evidence respecting the alleged transaction was resisted at the trial, and at the conclusion of the case a verdict was by consent taken for the demandant, subject to the opinion of the court whether the facts proved entitled the tenant to a verdict; and it was agreed that the court might draw such inferences from the evidence as the jury at the trial had authority to do.

Eccles for the demandant; *D. G. Miller* contra.
The authorities cited are referred to in the judgment.

DRAPER, J.—The question is, does the evidence given in this case sustain and establish the plea ?

The rule of law is, that a widow is entitled to dower out of all lands whereof her husband was seised (in fee, &c.,) during the coverture.

The exception applicable to this case is, that she shall not be endowed both of land given in exchange and of land taken in exchange, though her husband was seised of both ; but she may have her election to be endowed of which she will— Co. Lit. 31 b; Perk. sec. 319. The plea admits the seisin, which would give her the benefit of the rule, but it states an additional fact in order to bring her under the exception.

Mr. Crabbe, in his treatise on the law of real property, p. 379, thus explains the rule why the widow shall not be endowed both of the lands taken and those given in exchange: "If she were allowed dower out of both estates, and endowed of them, accordingly, then so soon as her dower was assigned out of her husband's land given in exchange, her endowment of those which were accepted by him in that transaction would be defeated by the entry of the owner of them previously to the exchange, under the implied condition annexed to exchanges by the law; so that the widow could not possibly enjoy permanent dower in both estates—See Bustard's case, 4 Co. 121. The law, therefore, in order to protect her against improvident exchanges by her husband of his lands, which might be injurious to the right of dower, permits her election to endowment out of either of the estates given or accepted in exchange, but does not allow her dower out of both."

The demandant has accepted dower, or rather a satisfaction for it, in consideration whereof she has released her dower out of the Zorra lands. These were her husband's lands; the lands which, according to the plea, he gave in exchange for the West Oxford lands. If the transaction between her husband and Fairbush had been what in law amounts to an exchange, the consequence of her taking her dower out of the Zorra lands would have been to give Fairbush a right to enter upon the West Oxford lands, and to avoid the exchange by force of the condition annexed by implication of law to such a conveyance; for "if there be father and son, and the father, being seised in fee simple of an estate, give it in exchange to a stranger for another estate, and then dies, the son afterwards marries and enters upon the estate taken in exchange; but the stranger, being evicted, enters upon the estate given by him in exchange to the father, Under these circumstances, the widow of the son will not be entitled dower of this last estate, because the son's seisin was entirely defeated upon the eviction of and entry by the stranger, in consequence of the implied condition annexed to all exchanges, that if either party be evicted of the thing received in exchange through the defect of the other's title, he shall

return to the possession of his own."—Crabbe, *ub. sup.*
citing Perkins, sec. 309.

All the authorities concur in stating that the word
" exchange" must be used between the parties in making
the exchange.   Since the Statute of Frauds, therefore,
the deed between the parties must contain that word, which
imports a special warranty in respect to the mutual consideration of the lands exchanged.   The necessity for using
the word " exchange,' is thus illustrated in the Touchstone,
page 295 : ." If A. by deed indented give to B. an acre of
land in fee simple or for life, and by the same deed B.
doth give to A. another acre of land in the same manner,
this cannot enure as an exchange.   So if an exchange be
made by word between two lands in one county" (which
might be before the Statute of Frauds), " and before their
entry indentures are made between them of the same lands
without words of exchange, and no livery of seisin is made,
this shall not pass by way of exchange."   And again, page
299 :   " If two do make an exchange by word of mouth,
and after, before either of them enter, they make indentures of the lands exchanged, and grant the same from
one to another, it seems hereby the nature of the exchange
is altered and the exchange determined."

If, then, the widow is to be deprived of her *primâ facie*
right to be endowed of all the lands whereof her husband
was seised during the coverture, it must be by reason of the
particular nature of the husband's title, of its being a title
by exchange, which has both a condition of re-entry and a
special warranty incident and annexed to it, because the
election of the widow is a consequence of the condition of
re-entry.

That the exchange of possession is insufficient by itself to
effect an exchange of the estates, will not, I suppose, be
denied, any more than that an exchange evidenced by words
only, and made without deed, is, since 29 Car. II. ch. 3,
inoperative and void.   It is true that in order to prove the
husband's seisin, if that be denied, the demandant is not
driven of necessity to produce and prove his title deeds.
She might, I apprehend, rest her case on proof that he died

in possession, or that he had been in possession as owner
twenty years and upwards, or, as was held in Lockman v.
Ness (5 O. S. 506), that her husband was in possession and
made a conveyance in fee simple. But in none of these
cases would any other legal inference or presumption arise
than that the husband was seized in fee simple; but when
it is endeavored to establish not merely that the husband
was so seized, but that he derived his seisin in such a manner—that is, *by such a form of conveyance*, for it amounts
to that—that the widow cannot, by reason of some act of
her own, which but for the conveyance to the husband
would have no such effect, claim dower by virtue of the
husband's seizin, the question to my mind assumes a very
different shape.

Suppose the defendant had pleaded a deed from Fairbush
to demandant's husband of the Oxford lands, and another
deed from the husband to Fairbush, in which the word
"exchange" was not used, but a money consideration was
stated, could he have supplied the want by averment that
the transaction was one of exchange—in the same manner as
in Vernon's case (4 Co. 1) the tenant pleaded to an action
of dower that the demandant's husband was seized of certain
lands in fee, and thereof infeoffed T., G. and others, and
their heirs, to the use of himself for life, and after his decease
to the use of demandant for her life, and *averred* that the
said estate for life so limited to the demandant was for her
jointure and in full satisfaction of her dower; and that after
the death of the husband the demandant entered into the land
so limited to her for her jointure, and agreed to it, in order
to bring the case within the statute 27 H. VIII. ch. 10? I
apprehend the defendant could not have supplied the omission in the deeds of the word "exchange" by any such averment. The contrary is expressly laid down in the Touchstone,
page 295, where it is said this word (exchange) is so individually requisite as it cannot be supplied by any other word,
" *neither will any averment that it was in exchange help in
this case.*" And this, in my humble judgment, renders it
unnecessary to labor to distinguish this case from those in
which the courts have held that a consideration which stands

with the deed, and is not repugnant to it, may be averred.
See Doe Milburn v. Salkeld (Willes 673) and the cases
therein cited; Gale v. Williamson (8 M. & W. 405), Rex v.
The Inhabitants of Cheadle (3 B. & Ad. 833), and Clifford
v. Turrill (9 Jur. 633).

But if the defendant could not by pleading the deeds, add
to them the word "exchange," or give them the effect which
that word would give by some express averment, can he by
pleading generally that the demandant's husband exchanged
the Zorra lands with Fairbush for the lands in West Oxford,
and by proving an exchange of possession, coupled with a
declaration, no matter how often repeated, of both those
parties that they had changed lands, effect the same end?

Suppose it was clear that no deed whatever had passed
between them, it will scarcely be contended that such declarations and change of possession supply the want; or suppose that deeds were before us in the ordinary form of bargain
and sale, for money consideration, made by each the other
of these parties for the lands they respectively owned: it
seems to me too clear to bear argument that the evidence in
such case would not avail to vary or add to, not the consideration, but the whole legal effect and incidents of the conveyance—See Goodtitle v. Otway (2 H. Bl. 516). I fully
recognize the principle of giving effect to the intention of
parties: *benignè faciendæ sunt interpretationes propter sim-
plicitatem laicorum, ut res magis valeat quàm pereat, et verba
intentioni non e contra debent inservire.* But this rule
applies to the construction of the instruments made by parties
and of the language used in such instruments, and the intent
which is apparent, though insufficiently expressed, on a consideration of the instrument itself. In the present case, I
do not see how any application of this principle can help;
for the only deed in evidence, which either the demandant's
husband or Fairbush have executed in pursuance of their
agreement, is the deed to Dodge of the Zorra lands. This
being taken as a fulfilment of the condition of the bond from
demandant's husband to Fairbush, may be fairly presumed to
be in accordance with it; and it is a common deed of bargain
and sale for a money consideration, negativing instead of

sustaining the defendant's allegation of an exchange ; and
Dodge may have taken the deed in this form advisedly.
The buildings and other improvements on the Zorra lands
may have been such that he did not desire to run the
possible risk of re-entry by demandant's husband if the
title to the West Oxford lands should prove defective ; and
the demandant's husband, by giving such a conveyance,
would destroy the previous parol bargain, as is expressly
stated in the passages cited from the Touchstone.   On the
whole, I feel constrained to hold that the alleged exchange
must be proved in its proper technical form and by deed ;
because, for the reasons given by Mr. Crabbe, it is only
upon such a title that the widow is put to her election as
the plea insists, and it is only by reason of a legal incident
to such a title that she can be barred.

In my opinion the plaintiff is entitled to the postea ; for
I think that the evidence not only fails to prove a title by
exchange in the demandant's husband, but, so far as it goes,
proves the contrary ; and then the case is simply that of a
widow claiming dower out of two several estates, of the
freehold and inheritance whereof her husband was seized
during the coverture.

BURNS, J.—The merits of the case upon the evidence,
if we were at liberty to consider it, appear to be with the
tenant ; but still we are called on to say whether in law the
demandant is entitled to retain the verdict.   It is urged on
her behalf that though the evidence may sustain the truth of
the plea, yet she is entitled to judgment, because the seizin
of her husband in the land in question stands admitted upon
the record ; and that fact alone entitles her to recover in a
court of law, if the other facts necessary to sustain the action
are not denied.   It is quite true the seizin of the husband is
admitted, as also the demandant's right to dower by reason
of her marriage ; but the question raised by the plea is,
whether that position is not displaced by the fact that such
seizin was acquired by virtue of other lands given in exchange
for that out of which dower is now claimed, and that the
demandant has elected to take and has obtained her dower

in the other land given by her husband in exchange. Two questions present themselves for consideration—first, whether such general mode of pleading be sufficient, without setting out in the plea the titles under which the husband was seized of the lands, and the description of conveyance by which the exchange was effected; and, secondly, if the general mode of pleading here adopted be sufficient, then by what species of evidence the same can be proved, and whether in this case, upon the production of the title, parol evidence can afterwards be received to shew a different tenure than imported by the conveyance. Previous to the Statute of Frauds (29 Car. II. ch. 3) an exchange could have been made by word without any writing, and of course could have been proved by parol. Vernon's case (4 Co. 1) shews that in pleading it was sufficient to aver facts which destroyed the demandant's right to dower; and such facts might at that time undoubtedly have been established by parol evidence. Mr. Thomas, in his note to that case, says: " there is nothing in the Statute of Frauds excluding averments, and it is the received opinion that whatever averments might have been made before that statute may be made now." I have always so understood the law to be; and therefore conclude that the plea is sufficient in point of form to bar the demandant, and that it was unnecessary for the tenant to set forth the species of conveyance by which the exchange was effected. Then it is to be considered how and what is the proper mode of establishing the truth of the plea. The title which the demandant's husband obtained for the land in question is not produced; so that we do not see whether the person who professed to transfer to him did so exchange or not. The probability is, that it does not so express the transaction, but that it is like the conveyance which the husband gave for the other land—a common, ordinary deed of bargain and sale, expressed to be for a money consideration. Taking the case upon the deed produced, then, as between the parties themselves to the conveyance, there can be no doubt that parol evidence would not be receivable to contradict or vary the terms thereof, and they would not be at liberty to aver that the transaction was an exchange in face of the conveyance importing the contrary.

The widow's right to dower does not depend upon the conveyance, but upon the seizin of her husband during coverture. Seizin is defined by Lord Mansfield, in Taylor v. Horde (1 Burr. 107), to be this : Seizin is a technical term to denote the completion of that investiture by which the tenant was admitted into the tenure, and without which no freehold could be constituted or pass." This seizin may be established by or be repelled by parol evidence, without production or proof of the title deeds. It is not a fact which necessarily depends upon the conveyances. Here the seizin of the husband is admitted upon the record ; and if the case had rested upon the evidence that the husband had obtained the land in question for the other, and that each had entered accordingly, I should have thought the plea well proved without the production or proof of the title deeds. The tenant, however, has proved the title which the demandant's husband gave for the other land, and the conveyance imports that the transaction was not an exchange. The question, then, is reduced to this, whether, after shewing a conveyance importing upon the face of it that the plea is not true, can he at the same time be allowed to prove by parol evidence that the transaction was different ? If the evidence offered were to vary or add to, or even to change the consideration mentioned in the conveyance, then, this litigation being between persons not parties to the conveyance, I think the tenant would be at liberty to shew the true state of facts. Many cases establish this proposition—See The King v. Scammonden (3 T. R. 474), The King v. Laindon (8 T. R. 379), Green v. Weston (Say. 209), The King v. The Inhabitants of Cheadle (3 B. & Ad. 833), Gale v. Williamson (8 M. & W. 405) ; see, also, the observations of Lord Lyndhurst upon what was stated by Lord Hardwicke in Peacock v. Morell (1 Ves. Sen. 128, that, unless the conveyance expressed to be for other considerations as well as a money consideration, parol evidence could not be received—Clifford v. Turrill (9 Jur. 633).

In the case before us the evidence is not offered to change or vary the consideration, but for the purpose of altering the construction of the conveyance, and saying that the husband did not hold by the tenure which he himself says he did.

The deed produced shews that the land said to be given in exchange was not so ; and, as an exchange must be mutual, if there were any mistake in that conveyance in respect of the mode of tenure, the tenant would be bound to shew, by production of the title of the land taken in lieu of it, that such mistake existed. His case does not rest upon any such proposition, that a mistake has been made, but it rests upon the proposition that, notwithstanding he has produced the conveyance, he is still at liberty to controvert the effect of it, by shewing the mode of tenure by which the husband held the land. The right of the demandant to dower being a presumption of law, as admitted by the pleadings on this record, might, I think, have been repelled by parol evidence, on the ground of being an extrinsic fact dependent on its own weight and authority ; but when the tenant shews, as he has done, that the husband's seizin is under a conveyance, importing that her right to dower is not only *presumptio juris*, but also *de jure*, then I do not see that he is at liberty to aver the contrary by parol. In Goodtitle v. Otway (2 H. Bl. 516) Mr. Justice Buller says : " I cannot find from any one case quoted at the bar that the court has received parol evidence in the case of a deed executed by the party himself, with a view of altering the construction of the instrument." Whenever the title is shewn, then the seizin of the party taking under it must be referable to such a seizin as the instrument confers ; and that tenure, I apprehend, cannot be varied or altered by parol evidence shewing that the parties did something else which might intend that the construction of the instrument should be such as that in operation of law a different tenure would be created. This last is the true effect of what is sought to be accomplished in this case, but I do not think it is consistent with authority to permit it. The plaintiff is therefore entitled to retain the verdict.

Judgment for the plaintiff (*a*).

(*a*) At the conclusion of the judgment, *Draper*, *J.*, mentioned that he had, in this case, conferred with the Chief Justice, before his leaving ; and that, so far as he had formed any opinion, he believed it was contrary to the judgment now given, and that *Burns*, *J.*, had, until very lately, agreed with the Chief Justice ; for himself, he had always thought the present opinion correct.

CUMMINGS ET AL V. MORGAN.

Chattel mortgage—Effect of, on timber made after execution.

The plaintiffs held a chattel mortgage from one C. of 700 pieces of timber, " together with whatever quantity of squared timber the said party of the first part may manufacture during the remainder of the season." The timber made after the execution of this mortgage was marked as it was got out with the plaintiff's mark, but remained in C's possession, and was seized there by the defendant, an execution creditor.
Held, that the plaintiffs could not recover for it under the mortgage.

INTERPLEADER ISSUE.—It was admitted that the plaintiffs were entitled to 700 pieces of timber under a bill of sale by way of mortgage from one Jacob Jea Cook to them, dated the 18th of February, 1853, in consideration of £400 advanced and to be advanced to him. The contest between the parties was in respect of a quantity of timber got out by the said Cook, and said to be delivered to the plaintiffs beyond the quantity mentioned. The mortgage was of these 700 pieces, " together with whatever further quantity of squared timber the said party of the first part may manufacture during the remainder of the season."

The defendant was an execution creditor of Cook, the *Fi Fa.* having been, delivered to the sheriff on the 20th of June, 1853.

At the trial, before *McLean, J.,* at the last spring assizes held at Belleville, it appeared that Cook got out upwards of 870 pieces of timber, 700 pieces of which were delivered in February, 1853, the residue in the spring. The timber was marked with the plaintiffs' mark as it was got out, and Cook considered it as delivered. The arrangement between the plaintiffs and Cook was, that Cook should take the timber to Quebec, where the plaintiffs were to sell it, and account for the proceeds. The plaintiffs might take the timber out of the possession of Cook at any time, and sell when and where they pleased. The timber, though marked with the plaintiffs' mark, remained in the possession of Cook afterwards just as it did previously, and the plaintiffs were no otherwise in possession than by the marking it with their mark. The timber was seized in the possession of Cook, but the defendant did not deny the plaintiffs' right to 700 pieces which were mentioned in the mortgage.

A verdict was taken for the plaintiffs, subject to the opinion of the court whether the plaintiffs could recover for the timber not included in the mortgage.

DRAPER, J.—Looking at all the circumstances of the case it appears to me clear that the plaintiffs had no right to any part of the timber made by Cook, whether made upon the 18th of February, 1853, the date of the assignment, or subsequently, except as mortgagees. There is no evidence to shew that any part of it was theirs absolutely, or that it was made for them as their sole property.

Their right to the 700 pieces which were made at the date of the assignment is not questioned by the defendant. The questions that arise seem therefore to be, whether the sub-sequently-made timber became subject as it was made, and marked to the provisions of the deed of assignment, which was by way of mortgage, so as to protect it for the plaintiffs' benefit against execution creditors; or if not (assuming the evidence and the facts to establish a parol assignment by way of mortgage), whether a parol mortgage of this subse-qently-made timber could be valid against such creditors.

We must look at our statutes 12 Vic. ch. 74, and 13 Vic. ch. 62, by the first of which every mortgage or conveyance intended to operate as a mortgage of goods and chattels made after the passing thereof, which shall not be accom-panied by an immediate delivery and be followed by an actual and continual change of possession of the things mortgaged, shall be absolutely void as against the creditors of the mortgagor, and as against subsequent purchasers and mortgagees in good faith, unless the mortgage or conveyance or a true copy thereof, together with an affidavit of the witness thereto of the due execution of the mortgage or conveyance, shall be filed as thereinafter directed. And the second statute amends the first section above quoted by adding to the end thereof—And that every sale of goods and chattels which shall not be accompanied by an imme-diate delivery and followed by an actual and continued change of possession of the goods and chattels sold, *shall be in writing*, and such writing shall be a conveyance under the provisions of the former act.

Notwithstanding the expression in the last Act as to conveyances, that they "shall be in writing," and the omission
thereof in the first act as to mortgages and conveyances
intended to operate as mortgages of goods and chattels, it
appears to me impossible to hold that a mortgage of chattels
made by parol only, unaccompanied by change of possession,
can be effectual as against creditors; for being by parol only,
neither the original mortgage nor yet a copy of it could be
registeréd, and to hold that because registration was in fact
impossible, therefore it became *unnecessary*, and that such a
mortgage would be valid without it, would be contrary to the
plain meaning of the legislature, and would afford a method
of evading the provisions of a most salutary act, intended to
prevent frauds. I should be more inclined to construe the
word " copy" as including a statement in writing of a mortgage made by parol, which might be verified by the affidavit of
a witness, as the term "*subscribing*" witness is not used, than
to conclude that a parol mortgage unaccompanied by change
of possession could be effectual against creditors notwithstanding the act—See Ausman v. Armstrong (11 U. C. R. 498.)

That a grant of goods which are not in existence, or which
do not belong to the grantor at the time of executing the
deed, is void unless the grantor ratify the grant by some act
done by him with that view after he had acquired the
property therein, is established by the case of Lunn v.
Thornton (1 C. B. 379), and in Short v. Ruttan (12 U. C.
Q. B. 79-84) the Chief Justice used the following language:
"As a general principle we take it to be clear, that an
assignment of personal property, whether absolute or by way
of mortgage, can only operate upon such property as was in
existence, and as the assignee had an interest in, at the time
of executing the assignment."

The whole tenor of the deed in the present case shews that
the only interest the plaintiffs were intended to take was as
mortgagees. It was only default that they were entitled
to possession, and it is consistent with its express language
that if there should be no default the mortgagor should not
be put out of possession. As to the 700 pieces of timber in
existence when the deed was executed no question arises ;

all turns, so far as the plaintiffs' claim is concerned, on the words "together with whatever further quantity of squared timber the said party of the first part" (the mortgagor ("may manufacture during the remainder of the season," and on the additional facts that the subsequently-manufactured timber was marked with the plaintiffs' mark as it was made, which the mortgagor treated as a delivery to the plaintiffs, and which, as between him and the plaintiffs, probably would be sufficient to give the latter a lien upon it till their debt was satisfied, or a right to take it into their own actual possession on default of the mortgagor.

But here the question arises between the mortgagee and a judgment creditor of the mortgagor, as regards property which cannot pass by the deed, because not in existence at its date; and because, though there was an act done (viz., the marking) by the grantor with intent to ratify the grant, and although the act coupled with the preceding agreement might constitute a mortgage by parol, yet there has been no actual and continued change of possession, nor any registration of any mortgage, written or parol, which could affect the subsequently-made timber.

In our opinion, the postea must be delivered to the defendant.

As to the case of Dunning v. Gordon (4 U. C. R. 450) cited in the argument, it is enough to observe that the statutes above referred to were passed since that decision, even if it were not otherwise distinguishable.

Judgment for defendant (a).

COOK v. FOWLER ET AL.

Replevin—14 & 15 Vic. ch. 64—Non-joinder.

Held, that under the circumstances of this case the plaintiff could have maintained trespass, and consequently that he could bring replevin.
In replevin non-joinder must be pleaded in abatement, and, when there is no such plea, the defendant cannot object that the evidence shews another person to be interested with the plaintff in the goods.

REPLEVIN for taking and detaining fifteen thousand feet of oak timber.

Pleas—1. Non cepit. 2. Timber not the plaintiffs, and

(a) In this case also, Mr. Justice Draper said that he had conferred with the Chief Justice, who concurred in the judgment now given.

issue thereon. 3. That the timber was the property of the defendant Fowler, and issue thereon.

At the trial, before *Macaulay*, C. J. C. P., at Sarnia, the plaintiff's evidence was to the effect that one C. A. Tompkins, an infant, owned a lot of land on which the timber in question had been cut by one Reynolds, who claimed to act under authority from the infant Tompkins, and who sold it to the defendant Fowler: that one Coverley, acting under a power of attorney from the infant's mother, sold it to the plaintiff subsequently to the sale to defendant Fowler. The power of attorney was put in and proved; and one Tyler, called as a witness for the plaintiff, swore that he had bought the timber from Coverley on behalf of the plaintiff, and gave other evidence tending to shew a partnership in the transaction between himself and the plaintiff.

The defendant's counsel moved for a nonsuit, on the grounds, first, that no property was shewn in the plaintiff, the power of attorney to Coverley being from Tompkins's mother, not from himself, and no authority to dispose of the infant's property shewn in her; and that, even if she had such authority, the power of attorney did not delegate it to Coverley, as that merely authorized the disposal of the mother's interest therein, and not the infant's: and secondly, that the property, if any, was in Tyler jointly with the plaintiff, and therefore the action should have been brought by them jointly, and that not having been done, the defendants were entitled to succeed on their second plea, at all events.

The learned judge directed the jury to find for the plaintiff, subject to the opinion of the court on the above points and the evidence, and also to find whether or not Tyler was a partner with the plaintiff in the transaction.

The jury found for the plaintiff, with £2 5s. damages; and that Tyler was such partner.

Leave was reserved to enter a verdict for the defendants, in case the court should so adjudge on the whole case.

Davis for the plaintiff.   *Becher* for defendants.

DRAPER, J., delivered the judgment of the court.

The questions for our decision arise upon the plea denying

the plaintiff's property in the timber, for the defendant gave
no evidence of any right or title in himself, in support of
the third plea.   The first point raised is as to the sufficiency
of proof of the plaintiff's title.   This was derived from
Coverley, and certainly Coverley had not under the power
of attorney any strict legal right to dispose of it, for in
the first place, the expressed power is to act in the name
and for the use and benefit of the widow, not of the
infant, whose right to the lands does not seem to have been
denied; and, in the second place, the widow, the infant's
mother, is not shewn to have been so appointed guardian of
the infant as to give her any authority over his estate.   For
all that appears, she was only guardian by nurture, which
would only give to her the custody of his person and the
care of his education.   But it appeared clearly enough that
Coverley, assuming to act for the infant, had obtained the
actual possession of the timber from Reynolds, against whom
the right of the infant was established by a verdict and
judgment; and that while thus in possession he sold it,
making himself, as I apprehend, responsible for the value to
the infant.   And looking at all the circumstances, I am of
opinion that, after obtaining the possession, he could have
maintained trespass as against any mere wrong-doer; and if
so possessed he was in a situation to sell to a *bona fide* purchaser for valuable consideration, which the plaintiff appears
to have been.   Upon this sale, and possession having been
delivered to the plaintiff as purchaser, the case falls within
the language of the first section of our replevin act; for
here are goods wrongfully taken, and here is a person who
could maintain an action of trespass for such taking, and in
every such case an action of replevin may by the express
words of the act be brought.   If it were not for this very
act the second plea would be bad, for it is a mere denial of
the plaintiff's property, without asserting it to belong to
any one else.   I am of opinion that, as to this objection, the
plaintiff is entitled to hold the verdict.

Then as to the second point, it is said that the defendant
may plead in abatement that the property was in the plaintiff
and a stranger (Co. Lit. 145 b.) ; and such a plea is generally

treated of as a plea in abatement, though, if it be so pleaded, it should shew the defendant entitled to a delivery, without which the force and effect of the replevin would not be taken away.—See Gilb. Repl. 162, 168. But in the present case no such defence is pleaded ; the objection is urged on the evidence, which shews that another party (Tyler) was a joint owner.

If this would under our statute constitute a defence at all, it appears to me that it should have been pleaded. Not being pleaded, I think the defendant cannot now urge it as a bar to the action. The case of Broadbent v. Ledward (11 A. & E. 209) has a strong bearing on this question, though there the action was detinue. The plaintiff has some right, both of property and possession, though another may be also entitled, while the defendants shew no right at all. No case has been cited to shew that such a course is open to the defendants, and that in replevin non-joinder can be objected without a plea in abatement ; and, as *Patteson, J.*, remarks, the rule as to the consequences of the non-joinder of parties as plaintiffs even in actions founded upon contract, is not satisfactory in principle, and ought not to be extended ; *a fortiori* not in actions of the nature of tort.

Postea to the plaintiff.

McLELLAN v. ROGERS.

Lease with right of purchase—Covenant for not conveying—Plea, that indenture avoided by rent in arrear.

Covenant on an indenture, excusing profert, by which the plaintiff demised certain land to defendant for a term of five years, and covenanted to convey to him in fee if he should pay £125 on or before a day named, *Breach*, that although the plaintiff offered the money before the day named, and requested a conveyance, yet the defendant refused.

Plea—after setting out the indenture in full, which contained a proviso that in case the rent or any part thereof should be in arrear for forty days, then the indenture and everything therein contained should be void— that before and at the time of the tender in the declaration mentioned the first year's rent was in arrear for forty days, whereby the indenture and the covenant to convey became void—Verification.

Held, on demurrer, plea good.

The plaintiff declared on an indenture dated the 27th of February, 1851, which indenture, sealed, &c., being in the possession of defendant, the plaintiff is unable to bring into court, whereby the defendant demised and leased to the plaintiff broken lots 10 and 11, in the third concession of West Gwillimbury, for five years, subject to a cesser of the term on condition in the indenture mentioned : and the defendant did thereby covenant to convey to the plaintiff on or before the 27th of February, 1856, by a good and sufficient deed, &c., the fee-simple of the said land, free from incumbrances, if the plaintiff should pay to defendant on or before the said 27th of February, 1856, £125, over and above all rent in the said indenture reserved, as by the said indenture will among other things more fully appear : that although the plaintiff did, before the 27th of February, 1856, to wit, &c., tender and offer to pay defendant the said sum of £125, over and above the rents, and did require the defendant to convey to the plaintiff, at the plaintiff's cost and charges, according to the true intent, &c., of the said indenture, yet the defendant wholly refused ; and so the defendant hath broken his covenant, to the plaintiff's damage of £1000.

Second plea.—That the indenture mentioned in the declaration as being in defendant's possession, the defendant now brings into court, and the same with all and singular the covenants, &c., is shewn to the court in the words following (setting it out in full, and being as far as is important to the question before the court, to the following effect)—that in consideration of the yearly rents and covenants on defendant's part to be paid and performed, the plaintiff demised and leased to defendant the premises stated in the declaration. *Habendum* to the plaintiff for five years from the 27th of February, 1851, subject to sooner determination under the proviso thereinafter mentioned, yielding, &c., every year to defendant the rent of £12 10s. on the 27th of February in each year, the first payment to be made on the 27th of February, 1852 ; and the plaintiff covenanted with defendant to pay the rent as aforesaid, and to pay all taxes, &c., which then were or should during the term become payable in respect of the premises, and to pay to the plaintiff the sum of £125 on or before the 27th of February, 1856, which said sum is to be over and above "the rent and taxes" reserved, or which shall have been paid or payable previous to such payment, and also over and above all taxes; which sum of £125, provided it is punctually paid, is to be accepted by defendant as the price of the premises. And the defendant covenanted with the plaintiff that the plaintiff, paying the yearly rent on the days, &c., and performing the covenants, &c., might peaceably hold and enjoy during the said term; and that if the plaintiff should pay to defendant on or before the said 27th of February, 1856, the said sum of £125 " over and above the rents and taxes" reserved, the defendant would, by deed of bargain and sale, or such other good and lawful deed as might be necessary for that purpose, at the costs of the plaintiff, convey the premises free from all incumbrances to the plaintiff in fee. Provided that if the rent or any part thereof should at any time during the term be in arrear for forty days next after, &c., whether demanded or not, or in case of breach or non-performance of any other covenants to be performed by the plaintiff (such as repairing, &c.), then in any such case the indenture and everything therein contained, and the term thereby granted, should cease, determine, and be absolutely void to all intents and purposes, and defendant should thereupon hold the premises utterly discharged of this lease. Which indenture being read, &c., the defendant says, that after the making thereof, to wit, on, &c., the plaintiff entered and took possession of, &c., under the said indenture; and while the plaintiff was so possessed, and before and at the time of making the tender in the declaration specified, the sum of £12 10s., being the rent reserved for the first year of the term ending on the 27th of February, 1852, was in arrear and unpaid for the space of forty days next after, &c., contrary to the force, &c., whereby the same indenture and everything therein contained, and the term ceased, determined, and became absolutely void, and the covenant to convey became and is absolutely void and no longer binding on defendant: verification.

Demurrer, for the following causes—1. That the plea is informal, setting forth the indenture and pleading that the new matter thereby shewn makes void the defendant's cove-

nant. 2. That the plea puts in issue a question of law for
trial by the jury. 3. That it offers as excuse for the breach
of defendant's covenant the non-performance by the plaintiff
of a condition precedent alleged to be contained in the
indenture mentioned in the declaration ; and the plea does
not state that the rent was not tendered, or that it was in
arrear against the will of the defendant. 4. That the plea
is double, as it relies on a breach of the alleged condition
precedent as an answer to the action, and offers two issues
thereon—first, That the covenant is void ; secondly, That
the matter pleaded discharges the defendant from performance thereof. 5. That the plea is argumentative. 6.
That it is uncertain whether the defendant relies on the
matter pleaded as a discharge, or that the covenant is
wholly void.

Joinder in demurrer, and notice of exception to the declaration, for variances between it and the indenture produced
and set forth in the plea.

Bell, for the demurrer, cited Stephen on Pleading, 5th ed.,
page 77 ; Jenkins v. Peace, 6 M. & W. 723 ; Snell v. Snell,
4 B. & C. 749 ; Newton v. Wilmot, 8 M. & W. 711.

McDonald, contra, cited 2 Co. 214 *a* ; 3 Co. 64 *a* ; Arnsby
v. Woodward, 6 B. & C. 519 ; Doe dem. Bryan v. Bancks,
4 B. & Al. 401.

DRAPER. J.—As regards the first ground of exception to
the plea. In arguing this ground of demurrer Mr. Bell
objected that the defendant should have demurred for the
alleged variance in omitting to notice a condition precedent,
and also that the setting out the indenture and new matter
in connection with its contents as avoiding the defendant's
covenant was an informal way of pleading.

There are many cases which shew that where want of
profert is excused by a party in his pleading, the other party
may set out the instrument. This was done in Hyde v. Watts
(12 M. & W. 254), where the defendant, in debt on common
counts pleaded an indenture, with an excuse of profert,
releasing defendant from the cause of action. The replication stated that the indenture was and is an indenture in the

words and figures following, setting it out in full, and concluding by stating a breach in non-performance of a matter
to be performed by defendant as a condition precedent to the
release.   The defendant rejoined, and there was a demurrer
to the rejoinder, on which the plaintiff had judgment.

In Trott v. Smith (10 M. W. 453) the plaintiff declared in
covenant on an indenture excusing profert on the ground
that the deed was in defendant's possession.   Defendant
pleaded, first, *non est factum ;* and in a second plea he set
out the indenture *in hæc verba,* and set up that the plaintiff
had become bankrupt, and that the cause of action had passed
to his assignees ; and 3rdly, averring that the indenture in
the declaration was the same as set forth in the second plea,
he pleaded a matter arising out of the indenture as so set
forth but not appearing in the declaration.   Both pleas were
demurred to, among other grounds, for not confessing and
avoiding, or traversing and denying the allegations in the
declaration ; and on argument it was insisted that the pleas
amounted to *non est factum,* though the objection was not
taken in that form in the special demurrer.   The court held
the pleas bad, but not on the formal objections.

In Bain v. Kirk (13 Q. B. 540, note), the declaration was
on a deed of which profert was excused on the ground that it
was in defendant's custody.   The defendant set out the whole
deed *in hæc verba,* and pleaded *non est factum.*   The point
raised was, whether a variance between the deed as stated in
the declaration and as set forth in the plea entitled defendant to a verdict.   The declaration stated an absolute covenant
to pay.   The deed set forth in the plea, it was contended,
made the payment dependent on the sufficiency of assets.
The point was not decided by the court.   But in North v.
Wakefield, in a note to which Bain v. Kirk is reported, it
was held, that where a deed is not set out on oyer, but is
pleaded according to its legal effect, *non est factum* puts in
issue, not only the execution, but the alleged construction of
the deed, though if the deed is set out on oyer and does not
support the construction put upon it in the previous pleading, the objection should be raised on demurrer:

Again, in Ricketts v. Loftus (14 Q. B. 482) the declara-

-tion stated that by deed, which being in defendant's custody
the plaintiff could not produce, &c. The plea set out the
deed verbatim, which appeared to be to the effect stated in
the declaration. The plea was specially demurred to, and
was upheld.

These cases, which were not referred to on the argument,
shew that the defendant has the sanction of precedents for
setting out in his plea a deed (of which profert has been
excused in the declaration because it was in defendant's
possession) with a view to founding his defence on some
matter apparent in or arising from its provisions. By
demurring the plaintiff admits the deed set out in the plea to
be that on which he sues. Then it was competent for the
defendant to plead any matter confessing and avoiding the
breach complained of, and the plea is properly concluded
with a verification. In this respect the plea is framed in a
similar manner to that in Ricketts v. Loftus.

In Trott v. Smith new matter also was pleaded, but the
plea concluded to the country ; but no objection was taken
to this conclusion, which may be questionable. The defendant, by setting out the deed in this manner, did not make it
part of the declaration, as would have been the case had it
been set out on oyer. He could not therefore have demurred
on the ground of variance. But having set it out, there
appears in it an express proviso and agreement that in a
certain event the deed and every matter and thing contained
in it should be void. Whether this event had happened or
not was a matter dehors the deed. If the defendant intended
to rely on it, he must necessarily state it in his plea, deducing
the legal conclusion that in such event the action failed.
He concluded properly with a verification, leaving it open to
the plaintiff to take issue on the fact, or admitting it to
demur in law. I do not understand the plea to urge the
non-performance of a condition precedent by way of answer
to the plaintiff, although on reading the deed as set out in
the plea that difficulty suggests itself. The defendant rather
appears to me to waive that and rely on the matter pleaded
as rendering the deed and all that is in it altogether void.
He does not say, "You cannot complain of my not conveying

becouse there was something to be done by you which is not done before you were entitled to call on me to convey ;" but he denies the right to sue, because on the facts alleged in his plea the deed has become wholly void. In this view which is, we think, the correct construction of the plea, the objection of duplicity fails ; and the same answer applies to the last objection.

On the whole we think the defendant entitled to judgment on the demurrer to his plea, and this renders it unnecessary to advert to the objections to the declarations on which I will only observe that such of them as are founded on variance between the deed stated in the declaration and that set out in the plea, are rested apparently on the mistaken assumption that by setting it out *in hæc verba* it is made part of the declaration, in the same manner as if set out on oyer. The law is clearly otherwise.

This judgment renders it unnecessary to grant a new trial which the defendant has moved for on the ground of excessive damages ; though I must say, for myself, that the facts proved on the trial incline me to consider that the defendant has little claim to any exercise of the equitable jurisdiction of the court in his favor.

Possibly a court of equity may relieve the plaintiff, although our judgment must be against him.—See Bowser v. Colby (1 Hare, 109).

Judgment for defendant on demurrer.

LAMPKIN v. THE ONTARIO MARINE AND FIRE INSURANCE COMPANY.

Fire insurance—Notice of loss and particulars of it—How waived—Unsatisfactory verdict.

Where notice of the loss and particulars of it are required by a policy of insurance, they may be waived by the conduct of the insurers.

In this case the declaratio₁ alleged that notice of the loss was given to the defendants forthwith, and an account of the particulars of the loss as soon as possible (such being the conditions of the policy); and issues were taken on these allegations. There were two separate policies, on a shop and on the goods contained in it. Both building and goods were destroyed. It appeared that the fire took place on the 13th of June, and the notices, both as to the shop and the goods, were given on the 13th of July. The defendants then entered into correspondence with the plaintiff as to furnishing better particulars, which were afterwards furnished; and they then refused to pay for the goods on account of some suspicious circumstances attending the fire, but they paid the amount insured on the house :

Held, that under these circumstances the defendants were precluded from objecting to the insufficiency of the notices, or to the time at which they were given

All the evidence on either side as to fraud having been fairly left to the jury, who found for the plaintiff, the court refused to interfere, though they would have been better satisfied with a verdict the other way.

COVENANT on policy of insurance for £500, dated 23rd of May, 1853, covering the plaintiff's stock of dry goods and groceries, and other articles usually kept in a country store, also shop furniture; the whole contained in a building of wood, two stories high, situated on lot No. 3 on the north side of the market square in the village of Port Dover in the occupation of the plaintiff.

Pleas.—1. *Non est factum.* 2. That the plaintiff was not interested in the property insured, as alleged. 3. That the property was not destroyed by fire in the manner alleged. 4. That the property was not duly described, and without concealment or misrepresentation, in conformity with the conditions attached to the policy. 5. That the plaintiff, on the occasion of the fire, did not use his best endeavors to save and preserve the property. 6. That the plaintiff did not forthwith after the loss give notice to the defendants, as alleged. 7. That the plaintiff did not, as soon after the loss as possible, deliver an account of the particulars of the loss. 8. That though the plaintiff did deliver an account of the particulars, yet the same was not signed or verified by his oath, as in the count alleged. 9. That the plaintiff did not make oath or declare the whole value of the said property or effects, or the interest of him the plaintiff therein, or in what general manner the buildings containing the same were occupied at the time of the loss, or how the fire originated, so far. as the plaintiff knew or believed, according to the conditions. 10. That the plaintiff was guilty of fraud, in this, that to defraud the defendants and cause them to pay a larger sum than the loss sustained on occasion of the fire, the plaintiff made and delivered tő the defendants a false and fraudulent account of the alleged loss : that he stated his loss to be £1500, and that insured goods to that amount had been burned ; whereas the loss did not exceed £300. 11. That the affidavit of the plaintiff in support of his claim was false : that he stated that goods were lost to over £1500, whereas he had not sustained such loss ; and that the affidavit was false in other particulars.

At the trial before *Burns, J.*, at the last assizes held at Toronto, it was admitted that the defendants had paid the first policy, which was upon the buildings.   It was agreed between the counsel on both sides that the questions which should be tried were.—1. Whether there was fraud in respect to the quantity of goods contained in the store at the time of the fire. 2. Whether the plaintiff gave the proper preliminary proofs respecting the loss.

The fire occurred on the night of the 13th of June, 1853, No one was in the building at the time, and there had not been any fire used for more than two weeks, as it was stated. The plaintiff and his wife occupied the rooms above the store as a dwelling house until about two weeks before the fire, when the plaintiff's wife had gone on a visit to London, and on her return to Port Dover she and the plaintiff boarded at an inn.   The plaintiff's clerk slept in the store, and he left for Buffalo at six o'clock in the evening before the fire, not intending to return. The plaintiff himself, the evening before the fire, had been with his wife to a place of amusement at Simcoe, and returned about ten o'clock.   The fire was discovered between one and two o'clock in the morning, and, when first discovered, the plaintiff was seen in the inn just as he came out of bed, asking where the fire was of which an alarm had been given.   He ran to the building, and when some person wished to enter one of the rooms to endeavor to save the goods, he said there was a loaded gun in the room, and it would be dangerous to go in. No report of a gun was heard. No one could say or give an account how the fire originated. No goods were saved, except some trifling articles of no value.

The plaintiff's affidavit, furnished to the company on the 11th of July, 1855, with his statement of the goods lost, was produced. The affidavit did not allude to the statement as being annexed, but it was annexed. In this the plaintiff stated that the amount of his purchases, from the time he began business, and which was proved to have been in November, 1852, was £2313 16s. 11d. The amount of his sales, including two invoices of goods sent by him to London, amounting to £261 4s. 10d., in the whole was £753 3s. 9d., and that deducted from his purchases left a sum of £1560 13s. 2d., which he claimed as being the value and amount of the goods destroyed by the fire. An affidavit of plaintiff's clerk was attached to the statement, also handed in to the company, verifying the amounts mentioned in the statement. The defendants had an agent residing at Port Dover; and after the affidavits and statement were delivered, the defendants, not being satisfied with respect to the quantity of goods claimed for, the agents framed certain questions to be answered by the plaintiff's clerk, who then was residing in the State of New York. These questions were answered on the 24th of September, 1853, and returned to the agent. A letter, dated 7th November, 1853, from the secretary of the defendants, addressed to Mr. Mitchell, to whom the policy had been assigned, was put in, and was as follows :

"I beg to acknowledge the receipt of your favour of the 5th inst., in which you inquire in what respect Mr. Lampkin has failed to satisfy the board. In reply, I would say that he has failed in several respects : he has not proved to our satisfaction that he had the quantity of goods on hand which he states in his affidavits: he has not furnished the magistrate's certificate which the policy requires : and, besides these, the circumstances attending the fire were so very suspicious as to lead to the general belief that the premises were burnt designedly. Such is the general opinion of residents at Port Dover ; and to shew that other companies agree with us in thinking this a case which ought to be resisted, I would mention that both the companies with whom Mr.

Lampkin effected insurance besides ourselves, have refused the payment of the respective sums claimed by him."

The plaintiff gave evidence of various parties from whom he had purchased goods, shewing that, between November, 1852, and the time of the fire, he had bought for the store at Port Dover goods equal in amount to that stated by him. Upon this point there was no room for doubt; and the question was, whether such amount of goods as stated by the plaintiff were or could have been in the building at the time the fire occurred. The plaintiff's clerk proved that the goods were sold in the ordinary way in country stores, with the exception of the two invoices of goods sent to London, which had been sent there to exchange for wool. He stated that no goods had been removed from the premises; but his statement of the quantities in the different parts of the building was not altogether satisfactory.

On the part of the defendants, it was objected that the plaintiff had not complied with the terms of the conditions of the policy as to notice to the company of the fire—that having occurred on the 13th of June, and the statements and affidavits having been sent in on the 11th of July, which was the first notice established, and therefore not notice *forthwith,* It was also objected that the statement sent in was not signed by the plaintiff as required; and no allusion was made in the affidavit to the statement, so as to incorporate it with the affidavit.

Leave was reserved to the defendants to have a nonsuit entered on these objections, if found to be fatal to the plaintiff.

The defendants then went into evidence to shew that it was not possible so many goods as claimed for could have been destroyed. The person who had been the former proprietor of the buildings, and who had carried on business there, stated that the premises would not hold more than from £700 to £900 worth of goods for such an establishment. He also proved that he had been in the store the afternoon before the fire, in order to purchase a pair of shoes, and he noticed that some of the shelves were empty, and that the plaintiff had a very small stock on hand, which consisted chiefly of boots and shoes lying on the counter. He said he would not give £500 for all the goods : but he was not in other parts of the building to see what might have been there. Other witnesses were called, who had been in the store a few days before the fire, and stated that the shelves were nearly empty and but few goods in the place. On the afternoon before the fire a case was observed standing in the store addressed to London, but whether it contained any thing was not known. After the alarm of fire was given, it was proved that the persons who went to try to save property could find very little, and as to silks, velvets, &c., nothing of them could be traced. On the part of the plaintiff it was endeavoured to be explained that Mrs. Lampkin, being a milliner, a great quantity of the goods consisted of articles in her line, which were much more expensive, and could be stowed away in much less space than ordinary goods. The agent of the defendants residing at Port Dover was in court but neither party examined him.

The jury found for the plaintiff, and £500 damages.

Vankoughnet, Q. C., obtained a rule to shew cause why a nonsuit should not be entered on the leave reserved, or why there should not be a new trial, the verdict being contrary to law and evidence. He cited Shaw v. St. Lawrence Mutual Insurance Company, 11 U. C. R. 73.

Hagarty, Q. C., shewed cause, and contended that the conduct of the defendants—as established by the documents required by them, and the answer to the application as to what the company intended to do—had waived any technical proof of other notice that a fire had destroyed the goods, and rendered it unnecessary to prove a signed statement of the loss. As to the merits, all the evidence which could be given was brought on both sides, and it was purely a question of fact for the jury. He cited Wing v. Hawly, 23 L. T. 120.

BURNS, J., delivered the judgment of the court.

Upon the merits of this case, as to the fact whether the quantity of goods claimed for as being in the shop, was in truth there when the fire occurred, we should have been better satisfied if the verdict had been for the defendants. There were many very suspicious circumstances strongly militating against the plaintiff's claim. The fact that shortly before the fire the plaintiff and his wife abandoned living in the apartments over the shop, and the further fact that the plaintiff's clerk left the establishment at six o'clock the evening before the fire, having no intention to return, and it not being shewn that the plaintiff contemplated employing another clerk, or that his business had become such that a clerk was unnecessary, combined with the evidence of persons who had been in the shop the day or two previous to the fire, and who stated that the shelves looked very empty, were such as to create great suspicion that all was not right, and it is not surprising that the defendants felt themselves called upon to resist the claim made upon them. On the other hand, the plaintiff proved very satisfactorily that the amount of goods purchased by him was fully equal to what he alleged. The only questions to be considered were, whether the purchased goods had all been carried to the shop, and no more had been removed or sold than proved. The plaintiff carried on business from November, 1852, to June, 1853. The evidence of the plaintiff's clerk certainly was not very sarisfactory in respect to the amount of goods remaining in the shop at the time of the fire. The case was fairly enough submitted to the jury, and of course the credit to be given to the witnesses rested with them. We feel that upon this point, inasmuch as the trial not only involved the plaintiff's character for honesty, but that if the defendants' suspicions be true the plaintiff would be subject to a criminal prosecution, we cannot, where the jury are the judges, and the case has been properly submitted to them, interfere.

With respect to the legal questions, little is to be found in the English works or reports on the subject of fire insurance and policies containing conditions similar to those in this case.

In an American work (Angell on Fire and Life Insurance) a chapter is devoted to the subject of the proofs requisite to establish preliminary matters. In the American courts, the subject of the requisite notice of loss by the assured, and the preliminary proofs of loss to be given in order to comply with the conditions of the policy, seem to have engaged attention more than in England. The result of the cases there is, that both notice of the loss and particulars of it may be waived by the insurers expressly, or by their conduct in dealing with the assured. That view seems to be reasonable and consistent with the law upon other subjects. For instance, an indorser of a promissory note or bill of exchange is only liable on certain conditions to be performed by the holder; yet the indorser may by his acts and conduct waive the performance of the conditions. The only English case I have been able to find, and none was cited in the argument, is Pim v. Reid, (6 M. & G. 1). As regards the points raised in the case before us, that case was only a Nisi Prius decision, but still it was that of an eminent judge, *Chief Justice Tindal*. The conditions of the policy were precisely similar to this case, and the third and fourth pleas like the sixth and seventh of this case. To support the affirmative of the third and fourth issues, the plaintiffs gave evidence of a notice of loss, and shewed that afterwards a correspondence took place between the insurance office and the plaintiffs, which it was contended amounted to a dispensation with the obligation to deliver a particular account of the loss. It was objected for the defendants, that even supposing the correspondence to amount to a waiver of the condition, which it was contended it did not, still the defendants were entitled to a verdict upon the fourth issue, which was formally taken upon the precise allegation of a delivery of a particular account of the loss as required by the conditions, as alleged in the declaration and as traversed by the fourth plea. *Chief Justice Tindal* overruled the objection, and the plaintiff had a verdict. The case came before the court upon another set of pleas which had been found for the defendant, whether upon them the plaintiffs were entitled to judgment *non obstante veredicto*. The defendants had not moved a cross rule upon the ruling of the Chief Justice at Nisi Prius; and after the decision of the court against the defendants upon the plaintiff's rule, the defendants moved for a new trial, but it was determined that the motion then came too late. If the Chief Justice's opinion had been expressly confirmed by the court, it must have been decisive of this case ; but I consider that the parties acquiesced in the ruling of the Chief Justice, because not only did they not move a cross rule but in the course of the argument on the pleas found in the defendants' favor the objection was not adverted to; and afterwards when it was found necessary that a writ of enquiry must be had, in consequence of the jury not having on the trial assessed the damages, the suit was compromised by the defendants paying the loss without costs. The opinion of Chief Justice Tindal is entitled to great weight, and, with a view which the American courts take upon the same subject, is, we think a sufficient guide to us. In the case before us the fire occurred on the 13th of June, and notice of the fire and particulars of loss were given in on the 11th of July. Instead of the defendants making any objections on the score that the notice of loss and the particulars of it were not in time, they enter into a correspondence with the plaintiff as to furnishing better particulars of the loss, which the plaintiff did furnish. Then, when again applied to, the defendants say that the suspicion with regard to how the fire occurred justifies them in declining to pay. After this and after the action was brought the defendants paid the amount of the buildings which had been insured under a separate policy, to the plaintiff. The due notice of the fire embraced the whole ; and if it were in time or waived as regards time of giving it in respect of the buildings, it would seem strange to hold it not waived as regards the goods in the same building. It is true the defendants might, in an action for the goods dispute whether notice and particulars of the loss of the goods were in time though they may have been satisfied to pay the amount of the policy upon the building ; but when the reason for declining to pay both in the first instance is placed upon the footing of questioning the *bona fides* of the plaintiff's conduct in respect of the fire, then is not the payment of the one policy strong evidence of the waiver of time and particulars of the loss in the other policy ? Taking the facts of the correspondence in respect to furnishing better evidence of the particulars, and not setting up the want of sufficient notice till the action brought, and then, after the action is brought, the payment of the amount insured upon the buildings into consideration we think it sufficient to hold that in law the defendants were precluded at the trial from disputing their liability upon the grounds alleged in the pleas.

We are of opinion, therefore, that the verdict should stand.

Rule discharged.

NELSON AND NASSAGAWEYA ROAD COMPANY V. BATES.

Joint stock road company—Action for calls—12 Vic. ch. 84—Instrument of incorporation registered before six per cent. paid—Irregularity cured by 16 Vic. ch. 190, sec. 55.

An instrument, under the provisions of 12 Vic. ch. 84, was signed by the defendant and others for the formation of a road company, the defendant agreeing to take three shares. The directors named met on the 27th of May. 1850, and called in four instalments, each of 10 per cent. on each share. The six per cent. required by the statute was at the same meeting paid by the promissory note of the directors to the treasurer, who then signed a receipt for the money and afterwards registered the instrument of incorporation. By the 20th of November, 1850, the treasurer had received by means of the call a sum equal to the six per cent., and he then destroyed the note. On the 13th of January, 1854, another call was made, payable by six instalments; and this action was brought for the four instalments of the first call, and the first three instalments due on the second.

Held, That the first call could not be recovered, for when it was made the six per cent. had not been paid (confirming Niagara Falls Road Company v. Benson (8 U. C. R. 307); but that the plaintiffs might recover the second call, for on the 13th of January the six per cent. had been actually paid; and the company having proceeded *bona fide* in the construction of their road, the irregularity in registering the instrument of incorporation before such payment was cured by 16 Vic. ch. 190, sec. 55.

DEBT for seven calls of ten shillings each, upon three shares held by defendant in the company. *Second count,* for interest.

Pleas—1. *Nunquam indebitatus.* 2. That at the time of the accruing of the causes of action in the declaration mentioned there was no such corporation as the Nelson and Nassagaweya Road Company. 3. That at the time of the commencement of this suit there was not, nor is, any such corporation as the Nelson and Nassagaweya Road Company : Issues.

The cause was tried at Hamilton in November, 1854 before *Draper, J.*

It appeared that an instrument, headed as required by the act 12 Vic. ch. 84 (schedule), was signed by the defendant and many other persons, dated 24th of January, 1850, in which the capital stock of the proposed company was stated to be £3000, and the defendant thereby agreed to take three shares, and five directors were appointed in that instrument.

On the 27th of May, 1850 (a sufficient number of shares having been subscribed to amount to £3000), the five directors met and passed a resolution to call in four instalments of the stock each of ten per cent. on each share, to be payable one on the 1st of September, one on the 1st of October, one on the 1st of November, and one on the 1st of December, 1850. Due notice, as required by law, was published in a newspaper of these four calls. At the same meeting at which the resolution for making four calls was adopted, it was considered how the six per cent. required by the fourth section of 12 Vic. ch. 84 should be paid. It was suggested, and at last determined on, that the five directors should sign a promissory note to their secretary and treasurer for the amount being £180; and upon this being done he signed a receipt for the money, and took the note. On the 26th of August, 1850, the treasurer took a memorial of and the instrument of incorporation together with his receipt for the instalment of six per cent., to the registrar of the county of Halton, who indorsed a certificate of the registration of such memorial on the instrument. The instalments called in were not punctually paid, and it was not before the 20th of November, 1850, that the treasurer received from such of the stockholders as did pay a sum equal to six per cent. on the capital stock of £3000. After receiving that amount he gave up or destroyed the note of £180, given to him by the directors. On the 13th of January, 1854, the directors passed another resolution to make six more calls of ten per cent. each, payable on the 1st of March, April, May, June, July, and August, 1854. This action was commenced when only three of the last six calls were due, and the plaintiff sought to recover these and the first four; in all seven calls. The whole road intended to be made according to the instrument was 24 miles long, and not quite six miles had been completed continuously. None of it had been constructed within the last two years. Besides the six miles (or thereabouts) there had been grading and cutting done on different parts of the line. The township council allowed parties residing on or near the plaintiffs' intended line of road to commute their statute labour for money and pay to it in aid of the company, and they also allowed statute labour to be performed on parts of the road not let out on contract by the plaintiffs.

For the plaintiffs it was also proved that the defendant had tendered for a contract to execute part of the road according to certain plans, &c., to be finished by the 1st of September, 1851. And it was insisted that, having signed the deed of incorporation and afterwards recognized the corporation as in existence by tendering for a contract with them, he should not be permitted to deny that they were a corporation, and that the evidence relative to the payment of the first instalment of six per cent." should not be received. And that at all events, all irregularities in the foundation of this and of similar companies were cured by the express words of the 16 Vic. ch. 190, sec. 55 ; and that the plaintiffs, complying with sec. 30 of 12 Vic. ch. 84, and sec. 18 of 16 Vic. ch. 190, were entitled to recover.

For the defendants it was insisted that the payment of six per cent. on the shares subscribed by each shareholder was necessary in order to fix him with liability or to authorize the company to treat him as a shareholder. That he might become satisfied the capital stock would be insufficient, or the work useless, if no more than the capital stock were to be laid out upon it, and therefore might withdraw at any time before paying the six per cent. ; and 16 Vic. ch. 190, sec. 4, was relied upon as favouring this construction. That it was not intended that a memorial should be registered but the instrument itself, which the legislature ought to keep to prevent its being altered, &c., and for the purposes expressed in 12 Vic. ch. 84. sec. 7, and in 13 & 14 Vic. ch 122, sec. 2. That at all events the directors could not meet and make calls until the six per cent. had been paid and the instrument registered. That admitting that it was not necessary each stockholder should pay six per cent. on his shares, still such an amount must be *bona fide* paid ; and the giving the note by the directors for the avowed purpose of getting the instrument registered and the company incorporated was fraudulent.

That the company had not complied with the requisitions of 12 Vic. ch. 84, sec. 21, and 16 Vic. ch. 190, sec. 27.

The following questions were submitted to the jury :

1. Whether, when the first four calls were made the instalment of six per cent. had been paid otherwise than by the note of the directors? The jury said, No.

2. Whether there had been any other payment than this note at the date of the registration of the instrument? They said, There had not.

3. Whether this note was paid by the directors, or in any other way than by moneys paid in by stockholders upon the calls made on the 20th of May, 1850? The jury said, The only payment was out of money so paid in by the stockholders.

4. About what date was there in the hands of the treasurer for the first time £180 (six per cent. on £3000,) the moneys of the plaintiffs? They said, About the 20th of November, 1850.

5. Was the promissory note of the directors given to elude the provisions of the statute, and in fraud of the stockholders? The jury said, It was.

6. Before or at what date was all the finished portion of the road exceeding five miles completed? The jury said, Before the 1st of January, 1853.

7. Have the plaintiffs made any number of miles, and if so how many since that date? They found the plaintiffs had not made any more road since.

The jury were directed to find for the plaintiff, subject to the opinion of the court on their finding and the whole law of the case. Leave was reserved to both parties to raise any exception which the facts and law might give rise to.

The jury found for the plaintiffs accordingly £11 19s. 11d. damages. In Michaelmas term the case was argued by *Connor*, *Q. C.*, and *Springer* for the plaintiffs ; and by *Start* for the defendant.

The following authorities were cited :—Niagara Falls Road Company v. Benson, 8 U. C. R. 307 ; The Eastern Archipelago Company v. The Queen, 2 El. & Bl. 856 ; The Stratford and Moreton R. W. Company v. Stratton, 2 B. & Ad. 513 ; The Ambergate, &c., R. W. Company v. Coulthard, 5.

Ex. 459 ; The North Western R. W. Company v. McMichael,
6 Ex. 271 ; The Waterford, &c., R. W. Company v. Dalbiac,
6 Ex. 443 ; The Agricultural Cattle Insurance Company v.
Fitzgerald, 15 Jur. 489, 16 Q. B. 432 ; The Thames Tunnel
Company v. Sheldon, 6 B. & C. 341 ; Stewart v. Gauty, 2 R.
W. Ca. 616 ; Rex. v. The Corporation of Carmarthen, 2 Burr.
869 ; Banwen Iron Company v. Burnett 8 C. B 431 ;
Mangles v. The Grand Collier Dock Company, 2 R. W. Cas.
359 ; Norwich, &c. Navigation Company v. Theobald, M. &
M. 151.

DRAPER, J.—If the statute 12 Vic. ch. 84, were still in
force, and the case were to be decided under its provisions,
I should adhere to the judgment of this court in the Niagara
Falls Road Company v. Benson (8 U. C. R. 307). I have
carefully considered the case of the London and Brighton
Railway Company v. Wilson (6 Bing N. C. 135), as well
as some other cases of a similar character. I think them
clearly distinguishable from the case we have already decided,
on this broad ground, that the creation of the plaintiffs into
a corporation was completely effected by the act of parliament, and the various powers given by the act were given
to a body corporate brought into present existence. Under
the 12 Vic. no corporation is erected, but a method is devised,
by pursuing and fulfilling the various portions whereof any
number of persons not less than five may become a corporation for the purposes in the act set forth, by such name
as they may see fit to adopt in their instrument or association and subscription. But each step pointed out in the
act as necessary to enable the corporation to be called into
existence is in the clearest language a condition precedent ;
and if any one of them were wholly omitted, then, though
a corporate name might be assumed and the corporate powers
might be exercised, yet there would be no corporation in
fact, and it would pe open to any one to contest it in a legal
proceeding, notwithstanding the 29th and 30th sections. which
contain almost precisely the same words as the act which
was under consideration in the case in 6 Bing. N. C. ; and
unless the application of this case be so restricted it will be

found to conflict with other decisions. The 55th section of the Imperial statute 7 & 8 Vic. ch. 110 does not differ materially from the language in the 29th and 30th sections of our statute 12 Vic. The Agricultural Cattle Insurance Company v. Fitzgerald (16 Q. B. 432) was an action brought upon this Imperial statute for a call and interest. The declaration stated the plaintiffs to be "a company completely registered, and which before the commencement of this suit had obtained a certificate of complete registration." The pleas were—1. *Nunquam indebitatus.* 2. That the plaintiffs were not, before or at the time of the commencement of the suit, a company completely registered *modo et formâ* : Issue. 3. That the plaintiffs were a company formed after the passing of the said act, but were not formed by any deed in writing under the hands and seals of the shareholders, as required by the said act ; to which the plaintiffs replied that they were formed by deed in writing as required. 4. That the plaintiffs were a company formed after the passing of the said act, but the deed did not contain the several requisite clauses directed by the statute. Replication.—That it did contain, &c. It was held not indispensable that the plaintiffs should produce the certificate of registration in order to establish that fact on these pleadings. But in giving judgment *Lord Campbell, C. J.,* observes, that a plea that the company had not obtained a certificate of complete registration before the commencement of the action would have been a goood bar, though he also says the plea of *nunquam inebitatus* does not put in issue the regular formation of the company, and under that plea the plaintiffs are entitled to a verdict on proving the due making of the calls, and that the defendant had due notice, and was a shareholder when they were made. Not one of these observations would have been called for if the defendant had been precluded from raising the question whether the plaintiffs had in fact become a corporation. Nor is this inconsistent with the decision in The Banwen Iron Company v. Barnett (8 C. B. 406), which in effect decides that when the certificate of complete registration by the proper officer has been granted under the 7th and 25th section of that act, it shall be proof conclusive, at all events against a shareholder in an action for calls, of the incorporation of the company ; for the 7th section expressly enacts, that, after such certificate shall be granted, it shall be taken as evidence of the proper provisions being inserted in the deed of settlement and of the performance of the conditions hereby required previous to the granting of such certificate, and the 25th section declares that on the complete registration being certified, such company and the shareholders shall be incorporated as from the date of such certicate by the name set forth in the deed of settlement.' I refer also to the Galvanized Iron Company v. Westoby (8 Ex. 17). Even with regard to companies incorporated by special act the effect of the clause commented on in the London and Brighton Railway Company v. Wilson against shareholders sued for calls, is not held to be so stringent as the janguage used in that case might appear to warrant. On this point I refer to the Waterford, &c., Railway Company v. Logan (14 Q. B. 672) and The West Cornwall Railway Company v. Mowatt (15 Q. B. 521).

There is one important distinction (not the only one) between the Imperial statute and our acts 12 Vic. ch. 84, and 16 Vic. ch. 190. By the former act the granting the certificate of complete registration, which operates to incorporate the company, is the act of a public officer not purely ministerial, for he has a discretion to withhold the certificate, though a mandamus will lie to him for not registering if he improperly refuses,—Reg. v. Whitmarsh (15 Q. B. 600). But in our acts the fulfilment of all conditions precedent is left to the parties getting up the company, and they are to take the original instrument and the treasurer's certificate to the registar, who is directed to register them. But the certificate of registry or the registration is not made evidence of anything beyond the mere fact of registration, as it is in the imperial act, nor is the company incorporated under our act by the registration merely or the certificate of it, as the 25th section of the imperial act provides ; but incorporation with us is gained by a compliance with the various requirements, of which registration is but one, and the previous payment of six per cent, to the treasurer is another.

We must consider then what bearing the 55th section of the 16 Vic. ch. 190 has upon the question, assuming for the moment that the plaintiffs would fail under 12 Vic. ch. 4. This section enacts that, notwithstanding any *irregularity* in the formation, registration, or management, and notwithstanding all the requirements of the former act may not have been strictly complied with, all such companies which shall have *bonâ fide* proceeded in the construction, &c., of any road shall be held to be duly organized, formed, registered, constituted, and managed under the same, anything therein contained to the contrary notwithstanding.

This section seems to me to imply that it was considered that even *irregularities* or an absence of *strict compliance* with the requirements of the 12 Vic. might give rise to serious, perhaps fatal, objections to companies which had *bona fide* proceeded with the construction of their undertaking. The relief is guardedly restricted to companies that have *bona fide* proceeded with the construction, &c., and it is not to affect the rights of any party (not excepting a shareholder) in any proceeding, action, or suit, pending when the act passed.

Even with regard to such companies as this clause was intended to relieve, I think we must hold that the legislature have not used the term " irregularity" as synonymous with " defect," or the phrase " notwithstanding all the requirements of the said act have not been strictly complied with" as equivalent to "notwithstanding some of the requirements of the act have not been complied with at all." It is observable that this term "requirements" is used in the 5th section of this act in reference to conditions in the preceding section almost the same as those contained in the fourth section of 12 Vic. ch. 84; and as used in the fifth section of the 16 Vic. it can have no other meaning than " conditions precedent."

I think it then clear that the legislature did not intend to absolve these companies from the consequence of defective performance or of absolute non-performance of a condition precedent. And this conclusion advances us another step in the inquiry—viz., under which head. must we range the giving of a promissory note by the directors to their treasurer for the six per cent. instead of the actual payment of the six per cent.; the obtaining the receipt of the treasurer for the payment as if actually made; and the procuring the registration of the original instrument and of the receipt, without which there could be no incorporation, which is to follow immediately after the registration as a consequence of the performance of the previous "requirements."

I have given my reasons (perhaps at unnecessary length) for upholding the judgment in the Niagara Falls Road Company v. Benson. In that case the sum of money equal to six per cent. on 450 shares (the whole number of shares being 1009) had been actually paid to the treasurer, who had given his receipt for it, which with the original instrument had been registered, but the money had been raised by discounting a note made by one director and indorsed by two others, and when this note arrived at maturity it was taken up by an appropriation for that purpose of funds of the company. The Chief Justice of this court observed, "When we see the funds so misapplied, the fair presumption is that what was done by the directors in July, was contemplated by the same directors in March, and that the money was only paid in to be taken out again, and was therefore only a colorable, not a real payment."

In the present case the money never came into the treasurer's hands at all until long after the first four calls were made—in fact, not until three of them were payable—while the registration was made nearly three months before the treasurer had this money in hand, though the payment should have preceded the registration. It is in effect as if the treasurer had given the receipt at the request of the directors without receiving anything, even a promissory note. There might have been some color for holding, that, where the money was actually in the treasurer's hands, the arrangement made was an irregularity; but I confess I am unable to view the present case in that light. Perhaps a strict compliance with the act would have rendered necessary a payment by each subscriber on his shares, instead of a payment by a number fewer than all the subscribers of a sum equal to six per cent. on all the shares. If so, this would have been a mere departure from the exact letter of the requirement, and would have been cured. But the non-payment of any part by any person is a total omission to comply with a requirement contained in the first and re-enacted in the latter act, and is not therefore, as I think, cured by the 55th section. And besides, the jury have expressly found that the promissory note was given by the directors to elude the provisions of the act, and in fraud of the stockholders, as in fact it would operate if it subjected them to liability for calls before the conditions precedent had been complied with. And I concur in the spirit of the finding; for a promissory note is not, in my opinion, a payment within the meaning of the act. If a note at one month or three months be a payment, why not at one year or three years?—and yet I do not see how the latter could be held as anything but a mere evasion of the act.

As to the first four calls, therefore, it appears to me the plaintiffs cannot recover. I have had a good deal more difficulty in coming to a conclusion as to those made on the 13th of January, 1854, and am even now not free from doubt as to the true solution of that question. But, setting aside for the moment any consideration of the defendant's subsequent acts, which were urged as concluding him from raising any objection to the plaintiff's right, I do not see at present that the plaintiffs cannot treat the defendant as a shareholder liable to pay these latter instalments.

It is no necessary consequence from the fact that the plaintiffs, not being legally a corporation on the 27th of May, 1850, when the resolution for the first four calls was passed; on the 26th of August, 1850, when the instrument of association was registered; or up to the 20th of November, 1850, when the instalment of six per cent. was first paid, may not from that day have become a corporation within the meaning of the several acts, especially referring to the fifteenth section of 16 Vic. ch. 190. On that day the requirements of the 12 Vic. were complied with, not regularly, nor strictly in the prescribed order. But they had subscribed stock sufficient in their judgment to complete the projected undertaking. They had executed such an instrument as the statute

required. They had paid to the treasurer six per cent. on
the capital intended to be raised ; and they had registered
their instrument of association together with the treasurer's
receipt. The statute limits no period from the taking the
first step within which all the subsequent preliminaries
must be complied with ; it only provides for the compliance
with all before the corporation is called into existence.

I see no reason for holding that a premature attempt to
commence operations before the conditions precedent were
complied with must prevent the shareholders from acquiring
a corporate capacity by a subsequent fulfilment of the various
requirements. Suppose, for instance, that while the 12 Vic.
was still in force every preliminary except registration had
been strictly fulfilled, and that, omitting to register, they had
made calls and endeavoured to enforce them by action. The
absence of registration would, in my opinion, have rendered
the calls illegal, and as a consequence the actions must have
failed. But I do not see that if they afterwards registered
and then made fresh calls, that the previous abortive proceedings would have formed an obstacle to the enforcing of
such calls. Or if they had registered, having previously
collected the six per cent. from each stockholder, but the
quantity of stock subscribed fell short of that which by the
instrument of association was stated to be requisite to complete the proposed undertaking, this would, as appears to
me, have been a defect fatal to their enforcing any calls.
But if, after failing in an attempt to recover such calls, the
original subscribers had increased the amount of stock taken
by them, or new subscribers had taken shares, making up
the amount stated, and a registry of such additional stock
was made, then again I do not see that, though an irregularity had taken place in the original proceeding, it would
not have been cured by the additional subscriptions and the
effect of the subsequent act. Or if calls were made without
the requisite notice, or to a larger amount at once than the
act permits, and suits brought to recover such calls were
defeated on that account, I do not suppose it will be contended that new calls correctly made could not be enforced.

Applying these suggestions to the present state of facts,

then, though I think it clearly irregular to register before the six per cent. was paid, and though I am strongly inclined to the opinion that the 12 Vic. contemplated a payment of six per cent. by each shareholder, still I do not think either difficulty insurmountable.

The latter is removed by the 16 Vic., the first section of which makes the act declaratory in all cases of doubt or ambiguity in the construction of the former ; and the fourth section enables the six per cent. to be paid by the company or any one of their members, or by the directors. And as to the former, when every requirement has been actually fulfilled, the order of fulfilment becomes, I think, immaterial; and though not in accordance with the statute—not a strict compliance—the irregularity was cured in favor of a company proved, as this was, to have *bona fide* proceeded in the construction of their work, by the fifty-fifth section of the 16 Vic. The registration would be, from the time the six per cent. was actually paid to the treasurer, a due registration, and the subsequent management would be confirmed. And thus the objections which lie to the first four calls would not exist as to those made since the payment of the six per cent.

I am of opinion there is nothing in the objections raised by the defendant founded on the twenty-first section of the 12 Vic. and the twenty-seventh section of 16 Vic. Both those sections are predicated on the assumption that the company had become a corporation, and on certain defaults they provided for the forfeiture of the corporate and other powers. But though the defaults may have occurred, still something more must take place before the forfeiture takes effect. Besides, the twenty-first section of 12 Vic. applies only to roads not more than five miles in length—the present road exceeding twenty ; and the twenty-seventh section of 16 Vic. provides, that if the road exceeds five miles, the company must complete in each year, after two years from their incorporation have expired, not less than five miles, under pain of forfeiture of their charter and of the corporate powers and authority thereby acquired, "so far as concerns the portion of such road which shall remain unfinished." No forfeiture has been pronounced, nor any step taken to procure any such judgment. The company have, it appears, finished five miles, and as to that no forfeiture could be incurred. The objection, therefore, fails entirely.

In my opinion the plaintiffs are entitled to retain so much of their verdict as the last three calls, with interest, amount to. If they consent to reduce the verdict to that sum this rule will be discharged; if not, we must grant a new trial without costs.

BURNS, J.—The subject naturally calls for an enquiry, *first*, what the rights of the parties are under the statute 12 Vic. ch. 84; and, *secondly*, whether such rights have been altered in any way by the statute 16 Vic. ch. 190.

First, then, was this body, calling itself a corporation under the 12 Vic. ch. 84, entitled to sue the defendants for calls, and can the defendant, under pleas of *nunquam indebitatus* and denying the existence of the corporation, question the right to do so? The fourth section declares and enacts that certain things must be done and completed before the persons joining together become a corporation, and not only must the treasurer's receipt for the six per cent. be registered, but the six per cent. must be paid to the treasurer. The mere registration is not made the act of incorporation, as is the case with companies in England under 7 & 8 Vic. ch. 110, but here all the matters specified are clearly conditions precedent. Under the English act the registrar is called upon to a certain extent to exercise an opinion whether the deed of settlement complies with the act, and when that officer has once granted a certificate of registration, then it is conclusive in an action for calls against a person who has signed the deed : The Banwen Iron Company v. Barnett (8 C. B. 406). Whether the judgment of the registrar can in any way be reviewed, in case of his having granted the certificate, does not appear to be settled. The case referred to is the one just cited—viz. Regina v. The Registrar of Joint Stock Companies—will be found in 15 Jur. 9. The Registrar had refused to register the deed, and the Court of Queen's Bench granted a mandamus to compel him to do so, and on demurrer to the return on the writ, the court decided that the proposed company was not a corporation within the meaning of the act. No officer or person is called upon by our statute to exercise any opinion previous to the association of persons becoming incorporated, and therefore the question is, whether it is not open to every person sued by the company to question the existence of it. If the company had been incorporated by act of parliament or charter, upon certain conditions to be performed, then it may be that if such conditions be not performed some proceeding is necessary, other than questioning the company's existence in an action for calls, to destroy its existence. The present case is quite different, however. Here the creative power is placed in the hands of the association, and certain things, as conditions precedent, are required to be done before the company can have any existence. It is not the case of the existence of a company with certain conditions to be afterwards performed, but it is with certain conditions first to be performed before any company can exist. Every person who subscribes does so in the first instance conditionally. The contract does not become perfected till all the conditions be complied with. It is not material to enter into the inquiry whether each individual should have paid six per cent. on his shares, for in this case it is found that in fact no money at all was paid when the deed was registered. I consider that the conditions in the act upon which persons associating together can become incorporated, are for the security of both subscribers and the public, and if so, I can see no distinction between the different classes in the right of questioning and denying the existence of the corporation. If the defendant had joined this company after the registration the case might be different, but being one of the original parties, I think he has a right to say that the contract he entered into was conditional, and that the conditions attached by the act not being performed, the company had no existence. The only question, as it appears to me, is, what is the proper mode to test the existence of the corporation ? If some officer or person were appointed to see that the company was to be incorporated *de facto*, and after a final completion it was questioned whether in truth the corporation was such *de jure*, then it would be reasonable that some other proceeding should be adopted than questioning the right in an action for calls. Under our act, however, I see no other way than that it must be thrown upon the court to determine, if the facts be admitted, or upon a court and jury if the facts be denied, whether the company is a corporation *de facto* as well as *de jure*, A person may by his conduct and dealings prevent himself from raising the question, but that is not so here. The defendant is only found to have signed the deed and done nothing more, and, as I have already said, that was only conditional. He might waive the conditions, perhaps, and prevent himself from denying the corporate existence, but the case presents no question of that kind.—See London and Brighton Railway Co. v. Wilson (6 Bing. N. C. 135 ;) The Waterford, Wexford, Wicklow, and Dublin Railway Co. v. Logan (14 Q. B. 672 ;) The Agricultural Cattle Insurance Company v. Fitzgerald (16 Q. B. 432 ;) Pitchford v. Davis (5 M. & W. 2). The power to sue for calls is given by the ninth section, and that power is to "any such company so to be incorporated as aforesaid." I suppose it would not be contended that a right to sue for calls existed upon the mere fact of a deed having been signed which was in conformity with the statute, without registration. Registration alone is not made the condition of the existence of the corporation, and if a subscriber could contest the existence of the corporation for want of registration, I can see no reason why he has not the same right when the other condition—viz., the payment of the six per cent.—has not been complied with. The right to sue depends upon the fact of being a corporation, and the right to be considered a corporation depends upon having first fulfilled the conditions. I do not see any other course the defendant has than to question the right as he does here, for if he could adopt any proceedings by or in analogy to *scire facias* to repeal a charter or *quasi charter*, the adoption of such a step must necessarily admit a corporation *de facto*, but that is the very point the defendant denies. We have already determined that giving and depositing a note with the treasurer by the directors is not a compliance with the statute, and I still think it was not. Then up to the passing of the statute 16 Vic. ch. 190, the plaintiffs were liable to have their corporate existence called in question by a shareholder disputing whether the conditions precedent to becoming a corporation had been performed.

Secondly. The next consideration is, what effect the statute 16 Vic. ch. 190 has upon the case. I do not consider that the 17th & 18th sections confer any right to sue for calls made at a time when the defendant would have a right to dispute the corporate existence. The language of those sections is precise enough as to what shall be sufficient in allegation and proof to entitle the corporation *prima facie* to maintain an action, but it does not appear to me that, because the legislature simplifies allegations and proofs in favor of the corporation, it follows as a rule that the defendant is abridged in his right of disputing his liability. The defendant is abridged in demanding proof of various formal matters, which previously must have been adduced to entitle the corporation to maintain a suit; but he is not deprived of his right to say either that he is not a member of the corporation liable to be sued, or to bring in question whether the conditions on which the association was to be a corporation have been performed. The fourth section makes the existence of the corporation to depend upon the same conditions as the former act did, and the 17th section gives the power to sue to such company so to be incorporated. If the remainder of the 17th section with the 18th section shall be construed to deprive the defendant of the right to question the existence of the corporation because the six per cent. on the capital had never been paid, it must equally be so as to whether registration had been made ; and then the case comes to this:—that the mere production of the defendants' signature to the instrument will oblige him to pay any calls, however illegally made, because the conditions are not performed.—The Galvanized Iron Co. v. Westoby (8 Ex. 17.) I do not think the Legislature ever contemplated abridging a party of the right to say his contract was conditional, and that the condition upon which he was to be liable has never been performed. Then it is to be considered what effect the fifty-fifth section, taken with the first and fourth sections, has upon the position of the plaintiff and the defendant. The instrument of agreement to become a corporation was registered in August, 1850, without the six per cent. being paid, but the six per cent. was subsequently paid in November, though no part of it was paid by the defendant. The first section declares that the companies, having formed themselves under the repealed act, may avail themselves of the provisions of this act as fully and effectually as if formed under the last act. Then the fourth section declares that the six per cent. may be paid by any one of the company or the directors. It is true that such payment must be made before registration, for the treasurer's receipt for the amount must be registered with the instrument. Then comes the fifty-fifth section, which was to cure irregularities in the formation, registration, and management of the company, and to prevent the existence being called in question because all the requirements of the former act had not been strictly complied with, provided the company shall have *bona fide* proceeded with the construction of the road. In this case, the company did so proceed. If the registration had been postponed till November, after the six per cent. had been actually paid, there can, I think, have been no question but it would have been regular, or if there had been a re-registry after the payment, then the only question would have been whether it was necessary that the defendant should have paid his six per cent. This is put at rest by the last act, and the only question is, whether the fifty-fifth section cures the registry. I am of opinion that it does, and that since the last act the company may be looked upon as legally constituted since November, 1850. The only remaining consideration is, whether these latter provisions can be looked upon as giving the company a legal right to sue for calls made at a time when they could not properly be made. If the plaintiffs can maintain the action for all the calls, then it must follow that the instant the last act passed the company could have sued without further notice to the defendant for the calls made at a time when, according to my view, the company had no existence. I do not think the legislature intended that result to follow, for they have been careful, by the proviso to the fifty-fifth section, to say that nothing in the act shall affect the rights of any party in any action or suit pending. If the action for the calls had been pending when the act passed, there can be no question that if the defendant would have been right in questioning the existence of the corporation because the six per cent. was not paid to him, that right would have been saved to him. The effect of the fifty-fifth section is, I think to legalize the formation, registration, and management of the company. Making a call I do not consider comes under any of these. After the company had become legalized, and though that in contemplation of law was to be carried back to the points enumerated, the directors should have made fresh calls before the corporation would have a right to sue. I look upon what the legislature has done as giving the company a right to call for the stockholders' engagements to be performed, and not that an immediate right of suit was conferred. So far as regards this question, it would have been rather absurd to have had one shareholder's rights to dispute his liability preserved because the suit for the call was pending, and yet in the case of another shareholder, who might be sued after the act passed, held to have no rights upon the same grounds because he was sued a day later. I apprehend the legislature meant, by legalizing the formation of the company and the registration of the instrument, to hold the parties bound to their engagements, but that would not enable the company to enforce the engagement in an illegal manner. I do not apprehend by the word *management* it was contemplated that a legal right to sue for calls was conferred if such right did not exist before. When the directors had a legal authority they should have called for the instalments again, as they may do yet.

For these reasons, I think the plaintiffs entitled to a verdict for the three calls in 1854.

LEYS ET AL. V. FISKIN ET AL.

Lease—Proviso not to assign—Forfeiture.

It was provided in a lease. that the lessor might re-enter, if the lessee " do, or shall at any time or times during the continuance of the said term, let, set, or assign over these presents, or the term, estate, or premises hereby granted, or otherwise part with his interest therein or thereto to any person or persons whatsoever," without the lessor's consent in writing. The lessee, on leaving the country for a time, rented the premises to one J., who was to go out when required.
Held, **no forfeiture.**

EJECTMENT for a house and lot, situated in Bond Street, in the city of Toronto. At the trial before *Burns, J.*, at the last assizes held in Toronto, it appeared that on the 25th of June, 1853, Mr. Francis Leys, by indenture, leased the premises to the defendant Fiskin for four years, commencing on the 17th of October, 1853, with a proviso, that if defendant should be guilty of a breach of any of the covenants therein contained on his part then it should be lawful for the said Francis Leys, his heirs, &c., to enter, and and again repossess, &c.

The following stipulation was contained in the indenture :

" If the said party of the second part, his &c., do, or shall, at any time or times during the continuance of the said term, let, set, or assign over these presents, or the term, estate, or premises hereby granted, or otherwise part with his interest therein or thereto, to any person or persons whatsoever, without the license or consent of the said party of the first part, his heirs, &c., in writing, under his- or their hand or hands, for that purpose first had and obtained, then and from thenceforth it shall and may be lawful to and for the said party of the first part, his heirs, &c., to enter into, and upon the said hereby demised premises," &c.

The action was brought on the part of the plaintiffs in consequence of an alleged breach of this stipulation. Francis Leys died about the middle of October, 1853, leaving the plaintiffs his children surviving him, some of whom were infants and some of them married women. The defendant Fiskin went to Scotland in the winter of 1853; and, before he left, the widow of Mr. Leys and he had some conversation about the premises. She asked him if he had done with the house, as he was going to Scotland, and he replied that he supposed it would make no difference to them if he got as good a tenant as himself. Since the defendant returned from Scotland, the widow saw him again, when he stated that the premises had been rented for some £80 or £85, but did not state to whom. That amount of rent included the use of his furniture which was left in the house. She stated she did not know how the defendant Jacques had got in, but he was in after Fiskin left for Scotland. The defendant Jacques was then called, who stated that his wife had made an agreement with Mr. Mitchell the partner in business with Mr. Fiskin, whom the witness did not know. What that arrangement was he did not know, except that his wife told him that they could occupy until next spring, subject, however, to go out when Mr. Fiskin required. No rent he said had been paid by him up to the time of the trial, but he supposed something would have to be paid.

The defendant objected, 1. That the evidence shewed nothing more than that Jacques was in taking care of Fiskin's furniture, and the house for him during his absence. 2. That under the covenant the sub-letting or assigning meant of the remainder of the term, and that such a holding as Jacques had did not operate as a forfeiture.

The learned judge reserved leave to the defendant to move to enter a nonsuit on the second point, but as to the first directed the jury to consider whether Jacques occupied the premises as a tenant, or was merely taking care thereof for Fiskin. It was admitted that Mr. Fiskin had paid the first half year's rent, commencing on the 1st of October, 1853, before the forfeiture which the plaintiffs contended for.

The jury found for the plaintiffs and damages £23.

McDonald obtained a rule to shew cause why the verdict should not be set aside, and a *verdict* (should have been a nonsuit) entered for defendant, or why a new trial should not be had.

Eccles shewed cause. He contended that if any of the points were found to be in the defendant's favor there should be a new trial rather than a nonsuit, because the plaintiffs were surprised by the evidence of the defendant Jacques, he not being able to state the terms upon which he held the premises.

In addition to the cases cited in the judgment, Roe v.

Sales, 2 M. & S. 289, and Doe v. Godwin, 4 M. & S. 265, were referred to.

DRAPER, J., delivered 'the judgment of the Court.

The case of Doe Pitt v. Hogg (4 D. & R. 226) seems to govern the present. In that case the covenant was not to grant any underlease whatever, nor to let, set, assign, transfer, and set over, or otherwise part with the premises demised, the lease, or the term *or any part thereof.* The alleged ground of forfeiture was, that the lessee deposited the lease with the brewers who supplied the house (which was a coffee house)- with beer, as a security for beer furnished by them. The court held that this was no forfeiture. *Abbott, C. J.,* said, " I am clearly of opinion that the effect of the covenant is only to restrain the lessee from *completely alienating* the legal interest in the premises to the prejudice of the landlord. And *Bayley, J.,* thought the case not distinguishable from Crusoe v. Bugby (2 W. Bl. 706, 3 Wils. 235.)

The language of the covenant in the present case is somewhat less stringent and therefore less favorable to the landlord's right to claim a forfeiture, for there is no express prohibition to *underlet,* and the words, " or any part thereof," are not used, and if they are read as applying to the term as well as to the premises, then the omission would furnish an additional argument against the maintenance of this action.

The case of Doe v. Worsley (1 Camp. 20) does not appear to have been cited in Doe v. Hogg; and I confess I feel it extremely difficult to reconcile the two decisions, or the latter with Roe v. Harrison (2 T. R. 425).

The case of Doe v. Carter (8 T. R. 57, 300) was clearly one of assignment in fact of the whole term, and therefore does not affect the present question.

Considering the clear and express language of the Chief Justice in Doe v. Hogg, which decision appears to have been acquiesced in ever since, and agreeing also in the general principle that the court should rather lean against than help a forfeiture, we are of opinion that the plaintiffs should not hold the verdict they have obtained, but that a nonsuit should be entered pursuant to the leave reserved. There was an error in the motion in this case, which asked to enter a verdict for the defendant. There is, however, no want of authority for the course we take in granting a nonsuit, notwithstanding this mistake—See Doe Lloyd v. Powell (5 B. & C. 308), Doe dem. Duke of Norfolk et al. v. Hawke (2 East. 481), Doe dem. Lockwood v. Clarke (8 East 185), Doe dem. Lloyd v. Ingleby (15 M. & W. 465).

BUFFALO, BRANTFORD, AND GODERICH RAILWAY COMPANY V. PARKE.

Buffalo, B. & G. Railway—By what acts governed—Evidence of calls—Gazette—Interval between calls—Proof of Defendant being a shareholder.

The Buffalo, Brantford, and Goderich Railway Company are to be treated as acting under 16 Vic. ch. 45, and not under the joint stock road acts —at all events, as regards shareholders who have taken their stock since the 16 Vic. was passed.

To prove a call made on the 15th of March, a *Gazette* of the 28th of May was put in, in which the notice bore date on the 15th of March. *Held*, insufficient, as the paper could not be taken as evidence of any notice prior to its own date.

The Railway Clauses Consolidation Act, 14 & 15 Vic. ch. 51, provides that no call shall be made " at a less interval than two months from the previous call." *Held*, that calls made on the 1st of September, 1st of November, 1st of January, &c., were bad.

Held, also, *per Burns, J.*, that the defendant's subscription to a list, stating the number of his shares, and the fact that he afterwards voted upon such stock, was *prima facie* evidence of his being a shareholder.

DEBT for calls on twenty shares of five pounds each, being five calls, each of twenty per cent. and for interest.

Pleas—1. *Nunquam indebitatus;* 2. That the defendant at the time of making the calls, was not a holder of the shares.

The case was tried at Goderich, at the fall assizes, in 1854, before the Chief Justice of the Court of Common Pleas. It appeared that the defendant subscribed for twenty shares in the capital stock of the corporation, which originally existed under 12 Vic. ch. 84, the act authorizing the formation of joint stock companies for the construction of roads and other works in Upper Canada, as amended by 13 & 14 Vic. ch. 72, which expressly extended the provisions of the former act to railroads (which extension to railroads was repealed by 14

& 15 Vic. ch. 121, saving the rights of the Brantford and Buffalo Joint Stock Railroad Corporation), and as further amended and extended by 14 & 15 Vic. ch. 122.

After the defendant had subscribed for these twenty shares the act 16 Vic. ch. 45 was passed by which the plaintiffs— then being "The Brantford and Buffalo Joint Stock Railway Company," were incorporated by their present name, and were expressly authorized to make and complete a railway from the Niagara river, near Fort Erie, in the township of Bertie, to the town of Brantford, and thence through Paris and Stratford to the waters of Lake Huron at the town of Goderich ; and by section four of this act certain clauses of the Railway Clauses Consolidation Act, 14 & 15 Vic. ch. 51, are expressly incorporated into this act. The defendant, it appeared, when applied to, did not deny his subscription for this stock, but refused to pay, stating objections to the manner in which the plaintiffs had carried on the under-taking and expended the funds ; and it was proved that he had voted, by virtue of a proxy under seal, in right of these twenty shares at a meeting of the shareholders held at Brantford, in June, 1854.

The Canada *Gazette* of the 28th of May, 1853, was put in, in which was a notice that, pursuant to a resolution of the board of directors, payment of the new issue of shares of the increased capital stock of the Buffalo,Brantford,and Goderich Railway Company was required to be made in five equal instalments—viz., 20 per cent. on or before the 1st day of May then next ; 20 per cent. on or before the 1st day of July then next ; 20 per cent. on or before the 1st day of September then next ; 20 per cent. on or before the 1st day of November then next ; and 20 per cent. on or before the 1st day of January, 1854. This notice was dated 15th of March, 1853.

The defendant's counsel objected—1. That no resolution of the Company under their seal, nor any resolution to make calls was proved.

2. That the defendant was not bound by the subscription in the stock-book, because no such instrument as is required by the statute 12 Vic. ch. 84, constituting the original asso-ciation, pas proved; and that the stock-book put in was not

headed by a copy of the resolution for extending the original capital under the hand of the president and the seal of the Company and as required by 14 & 15 Vic. ch. 122, sec. 2.

3. That the defendant's having given a proxy under seal did not estop him from denying that he was a shareholder; and that the proxy at all events, did not shew what number of shares the defendant held.

4. That there was no sufficient proof of calls, the notice being under 14 & 15 Vic. ch. 51, sec. 16, subsecs. 10 and 24, only inserted in the *Gazette*, and not in a local paper, as required by 12 Vic. ch. 84.

5. That it was necessary under 12 Vic. ch. 84. sec. 30, to prove not only notice of the call, but that it was in fact made.

6. That two calendar months did not intervene between the calls, assuming that they were properly made under 14 & 15 Vic. ch. 51.

The plaintiffs' counsel answered—That the statute 14 & 15 Vic. ch. 51 governed the plaintiffs' proceedings since the incorporation of the Company, the defendant having subscribed his stock since the statute 16 Vic. ch. 45; that no resolution under seal was therefore necessary; and that the defendant, having voted by proxy, could not be permitted to deny he was a shareholder.

The learned Chief Justice held that the statutes 12 Vic. ch. 84, 13 & 14 Vic. ch. 72, and 14 & 15 Vic. ch. 121 & 122, no longer governed this corporation; but that they were regulated by 14 & 15 Vic. ch. 51, and 16 Vic. ch. 45: that by section six of this last act the governing body—*i. e.*, the directors—had power to extend the capital stock of the Company to £1,000,000 without a vote of the shareholders: that the notices in the *Gazette* in themselves amounted to a call, rendering it unnecessary to prove any resolution to make calls. He considered the evidence of the first call insufficient, there being no proof of sufficient length of notice of that call given; but that there was sufficient proof of the remaining four calls: that there was a lapse of two calendar months between each call within the meaning of the act—though he thought this point open to question: that the defendant by giving a sealed proxy admitted himself to be

a shareholder—at all events, so far as to obviate the necessity of more formal proof, though this might not be conclusive
upon him so as to prevent his proving the contrary.

The jury, on this direction, gave the plaintiff a verdict for
the four last instalments, with interest, amounting to £85
12s. 8d.

In Michaelmas term D. G. Miller obtained a rule nisi for
a new trial, on the law and evidence, and, for misdirection.

In the same term Becher shewed cause. He objected that
the defendant should not now be heard to urge that all the calls
were bad because made at the same time, as no such objection
was made at the trial but only that there was not an interval
of two months between each call; that as the defendant subscribed for shares after the 16 Vic. ch. 45, was passed, he
could not go back to objections arising under the provisions
of the 12 Vic. ch. 84, or the acts amending or extending that
act; that the Gazette is made conclusive evidence of the calls
being made, by the 24th subsection of sec. 16, of 14 & 16 Vic.
ch. 51.

C. Robinson, with him, cited Lester v. Garland, 15 Ves.
Jun. 248; Ambergate Railway Co. v. Coulthard, 5 Ex. 459;
Robinson v. Waddington, 13 Q. B. 753.

Eccles supported the rule, citing Gas Co. v. Russell, (6 U.
C. R. 567).

DRAPER, J.—We agree with the learned Chief Justice of
the Court of Common Pleas in the opinion expressed by him
at the trial, that this corporation must be treated as acting
under the 16 Vic. ch. 45 and the Railway Clauses Consolidation Act—at all events as respects the defendant, who did
not subscribe until after the 16 Vic. was passed.

Under the Railway Clauses Consolidation Act, thirty days'
notice at the least must be given of each call, and no call
can be made "at a less interval than two months from the
previous call"—(Sec. 16, subsec. 10). The plea of nunquam
indebitatus puts the plaintiffs to proof of calls primâ facie
legal—i. e., calls of which sufficient notice has been given;
and, if more than one call, that each subsequent call is not
required to be paid at an interval of less than two months
from the previous call.

The *Gazette* of the 28th of May, 1853, is the earliest put in. The notice therein contained bears date on the 15th of March, 1853, and would therefore if the call were proved to have been made on that day, shew more than thirty days' notice of the first call, which was made payable on the 1st of May, 1853; but there was no other proof of the call than this *Gazette*, and in our opinion it cannot be considered as giving notice anterior to the date of its publication, nor as being evidence of any notice of an earlier date than the date of the *Gazette* itself. We concur therefore, in holding that there was no evidence of notice of the call which was made payable on the 1st of May, 1853.

The next call—and which for the purpose of the rule we must consider as the first--was made payable on the 1st of July, 1853. The notice in the *Gazette* of the 28th of May next preceding was sufficient as well for this as for the three subsequent calls. But they were made payable respectively on the 1st of September and the 1st of November, 1853, and the 1st of January, 1854. The objection raised to them is, that there was not the required interval of two months, which means calendar months, from each previous call.

In our opinion this objection must prevail. As long ago as the case of Lester v. Garland (15 Ves. Jr. 248) it was said by the Master of the Rolls that the day of an act done and an event happening ought in all cases to be excluded rather than included. In Robinson v. Waddington (13 Q. B. 753) it was held that in construing 2 W. & M. ch. 5, sec. 2, which authorized the sale of goods distrained within five days next after the taking, the days must be calculated as the rule now is in other cases, inclusively of the last and exclusively of the day of taking. The cases up to that time were brought under the notice of the court by the counsel, and the court (*Lord Denman* apparently with reluctance considered the rule to be established as was stated in Young v. Higgon (6 M. & W. 49); in which it was held that, in the computation of the calendar month's notice to a justice, the day of giving the notice and the day of suing out the writ are both to be excluded. The principle is further illustrated by the case of The Queen v. The Aberdare Canal Company (14 Q. B. 854), where a statute enacted that no meeting of the commissoners should be held unless notice of the time, &c., of such meeting should be given at least sixteen days before such mreting. The notice in question was for a meeting to be held in February 12th. The notice was dated, and was published in a newspaper, on January 27th, and it was held to be insufficient.

According to these authorities, the day on which a previous call is payable must be excluded from the computation. The 1st July being therefore excluded, how can it be said there was an interval of two months between the day and the 1st of September? The calls should not have been made payable until the 2nd of that month. As suggested by *Parke, B.*, in Young v. Higgon, reduce the time to one day, and read the statute as requiring an interval of one day from the previous call before a subsequent one can be made; then if a call were payable on the first of July, could a second be made for the 2nd? and yet, if not, the present case fails.

The rule, therefore, for a new trial must be made absolute without costs, unless the plaintiffs reduce their verdict to the amount of the instalments due 1st of July, 1853, and interest.

There were three other actions brought by these plaintiffs against Black, Smith, and Clarke, respectively, in each of which the plaintiff took a verdict by consent upon an understanding that if a new trial were given in the case in which we have just pronounced judgment, there should be a new trial on the same terms without motion.

I am not sure whether our judgment properly applies to all those cases. It may be that only the first instalment is recovered in some or all of them; in which case, in our opinion, the plaintiffs would be entitled to retain their verdict if the first instalment is taken to mean that which was payable on the 1st of July, 1853.

The learned Chief Justice of this court, with whom we conferred before his departure, has authorized me to say that he concurs in our judgment.

No objection was urged by the defendant that the proof given did not sustain the declaration, in this, that the declaration is for four calls, and the notice in the *Gazette* seems capable of the interpretation that the whole amount of each share was called for, but that the call was payable by five instalments. Such a distinction has been noticed in some of the English cases.

BURNS, J.—I entirely agree with my brother *Draper* in the judgment he has pronounced, and I merely would add to it a few remarks upon another point. A question was made at Nisi Prius as to the mode of becoming, and how to prove that the person was a shareholder,—it being contended that it should have been shewn the defendant had become such shareholder under seal. There is nothing in the statute 12 Vic. ch. 84 requiring the instrument signed by shareholders to be sealed; but supposing there were, yet this defendant became a shareholder of the Company under the statute 16 Vic. ch. 45, which incorporates into its provisions the General Clauses Consolidation Act, 14 & 15 Vic. ch. 51. The seventh section of this latter act defines a shareholder to mean *every subscriber to or holder of stock in the undertaking*. The case of the West Cornwall Railway Co. v. Mowatt (15 Q. B. 521) shews what is *primâ facie* evidence of being a shareholder, and that upon such being shewn, it is for the defendant to rebut it. The evidence here is, that the defendant subscribed to a list stating the number of shares he took in the undertaking, and he afterwards voted upon the stock at the election of directors. That is sufficient.

The plaintiffs are entitled to recover the one call of which there was a sufficient notice; and with regard to the rest, if no other evidence can be offered than we have seen, they will have to retrace their steps and make proper calls.

Rule accordingly.

THE COUNTY OF SIMCOE AGRICULTURAL SOCIETY v. WADE.

Purchase of animal for a special purpose—Implied warranty.

The plaintiffs, an agricultural society, wishing to purchase a bull for breeding purposes sent their agent to the defendant, who gave him the choice of two which he had for sale. The agent chose one on his own judgment; and the defendant gave no express warranty except as to pedigree; but he was aware that the bull was purchased for the purpose of getting stock.
Held, that there was no implied warranty of the bull's fitness for the purpose for which he was required

ASSUMPSIT.—*Declaration*—That the defendant was possessed of a bull, and the plaintiffs were desirous of purchasing the same and keeping it to be used as a stock-getter, in case it was fit for that purpose, of which the defendant had notice; and thereupon in consideration that the plaintiffs would buy the said bull of the defendant for £50, the defendant promised that the said bull was fit for the purpose of getting stock: that the plaintiffs did buy, and the defendant sold, the bull to be used for such purpose. *Breach:* that the bull was not at the time of making the promise, nor afterwards, fit, &c.; but was unfit and incapable, and of no use and value in that behalf.

Plea—Non-assumpsit.

At the trial, before *Draper, J.*, at Barrie, in October, 1854, it appeared there had been some correspondence between the plaintiffs' secretary and the defendant, the particulars of which were not satisfactorily made out, as the letters were not produced. But in consequence of it the plaintiffs sent an agent to purchase a bull of the defendant, and the defendant gave the agent a choice of two which he had for sale. The defendant gave no express warranty except as to pedigree. The agent selected one on his own judgment, it being understood that the object of buying was to put him to cows in the county of Simcoe. This took place in May, 1853; and the bull was brought from the defendant's and put in charge of a person, who was called as a witness, and proved that though twenty-one cows were put to the bull, and some of them repeatedly, none proved with calf. This was corroborated by other witnesses, one of whom however, swore that he believed the bull had been twitched—an operation which he described, and which would destroy the procreative power of the animal, and he said he thought this had been done after the bull came into the plaintiffs' possession. The defendant called no witnesses.

The jury were told if there was an express warranty, to find for the plaintiff; if not, to inquire whether the defendant sold the bull without fraud or concealment, believing him, but neither promising nor warranting that he was, *aptus procreando,* leaving the plaintiffs to exercise their own judgment in the purchase—in which case the defendant would not be liable even if he knew the very object of the plaintiffs in buying the bull, which question they were asked to express an opinion on.

The jury gave a verdict for the defendant, saying that the defendant knew the purpose for which the plaintiffs made the purchase.

At the close of the plaintiffs' case the defendant's counsel had moved for a nonsuit, which was not granted, though leave was reserved to move.

Eccles obtained a rule nisi for a new trial, to which *J. D. Armour* shewed cause, citing Burnby v. Bollett, 16 M. & W. 644; Sutton v. Temple, 12 M. & W. 52; Hart v. Windsor, 12 M. & W. 68; Chanter v. Hopkins, 4 M. & W. 399; Parkinson v. Lee, 2 East 314; Grey v. Cox, 4 B. & C. 108; Story on Sales, 392, sec. 374; Jones v. Bright, 5 Bing, 533.

Eccles, contra, cited Brown v. Edgington, 2 M. & Gr. 279.

BURNS, J.—The jury have found that the defendant did know the purpose for which the plaintiffs wanted the bull in question, but it does not appear to me that such finding makes any difference as to the liability upon the evidence. It is not pretended there was any express warranty, and the only point to be decided is, whether an implied warranty in law arises upon the facts proved, with the finding of the jury that the defendant knew the purpose for which the plaintiffs wanted the bull. The witness whom the defendant sent to procure the bull says that the defendant exhibited to him two bulls, and he, the witness, made his own selection; and that the defendant warranted nothing except the animal's pedigree. No representation is proved to have been made by

the defendant; and so far as the particular animal is concerned, the purchase was made entirely upon the judgment
of the person sent by the plaintiffs to make the selection. If
any implied warranty could be held to exist, it must have
applied to the other bull as much as the one selected. If the
defendant, knowing the purpose for which the plaintiffs
wanted the bull, had represented the one selected as the most
proper for the plaintiffs, or if the agent had acted upon the
defendant's judgment in the selection, possibly there might
have been cause to complain. Though the defendant did
know the purpose for which the animal was wanted, yet if he
said and did nothing to induce the plaintiffs to purchase, I
take it there is no implied contract. This seems to me to be
the result of the cases, and is well exemplified by the language of *Maule, J.*, in Keats v. Earl Cadogan (10 C. B. 596):
" If a horse dealer contracts to sell a gentleman a horse fit
to carry him, and he sells him one which he knows to be unfit
for the purpose, he does not perform his contract. But if a
man buys a horse generally, the seller will not be responsible,
although, knowing that his customer wanted the horse for his
own riding, he sells one which will not carry him." In this
case, taking the finding of the jury against the defendant as
to his knowledge, then he exhibited his stock to the plaintiffs'
agent generally, leaving him to make his own selection and
act on his own judgment. It appears to me it is impossible
to say otherwise upon the facts proved here than that it was
a general sale. Should I have thought, however, that it was
a special sale for a special purpose, still the question would
remain, whether in a case like the present, whether the seller
must necessarily be as ignorant as the buyer of the fitness of
the bull for the purpose required, and knowing also that such
fitness could not be ascertained until the course of nature
developed the truth, I should be inclined to hold that no
implied warranty accompanied the sale. The manufacturer
of an article is bound to know the quality of what he manu-
factures; and the seller of a horse, if he sells for the purpose
of carrying or driving, is bound to know that the horse
possesses the qualities for the purposes of which the sale is
made; and it is upon this principle there is held to be an

implied contract in such cases. In a case where knowledge could not by possibility of nature exist, it would seem absurd to say the seller was bound to know that which futurity alone could disclose. In such cases it appears much more reasonable to hold that if a purchaser wishes to protect himself he should take an express undertaking.

DRAPER, J.—I continue to think the direction to the jury was right, and that they have rightly found for the defendant. The case is one of contract. The plaintiffs aver they wanted to buy a bull for the purpose of getting stock, and that the defendant knew this, and sold them a bull, and promised that the bull was fit and capable for the purpose required. The fact that the plaintiffs bought the bull in question of the defendant was not disputed at the trial. The *breach* of the alleged contract is not put in issue, for the only plea is *non-assumpsit*, which only denies the contract alleged. Upon the evidence it is clear there was no *express* contract that the bull would turn out capable of getting stock. The only question is, whether, because the defendant knew the purpose for which the plaintiffs made the purchase, he must be taken *impliedly* to have contracted that this animal was capable of effecting that purpose. The verdict establishes that there was neither fraud nor concealment on the defendant's part, and the evidence shewed that the animal was selected by the plaintiffs' agent; and that, though there was a warranty of pedigree, there was no other express warranty either asked or given. The plaintiffs' agent acted on his own judgment. This fact excludes the application of that class of cases which proceed on the ground that an examination of the thing sold is from its nature or situation at the time of sale impossible, such as Gardner v. Gray (4 Camp. 144).

The case of Jones v. Bright (5 Bing. 533) is distinguishable. There the article (copper sheathing) was purchased from the defendant, the manufacturer, who knew that it was required for sheathing a ship. It turned out bad, and in an action on the case in the nature of deceit it was held that the plaintiff should recover damages. Gray v. Cox (4 B. & C. 108), so far as it is an authority, is open to the same answer; Brown v. Edgington (2 M. & G. 279), which was on a sale of rope for a particular purpose, is of the same class.

But these and other cases (see Chanter v. Hopkins, 4 M. & W. 399 ; Shephard v. Pybus, 3 M. & Gr. 868) lead to the conclusion, that if the purchaser specifically describes the identical articles he requires, or selects what he wants, relying on his own judgment of its fitness for the purpose to which he intends to apply it, the mere fact that the vendor knows the use for which it is designed will not raise an implied warranty that it is fit for that purpose :—that is, in other words, if the purchaser has as full an opportunity of exercising his judgment upon the quality of the article as the vendor has, and there be no fraud, the purchaser takes the risk of latent defect; but if the purchaser states that he relies on the seller's judgment, by informing him that he requires an article for a particular purpose, and the seller undertakes to furnish *such* an article, the transaction carries with it an implied warranty.

Applying these principles to the evidence called by the plaintiffs : their own agent proved that he went to the defendant and selected the bull in question on his own judgment, the defendant being aware of the object of the plaintiffs in purchasing, and expressly warranting the pedigree of the animal, but not warranting or being asked to warrant anything more, and acting (as the jury by their verdict declared) without fraud or concealment. In my opinion, at the trial and now, this brings the case within the principle of those decisions in which it has been held that the law does not imply a warranty, and therefore the contract alleged in the declaration was not proved.

Besides the cases above noted, I refer to Bluett v. Osborne (1 Stark N. P. C. 384), Parkinson v. Lee (2 East 314), Burnby v. Bollett (16 M. & W. 644), Sutton v. Temple (12 M. & W. 52), Dickson v. Zezinia (10 C. B. 602).

I have not founded my decision upon any distinction between articles the produce of nature and those the produce of art, though I do not wish to be understood as deciding anything against such a distinction being under particular circumstances maintainable. Reference was made by Mr. Eccles to several *dicta* in various decisions alluding to the sale of horses, where the buyer explained that he was buying for a particular purpose, and the animal was selected and sent by the seller as fitted for that purpose, shewing that a warranty would be implied. I agree to that extent. But the present case much more closely resembles that put by Maule, J., in Dickson v. Zezinia (10 C. B. 610); "If a man sell a horse and warrant it to be sound, the vendor knowing at the time that the purchaser wants it for the purpose of carrying a lady, and the horse, though sound, proves to be unfit for that particular purpose, this would be no breach." For here there was a specific warranty, namely, of pedigree; and, as is said in the same case, "*expressum facit cessare tacitum*," and an implied warranty on another point would therefore on this ground also seem excluded.

Rule discharged.

CAUGHILL V. MARIA TEAL, EXECUTRIX OF JOHN B. TEAL.

Sci Fa.—Practice—Appropriation of payments.

Sci. Fa. on a payment alleged to have been recovered against the defendant, executrix, &c. (not *as* executrix) for £250. *Plea*, payment. The defendants proved payments to about £130. An account was produced by the plaintiff shewing due at testator's death £76 7s. 4d. This was carried forward, and the account continued for some time against the defendant, leaving a balance due altogether of £196 12s. 1d. The defendant contended that, as the payments proved exceeded the amount due by testator at his death, she was entitled to a verdict ; but

Held, That the statement in the *Sci. Fa* did not amount to an allegation that the defendant was sued in her representative character, the word *executrix* being mere description; and that the plaintiff was therefore entitled to a verdict on the issue, only half the amount of the judgment having been proved to be paid.

Semble, That on such issue the plaintiff should have taken a verdict merely that the judgment was unsatisfied, not for any specific sum ; and that a verdict so taken would not prevent the defendant from obtaining relief if the execution on the judgment should be endorsed for more than the sum due.

Scire Facias on a judgment for £250, recovered against the defendant, executrix, &c., of John B. Teal, deceased. *Plea,* payment by defendant as executrix; on which issue was joined.

The trial took place in January, 1855, at Toronto, before McLean, J.

The issue being on the defendant she called a witness, who proved that in 1852 he paid to the plaintiff for defendant various sums, all of which were included in a receipt put in : " Received from J. H. Jones £80 currency on mill rent. Vienna, Sept. 18, 1852 :" signed by plaintiff for defendant. Mr. Jones further stated that in 1853 he paid the plaintiff £52 on account of defendant : that he was indebted to defendant at the time he paid these moneys, as he had rented a mill from her in May, 1852. An account was produced on cross-examination of this witness by the plaintiff's counsel, and shewn to him. He stated that the plaintiff had in his presence shewn the account to defendant, who objected to some items, about £16, which items the plaintiff consented to strike out, but no specific balance was agreed upon. The defendant stated that the plaintiff was willing to take her note endorsed by Jones for any balance due, but Jones declined endorsing. This account began on the 28th of September, 1850, against the testator. The last charge against him was on the 29th of March, 1851. Credit was given for payments, and it was closed thus—"Balance due at J. B. Teal's death, £76 7s. 4d." Then an account was opened headed " Mrs. John B. Teal, Dr.," the first item of which was in 1851, April 9th—amount forwards £76 7s. 4d., and was continued to December 27th, 1852, when the debit side amounted to £312 7s. 5d., and credit was given for £115 15s. 4d., leaving a balance claimed of £196 12s. 1d.

The defendant's counsel contended that this £115 15s. 4d. must be referred to the first items of the account, including the debt of the testator, and could not be applied to defendant's own personal account. The learned judge said that as the defendant's counsel admitted the judgment, and that a verdict must be rendered against the defendant, he (the learned judge) did not see how the amount of the verdict could affect his case : that if the first items must be considered as discharged by the payments made, then the defendant, or the parties interested in the estate, must apply to the court to have satisfaction entered on the judgment, which stood admitted to be for £250. .

The jury gave the plaintiff a verdict for £210 12s. 1d.,

made up according to the figures at the foot of the account of the balance £196 12s. 1d., less £16, the amount which, according to the evidence, the plaintiff agreed to deduct, adding for interest £30.

Eccles obtained a rule nisi for misdirection, contending in substance that as the plaintiff's own account shewed that the testator only owed £76 7s. 4d., and as this was a *Sci. Fa.* to revive a judgment against the defendant as executrix, it must, in the absence of anything to the contrary, be assumed that, though the judgment was for £250, there was only £76 7s. 4d. due upon it, and then the payments proved by Jones overbalanced it; and, though it is true the defendant is upon the account produced largely indebted to the plaintiff, yet he has not sued her for that debt, but only brings *Sci. Fa.* on the judgment.

Leith, contra, insisted that it appeared the payments were on the evidence shewn to be payments from defendant's own moneys, and not out of the estate, and therefore they were applicable to her own debt.

DRAPER, J., delivered the judgment of the court.

The judgment recited in the *Sci. Fa.* is against the defendant, executrix, &c., not *as* executrix. She pleads that she, *as* executrix, paid and satisfied the plaintiff, &c. There is nothing to shew when the judgment was entered, or that the sum named in it was not the true debt, or that it was recovered against defendant as executrix. The statement in the *Sci. Fa.* that the plaintiff recovered against the defendant, " executrix of the last will, &c.," does not amount to an allegation that she had been sued in her representative character.—Henshall v. Roberts (5 East 150), Walker v. Covert (5 O. S. 58). Then, if the judgment stated in the *Sci. Fa.* is one recovered as against the defendant individually, the word " executrix" being read as mere addition or description, the case amounts to this.—*Sci. Fa.* is brought on a judgment recovered against the defendant for £250. She pleads payment, and shews payments of about half that sum. The plaintiff is clearly entitled to a verdict on the issue. The question discussed on the argument, as to the application of the payments, does not arise. It is true the plaintiff has on this issue taken not merely a verdict that the judgment is unsatisfied, but for a specific sum. But this appears to us of no consequence, and will not, we apprehend, bar the defendant from applying to the court for relief, if the execution to be sued out under the judgment in this case is endorsed for too much, and the plaintiff endeavours to levy more than remains due. In entering judgment on this *Sci. Fa.* I do not see, according to the usual forms, how any notice can be taken of the verdict for damages, nor indeed with what object the plaintiff took a verdict in that form.—See Henriquez v. Dutch West India Co. (2 Str. 807), Knox v. Costello (3 Burr. 1791).

Rule discharged.

In Re Township Clerk of Euphrasia.

A mandamus to a clerk of a municipality to furnish a copy of a by-law was refused, where it did not appear that the demand was accompanied by an offer of his fee.

Cosens moved for a mandamus absolute in the first instance, commanding the township clerk to give to Dickenson Fletchers a properly authenticated copy of a certain by-law.

Draper, J.—The proof of the existence of such a by-law is not very distinct; and though there is an affidavit of a demand of a certified copy of a by-law passed on or about the 7th of November last, for raising the taxes of said municipality for the year 1854, and of the clerk's refusal, it is not shewn that there was any tender or offer to pay the clerk his fees. The 12 Vic., ch. 81, sec. 155, makes it the duty of the clerk, upon such application as is stated, " and upon payment of his fee therefor," within a reasonable time, to furnish a copy. Without this is done, we think we ought not to order the clerk to deliver a copy.

BENS V. GILBERT STOVER, DAVID STOVER, AND GILBERT
STOVER, JR.

Practice—Mistake—Application for new trial made in wrong court—Agreement—Variance.

An application for a new trial made in this court was referred to the C. P. as the record had been returned there, and the case, which had been tried before the Chief Justice of the C. P., was not to be found in his note-book of trials from this court. A rule *nisi* was then obtained in proper time in the C. P. and enlarged until the next term, and in the meantime it was discovered that the record had been by mistake endorsed in C. P.

Under these circumstances the application was entertained in this court on the return of the rule.

The declaration stated an agreement to pay to three persons, and the agreement when produced was to pay half to one and half to the two others :—
Semble, per *Draper, J.,* no variance.

COVENANT on an agreement made between the plaintiff and the three defendants, by which it was alleged in the declaration that the plaintiff agreed with defendants to pay them £1 10s. for every one thousand feet of lumber, to be delivered as in the agreement mentioned. *Breach,* non-delivery.

At the trial, before *Macaulay,* C. J., at St. Thomas, the agreement was produced, and by it the plaintiff agreed " to pay the said parties of the first part at the rate of £2 10s. per thousand feet, one-half to be paid to Gilbert Stover, Senior, and the other half to D. and G. Stover, Junior, as the lumber may be delivered from time to time."

On the defence a variance was objected, that the declaration stated the payment was to be made to the then defendants, whereas by the agreement the payment was to be one-half to Gilbert Stover, Senior, the other half to the other two defendants. The objection was overruled; but the learned Chief Justice directed the jury to find specially whether the execution of the agreement produced was proved to their satisfaction, and on their finding that it was he directed that finding to be specially endorsed on the record ; and he left to the jury to enquire whether the defendants had failed to deliver the lumber according to their contract ; whether the plaintiff had over-paid them ; and in reference to both questions to take into consideration the evidence given on behalf of the plaintiff of a settlement between the parties, which evidence was not contradicted by the defendants. The jury found for the plaintiff, damages £114 5s. 4d.

By some oversight the Nisi Prius record had been endorsed as if the action was brought in the Court of Common Pleas, and a motion was made in due time in that court, and a rule there granted for a new trial on the ground that the verdict was against law and evidence for the admission of improper evidence, for misdirection, and upon affidavits. This motion was not made in the Common Pleas, until an application had been made in this court, when in consequence of the record being returned to the Court of Common Pleas, and of the learned Chief Justice of that Court not having included the case in his note-book of trials on record from this court, the defendant's counsel were referred to the Common Pleas, and got the rule *nisi* there; and the rule having been served was enlarged by consent until Hilary term. In the mean time the mistake was discovered, and the plaintiff's counsel having refused to argue that rule in this court.

D. G. Miller, for defendants, obtained a rule *nisi* in Hilary term to make the rule granted by the Common Pleas under the mistake a rule of this court, and to file here all the papers used in that court, on the motion, (the Court of Common Pleas permitting the defendant to withdraw them from their files for that purpose,) and for a new trial on the same grounds as were taken in the other court.

Leith shewed cause, objecting : First, That a rule of the Court of Common Pleas could not be made a rule of this court, Secondly, That as a rule *nisi* for a new trial in this court, it had been applied for and obtained too late, this rule having been asked for and granted in the second term after verdict. He also shewed cause on the merits, filing affidavits in answer to those filed by the defendant.

DRAPER, J., delivered the judgment of the court, &c.

We think that we should probably have found it competent for us to have granted a new trial, even if, in order to decide on the merits of the application, we were obliged to resort to the rule granted in the Common Pleas as the foundation of our proceeding—(See Piggott v. Kemp (2 Dowl. 20.) But we do not doubt the *power* of the court to entertain a motion for a new trial at any time before judgment is actually entered; it is a matter of discretion, under the particular circumstances, and I have known that discretion exercised, though very sparingly, after the four days had expired. There is also English authority recognising the principle—Birt v. Barlow (Doug. 171), Rex v. Gough (Doug. 797), Rex v. Holt (5 T. R. 436), Thomas v. Edwards (1 Cr. M. & R. 382). The defendant's counsel applied here in due time, and owing to the error about the record was sent to the wrong court, who granted him a rule : under such peculiar circumstances we ought not, in our opinion, to refuse to examine into the case to see if any injustice has been done.

Upon examining the evidence and the affidavits on both sides, we are clearly of opinion that there is no ground for a new trial; and on the return of this rule Mr. Miller did not press any exception to the charge of the learned Chief Justice, or renew any objection to the admission of evidence. The objection of variance was removed at the trial by the manner in which the question respecting the agreement was submitted to the jury, and their finding thereon endorsed on the record. For myself, I will add, that I think the objection was not tenable ; that the payment was contracted to be made to the three defendants, and was properly so stated in the declaration, the paying one particular portion to one defendant, and the residue to the other two, was a mere arrangement of the mode in which payment to the *three* might be made.

Rule discharged.

DOE DEM. HAY V. HUNT.

In ejectment under the old form, where the lessor of the plaintiff died before the trial,—*Held*, that no *sci. fa.* was necessary, but that judgment might be entered, and a writ of possession obtained.

Read obtained a rule *nisi* to rescind an order of *Burns*, J., discharging a summons for restoring the defendant to the possession of the premises, out of which he had been turned on a writ of *Hab. fac. poss.*, issued in this cause ; and that the defendant should be restored to possession : or for a writ of restitution. The ground of the application was that after the commencement of this action, and before the trial, the lessor of the plaintiff died.

M. Vankoughnet shewed cause. The authorities cited are sufficiently noticed in the judgment.

DRAPER, J., delivered the judgment of the court.

It is conceded by the form of the application that, the judgment is regular. In Adam's treatise on ejectment, 2nd ed., 283, it is said : " The death of the lessor of the plaintiff, although he be only tenant for life, will not abate the action, nor can it be pleaded *puis darrein continuance*, because the right is supposed to be in his lessee (the plaintiff;) who may proceed for the damages occasioned by the supposed ouster, although he cannot obtain possession of the land." Thrustout dem. Turner v. Grey (Str. 1056) is cited; and, as regards the proceeding where the lessor of the plaintiff is only tenant for life, it sustains the position. If, therefore the words "although he" (the plaintiff) " cannot obtain possession of the land," are limited to such a case, they do not affect the present case, where the lessor of the plaintiff was seised in fee.

On the other hand, in Watson on Sheriffs, page 217, it is said: "In ejectment, the plaintiff and defendant being merely nominal, even if real persons, execution might issue, notwith- standing their death, without a *sci. fa.;* and it seems that, after the death of the lessor of the plaintiff, a writ might be issued and executed—at all events, if it bear teste in his lifetime"—citing Tidds' Pr., 8th ed., 1171-2; Doe dem. Beyer v. Roe (4 Burr. 1970), in which case the writ was tested before the death of the lessor of the plaintiff, though issued after ; the court rested the judgment mainly on that ground, but observed, that the ejectment was brought by John Doe, and "the defendant does not shew that John Doe, *the plaintiff in this action is dead.*"

There can be no doubt that the action may proceed to judgment, notwithstanding the death of the lessor of the plaintiff. Thus in Thrustout v. Bedwell (2 Wils. 7) the lessor of the plaintiff died before the assizes. The case, how- ever, went on, and the plaintiff was nonsuited because the

defendant did not confess lease, entry, and ouster. It was
held that the lessors's executor could not tax the costs on the
consent rule against the defendant—not, however, on the
ground that the action had abated, but from the merely personal nature of the undertaking in the consent rule. On the
same principle, in Doe v. Grundy (1 B. & C. 284), where
the lessor of the plaintiff died before the trial but after the
commission day, and the cause was tried, and the plaintiff
was nonsuited on the merits, the court held that his executor was not liable to pay the costs. So in Doe v. Cozens
(9 DowL 1040) the death of the lessor of the plaintiff after
verdict, and pending a rule for a new trial, was held to
afford no ground for staying the proceedings, or for ordering that the plaintiff should find security for costs. On the
argument of the rule for a new trial in this cause (1 Q. B.
426), it was said by the defendant's counsel *arguendo*, "perhaps in strictness the action would not abate, as it could
not be said that the nominal plaintiff had died." The court
apparently acquiesced in the admission. So in Doe dem.
Lord Egremont v. Stephens (2 D. & L. 993), a verdict was
taken subject to the opinion of the court on a special case,
and before the terms of that could be settled, the lessor of
the plaintiff died. The court held that this fact afforded no
ground for setting aside the verdict or for staying the proceedings, though the court would under the circumstances
compel the plaintiff to find security for costs. And Mr.
Archbold, in his new practice (ed. of 1847), cites this case
as shewing that the only effect of the death of a sole lessor
of the plaintiff in ejectment is, that the defendant may
obtain security for costs.

It seems therefore so far clear, and it was so agreed on
moving and supporting this rule, that the plaintiff's judgment is right.

That being conceded, the question is, why he may not
issue execution? The defendant's whole ground of resistance
to this course is, that the lessor of the plaintiff died before
the judgment was entered; for if the judgment be regular,
it becomes indifferent at what earlier stage of the proceedings he died.

It does not appear to me that Thrustout v. Grey is an

authority for this position, for there the lessor of the plaintiff
was only tenant for life; consequently the plaintiff, his
lessee, could not have a right to possession longer than the
lessor had; and although, on the record, a longer term
might have been set out, and by the judgment recovered,
yet the court in such a case would treat the action as it
really is (or was before our recent statute), as a fictitious
action, and would limit the plaintiff to the right of his
lessor; and therefore the court say in that case the possession could not be obtained.   Whether the reason given for
allowing the plaintiff to proceed,—namely, for " damages
and costs"—be a sound one, is another question.   According
to the case of Thrustout v. Bedwell, the executor of the
lessor of the plaintiff could not recover costs, either by
action or attachment, the undertaking in the consent rule
being merely personal as between the parties to it; but
that was when the defendant did not appear to defend, and
so the only remedy was on the consent rule; whereas if a
verdict were recovered the court seem to have thought
John Doe might recover his costs, though the title having
expired he could not get possession.

In Chitty's Archbold (2nd vol. 768, 7th ed.), it is said:
" If the lessor of the plaintiff die after the teste of the writ
of *habere*, but before it is actually sued out, it is not necessary to revive the judgment by *Scire Facias;* and as he is
not a party to the record it seems no *Scire Facias* would
be necessary if he dies before the teste of the writ, although
this appears doubtful," citing Doe Beyer v. Roe, in which
case, according to the fact stated, as the writ bore teste before the day of the death of the lessor of the plaintiff, it was
clearly regular, and would have been so in any form of action.
The court say : " This is an ejectment brought by John
Doe, and the defendant does not shew that John Doe, the
plaintiff in this action is dead"—and then go on to say the
writ is at all events regular.   This case, though not an
authority to shew that if the writ had been tested after the
lessor of the plaintiff died it would have been regular, is
certainly no authority for the contrary position.

In Doe Byne v. Brewer (4 M. & S. 300) the court held

that the lessor of the plaintiff could not release the action, and this authority was acted on in this court in Doe Boyer v. Claus (3 O. S. 146). Lord Ellenborough observed: "Looking to the record we must consider those as real parties to the action who are parties upon the record, and the real parties alone are qualified to release the action." I do not see why the same rule should not apply here. It is not pretended the lessor of the plaintiff was not tenant in fee, and therefore could grant a term extending beyond the period of his life. It is established by the verdict and judgment that the defendant was a trespasser, unlawfully in possession. If Thrustout v. Grey mean anything, it must mean that John Doe might, if he got a verdict, enter judgment, which in form would be for the term, and for damages and costs, and that John Doe might levy the costs though he could not get possession. John Doe might bring trespass for mesne profits, although his lessor was dead, and might recover damages and costs. Even if, as between the party who has actually had possession delivered to him and some other party, there may be a question of right, what is that to the defendant? he is found to have had no right at the trial, and he shews no new right accruing in consequence of the death of the lessor of the plaintiff.

We are therefore of opinion that no *Scire Facias* was necessary in this case, and that the execution by *hab. fac. poss.* was regular. The result might possibly have been different, if the action had been brought under our late act. This may be one unforeseen change in the practice in ejectment thereby created. It is right, however, for me to say that my impression during the argument was quite the other way, and that I believe the learned Chief Justice of this court was in favour of the application.

REGINA EX REL. BLAISDELL v. ROCHESTER.

Contested election—Summons issued by Judge of the C. C.—Necessity of filing papers weth D. C. C.—Affidavit and recognizance.

A county judge issued his fiat for a *quo warranto*, and the papers remained with him, but were handed to the defendant's solicitor, before the return day, for perusal. *Held* sufficient, and that it was not necessary that they should have been filed with the Deputy Clerk of the Crown before the summons issued.

Semble, that the relator's attorney may act as commissioner to take the recognizance and affidavit.

The judge of the county court of the county of Carleton granted his fiat for a writ of summons in this case, under the 16 Vic. ch. 181, sec. 27, and he made the writ returnable at his own chambers at a specified day. The statement of the relator with his affidavit, and the recognizances with the affidavit of justification, were all left with the learned judge, and his fiat was taken to the office of the deputy clerk of the crown and left there, and that officer issued the writ. Before the return of it the defendant's solicitor obtained a perusal of all the papers from the judge, and before or perhaps on the return day the relator's solicitor and the defendant and his solicitor appeared before the judge, and on the defendant's part the following objections were taken as a ground for setting aside the proceedings :—

1st. That the recognizance does not appear to have been taken at a place within the authority of the commissioner.

2. That the papers were not filed in the court of Queen's Bench according to the notice, which stated that they were filed "in this court," according to the form given by the rules.

3. That the name of the relator to the affidavit verifying his statement is obliterated, and no certificate explaining the fact.

4. That some of the papers are not according to the form prescribed by the rules.

5. That the recognizance and affidavit are irregular being taken by the commissioner, who was also attorney for the relator.

The learned judge declined to give way to any of these objections.

On a subsequent day the parties again appeared, and the

papers *then* were all duly filed with the Deputy Clerk of the Crown. The defendant declined to answer, admitting that his name was not on any of the collectors' rolls for the proper amount, whereupon the learned judge gave judgment against him.

The papers having all been returned here, *Eccles* moved for a rule *nisi* to set aside the judgment and proceedings relying on the second and fifth objections above noted.

DRAPER, J., delivered the judgment of the court.

As to the second objection, there was no rule infringed by the absence of a formal filing of the papers in the deputy clerk's office before the writ of summons issued. The papers remained with the judge who granted the summons, and the defendant sustained no prejudice by this, for it appears his solicitor saw them and had full opportunity to examine them before the writ was returnable.

And as to the fifth objection, the proceeding is analogous to the suing out a writ of *capias* on an affidavit taken before the commissioner, who afterwards acts as the plaintiff's attorney in suing out the writ. These objections were in the discretion of the learned judge, who had the best opportunity of judging whether the case was such as to render it proper to give any weight to it. It cannot be said that any positive rule of law or practice governed the point, and we see no reason whatever to suppose that any injustice has been done by the decision.

Even if we doubted the strict regularity of the proceeding objected to, on the ground of the commissioner being also the attorney, we should be slow to interfere unless a very strong necessity for so doing was made out. But in this case the defendant raises nothing but technical objections; when they are overruled he declines making a defence, and admits he cannot deny the truth of the alleged want of qualification which is objected to his election. On the merits we see no reason to interfere with the judgment, and that being so, we should be establishing a bad precedent if we were to encourage appeals in cases of this description upon mere questions of formal practice, and upon

merely technical objections should set aside a judgment
well founded on the real merits of the case.

Rule refused.

VANCE v. RUTTAN.

Lease—Goods seized under fi. fa.—Landlord's claim for rent.

Premises were let for a year at a rent of £75, to be paid on the first day of
May ; and it was agreed that if the tenant should leave before the first of
May, then the rent was to become payable immediately. The tenant did
leave on the Saturday before the first of May, and on Monday the goods
were seized under execution.
Held, that the landlord was entitled to his rent from the sheriff.

CASE for false return to a *fi. fa.*, complaining that the
sheriff made £140 13s. 10d., besides fees and expenses, and
paid the plaintiff only £115 12s. 5d., and returned *nulla
bona* as to the residue. *Plea*, not guilty.

At the trial at Toronto, in January, before *McLean*, J., it
was admitted that defendant had levied £140 13s. 10d., and
had only paid over £115 12s. 5d.; and that unless the
defendant was justified in paying a year's rent of the premises
occupied by Herschberg, the execution debtor, and upon
which premises the levy was made, the plaintiff was entitled
to recover. The landlord of the premises was called as a
witness, and swore that in October, 1853, he let them to
Herschberg for a year, at a rent of £75, to be paid on the
first of May then next. Herschberg claimed that if he should
leave before the year was up, he might let for the residue of
the year. The landlord agreed, if the premises were let only
as a dry goods store ; and he swore it was agreed that if
Herschberg left the premises *before* the first of May, 1854,
the rent was to become payable immediately on his leaving.
Herchberg ran away about the first of April, leaving his wife
behind him. She left on a Saturday before the first of May,
and on the Monday following the sheriff entered and levied.
Herschberg did not return again, and left the rent unpaid,
and the landlord claimed and obtained it from the sheriff.
The sheriff afterwards sold the residue of Herschberg's term.
The learned judge in effect directed the jury that if they
believed this witness they should find for the defendant ; for
then, on Herschberg quitting, and his family leaving also

after him; the event happened which entitled the landlord to claim his rent, immediately, instead of waiting, as otherwise stipulated, to the 1st of May. The jury found for defendant.

McMichael moved for a new trial 'on the law and evidence, and for misdirection.

DRAPER, J., delivered the judgment of the court.

We think the charge substantially correct. The term was created for a year from October, 1853. The rent reserved was made payable on the 1st of May, 1854, with a further stipulation, that if Herschberg went away before that day the rent should be payable immediately. He did go away, and was followed by his family, quitting the premises before the 1st of May, though leaving his goods. None of them have ever returned since. Then, if the landlord's statement be true, the event happened which gave him a right to immediate payment. No exception appears to have been taken to the manner in which the question was submitted to the jury, and their verdict appears to us in accordance with the substantial justice of the case.

Rule refused.

FELLOWES v. HUTCHISON.

Malicious prosecution—Opinion of counsel.

Case for maliciously and without reasonable or probable cause, preferring a charge of felony
The learned judge directed the jury to enquire whether the defendant had laid a *bona fide* statement of the material facts of the case before counsel, and whether he acted *bona fide* on the opinion so obtained, saying that if, so, that was reasonable and probable cause.
Held, that such direction was right.

CASE for maliciously and without reasonable or probable cause accusing the plaintiff, before George Gurnett, Esq., with having forcibly taken possession of a schooner of defendant's, called the "Hebe," with the felonious intent of appropriating it to plaintiff's own use; and procuring a warrant to be issued, and the plaintiff to be arrested, and to be forced to find bail, and causing the plaintiff to be brought before said justice of the peace to be examined concerning the said supposed crime, when the charge was dismissed. *Second count* for slander, in saying that the plaintiff and another person forcibly took possession of a schooner of defendant's with the felonious design of appropriating it to their own use, thereby meaning that the plaintiff was guilty of feloniously taking away the said schooner. *Plea*, not guilty.

Tried at Toronto, before *McLean, J.* Verdict for defendant. *Dempsey* moved for a new trial for misdirection.

DRAPER J., delivered the judgment of the court.

It seems perfectly clear that there was no actual sufficient ground for preferring a charge of felony against the plaintiff, and if at the time of preferring this charge the defendant knew (and there is evidence tending to the conclusion) that the plaintiff had taken possession of the schooner under a claim of right, and *bona fide*, though in error, there was no probable cause for the accusation.—See James v. Phelps (11 A. & E. 483.) But for the evidence given by Mr. M. C. Cameron, there would seem little doubt but that the plaintiff had a good case on the first count to go to the jury. The law certainly is, that if a party lays all the facts of his case fairly before counsel, and acts *bona fide* on the opinion given by that counsel, however erroneous the opinion, he is not liable to this action—*per Bayley, J.*, in Ravenga v. Mackintosh (2 B. & C. 597. See, however, Hewlett v. Cruchley (5 Taunt. 280.) The learned judge reports that in substance he directed the jury to enquire whether the defendant did lay a *bona fide* statement of the material facts of the case before counsel for his opinion, and whether he acted *bona fide* on the opinion so obtained, saying, that if so, that was reasonable and probable cause.

Such a direction is in our opinion right, and we therefore think there should be no rule.

Rule refused.

ROSSIN ET AL. v. WHITE ET AL.

Promissory note—Pleading.

Declaration on a promissory note against the maker, the payee, and second endorser. *Plea*, by the payee and second endorser, that they did not endorse the said promissory note in manner and form.
Held, on demurrer, plea bad.

The plaintiffs declare that George W. White made his promissory note, dated 31st of July, 1854, for £46 4s. 9d., payable at three months to the order of defendant, Jacob Rikley; that the defendant Rikley endorsed and delivered the note to defendant William McCracken, who endorsed and delivered the note to the plaintiffs. The declaration contained the usual averments of presentation, non-payment, and notice to the endorsers; by reason whereof the defendants became jointly and severally liable to pay.

The defendants Rikley and McCracken joined in a plea, "that they did not indorse the said promissory note in manner and form in the declaration alleged."

Demurrer—That the plea is joint, not several, whereas each defendant should alone have denied his own endorsement; that the declaration does not assert a joint endorsement, which is what this plea denies. 2. That the plea is an argumentative denial of the endorsement by each of the defendants. 3. That it contains a negative payment, with the admission of the endorsement by one of defendants. 4. That the plea is double and multifarious (not stating in what the duplicity consisted), and tenders an immaterial issue.

Hector Cameron, for the demurrer, cited Hawke v. Salt, 3 C. P. 97.

McIntyre endeavoured to sustain the plea, by insisting that it might, by the aid of the words "in manner and form, &c.," be read distributively as a traverse by each defendant of his own endorsement; he cited The City Bank v. Keller et al., 2 C. P. 508 ; Tompkins v. Scott, 9 U. C. R. 103.

DRAPER, J., delivered the judgment of the court.

We think this case undistinguishable in principle from that of Hawke v. Salt (3 C. P. 97), which was a joint action against the maker and two endorsers of a promissory note, brought as this is, by virtue of our Provincial statutes 5 Wm. IV. ch. 1, 3 Vic. ch., 8, and 13 & 14 Vic. ch. 59; and in which *Chief Justice Macaulay* stated in conclusion that in such an action, where the defences of the several defendants clash, or the facts are not equally adapted as a defence to all parties, they should plead separately.

Now treat this plea as separately pleaded by each defendant, and it amounts to a denial by each that either he or the other defendant endorsed the note in question; and this is the utmost limit we can go (further than I am prepared to hold we ought to go) in support of the plea. The payee and first endorser denies the endorsement alleged to have been made by him which he may do, and he also denies the endorsement to the plaintiff by his (the payee's) endorsee— which would make the plea double, and is tendering a traverse immaterial to his defence; unless indeed it appeared that he had endorsed in some special manner, rendering proof of the second endorsement necessary to charge him. The second endorser denies his own endorsement, and also that of the first endorser, which latter he admits by the act of endorsing; so that if his own endorsement be proved, the other endorsement is proved also, and as against him conclusively, even though it might be a forgery. This would also make the plea double, and is denying a fact which it is not competent for him to deny.

To use the language of the Chief Justice, in Hawke v. Salt, if the plea is bad in part, or as to one of the defendants, it is bad altogether; and a latter part of that judgment affords an answer to the point contended for by Mr McIntyre; namely, that we may read this plea as a separate denial by each defendant of his own endorsement, and of nothing else. The words import nothing of the sort; they deny that *they*—i.e., the two defendants—endorsed. It was material for each of them to deny his own endorsement, and immaterial for the payee to deny the subsequent endorsement, as for all that appears the payee endorsed in blank (and not specially); while it was material for the second endorser to deny his own endorsement, and he could not deny that of the payee against the admission by his own endorser.—*Vide tamen,* 13 M. & W. 450; 8 Q. B. 473.

We think the plaintiff is entitled to judgment. As the plea reads, the two defendants say they did not endorse. The obvious meaning is that they did not jointly endorse, and then the plea is bad, for the declaration does not so allege; or by a somewhat forced construction the plea may mean that the defendants unite in denying that they separately endorsed, *i. e.*, each defendant denies his own and the other's endorsement. This is also bad, for the reasons above given. The only remaining method of construing the plea is to reject the plain construction of its terms, which we have no right to do, or to reject a portion of the allegation of each defendant; namely, so much as relates to the endorsement by the other defendant; against which rejection the judgment in Hawke v. Salt affords clear and satisfactory authority.

Judgment for plaintiffs on demurrer.

REGINA v. ROSE.

Boundary line commissioners—1 Vic. ch. 19 ; *3 Vic., ch.* 11—*Form of judgment—Omission to file.*

Held, That the minute of the boundary line commissioners, produced in this case, could not be considered a judgment within the meaning of the 3 Vic., ch. 11, and that the defendant should therefore have been permitted to give evidence contradicting such minute.

The second section of this act, which provides that every such judgment shall be filed, is directory only, and the omission to file will not affect the validity of the judgment.

NUISANCE.—The indictment charged that the defendant Silas Rose, on the 1st of May, 1854, in the township of Oxford, in the county of Grenville, obstructed a certain road, called the side-line road, between lots 20 and 21 in the first concession of the said township, the road being a common highway, and by obstructions placed across the road prevented the same from being used.

The case was tried at the last assizes held at Brockville, before *McLean, J.*, and the evidence to sustain the charge was as follows :—In 1842 one Jehiel Hurd complained to the board of boundary commissioners for the District of Johnstown, and requested that they would hear and determine all matters in dispute between himself and certain persons, of whom the defendant was not one named by him, touching the line between lots Nos. 20 and 21, in the first concession of Oxford, and also the line in the centre of lot No. 20. A parcel of papers were produced, shewing that the commissioners had a meeting upon the notice and requisition, and had taken evidence upon the subject of the line between the lots 20 and 21 ; and a memorandum of minutes of what the commissioners called a judgment was made on the 22nd of July, 1842. These papers were not produced from the registry office of the county of Grenville, but were said to have been left at the registry office for the county of Leeds, though not filed or entered of record in the latter office.

The minute of the commissioners was in the words and figures following :—

" <i>Minutes of the judgment.</i>

" Find post between 20 and 21, marked 20 on west side, an original post; find the line running thence to rear of concession, parallel with boundary line of township, to be the boundary between lot 20 and allowance for road on east thereof; stone monuments to be placed at front and rear of said line, also at centre of lot 20, and at the rear of said centre ; following costs reasonably incurred and awarded as within.

" <i>Kemptville, 22nd July,</i> 1842.

O. R. G.

J. B.

R. F. S."

Mr. <i>Steel</i>, the commissioner who was examined, stated that the parties were heard, and the commissioners came to a conclusion, and signed a paper, of which the foregoing is a copy, with their initial letters, intending afterwards to draw up a formal and extended judgment. Evidence was adduced to shew that stone monuments had been placed under the directions of the commissioners, and that the road between lots 20 and 21 had been laid out on the east side of the line so said to be established by the commissioners. Statute labor had been done for some six or seven years, and the road had been used by the public for some twelve years, until the month of May last, when the defendant obstructed it by fencing it up.

The objections raised by the defendant at the trial were as follows: First, that there was no evidence to shew that the boundary commissioners were required to ascertain the lines in question by any one who owned the land, and who had authority by law to ask their interference in establishing a line. Secondly, that the instrument produced is not a decree or judgment of the commissioners. Thirdly, that there is no decision where the western limit of 21 is.

These objections were overruled by the learned judge, and then the defendant tendered evidence to show that the allowance for road was on the west side of the line ascertained by the commissioners as the east line of lot No. 20, which the learned judge rejected, considering that the commissioners had determined the matter, and that such determination was binding, unless appealed against; and he therefore directed a verdict of guilty to be entered; and reserved the considerations of the case upon the objections made for the judgment of this court, and also further whether the evidence tendered should have been received.

The case was argued by *Freeland* for the crown, and *Richards* for defendant.

BURNS, J., delivered the judgment of the court.

The statute 1 Vic. ch. 19, as amended by 3 Vic. ch. 11, is the statute which governs this case, so far as the same is to be governed by the decision of the boundary commissioners. The second section of the latter act enacts that the judgment and final decision of the commissioners shall be filed with the registrar of the county where such boundary commissioners shall be situate. We do not consider it necessary to the validity of the judgment that it should be filed with the registrar of the county. We cannot but see the legislature intended it should operate as a notice in some way, for some purpose, and in that way the provision with respect to filing it in the registry office has importance. The first section of the first mentioned act enacts that the acts, orders, judgments, and decrees of the commissioners shall be final and conclusive between the parties, their heirs and assigns, except in case of appeal to be brought within the time limited. By the 17th section an appeal lies to the Court of Chancery or the Court of Queen's Bench. All these provisions shew that it is necessary that the judgment or final decision of the commissioners should shew upon the face of it who were the parties litigating the dispute, that it may be seen who are to be bound, also whether the parties who are to be bound appeared, or were summoned and made default. The judgment to be filed with the registrar should be so drawn up in form as that either the parties named in it, or some person whose rights would be affected by it, could bring the matter before the courts named, to be heard upon appeal. Now when we look at the memorandum herein set out, not one of the requisites which would be expected to be found in a final judgment or decree of a court, or board of commissioners acting as a court, is to be found. In order to understand the meaning of it, even as regards the signatures, or to know who the commissioners are, parol evidence must be resorted to. The township is not stated or mentioned in which the line is determined, and resort must be had to other documents and parol evidence to connect those documents with what is said to be a judgment. The legislature never surely meant, if a person desired to appeal from a judgment or final decision of the commissioners, that he should be obliged to furnish the court with evidence as to the meaning of the initials, such as O. R. G., and J. B., and R. F. S., and also how to apply the different figures and contractions in the minute set forth. Suppose such instrument as furnished in the present case to be properly filed, it may well be asked what information would be derived from it, as to what township the line was in which Messrs. O. R. G., and J. B., and R. F. S., professed to settle, or between what parties, or whether the parties appeared or made default. It is quite too absurd to suppose the legislature ever intended that such a document as produced should be final and conclusive, and bind the rights of parties to whom it affords no information whatever. We cannot hold this to be a judgment or decree within the meaning of the act.

There was evidence offered at the trial, independent of what was considered to be the decision of the commissioners, which might have been sufficient *prima facie* for the purpose of calling upon the defendant to prove why and wherefore he interfered with a road which had been a travelled road for a number of years, and upon which statute labor had been done. When the defendant offered to prove the line to be as he contended for, his evidence was rejected. The case has not been heard upon the merits, and possibly it may be that the defendant, by his conduct or acquiescence, has dedicated the piece of land in question for the road. The matter has been assumed against the defendant upon the idea that a judgment of the boundary commissioners bound his rights or prevented him from asserting what he now contends for. Without meaning to say the opinion which the commissioners endeavoured to perfect into a judgment may not be quite correct and that perhaps the defendant may be liable to be indicted for obstructing a road which his own act and acquiescence may have dedicated to the public, it is sufficient to say that, as he was prevented from going into evidence on the ground that he was bound by a decision which, in our opinion was not such a judgment as the statute contemplates. we cannot support the conviction.

The same course should be taken as was done in Regina v. Spence (11 U. C. R. 31)—viz., the judgment must be arrested, so that a fresh indictment may be preferred if the parties be so advised.

Judgment arrested.

WILMOT V. JARVIS.

Warehouseman—Liability of, for insufficiency of his building.

A person sending goods to be warehoused has a right to expect that the building in which they are placed shall be reasonably fit for the purpose, but he has no right to expect more than ordinary and average care in that respect, and it is only in the absence of such care on the warehouseman's part that he will be liable.

The fact of the building having fallen from a defect in the foundation is not conclusive evidence against the warehousman, for that might happen without any negligence on his part.

CASE—The declaration stated that the defendant was a warehouseman, and that the plaintiff delivered to him 12,000 bushels of wheat, to be safely and securely warehoused, for certain reward to be paid by the plaintiff to the defendant, and to be re-delivered on request; and that it was the defendant's duty to take care of and re-deliver the said wheat to the plaintiff on request. *Breach*, that the defendant took so little and such bad care, that through the negligence, carelessness, and improper conduct of the defendant, the wheat became damaged, injured, and wholly lost to the plaintiff. *Second count*, averring more generally that the defendant had the care of 12,000 bushels of wheat of the plaintiff's, and it was the defendant's duty to take care thereof; yet the defendant did not take due and proper care, and the wheat in consequence was wholly lost to the plaintiff. *Pleas*—1. Not Guilty. 2nd. That the plaintiff did not deliver to defendant the wheat, &c. 3rd. To second count, that he had not the care of the said wheat, &c.

The case was tried at Toronto, in January, 1855, before *McLean, J.* It was admitted that the defendant received as warehouseman 9042 $\frac{25}{60}$ bushels of wheat belonging to the plaintiff. The question in dispute was as to the liability of the defendant for the damage to and loss of this wheat. It had been in a store-house erected by the defendant upon piles driven in the bay at Toronto. This store-house was large enough, according to the testimony, to hold 50,000 bushels of wheat, and there was but little stored in it except the plaintiff's wheat, when the piles gave way, falling to the westward, and the store-house fell over bodily into the water. On the part of the plaintiff evidence was given to shew that the foundation was wholly insufficient in this respect; that at the south end there was only two feet or so of earth or mud, through which the piles were driven on to the solid rock; that although the piles were sufficient to bear the weight as long as they maintained their perpendicular, yet they had not sufficient support to do this They had been driven in the winter time, and when the ice moved the piles had moved also, shewing that they could not resist the pressure of the floating ice; that it was necessary, in order to give the piles support and protection, that there should be cribs of timber filled with stone, and sunk in proper places for that purpose. An engineer and architect was called, who proved that before the frame of the store-house was put up he was called on by the then partner of defendant to report upon the wharf and store-house foundation, who told the partner not to go on with raising the store-house, as the foundation was insecure. At that time they were putting a crib at the south end. No engineer was employed by the defendant, so far as appeared, to superintend the driving of the piles, or to ascertain the sufficiency of the foundation, for he would not recognize or have anything to do with him.

The learned judge told the jury that it was the first duty of a warehouseman to provide a sufficient building to receive and secure any property received to be stored, and that, if a warehouse falls down from any defect in the building or foundation, the party will be liable for the injury sustained in consequence ; that if the falling is occasioned by any storm or convulsion of nature, he would not be so liable ; that in this case the store-house had been erected by the defendant, and he was bound to make and have it sufficient for storing such property as he received ; that the fact of the building, intended to store so large a quantity as 50,000 bushels of wheat, falling with less than 10,000 bushels in it, was of itself evidence to shew the insufficiency of the building.

The defendant's counsel excepted, that the liability of a warehouseman was stated too largely. The jury found for the plaintiff £2106 9s. 6d. damages.

Vankoughnet, Q. C., moved for a new trial on the ground of misdirection. He complained that the charge amounted to this—that the defendant was bound at all hazards to have a sufficient warehouse, and was answerable against latent defects ; that the distinction between the liability of a common carrier and a warehouseman was not sufficiently kept in view or presented to the jury. He cited Cairns v. Robins 8 M. & W. 258 ; Earside v. The Trent Navigation, 4 T. R. 581 ; Hyde v. The Trent Navigation, 5 T. R. 389 ; *In re* Webb et al., 8 Taunt. 443.

Hagarty, Q. C., shewed cause, and cited 2 Kent's Com. 565 ; Leck v. Maestaer, 1 Camp. 138; Gow. N. P. 30; Dakin v. Brown, 8 C. B. 92 ; Clayards v. Dethick. 12 Q. B. 439.

DRAPER, C. J., delivered the judgment of the court.

Upon the best consideration we can give this case, we are of opinion there should be a new trial. We by no means desire to have it understood that we have adopted any conclusion that the plaintiff may not ultimately be entitled to recover ; but as it appears to us there was a miscarriage in the manner in which the case went to the jury, and they may have been very erroneously impressed with the nature of the defendant's liability from observations made in the charge. though such observations would not have misled any one acquainted with the rules and principles of law applicable to the case.

The defendant is a bailee; the bailment is of that character which is both for the benefit of the bailor and bailee, and falls within the class of *locatio operis faciendi*, with regard to which it is well established that an ordinary and average degree of diligence is sufficient to accept the bailee from responsibility—Jones on Bailments, 132–3, 136, 1 Smith L.C. 104; or, as expressed by Chancellor Kent—"A warehouseman, or depositary of goods, being bound only for ordinary care is not liable for loss arising from accident when he is not in default, and he is not in default when he exercises due and common diligence ; but he is bound to see that the place in which the articles deposited with him are kept is fit and properly secured for their reception and safety."—(2 Kent Com. 565). I have quoted the whole sentence because, as I understood on the argument, it had been cited and relied upon by the plaintiff's counsel at the trial. At the same time, I must say that if the latter branch of it were taken without the former—*i. e.* without the words "he is not in default when he uses common diligence"—so that it would apparently amount to an unqualified assertion that the warehouse must be secure against defects even latent, I should not be able to subscribe to its accuracy.

We disclaim all idea that the party who sends his goods to be warehoused is to enquire into the fitness or safety of the building where they are to be received. He has a right to expect that the building will be reasonably fit for that purpose; that there shall be no gross negligence, either in that respect or in protecting the goods against spoliation or destruction. But he has no right, in our opinion, to expect anything beyond ordinary and average care in the one particular more than in the other; and the question for the jury and on which the defendant's liability depends in law, is, whether the evidence shews a want of that ordinary and average care ; that the warehouse fell from any defect in the building or foundation does not by itself determine this question, because that might happen, not only without gròss negligence on the defendant's part, but without any negligence at all.

We think, therefore, there should be a new trial without costs.

Rule absolute (a).

THOMAS FITZPATRICK AND HIS WIFE V. THE GREAT WESTERN RAILWAY COMPANY.

Pleading—Case for injury caused by railway collision—Statement of cause of action.

Declaration in case stated that the plaintiff, being pregnant, at the request of defendants became a passenger in one of their carriages, to be safely conveyed by them for reward ; that the defendants received her as such passenger, and it was their duty to use due care in conveying her, yet the defendants, not regarding, &c., so negligently conducted themselves that a collision took place with another train, by means whereof the carriage, in which the plaintiff was, was broken, &c., and thereby the plaintiff was much affrighted and alarmed, whereby she became sick, sore, and disordered, and so continued from thence hitherto, and thereby also, *by reason of the terror and alarm occasioned to her by the said collision*, and of such sickness caused thereby, she had a premature labour, and bore a still-born child.

Held, on general demurrer, that a sufficient cause of action was disclosed.

CASE—The declaration stated that the plaintiff Sarah, being pregnant and with child, on the 10th of November, 1854, at the request of defendants, became a passenger in one of their carriages, to be in that behalf by them safely and securely carried and conveyed on a journey, to wit, &c., for reward ; and the defendants received the plaintiff Sarah as such passenger ; and thereupon it became and was the duty of the defendants to use proper care and skill in and about the carrying and conveying the said plaintiff Sarah ; nevertheless the defendants, not regarding their duty, did not use due and proper care, but took so little care, and so negligently and unskilfully conducted themselves in and about the carrying and conveying the plaintiff on her journey, and in and about the conducting, managing, and directing the carriage in which she was passenger, &c., that a collision with another train of the defendants took place, and the train of carriages, in one of which the plaintiff Sarah was, ran with great violence upon and against the other train, by means whereof

---

(a) This case was again tried at Toronto, May, 1855, before *Burns, J.*, and resulted in a verdict for the plaintiff with only £1,000 damages, which was not moved against.

the first mentioned train was injured, and the carriage, in which the plaintiff Sarah was, was broken, &c., *and thereby* the plaintiff Sarah was much affrighted, terrified, and alarmed, *whereby* she became sick, sore, and disordered, and so continued *from thence* hitherto; during which time, she suffered great pain and anguish, insomnch that her life was endangered, and *thereby also, by reason of the terror and alarm* occasioned to her by the said collision, and of such sickness caused thereby, she had a premature labour, and bore a still-born child.

General demurrer—that the declaration shews no ground of action, or any breach of duty or negligence on the part of the defendants causing any such injury to the plaintiff Sarah; that the breach is inconsistent with the contract to carry safely and securely; that for anything that appears the said Sarah was carried safely and securely; that the fright, terror, and alarm of the said Sarah, and the alleged consequences as stated in the declaration, are not causes of action for which the plaintiff can recover.

Becher for the demurrer.   *Paterson* contra, cited Westbtook v. Australian Navigation Company, 24 Eng. Rep. 327; Burnett v. Lynch, 5 B. & C. 609.

DRAPER, J., delivered the judgment of the court.

The demurrer admits the negligence complained of, that the carriage, in which the plaintiff Sarah was riding, was owing to such negligence and a collision with another train driven in, broken and crushed, whereby she was much affrighted, terrified, and alarmed, whereby she became sick, sore, and disordered, and so continued from thence hitherto, &c.

The question is, whether the statement discloses a cause of action sufficient on general demurrer. We think it does. What may be offered in evidence under this statement, and whether it can be so maintained by proof as to entitle the plaintiff to a verdict, is quite a different question from that presented now for our decision. We look upon the statement in the part of the declaration we have noticed as referring the sickness, &c., of the plaintiff in point of time to the time of the collision, and the injury thereby of the carriage in which plaintiff was. It is as if the complaint was, " I was in your carriage, in which you undertook to convey me with proper care. By your want of care, a collision took place, and the carriage was crushed whereby I became sick, sore and disordered, through the fright and terror your negligence gave rise to, and I have continued in that state from thenceforth hitherto, *i.e.* from the time of that collision." May not the plaintiff prove an inward injury or disorder as well as an external wound or bruise ? The only difficulty suggested is the introduction of the statement of alarm and affright, as if preceding and occasioning the sickness and disorder. But, in our opinion, we are not bound to read the declaration in that manner. We may, we think, consider the fright and commencement of the sickness, &c., to be alleged as simultaneous ; and if, as we do not doubt, the declaration would be good without stating the affright, but stating only the sickness, &c., as the result of the defendants' negligence, we do not see that the addition of this statement makes it demurrable.

There must be judgment for the plaintiffs on demurrer.

If desired, the defendants may withdraw their demurrer, and plead, on payment of costs, and on consenting to admit at the trial the negligence, &c., necessary to sustain the action, requiring only proof of such consequential damage as is admissible under the declaration.

- Judgment for plaintiffs on demurrer.

MUNRO ET AL. V. GREY.

Evidence to support title under sale for taxes—Several lots in same grant— What portion to be sold for arrears.

EJECTMENT—The defendant claimed under a Sheriff's deed, under a sale for taxes, but there was no proof that any taxes were imposed or in arrears except an extract from the treasurer's book, by which it appeared that the taxes on the lot in question had been paid up to 1828. *Held* insufficient, and that the plaintiff must recover.

Semble, that where several lots are included in one grant, but described by separate numbers, a portion of each lot must be sold to pay the taxes due upon such lot, and not a portion of the whole block, beginning at the boundary from which the lots are numbered, for the taxes due upon the whole.

EJECTMENT for 48 acres of lot No. 16, 1st con., Rideau Front of Nepean, beginning at the front angle of the said lot, on that side from whence the lots are numbered, and measuring backward, lacking a portion of the width corresponding in quantity with the proportion of said lot in regard to its length and breadth.

At the trial at Bytown, before *McLean, J.*, the plaintiff put in a grant under the Great Seal, dated the 17th day of May, 1802, to Lilly Fraser, for 600 acres of land, being lots 14, 15, and 16, 1st con. and broken front of Nepean ; a deed dated 6th of May, 1832, from Lilly Fraser to Grace Munro, wife of Hugh Munro for lots 15 and 16, 1st con., and broken front of Nepean. A power of attorney from Grace Munro to one Stephen Collins was put in, and a deed from Grace Munro to her Majesty, dated 30th of Jan., 1840, for nine acres of land covered with water, part of No. 14, 1st con. Nepean, executed by Stephen Collins's attorney. A good deal of evidence as to Stephen Collins's conduct in the matter and Hugh Munro's statements on the subject was given. the relevancy of which was not very clear. But it appeared in the course of this evidence that Collins had asserted a title to 48 acres of lot No. 16 (in question), on a purchase at a sheriff's sale for taxes, and that the 48 acres had been surveyed, excluding the drowned land conveyed to her Majesty by the deed of 30th of January, 1840, which it would appear from the evidence, would fall within the description in the declaration It further appeared that the defendant had gone into possession under Collins, who was since dead.

On the defence, a deed dated 19th of February, 1839, was proved, from the then sheriff of the district of Bathurst, in which district the township of Nepean was situated, by which in consideration of £4 2s. paid by Stephen Collins, being the purchaser at public auction of the parcel of land thereinafter mentioned, the sheriff did grant, bargain, and sell unto Stephen Collins in fee, 48 acres of lot No. 16, 1st concession of Nepean, on the Rideau, described verbatim as in the declaration. Also, an extract from the treasurer's books proved by a witness who had compared it with the original, as follows :—

Township.	Lot.	Con.	Years.	Acres.	Amount. £. s. d.	Acres. Sold.	To whom Sold.	When Redeemed.	By whom Redeemed.	Sold 20th Dec.
Nepean. R. F.	16	1	8	200	3 14 6	40	Captain Collins.	Cer. given 21st Dec. 1838.		Dec. 1837

1ST CON. RIDEAU, TOWNSHIP OF NEPEAN.

Name.	Lot.	Acres.	Years.	1634.	1835.	1836.
Lilly Fraser.	16	200	1820.	Sold.	Sold.	Sold.

			1822	1823	1824	1825	1826	1827	1828	1829	1830	1831	1832	1833
Lilly Fraser.	16	200	Pd.	Pd.	Pd.	Pd.	Pd.	Pd.	Pd.	—	—	—	—	—

The defendant's counsel contended that this extract was sufficient evidence to shew the liability of the lot to be sold for taxes in arrears. He had no proof of the schedule from the Surveyor General to shew that the lot was described, or how, but he urged that the patent was sufficient evidence of the description of the lot. The learned Judge was of opinion that this was so, but that it proved that lots 14, 15, and 16' were granted in a block, in which case that portion of the land next to the boundary from which the lots were numbered would be liable for the taxes on the whole, and no part of No. 16 would be saleable until all 14 and 15 were sold, as there was no evidence to shew that at the time of the alleged sale for taxes it was liable to be sold for the amount due on it alone. Proof of the acquiescence of Munro in this sale was offered, but rejected, it not being under seal. And the learned judge held that the defendant must fail in the absence of all proof necessary to shew the sale to have been legal, as there was no proof that any taxes were imposed, or that any were due on the lot in question.

The jury, on this direction, found for the plaintiff Munro.

Eccles obtained a rule *nisi* to set aside the verdict, for misdirection, and the rejection of evidence.

Hagarty, Q. C., shewed cause—citing Doe v. Edwards, 5 U. C. R. 594; Stafford v. Williams, 4 U. C. R. 488.

DRAPER, J., delivered the judgment of the court.

If it were necessary in order to uphold the verdict which the plaintiff has obtained, to determine that where three lots of land are included in one grant to the same individual, and are described therein as lots 14, 15, and 16, that in any sale for taxes accruing due upon lot No. 16, (no arrearage appearing on the other lots) a portion of No. 14 must be sold, because that lot would commence at the front angle of the block composed of these three lots so granted, on that side from which the lots are numbered, I must confess that, as at present advised, I must hold that the verdict could not be supported.

But as we agree entirely with the directions of the learned judge, that there was no sufficient legal evidence that any taxes were eight years in arrear upon lot No. 16, and as without such evidence the defendant fails, and as consequently the question first adverted to becomes entirely unimportant, we think the plaintiff should retain his verdict.

The conduct of Stephen Collins, the purchaser at the sheriff's sale, if truly stated, is highly reprehensible, and it would be a matter of regret that it should be successful. It appears somewhat singular that the officers of H. M's. Ordnance in charge of the Rideau Canal should have been advised that a surrender of land, the property of a married woman, could be effectually made by an attorney appointed by her during coverture, and particularly when that power of attorney contains only an authority to receive compensation for damage by overflowing land, and to acquit and discharge such damage. The formalities required to enable a married woman to convey her real estate seem to have been overlooked. But if we rightly understand the evidence, the deed from the sheriff, dated a year before that surrender, covered the nine acres surrendered; so that when Collins directed the surveyor to lay out for him 48 acres over and above the nine acres mentioned in the surrender, he was claiming more land than he would have had a right to, even if the sale for taxes were upheld. As the plaintiff, however, limits his claim to 48 acres of land, described exactly as the land in the sheriff's deed is described, no question on this point would arise.

Rule discharged.

McLELLAN V. ROGERS.

Practice—Amendment after demurrer.

Where contingent damages had been assessed on a demurrer to a plea, and judgment was afterwards given for the defendant, the court refused leave to the plaintiff to reply *de novo*, no distinct affidavit of merits being filed.

Bell obtained a rule *nisi* in this cause, upon reading the copies of the pleas and the papers filed, for leave to the plaintiff to amend, by withdrawing the demurrer, and replying *de novo* to the defendant's second plea. There was an affidavit verifying the copies of the pleadings and demurrer, and an affidavit of the plaintiff that the lease in question in the cause (referring to that set out in the defendant's second plea) was made for the purpose of securing a money loan to him by defendant : that at the time of making the same the defendant retained in his own hands, with the deponent's assent, a portion of the £125, (the amount named as the loan to be repaid by the plaintiff, and secured by said lease), sufficient to cover the rent by said lease reserved for the first two years of said term ; which fact the plaintiff "thinks he will be able to establish by clear proof," if he is allowed the opportunity of another trial.

. In answer, *McDonald* filed the defendant's affidavit, denying the allegations in the plaintiff's affidavit, and stating that the plaintiff never paid anything for the land in the lease mentioned, except with money furnished by defendant: that before the making of the lease and the conveyances therein mentioned, both plaintiff and defendant endeavoured to get the land sold, in order that the defendant might get his money, but as no sale could be effected, it was agreed as in the said lease contained: that it was the true intent of both parties that the land should become defendant's property, but the privilege of purchasing was reserved to the plaintiff : that the conveyance to the defendant and the lease to plaintiff were made for the express purpose, and upon the joint instructions of the plaintiff and defendant, in order that there should be no question as to a loan or security : that it is untrue that any sum of money was retained by defendant in his own hands, or that any portion of the £125 formed any part, in anticipation or ortherwise, of the rents in the lease named. That no tender of any rent was made to the defendant, except that mentioned in evidence on the trial of this cause. .

McDonald further objected that this application came too late. The cause had been tried at the October assizes, on the pleadings as they now stand ; the plaintiff had a verdict with £500 damages on the first issue, and contingent damages on the demurrer. In the term following the demurrer was argued, and on the first day of the present term the court gave judgment against the plaintiff, and refused the defendant's rule, granted in the preceding term for a new trial, as become unnecessary (*a*). He cited Smith v. London, &c., R. W. Co. (7 C. B. 782), where, after "very reluctantly" giving judgment against a plea, the court refused the defendant leave to amend. *Wilde*, C. J., saying that he was for adhering strictly to the general rule not to allow an amendment after judgment ; and *Creswell*, J., adding, " If you had only taken the hint when we paused to deliberate, you would perhaps have been in time." And he distinguished the present case from Maxwell v. Ransom (1 U. C. R. 281). He also referred to Robinson v. Raley (1 Burr. 316).

Bell, contra, relied upon Breakenridge v. King (4 O. S. 297) ; where the court, after the trial of an issue in fact and an assessment of contingent damages on a demurrer to two of the defendant's pleas, allowed an amendment where the demurrers were not frivolous, and the demandant would have been barred of her claim to dower.

DRAPER, J., delivered the judgment of the court.

We think in this court we must treat Breakenridge v. King as settling the rule of amendment. I must confess I think it goes beyond any authority in the English courts, where after judgment on demurrer the rule is never to allow an amendment. Even after argument, the court is very reluctant to allow a party to amend—in one case saying, " We never allow an amendment after argument"—Skuse v. Davis (10 A. & E. 640) ; for, as is well observed in 1 Smith L. C. 247, " if it were to become usual so to do,

---

(*a*) See the demurrer, reported *ante* page 571.

great encouragement would be afforded to frivolous and experimental demurrers; since parties would take the chance of succeeding upon argument of any legal objections which might occur, knowing that in case of failure they would be allowed to amend, and go to trial on the facts." I am afraid that our own experience affords proof of the justice of this remark. The law is very clearly stated by *Tindal*, C. J., in Bramah v. Roberts (1 Bing. N. C. 481) : " The law of Westminster Hall, I believe, ever since it stood in the place where it now stands, has been, that if a party thinks proper to rest his defence or his case upon a point of law raised upon the record, he either must stand or fall upon the point so raised. I do not mean to say that a case may not arise where a point being so taken, a party may, even after judgment, apply to the court to amend ; but, according to the advice of Lord Coke, you ought never to rely upon a point of law when the facts are in your favour. Although there are excepted cases which will always be attended to, I should expect, after an argument has been heard and judgment given for the plaintiff, at least a distinct affidavit of merits from those who make the application."

When we look at the second plea, it is obvious that unless the plaintiff can take issue on some of its averments, the proof of which will lie on himself, he must fail in this action. For the contract of the parties must govern the court, and it is part of their contract that the plaintiff's right of purchase shall depend on his performance of certain acts in the nature of conditions precedent. That being so, we should, we think, in the language of *Tindal*, C. J., expect a distinct affidavit of merits. Now the plaintiff's affidavit is not at all strong as to his expecting to be able to prove what he states, and on the other hand, the defendant's denial is most distinct and unequivocal.

Without, therefore, in the slightest degree impugning the authority of Breakenridge v. King, we do not think this a case in which, in the exercise of sound discretion, we should grant the amendment.

Rule discharged.

GREAT WESTERN RAILWAY COMPANY V. MILLER.

Arbitration—Revocation of submission.

Where the company had entered into possession of lands without consent of
the owner, and held them for some time, and an arbitration was agreed
on, by which it seemed probable that the price would be fixed at a sum
very much larger than the company would be willing to pay:
Held, that the company could not be allowed on this ground to revoke the
submission.

The Great Western Railway Company, on the 18th of
December, 1854, obtained a judge's summons to shew cause
why the submission made between the said company and
Andrew Miller should not be revoked, on grounds disclosed
in papers and affidavits filed; and that all proceedings should
in the meantime be stayed.

The application was grounded upon the 7 Wm. IV. ch. 3,
sec. 29, which enacts " that the power and authority of any
arbitrator or umpire, appointed by or in pursuance of any
rule of court, or judge's order, or order of Nisi Prius, in any
action now brought, or which shall be hereafter brought, or
by or in pursuance of any submission to reference containing an agreement that such submission shall be made a
rule of His Majesty's Court of King's Bench, shall not be
revocable by any party to such reference without the leave
of the court by which such rule or order shall be made, or
which shall be mentioned in such submission, or by leave
of a judge, and the arbitrator or umpire shall and may, and
is hereby required to proceed with the reference notwithstanding any such revocation, although the person making
such revocation shall not afterwards attend the reference."

The submission was made under the seals of both parties,
and bore date the 7th of February, 1854. It recited that the
company had set out and taken, for the use of their road, a
portion of Miller's lands (describing them), together with
the rights, privileges, advantages, and appurtenances thereto
belonging; and that disputes existed between the parties as
to the value of the land, privileges, advantages, and appurtenances so set out and taken, and as to the amount of damages the said Miller might sustain by reason of the same
being taken from him; and it submitted these differences to
the arbitration of three persons, according to the several acts

of Parliament in that behalf, or a majority of them; and the award of the arbitrators, or a majority of them, if made in writing under their hands, ready to be delivered to the parties by the 31st of March, 1854, shall be binding and conclusive on the parties.

The arbitrators had power to enlarge the term for making the award, and to examine the parties and witnesses on oath, and the submission might be made a rule of this court.

In support of the application affidavits were filed—1st, of Mr. Hatt, that the arbitrators had had sundry sittings; that on several occasions during the pendency of the arbitration Miller stated his willingness to part with the property in question, which he considered worth a large sum of money, and stated he would give the company a considerable sum if the company would not take his property, though deponent thought Miller's only object was thereby to enhance the value in the opinion of the arbitrators.

2nd. The affidavit of Mr. O'Reilly, the company's solicitor, that he had been served a few days before the 16th of December, 1854, with an appointment, signed by two of the arbitrators, that the 20th December, 1854, was appointed peremptorily to proceed with the matters referred, when the arbitrators, or such two as should be present, would hear all further allegations and proof, and make up their valuation, and award without further hearing or adjournment; that the directors of the company were desirous of abandoning all claim to the land in question, in consequence of the alarming price put upon the property by certain of Miller's witnesses; that he believed the value of the property would be very trifling if the railway had not been built; that he believed its actual value, that is the price it would sell for at public auction, bore a small proportion to the price named by these witnesses; that he had on behalf of the company proposed to Miller and his solicitor to abandon all claim to the property, and pay the costs up to this time, which offer was declined; that Miller was endeavoring to force the company to take the property at such price as he could induce the arbitrators to put upon it, and though he valued the property at an inconsiderable amount, he had felt unsafe (from the experience of other awards) to advise the company to let an award be made if they could help it.

3rd. The affidavit of C. J. Brydges, managing director of company, that the directors were desirous of withdrawing all claim to the property in question, in consequence of the alarming amount at which it was possible or probable it might be valued : that he had been informed and believed that some of Miller's witnesses valued it at £20,000, when the board of directors would not feel justified in paying over £2,000 : that in his opinion the property would be of trifling value if the railways and works of the company had not been built, yet he was fearful that the fact that the larger portion of the value of the property was derived from the works, &c., of the company might not be regarded in this arbitration : that until within a few months past Miller had strenuously opposed the company taking his property on any terms, but as the defendant believed, Miller was then endeavoring to force on the arbitrators, in order to compel the company to take the property at such valuation as the arbitrators could be induced to put upon it; that a water tank had been placed on the property by the company, but it had done no injury to it, and could be removed in a few days.

It was further shewn that the arbitrators were authorized to enlarge the time for making their award until the first of May, 1855, without prejudice to the application.

In opposition to the motion, an affidavit of Miller was filed, stating that in 1847, in contemplation of the increased value which would accrue to the property now in question by the construction of the railway he let the company have a piece of land adjoining it at a mere nominal value, and then made an agreement with Mr. Hatt, at that time a director and agent for the company in obtaining lands necessary for their railway, to the effect following :—that in case the company constructed their railway between Windsor and the Niagara river, he (Miller) would, at the request of the company or their agent, and in consideration of six shares of the capital stock of the company, convey to them in fee a certain piece of land, and granted to the company the right of way for the road over such land ; " and the said company do hereby covenant and agree not to interfere with or obstruct the said Miller in his claim or right to the water found lying north and east of the starting point" in the description of said land; that he did make a conveyance of said piece of land, and the company now occupy it for their track and part of their depot ground; that in the fall of 1853 he was informed by Mr. Hatt, then the solicitor of the company, that they had taken the land and privileges now in question; that he (Miller) protested against this as a violation of the agreement, and told Hatt his estimate of the value was £30,000; that Hatt said the company must have the land, and that, unless Miller and the company could agree on the value, or appoint an arbitrator, the company would take steps to appoint an arbitrator for him; that Miller, after taking legal advice as to the right and power of the company, signed the submission to arbitration; that depending on the company holding the land at the valuation to be fixed by arbitrators, he engaged in transactions subjecting him to heavy pecuniary liability; that the company had had possession of the property for more than a year, in consequence of which Miller did not press his claim on the government for water frontage; that from the depressed state of the money market the property was not so saleable now as it was a year ago; that the first meeting of the arbitrators was on the 26th of June last, when Miller submitted his case, and called his witnesses, and the subsequent adjournments were made for the accommodation of the company, and at the instance of their solicitor. The application was referred to the full court, and was argued during this term by *Galt* for the company, and *Freeman*, contra.

DRAPER, J., delivered the judgment of the court.

The setting out and ascertaining what lands are required for the railway, or the conveniences thereof, is the act of the company. They are authorized to contract, compound, &c., with the owners of lands they may require, and in case of disagreement, either on the value of the lands and tenements or private privileges proposed to be purchased, or the amount of damages, an arbitration is provided for, which is in fact

compulsory on the owner, for if he be unwilling to appoint
arbitrators a mode is provided by which it may be done without his concurrence.   The obligation on the company is to
pay the sum awarded for compensation within three months
from the time of the award being made ; in default whereof
their right to assume any such property shall wholly cease,
and it shall be lawful for the proprietor to resume his occupation, and possess fully his rights and privileges in respect
thereof, free from any claim or interference of the company.

This provision for arbitration is interfered with, however,
by the latter act, passed 22nd of April, 1853, 16 Vic., ch. 99,
the fifth section of which enacts that, notwithstanding any
former acts, in case disputes shall arise between the company
and the owner or occupier of any land or privilege appertaining thereto, which may have been taken or which shall
be required or taken by the company, as to the value of the
land so taken and the privilege appertaining and damages
done thereto, the company may tender to such owner or
occupier such sum as compensation as the company may
think fit; and in case an arbitration or suit be had thereon,
by reason of the owner or occupier refusing the compensation tendered, and no greater sum be allowed by the arbitrators, or by a jury empanelled to try, the owner or
occupier shall pay the costs of the arbitration or suit ; and
if a greater sum than the compensation tendered be allowed,
then the company shall pay the costs and the additional
sum allowed.   The sixth section allows the company, after
such tender and a refusal thereof, to pay the sum tendered
into court, and thereupon the company may take immediate
possession of the land, &c.   The tenth section expressly
limits the bringing of actions for indemnity for any damage
or injury sustained by reason of the railway to six months
next after the time of such damage sustained, or if there
be a continuation of damage, to six months after the doing
or committing such damage shall cease.

In this case the company took possession of Miller's lands
apparently against his will.   The precise date is not given ;
it was, however, some time in the fall of 1853, and therefore
several months after the last mentioned statute was passed,

Under the original charter they were permitted to enter (section 5) before ascertaining or paying the value. The latter act seems to restrict this power until after tender and payment into court. However, they did enter without having made (so far as is disclosed to us) any tender, or paying any sum into court, and aware that Miller set a very high value (possibly an extravagant one) on the property. They then, according to Miller's affidavit, compelled him to appoint an arbitrator by resorting to the means provided by their first act in case of his refusal, and the submission is entered into on the 7th of February, 1854, and has been enlarged from time to time. Before August last, Miller's witnesses were examined, and subsequently enlargements were made at the company's instance. In December last two of the three arbitrators gave the company notice that it was their intention to proceed and dispose of the matter on the 20th of that month; and then, apparently in consequence of this notice, the company's solicitor apprises Miller's solicitor of the company's desire to abandon the land, paying the costs of the arbitration up to that date (13th December), and to revoke the submissions, and this proposal being declined, the summons for leave to revoke was obtained on the 18th of December.

The sole ground for the application is that the company's officers anticipate the arbitrators will fix the value of the property they have taken at a much higher sum than they are willing to pay. I treat as unimportant the statement of Miller's unwillingness to let the company have his land at first, and his present urgency to compel them to pay for it. It may be replied that the company were on their part equally urgent to take it, in the first instance, and only cooled down when they found the value stated by Miller's witnesses to be ten times what they wished to give. In the meantime, however, they keep possession, only offering to surrender it just before making this application, and then making no tender of amends for the use and occupation; and moreover, all this results from their own voluntary act in entering on Miller's property.

It is not suggested that there is any reason to apprehend

partiality or any sort of unfairness on the part of the arbitrators, nor even misconduct in receiving evidence or rejecting it, or in going into matters not submitted to them. I gather rather that the apprehension is that the arbitrators will act upon the evidence offered to them by Miller, and that the company do not expect to be able to shake that evidence, or to shew that it is unfounded, at least not to such an extent as will meet their own views. But let us assume this motion should be granted, in what position will it place the other party? The company will not, I presume, submit the question again to arbitration (for that would be inconsistent with what they are advancing); and though the last statute speaks of the damages being ascertained by a jury empanelled to try, that, in the first place, is where there has been a tender; and, secondly, I see no method pointed out for empanelling such a jury. So that, unless Miller could bring an action founded on their entry as a wrong, or a special action on the whole case, he might be remediless. He would probably have the effect of the tenth section of the last act to contend against; and it might also be urged as an argument against his claims, that the court had sanctioned a revocation of the submission. I see no ground to justify us in relieving the company for the purpose of putting him in a disadvantageous position, or even in subjecting him to a risk of it.

If the price of the land were ascertained, it may be that, by withholding payment, and abandoning the land, the company could not be compelled to take it and pay the ascertained price. If that is so, our refusal to interfere will add very little to the expense which they will incur. It may be, however, on the other hand, that the price being ascertained, they will be compelled to complete the purchase. If so, then it will only be because that is the equitable and just consequence of their own acts, and then certainly we ought not to interfere to deprive Miller of a just right.

In our opinion the rule to revoke the submission should be refused.

HENRY SMITH V. PATRICK ROONEY.

Appeal—County Court—Practice.

A county court judge arranged with the bar of his county "to transact all term business in vacation," and acting under such arrangement set aside a verdict and judgment after the term succeeding the assizes in which the verdict was rendered.

An appeal from his decision was allowed with costs, such arrangement being contrary to the express words of the statute.

APPEAL from the County Court of the county of Perth. This was on action of replevin, tried at the last November sittings, when a verdict was found for the defendant.

On the fourth of December following (the first day of the county court term) a notice was served on Mr. E. F. Ryerson, agent for defendant's attorney, that a motion would be made to set aside the verdict, " to-morrow, on the return of *Charles Robinson,* Judge of this Honorable Court, or so soon thereafter as counsel can be heard ;" and this notice, with affidavit of service, was filed on the following day with the clerk of the court. The judge not having returned on the 16th of December judgment was signed, and on the 18th a notice was served on Mr. Ryerson apprising him that on the return of the judge a motion would be made to set aside the judgment, and on the 20th of December a summons was obtained, on which an order was made on the 5th of January to set aside the judgment.

On the 20th a rule *nisi* was also issued for a new trial, which was afterwards made absolute.

Mr. Ryerson stated in his affidavit filed in opposing these applications, that he had no authority in this cause to bind the defendant's attorney, or make any arrangement or terms whatever for him, and that his duties were confined to transmitting, serving, and filing papers in this cause.

The learned judge, in transmitting the papers, reported that the verdict was perverse, and that the order to set aside the judgment, and the rule for a new trial, were made in vacation, he " having made an arrangement with all the legal practitioners in the county of Perth, and among the rest with Mr. Ryerson, agent for the defendant's attorney, to transact all term business in said court in vacation."

The defendant appealed, on the ground, amongst others, that the term next after the verdict having elapsed without any proceeding taken by the plaintiff to set aside the verdict, such verdict could not afterwards be set aside.

Leith, for the appeal.

C. Robinson, contra.

8 Vic., ch. 13, sections 37, 42, 43, were referred to.

DRAPER, delivered the judgment of the court.

We are of opinion that it is impossible to sustain the proceedings appealed against.

The court would not (unless, perhaps, under some extreme circumstances) listen to a party applying against proceedings taken in a cause by his own express consent : as where a particular step was agreed on, or a particular objection was waived. But this is not a case of that description. The consent spoken of does not appear to have been to a particular step in a cause, or even to be limited to a particular cause, but is described by the judge in his return as an arrangement made " with all the legal practitioners in the county of Perth, and among others with Mr. Ryerson, agent for the defendant's attorney, to transact all term business " in the county court in vacation. Except for this statement there is nothing to shew any such consent or arrangement. It does not appear in any affidavit, nor is the summons to set aside the verdict on the judgment drawn up upon any such affidavit, nor does that summons refer to anything, except to what took place at the trial, as its foundation.

Then it amounts to this : the statute fixes a term for the county court, and enacts that no motion for a new trial or nonsuit *shall be entertained* after the rising of the court on the second day of the term, and that the party obtaining a verdict may enter his judgment on the third day of the next ensuing term.

The judge and the members of the bar of the county court enter into an arrangement to disregard the statute wholly, and to transact term business in vacation. And in pursuance of such arrangement a judgment entered regularly, and at the time authorized by the statute, is set aside in vacation, and a motion for a new trial is entertained and a new trial granted, not only after the second day, but after the expiration of the term next after the verdict is rendered. Even in this court, where it is only a matter of practice regulated by the court itself, and not fixed by express legislation, it is only under very peculiar circumstances that we hear a motion for a new trial after the four days. In the present case we think the rule for a new trial appealed against was beyond the authority of the court, as expressly limited by the act, and that there is no legal ground for setting aside the judgment apparent on the paper transmitted to us, even if it were competent to the judge to exercise such a power in vacation.

The appeal must therefore be allowed with costs, and the rule for setting aside the judgment and verdict discharged and set aside.

Judgment below reversed.

Rutledge v. The Woodstock and Lake Erie Railway and Harbour Company.

Burgess v. the same.

Woodstock and Lake Erie Railway Company—10 & 11 *Vic. ch.* 117, *secs.* 8, 11, 15— *Damage caused by throwing down fences to enter on lands.*

The declaration charged that the defendants were in course of making their railway through the plaintiff's close, and of fencing off the said close from their line of road, and that during such time they ought to have kept up the plaintiff's fences, and to have so conducted themselves in and about the fencing off the railway from said close that the plaintiff's crops sho uld not be injured by their default:—Yet the defendants threw down the plaintiff's fences between the said close and the line of railway, and permitted them to remain prostrate for an unreasonable time, and so misconducted themselves in fencing the said line, and neglecting to erect such fences, that cattle got in and destroyed the plaintiff's crops.

It appeared from the evidence that the injury complained of, the destruction of the plaintiff's crops, must have been occasioned by the first breaking down the fences for the purpose of entry (which was authorized by the 10 & 11 Vic. ch. 117, sec. 11), and before a reasonable time had expired for fencing in the line (as the defendants were bound to do under the 15th section).

Held, therefore, that the plaintiff could maintain no action, but must proceed by arbitration under section 3.

CASE.—The declaration stated that the plaintiff, before and at the time of committing, &c., was possessed of lot number 13 in the 2nd concession of Norwich, and that the defendants were in course of making a railway through the said close, and of fencing off the said close from the line of the said railway, and defendants during all the said time ought to

have kept up the fences of the plaintiff, and to have conducted themselves in and about the fencing by the defendants of the said line of railway from the said close, and
the growing crops of the plaintiff in the said close should
not have been exposed or injured by the default of defendants. Yet the defendants, well knowing, &c., but contriving,
&c., whilst the plaintiff was so possessed, and on divers other
days, &c., threw down the fences of the plaintiff between the
said close and the said line of railway, and wrongfully permitted said fences to remain prostrate for an unreasonable
space of time, and so misconducted themselves in and about
the fencing up of the said line of railway, and by neglecting
and delaying to erect the said fences last mentioned within
a reasonable time, that divers cattle, for want of a fence, and
by reason of defendants' neglect and default, went into the
plaintiff's close, and eat up and damaged the grass, grain,
and herbage of the plaintiff, and thereby for a long time
continued to hinder and obstruct the plaintiff in the use
and enjoyment of his close. *Second count*, for obstructing
a certain right of way of the plaintiff's over the said close.

Plea—Not guilty, by statute.

The trial took place at Woodstock, in November last, before
Robinson, C. J. The plaintiff proved his possession of the
close mentioned in the declaration, and that the defendants'
railway crosses it obliquely through the field; that defendants' men were employed there since the 1st of June, 1854.
The line was laid out about a year before the trial. The
defendants took down the plaintiff's fences in the line of their
road in four places. They let down the line fences between
the plaintiff and his neighbour, so that the neighbour's cattle
got into the plaintiff's wheat, as well as letting in the plaintiff's own cattle, whereby 18 acres of fall wheat and one
acre of peas were destroyed. The defendants put down the
plaintiff's fence the whole width of the railway. Up to the
time of the trial the defendants had not fenced off their railway track. This was the whole evidence given, excepting
as to the value of the crops destroyed.

The defendants' counsel objected that the action was
grounded on an assumed obligation of the defendants to

uphold the plaintiff's fences along their line of railway until they had fenced off their road, and that no such obligation arose, and that the damage was of that character which under the act of incorporation it was provided should be settled by arbitration. Leave was reserved to move for a nonsuit, and the plaintiff had a verdict for £47.

BURGESS V. THE SAME DEFENDANTS.

This was a similar action tried immediately after the foregoing, in which the pleadings were similar and the evidence not so strong. The plaintiff had a verdict for £30, with leave reserved to move for a nonsuit.

Galt moved in both cases accordingly, in Michaelmas term; and in this term *D. G. Miller* shewed cause.

Connor, Q. C., and *Galt,* contra, cited Bradley v. Great Western Railway Company. 11 U. C. R. 220; The Governor & Company of British Cast Plate Manufacturers v. Meredith, 4 T. R. 794; Grocers Company v. Donne, 3 Bing. N. C. 34; Boulton v. Crowther, 2 B. & C. 703; Sutton v. Clarke, 6 Taunt. 29; Kerby v. the Grand River Navigation Company, 11 U. C. R. 334.

DRAPER, J., delivered the judgment of the court.

The Company are authorized by the 11th section of 10 & 11 Vic. chap. 117, to explore the country between Woodstock and Port Dover, &c., and to take, &c., for the use of them and their successors, the line and boundaries of a railroad, &c.; and for these purposes the company their agents, servants and workmen, are authorized to enter on the lands of any person or body, to survey and take levels, set out and ascertain such parts as they shall think necessary for making the railroad, &c.; and after a variety of other powers, the act empowers them to construct, make, and do all other matters and things which they shall think necessary and convenient, &c., for the said railroad, &c.; they the said company doing as little damage as may be in the execution of the several powers to them hereby granted, *and making satisfaction in manner herein mentioned for all damages to be sustained by the owners* or occupiers of such lands, tenements, and hereditaments.

This clause appears to us to relate to those damages which are occasioned by the making use of the powers conveyed by the proceeding portion of the section.

Then what is the "manner herein mentioned?" The third section of the act is the one which points this out, It authorizes the company to contract, compound, &c., with the owners of any land on which they may determine to construct their road, either by purchase or for the damage which such owner may be entitled to recover from the company in consequence of the road being constructed upon his lands; and in case of disagreement between the company and the owner a reference to arbitration is provided for. This clause does not in our opinion reach damages for an injury such as complained of in this action—1st. because the terms used in the act—damages which the owner never may be entitled to receive from the company in consequence of the road being made and constructed on his lands—appear to us to point to damages to the value of the estate, its convenience of occupation, &c.—damages of a character which may like the value of the land taken, be estimated at once and conclusively. 2ndly. Because the 12th section of the act prevents the company interfering with or encroaching on any fee simple, or other fee, right, or private easement, without permission first had and obtained, either by consent of the owner, or by virtue of the reference authorized by this act; and if the reference or consent is to precede the interference with the property, we do not see how damages of the character sued for in this action could be included.

Upon this view, a damage caused by entry on the land to take possession of the railway track, and for the purpose of such entry throwing down the fences of the plaintiff where they crossed and obstructed the land on which the railway was intended to be constructed, would not come under the third section, but within the eleventh.

Then, is this the kind of damage to recover which this action is brought? The declaration stated that the defendants were in the course of making a railway through the plaintiff's close (which apparently shews that whatever was necessary to give the right to enter and commence their work had been done, either by consent or reference as stated in the twelfth section.) Then, it is stated that during all the said time they ought to have kept up the plaintiff's fences, and to have conducted themselves about the fencing their line of railway from the plaintiff's close, and that his grass and growing crops should not have been exposed by their default. Yet the defendants threw down plaintiff's fences between the close and the line of railway, and wrongfully permitted those fences to remain postrate, and so misconducted themselves about fencing up the line of railway, and by neglecting and delaying the erection of the last mentioned fences in a reasonable time, that divers cattle, &c., entered the plaintiff's close and destroyed his grass and crops, &c.

It appears to us that the declaration, though not very clearly expressed, complains of two wrongs, or rather perhaps of one damage resulting from two causes:—1st. From the throwing down of the plaintiff's fences. 2nd. From omitting to put up such fences as it was the defendants' duty to erect. This duty arises under the fifteenth section of the act, which enacts that the company shall "erect and maintain sufficient fences upon the line or the route of their said single or double railroad or way." Upon a similar clause in another act, this court has decided that such a company is bound to put up fences within a reasonable time along their line of road while it is in progress.—Bradley v. Great Western R.W. Co. (11 U. C. R. 220.) The facts of these two causes of damage seems to us to be clearly within the eleventh and third sections. The throwing down of the plaintiff's fences to occupy the railway track and work upon it is authorized by the statute. It is therefore not a wrong, but it may occasion damage, for which compensation must be made in the manner pointed out in the third section. The second is a breach or neglect of duty, for which an action will lie.

We must then go to the evidence. This shews that early in June, 1854, the company's workmen entered on the land, and threw down such fences (four in all) of the plaintiff's as intersected the line of railway, thus inevitably exposing his wheat and other grain, through which the line of railway passed, to destruction. The action was begun on the 16th of

September following. We think we must notice, that in June the plaintiff's wheat must have been in an advanced state, within say two months of the harvest. Simultaneously with the defendants' entry, the reasonable time for erecting the fences on the line of their railway began to run. It is not for the court to determine when that time would expire, for that is a question for the jury, but it is obvious from the evidence that the destruction of the plaintiff's wheat must have been occasioned by the first throwing down of the plaintiff's fences, thus exposing his fields to trespass and injury; and it appears a reasonable conclusion that this, the only damage complained of or proved, must have been consummated before a reasonable time for the discharge of the duty of fencing the line of the railway had expired.

It is true that the declaration alleges, as a part of defendants' duty, that they should have kept up the plaintiff's fences, and charges as a breach that they permitted the fences they threw down to remain postrate for an unreasonable time. The plea of not guilty by statute (sec. 31) puts this in issue, both inducement and breach. The evidence shews no unnecessary throwing down the fences : that is, no fences thrown down other than those which intersected the line of railway ; and there certainly is no duty imposed, that we can find, to replace those fences. Neither does the statute any where impose the obligation of maintaining any fence of the plaintiff's ; so that it might be open to question whether the duty alleged in that respect, and the breach of *that* duty, and the consequent damage, are not so inseparably mixed as to make the whole statement bad.

Without so deciding, however, it appears to us that, taking the more favourable view of the plaintiff's case, it establishes an injury and loss from an act which the eleventh section authorized, and that compensation for such a loss is to be sought, not by action, but by the arbitration directed in the third section, and that upon the evidence the question of damage arising from the defendants' neglect to fence their line of railway after the expiration of a reasonable time does not arise.

Several decisions were cited by the defendant's counsel

during the argument, with the view of bringing this case within the principle, that when parties have a public trust or duty to execute, and act according to the best of their skill in the performance of it, and within their power, they are not liable to an individual for a consequential injury, though that individual may be otherwise without remedy. We are not prepared to apply that principle to the case of a railway company incorporated at their own request and for their own benefit, however largely public convenience may be benefited by their successful operation. But we think that where a statute legalizes an act which otherwise would be unlawful, and expressly provides that compensation for damage resulting from that act is to be made in the manner therein mentioned, the only remedy for such damage must be sought in the mode the act prescribes. In our opinion, therefore, the rule should be made absolute.

Rule absolute.

Tyrrel v. Gamble.

Special contract—Common counts.

When there is a special contract for work and labour, it must be distinctly shewn that such contract has been rescinded before a recovery can be allowed upon the common counts for work specified in it.

Assumpsit—for goods sold and delivered, work and materials, money lent, paid, and received, and on account stated.

Pleas—Non-assumpsit, Payment, and Set off. The cause was tried at Toronto, in January, 1855, before *McLean, J.*

It appeared that on the 12th of February, 1853, the defendant had entered into an agreement in writing with one W. Fisher for putting up a pier at the mouth of the Humber, which work Fisher commenced, but failed in completing. On the 3rd of May, 1854, the plaintiff signed and sealed an instrument, as follows :—"I hereby propose and agree to construct a store-house 40 + 60, and also to complete the wharf at the mouth of the river Humber, for William Gamble, Esq., according to the specifications dated this day, for the sum of £375 currency, payments to be made in cash, as the work progresses, fiften per cent. being kept back until the work is complete. The whole to be finished on or before the

1st day of August, provided the materials are provided. I
also agree to allow £11 for timber all ready hewn." Under
which the defendant signed and sealed the following:—"I
agree to accept the above proposals, and make the payments
as above stated, and supply the materials as above mentioned." The specifications were as follows:—"The store-
house to be framed with six bents 12 feet from centre to
centre, with two beams in each bent, and a stoop with shed
roof on each side 10 feet wide and 60 feet long, the under
part of the store to be enclosed 40 feet square, leaving ten
feet all round an open space. The two upper floors to be
laid with inch boards double. The building to be all sheeted
on the out side with inch boards well nailed, and then sided
with half inch siding, and roof to be well shingled, and one-
flight of open stairs with pine rail made and fixed; also large
doors made and hung at each end of the store and at each
side, for teams to drive through. The wharf to be completed
to the shore, with (eleven say) more cribs the same size as
the cribs at present sunk, and the cribs that are present
sunk to be levelled up so as to make the whole of the wharf
and pier-head four feet above the level of the water as established at time contract was made with Fisher; the string
pieces to be flatted and five in width, sized down on all the
cribs, and then all planked with three or four inch pine plank,
the whole completed according to the agreement for the same
as entered into with one Wm. Fisher, former contractor,
appended hereto, and the store-house to be finished with win-
dows and shutters, and ports for grain, and trap doors for
hoisting in centre of the building."—Signed and sealed by
the plaintiff. Annexed to these specifications were the following "General conditions"—"The contractor is to do
all the carpenter and joiner work of the store-house, and also
to raise the same, and finish the whole in a good, sound
and workmanlike manner, and to frame all the cribs for the
wharf, and to put them to their proper places, and to raise
all to a proper level, and to perform the whole of the work
so far as putting the timber together and planking. The
proprietor is to furnish all the timber for the store-house and
wharf convenient on the beach, and also all lumber, nails,

spikes, and all other materials required for the work on the spot, and to provide the stone and put them into the cribs as they are required." Signed and sealed by plaintiff.

The particulars of the plaintiff's demand included a small claim for a matter wholly independent of this contract. The particulars claimed £185 for amount of work done up to the 12th of August, according to the contract; stating the contract price for the wharf when finished to be £219 and £30 for work done to the storehouse up to the same date stating the contract price to be for that building complete £145. The residue of his claim the sum total of which was £378 14s. 5d., was for extra work, part of it, as was alleged, being work done by the plaintiff in getting timber and stone, which the defendant should have brought to the spot, whereas the plaintiff had to fetch both certain distances. According to the testimony of one of the plaintiff's witnesses, the plaintiff and defendant met together on the wharf, which as that witness said, the plaintiff could have finished for £30, if the materials had been there. It was then agreed between the plaintiff and defendant that it would be better to stop the work until stone could be got in, and the work was discontinued, and was not resumed till the 16th of October following. On the 9th of October, two persons (both called) went to defendant at plaintiff's request, to tell defendant that the plaintiff could not go on with the work on the old terms. Defendant answered he knew the bargain that was between him and the plaintiff, and further said he would meet the witnesses down at the wharf, and see what was to be done. He did meet them, one of them being a foreman newly appointed by the plaintiff. Nothing more was said about the terms on which the work was to go on, but the defendant gave directions for the work to proceed, by levelling up the cribs which had partially sunk since August. On one occasion defendant stated to plaintiff's foreman that some work he required should be done according to the old contract, and the foreman said he would speak about it to the plaintiff. The plaintiff told the foreman to state to defendant that it was immaterial to him, plaintiff, that the work would be more expensive if done according to the old contract, and that he,

plaintiff, would charge for all the extra trouble ; that he had
levelled the work once, but would not do it again, except by
day's work.   On this being stated to defendant, he made no
reply, but gave the foreman some directions.

According to Fisher's contract, the work was to be done to
the full satisfaction of the defendant or his engineer, according
to the particulars therein set forth.   Plaintiff gave a good
deal of evidence as to the value of the work done by him, for
which he claimed to be paid *dehors* the contract, while on
the defendants' part it was objected that the plaintiff should
have declared on the contract, or. at all events that as to all
work specified by or coming within the true meaning of the
contract, the defendant was only liable at the rate the contract specified.   This was overruled.   A great point in
dispute between the parties, and on which there was much
contradictory evidence, was whether the defendant supplied
materials as they were required, and whether the plaintiff
was not hindered in getting on with the work for want of
them, and whether the plaintiff himself did not procure a
considerable quantity of stone requisite for loading the cribs,
the defendant failing to do so.   The defendant called
evidence to rebut the statements of witnesses on these points;
and to shew that the defendant, on the 9th of October,
expressed himself more clearly and decidedly that he expected the plaintiff to complete the work as specified in the
contract.   He also called witnesses to prove that a good deal
of the work was very badly and insufficiently executed,
rendering further outlay necessary to make the wharf complete and secure.   As to the storehouse, the plaintiff did not
pretend to have done more than a part of the framing.

The learned judge told the jury that unless the contract
was abandoned, the plaintiff could only recover for work done
within its terms according to the price agreed upon; that at
the time of suspending the work there was no agreement to
abandon the contract so far as the evidence shewed; and he
commented on facts tending to shew that in October, the
plaintiff was aware that the defendant considered the work
was going on under the contract; and directed that that portion of the claim which was for levelling the cribs, which

had sunk or got out of place, was clearly within the contract of the plaintiff, and should not be allowed for as claimed. The jury, however, gave the plaintiff a verdict, and £136 9s. 6d. damages.

In Hilary term last *Vankoughnet*, Q. C., obtained a rule *nisi* to set aside the verdict as being against law and evidence, and for misdirection—complaining that the learned judge should not have permitted the plaintiff to go to the jury on this declaration on any matter which came within the contract, as for any such matter the contract should have been declared upon.

Hagarty, Q.C., argued that the contract could not be sued upon ; it had been waived, at all events as to time. Both of the counsel went at length into the evidence as to the quantity and character of the work done, and the right of the plaintiff to recover, without reference to the legal objection.

Burns, J., delivered the judgment of the court.

Because the work which the defendant had agreed to do was not completed by the time mentioned in the agreement, it is said no declaration could be framed to meet the plaintiff's demand. This proposition must depend upon the fact whether the plaintiff has or not completed his part of the agreement. If he has not, and the fault proceeds from himself, then it only proves that he has not done that which entitles him to maintain an action ; but if the fault proceeds from the defendant, then the plaintiff would be entitled to recover for what work he has done. The plaintiff did not engage to finish the wharf and store-house positively by the 1st of August, 1854, but only to do so, provided the materials were furnished. The defendant was to furnish all the materials for the work, and if he did not furnish them in time, so that the plaintiff could complete his undertaking by the 1st of August, then of course the plaintiff must have a reasonable time after that to complete his undertaking. If the defendant did not furnish the materials in proper time, or after the same were demanded, of course the plaintiff would not be bound beyond a reasonable time, and he might place himself in a position to rescind the contract, and either

be enabled to maintain an action for work and labour for the
value of the work-done, or an action against the defendant
for breach of the agreement. Such, however, is not the
plaintiff's complaint, nor does the evidence support such a
case. Time clearly was not of the essence of the contract,
nor did it form an ingredient in the consideration, beyond
limiting the time for completion of the undertaking on the
defendant desiring it by furnishing the materials. If it be
true that the work was suspended by the mutual understanding of the parties till October, and then that the
defendant furnished the materials and the plaintiff went on
with the work, the contract was still subsisting and not put
an end to. There would be no difficulty in framing a
declaration to meet the case, if the plaintiff, upon the
mutual understanding, had subsequently completed his
contract. He did not complete it, and it is clear from the
evidence that the defendant did not abandon it. The plaintiff could not put an end to it merely from his own choice
or disposition to do so, unless the defendant were in fault,
and had so placed the matter as enabled the plaintiff to
rescind the contract. The weight of evidence shews that
the suspension of the work was rather for the convenience
of both parties. But, suppose it were for the convenience
of the defendant alone, yet if it were assented to by the
plaintiff; it would not be in his power to rescind the contract, because he afterwards changed his mind, or because
circumstances had caused the prices of labour to be higher,
before the plaintiff again resumed the work. The plaintiff
sending persons to the defendant to say he would require
other and different prices for doing the work, and the
defendant saying nothing in answer thereto, but that he
knew his contract, affords no evidence in itself that the
contract was at that time rescinded; because, to make such
evidence of service in the plaintiff's favour, it should be shewn
that the contract had previously been rescinded. The defendant being present, superintending the work, subsequently,
affords no evidence that there was a new or fresh contract
between the parties, because we see that from the contract
originally between the defendant and Fisher he had the
right to give directions respecting the work himself, or

employ an engineer. Under these circumstances, the proper
question for the jury was, in the first place, to say whether
the contract was rescinded or not, for if not rescinded, then
the action for work and labour could not be sustained. The
great danger to parties depending upon and relying on
their written contracts of allowing such loose evidence to
sustain a case, where the contract has not been completed,
to enable a plaintiff to recover on the common demand for
work and labour, should induce us to scrutinize the evidence
well. If a jury shall say in this case that the contract
was not rescinded, then we have no hesitation in saying the
law protects the defendant from being liable in this form of
action. A jury should be distinctly asked to pronounce
upon that point; and as the weight of evidence seems to
be with the defendant in that respect, we feel bound to
grant him a new trial; costs to abide the event.—See
Barnaby v. Harding (8 Ex. 822), Mawman v. Gillett (2 Taunt.
325, in the note), Crosthwaite v. Gardner (21 Law J. Q. B.
356, 12 Eng. Rep. 474).

Rule absolute (a).

In re Reist v. The Grand Trunk Railway Company.

A mandamus was refused to compel a railway company to make crossings
at a particular place, under 14 & 15 Vic. ch. 51, sec. 13.

M. C. Cameron applied for a mandamus to compel the
company to construct crossings at certain points where
the railway passed through the applicant's farm.—14 & 15
Vic. ch. 51, sec. 13; York and North Midland R. W. Co. v.
The Queen, 1 Ell. & Bl. 858; Sadd v. Maldon, Witham
and Braintree R. W. Co., 6 Ex. 143; Cother v. Midland
R. W. Co., 11 L. J. Ch. 235; Tapping on Mandamus, 303,
were referred to in support of the application.

The rule was refused on the ground that, though a mandamus might perhaps go to make crossings, if the company

---

(a) This case was again tried in June, 1855, before *Richards*, J., at
Toronto, and resulted in a verdict for the plaintiff with only £9 damages,
which was not moved against. The evidence was in all material respects
the same as at the first trial.

had refused altogether to do so, yet the court would not take upon themselves to say as a matter of fact what are the proper places to make them at, as asked for here : the affidavits shewing that the company wished to make the crossings at particular places, but that the applicant wished them elsewhere.

Rule refused.

During this term, the following gentlemen were called to the bar :—F. EVANS CORNISH, HENRY MACPHERSON, SAMUEL B. HARMAN, WILLIAM DAVIS ARDAGH, and SAMUEL J. LANE.

A DIGEST

OF

ALL THE REPORTED CASES

DECIDED IN THE

COURT OF QUEEN'S BENCH,

FROM HILARY TERM, 17 VICTORIA, TO
HILARY TERM, 18 VICTORIA.

ACTION.

See COMMISSIONERS FOR INDIAN AFFAIRS.—CONTRACT, 2.—MUNICIPAL CORPORATIONS, 3.—PLEADING, 14.—TAXES, 1.—TRESPASS, 2.

Action for prosecuting false claim to land—Heir and devise commission, false affidavit used before.]—An action will not lie for knowingly prosecuting a false claim before the heir and devisee commission, to the plaintiff's injury and with knowledge of his claim.

One M., in 1839, having a right of purchase of a lot from the Crown, mortgaged to DeB. to secure payment of a sum by instalments, the last of which would fall due in 1849. Soon after this mortgage, M. gave to B. a bond for a deed on certain conditions to be fulfilled by B., who took possession. In 1850 the plaintiff went in under an agreement for purchase from B., who had not fulfilled the conditions of his bond. In 1851 the defendant took an assignment of DeB.'s mortgage, and in the same year he claimed before the heir and devisee commission, making the usual affidavit of ignorance of any adverse claim, and obtained a patent. The plaintiff thereupon brought an action on the case, alleging, in the first and second counts of his declaration, that the defend-

ant, maliciously contriving and intending to injure him, represented himself as assignee of the original nominee of the Crown, and claimed as such before the heir and devise commission; and in order to defraud the plaintiff, and not having himself any well founded claim, and knowing the plaintiff's claim, made affidavit that he was not aware of any adverse claim, and procured his own claim to be allowed—whereby, &c. The third and fourth counts, founded on the statute 32 Henry VIII, ch. 9, were for buying M.'s pretended right, the defendant being in possession claiming title. *Held,* that on the evidence the allegations were not supported; and that, admitting them all to be true, no ground of action would be shewn. *Shields* v. *DeBlaquiere,* 386.

ADMISSION.

Agreement to admit deeds, a waiver of objections — Estoppel — Registry laws.]—Where the defendant's attorney had agreed, in an action of ejectment, to admit deeds by the production of memorials without accounting for the deeds, and to admit the execution of such deeds as the plaintiff might produce, without proof by a subscribing witness—

Held, that it could not be objected at the trial that a memorial signed by the grantee was no evidence of the deed. *Rutledge v. McLean,* 205.

AFFIDAVIT.
See MUNICIPAL ELECTIONS.

AGREEMENT.
See ASSIGNMENT.—CHATTEL MORT-GAGES, 1.—CONTRACT.—DEED, 1.—TRESPASS, 2.

Agreement— Construction— Necessity of request—Issue on defendant's readiness to perform.]—1. The defendant made the following agreement in writing :—" Within three months, and when desired by him, I promise to pay Moses C. Nickerson " (the plaintiff) " or bearer, £50 currency, in such stone and marble-work as he may want, at cash price, delivered at Port Dover, value received, with interest." *Held,* That the plaintiff was bound to prove notice to the defendant of the kind of stone or marble-work required, and when it was to be delivered, and until such request there could be no default. *Quare,* Whether a plea, that after the making of the agreement, and within three years from the date thereof, the plaintiff was, and still is ready and willing to perform the agreement, would raise a material issue. *Semble,* That the defendant, on a proper demand, would have been bound to carry out the agreement, even after the expiration of the three years. *Nickerson v. Gardner,* 219.

Agreement—Rescision of— Right to sue on the common counts.]—2. In March, 1852, the plaintiff and defendant made an agreement in writing, by which the plaintiff was to build a cottage for the defendant, and to complete it by the 1st of November, for £212 10s., of which part was to be paid on the completion of the building, and the remainder at the times specified in the agreement. The defendant requested the plaintiff to postpone the work, and it was in consequence not commenced until August, 1853, and finished in March, 1854. It was not shewn that any new agreement had been made; but it appeared that, as wages and materials had increased in price, the plaintiff, when asked to proceed with the work in 1853, objected to being bound by the old agreement, and the defendant then promised to pay £100 at the completion of the building, and the whole sum if he could, saying he would probably pay the whole. *Held,* That the first contract was clearly at an end, and that the plaintiff was not bound to declare specially on the subsequent promise, but might sue upon the common counts. *Havill v. Freeman,* 223.

Agreement — Accidental fire — Rights of parties.]—3. The defendant agreed with the plaintiff to saw for him at a certain price whatever logs should be delivered at the plaintiff's mill, the plaintiff to draw away the lumber as soon as possible after it was cut: the defendant also agreed to deliver at Port Perry, within a reasonable time, any lumber cut by him under the agreement after the 1st of March. Some lumber was cut before the first of March and drawn away by the plaintiff; some was also cut after the first of March, and this was destroyed at the mill by an accidental fire in June following. The jury found that of the latter portion the defendant might have delivered about 40,000 feet before the fire. *Held,* that the plaintiff was entitled to recover the value of the lumber so destroyed and which might have been delivered, and that the defendant was entitled to be paid for sawing this lumber as well as that drawn away by the plaintiff. *Schofield v. Town, and Town v. Schofield,* 439.

AMENDMENT.

After demurrer.]—Where contingent damages had been assessed n demurrer to a plea, and judgent was afterwards given for der endant, the court refused leave to he plaintiff to reply *de novo*, no istinct affidavit of merits being led. *McLellan* v. *Rogers*, 651.

APPEAL.

See INDICTMENT.

APPROPRIATION OF PAYMENTS.

See PAYMENT—SCI. FA.

RBITRATION AND AWARD.

See PLEADING, 8.

Appointment of third arbitrator.] 1. A submission under a rule of eference was to K. and M., and uch person as they should appoint. he affidavits were contradictory as to the fact of a verbal appointment of C. as third arbitrator, and there was no proof of any appointment in writing ; but it was sworn that he was chosen by the defendant, as one of two persons proposed by the plaintiff, and that he sat with the others, and voted in the defendant's presence without objection. The court, under these circumstances, refused to interfere against an award made by K. & C. *Osborne* v. *Wright*, 65.

Award as to compensation for lands taken—Excessive valuation—9 Vic. ch. 81, sec. 26—Submission by married woman—Land owned by several devisees—Reservations or conditions in award—Form of such awards, and principles on which the court will interfere with them.]—2. The court in this and the succeeding cases set aside the awards, made under 9 Vic. ch. 81, as to compensation to be paid to parties whose land was required for the Great Western Railway ; the sum awarded being so excessive as to shew clearly that the arbitrators

had disregarded the direction of the statute, to consider the benefit conferred on the property as well as the damage done. The fact of one of the parties having an interest in the land being a married woman was held no objection to the award, for it was known to the company when they agreed to the submission, and both she and her husband were willing to convey their interest in accordance with the award. The following proviso was inserted in the award : " It being understood that the Great Western R. R. Co. shall construct and maintain a public water tank south of the railway, sufficient at all times to supply the inhabitants of the front of said lots 79 and 80 with water from the Detroit river, and shall keep open Ferry-street at its present width." —*Held*, That the company could not object to the award on this ground. It was expressed in the award that the land should be subject to the reservation of the Bordage road expressed in the patent to F. B. of the said land, and to any public or private right, excepting the right of the parties submitting to the arbitration, in respect of Water-street and River-street having been laid out on a certain plan. —*Held*, also, no objection. Where the parties interested in the land were devisees under a will, it was held unnecessary to state in the award how much each was to receive ; for the money might be paid to the executors, and left to them to divide. *Semble*, That as the submission to arbitration in matters of this description is in a measure compulsory, the court might interfere to prevent injustice where they would hesitate to do so in an ordinary case. [For suggestions as to the proper form of award in these cases, see the conclusion of the judgment of the Chief Justice.] *Great Western Railroad Company* v. *Baby et al.*, 106.

Compensation for matters not within the submission—Reservation of right to cross the track.]—**3.** In this case the arbitrators awarded a certain sum for the defendant's interest in the land as lessee, " and for the lumber taken by the said company now piled upon that part of the wharf taken by the said company." The award then proceeded to say, " we have taken it for granted, in making this award, that the said C. H. shall have the right to cross the railway track from one part of his property to another." *Held,* That the arbitrators had no power to award compensation for the lumber; and that the provision as to the right to cross was objectionable as not being sufficiently definite or certain. *Great Western Railroad Company* v. *Hunt,* 124.

Uncertainty—Excessive compensation.]—**4.** The award in this case also was held bad, for want of certainty and definiteness in the provisions respecting the right to cross the track and the manner of doing so. It appeared, too, that the sum awarded was excessive. *Great Western Railroad Company* v. *Dougall,* 131.

Sum awarded excessive—Reservation of right to cross.]—**5.** This award also was objectionable for the excessive compensation given. It contained the following reservation :—" Reserving to Dodds the right to cross the railroad line from one portion of the said land to the other." *Held,* That the arbitrators had no right to make an absolute reservation as this assumed to be, and that, even if they had, so indefinite a provision would have been a void exercise of their authority. But *semble,* that such reservation, being unauthorized and void, would not necessarily invalidate the whole award. *Great Western Railroad Company* v. *Dodds,* 133.

Award under 16 Vic. ch. 183, sec. 33—No notice of meeting given to was agreed that the timber then made and all that might thereafter be made, should be delivered to the plaintiff as security, and in proof of such delivery should be marked as specified, and that it should be rafted to market under W.'s directions. The timber was seized under an execution by the defendant as sheriff; and the plaintiff, claiming under this deed, replevied. *Held*, that W. could not be looked upon merely as agent of the plaintiff, and the timber regarded as the plaintiff's from the first, for that would be inconsistent with the terms of the deed. *Held* also, that the statute requiring registration could apply only to that part of timber in existence as timber and owned by W. at the execution of the instrument, but that it clearly applied to that portion, and therefore for want of registration the deed must be held void altogether; but, at all events, it could have operated to pass only that part of the timber which was made and capable of delivery at the time of its execution, and such as being made afterwards was delivered to the plaintiff and marked for him. *Short* v. *Ruttan*, 79.

ATTACHMENT.

See WARRANT.

ATTORNEY.

See COSTS.—MUNICIPAL ELECTIONS.

Plaintiff's name used without authority—Attorney ordered to pay costs.]—Where an attorney had made use of the plaintiff's name in a suit without his consent, he was ordered to repay to such plaintiff the costs which he had been obliged to pay to the defendant on failure of the suit. *In re Henderson* v. *McMahon*, 288.

BANKRUPTCY.

See INSOLVENT AND INSOLVENCY.

4 r—VOL. XII. Q. B.

BILLS OF EXCHANGE AND PROMISSORY NOTES.

"Port Hope, December 8, 1853.
" £228 7s 6d.

" Three months after date, pay to the order of William Thompson, at Port Hope, the sum of two hundred and twenty-eight pounds seven shillings and six pence, currency, for value received.

Signed, "JOHN THOMPSON."

1. *Held*, not a promissory note. *Forward et al* v. *William Thompson and John Thompson*, 103.

Presentment—Pleading.]—2. Assumpsit against the maker and endorser of a promissory note. The first count alleged that the maker had absconded, and was absent from Canada when the note fell due. The second count averred as an excuse for presentment the absence of the maker and the plaintiff's inability to find him. *Pleas*, to the first count—1st, That the note was not duly presented for payment; 2nd, That it was not duly presented at the maker's last place of abode. To the second count, that the maker's last place of abode was well known to the plaintiffs when the note fell due. *Held*, on demurrer, pleas bad. *Forward et al.* v. *John Thompson and Wm. Thompson*, 194.

Declaration on Promissory Note—Special Demurrer.]—3. Endorsee against maker of a note. The declaration alleged that the defendant thereby promised to pay to certain persons trading under the name, style and firm of W. B. Clark & Co., and that the said persons so trading, &c., by and under that name and style, *then* duly endorsed the said note to the plaintiffs. *Held*, on special demurrer, that it sufficiently appeared when the note was endorsed, and that the endorsers were sufficiently described. *Gooderham et al.* v. *Garden*, 521.

Promissory notes—Special demurrer—Pleading.]—4. Declaration on two promissory notes, including both in one count, and averring that the payee *afterwards duly endorsed the said notes respectively* to the plaintiff, and that defendant (the maker) did not pay the amount of the said notes, although they were duly presented for payment, &c. *Held,* on special demurrer, bad. *Beaty* v. *Jarvis,* 540.

Promissory note — Indictment — Forgery—10 & 11 Vic., ch. 9.]—5. A forged paper purporting to be a bank note is a promissory note within the meaning of the statute: and it is equally so if there is no such bank as that named. *Regina* v. *McDonald,* 543.

Promissory note—Pleading.]—6. Declaration on a promissory note against the maker, the payee, and second endorser. *Plea,* by the payee and second endorser, that they did not endorse the said promissory note in manner and form. *Held,* on demurrer, plea bad. *Rossin et al.,* v. *White et al.,* 634.

BILL OF SALE.
See ASSIGNMENT.

BIRDSALL'S LINE.
See BOUNDARY.

BOND.
See DOWER, 1.—USURY.

BOUNDARY.
See POSSESSION.

16 *Vic. ch.* 228, *sec.* 1—*Limit tween* 12 & 13, 1*st. Con. Monaghan* —*Birdsall's line.*]—*Held,* that under 16 Vic. ch. 228, sec. 1, Birdsall's line, as laid out on the ground, must govern as the allowance for road between lots twelve and thirteen along their whole extent, and not merely up to park lot ten on lot thirteen ; and that it was immaterial whether such line was correctly described in the statute. *Otty* v. *Davis,* 454.

BOUNDARY-LINE COMMISSIONERS.

1 *Vic. ch.* 19 ; 3 *Vic. ch.* 11—*Form of judgment—Omission to file.*]—*Held,* that the minute of the boundary-line commissioners produced in this case could not be considered a judgment within the meaning of the 3 Vic. ch. 11, and that the defendant should therefore have been permitted to give evidence contradicting such minute. The second section of this act, which provides that every such judgment shall be filed, is directory only, and the omission to file will not affect the validity of the judgment. *Regina* v. *Rose,* 637.

BY-LAW.
See MANDAMUS, 5—MUNICIPAL CORPORATIONS.—TAXES, 1.

BUFFALO, BRANTFORD, AND GODERICH RAILWAY COMPANY.
See RAILWAYS AND RAILWAY COMPANIES, 1.—TIME (COMPUTATION OF).

By what acts governed.]—The Buffalo, Brantford, and Goderich Railway Company are to be treated as acting under 16 Vic., ch. 45, and not under the joint stock road acts —at all events, as regards shareholders who have taken their stock since the 16 Vic. was passed. *Buffalo, Brantford, and Goderich Railway Company* v. *Parke,* 607.

CANADA COMPANY.
See TRESPASS, 2.

CASE.

Action on the,]—See " Action."

CERTIORARI.

Indictment—Certiorari.] — After an acquittal in a criminal case the court refused a *certiorari* to remove the indictment with a view of applying for a new trial; or to stay the entry of judgment, so that a new indictment might be preferred and tried without prejudice. *Regina v. Whittier*, 214.

CHATTEL MORTGAGES.

See ASSIGNMENT.

Second mortgage by mortgagor without first mortgagee's consent— Entry by first mortgagee thereupon —Trespass.]—1. The plaintiff mortgaged certain goods to defendant, with a proviso for redemption on payment of £125 on 20th of October, and an agreement that the plaintiff should account to defendant for the price of the goods, or any part thereof, sold by him in the course of business before the day for payment of the mortgage money; and that in case of default, or in case plaintiff should attempt to sell or dispose of the goods without defendant's consent first had in writing, it should be lawful for defendant to enter and take said goods. On the same day the defendant gave the plaintiff a writing, authorizing him to sell goods that day mortgaged to him, "and to continue selling the same until further notice in writing, subject nevertheless to the proviso of the said bill of sale in other respects." The plaintiff, on the 17th of October, mortgaged the same goods to one C. to secure a debt. *Held*, a violation of the agreement between the plaintiff and defendant, and that the defendant was entitled to enter and take possession of the goods. *Closter v. Headley*, 364.

Who may take saw-logs mortgaged and afterwards made into lumber.]—

2. A person advancing money belonging to others, but for which he himself is responsible, may legally take a chattel mortgage for it in his own name. A mortgage on saw logs will bind the lumber into which they are sawn, but the mortgagee must prove that such lumber was made out of the logs mortgaged. *White et al. v. Brown*, 477.

Effect of, on timber made after execution.]—3. The plaintiffs held a chattel mortgage from C. of 700 pieces of timber, "together with whatever quantity of squared timber the said party of the first part may manufacture during the remainder of the season." The timber made after the execution of this mortgage was marked as it was got out with the plaintiff's mark, but remained in C.'s possession, and was seized there by the defendant, an execution creditor. *Held*, that the plaintiffs could not recover it under their mortgage. *Cummings et al. v. Morgan*, 565.

COLLISION.

See NAVIGATION—PLEADING, 14.

COMMISSIONERS FOR INDIAN AFFAIRS.

See BOUNDARY-LINE COMMISSIONERS.

2 Vic. ch. 15, *sec.* 5—14 & 15 *Vic. ch.* 54, *sec.* 5.]—An action against Commissioner of Indian Affairs fo seizing and selling lumber cut o Indian land must be brought withi six months from the seizure, no from the sale. *Jones v. Bain*, 550

COMMISSIONERS TO TAK AFFIDAVITS.

See MUNICIPAL ELECTIONS.

COMMON COUNTS.

See AGREEMENT, 2.

COMMON SCHOOLS.

Authority of School Trustees—16 Vic. ch. 185, sec. 6,]—1. Two of the trustees of a school section are not competent to act in all cases without consulting the third; nor can the whole body, without any reference to the freeholders, determine upon the site for the school-house, and purchase it, and impose a rate to meet the expense. *Orr* v. *Lawrence Ranney, Thomas Randle, and William Beattie*, 377.

Alteration of school section—Election of new trustees.]—2. An alteration of the boundaries of a school section under 13 & 14 Vic. ch. 48, sec. 18, subsec. 4, does not make it necessary to call a school section meeting and appoint new trustees. The trustees in this case proceeded to collect the rate by action instead of by warrant, as provided by 13 & 14 Vic. ch. 48, sec. 12, sub-secs. 2, 7, 8; and *semble per Draper, J.,* that the appeal might have been dismissed on this ground; but the objection was waived, *The Chief Superintendent of Common Schools for Upper Canada, Appellant, in a cause of the Trustees of School Section No. 2, in the Township of Moore,* v. *William McRea,* 525.

3. Under 13 & 14 Vic. ch. 48, school trustees are authorized to levy a rate for the erection of a school house in their section. *The Chief Superintendent of Schools, Appellant, in re John A. Kelly* v. *Charles Hedges et al.,* 531.

—•—

COMPUTATION OF TIME.

See TIME (COMPUTATION OF.)

—•—

CONDITION.

See DEED, 2.

CONTRACT.

See AGREEMENT. — ASSIGNMENT. CORPORATIONS. — GUARANTEE. MONEY HAD AND RECEIVED. PLEADING, 5.—WARRANTY.

Sub-contract for work on railro —Extra work—Reference to origin contract.] — The defendants, wi other persons, had entered into a agreement with the Great Weste1 Railway Company to make and co plete certain sections of the railwa Their agreement was to do the sev ral descriptions of work in accor ance with the plans and specific tions furnished by the Company engineer, and for the prices co tained in a schedule, all of whi were annexed to the agreemer In these were contained, amo other things, a full detail of t manner in which the culverts we to be made, and the kind of sto to be used, &c. It was also p1 vided that, if the engineer shou so direct, embankment might substituted for trestle work piling, at any point, and vice ver: without any extra allowance the for. The plaintiff afterwards e tered into an agreement under se with the defendants to furnish materials necessary to build a complete all the arched culve required on one of the sectio included in their contract with t Company; "and that the sa shall be done in strict accordan with the plans, specifications, a directions of the engineer of t Great Western Railway Compa having charge of the same." T agreement was signed "S. Farw & Co." by Farwell, one of t defendants. The plaintiff was p ceeding with the constructi n the culverts, when the Compan engineer in charge decided up having a description of mason w(superior to and different from t specified in the defendants' origi contract with the Company; and c of the defendants then desired the plaintiff to go on with the work as required, and promised to pay the additional expense incurred by the change. The plaintiff sued on the common counts for the value of the work as done upon that undertaking not under the contract. *Held*, that although it was stipulated that he should abide by the directions of the engineer, the plaintiff might refer to the defendants' original contract with the company, to shew what kind of work was contemplated by his agreement, and that he was entitled to recover under the common counts for extra work ; for as the plaintiff's contract was evidently made with reference to that under which the defendants were acting, it would be impossible, without looking at both, to put a just construction on their agreement. *Quœre* whether the contract with the plaintiff, as executed by Farwell, could bind the other defendants. *Logan* v. *Stranahan et al.*, 15.

Right of action.]—2. A contracted with defendants to perform certain work, and B. entered into a bond as his surety. It appeared that B. was in fact the principal, and did the work, and that A. had tendered and taken the contract for him, and had executed a writing assigning to him all his interest in the proceeds. *Held*, that B. could have no right of action against the defendants. *Ferris* v. *The Municipality of the township of Kingston*, 436.

CORPORATIONS.

See JOINT STOCK COMPANIES.

Corporation—Necessity for contract under corporate seal.]—Where work done for a corporation is such as was evidently contemplated by their character, and they have accepted and availed themselves of it, they cannot refuse to pay on the ground that there was no contract under seal. *Held*, therefore, that the Hamilton and Gore Mechanics' Institute were liable to the defendant for services rendered by him as an architect upon a verbal agreement, in preparing plans and superintending the erection of a hall for their accommodation. *Draper, J.*, dissenting on the ground that—as there was nothing in the defendants' charter to bind them by any particular form of contract, and the claim was not one for small or ordinary services which might constantly be required —the case could not be held within any of the recognized exceptions to the general rule, which required a contract under the corporate seal. *Clark* v. *The Hamilton and Gore Mechanics' Institute*, 178.

COSTS.

See ATTORNEY.—NEW TRIAL, 1.

13 & 14 Vic. ch. 53, sec. 78—Set off of defendant's costs against plaintiff's verdict.]—The 13 & 14 Vic. ch. 53, sec. 78, enacts, that in any suit which might have been brought in a division court, unless the judge shall certify as therein mentioned, so much of the defendant's costs as shall exceed the costs which would have been incurred by him in the division court shall be set off by the master, in entering judgment *against the plaintiff's costs*, and the defendant shall be entitled to execution against the plaintiff when the costs so set off shall exceed the plaintiff's verdict and division court costs. *Held*, that under this provision the defendant might set off the excess of his costs of defence above his own and the plaintiff's division court costs, against the plaintiff's verdict — *Draper, J.*, dissenting. *Held*, also, That the plaintiff's attorney, having advanced to the plaintiff the amount of the verdict, could have no lien so as to deprive the defendant of the benefit of the statute. *Cameron* v. *Campbell*, 159.

COUNTY COURT.

See MANDAMUS, 2, 3.

COVENANT.

See DOWER, 1.—PLEADING, 8.

CRIMINAL LAW.

e BILLS OF EXCHANGE AND PRO-
MISSORY NOTES, 5.—BOUNDARY
LINE COMMISSIONERS.— CERTIO-
RARI.—INDIAN LANDS.— INDICT-
MENT.

CROPS.

See EXECUTOR.

DAMAGES.

easure of.]—See " Agreement,"
3.—" Detinue."

mallness of]—See "New Trial," 1.

DEATH.

lessor of plaintiff before trial.]—
See " Ejectment," 2.

DECLARATIONS.

nder 5 & 6 Will. IV. ch. 62.]—
See " Evidence," 1.

DEED.

ee ADMISSION.— DETINUE.—RAIL-
WAYS AND RAILWAY COMPANIES,
1,—REGISTRY AND REGISTRAR.

*Ejectment—Construction of deed
Revocation of will—Misdirection.*
1. In January, 1841, B made his
ll, devising to his daughter, the
fe of the defendant, the land in
estion, in fee. In July following
, and the defendant and his wife
ecuted a deed reciting the will,
d stating that the parties had
utually agreed that the defendant
d his wife should come upon the
nd, and have, hold, occupy, pos-
ss, and enjoy it, without the in-
rruption or denial of him the said
B., his heirs or assigns, so long as
the defendant and his wife should
support the said B. and his wife in
the manner described. The deed
then set out, that in consideration
of the will, and that the said B. did
put the defendant and his wife in
possession, they had agreed to
maintain the said B. and his wife
during their natural lives ; and that
if the defendant and his wife should
keep their agreement, then the land
was to become the property of the
said defendant and his wife, their
heirs and assigns for ever. B, lived
with and was supported by the
defendant and his wife until his
wife died in 1847. He afterwards
married again, and in July, 1850, a
few days before his death, made
another will, revoking all former
wills, and directing his executors
to sell all his land, and to divide
the proceeds equally among his
four daughters. The defendant
had made considerable improvements on the farm during his occupation. *Held,* on ejectment brought
by one of the four daughters, that
the deed passed no estate of inheritance, and that nothing contained
in it could operate as an estoppel
on the devisees under the second
will. It gave only a right to occupy until the testator's death, with
the assurance that if the agreement
were kept by defendant and his
wife, he would make no alteration
in his first will. *Held,* also, that it
should not have been left to the
jury to find whether the testator
was of sound mind when he made
the second will, or whether any
coercion had been used in obtaining
it, for there was no evidence to impeach the will on either of these
grounds. *Quære,* whether the defendant, having kept the condition
on his part, would have any remedy
against B.'s representative for
breach of the agreement. *Throop
and wife v. Edmonds,* **33.**

Condition void as repugnant to the premises]—2. The defendant claimed under a deed in fee, in which after the habendum, was contained a proviso that the conveyance should be void, and the estate reverted to the grantor, if the grantee should make default in performing the covenant thereinafter contained. This covenant was, that the grantee should cultivate the land during the life of the grantor for his benefit. *Held,* that the proviso was void as being inconsistent with the grant, and therefore that the defendant was entitled, notwithstanding the grantee's covenant had been broken. *Brown* v. *Stuart,* 510.

DEMAND OF PERUSAL AND COPY OF WARRANT.

See WARRANT.

DEMURRER.

Notice of exceptions to the declaration having been duly served by the defendant, were omitted by the plaintiff in the demurrer books entered by him. The court refused to give judgment in favor of defendant, as allowed by rule of court, the plea being clearly bad, but allowed the exceptions to be argued. *Semble,* that such cases will in future be struck out of the paper, *Curry* v. *McLeod,* 545.

DESCENT.

See WILL.

DETINUE.

Detinue for a deed—Evidence—Measure of damages,]—Detinue for an indenture of bargain and sale. *Pleas*—1. Non detinet ; 2. That the deed was not the plaintiff's. The jury found that the indenture was delivered by one A. to the defendant, to be delivered to the plaintiff after A.'s death, on condition that he the (the plaintiff) should keep A. until his death, and should pay his debts ; and that the plaintiff had not maintained A., but after his death was ready to pay his debts. The defendant, who was one of A's creditors, had refused to accept his debt from the plaintiff, and had destroyed the deed. *Held,* that on these facts and pleadings the plaintiff could not recover ; for as to the first plea, the writing being delivered to the defendant merely as an escrow, was not in fact a deed as described in the declaration ; and, as to the second plea, the plaintiff had forfeited his right by a breach of one of the conditions. *Semble,* that in tuch cases where the plaintiff shews himself entitled to the deed, but the defendant intending to do right has given it up to another, the damage should be left as a question for the jury under the circumstances, and should not as of course be the value of the land. *Reynolds* v. *Waddell,* 9.

DEVISE.

See WILL.—EXECUTORS.

DISCONTINUANCE.

See LIMITATIONS (STATUTE OF).

DISSEIZIN.

See EVIDENCE, 2.

DIVISION COURTS.

See COSTS—WARRANT.

Jurisdiction of Division Courts—13 & 14 Vic. ch. 53.]—1. The jurisdiction of the division courts does not extend to persons residing out of the county. *Dulmage* v. *The Jydge of the County Court of Leeds and Grenville,* 32.

Order for trial of Division Court suit under 16 Vic. ch. 177, sec. 9—Prohibition.]—2. On an application for a writ of prohibition the question was, by whom the order referred to in **16 Vic. ch. 177**, sec. 9, should be granted, whether by the judge who would ordinarily have cognizance of the suit, or by the judge in whose court it is desired to sue under such order. The court considered the point to be doubtful and the writ was therefore refused, and the applicant ordered to declare in prohibition. *Bongard* v. *Mc-Whirter*, 143.

DOWER.

Inchoate right to dower no breach of covenants for seizin or quiet enjoyment— Variance between bond as pleaded and as set out on oyer.]—1. The plaintiff declared on the covenants for seizin and quiet enjoyment contained in an ordinary conveyance of land, alleging as a breach the prospective claim for dower of the defendant's wife. The defendant pleaded, that at the making of the said indenture it was agreed between the plaintiff and defendant that the plaintiff should convey certain lands to the defendant in exchange for the lands by the said indenture conveyed, and that the prospective claims to dower of their respective wives should be wholly provided for by a separate instrument, to be taken as part of the said indenture, and to form a distinct provision between the plaintiff and defendant as the said respective contingent claims to dower including the claim of defendant's wife, and thereby excluding it from the operation of the covenants declared on : that thereupon the plaintiff, by his certain writing obligatory, after reciting the said respective conveyances in exchange as aforesaid *and the said agreement*, agreed with the defendant that the said prospective claims to dower, including the claim in the declaration mentioned, should be exclusively and completely provided for as a separate matter, not included in the covenants declared on ; and that as soon as the defendant's wife should bar her dower in the lands conveyed by the said indenture, the plaintiff's wife should release her dower in the lands convey in exchange as aforesaid ; and the defendant averred that the claim in this action was covered and provided for by the said writing obligatory and excluded from the covenants in the declaration. The plaintiff craved oyer, and the instrument as set out appeared to be a bond in £100 given by the plaintiff to the defendant, reciting the conveyances in exchange mentioned in the plea, and that it had been agreed that the plaintiff's wife should bar her dower as soon as the defendant's wife had released hers, and conditioned to be void if this was done ; but nothing was said of any further agreement that such dower should be excepted from the covenants in the deed executed by the defendant as stated in the plea. *Held*, on demurrer, plea bad, for not describing the bond correctly as regards the recital, or setting it out according to its legal effect ; but the court gave judgment for the defendant, on the ground that a prospective claim to dower is no breach either of the covenant for seizin or quiet enjoyment. *Quære*, however, whether the intention of the parties did not sufficiently appear from the bond, to enable the court to stay proceedings in this action as being against good faith, unless the plaintiff would swear that the agreement was not such as alleged by the defendant. *Quære*, also, whether, taking the bond and award together as one instrument, the covenant might not be read as containing an exception of the claim for dower, *Thornhill* v. *Jones*, 231.

13 & 14 Vic. ch. 58—Offer to assign—Plea of tout temps prist, effect of, as to damages and costs.]—2. *Dower*—The tenant pleaded *tout* temps prist. The plaintiff replied, denying the readiness of the demandant to assign,and averring a demand under the 13 & 14 Vic. ch. 58, and a refusal. The tenant traversed the refusal. It appeared that after receiving the demand the tenant gave a written notice to the demandant that he was willing to assign her dower. In pursuance of this notice the tenant the demandant's husband met on the ground, and the tenant then offered what he considered a third, and put up pickets to mark the boundary. The husband, however, refused this, and would not say what particular portion the demandant wanted or would take. The parties then separated, and this action was brought. *Held*, that the offer proved was sufficient, and that a verdict was therefore rightly found for the tenant. *Draper*, J., considered that the late statute was not intended to interfere with any right to costs existing under the old practice, or to render necessary a demand in cases where the demandant would before have been entitled to costs without it ; that the plea of *tout temps prist* admitted a right to damages from the commencement of the suit to the issuing, if not to the execution of the writ of enquiry, without any suggestion that the husband died seised ; and that on these pleadings, therefore, the demandant might strictly have recoverd such damage, and consequently the costs ; but as this was not insisted on at the trial, and the verdict was just, he concurred in refusing to interfere. As to the practice and pleadings in dower, under the late act, see the judgments of *Draper* and *Burns*, JJ., *Bishoprick and Wife* v. *Pearce*, 306.

13 & 14 Vic. ch. 58—*Damages—Costs*.]—3. *Dower*—There was no suggestion in the declaration that the husband died seised, and no claim for damages. The tenant

pleaded *tout temps prist*. *Replication*, A demand and refusal. *Rejoinder*, taking issue on the refusal. It was proved that after demand served on the tenant, under 13 & 14 Vic. ch. 58, sec. 5, he went to the demandant's attorney and said that he was ready and willing to assign dower whenever she would come for it, to which the attorney replied that the tenant must take his own course. The jury found for demandant and 1s. damages; and a rule having been obtained for a new trial—*Held*, per *Draper*, J., and *Burns*, J., that such rule should be discharged. Per *Draper*, J.—That by pleading *tout temps prist* the tenant had admitted a right to damages, at least from the bringing of the action, which would carry costs. Per *Burns*, J.—That the offer proved was insufficient, and in effect amounted to a refusal, and the demandant should therefore have costs ; but that there could be no damages, as the husband was not proved to have died seised. *Robinson*, C. J., dissenting, on the ground that the evidence shewed no such refusal as could do away with the effect of the offer proved, and that the offer was sufficient under the statute to exempt the tenant from costs. *Quin* v. *McKibbin*, 323.

Non-tenuit—Ne unques seisie.]— 4. W. C. died seised in fee of the land in question, having devised the same to his wife for life, and after her death to his son, the demandant's husband, in fee. The testator's widow, the devisee for life, died before the demandant's husband, and during her life his interest was sold under a *fi. fa.* against lands, and conveyed to one J., who, having recovered possession, sold to the tenant, who mortgaged back again to J., but continued in possession. It was not shewn whether all the mortgage money had been paid or not ; but the time for payment of several of the instalments had not arrived. *Held*, that the demandant could not succeed, for the tenant was not tenant of the freehold, but the mortgagee : nor was the husband ever so seised as to entitle his widow to dower, for his reversionary interest was sold during his life time. *Cumming* v. *Alguire*, 330.

Inchoate right to, no breach of covenant for seizin.]—5. A. executed to B. two deeds in fee of certain lands, containing the usual covenants for seizin. The wife of M. from whom A. had purchased, afterwards brought an action of dower against B., and B., having compounded with her, and obtained a release, sued A. on the covenants for seizin contained in his deeds. This action was brought more than twenty years after the execution of one of the deeds. *Held*, confirming Thornhill v. Jones, ante page 231, that the claim for dower, being inchoate at the execution of the deeds, constituted no breach of the covenant for *seisin* ; and on that ground it would have been proper to arrest judgment ; but a verdict having been found for the plaintiff on a plea of the Statute of Limitations, contrary to the evidence, a new trial was granted. *Dack* v. *Currie*, 334.

Exchange—Evidence—Dower.]— 6. Plea, the husband exchanged other lands with one F. for the lands in question, and that the demandant elected to be endowed of such other lands. To prove this exchange, an ordinary deed of bargain and sale of the other lands was produced, executed by demandant's husband, for an expressed consideration of £600 ; and it was shewn clearly by parol evidence that the transaction between F. and the husband was in fact an exchange. *Held*, that such evidence could not avail ; that the exchange must be proved in proper technical form, and by deed;

and that the demandant was therefore entitled to succeed. *Towsley* *Smith*, 555.

— ◆ —

EJECTMENT.

See EVIDENCE, 2.—NEW TRIAL,

1. The jury having found a ge eral verdict for the plaintiff, thoug the defendant was in fact entitle to the part he had cleared—*Hel* that this was not ground for a ne trial, but for an application to r strain the plaintiff from taking po session of such part. *Ferrier* *Moodie*, 379.

2. In ejectment under the o form, where the lessor of the plai tiff died before the trial—*Held*, th no *Sci. Fa.* was necessary, but th judgment might be entered, and writ of possession obtained. *D* *dem. Hay* v. *Hunt*, 625.

ELECTIONS.
See MUNICIPAL ELECTIONS.

ESTATE.
See DEED—WILL.

ESTOPPEL.
See DEED, 1.— INSURANCE—PLEA
ING, 4.

Sale by sheriff— Estoppel on clai ants]—1. Where the sheriff und a *fi. fa.* seized and sold certain goo claimed by the plaintiffs—*Held*, th the fact of one of the plainti having attended and bid at the sa did not estop them from compla ing of the seizure of the goods their own. *Lines et al.* v *Gran* 209.

2. A bailee of goods is not est ed from disputing the bailo title. *White et al.* v. *Brown*, 4

EVIDENCE.
See ADMISSION—CONTRACT—GU
ANTEE—LIMITATIONS (Statute
—MALICIOUS PROSECUTION–PA
NERS AND PARTNERSHIP—PLE

ING, 2, 3—TAXES, 2—WORK AND LABOUR.

Declarations under 5 & 6 *Wm. IV. ch.* 62.—1. In support of a claim for work and labor, in an action of assumpsit, the plaintiff produced declarations of witnesses, taken under the Imperial acts 5 & 6 Wm. IV. ch. 62, purporting to be taken before one Alexander Dick, a justice of the peace in Glasgow, and annexed to each declaration was his certificate to that effect, under his hand and seal. The signature of the justice was not authenticated in any way, nor was it proved that he held the office, or that the plaintiff, at the time of the declaration made, was resident in Great Britain or Ireland. These declarations were not transmitted under the seal of the justice, but brought into court by the plaintiff's attorney. *Held,* that such evidence could not be received.

The court remarked upon the great want of caution apparent in the provisions of the statute above mentioned. *Smith* v. *McGowan,* 270.

Ejectment on sheriff's deed—Proof of judgment—Disseisin.]—2. Where ejectment is brought on a sheriff's deed against a stranger to the execution debtor, it is necessary to prove the judgment on which the execution issued :—but

Quære—per *Draper,* J.—Where the judgment debtor is the tenant in possession, a stranger to the judgment debtor and to the tenant comes in to defend—whether any more need be proved against such defendant than would have been required against the actual tenant ; or whether an application must be made under 14 & 15 Vic., ch. 114, sec. 2.

It was contended on the argument that a mortgage under which plaintiff claimed part of the premises, could vest no interest, defendant being then in adverse pos-

session ; but *held,* that this objec tion should have been taken at th trial, and the fact of disseisin left t the jury ; and *semble,* that the ev dence was against such exceptio *Perry* v. *Maurice Piquott,* 372.

16 *Vic. ch.* 19 — *Verdict taken p confesso* — *Rejection of evidence - Power of court to review judge's d cision.*] — 3. A defendant havin been notified (under 16 Vic. ch. 1 to attend as a witness for the plai tiff, did not appear, and the learne judge at the trial ordered a verdi *pro confesso* to be taken against hi declining to hear evidence tendere in support of the plea. The cou afterwards refused to disturb th verdict, as it was not shewn clearl that any injustice had been don *Quære,* however, whether the ev dence tendered should not hav been received ; and whether th court have power under this statu to review the decision of the judge Nisi Prius. *McGann* v. *Keyes,* 42

Proof of foreign judgment—13 14 *Vic. ch.* 19, *sec.* 1.]—4. To prove judgment of the Supreme Court the State of New York, held Watertown, in the county of Jeffe son, a copy of the roll was pr duced, certified by the *county cle* under the seal *of the county—Hel* insufficient. *Woodruff* v. *Wallin* 501.

EXCHANGE.

Evidence of.]—*See* DOWER, 6.

EXECUTION.

See LANDLORD AND TENANT, 2
POUNDAGE.

EXECUTORS.

See WILL.

Share of crop sown in testato lifetime, and reaped after his dea — Whether it goes to his executo or to the devisee of the land.]—M.

the spring of 1852, agreed by parol with A. to work his farm on shares, and put in a crop of rye. In December, 1852, A. entered into a written agreement with G. to rent the farm to him for three years; and in January, 1853, A died, leaving a will. M. in 1853. with the assent of G., reaped the crop which he had sown in the previous year. *Held*, that the share of such crop to which A. would have been entitled, must go to the devisee of the land, and not to the executors. *Tubbs et al., Executors of John Morgan v. Thomas Morgan*, 151.

FALSE RETURN.
See PLEADING, 7.

FENCES.
See RAILWAYS AND R.W.COMPANIES, 3, 4, 5—WOODSTOCK AND LAKE ERIE R. W. AND HARBOUR CO.

FIRE.
Accidental loss by]—*See* " Agreement," 3—"Nuisance"—"Pleading," 8.

FOREIGN JUDGMENT.
See EVIDENCE, 4.

FORFEITURE.
See LEASE.

FORGERY
See BILLS OF EXCHANGE AND PROMISSORY NOTES, 5.

GRAND RIVER NAVIGATION COMPANY.
Liability of, for consequential injuries—2 Wm. IV. ch. 13.]—1. The Grand River Navigation Company, under their act of incorporation, are not liable in an action at law for consequential injuries arising from works erected by them on the Grand River, or on lands in the vicinity of the persons injured. *Young v. The Grand River Navigation Co.*, 75.

2 *Wm. IV. ch.* 13—*Liability for obstructions to Navigation*]—2. The Grand River Navigation Company are liable under their charter for injuries caused by obstructions in any part of the natural channel, and not merely for such as occur in the artificial channels or works constructed by them. *Phelps v. The Grand River Navigation Co.*, 245.

GREAT WESTERN RAILWAY COMPANY.
See ARBITRATION AND AWARD, 2— RAILWAYS AND R. W.Co.s., 2, 3, 4.

GUARANTEE.
See PAYMENT.

Consideration—Acceptance— Defendant failing to attend as witness, effect of, on his affidavit filed in term.]

" MR. THOMAS MASON,

" DEAR SIR,—In answer to your favor of this date, I beg to say I will pay whatever sum you may agree upon to pay for an omnibus, if you should find one to suit you, so soon as the same is delivered to you in Hamilton ; and this may be considered as a guarantee to the party from whom you may purchase. I remain yours very truly, (Signed) ." SAMUEL MILLS."

Held, that this, though addressed only to T. M., would attach at once as a guarantee in favor of any party who might furnish the omnibus ; and that no further proof of acceptance or of consideration was required. The defendant having been notified, failed to attend as a witness. *Held*, therefore, that no attention should be given to his affidavit impeaching the correctness of the verdict. *Manning v. Mills*, 515.

EIR AND DEVISEE COMMISSION.

See ACTION.

HIGHWAY.

ee PLEADING, 2—RAILWAYS AND R. W. Co s., 2.

Trespass, qu cl. fr.]—The defenant justified on the ground that he plaintiff had wrongfully enlosed a government allowance for oad, and that the grievances comlained of were committed in reoving the obstruction. It was lleged in the declaration that this overnment allowance had never een used, but had been in plainiff's possession since 1816, another oad parallel to it having been ravelled on instead. *Held*, plea, ad, as under 9 Vic. ch. 8 such overnment allowance could only e opened by order of the muniipal council. *Curry v. McLeod*, 45.

INDIAN LANDS.

See COMMISSIONER FOR INDIAN AFFAIRS.

No new trial under 14 & 15 *Vic. h.* 13—*Indictment under* 13 & 14 *ic. ch.* 74. *for purchasing land rom Indians without the consent f government—To what lands the ct extends — Scienter — Variance etween indictment and proof as to ands purchased—Meaning and obect of the statute.*]—The court has o power to order a new trial in a riminal case reserved under 14 & 5 Vic. ch. 13; but only to decide pon any legal exceptions raised, nd whether there was legal evience to sustain the indictment, aking it in as strong a sense gainst the defendant as it will ear, and supposing the jury to ave given credit to it to its full xtent. The 13 & 14 Vic. ch. 74, rohibits the buying or contracting o buy from Indians, not merely

any lands of which they are in actual possession, but any lands held by the government for their use or benefit ;—but *Quære*, whether the clauses of the act relating to trespasses on Indian lands extend to any lands not actually possessed by them. *Held*, that the indictment in this case, after verdict, sufficiently averred the lands purchased by the defendant to be Indian lands—*i. e.*, lands held by the crown for them ; and *Quære*, whether the act extends only to lands so held, or as well to the lands purchased by Indians from individuals. A guilty knowlege on defendant's part sufficiently averred in the indictment. *Held*, also, that no variance was shewn between the land described in the indictment and that which the defendant was proved to have contracted for. *Held*, also, no objection that the purchase was alleged to have been from certain Indians named, whereas it was in fact from the tribe through their council. *Held*, also, that the evidence in this case was sufficient to sustain the conviction. *Semble*, that the meaning of the statute is, that no one shall attempt to bargain with the Indians for the purchase of their lands, until he has first obtained the consent of government, and that it is therefore contrary to the act to make even a conditional agreement, subject to their approval. The proposal should be made to government in the first instance. *Regina v. Baby*, 346.

INDICTMENT.

See BILLS OF EXCHANGE AND PROMISSORY NOTES—INDIAN LANDS.

Quarter Sessions—Order to pay costs of appeal—Indictment for disobedience of.]—1. The Court of Quarter Sessions have no authority to order a person to pay any part of the costs of an appeal to them from a conviction, after he has been acquitted on such appeal, or to convict him of an offence for disobeying such order. *Regina* v. *Orr*, 57.

Indictment — Right of jury to find general verdict of acquittal—Certiorari.]—2. On an indictment for nuisance judgment had been arrested, and a second trial had, in order to take the opinion of the jury on a particular question which the court thought material. The jury upon the second trial found a general verdict of acquittal without answering such question, which was submitted to them by the judge. The indictment had not been removed by *certiorari;* and *held*, therefore, that this court could not interfere by staying the entry of judgment until a new indictment could be preferred. *Semble,* that the jury had a right to find generally as they did. *Regina* v. *Spence*, 519.

INNS.

See MUNICIPAL CORPORATIONS. 1, 2, 4.

INSOLVENT AND INSOLVENCY.

Bankruptcy and Insolvent Debtors' Acts, 7 Vic., ch. 10; 8 Vic., ch. 48— Construction of.]—*Quære,* whether a person having failed before the passing of the Bankruptcy Act, but continuing a trader, and unable to meet his engagements, after that act had come into force, and being therefore in a position to avail himself of its provisions, could, notwithstanding, take advantage of the Insolvent Debtors' Act. *Semble,* per *Draper* and *Burns*, JJ., that he could not. Per *Robinson*, C. J., that he could. But *held*, that a final order obtained under the above circumstances was conclusive, and not to be questioned in an action brought for a debt barred by it. *Stevenson* v. *Green*, 290.

INSPECTORS OF LICENSES.

See MANDAMUS.

INSURANCE.

Fire Insurance--Notice of loss and particulars of it — How waived—Unsatisfactory verdict.]—Where notice of the loss and the particulars of it are required by a policy of insurance, they may be waived by the conduct of the insurers. In this case the declaration alleged that notice of the loss was given to the defendants forthwith, and an account of the particulars of the loss as soon as possible (such being the conditions of the policy); and issues were taken on these allegations. There were two separate policies, on a shop and on the goods contained in it. Both building and goods were destroyed. It appeared that the fire took place on the 13th of June, and the notices, both as to the shop and the goods, were given on the 13th of July. The defendant then entered into correspondence with the plaintiff as to furnishing better particulars, which were afterwards furnished; and they then refused to pay for the goods on account of some suspicious circumstances attending the fire, but they paid the amount insured on the house. *Held,* that under these circumstances the defendants were precluded from objecting to the sufficiency of the notices, or to the time at which they were given. All the evidence on either side as to fraud having been fairly left to the jury, who found for the plaintiff, the court refused to interfere, though they would have been better satisfied with a verdict the other way. *Lambkin* v. *The Ontario Marine and Fire Insurance Company*, 578.

INTEREST.

See USURY.

JOINT STOCK COMPANIES.

See BUFFALO, BRANTFORD, AND GODERICH R. W. CO.—GRAND

RIVER NAVIGATION Co.—GREAT WESTERN R. W. Co.—SANDWICH AND WINDSOR ROAD Co.

Action for calls—12 Vic. ch. 84—Instrument of Incorporation registered before six per cent paid—Irregularity cured by 16 Vic., ch. 190, sec. 55.]—An instrument, under the provisions of 12 Vic., ch. 84, was signed by the defendant and others for the formation of a road company, the defendant agreeing to take three shares. The directors named met on the 27th of May, 1850, and called in four instalments, each of ten per cent. on each share. The six per cent. required by the statute was at the same meeting paid by the promissory note of the directors to the treasurer, who then signed a receipt for the money, and afterwards registered the instrument of incorporation. By the 20th of November, 1850, the treasurer had received, by means of the call, a sum equal to the six per cent., and he then destroyed the note. On the 13th of January, 1854, another call was made, payable by six instalments ; and this action was brought for the four instalments of the first call, and the first three instalments due on the second. *Held*, that the first call could not be recovered, for when it was made the six per cent. had not been in fact paid (confirming Niagara Falls Road Company v. Benson, 8 U. C. R. 307) ; but that the plaintiffs might recover the second call, for on the 13th of January the six per cent. had been actually paid : and the company having proceeded *bonâ fide* to the construction of their road, the irregularity in registering the instrument of incorporation before such payment was cured by 16 Vic. ch. 190, sec. 55. *Nelson and Nassagaweya Road Company v. Bates,* 586.

JUDGMENT.

See EVIDENCE, 2, 4.

LANDLORD AND TENANT.

See RAILWAYS AND RAILWAY COMPANIES, 1.

Rent, when payable quarterly or yearly—Inconsistent verdicts on same evidence.]—1. *Held*, under the facts set out in this case, that it was properly left to the jury to say whether the rent was to be paid quarterly or yearly, and that they were supported by the evidence in finding it payable quarterly. Different verdicts having been rendered in two cases on the same evidence, the court granted a new trial, with costs to abide the event, in the case in which they considered the finding to be least supported. *Wilson v. McNamara,* 446.

Lease—Goods seized under fi. fa.—Landlord's claim for rent.]—2. Premises were let for a year at a rent of £75, to be paid on the first of May ; and it was agreed that if the tenant should leave before the first of May, then the rent was to become payable immediately. The tenant did leave on the Saturday before the first of May, and on Monday the goods were seized under execution. *Held*, that the landlord was entitled to his rent from the sheriff. *Vance v. Ruttan,* 632.

LEASE.

See LANDLORD AND TENANT—PLEADING, 13—TRESPASS.

Proviso not to assign—Forfeiture.]—It was provided in a lease, that the lessor might re-enter, if the lessee " do, or shall, at any time or times during the continuance of the said term, let, set, or assign over these presents, or the term, estate, or premises hereby granted, or otherwise part with his interest therein or thereto to any person or persons whatsoever," without the lessor's consent in writing. The lessee, on leaving the country for a time, rented the premises to one J., who was to go out when required. *Held*, no forfeiture. *Leys et al* v. *Fiskin et al.*, 604.

LIBEL.
On title to land.]–See "Pleading," 4.

LICENSE.
See RAILWAYS AND RAILWAY COMPANIES, 1.

LIEN.
See COSTS.

LIMITATIONS (STATUTE OF).
See POSSESSION.

4 *W. IV. c. 1—Discontinuance—Land in question forfeited for plaintiff's treason.*]—1. EJECTMENT.–The plaintiff in 1814, being charged with high treason, fled from the province, leaving his family on the property in question, and they afterwards joined him in the enemy's country, *Held*, that the circumstances of his leaving should have been considered by the jury as conclusive of an intention to abandon the possession ; and that it could not be said that leaving his family in possession was the same as remaining himself, that the discontinuance commenced when they left, and that, being abroad then, the plaintiff was entitled to the benefit of the disability. It was shewn by affidavits, in moving for a new trial, that the plaintiff had in fact been attainted for treason, and the land in question forfeited to the crown, and on this ground the court granted the defendant a new trial on payment of costs. *Butler and McNeil* v. *Donaldson*, 255.

Writs not properly continued—12 Vic. ch. 63, sec. 25]—2. In an action on a promissory note, due 4th September, 1847, the original writ issued on the 15th April, 1853, and was returned *non est inventus*, and filed

3rd Sept. 1853. On the same day an alias writ was issued, which was also returned *non est inventus*, but was not filed until the 12th May, 1854 ; nor was any memorandum endorsed on it, specifying the date of the first writ. A pluries issued on 12th May, and was served on 31st July. *Plea*, the Statute of Limitations. *Held*, that the directions of the 12 Vic. ch. 63, sec. 25, not having been complied with, the defendant was entitled to succeed.—*Ford* v. *McGoey*, 505.

LUMBER.
See CHATTEL MORTGAGES, 2, 3.

MAINTENANCE (STATUTE OF).
See ACTION.

MALICE.
See PLEADING, 9.

MALICIOUS PROSECUTION.
Opinion of counsel.]—*Case* for maliciously and without reasonable or probable cause preferring a charge of felony. The learned judge directed the jury to inquire whether the defendant had laid a *bona fide* statement of the material facts of the case before counsel, and whether he acted *bona fide* on the opinion so obtained, saying that if so, that was reasonable and probable cause. *Held*, that such direction was right. *Fellowes* v. *Hutchinson*, 633.

MANDAMUS.
Inspectors of licenses — Jurisdiction of.]—1. The court refused to interfere by mandamus to compel the inspectors of licenses to examine a certain house fitted up by the applicant as a saloon, and to grant him the proper certificate, if he should be found to have complied with the by-law of the municipality in that behalf. *In re Baxter* v. *Hesson et al.* 139.

County Court.]—2. A mandamus will lie to the judge of the County Court, commanding him to hear and determine a matter, but not to correct his judgment when given. *In re Burns* v. *Butterfield*, 140.

County Court.]—3. A mandamus will not lie in the judge of a county court to reverse his decision on a point of practice. *In re Woods* v. *Reunett*, 167.

12 *Vic. ch.* 81—*Mandamus to M. C. to make road.*]—4. *Semble*, that under the facts of this case there was clearly a duty incumbent on the Municipal Council, under 12 Vic. ch. 81, sec. 37, to make the road which they were desired to make. The court, however, granted only a mandamus nisi, in order that any question raised upon the return might be disposed of formally. *In re the Municipality of the township of Augusta and the Municipal Council of the United Counties of Leeds and Grenville*, 522.

5. A mandamus to a clerk of a municipality to furnish a copy of a by-law was refused, where it did not appear that the demand was accompanied by an offer of his fee. *In re Township Clerk of Euphrasia*, 622.

6. A mandamus was refused to compel a railway company to make crossings at a particular place, under 14 & 15 Vic. ch. 51, sec. 13. *In re Keist* v. *The G. Trunk R. W. Co.*, 675.

MARRIED WOMAN.
See ARBITRATION AND AWARD, 2.

MEASURE OF DAMAGES.
See AGREEMENT, 3.

MEMORIALS.
See ADMISSION.

MISDIRECTION.
See DEED, 1.—NEW TRIAL, 5.

MISJOINDER.
The plaintiff complained of defendant for entering wrongfully into

a close, of which the plaintiff averred himself to be in possession, and pulling down the fences, &c. ; and a count for this cause of action was framed in case, and joined with a second count in trover. *Held*, a misjoinder, the first count being substantially for a trespass. *Curry* v. *McLeod*, 545.

MISNOMER.
See MUNICIPAL CORPORATIONS, 3.

MONAGHAN (TOWNSHIP OF).
See BOUNDARY.

MONEY HAD AND RECEIVED.
See TAXES.

Agreement for sale of land—Conveyance by vendor to railway after agreement—Rescission of contract—Money had and received.]—The plaintiff purchased from defendant, who held a bond for a deed from one C., his right to certain land. Before the purchase money was paid up by the plaintiff, and after the defendant had obtained his deed from C., he conveyed to the Great Western Railway Company a small part of the lot for their road. It appeared that the railway had been surveyed before the sale to the plaintiff ; that the plaintiff had taken and for some time held possession of the land under his agreement ; and the defendant declared that he was ready to convey to the plaintiff, on receiving what was due, giving him credit on account for the sum paid by the railway company. *Held*, that under these circumstances, the plaintiff could not treat the contract as rescinded, and recover the amount paid by him, with interest, in an action for money had and received. *Reynolds* v. *Crawford*, 168.

MORTGAGE.
See CHATTEL MORTGAGES.

MUNICIPAL CORPORATIONS.

See MANDAMUS, 1, 4, 5.

Sale of spirituous liquors in taverns —By-law to limit the number of taverns to one, held unreasonable— 13 & 14 Vic. ch. 65. sec. 4—16 Vic. ch. 184, sec. 4.]—1. The Municipality of the Township of Darlington passed a by-law, enacting, I. That the number of taverns which should receive license to sell wines and spirituous liquors in the municipality should not exceed one. II. That the sum to be paid by any person who should obtain a license to keep such tavern should be £10 annually, above the duty imposed by the Imperial or Provincial statute for such license. IV. That the person receiving such license should be subject to the following regulations, amongst others : 2. That no innkeeper shall sell or permit the drinking of any intoxicating liquors on the Sabbath day, except in case of sickness, or to travellers. 4. That no innkeeper shall sell intoxicating drink to any apprentice or minor, without the permission of his legal protector ; nor shall he sell to any habitual drunkard, after being forbidden so to do by any relative or friend of such drunkard. 6. That no innkeeper shall be allowed to sell, give, loan, barter, or dispose of in any way, any intoxicating liquors after the hour of ten o'clock at night, or before five in the morning, travellers excepted. By a subsequent by-law, the fee to be paid for the license was increased to £25. It appeared by the affidavits that a by-law to prohibit absolutely the sale of spirituous liquors, &c., had been submitted to the electors, but not passed, as a sufficient number did not attend the meeting— that this by-law had not been so submitted—and that the township of Darlington contained a population of six thousand. *Held*, that first enactment was bad, as amount-

ing in effect to a total prohibition, and being therefore an attempt to evade the provisions of 16 Vic. ch. 184, sec. 4, by which no such by-law can be passed without the assent of a majority of the electors : —That the second enactment was also bad, being inseparably connected with the first. That the second, fourth, and sixth regulations, were beyond the jurisdiction of the municipality to impose. *Held*, also, that the second by-law was bad, as the fee imposed exceeded £10, and no reference had been made to the electors. *In re Barclay and the Municipality of the Township of Darlington*, 86.

By-law to prohibit absolutely the sale of liquors, &c.—Approval of electors.]—2. By-laws for prohibiting the sale of spirituous liquors, &c., which, under 16 Vic. ch. 184, sec. 4, require to be submitted to the electors, must be adopted and approved of by a majority of all the qualified municipal electors of the municipality, not merely by a majority of those who may attend at the meeting called to consider such by-law. Where the by-law which provided for calling such meeting assumed that the approval of th majority of the voters present would be sufficient : *Held*, that it was nevertheless proper to move against the then proposed by-law, after it had been passed on such approval, and not against that which laid down the improper course of pro ceeding. *In re McAvoy and th Municipality of Sarnia*, 99.

Resolutions]—3. The court has n jurisdiction over resolutions of Mu nicipal Corporations, to set aside summarily in the sam manner as by-laws. *Cæsar an the Municipality of Cartwright*, 341

Corporation—Liability of, for in juries caused by construction of sewe — Corporate seal — Misnomer Pleading.]—4. *Held*, that a muni cipal corporation were liable for injuries committed in the construction of a sewer under the superintendence of their engineer, the work having been accepted by them, though no authority or contract was shewn under the corporate seal. *Held* also, that an inaccuracy in the corporate name was immaterial after verdict, the identity of the corporate body being clear. *Held* also, that the injury complained of was sufficiently alleged in the declaration to be a wrongful act. *Farrell v. The Mayor and Town Council of the Town of London*, 343.

By-law—Tavern licenses—Sale of spirituous liquors—Imprisonment on failure to pay fine.]—5. The Municipality of Otonabee passed a by-law on the 25th of March, 1854, enacting: 1. That there should be a license issued for one inn only where spirituous liquors should be sold, and that such inn should be in Peterborough East. 2. That persons applying for a license to keep such inn should produce a certificate from four municipal electors residing in the locality where such house was to be kept of his honesty and good moral character, and a certificate from the township treasurer that he had deposited a bond with such treasurer, made in favor of the reeve and his successors, approved by the councillors of the ward in which such tavern should be situated, binding him in £50, with two sufficient sureties in £25 each, to abide by all the by-laws of the township council for the regulation of such houses. 4. That all tavern-keepers obtaining license under this by-law should shut up their bar and bar-room at 10 p.m., and keep it closed on Sunday, and should not give or sell liquors to any person in a state of intoxication. 6. That persons wilfully neglecting,

refusing, or failing to comply with the provisions of the preceding clauses of this by-law, or selling by retail without license, should be liable to a fine of £5, or failing to pay the same, to twenty days' imprisonment. 9. That there should be one shop license, and no more, granted within the said municipality, and that such license should be granted to one of the store-keepers in the village of Keene. The reeve of the township swore that the by-law was passed, because 244 out of the 480 electors had expressed themselves in favor of limiting as much as possible the sale of spirituous liquors; and that at the last election three out of the five were returned on the understanding that they would support such a measure. *Held*, that these facts could not affect the question; that the first and ninth sections of the by-law, and so much of the sixth as related to imprisonment of offenders fined on failure to pay, must be quashed; and that the second and fourth sections were good. *In the matter of Greystock and the Municipality of Otonabee*, 458.

Township of North Dumfries—Exempted from debt for Guelph and Dundas road—14 & 15 Vic. ch. 5, sec. 8.]—6. By the 14 & 15 Vic. ch. 5, the county of Waterloo is made to consist of certain townships, including North Dumfries, which before formed part of the county of Halton. The 8th section provides that the townships named, in which North Dumfries is not included, shall be responsible for their share of the debt for building the Guelph and Dundas road. This debt had been incurred by the former district of Wellington, which embraced all the townships mentioned in sec. 8, except Dumfries. *Held*, that the Municipal Council of Waterloo could not impose a rate on Dumfries to pay such debt, the omission of that township in the 14 & 15 Vic shewing clearly that it was not intended to be liable. *In the matter of the Municipality of the Township of North Dumfries and the Municipal Council of the County of Waterloo*, 507.

MUNICIPAL ELECTIONS.

Summons issued by Judge of the C. C.—Necessity of filing papers with D. C. C.—Affidavits and recognizance.]—A county judge issued his fiat for a *quo warranto*, and the papers remained with him, but were handed to the defendant's solicitor, before the return day, for perusal. *Held* sufficient, and that it was not necessary that they should have them filed with the Deputy Clerk of the Crown before the summons issued. *Semble*, that the relator's attorney may act as commissioner to take the recognizance and affidavit. *Regina ex rel. Blaisdell* v. *Rochester*, 630.

NAVIGATION.

See GRAND RIVER NAVIGATION Co. *Collision of steamers — Plaintiff not provided with lights, as required by 14 & 15 Vic. ch. 126, sec. 1— Effect of such neglect, under sec. 11.*] —Case for injury caused by a collision. It appeared that the plaintiff's steamer had only one of the lights required by the statute, which was not seen by defendants, and that the defendants' steamer was properly provided with lights, which were discerned in good time. The learned judge stated to the jury that he had no strong impression of the right on either side, and left it to them to say, upon all the evidence, who was to blame for the accident. A verdict was found for the plaintiff. *Held*, that sufficient weight had not been given to the fact that the plaintiff's boat was without the lights required by the statute; that the evidence tended

to shew the accident to be in, som degree attributable to such default and that a new trial should be ha to determine whether it was so not, for if it were, the act woul be conclusive against the plaintiff recovery. *Gildersleeve* v. *Bonter al.* 489.

NEGLIGENCE.

See NAVIGATION—RAILWAYS & W. Co.'s, 3, 4—WAREHOUSEMA

NEW TRIAL.

See CERTIORARI. — DEED, 1 EJECTMENT, 1.— GUARANTEE. INDIAN LANDS. — INSURANCE. LANDLORD AND TENANT, 1. LIMITATIONS (STATUTE OF). PRACTICE.—WILL.

Too small damages.]—1. Whe the damages given were complain of as being too small, a new tri was granted with costs to abide t event—viz., the event of the plai tiff's recovering more than t amount of the first verdict. *Jon et al.* v. *McDowell*, 214.

2. Where two new trials ha been granted in order to dispose the question on its merits, t court will not be disposed at t last trial to consider technical o jections taken as grounds of no suit. *Wafer* v. *Burns*, 384.

Ejectment—New trial on conditi of receiving evidence from judg notes.]—3. Ejectment for a hou and small lot of land adjoining. appeared that, as to the hou notice to quit had been given t late, but that the plaintiff was e titled to the land. The jury fou in his favor for all the premis *Ordered*, that unless the plain would confine his judgment to t land, defendant should have a n trial; but as one of the plainti witnesses lived at a distance, was imposed as a condition t his evidence, given at the last tri should be read from the judg notes. *Conley* v. *Lee*, 456.

4. A new trial will not be granted or the discovery of new evidence, nless such evidence is specifically hewn in the affidavits. *White et l. v. Brown*, 477.

5. A new trial will not be granted or a misdirection as to the right to egin, unless it appears that injustice may have been occasioned y it. *McDonald v. McHugh and ife, Administratrix of John Kelly*, 03.

NON-JOINDER.
See REPLEVIN, 2.

OTICE TO EXAMINE PARTY AS WITNESS.
See EVIDENCE, 3.—GUARANTEE.

NUISANCE.
ee INDICTMENT, 2.—RAILWAYS AND R. W. COMPANIES.

NUL TIEL RECORD.
When *nul tiel* record is pleaded he issue is complete, and no replication or entry on the record is necessary, but the court may give ay of trial by the record. *Jones . Ruttan*, 202.

ONTARIO, SIMCOE & HURON R. R. CO.
See RAILWAYS AND R. W. COMPANIES, 5.

OPINION OF COUNSEL.
See MALICIOUS PROSECUTION.

PARTNERS AND PARTNER-SHIP.
Evidence of dissolution.] — The plaintiff sued M. and B. upon a promissory note signed M. & Co., made by M., dated 10th October, 1853. For the defence, a deed of dissolution of partnership between M. and B. was proved, dated 25th May, 1853, and three *Canada Gazettes* giving notice of such dissolution, the first dated 25th June, 1853. It was not shewn that the plaintiff ever knew of B. being a partner, and the note was made at Port Hope, where M. and B. had carried on business, but B. lived in Montreal. *Held*, that a verdict should have been found for defendants. *Quære*, as to what is sufficient notice of a dissolution of partnership. *Dalring v. Magnan & Bourdreau*, 471.

PAYMENT.
See PLEADING, 12.—VARIANCE.

Guarantee—Appropriation of payments.]—In April, 1850 R. became security to the plaintiffs for S. to the extent of £100. and S. thereupon received goods from them to the amount of £151. In April S. desired to make a further purchase. R. wrote to the plaintiffs becoming security to the extent of £75, and in his letter he said, " I understand from S. that he has paid you £75 on account of the £100." The plaintiffs sent no answer, but supplied the goods required. The £75 had been paid by S., and in his letter enclosing it he said, " I send you £75 on account of goods bought by me, being one-half of the whole." *Held*, that R. was entitled to have the whole of this payment credited against the £151 secured by his first guarantee, and that the plaintiffs could not appropriate it to any part of the debt of S. for which R. was not liable. *Lyman et al. v. Miller*, 215.

PLEADING.
See AGREEMENT, 1, 2.—BILLS OF EXCHANGE AND PROMISSORY NOTES, 2, 3, 4, 6.—DOWER.—MISJOINDER.— MUNICIPAL CORPORATIONS,3.—NUL TIEL RECORD. REPLEVIN, 2.—SCI. FA.—TRESPASS, 1.—USURY.—VARIANCE.—WARRANT.—WOODSTOCK & LAKE ERIE R. W. & HARBOR CO.—WORK & LABOR.

Principal and surety—Discharge of surety.—1. *Debt* on bond against a surety for the performance by W. R. of his duties as agent for the plaintiffs. *Breach*, the conversion by W. R. to his own use of money received for the plaintiffs. *Plea*— That after the breach the plaintiffs and W. R. accounted together respecting the indebtedness of the said W. R. to the plaintiffs, *as such agent and otherwise*, and on such accounting the said W. R. was found indebted to the plaintiffs *as such agent* in £4462 8s. 1d.; that the said W. R. then immediately executed and delivered to the plaintiffs a mortgage of certain lands to secure the payment ot his said indebtedness, in which said mortgage the said W. R. covenanted to pay the plaintiffs the said sum on certain days and times therein mentioned, whereby the said indebtedness of W. R. became merged in the said specialty, and the time of payment thereof postponed and delayed without the consent of the defendant; by reason whereof the said defendant became absolutely discharged from the said debt above demanded, and damages, &c. *Held*, on demurrer, plea bad, as not shewing that the consideration for which the mortgage was taken would include everything that could be proved under the declaration against the defendant as surety. *Commercial Bank v. Muirhead*, 39.

Obstruction of road—Pleading—Evidence.]—2. In an action on the case for obstructing a road, the plaintiff declared that he was possessed of a certain close, and *by reason thereof* was entitled to a certain way, and he charged the defendant with obstructing the said way while he (the plaintiff) was so possessed of the said close, and so entitled to the said way as aforesaid. The defendants traversed the right of way set up. *Held*, that upon these pleadings the plaintiff was bound to shew an ease-

ment as alleged in the declaration, and could not proceed for the obstruction ot a public highway; and even if he could, it would have been fatal to his case that no special damage was alleged, without which he could have no right of action as a private individual. *Fisher v. The Municipality of Vaughan*, 55.

Case for overflowing land—Pleading—Evidence.]—3. Case for overflowing the plaintiff's land, by penning back the water of a stream running through it, and thence over the land of the defendant. The second count charged that one H. wrongfully erected a dam across the stream on the defendant's land, which occasioned it to overflow the plaintiff's land, and that the defendant wrongfully kept up the said dam so wrongfully erected by H., whereby the water had been injuriously penned back upon the plaintiff's land. *The third count* stated that one H. had erected a dam ten feet high on defendant's close (not alleging this to be a wrongful act); that one T. wrongfully raised and increased in height and width the dam built by H., by means whereof the water was obstructed and penned back and overflowed the plaintiff's land; and that the defendant had wrongfully kept up and maintained the dam so wrongfully increased by T. The defendant pleaded not guilty to the whole declaration, and to the second count a prescriptive right for the use of a certain mill on his lot. The jury found for the defendant. *Held*, that on these pleadings the defendant was entitled to retain his verdict on the third count, as well as on the second; for the plea of not guilty put in issue the erection of a dam by H., charged in the second count, as well as the continuance of it by the defendant; and the gist of the action, and the substantial point involved in both counts, was not the erection of the dam, but the wrongful penning back of the water, which was decided in the defendant's favor by the verdict on the third count. *Nigh* v. *Sowerwine*, 67.

Libel on title to land—Justification—Estoppel.]—4. Case for libel in publishing a printed notice denying the plaintiff's title to certain land, of which the declaration alleged that he was seized in fee, and which he had advertised for sale, and stating that one C. J. had the title, and that a suit was pending in Chancery to establish her undoubted right. Second plea—That the plaintiff was not, at the said time when, &c., seized as of fee of or in the land, or any part thereof. Third plea—That the matters published by the defendant were at the said time when, and still are true in substance and effect, Fourth plea—That the said C. J. had and still has an undoubted right to the land ; and that the defendant so believing, as her agent, and at her request. published the notice, to protect her right, and without malice. The fifth plea alleged that the plaintiff's only title was by virtue of an indenture of mortgage executed to him by one K., who was then seized in fee ; that the said indenture was given to secure usurious interest ; that the said K. died intestate, and his heir gave to the said C. J. full license to enter on and occupy the said land during her life ; and thereupon the defendant, as her agent, published, &c. (as in the fourth plea). The plaintiff replied, by way of estoppel, a verdict and judgment in an action of ejectment brought by him against the defendant and one E. Y., to recover possession of this land, in which it was found by the jury that the said indenture was not illegal or usurious. *Held*, on demurrer, second plea good ; third plea bad,

as too general ; fourth and fifth pleas bad, for omitting to justify the statement that a chancery suit was pending, that being a very material part of the libel. *Semble*, that the replication to the fifth plea shewed an estoppel. *Mair* v. *Culy*, 71

Assumpsit—Plea not answering the whole breach.]—5. Assumpsit on a contract to make and furnish a steam-engine and boiler, and that the said boiler should be made of good and sufficient materials, and should be reasonably fit and proper for the said engine, and the reasonable and proper working and use thereof. *Breach*—That the boiler furnished was not made of good and sufficient materials, and was not reasonably fit and proper for the said engine, and the reasonable and proper working and use thereof. *Plea*—That the said boiler was made of good and sufficient materials. *Held*, on demurrer, plea bad, as not answering the whole breach. *Abel* v. *Leonard*, 192.

Account stated — Pleading.]—6. Assumpsit on account stated for £1,200. *Plea*—That after the cause of action accrued, and before the commencement of the suit, the plaintiff and defendant together of all concerning the causes of action in the declaration mentioned, and of and concerning certain other demands of the plaintiff against the defendant, and of the defendant against the plaintiff ; and on such accounting the defendant was found indebted to the plaintiff in £800, and no more, which sum the defendant promised and hath been and is ready to pay. *Held*, on demurrer, plea good. *Beattie* v. *Hatch*, 195.

False return to Fi. Fa. of goods on hand for want of buyers.]—7. Case for falsely returning to a *Fi. Fa.* goods on hand for want of buyers, when the defendant might have levied the amount. *Pleas*—1. That no such writ of *Fi. Fa.* was duly sued out, as in the declaration alleged ; 2. That the defendant did take goods out of which he could have levied the sum directed to be levied, which goods remained and still remain in his hands for want of buyers. *Held*, on demurrer, both pleas bad. *Jones* v. *Ruttan*, 202.

Covenant for not rebuilding after fire—Plea of former recovery of prospective damages for the whole term—Award between plaintiff and third party.|—8. Covenant against the executors of a lessor for not rebuilding after loss by fire. 2nd *plea—* That after the said fire the defendants, as executors, were sued in a former action by the plaintiff on the covenant; that the plaintiff at the trial claimed to recover prospective damages for the whole term in the lease ; that the defendants, not intending to rebuild, assented to this ; that the jury were therefore directed to give and did give damages accordingly , and that the defendants, in consequence of the understanding at the trial, made no attempt to disturb the verdict, but allowed judgment to be entered, and considering that full damages had been given, did not rebuild ; that the damages then given far exceeded all damages sustained up to the time of that action ; and that, in consequence of the matters above mentioned, this action is prosecuted fraudulently and wrongfully against the defendants. The third plea set up an award as to the damages sought to be recovered between the plaintiff and one G.M., who, it was averred, was assignee of the premises under the will of the plaintiff's lessor for a term in the said will mentioned ; but it was not averred that the plaintiff had obtained satisfaction through this award. *Held*, on demurrer, second plea bad, at least in point of form; third plea bad, as shewing no de-

fence. *Proudfoot* v. *Trotter et al* executors of *John McGill*, 226.

9. In an action for enforcing judgment in itself regular, b which has been satisfied, mali and want of probable cause mu be alleged in the declaration. *Au* v. *Armstrong*, 385.

Case for obstruction of watercour —Plea held bad as an argumentati traverse of defendant's alleged right —10. *Harris* v. *Fraser*, 402.

Accord and satisfaction — U certainty — Demurrer.] — 11. A sumpsit on the common count *Plea*—That after the making of t promises, and before the commenc ment of this suit, it was agreed th defendant should sell to plainti and plaintiffs then and there boug of defendant, 20 shares of stock a certain steamer ; and that defe dant should hold such shares f plaintiff's use, and transfer them the plaintiffs when required ; a that the plaintiffs should then a there accept the said agreement defendant, and the said shares to be transferred, in full satisfacti and discharge of the said promise that in pursuance of such agre ment, and ever since the maki thereof, defendant had held and st holds such shares for the use of t plaintiffs, and hath always be and still is ready to transfer the when required. *Held*, on demurr plea bad, because it was not shev whether the alleged agreement w before or after the breach of t promise sued on. *Ross et al. Heron*, 467.

Payment of a less sum in sat faction of a greater.]—12. Plea payment and acceptance of a le in satisfaction of a larger sum he bad. *Quære*, whether a plea th the demand sued for was of an u liquidated nature, and was disput either wholly or in part, and that was agreed that plaintiff should] ceive a less sum in satisfaction his alleged cause of action, could be supported. *Holmes* v. *McDonell*, 469.

Lease with right of purchase—Covenant for not conveying—Plea, that indenture avoided by rent in the arrear.]—13. Covenant on an indenture, excusing profert, by which the plaintiff demised certain land to defendant for a term of five years, and covenanted to convey to him in fee if he should pay £125 on or before a day named. *Breach*, that although the plaintiff offered the money before the day named, and requested a conveyance, yet the defendant refused. *Plea*, after setting out the indenture in full, which contained a proviso that in case the rent or any part thereof should be in arrear for forty days, then the indenture and everything therein contained should be void—that before and at the time of the tender in the declaration mentioned, the first year's rent was in arrear for forty days, whereby the indenture and the covenant to convey became void—Verification. *Held*, on demurrer, plea good. *McLellan* v. *Rogers*, 571.

Case for injury caused by railway collision — Statement of cause of action.]—14. Declaration in case stated that the plaintiff, being pregnant, at the request of defendants became a passenger in one of their carriages, to be safely conveyed by them for reward ; that the defendants received her as such passenger, and it was their duty to use due care in conveying her, yet the defendants, not regarding, &c., so negligently conducted themselves that a collision took place with another train, by means whereof the carriage, in which the plaintiff was, was broken, &c., and thereby the plaintiff was much affrighted and alarmed, whereby she became sick, sore, and disordered, and so continued from thence hitherto, and thereby also, *by reason of the terror and alarm occasioned to her by the*

said collision, and of such sickness caused thereby, she had a premature labour, and bore a still-born child. *Held*, on demurrer, that a sufficient cause of action was disclosed. *Thomas Fitzpatrick and his Wife* v. *The Great Western Railway Company*, 665.

POSSESSION.

See LIMITATIONS (STATUTE OF), 1.— TRESPASS, 2.

Boundary—Right by possession according to division line agreed on —Extent of such right.]—1. If two parties owning respective halves of a lot, agree to a division line which is not the true boundary, and one party clears a portion of land according to such line, and obtains a right by possession to such portion, this will not give him any right by constructive possession to the whole as if this line were carried out. *Ferrier* v. *Moodie*, 379.

Trespass—Proof of possession— Erroneous survey.] — 2. Trespass *quare clausum fregit*, describing the *locus in quo* by metes and bounds and as part of " what has heretofore been known as lot 15, 1st concession, Delaware." The defendant gave no evidence of title. The plaintiff claimed by virtue of his possession, and it appeared that more than twenty years ago, relying on an erroneous survey, he had fenced in a part of the defendant's lot 14 in the broken front concession. This fence, if continued, would have included the part in question, but it had never been extended to any part of lot 14, in the 1st concession. *Held*, that the plaintiff could not be considered as having any such possession of the *locus in quo* as would entitle him to recover. *Weld* v. *Scott et al.*, 537.

POUNDAGE.

Sheriff's right to poundage.] Where the sheriff, under a writ o

Fi. Fa., seized goods sufficient to cover the claim, and afterwards withdrew from the possession, in obedience to a judge's order founded upon an undertaking of the defendant to give credit for the amount of the levy on an execution which he held against the plaintiff. *Held,* that the sheriff was entitled to poundage. *Thomas, Sheriff, &c.,* v. *Cotton,* 148.

PRACTICE.

See AMENDMENT. — CERTIORARI — DEMURRER. — EJECTMENT. — INDICTMENT, 2.—LIMITATIONS (STATUTE OF), 2.—MANDAMUS, 2, 3, 5. —MUNICIPAL ELECTIONS.—NEW TRIAL — NUL TIEL RECORD — WILL

Mistake — Application for new trial made in wrong court.]—1. An application for a new trial made in this court was referred to the C.P., as the record had been returned there, and the case, which had been tried before the Chief Justice of the C. P., was not to be found in his note-book of trials from this court. A rule *nisi* was then obtained in proper time in the C. P., and enlarged until the next term, and in the meantime it was discovered that the record had been by mistake endorsed in C. P.. Under these circumstances the application was entertained in this court on the return of the rule. *Bens* v. *Gilbert Stover, David Stover, and Gilbert Stover, Jr.,* 623.

Appeal — County Court — Practice.] — 2. A county court judge arranged with the bar of his county "to transact all term business in vacation," and, acting under such arrangement, set aside a verdict and judgment after the term succeeding the assizes in which the verdict was rendered. An appeal from his decision was allowed, with costs, such arrangement being contrary to the express words of the statute. *Smith* v. *Rooney,* 661.

PRETENDED TITLE.

See ACTION.

PRINCIPAL AND SURETY

See CONTRACT, 2. — PAYMENT. PLEADING, 1.

PROHIBITION,

See DIVISION COURTS, 2.

PROMISSORY NOTES.

See BILLS OF EXCHANGE AND PR MISSORY NOTES.

QUARTER SESSIONS.

See INDICTMENT.

QUIET ENJOYMENT.

Covenant for.]—See "Dower," 1

QUO WARRANTO.

See MUNICIPAL ELECTIONS.

RAILWAYS AND RAILWA' COMPANIES.

See ARBITRATION AND AWARD, 2, 4, 5, 8.—BUFFALO, BRANTFOR AND GODERICH R. W. Co —Co TRACT, 1 —GREAT WESTERN W. Co.—MANDAMUS, 6. — MONE HAD AND RECEIVED.—PLEADIN 14.—TIME (COMPUTATION OF). WOODSTOCK AND LAKE ERIE W. AND HARBOR Co.

Brantford & Buffalo R. R. Co. Construction of deed taken by Right to enter upon lands—Licen not revocable—Plaintiff not in position to maintain trespass — 1 Vic., ch. 84, 16 Vic, ch. 45.]— On the 26th of October, 1852, th Buffalo and Brantford Joint Stoc Railroad Company, took a dee from the plaintiff's father, by whic in consideration of the benefi which would result to him from th construction of the road, and £27 10s., he agreed "to allow an permit the said Company forthwit to take, occupy, possess, and enjo of and through" the land in que tion. It appeared that the plainti had no title to the land, but had merely been allowed by his father to occupy it : that he had admitted in presence of his father that it was with his father, and not with him that the Company must settle ; and that he had worked under the defendant, a contractor with the Company, in making the fence along the line through this land. After the deed, the plaintiff and his father forbade the defendant from entering. The defendant entered in December, 1852, for the purpose of making the railway, and the fences along the line being insufficient, the plaintiff's wheat was injured by cattle getting in. For these injuries he sued in this action of trespass *quare clausum fregit.* The jury found for the plaintiff and £25, on the ground, as they stated, that the defendant had been forbidden to enter upon the premises before any work was done.

The Company was established under the general act 12 Vic., ch. 84, and the deed was taken while under that act ; but before entering they were placed under " The Railway Clauses Consolidation Act," by 16 Vic., ch. 45. *Held* (treating the question as between the Company and the owner)—*First*, That the deed taken was more than a mere agreement as to the price ; the effect of it was to give the Company permission forthwith to take and occupy a right of way through the land, of the ordinary width of the road.—*Secondly*, That the Company having by their agreement previously made a right to enter *forthwith,* the 14 & 15 Vic., ch. 51, sec. 11, sub-sec. 2, would not apply. *Thirdly*, That the Company could enter forthwith, though they had not paid or tendered the money— that not being a condition precedent according to the deed, and there being nothing in the 12 Vic., ch. 84, to prevent it ; and therefore that they could not be considered

trespassers. *Held,* also, as to th plaintiff, that the verdict was wron taking the reasons given by th jury ; for looking upon the dee merely as a license, it was acte upon the moment the Compan entered into contracts for the wor on which they would be liable t others, and was therefore not rev cable.—Secondly, That on leg grounds, independently of his ow conduct, which in justice shoul estop him, the plaintiff could n maintain trespass against any on claiming under the Company ; fc he was not at any time more than tenant at will, and the deed dete mined the will and left him tenar at sufferance only, with a right 1 enter and remove the crop. *Nelso* v. *Cook,* 22.

G. W. R. W. Co.—Width bridges to be erected when highwa crossed.] — 2. A railway compan by their charter were bound to r store any highway intersected b their track " to its former state, in a sufficient manner not to impa its usefulness." They constructe their road across a street in t city of Hamilton, which was sixt six feet wide, and connected t street again by a bridge across t track forty feet two inches in widt *Held,* that the jury might with pr priety find this to be a sufficie compliance with the act, and th the defendants were not necessaril guilty of a nuisance because t bridge was not of equal width wi the street crossed. *Regina* v. *Gre Western Railroad Co.,* 250.

G. W. R. W. Co.—Duty to ere fences—Negligence in not slackenii speed at crossings.]—3. The Gre Western Railway crosses a hig way on a level, and one of the trains going at its usual rate speed ran into and killed two cow which were passing along the hig way at their usual pace, but wit out an attendant. The owner the cows sued the company in an action on the case, founding his claim to damages solely on the ground of their neglect in not slackening speed at the crossing. It appea.ed in evidence that the track was not fenced. *Held*, 1st. That if the company were bound to fence in their road where the accident occurred, it was by their default the cows got upon the track, and therefore they could not object that the cows were not legally on the highway.—2ndly, That if the company were not bound to fence, still they were guilty of negligence as charged in the declaration, and therefore as against them the cows were legally there. *Semble*, that the effect of the 9th clause of 4 Wm. IV. ch. 29, is to oblige the Company to erect fences, and to place gates where their road crosses highways, and to have such gates properly watched and attended. *Semble*, also, that this clause extends to all parts of the road, as well west as east of London. *Renaud v. The Great Western Railway Co.*, 408.

G. W. R. W. Co.—Obligation to fence.]—4. The declaration averred that it was defendants' duty to keep up sufficient fences along their line of railway, and that by the neglect of such duty the plaintiff's mare, which was lawfully depasturing on the adjoining land, got upon the track and was killed. No negligence was charged against defendants in the management of their train. It was proved that the mare had escaped from her stable on another farm, and was trespassing on the lot from which she got upon the railway. *Held*, (confirming Dolrey v. Ontario, Simcoe & Huron R. R. Co., 11 U. C. R. 600), that the plaintiff could not recover; the defendants being bound to fence only as against the owner of the adjoining lands. *Gillis v. Great Western Railway Company*, 427.

12 *Vic.*, *ch.* 196, *sec.* 18—*Oblig tion to fence—Request—Insufficie fence put up by plaintiff himself.*] 5. The defendants by their chart 12 Vic. ch. 196, sec. 18, are bou to fence off their railway from tl adjoining lands, in case the owne of such lands shall at any time desire.

The plaintiff, owning adjoini lands, made a verbal request defendant's resident engineer erect a fence, and as this was n done, he put up a slashed fence 1 himself, and some bars in it bei left down, his cows got on the tra and were killed. *Held*, first, th the request made was sufficient. *Secondly*, That the fact of t plaintiff having erected an insu cient fence for himself, and ne lected to put up the bars, could r dispense with the duty impos upon the company, or affect right to compensation. *Wilson The Ontario, Simcoe, and Hur Railroad Union Co.*, 463.

———

RECITAL.

See REGISTRY AND REGISTRAR.

———

REGISTRY AND REGISTRA

See ADMISSION.—ASSIGNMENT.

The plaintiff proved a deed himself from D., dated 3rd of Ju 1851, registered on the 7th of t same month. The defendant in an instrument under seal, da 3rd of June, 1847, between one and D., reciting that differen had arisen between them, and t M. had brought ejectment to cover possession of this lot, "belo ing to the said M.," and in c sideration of M, withdrawing 1 record, D. agreed that the lot sho be valued by certain parties, a covenanted to pay to M. or sec by mortgage on the land whate that value might be. No valuat was made. *Held*, this agreem being unregistered, that the reci in it could not affect the plaintiff's title. *Rutledge* v. *McLean*, 205.

RENT.
See LANDLORD AND TENANT.

ROAD COMPANIES.
See JOINT STOCK COMPANIES.

REPLEVIN.
See ASSIGNMENT.

Replevin under 14 & 15 *Vic., ch.* 64—*Value of goods, how to be ascertained.*] — 1. Goods seized under an execution in the hands of the debtor were replevied, under 14 & 15 Vic., ch, 64, by S. claiming under an assignment from such debtor. S. failed in the action of replevin ; and in this suit, brought by the sheriff on the replevin bond, the defendants suffered judgment by default, and a verdict was rendered for the penalty. The jury having found at the trial the value of the goods, the court ordered proceedings to be stayed on payment of such value into court, together with the costs. *Quære,* as to the proper method of ascertaining the value. *Ruttan, Sheriff,* v. *Short, et al.*, 485.

Replevin—14 & 15 *Vic., ch.* 64—*Non-joinder.*]—2. *Held,* that under the circumstances of this case the plaintiff could have maintained trespass, and consequently that he could bring replevin.

In replevin non-joinder must be pleaded in abatement, and, when there is no such plea, the defendant cannot object that the evidence shews another person to be interested with the plaintiff in the goods. *Cook* v. *Fowler et al.*, 568.

REQUEST.
See AGREEMENT, 1.

RESCISSION OF CONTRACT.
See WORK AND LABOUR.

RESOLUTIONS.
See MUNICIPAL CORPORATIONS, 3.

RIGHT TO BEGIN.
See NEW TRIAL, 5.

ROAD.
See HIGHWAYS.—MANDAMUS, 4.

ROAD COMPANIES.
See JOINT STOCK COMPANIES, — SANDWICH AND WINDSOR ROAD Co.

SALE.
See TAXES.—VENDOR AND VENDEE.

SATISFACTION.
See PLEADING, 11, 12.

SANDWICH AND WINDSOR ROAD COMPANY.

Sandwich and Windsor Road Co. —*Limits of their road.*] — *Held,* upon the special case stated, that the defendants, a joint stock road company, incorporated under 12 Vic., ch. 84, had no authority to construct their road through the town of Windsor, or beyond the entrance of the town from Sandwich—the road which they were authorized to make being described in their instrument of incorporation filed under the act as a road from the town of Sandwich to the town of Windsor. *Secondly,* That as no limits had been assigned to the town of Windsor when the defendants were incorporated, the court would look to what the proprietor of land on which a part of what was commonly called Windsor stood had designated Windsor on a plan which he had filed in the Registry office, aud referred to in giving deeds : and to the popular understanding as to what constituted Windsor; and that, taking these facts as guides. it was quite clear that the road had been extended into the town, and a tollgate placed within the limits. *Thirdly,* That it was immaterial that at a public meeting held in Windsor, it had been resolved to make no opposition to the road, for this could not bind the plaintiff. *Dougall* v. *The Sandwich and Windsor Plank and Gravel Road Company*, 59.

SAW LOGS.

See CHATTEL MORTGAGES, 2.

SCHOOLS.

See COMMON SCHOOLS.

SCIRE FACIAS.

See EJECTMENT, 2.

Sci. Fa. — Practice — Appropriation of payments]—*Sci. Fa.* on a payment alleged to have been recovered against the defendant, executrix, &c., (not as executrix) for £250. *Plea*, payment. The defendants proved payments to about £130. An account was produced by the plaintiff shewing due at testator's death £76 7s. 4d. This was carried forward, and the account continued for some time against the defendant, leaving a balance due altogether of £196 12s. 1d. The defendant contended that, as the payments proved exceeded the amount due by testator at his death, she was entitled to a verdict; but—*Held*, That the statement in the *Sci. Fa.* did not amount to an allegation that the defendant was sued in her representative character, the word *executrix*, being mere description; and that the plaintiff was therefore entitled to a verdict on the issue, only half the amount of the judgment having been proved to be paid. *Senble*, That on such issue the plaintiff should have taken a verdict merely that the judgment was unsatisfied, not for any specific sum; and that a verdict so taken would not prevent the defendant from obtaining relief if the execution on the judgment should be endorsed for more than the sum due. *Caughill* v. *Maria Teal, executrix of John B. Teal*, 619.

SEAL.

See CORPORATIONS.—MUNICIPAL CORPORATIONS, 3.

SEIZIN.

See DOWER, 1, 4, 5.

SET OFF.

See COSTS.

SHERIFF.

See PLEADING, 7.—POUNDAGE.

SHERIFF'S DEED.

See TAXES, 2.

14 & 15 Vic., ch. 5, sec. 12—Sheri of Oxford, sale by, of lands in Oa land after 1st January, 1852.] Under a *Fi. Fa.* issued upon jud ment entered in November, 185 the sheriff of the county of Oxfo in 1853, conveyed certain lands i the township of Brant, reciting the deed that they had been seize in December, 1851. By 14 & 1 Vic., ch. 5, which came into for on the 1st of January, 1852, t township of Oakland was annexe to the county of Brant, but by t 12th clause it was enacted that a proceedings in any court at t time when the act should con into effect, might be continued trial and judgment in such cou and such judgment might be ex cuted as if the act had not be passed. *Held.* that under this pr vision the sheriff was authoriz to convey as he had done. *Shenst* v. *Baker*, 175.

SHERIFF'S SALE.

See ESTOPPEL, 1.

SHIPS.

See NAVIGATION.

SLANDER.

See PLEADING, 4.

SPECIAL CONTRACT.

See WORK AND LABOUR.

SPIRITUOUS LIQUORS.

See MUNICIPAL CORPORATIONS, 1,2,5.

STATUTE OF LIMITATIONS.

See LIMITATIONS (STATUTE OF).

STATUTES (CONSTRUCTION OF).

See TAXES, 1.

32 H. VIII. ch. 9.—See " Action."

2 W. IV. ch. 13.—See "Grand River Navigation Co."

4 W. IV. ch. 1—See " Limitations (Statute of))."

4 W. IV. ch. 29.—See "Railways and Railway Companies," 3.

5 & 6 W. IV. ch. 62.–See "Evidence," 1.

1 Vic. ch. 19.—See " Boundary Line Commissioners."

3 Vic. ch. 11.—See "Boundary Line Commissioners."

7 Vic. ch. 10.—See " Insolvent and Insolvency."

8 Vic. ch. 13.—See " Practice," 2.

8 Vic. ch. 48.—See " Insolvent and Insolvency."

9 Vic. ch. 8.—See " Highway."

9 Vic. ch. 81.—See " Arbitration and Award," 2.

10 & 11 Vic. ch. 9.—See "Bills of Exchange and Promissory Notes," 5.

10 & 11 Vic. ch. 117.—See " Woodstock and Lake Erie Railway and Harbor Co "

12 Vic ch. 63.—See " Limitations (Statute of) "

12 Vic. ch. 74.—See " Assignment."

12 Vic. ch. 81 —See " Mandamus," 4.

12 Vic. ch. 84 —See " Joint Stock Companies"—" Railways and Railway Companies," 1.

12 Vic. ch. 196.—See " Railways and Railway Companies," 5.

13 & 14 Vic. ch. 19.—See " Evidence," 4.

13 & 14 Vic. ch. 48.—See " Common Schools," 2, 3.

13 & 14 Vic. ch. 53.—See "Costs"—" Division Courts," 1.

13 & 14 Vic. ch. 58 —See "Dower,"2, 3.

13 & 14 Vic. ch. 62.—See "Assignment."

13 & 14 Vic. ch. 65.—See " Municipal Corporations, 1, 5.

13 & 14 Vic. ch. 74. — See " Indian Lands."

14 & 15 Vic. ch. 5.—See " Municipal Corporations," 6.

14 & 15 Vic. ch. 6.—See "Will."

14 & 15 Vic. ch. 13.—See " Indian Lands"—" Sheriff's Deed."

14 & 15 Vic. ch. 51.—See "Mandamus," 6—" Railways and Railway Companies," 1 —" Time (Computation of)."

14 & 15 Vic. ch. 54.—See "Commissioners for Indian Affairs "

14 & 15 Vic. ch. 64.—See " Replevin."

14 & 15 Vic. ch. 114.—See " Ejectment"—" Evidence," 2.

14 & 15 Vic. ch. 126.—See "Navigation."

16 Vic, ch. 19.—See " Evidence," 3.

16 Vic. ch. 80.—See " Usury."

16 Vic.ch.177.—See"Division Courts,"2.

16 Vic. ch. 183.—See " Arbitration and Award," 6—" Taxes," 1.

16 Vic. ch. 184.—See "Municipal Corporations," 1, 2.

16 Vic. ch. 185.—See"CommonSchools'1.

16 Vic. ch. 190.—See "Joint Stock Companies."

16 Vic. ch. 228.—See " Boundary."

SUB CONTRACT.

See CONTRACT, 1.

SURETY.

See CONTRACT, 2.—PRINCIPAL AND SURETY.

TAVERNS.

See MUNICIPAL CORPORATIONS. 1, 2, 5.

TAXES.

16 *Vic. ch.* 183, *sec.* 11, *construction of*—"*Herein contained*," *in the last clause construed to apply to that clause, only— Money had and received.*]—The plaintiff paid certain taxes imposed by a by-law of a district council. This by-law was afterwards decided to be illegal in an ejectment brought by this plaintiff to contest the validity of the sale of his lands for these taxes, but it was not quashed by the court, because before the application was made for that purpose it had been repealed by the council who passed it. The plaintiff then brought this action for money had and received, &c., to recover back what he had paid. During the pendency of this

suit a statute was passed (16 Vic. ch. 183) which enacted that taxes imposed under certain by-laws, of which this was one, should be valid, and that any such taxes that had been paid should not be recovered back, and, notwithstanding the informality of the by-law, should remain chargeable against the land; and (in the eleventh clause) that when lands had been sold for such taxes, and the owner should neglect to redeem them under the privilege given by the act, the sale should be confirmed, " Provided that nothing *herein contained* shall be held to make valid the title to any lands which shall have been adjudged to be invalid by any court of competent jurisdiction, or in any way to make void any judgment in any of the superior courts of Upper Canada, or to affect any suit pending therein in which the validity of any such by-law may have been called in question." *Held*, that the words "herein contained" must be applied only to the cause in which they occur, and not to the whole act—that being in this case the reasonable, and in general the more obvious, though not the inevitable construction ; for otherwise, either the absurdity would result, that as the plaintiff's recovery back would cancel the payment, the land under the provisions of the statute would become chargeable with the same sum :—or the plaintiff, having paid the taxes to avoid a sale, would be in a better position than those who had not paid, or whose lands had been sold, which could not have been intended. The action being defeated by the statute, it was unnecessary to determine the point argued—whether money had and received would lie under the circumstances in which the payment was made. *McGill v. The Municipal Council of Peterborough and Victoria*, 44.

Evidence to support title [und sale for taxes—Several lots in t same grant—What portion to be so for arrears.]—2. EJECTMENT.—T defendant claimed under a sheriff deed under a sale for taxes, b there was no proof that any tax were imposed or in arrear, exce an extract from the treasurer book, by which it appeared th the taxes on the lot in question h been paid up to 1828. *Held*, i sufficient, and that the plaint must recover. *Semble*, that whe several lots are included in o grant, but described by separa numbers, a portion of each l must be sold to pay the taxes d upon such lot, and not a portion the whole block, beginning at t boundary from which the lots a numbered, for the taxes due up the whole. *Munro et al. v. Grey*, 64

TERRITORIAL DIVISIONS

See SHERIFF'S DEED.

TIMBER.

See ASSIGNMENT.—CHATTEL MOR GAGES, 2, 3.

TIME (COMPUTATION OF)

See COMMISSIONERS FOR INDIAN AFFAIRS.

The Railway Clauses Conso dation Act, 14 & 15 Vic. ch. 5 provides that no call shall be ma " at a less interval than two mont from the previous calls." *Hel* that calls made on the 1st of Se tember, 1st of November, 1st January, &c., were bad. *Buffa Brantford, and Goderich Railw Company v. Parke*, 607.

TITLE.

See DOWER, 1, 5.—PLEADING, 4. POSSESSION.—REGISTRY AND R GISTRAR.

TREASON.

See LIMITATIONS (STATUTE OF)

TREES.

See TRESPASS, 1.

TRESPASS.

See CHATTEL MORTGAGES, 1.—MIS-JOINDER.— RAILWAYS AND R.W COMPANIES, 1.

Pleading.—Trespass.] — 1. The plaintiff charged the defendant with *cutting down* and carrying away trees. It appeared the plaintiff had leased the land to the defendant's brother, making no reservation or mention of the trees. *Held*, that on this declaration the plaintiff could not recover. *Roys* v. *Cramer*, 165.

Purchase of growing timber—Right of purchaser to bring trespass qu. cl. fr.]—2. The plaintiff had purchased from the Canada Company all the merchantable timber on a certain lot, and held a letter from them (set out below) authorizing him to enter upon the land and mark whatever trees he might choose, and afterwards to cut and carry them away. *Held*, that he had not such a possession as would enable him to bring trespass *quare clausum fregit. Quære*, what remedy he could have for trespasses on the land:—whether he could support an action on the case against the trespasser for interfering with his privilege; or would be compelled to look to the company, treating their letter as an agreement. *Perry* v. *Buck*, 451

USURY.

Pleading — 16 Vic. ch. 80 — Meaning of "legal interest."] — Debt on bond. Plea—That the defendants owed the plaintiff £800, and gave their notes for that sum, payable by instalments, *with legal interest;* that it was agreed that the defendants

4 *x*—VOL. XII. Q.B.

should pay certain sums, by way of bonus and usurious interest, in addition to *the said legal interest;* and that the bond sued on was given to secure such payments. *Held*, on demurrer, plea good; for the court would intend that by the words "legal interest" six per cent. was meant, and therefore the bond was shewn to be wholly void. *Nourse* v. *Goodeve et al.*, 198.

VARIANCE.

See INDIAN LANDS, —MUNICIPAL CORPORATIONS, 3.

The declaration stated an agreement to pay to three persons, and the agreement was to pay half to one and half to the two others : — *Semble*, per *Draper J.*, no variance. *Bens* v. *Stover et al.*, 623,

---

VENDOR AND VENDEE.

See MONEY HAD AND RECEIVED.—WARRANTY.

WAREHOUSEMAN.

Liability of, for insufficiency of building.]—A person sending goods to be warehoused has a right to expect that the building in which they are placed shall be reasonably fit for the purpose, but he has no right to expect more than ordinary and average care in that respect, and it is only in the absence of such care on the warehouseman's part that he will be liable. The fact of the building having fallen from a defect in the foundation is not conclusive evidence against the warehouseman, for that might happen without any negligence on his part. *Wilmot* v. *Jarvis*, 641.

WARRANT, (DEMAND OF PERUSAL AND COPY OF.)

Demand of perusal and copy of warrant, under 16 Vic. ch. 177 sec. 14.]—The provisions of 16 Vic. ch.

177, sec. 14 do not apply in an action against a bailiff acting under a warrant of attachment or execution from a division court, where the wrong complained of is the misconduct of the defendant, and not anything illegal in the writ itself, or in the act of granting it. But in this case the defendants could not have availed themselves of the statute, for the general issue was not pleaded "by statute," and it did not appear on the plaintiff's case that the defendants were acting in the execution of any process. *Sayers* v. *Findlay, Stafford, and Purdy,* 155.

WARRANTY.

Purchase of animal for a special purpose—Implied warranty.]—The plaintiff's, an agricultural society, wishing to purchase a bull for breeding purposes, sent their agent to the defendant, who gave him the choice of two which he had for sale. The agent chose one of his own judgment, and the defendant gave no express warranty except as to pedigree, but he was aware that the bull was purchased for the purpose of getting stock. *Held,* that there was no implied warranty of the bull's fitness for the purpose for which he was required. *The County of Simcoe Agricultural Society* v. *Wade,* 614.

WATERCOURSE.

See PLEADING, 3, 10.

WILL.

See DEED, 1.—EXECUTORS.

Construction of—Term vested in executors—Descent under 14 & 15 Vic. ch. 6.]—R. died in 1847, having devised to T. the defendant's son, the land in question. He also devised to on B. another lot of land not quite paid for, declaring it as his wish that the land devised to T. should remain in the hands of his executors until a deed should be obtained for the lot left to B., and the executors were to make the necessary payments from the rents of his real and personal estate. It was proved that the land devised to B. had been paid for, but the deed had not been obtained, as there were rival claimants, and the vendor required indemnity. *Held,* that the land devised to T. would vest on payment of the money for B.'s lot, though the deed had not been executed. Both plaintiff and defendant claimed by deed from T.'s sister, the plaintiff having the first conveyance It was not distinctly proved at the trial, when T. died, nor was it left to the jury to find whether he died before or after the first of January, 1852, when the 14 & 15 Vic., ch. 6, came into force—this point having escaped attention. If he died before then the defendant would be entitled, as claiming under his sister, who would be his heiress—if after, the defendant would be entitled as his mother, in preference to his sister. A new trial was therefore ordered, with costs to abide the event in order to give the plaintiff an opportunity of establishing his case on this point. *Bekett* v. *Foy,* 361.

WINDSOR AND SANDWICH ROAD CO.

See SANDWICH AND WINDSOR ROAD COMPANY.

WITNESS.

See EVIDENCE.—GUARANTEE.

WOODSTOCK AND LAKE ERIE R. W. AND HARBOUR CO.

Woodstock and Lake Erie Railway Co.—10 & 11 Vic. ch. 117, secs. 3, 11, 15 — Damage caused by throwing down fences to enter on lands.]—The declaration charged that the defendants were in course of making their railway through the plaintiff's close, and of fencing off the said close from their line of road, and that during such time they ought to have kept up the plaintiff's fences, and to have so conducted themselves in and about the fencing off the railway from said close that the plaintiff's crops should not be injured by their default, yet the defendants threw down the plaintiff's fences between the said close and the line of railway, and permitted them to remain postrate for an unreasonable time, and so misconducted themselves in fencing the said line, and neglecting to erect such fences, that cattle got in and destroyed the plaintiff's crops. It appeared from the evidence that the injury complained of—the destruction of the plaintiff's crops—must have been occasioned by the first breaking down the fences for the purpose of entry (which was authorized by the 10 &

11 Vic. ch. 117, sec. 11), and befor a reasonable time had expired fo fencing in the line (as the defend ants were bound to do under the 15t section). *Held,* therefore, that th plaintiff could maintain no action but must proceed by arbitration un der section 3. *Rutledge* v. *The Wood stock and Lake Erie Railway an Harbor Co.; Burgess* v. *the same,* 668

WORDS (CONSTRUCTION OF).

"Herein contained."]—See Taxes,]
"Legal Interest."]—See Usury.

WORK AND LABOR.

Sepcial contract—Common counts. —When there is a special contrac for work and labor, it must be dis tinctly shewn that such contrac has been recinded before a recover can be allowed upon the commo counts for work specified in i *Tyrrell* v. *Gamble,* 669.

Lightning Source UK Ltd.
Milton Keynes UK
UKHW010801280219
338010UK00004B/183/P